The Columbia Anthology of Modern Chinese Literature

MODERN ASIAN LITERATURE

The Columbia Anthology of Modern Chinese Literature

SECOND EDITION

Joseph S. M. Lau and Howard Goldblatt, editors

COLUMBIA UNIVERSITY PRESS
NEW YORK

Columbia University Press
Publishers Since 1893
New York Chichester, West Sussex

Library of Congress Cataloging-in-Publication Data
The Columbia anthology of modern Chinese literature / Joseph S.M.
Lau and Howard Goldblatt, editors. — 2nd ed.
p. cm. — (Modern Asian literature series)
Includes bibliographical references and index.
ISBN-13: 978–0–231–13840–6 (cloth: alk. paper)
ISBN-13: 978–0–231–13841–3 (pbk.: alk. paper)
ISBN-10: 0–231–13840–7 (cloth : alk. paper)
ISBN-10: 0–231–13841–5 (pbk. : alk. paper)
ISBN-13: 978–0–231–51100–1 (e-book)
ISBN-10: 0–231–51100–0 (e-book)
1. Chinese literature—20th century—Translations into English.
I. Lau, Joseph S. M., 1934– . II. Goldblatt, Howard, 1939– .

PL2658.E1C64 2006
895.1′08005—dc22

2006019770

∞

Columbia University Press books are printed on permanent and durable acid-free paper.
Printed in the United States of America
c 10 9 8 7 6 5 4 3 2 1
p 10 9 8 7 6 5 4 3

CONTENTS

PART FIVE

Poetry, 1949–1976

PREFACE TO THE SECOND EDITION

Ten years seems just about right when it comes to revising a modern anthology—making it more modern, as it were. As editors we have been gratified by the acceptance of our work by reviewers, teachers, and readers, encouraged by their enthusiastic responses. Where that enthusiasm has been tempered with criticism, most often owing to omissions, we have taken note and have filled in the blanks as best we could.

The beginnings remain as they were in the first edition: Lu Xun may not have been the first to write a "modern" story, but modern Chinese literature truly begins with him. From there, however, previous readers will note changes in virtually all periods and in all genres, and first-time users will benefit from a smoother, more fully inclusive overview of Chinese fiction, poetry, and prose from the twentieth, and a bit of the twenty-first, centuries. Additions have been made in colonial and post–WWII Taiwan, the first seventeen years of the People's Republic, the Cultural Revolution era, and, most prominently, writing of the post-Tian'anmen period. We have included an essay by a Taiwanese indigenous writer, a story with a homosexual theme, and, for the first time, excerpts from novels (both by women, one by an established stylist, the other by a counterculture teenager). New stories by Huang Chunming and Mo Yan have replaced those by these authors in the first edition. There has been a price, of course: we have had to make the difficult decision to delete some pieces,, but restrictions on length made that unavoidable. Readers are encouraged to consult the first edition for selections that did not make the cut (some are listed as "missing" in the introduction, which has otherwise not been altered); permission is herein granted to photocopy deleted selections for classroom use without charge.

Finally, in order to contextualize a century of writing in the Chinese language, the reader is urged to consult Bonnie S. McDougall and Kam Louie, *The Literature of China in the Twentieth Century* (Columbia University Press, 1999).

ACKNOWLEDGMENTS

The editors are grateful to friends and colleagues whose generous support made this anthology possible. The greatest debt is owed to contributors whose translations have made this high-quality literature from China available to Anglophone readers.

We also gratefully acknowledge financial support from the China Times Foundation; many favors from William S. Tay, Eva Hung, D. E. Pollard, and Janice K. Wickeri; and the editorial guidance of Jennifer Crewe at Columbia University Press.

Joseph Lau would like to thank the Chiang Ching-kuo Foundation for a grant for research on contemporary Chinese fiction. Thanks are also due to C. T. Hsia and Leo Ou-fan Lee, co-editors of *Modern Chinese Stories and Novellas: 1919–1949*, for use of material that first saw print there. To Chuang Liang-yu of the Ching Leng Foundation, and Lam Shan Muk of the *Hong Kong Economic Journal*, he owes a debt that cannot be adequately expressed in words. Their degree of interest and concern for this project since its inception is commensurate with the warmth of their friendship.

As editors who admit to their own biases and limitations, we realize that some readers may be disappointed by the absence of their favorite author or selection. We hope, however, that the quantity, quality, and diversity of our selections will ease their concerns and supply them with much good reading.

INTRODUCTION

Anthologies of modern Chinese literature in English translation are normally restricted to specific genres, locales, or periods. Until now, no comprehensive anthology covering representative works in the major genres from all three principal venues (China, Taiwan, and Hong Kong) for the entire modern period has yet been published.

That this anthology makes its appearance more than a decade after the Fourth Congress of Chinese Writers (1979) has turned out to be a blessing. Back in the mid-1930s, when Edgar Snow was gathering material for his *Living China: Modern Chinese Short Stories* (1937), he had to allow that "even if contemporary China has produced no great literature, there must be much of scientific and sociological interest, and for utilitarian purposes alone it ought to be made available to us."

If Snow were to do the selections today, he would not need to make any such allowances, for the kind of fiction and, for that matter, poetry that has emerged from China since the early 1980s needs no apologies. The new generation of writers, though no less concerned about the salvation of the country than their predecessors, have identified their own genius by severing ties with the critical-realist mode so fashionable during the 1920s and 1930s. The Chinese writers of the post-Mao era have entered a brave new world of narrative possibilities that enables them to circumvent political taboos and illuminate the realities of China through forms and techniques as diverse as parable, farce, modernism, avant-gardism, and, more recently, magical realism.

Modern Chinese literature is very much a barometer of the social, political, and historical conditions of its times. China's defeat in the Opium War (1839–1842) has generally been regarded by historians as the beginning of the end of imperial China. For the Chinese, who thought of their nation as the Middle Kingdom, the humiliation of being vanquished by British gunboats turned out to be more than a shattering experience. They began to realize, perhaps for the first time in their history, that their country was backward not only in science and technology but in social and political institutions as well. Confucianism, insofar as it was identified as China's state religion, coterminous with the concepts of altruism, compassion, and benevolence, was bankrupt precisely because it was perceived to be the very source of backwardness and resistance to change.

Years before Lu Xun published his first stories, a note of despair and resignation had been sounded in the works of the late-Qing novelists. Liu E (1857–1909), for example, ominously likened the fate of old China to a ship adrift on a turbulent sea in his novel *The Travels of Lao Can* (1907). Equally indicative of the temper of the times is *A Flower in a Sinful Sea* (1894) by Zeng Pu (1872–1935), who published his novel under the pen name The Sick Man of East Asia. China in his narrative is the Island of Happy Slavery, destined to sink into the Sea of Sin. Such apocalyptic visions are certain to have prompted Lu Xun to refer to China in 1922 as an "iron house without windows, absolutely indestructible, with many people fast asleep inside who will soon die of suffocation." Though the Manchu empire was overthrown in 1911, things did not improve much during the early Republican years. As we see in Ba Jin's "Dog" (1931), the self-image of the Chinese is one of pity and disgust. This tale, though artistically crude, serves as a yardstick to measure the degree of progress China made over the next decades in altering its status from a semicolonial state to an autonomous polity.

It is generally agreed that modern Chinese literature begins with Lu Xun. Appropriately, he called his first collection of stories, written between 1918 and 1922, *Call to Arms*. Burning with a zeal to expose the evils of feudal society, Lu Xun introduced an iconoclastic fervor that came to characterize the defiant spirit of May Fourth writers in "a nation afflicted with a spiritual disease and therefore unable to strengthen itself or change its set way of inhumanity," in the words of C. T. Hsia.

Smarting from the fiasco of the failed Boxer Uprising (1900), leading Chinese intellectuals of the May Fourth era were more convinced of the superior nature of Western civilization than were their late-Qing counterparts. They believed that China stood no chance of rejuvenation unless its hopelessly archaic political systems and social institutions were completely overhauled. Indeed, confidence in the health of traditional Chinese culture had sunk so low that drastic calls for Westernization, such as the Latinization of the Chinese language, were made issues of the day.

In the writings of the May Fourth period, modern China is modern only because it is coeval with the modern world, for it is still plagued by the bugbears of poverty, ignorance, lethargy, cowardice, selfishness, hypocrisy, cruelty, superstition, and corruption. By looking China's problems squarely in the eye, May Fourth writers defined the character of modern Chinese writing by their engaged spirit and an openness to trenchant self-criticism.

Not all Republican-era writers, to be sure, were interested in addressing the immediate concerns of the day—to the benefit of thematic diversity. Such diversity can be seen by comparing the respective thematic concerns of representative writers. For example, in the first period we have in Wen Yiduo a poet so despairing of China's stagnation that he likens it to "Dead Water" (1926). Dai Wangshu's stirring poem "Written on a Prison Wall" (1942) evokes the patriotic sentiments of his ancient predecessor Qu Yuan (340?–278 B.C.). In contrast, Xu Zhimo's love protestations and Li Jinfa's enigmatic ruminations strike us as otherworldly for their self-regarding propensities.

A similar variety of themes can be found in early fiction. While most of the May Fourth writers after Lu Xun tie feudalism to cannibalism and devote themselves one way or another to the cause of national salvation, Xu Dishan, as is evident in "The Merchant's Wife" [missing], appears to be more concerned with the salvation of the heroine's soul than with the glaring inequities that reduce her to her present misery. Shen Congwen, on the other hand, tests the possibilities of happiness for the woman after whom the story "Xiaoxiao" (1929) is named. She is situated in a patriarchal society governed by the rules of expediency and the impulse of charity, a natural order free from established moral dogmas and assumptions.

Writers of the first period are relatively free to indulge in personal interpretations of reality. Since the establishment of the People's Republic in 1949, however, writers have been denied the luxury of such individualist expression. Their perception of reality must conform to prescriptions laid down by Mao Zedong in his "Talks at the Yan'an Forum on Literature and Art" in 1942. People are divided into separate classes as antagonistic groups in society, according to Mao, and there will be no genuine love of humanity until classes are eliminated all over the world. Mao made it imperative that literature function in the service of politics.

With politics in command, much of the People's Republic of China (PRC) writing between the early 1950s and mid-1970s takes on a measure of the exemplum. The positive heroes and heroines in these staple outputs are invariably fearless, sexless, selfless, and untiring, ever ready to lay down their lives for the glory of the socialist cause. In Shi Ying's poem "The Mountain Girl Likes to Talk" (1963) we have a paradigm:

> Where is the home of the mountain girl?
> In the office of the production team,

At the broadcasting station of the village,
In the classroom of the village school . . .
She lives at all these places . . .
In the morning she goes home to the production team office,
Picks up the phone, and starts talking into it;
At noon she goes home to the broadcasting station to announce
The approaching storm of heavy snow and high winds at night;
But at night she goes home to the village school classroom,
Where an advanced class listens to her talk on a new poem.
A telephone messenger, a broadcaster, and a teacher,
All three rolled into one is she . . . [1]

One who lives at all these places has no "room of her own," and since she works three shifts respectively at the production team, the broadcasting station, and the village school, it is hard to imagine how she might have any time left for herself. She embodies all the qualities of a Chinese Communist exemplary heroine. Burdened with such ideological expectations, the literature of the Maoist era, particularly during the catastrophic years of the Cultural Revolution (1966–1976), cannot be expected to impress as a self-sufficient aesthetic entity, since its primary function was to celebrate the accomplishments of the new society.

However, one of the virtues of literature lies in its ability to create alternative worlds. But for the appearance of a number of gifted poets and fiction writers in Taiwan and Hong Kong, modern Chinese literature from the 1950s to the 1970s would have remained a closed world in which individual voices were summarily stifled. The Nationalist Government under Chiang Kai-shek was, of course, no model of democracy. By governmental decree, virtually all literature of the 1930s and 1940s from the mainland was proscribed, even though such measures did not inhibit aspiring writers from reading Lu Xun and other major underground figures, at considerable personal risk. Fortunately the government did not go so far as to follow Mao in proclaiming its version of the "Commandments" for writers to observe. Hence the possibility of alternate worlds, so long as such worlds were insulated from Communist evangelism.

In such a political climate, it is easy to see why young poets on Taiwan had to take a historical return—to the first flowering of modernist verse in the early 1930s, exemplified in the pioneering work of such Shanghai-based poets as Ji Xian and Dai Wangshu, who were associated with the journal *Xiandai* (*Les contemporains*). The self-reflexivity incidental to this mode of writing and its assumptive indifference to history and tradition liberated the Taiwan modernists

1. Kai-yu Hsu, ed., *Literature of the People's Republic of China* (Bloomington: Indiana University Press, 1980), p. 732.

from the burden of quotidian existence. It allowed their imaginations to soar beyond the confines of geography, nationality, race, even culture itself. Whatever their obsessions, each achieved a technical sophistication and stylistic finesse seldom realized in the work of their mainland counterparts during that period. By accentuating the unconscious and the mythopoeic, the Taiwan modernists affirmed the primacy of individual instincts over the collective consciousness, which define the Everyman in PRC literature during this period.

Few fiction writers from the mainland are represented in the second period. As with poetry, one must turn to Taiwan writers for samples of alternative worlds in fiction. Unlike poets, however, Taiwan novelists of this period did not strive to practice the art of modernism. Modernist strains, to be sure, are evident, but by and large, it can be said that Taiwan writers of the 1950s and 1960s stayed within the bounds of realistic and satirical writing of social conscience.

The Great Proletarian Cultural Revolution came to a close with Mao's demise in 1976. Encouraged by Deng Xiaoping's message to the Fourth Congress of Chinese Writers and Artists in 1979, calling for an "emancipation of thought" and the "smashing of spiritual shackles," new writing by daring young poets began to appear almost overnight. What strikes the reader more than the refreshing absence of sociopolitical dogma is the passion in asserting the sanctity of the self in artistic creations. As Gu Cheng explains to his father, Gu Gong: "The purpose behind portraying the world is to portray 'the self.' Your generation sometimes wrote about 'the self,' but this 'self' was always described as 'a pebble used to build roads,' a 'gear valve,' or 'a screw.' Is this 'self' human? No, it's only machinery."[2]

Refusing to be just a pebble, a gear valve, or a screw, the New Age poets cast off the service-oriented role of "cultural worker" that their immediate predecessors were obliged to play. For this reason, the generation of poets catapulted to national fame in the early 1980s, such as Bei Dao, Gu Cheng, Shu Ting, and Yang Lian, are bona fide artists, in that poetry for them is a medium for expressing individual visions and convictions rather than a vehicle for propagating certified truths. Much of their writing has been considered "misty" (*menglong*), a euphemism for obscurity. In point of fact, "misty poetry" has been a time-honored tradition in modern Chinese literature since the May Fourth era, as can be seen in the symbolist compositions of Li Jinfa. Of the Taiwan poets selected for this anthology, it must be conceded that Ye Weilian's metaphysical lines are no less "misty" than those of his peers in the PRC.

Obscurity denotes intense subjectivity of emotions on the part of the poet. For pioneers of the "misty art," ambiguity may be just a form of stylistic experimentalism. With the post-Mao obscurists, however, "mistiness" can be as much

2. Helen F. Siu and Zelda Stern, eds., *Mao's Harvest: Voices from China's New Generation* (New York: Oxford University Press, 1983), p. 13.

a preferred form of artistic expression as it is a measure of expedient politics to dodge the criticism of die-hard conservatives. The amorphous texture of their poems lends itself to multiple interpretations, the very stuff alternative worlds are made of.

In the words of Leo Ou-fan Lee, post-Mao Chinese poetry is energized by "a diversity of extreme sensibilities, a polyphony of new voices clamoring to be heard, a raw energy and a defiant spirit that can no longer be contained by any official campaigns. Given more time, China's younger poets will surely bring out a rich and varied harvest of poetic creation, the likes of which has not been witnessed during the past forty years" (*Red Azalea*, xxvii).

Equally impressive are the achievements of fiction writers in post-Mao China. Like the misty poets, the new-breed writers who attained national prominence in the mid-1980s are in their late thirties or early forties. Like "misty" writing, their texts can be just as resistant to formulaic interpretations. But whatever label is applied to identify the genius of their art, be it modernism, surrealism, or magical realism, they have at least one thing in common: their unceremonial representation of the human condition in present-day China.

Can Xue's is allegorically a claustrophobic miniaturist world of depravity and bestiality in which the protagonists behave like cornered animals in the heat of mutual laceration. Mo Yan, on the other hand, is noted for his unrestrained celebration of passion and his ties to the earth. Sex and violence often figure in his fiction as metaphors to reinvigorate the frayed nerves of the Chinese race, at times coming off paradoxically as modern agents of catharsis. In his own way, Han Shaogong is also concerned about Chinese racial quality: like Mo Yan, he believes that the mentality that spawned the atrocities of the Cultural Revolution represents a retrogression from civilization to barbarity on the part of his fellow countrymen. It is a sign of racial degeneracy. In "Woman Woman Woman," a novella too lengthy to include in this anthology, the putative heroine undergoes a cycle of counter-evolution, reduced to a fishlike "thing" in the end.

Such imagination of disaster signals a disquieting departure from the ameliorative optimism that characterizes, however grudgingly, most of the May Fourth writers. Lu Xun's madman has undergone several generic incarnations, but in the hands of the new generation of writers, he seems to have lost his power to plead the cause of the children. However, the apparent indifference to immediate social issues by these young writers need not be construed as an instance of muted conscience. It may be that, being brought up among the ruins of the Cultural Revolution on a steady diet of Socialist evangelism, they have now, thanks to a more tolerant political ethos, learned to live the life of the *étranger*, committed to no cause other than the sanctity of their art. Such unsentimental, nearly cynical, views of reality are common to their Taiwan and Hong Kong counterparts. Zhang Dachun's performance in "Lucky Worries About His Country," for instance, is remarkable not only for its amazing acrobatics of sardonicism but even more significantly for its unmistakable attempt at demythification. Sacred cows are an endangered species in post-Chiang Taiwan.

The Chinese fictional world has never witnessed such a diversity of themes, multiplicity of perspectives, or plenitude of "defamiliarized" emotions and sensibilities as have surfaced during the past few decades. Not all post-1980 fiction is necessarily modernistic, surrealistic, or "absurd," to be sure. In Chen Cun, for instance, the conventional storyteller's social instinct and narrative style are still alive; what appears to be missing is the wonted promise of millennium. In the hands of Qiao Dianyun [missing], humor is satirically black and savage. If illicit passion, in the memorable words of Denis de Rougemont, "means suffering," it is hard to find support in Zhu Tianwen's "Fin de Siècle Splendor." Perhaps feminism has redefined relationships between the sexes, or perhaps men and women are affected differently by the fin de siècle syndrome; whatever the case, it is clear that affairs become truly "casual" and guilt-free. Tie Ning's "Octday" does not deal with adultery, but the way the heroine takes her destiny into her own hands is a good measure of the progress Chinese women have made toward independence since the days of Ling Shuhua or Zhang Ailing. Such progress would not have been possible if the writers had not been allowed to go about their business as self-willed individuals. The existence of alternative worlds presupposes the autonomy of writers. It is gratifying to note that in the hands of the new generation, literature has finally vindicated itself as an independent artistic enterprise.

In their own way, the essays included in this volume also offer glimpses into the alternative worlds of modern Chinese literature. Whether it is in the *zawen* (topical essay) or *xiaopinwen* (familiar essay) form, the essay is happily an open form of composition, an ideal medium for transmitting personal impressions or reflections. Topical essays, in the useful description of D. E. Pollard, "are a vehicle for argument: they convey the author's reactions to (usually animadversions on) current events, issues and pronouncements, and past and present practices, personages, creeds: anything under the sun, in fact, so long as the thing has some relevance to the here and now."[3]

The familiar essay, on the other hand, is a natural form for the display of wit, humor, insight, erudition, intimate sentiments, personal quirks, and prejudices. One practical way to appreciate the characteristic differences between these two types of essay is to examine the "worlds" of the Zhou brothers, acknowledged masters of the two forms. Whatever topic Lu Xun (Zhou Shuren) elects to discuss, be it the kitchen god or the emperor, he often ends up using the past to "animadvert on" the present. In contrast, Zhou Zuoren's familiar

3. D. E. Pollard, "Translator's Introduction: Four Contemporary *Zawen*," *Renditions* 31 (Spring 1989): 148–150.

essays, such as "Reading on the Toilet" (1936), appear more leisurely and personal.

What should be noted in this connection is that some of our essayists are crossbred. Since form is dictated by content, a topical writer is always ready to switch style when the material at hand calls for a familiar expression. Lu Xun, for example, has written a number of essays so devoid of his habitual sarcasm and acerbity that they can be more appropriately placed in the category of familiar essay. In making the selections for this anthology, we have placed a higher priority on the familiar essay, for we believe that the casual, sensible, and commonsensical nature inherent in this form will be more appealing to the general reader.

Quantitatively and qualitatively, the golden age of the essay was the 1920s and 1930s. Topical essays all but disappeared in China during the Maoist era. Since these essays have a vested interest in "hostile contradictions," as Pollard has put it, their existence would be hard to justify in a new society where all contradictions are presumably eliminated. But familiar essays did not fare much better in an era in which the entire country was engaged in Socialist construction; it is hard to believe that this type of essay, which makes a virtue of wishful indulgence, would be allowed to flourish.

It is small wonder, then, as with poetry and fiction, that the most successful practitioners of this genre from the 1950s to the 1970s were those who published in Taiwan. Among the veterans, Lin Yutang and Liang Shiqiu remained active after 1949 in the United States and Taiwan, respectively. For this reason, we have included their works of both the first and the second periods, with a view to demonstrating the continuum as well as the vitality of the familiar-essay tradition. They have worthy successors in Yu Guangzhong and Yang Mu, who, like the May Fourth masters, not only are at home in classical Chinese but are also comfortable in Western literature.

Except for Dong Qiao's piece [missing], which further attests to the undiminished vigor of the genre, the rest of the entries in the last period cannot formally be considered familiar essays. Each account confides a spiritual trauma related to the calamities of the Cultural Revolution. With Ba Jin and Wen Jieruo, the suffering is all the more intense because the authors are witness to the deaths of loved ones after being savaged by Red Guards.

We regret that space constraints have precluded the inclusion of drama. The best dramatic works are, unfortunately, multiple-act plays, and excerpts of any literary piece permit no more than a fragmented experience. Since most of the major plays of this century have been translated into English, it would be a disservice to the appreciation of modern Chinese drama if they were presented in truncated form. For the same reason, we have included no excerpts from novels. Many of the best have been, and will continue to be, translated in separate volumes for Western readers.

BIOGRAPHICAL SKETCHES

While Pinyin spellings have been used throughout, preferred or commonly used spellings for the names of writers from Taiwan, Hong Kong, etc., are given before their dates or in the text.

AI QING (1910–1996) At nineteen, Ai Qing (Jiang Haicheng) went to France to study painting, supporting himself by painting porcelains. The works of the French symbolists and other Western poets changed the interest of his pursuits, and he decided to become a poet rather than a painter. Returning to Shanghai in 1932, he joined the League of Left-Wing Artists. Found to be harboring "incendiary ideas," he was detained for a number of months in the French concession. Adopting the pen name Ai Qing, he wrote poetry in prison. His reputation has suffered in recent years for his attack on the so-called "misty" poets of the late 1970s, who have now become internationally famous.

ALAI (1959–) Born in what is now Sichuan Province, Alai comes from a Tibetan peasant family. After graduating from a normal college, he taught primary school in a rural village. His writing career began in the early 1980s as a poet, but he turned to fiction, producing several volumes of short stories. His first novel, *Chenai luoding* (translated into English as *Red Poppies*), won a major national award; he has followed that with a series of novellas set in contemporary Tibet and dealing with Tibetan history and culture.

BA JIN (1904–2005) Ba Jin (Li Feigan) was catapulted to national fame with the publication of his first major novel, *Family* (1933). However, his popularity with young readers in the 1930s did not rest so much with his craft as with the humanitarian impulses that identify his writing. He once openly confessed that he was not an artist, since he had little patience for such matters as style and technique. He was interested in speaking for the demeaned and injured—in his own words, to "strike a blow against darkness." The story "Dog" is as historically significant as Yu Dafu's "Sinking." Melodramatic in tone, it is nonetheless a powerful allegorization of a once proud people that has gone to the dogs.

BAI QIU (Pai Ch'iu, 1937–) Bai Qiu (He Jinrong) was a primary-school student in Taiwan under the Japanese occupation. When the island was returned to China in 1945, he was literate only in Japanese. Yet he marked his first triumph in Chinese writing with *Death of the Moth* (1959). Though associated with the Modernist School and the Blue Stars Society during the early stages of his career, Bai Qiu found his independent voice in the sixties in *Bamboo Hat*, a magazine established to promote nativist sentiments in Taiwan poetry. He is now a professional interior designer.

BAI XIANYONG (Pai Hsien-yung, 1937–) Bai Xianyong's family background affords him privileged insights into the disinherited dramatis personae of Republican China that he portrays: he is the son of General Bai Chongxi. After the Communist takeover in 1949, he moved with his family to Taiwan. He holds a degree in Western literature from National Taiwan University and a master's degree in fine arts from the University of Iowa. Now professor emeritus of Chinese at the University of California, Santa Barbara, he is considered by some to be the preeminent stylist of his generation. His novel *Niezi* (translated into English as *Crystal Boys*) gained fame as a major work dealing with homosexual themes.

BEI DAO (1949–) Though better known as a *menglong*, or "misty" poet, Bei Dao (Zhao Zhenkai) is also a noted story writer whose writing is nurtured by mixed feelings of anxious anticipation and muted fury. A Red Guard at the beginning of the Cultural Revolution, he began writing poetry in 1970. His poems first appeared in *Today*, a typescript magazine that he cofounded in Beijing. With Gu Cheng and Yang Lian, Bei Dao is one of the most frequently translated Chinese poets. Since 1989 he has lived in involuntary exile in the West. He is currently a professor of creative writing at the University of Notre Dame.

BIAN ZHILIN (1910–2000) Bian Zhilin graduated in Western literature from Beijing University in 1933. His early poems are dense with loving images of the ancient capital. When war with Japan broke out, he worked with northwestern youth groups in their Resist Japan campaigns. As the poet became more involved with the exigencies of the times, so did his poetry. He joined the Communist Party in 1956. Bian also translated from English and French literature.

CAN XUE (1953–) Can Xue (Deng Xiaohua)'s imagination of disaster can be understood only in parabolic terms. "Hut on the Mountain," arguably one of the most enigmatic pieces of post-Mao fiction, thrives on the nature of its thematic indeterminacy. Can Xue, whose family was a target of the Anti-Rightist Campaign in 1957, suffered much during the Cultural Revolution. Many of her stories have been translated into English.

CHEN CUN (1954–) In China, Zhang San (Zhang the Third) is often mentioned in the same breath as Li Si (Li the Fourth) to designate the nondescript Everyman. A dry, laconic language with deliberate repetitious lapses is used to narrate a Sisyphean existence. Though the protagonist is habitually referred to as Zhang San, the tone in "A Story" differs discernibly from other Zhang San stories, if only because the subject it confronts is insufferably violent.

CHEN JINGHUA Little is known about Chen, a commune member during the Cultural Revolution.

CHEN KEHUA (1961–) A practicing ophthalmologist, Chen began writing poetry in 1976 and has won several awards for his work.

CHEN RUOXI (Ch'en Jo-hsi, 1938–) Born in Taiwan into a proletarian family, Chen (Chen Xiumei) majored in Western literature at National Taiwan University. Upon graduation, she furthered her studies at Mount Holyoke College and Johns Hopkins University. In 1966, after obtaining her M.A. degree, she left for Nanjing, where she taught English until 1973, during the Cultural Revolution. "The Tunnel" offers a glimpse of Chinese life in those days. After leaving China, Chen stayed in Hong Kong for a year before emigrating to Canada and later to the United States. Her stories recollecting the experiences of her years in China have been translated into English as *The Execution of Mayor Yin*.

CHEN YINGZHEN (Ch'en Ying-chen, 1936–) Chen Yingzhen (born Chen Yongshan) graduated from Tamkang College in 1960. He was convicted on charges of "subversive activities" by the Nationalist government in 1968 and given a ten-year sentence. The death of Chiang Kai-shek in 1975 brought about an amnesty, and Chen was released in September of that year. His fiction of the 1960s, as represented by "My Kid Brother Kangxiong," is dominated by narcissism and nihilism, bearing testimony to the author's loss of faith in the capitalist order in general and disenchantment with the Nationalist government in particular.

CHUN SUE (Chun Shu, 1983–) "Born at the Right Time" was published as chapter 2 of the "linglei" (counterculture) novel *Beijing Doll* (*Beijing wawa*), written when the author was seventeen. A best seller in China, the novel chronicles the sexually promiscuous rock 'n' roll lifestyle of a high school dropout.

DAI TIAN (Tai Ti'en, 1937–) Dai (Dai Chengyi) spent his childhood in Mauritius. He came to Taiwan in 1957 to study in the Department of Western Languages and Literatures at National Taiwan University. Like many of his contemporaries, he attended the University of Iowa's International Writing

Program. He has served as editor of the book section of the Chinese edition of *Reader's Digest*. At present he is chief editor of the *Hong Kong Economic Monthly*.

DAI WANGSHU (1905–1950) Dai Wangshu (Dai Chaocai)'s earliest publications during his high school days "amount[ed] to little more than a couple of humorous anecdotes in dialogue form" (Gregory Lee). It was only as a student at Shanghai University that he turned to writing poetry. He became so enamored of the French language that he decided to study in France (1932–1935). After the outbreak of the Sino-Japanese War in 1937, Dai took refuge in Hong Kong, where he served as an editor of a leading newspaper. After the British Colony fell to the Japanese, Dai was imprisoned and tortured for his anti-Japanese sentiments.

DING LING (1907–1986) Following the death of her father when she was four years old, Ding Ling (Jiang Bingzhi) learned her lessons in modern Chinese womanhood from her independent mother. After spending a year at Shanghai College, in 1924, Ding Ling left for Beijing, where she met her future husband, Hu Yepin, one of five Communist martyrs shot by the Nationalist police on February 7, 1931. The author's outspokenness about the stark realities of Yan'an life became the cause of her downfall during the Anti-Rightist Campaign in 1957. She was rehabilitated in the late 1970s.

FENG ZHI (1905–1993) Feng Zhi began writing for literary journals as a student at Beijing University. From 1930 to 1935 he was in Germany studying literature and philosophy. A devotee of the sonnet form, Feng distinguished himself as a "story poet" during the early stages of his career. After his return from Germany he taught at a number of universities. He joined the Communist Party in 1956 and was appointed director of the Foreign Literature Institute at the prestigious Academy of Social Sciences in 1964.

FENG ZIKAI (1898–1975) Essayist, painter, and translator. Feng's brush drawings won a large and affectionate following among children in the 1930s. After graduating from Hangzhou First Normal School, he went to Japan in 1921 to study Western painting and music. He taught at a number of universities from 1939 to 1943, then devoted most of the 1950s to writing and translating.

GAO XINGJIAN (1940–) Gao was born in 1940 in Jiangxi Province, where he went to school. He earned a university degree in French at Beijing University and began his writing career soon after, gaining fame as the author of avant-garde dramas, most notably the play *Bus Stop*. In 1987, he chose exile in France, where he completed his novel *Soul Mountain* (1990). That was followed by the novel *One Man's Bible* (1999). In 1992 he was named a Chevalier de l'Ordre des Arts et des Lettres by the French government. In 2000 he was awarded the Nobel Prize for Literature. He is a playwright and painter as well as a fiction writer and critic. He lives in Paris.

GU CHENG (1956–1993) One of the well-known "misty poets," Gu Cheng was the son of Gu Gong, also a poet. During the Cultural Revolution, the Gu family was sent down to the countryside, where Gu Cheng worked as a swineherd for four years. His first poems were published in *Today*. A member of the Chinese Writers Association, after the Tian'anmen Square crackdown in 1989 he and his wife took up residence in New Zealand, where he committed suicide in 1993. His poetry has been translated into many Western languages.

HAN SHAOGONG (1953–) Streaks of pessimism are evident in Han Shaogong's works, particularly "Ba Ba Ba" (1986) and "Woman Woman Woman" (1986), in which the Chinese race is seen to be on the threshold of degeneration. Han's narrative technique has been likened to the magical realism of Gabriel García Márquez. He has lived on Hainan Island since the 1989 Tian'anmen Square crackdown.

HE QIFANG (1912–1977) He Qifang received a sound education in the Chinese classics at home. In 1931 he was enrolled at Beijing University as a student of philosophy, and it was during this period that he began writing poetry and essays. In the summer of 1938, a year after the outbreak of the Sino-Japanese War, He journeyed from Chengdu to Yan'an, became a member of the Communist Party, and began teaching at the Lu Xun Arts Institute. He was sent down to a "Cadre School" for re-education in the countryside during the Cultural Revolution.

HUA TONG Hua Tong is the pen name of Lin Zhengyi, a writer attached to the military. He was several years older than the urban youth generation, and was not himself rusticated. He lives in Liaoning Province.

HUANG CHUNMING (Huang Ch'un-ming, 1935–) Huang has been a rebel since childhood when, unable to bear the hardships of living with a stepmother, he ran away from home. He attended Taipei Normal College to prepare himself for a teaching career, only to be dismissed for "unruly behavior." Huang's childhood experiences have nurtured his deep sympathy for the weak and downtrodden. His most memorable characters are country folk or urbanites with no intellectual pretensions.

HUANG GUOBIN (Wong Kwok-pun, 1946–) In order to read Western poetry in the original, Huang learned French, German, Italian, and Spanish. He holds a B.A. in English from the University of Hong Kong and a Ph.D. from the University of Toronto. In addition to ten collections of poetry, he is the author of three volumes of poetry criticism. He is at present a senior lecturer in translation at Hong Kong's Lingnan College.

JI XIAN (Chi Hsien, 1913–) Ji Xian (Lu Yu)'s earliest pen name was Lu-yi-shi ("Louis" in transliteration). An advocate of wholesale Westernization in modern Chinese poetry, he was looked upon as a high priest of modernism in Taiwan poetry in the early fifties, after leaving Shanghai in 1948. Ji Xian taught middle school until his retirement in 1974 and now lives in California.

LAI HE (Lai Ho, 1894–1943) The first modern writer in Taiwan, he received a traditional education in the Chinese classics before attending medical school and starting a career as a doctor. He spent several years in Amoy, on the mainland, where he was influenced by the May Fourth movement. He fell afoul of the Japanese colonial administration in Taiwan, was imprisoned, and died soon after his release. Although his published output was relatively sparse (fifteen stories, thirteen modern poems, and sixteen essays), he has been called the "Father of Taiwan's new literature."

LAO SHE (1899–1966) Lao She (Shu Qingchun) is best known to the West for his novel *Camel Xiangzi* (1938) (translated by Evan King as *Rickshaw Boy* in 1945). Born into an indigent Manchu family in Beijing and orphaned as a child, Lao She left China in 1924 to teach Chinese at the University of London. There he produced three works that distinguished him as a novelist of earthy humor and sardonic wit. He continued writing with renewed energy after his return to China in 1930. From then until 1937, when China went to war, he wrote a number of novels that secured his position as one of the leading novelists of his time. Lao She died at the hands of the Red Guards on August 24, 1966.

LI ANG (1952–) Considered "the most consistent, successful, and influential writer of sexual fiction in Chinese" (Howard Goldblatt 1990), Li Ang (Shi Shuduan) is the author of *The Butcher's Wife* (1985), a novella that "shows the influence of the modernist aesthetic in its highly sensational treatment of such primitive instincts as hunger and lust." After graduating from the College of Chinese Culture, she earned a master's degree in drama at Oregon State University. Li Ang, author of several influential novels, teaches at her Taiwanese alma mater.

LI JINFA (Li Shuliang, 1900–1976) Li Jinfa caught his Chinese readers' attention by his pen name, which is literally Li the Blond Hair. After finishing middle school in the British system in Hong Kong, Li went to France in 1919 to study sculpture. Influenced by French symbolist poets such as Baudelaire and Verlaine, he began writing poetry in 1920. Regarded as an eccentric by his contemporaries, Li bequeathed a viable legacy to later poets by his pioneering experiments in modernist poetry.

LI RUI (1950–) Like the majority of young Chinese writers who emerged onto the literary scene in the mid-1980s, Li Rui had no formal education beyond middle school. In 1969 he was sent down as an "educated youth" to Shanxi for a different kind of education. The material for "Electing a Thief" is drawn from his experience and observation of life in Liangshan, where he lived for six years. His most significant work to date is the historical novel *Jiuzhi* (translated into English as *Silver City*).

LIANG SHIQIU (Liang Shih-ch'iu, 1901–1987) A prominent essayist, Liang Shiqiu (Liang Zhihua) was also the translator of the complete works of Shakespeare, a project that took thirty-seven years to complete. He attended the University of Colorado as a senior in the English department, then spent a year each doing research at Harvard University and Columbia University.

He returned to China, where he served as chairman of the English departments at Beijing University and Beijing Normal University. Liang followed the Nationalist government to Taiwan in 1949 and taught at Taiwan Normal University until his retirement in 1966.

LIN YUTANG (1895–1976) To Western readers Lin Yutang is the author of such popular books as *My Country and My People*, *The Importance of Living*, and *The Importance of Understanding*. A bilingual author, Lin graduated from Shanghai's St. John's University. He taught at Qinghua University and Beijing University before pursuing graduate work at Harvard in the United States and Leipzig in Germany, where he obtained his doctorate. He came to the United States after China declared war on Japan, staying until 1954, when he was appointed chancellor at Nanyang University in Singapore. He spent the last years of his life in Taiwan and Hong Kong.

LING SHUHUA (1904–1990) Ling Shuhua's father was a scholar-poet and ranking mandarin in the last days of the Chinese empire. Her mother was the fourth of five concubines. Ling's first stories were published in *Contemporary Review* while she was a student of English literature at Yanjing University. After World War II she took up residence in London with her diplomat husband, Chen Yuan. "The Night of Midautumn Festival" shows her psychological understanding of protagonists caught between claims of personal loyalty and marital priorities.

LIU HENG (1954–) Liu Heng (Liu Guanjun) was brought up in the midst of the Cultural Revolution. After graduating from high school, he was sent as an "educated youth" to work in the countryside. He also served in the army. "Dogshit Food" was a national award-winning story in China in 1985–1986. The movie *Ju Dou* was based on Liu's 1988 novella *Fuxi Fuxi*. His novels *Black Snow* and *Green River Daydreams* have been well received in the West. Liu is currently an editor of *Beijing Literature*.

LIU YICHANG (1918–) A veteran editor and writer, Liu Yichang (Liu Tongyi) graduated from Shanghai's St. John's University. Before settling in Hong Kong in 1957, he lived and worked in Singapore. He has published several volumes of essays, short stories, and novels and is at present editor of the magazine *Hong Kong Literature*.

LU XUN (1881–1936) Lu Xun (Zhou Shuren) is the most famous and influential of modern Chinese writers. Appalled by the practice of traditional Chinese medicine, he studied Western medicine in Japan, where he discovered that what his fellow countrymen needed was not so much physical health as spiritual awakening. As a first step he and his younger brother, Zhou Zuoren, published a two-volume set of translations from European writings, only to be deeply distressed by its poor reception. In 1909 he returned to China, where, at the insistence of an editor friend, he resumed writing. His first story, "The Diary of a Madman" (1918), was a landmark in modern Chinese fiction for its savage commentary on traditional Chinese culture and society.

A prolific *zawen* (topical essay) writer, Lu Xun was also a pioneer scholar of traditional Chinese fiction.

LUO FU (Lo Fu, 1928–) Luo Fu (Mo Luofu) graduated from the Department of English of Tamkang College. He was a Navy broadcasting reporter and a liaison officer in Taiwan and in Vietnam. He is most readily identified with *Death in the Stone Cell* (1964), a collection of poems that puzzled as much as dazzled his contemporaries with its savage imagery and uncompromising obscurity. Luo Fu was a founder of the *Epoch Poetry Quarterly*, which exerted tremendous influence on Taiwan's young poets.

LUO QING (Lo Ch'ing, 1948–) Luo Qing (Luo Qingzhe) is a professional painter. He launched his poetic career with a collection titled *Six Ways of Eating Watermelons* in 1972. After college in Taiwan, he received an M.A. from the University of Washington in comparative literature. He is at present on the faculty of National Taiwan Normal University.

LUO ZHICHENG (Lo Chih-cheng, 1955–) Born in Taipei, Luo studied philosophy at National Taiwan University. He received his Ph.D. from the University of Wisconsin, Madison. An active figure in media business, he heads a publishing house in Taiwan. Since 1975 he has published seven collections of poetry.

MAO DUN (1896–1981) Mao Dun (Shen Yanbing)'s literary career took a bureaucratic turn after the establishment of the People's Republic of China in 1949. Appropriate to his positions in various governmental and cultural organizations, including a lengthy tenure as minister of culture (1949–1965), his post-1949 output consisted mostly of speeches, reports, directives, or brief comments on literature. Yet there is no question about his place as one of modern China's top novelists, by virtue of his pre-1949 accomplishments. "Spring Silkworms" has as its theme the bankruptcy of the rural economy and the futility of individual effort in competing for survival with foreign industry.

MO YAN (1955–) Mo Yan (Guan Moye) is of peasant stock from Shandong Province. Before joining the People's Liberation Army in 1976, he worked part-time at a linseed oil factory. He graduated from the literature department of the Armed Forces Cultural Academy in 1986 and became a member of the Chinese Writers Association that same year. He began to win national recognition in the mid-1980s with such stories as "The Crystal Carrot," but it was his first novel, *Red Sorghum*, that established his international reputation. The movie version of this work was named best film at the Berlin Film Festival in 1988. In recent years, he has published a string of powerful novels, historical and contemporary, for which he has been awarded several international prizes.

MU DAN (1918–1977) Mu Dan (Zha Liangzheng) graduated from National Southwest Associated University in 1940. From 1949 to 1952 he was a graduate student in the Department of English at the University of Chicago.

Returning to China in 1953, he taught at Nankai University. Branded an "anti-revolutionary" for publishing "Nine Schools of Thought Compete to Bloom" in *People's Daily*, he suffered a salary cut and a demotion in rank. He was posthumously rehabilitated in 1979.

QIU MIAOJIN (Ch'iu Miao-chin, 1969–1995) Born in central Taiwan, Qiu graduated from the National Taiwan University Department of Psychology and continued her studies in Paris. Though she lived a short life, she left a rich corpus of fiction that expresses a lesbian's views of love and hate. *Letters from Montmartre* was published a year after her suicide in France.

SHEN CONGWEN (1902–1988) Born of Miao (Hmong) ancestry in West Hunan in 1902, Shen Congwen was at once an established novelist, a university professor, and in later years, an expert on ancient Chinese costume. Yet he had little formal education. After serving in the army, he went to Beijing at the age of twenty to seek his fortune in a literary career. His varied experience as a soldier and his personal knowledge of the simple virtues of China's aboriginal tribes were great assets to his writing. "Xiaoxiao" effectively demonstrates the author's unique style and personal conviction regarding the possibility of living a moral life on one's own terms. After 1949 Shen gave up fiction and devoted himself to historical research. His *Researches Into Ancient Chinese Costume* (1981) has been acclaimed as a pioneering study.

SHI ZHECUN (1905–2003) Shi Zhecun's fictional work departs in large measure from the main current of modern Chinese fiction in that his material has little to do with the harsh realities of his time. He is not a typical writer who, in the famous phrase of C. T. Hsia, is "obsessed with China." In "One Evening in the Rainy Season" he is obsessed, to be sure, but with the nervous manifestations of the individual psyche suffering from repressed sexuality or thwarted desire. For this he is often identified as a "decadent" writer. He studied French literature in college and edited the monthly *Les contemporains*. Shi gave up creative writing for a university career after 1937.

SHU TING (1952–) Shu Ting (Gong Peiyu)'s junior high school education was disrupted and she was sent to the countryside during the Cultural Revolution. In the early 1970s, she supported herself with a number of odd jobs, including assignments in textile and lightbulb factories. She is now a member of the Chinese Writers Association and has traveled extensively in Europe and the United States.

SU TONG (1963–) Su Tong (Tong Zhonggui), a graduate of Beijing Normal University, currently works as an editor in Nanjing. One of his stories, "Wives and Concubines," was adapted for the movie *Raise the Red Lantern*. *Rice*, a novel, was awarded the 1991 Mao Dun Prize for fiction. His most recent translated work in the historical novel *My Life as Emperor*.

SYMAN RAPONGAN (1957–) Born on Taiwan's Lanyu Island as a member of the Tao tribe, he was previously known by his Chinese name, Shi Nulai. A graduate of the Department of French Literature at National Qinghua

University, he became a schoolteacher and served as a member of the Taipei Municipal Aboriginal Affairs Committee. He began writing fiction and essays in 1992, for which he has received important literary prizes.

TIE NING (1957–) Tie Ning began writing diaries when she was a second-grade student. A voracious reader, she read a great many literary classics in her childhood. She graduated from high school in 1975 and joined the Communist Party in the same year. She is a member of the Chinese Writers Association. Written from a feminist perspective, "Octday" lampoons an old-fashioned social attitude that automatically regards the woman as victim in a divorce.

WANG ANYI (1954–) Born in Nanjing, Wang moved with her mother to Shanghai in 1955. She spent much of the Cultural Revolution in rural Anhui Province. She has been a performer and an editor, but is now a full-time writer, among the most prolific, popular, and respected in contemporary China. Her stories and novels, normally set in Shanghai, are known for their keen evocation of place and lifestyle. The novel *Changhen ge* (*A Song of Everlasting Love*), which follows the life of a 1930s beauty contest winner and makes the city of Shanghai come alive, has become a modern classic. "Nanny" is the opening chapter of her 2000 novel of Shanghai citizens, *Fuping*.

WANG MENG (1934–) Wang became a member of the Communist Party in 1948, at the age of thirteen. An idealist, he published "A Newcomer to the Organization Department" in 1956, a story exposing bureaucratic incompetence and corruption. "Interfering in Life and Searching for Truth" had him in deep water, and he was exiled to a Uighur peasant village for twenty years. He made a remarkable comeback after 1976: appointed minister of culture in 1986, he was dismissed after the Tian'anmen Square crackdown in 1989 for his liberal views on art and politics. He continues to write.

WANG RUOWANG (1917–2001) A native of Jiangsu Province, Wang spent several years in a KMT prison after joining the League of Leftist Writers in 1933. Twenty years later, under the new government, he served as deputy editor in chief of *Literature Monthly*, which he published essays and other pieces that resulted in his being labeled a rightist. He suffered grievously during the Cultural Revolution, after which he was appointed to the board of the magazine *Shanghai Literature*. In 1987 he was expelled from the Communist Party.

WANG XIAOLONG (1954–) Wang Xiaolong founded the Experimental Poetry Society in 1980. In the words of Edward Morin, "The purview he communicates in poetry has been termed 'non- emotionalization.' With philosophical underpinnings in existentialism, he suggests that man has no privileged place in the universe and may be living a life no more meaningful than an insect's."

WANG XIPENG Little is known about Wang, a commune member during the Cultural Revolution.

WANG ZENGQI (1920–1998) Wang Zengqi studied Chinese literature with Shen Congwen at National Southwest Associated University from 1939 to 1943. His first published work of fiction was in fact an exercise in Shen's class. He was appointed editor of *Beijing Literature* in 1950 and *Folk Literature* in 1955. Wang, who has published three volumes of short stories, is also a well-known essayist.

WANG ZHENHE (Wang Chen-ho, 1940–1990) Educated at National Taiwan University, Wang Zhenhe attended the University of Iowa's International Writing Program from 1972 to 1973. With "An Oxcart for a Dowry" he distinguished himself from other Taiwanese writers by using a local dialect largely invented to achieve a comic effect. In the author's own translation, the characters' names are "rendered" into English equivalents rather than transliterated. Thus, Wangfa becomes "Prosperity," Jian becomes "Screw," and Ahao is "Nice." For the sake of consistency and faithfulness, in this version the personal names have been romanized and some missing sentences restored. His novel *Rose, Rose, I Love You* is one of the finest comic satires ever written in Chinese.

WEN JIERUO (1927–) Wen Jieruo attended primary school in Tokyo from 1934 to 1936. After returning to Beijing, she was placed in a Japanese primary school until 1940. She graduated from Qinghua University in 1950 with a degree in Western literature. Wen and her husband, the journalist Xiao Qian (1910–1999), suffered greatly at the hands of Red Guards during the Cultural Revolution. "Living Hell" is a chapter from her memoirs about that catastrophe.

WEN YIDUO (1899–1946) Wen Yiduo was given a solid classical Chinese education by his parents and tutors before being exposed to Western literature as a student at Qinghua University. From 1922 to 1925 he studied painting in the United States, an experience tempered by his impressions of racial prejudice. He returned to China determined to spearhead social and political changes to better the common lot of his countrymen through literature. He died a victim of political assassination for his outspokenness.

WONG MAN (1971–) Born in Wuhan, Hubei, Wong came to Hong Kong in 1986 and began writing poetry two years later.

WU ZHUOLIU (Wu Cho-liu, 1900–1976) Born into a Hakka scholar-gentry family in Xinzhu, Taiwan, Wu graduated from a normal college and became a teacher. He resigned as a result of a futile protest against a Japanese supervisor and traveled to the Chinese mainland, where he worked as a reporter. Upon his return to Taiwan, he continued working as a reporter; his short stories often have a distinctive journalistic flavor. Wu wrote fiction for more than three decades; his most famous work, the anti-Japanese novel *Yaxiya de gu'er* (1943–1945) has appeared in English as *Orphan of Asia*.

WU ZUXIANG (1908–1994) Wu, a professor of Chinese literature at Beijing University, was active in literary research and criticism from the early 1940s. One of the most gifted writers of the 1930s, he is remembered by a handful of stories that have set a standard for excellence in modern Chinese fiction. From Lu Xun onward, many Chinese writers have dealt with the suffering of Chinese peasants at the hands of rapacious landlords and corrupt government officials. But no one comes close to Wu in his mastery of savage irony and an ability to translate incidents of class antagonism into metaphors of cannibalism.

XI CHUAN (1963–) Xi Chuan (Liu Jun), born in Jiangsu Province, graduated from the English department of Beijing University in 1985. After working as an editor at *Globe* magazine, he became a teacher of English and classical Chinese literature at the Central Institute of Fine Arts. Through his published poetry, essays, and translations in official and unofficial, mainstream and avant-garde outlets, he has become a major presence in contemporary PRC poetry. He is an editor at the New China News Agency.

XI XI (1938–) Xi Xi (Zhang Yan) was born in Shanghai. After graduating from Hong Kong's Graham College of Education, she taught school until 1979, then turned to full-time writing. Publications include a novel and a number of collections of essays, stories, and poetry. Her sensitive reading of the female psyche is acutely registered in "A Woman Like Me," which was awarded the first prize for fiction by Taiwan's *United Daily* in 1982.

XIA YU (HSIA YÜ, 1956–) Xia Yu was born in Taiwan, but now divides her time between Paris and Taipei. She received a B.A. in film and drama from National Arts College, and has worked in television and theater. She makes a living as a lyricist and translator, and is the author of four volumes of poetry.

XIAO HONG (1911–1942) Xiao Hong (Zhang Naiying) was born to a landlord family in Heilongjiang, Northeast China. She rose to eminence by virtue of her first novel, *The Field of Life and Death* (1935). The story "Hands" is the most artistically accomplished of Xiao Hong's short fiction. From 1936 to 1940, the early years of the Sino-Japanese War, she led the somewhat bohemian existence that characterized most of her adult life. She died in a Hong Kong hospital on January 22, 1942, slightly over a month after the British Colony fell into Japanese hands.

XIAO WENYUAN (1933–) Xiao Wenyuan graduated from the Chinese Department of Nankai University in 1956 and is at present a research fellow of Tianjin's Writers Association. His publications include fiction, essays, and poetry.

XIONG HONG (Hsiung Hung, 1940–) Considered one of Taiwan's best lyricists, Xiong Hong (Hu Meizi) published her first poems when she was fifteen. "She is the poet of the light touch and is often labeled by critics a member of the School of Elegance," in Chi Pang-yuan's words. She graduated from National Taiwan Normal University with a B.A. in fine arts and, in 1974, attended the International Writing Program at the University of Iowa.

XU ZHIMO (1895–1931) Considered by some the greatest poet of his generation, Xu Zhimo could also be the most romantic. As noted by Kai-yu Hsu, "In the barely ten years of his productive (and prolific) life, he championed a total liberation of man's soul, a complete realization of man's pursuit of beauty, and an unreserved surrender of oneself to love." Educated at Columbia and Cambridge universities, Xu died in a plane crash en route from Shanghai to Beijing.

YANG LIAN (1955–) Yang Lian was born in Bern, Switzerland, while his parents were at the Chinese Embassy there. Sent down to the countryside during the Cultural Revolution, he began to write "modernist" poetry in 1976. His early poems were published in the magazine *Today*. Some of his poetry collections were banned in early 1987. Since the 1989 Tian'anmen Square crackdown, Yang and his family have lived as self-exiles in New Zealand, Australia, and Europe.

YANG MU (1940–) Few poets in Yang Mu (C. H. Wang)'s generation have enjoyed his fame as an essayist. Along with Yu Guangzhong, he is considered one of the finest poet-essayists in modern Chinese literature. A graduate of Tunghai University in Taichung, Taiwan, he has an M.F.A. from the University of Iowa and a Ph.D. from the University of California, Berkeley. He has been professor of Chinese and comparative literature at the University of Washington and dean of arts at Taiwan's Tunghua University. He is now at the Academic Sinica.

YE SHAOJUN (1894–1988) Known later in his career as Ye Shengtao, Ye Shaojun is noted for his characterization of the "unheroic hero" in language that appears plain and reserved, yet is taut with emotional undertones. His fondness for understatement belies his passionate commitment to bettering the plight of the poor and the oppressed. His was a China plagued by the bugbears of superstition, ignorance, moral inertia, residual feudalism, and an anachronistic value system. Such legacies of his benighted country are most effectively dramatized in "A Posthumous Son."

YE WEILIAN (1937–) Ye Weilian (known in the West as Wai-lim Yip) made a name for himself as a poet during the late 1950s when he was a student of English at National Taiwan University. After earning an M.A. at National Taiwan Normal University, he continued his studies in the United States, obtaining an M.F.A. and the Ph.D. from the University of Iowa and Princeton University, respectively. He is at present professor of comparative literature at the University of California, San Diego.

YIP FAI (1952–) Yip Fai is the pen name for Yip Tak Fai. He has been a freelance writer for more than thirty years and has edited several poetry journals. He is the general manager of a newspaper publisher.

YU DAFU (1896–1945) What sets Yu Dafu apart from his contemporaries is, as is evident in "Sinking," a frank recognition of the extent to which human behavior can be affected by the sex drive. Among May Fourth writers, no one went further in treating sexuality as a serious matter for contemplation. The suicide of the autobiographical hero, to all appearances a self-pitying paranoid, takes on a parabolic meaning when he attributes the cause of his suffering to the general debilities and impotence of China. In line with the fashion of the day, Yu Dafu received his college education in Japan. Considered a decadent writer for his escapist sentiments, he made a fresh impression when the Sino-Japanese War broke out (1937) by joining the national front against Japanese aggression, working as a newspaper editor in Singapore. When that city fell into Japanese hands in 1942 he fled to Sumatra, where he continued his patriotic activities until the Japanese military police tracked him down and killed him.

YU GUANGZHONG (Yu Kwang-chung, 1928–) Poet, essayist, critic, and translator, Yu Guangzhong is one of the most prolific and acclaimed writers in Taiwan. He went there as a refugee college student from the mainland in 1950 and completed his study in Western literature at National Taiwan University. He holds an M.F.A. from the University of Iowa. Twice a Fulbright visiting professor of Chinese literature in the United States, Yu is at present professor of Western literature at National Sun Yatsen University in Kaohsiung, Taiwan.

YU HUA (1960–) After graduation from high school in 1977, Yu Hua performed dental services for five years before turning to writing. His first efforts were published in 1984, but it was only after the appearance of "On the Road at Eighteen" in 1986 that he began to win critical acclaim. He is the author of the novel-cum-movie *Huozhe* (*To Live*).

YUAN QIONGQIONG (Yuan Ch'iung-ch'iung, 1950–) A graduate of Provincial Tainan Commercial and Vocational School in Taiwan, Yuan began writing in 1967. Though she also wrote poetry under the pen name Zhu Ling in the early years, she is more established as a writer of short fiction. Her celebrated piece "A Room of One's Own" won the prestigious *United Daily* literary award in 1980. She is at present a freelance TV scriptwriter in Taiwan.

ZHANG AILING (1921–1995) Known to Western readers as Eileen Chang, Zhang was seldom mentioned in histories of modern Chinese literature published in the 1970s. If not for C. T. Hsia, who considers her "the most gifted Chinese writer to emerge in the forties" and devotes the longest chapter in his *History of Modern Chinese Fiction* to assessing her accomplishments, she might have remained an obscure writer. Zhang's work is valued for its psychological insights. She had a fine command of English and translated a number of her own works into English. In 1955 she emigrated to the United States, where she lived in seclusion until her death.

ZHANG CUO (Chang Ts'o, 1943–) Known in the West as Dominic Cheung, Zhang Cuo (Zhang Zhen'ao) graduated from National Cheng-chih University in Taiwan and did postgraduate work at the University of Washington, where he obtained his doctorate. Zhang Cuo's "personal life as well as his lyrics are characterized by the search for a national and personal identity, which is often lost in the tragic historical experiences of China" ([Dominic]

Cheung, *Isle*, 139). A leading poet of his generation, he is a professor of comparative literature at the University of Southern California.

ZHANG DACHUN (Chang Ta-ch'un, 1957–) Zhang graduated from Taiwan's Fu Jen University and worked for a number of years as a reporter and editor for *China Times*. A skilled writer, Zhang has produced volumes of fiction for popular consumption. On the other hand, he has also written thought-provoking stories that have won critical acclaim. "Lucky Worries About His Country" shows Zhang's writing at its satirical best. Zhang now makes his living as a freelance writer and TV host.

ZHANG TIANYI (1906–1985) A keen but uncynical observer of "the animal called man," Zhang was a short-story writer of the thirties who excelled in satire and the comic art. Though he embraced the Marxist doctrine, his best works were seldom vitiated by simplistic subscription to fashionable leftist dogmas predicated on rebellion and protest. Thus, in spite of the fact that tension exists between the classes in "Midautumn Festival," it is not presented to the reader in a tendentious fashion. Instead, the reader is invited to witness the foibles, follies, and essential meanness of which human beings are capable. Zhang also wrote children's literature.

ZHENG CHOUYU (Cheng Ch'ou-yü, 1933–) Though a Northerner, Zheng (Zheng Wentao) entrances his readers with lyrical evocations of the South. He is one of the few poets in Taiwan whose collections of poetry have made the best-seller lists. A graduate of Taiwan's Chung-hsing University, Zheng worked for a number of years at Keelung's Harbor Bureau before attending Iowa's International Writing Program in 1968. He now teaches Chinese at Yale University.

ZHENG MIN (1920–) Zheng earned a degree in philosophy from National Southwest Associated University in 1943. She did graduate work at Brown University and obtained an M.A. in English literature in 1951. She returned to China in 1959 with her husband, an engineer, only to be harassed by officials who took them to be American spies. She taught English literature at Beijing Normal University until her retirement. After giving up her creative career for two decades, she resumed writing poetry in the 1980s.

ZHENG QINGWEN (Tzeng Ching-wen, 1932–) Born in Taoyuan, northern Taiwan, Zheng graduated from the Department of Commerce of National Taiwan University and worked for years as a banker. After retirement, he became a full-time writer, and his fiction has received many awards; a translation of his short stories, *The Three-Legged Horse*, was a recipient of the Kiriyama Pacific Rim Prize for fiction. His work can be divided into two streams: that which takes traditional Taiwanese village life as a backdrop and that which concerns life in contemporary urban society; in both it is the human psyche that concerns him the most.

ZHOU MENGDIE (Chou Meng-tie, 1920–) Zhou Mengdie's personal name is as allusive as his poetry. "Mengdie" is butterfly dream, a famous parable by the philosopher Zhuangzi about identity. A normal-school graduate, Zhou toyed with the idea of becoming a monk before enlisting in the Nationalist Army. He came to Taiwan in 1950 and has become a devout Buddhist.

ZHOU ZUOREN (1885–1967) Zhou Zuoren's works were banned in Taiwan and mainland China until only recently, due to "Japan connections" during World War II. He held a series of important posts in Beijing under Japanese occupation, including a deanship of the College of Humanities of Beijing University. At the end of the war, he was sentenced to ten years in prison by the Nationalists but was released by the Communists in 1949. Though his reputation is overshadowed by that of his brother, Lu Xun, he is one of the most accomplished and prolific essayists of his time.

ZHU TIANWEN (Chu T'ien-wen, 1956–) Zhu Tianwen is the daughter of the veteran novelist Zhu Xining. Allegedly a decadent work about the "Beautiful People" of contemporary Taiwan, "Fin de Siècle Splendor" is also a muffled lament about the transience of life and the fragility of youth and beauty. Zhu holds a B.A. in English from Tamkang University. Her novel, *Life of a Desolate Man*, which chronicles the lives of Taiwanese caught up in the AIDS pandemic, gained an international reputation. In addition to fiction, Zhu also writes film scripts.

ZHU ZIQING (1896–1948) Though Zhu Ziqing made his debut in the literary world as a poet in the early 1920s, he is better known as a leading essayist. Educated at Beijing University, he was appointed professor of Chinese literature at Qinghua University in 1925. In addition to research on classical Chinese literature, he published a number of essays that were so well received they were adopted as high school texts. From 1931 to 1932 he studied linguistics and English literature in London.

PART ONE

Fiction, 1918–1949

Lu Xun (1881–1936)

PREFACE TO THE FIRST COLLECTION OF SHORT STORIES, *CALL TO ARMS*

Translated by Yang Xianyi and Gladys Yang

When I was young I, too, had many dreams. Most of them came to be forgotten, but I see nothing in this to regret. For although recalling the past may make you happy, it may sometimes also make you lonely, and there is no point in clinging in spirit to lonely bygone days. However, my trouble is that I cannot forget completely, and these stories have resulted from what I have been unable to erase from my memory.

For more than four years I used to go, almost daily, to a pawnbroker's and to a medicine shop. I cannot remember how old I was then, but the counter in the medicine shop was the same height as I, and that in the pawnbroker's twice my height. I used to hand clothes and trinkets up to the counter twice my height, take the money proffered with contempt, then go to the counter the same height as I to buy medicine for my father, who had long been ill. On my return home I had other things to keep me busy, for since the physician who made out the prescriptions was very well known, he used unusual drugs: aloe root dug up in winter, sugar-cane that had been three years exposed to frost, twin crickets, and *ardisia* . . . all of which were difficult to procure. But my father's illness went from bad to worse until he died.

I believe those who sink from prosperity to poverty will probably come, in the process, to understand what the world is really like. I wanted to go to the

J— school in N—,[1] perhaps because I was in search of a change of scene and faces. There was nothing for my mother to do but to raise eight dollars for my traveling expenses, and say I might do as I pleased. That she cried was only natural, for at that time the proper thing was to study the classics and take the official examinations. Anyone who studied "foreign subjects" was looked down upon as a fellow good for nothing, who, out of desperation, was forced to sell his soul to foreign devils. Besides, she was sorry to part with me. But in spite of that, I went to N— and entered the J— school; and it was there that I heard for the first time the names of such subjects as natural science, arithmetic, geography, history, drawing, and physical training. They had no physiology course, but we saw woodblock editions of such works as *A New Course on the Human Body* and *Essays on Chemistry and Hygiene*. Recalling the talk and prescriptions of physicians I had known and comparing them with what I now knew, I came to the conclusion that those physicians must be either unwitting or deliberate charlatans, and I began to sympathize with the invalids and families who suffered at their hands. From translated histories I also learned that the Japanese Reformation had originated, to a great extent, with the introduction of Western medical science to Japan.

These inklings took me to a provincial medical college in Japan. I dreamed a beautiful dream that on my return to China I would cure patients like my father, who had been wrongly treated, while if war broke out I would serve as an army doctor, at the same time strengthening my countrymen's faith in reformation.

I do not know what advanced methods are now used to teach microbiology, but at that time lantern slides were used to show the microbes, and if the lecture ended early, the instructor might show slides of natural scenery or news to fill up the time. This was during the Russo-Japanese War, so there were many war films, and I had to join in the clapping and cheering in the lecture hall along with the other students. It was a long time since I had seen any compatriots, but one day I saw a film showing some Chinese, one of whom was bound, while many others stood around him. They were all strong fellows but appeared completely apathetic. According to the commentary, the one with his hands bound was a spy working for the Russians, who was to have his head cut off by the Japanese military as a warning to others, while the Chinese beside him had come to enjoy the spectacle.

Before the term was over I had left for Tokyo, because after this film I felt that medical science was not so important after all. The people of a weak and backward country, however strong and healthy they may be, can only serve to be made examples of, or to witness such futile spectacles; and it doesn't really matter how many of them die of illness. The most important thing, therefore, was to change their spirit, and since at that time I felt that literature was the

1. The Jiangnan Naval Academy in Nanjing.

best means to this end, I determined to promote a literary movement. There were many Chinese students in Tokyo studying law, political science, physics and chemistry, even police work and engineering, but not one studying literature or art. However, even in this uncongenial atmosphere I was fortunate enough to find some kindred spirits. We gathered the few others we needed, and after discussion our first step, of course, was to publish a magazine, the title of which denoted that this was a new birth. As we were then rather classically inclined, we called it *Xin Sheng* (*New Life*).

When the time for publication drew near, some of our contributors dropped out, and then our funds were withdrawn, until finally there were only three of us left, and we were penniless. Since we had started our magazine at an unlucky hour, there was naturally no one to whom we could complain when we failed; but later even we three were destined to part, and our discussions of a dream future had to cease. So ended this abortive *New Life*.

Only later did I feel the futility of it all; at that time I did not really understand anything. Later I felt if a man's proposals met with approval, it should encourage him; if they met with opposition, it should make him fight back; but the real tragedy for him was to lift up his voice among the living and meet with no response, neither approval nor opposition, just as if he were left helpless in a boundless desert. So I began to feel lonely.

And this feeling of loneliness grew day by day, coiling about my soul like a huge poisonous snake. Yet in spite of my unaccountable sadness, I felt no indignation; for this experience had made me reflect and see that I was definitely not the heroic type who could rally multitudes at his call.

However, my loneliness had to be dispelled, for it was causing me agony. So I used various means to dull my senses, both by conforming to the spirit of the time and turning to the past. Later I experienced or witnessed even greater loneliness and sadness, which I do not like to recall, preferring that it should perish with me. Still my attempt to deaden my senses was not unsuccessful—I had lost the enthusiasm and fervor of my youth.

In S—[2] Hostel there were three rooms where it was said a woman had lived who hanged herself on the locust tree in the courtyard. Although the tree had grown so tall that its branches could no longer be reached, the rooms remained deserted. For some years I stayed here, copying ancient inscriptions. I had few visitors, there were no political problems or issues in those inscriptions, and my only desire was that my life should slip quietly away like this. On summer nights, when there were too many mosquitoes, I would sit under the locust tree, waving my fan and looking at the specks of sky through the thick leaves, while the caterpillars which came out in the evening would fall, icy-cold, onto my neck.

2. Shaoxing.

The only visitor to come for an occasional talk was my old friend Jin Xinyi. He would put his big portfolio down on the broken table, take off his long gown, and sit facing me, looking as if his heart was still beating fast after braving the dogs.

"What is the use of copying these?" he demanded inquisitively one night, after looking through the inscriptions I had copied.

"No use at all."

"Then why copy them?"

"For no particular reason."

"I think you might write something. . . . "

I understood. They were editing the magazine *New Youth*,[3] but hitherto there seemed to have been no reaction, favorable or otherwise, and I guessed they must be feeling lonely. However, I said:

"Imagine an iron house without windows, absolutely indestructible, with many people fast asleep inside who will soon die of suffocation. But you know since they will die in their sleep, they will not feel the pain of death. Now if you cry aloud to wake a few of the lighter sleepers, making those unfortunate few suffer the agony of irrevocable death, do you think you are doing them a good turn?"

"But if a few awake, you can't say there is no hope of destroying the iron house."

True, in spite of my own conviction, I could not blot out hope, for hope lies in the future. I could not use my own evidence to refute his assertion that it might exist. So I agreed to write, and the result was my first story, "A Madman's Diary." From that time onward, I could not stop writing, and would write some sort of short story from time to time at the request of friends, until I had more than a dozen of them.

As for myself, I no longer feel any great urge to express myself; yet, perhaps because I have not entirely forgotten the grief of my past loneliness, I sometimes call out, to encourage those fighters who are galloping on in loneliness, so that they do not lose heart. Whether my cry is brave or sad, repellent or ridiculous, I do not care. However, since it is a call to arms, I must naturally obey my general's orders. This is why I often resort to innuendoes, as when I made a wreath appear from nowhere at the son's grave in "Medicine," while in "Tomorrow" I did not say that Fourth Shan's Wife had no dreams of her little boy. For our chiefs then were against pessimism. And I, for my part, did not want to infect with the loneliness I had found so bitter those young people who were still dreaming pleasant dreams, just as I had done when young.

It is clear, then, that my short stories fall far short of being works of art; hence I count myself fortunate that they are still known as stories, and are even being

---

3. The most influential magazine in the cultural revolution of that time.

compiled in one book. Although such good fortune makes me uneasy, I am nevertheless pleased to think they have readers in the world of men, for the time being at least.

Since these short stories of mine are being reprinted in one collection, owing to the reasons given above, I have chosen the title *Na Han* (Call to Arms).

1922

A MADMAN'S DIARY

Translated by Yang Xianyi and Gladys Yang

Two brothers, whose names I need not mention here, were both good friends of mine in high school; but after a separation of many years we gradually lost touch. Some time ago I happened to hear that one of them was seriously ill, and since I was going back to my old home, I broke my journey to call on them. I saw only one, however, who told me that the invalid was his younger brother.

"I appreciate your coming such a long way to see us," he said, "but my brother recovered some time ago and has gone elsewhere to take up an official post." Then, laughing, he produced two volumes of his brother's diary, saying that from these the nature of his past illness could be seen and there was no harm in showing them to an old friend. I took the diary away, read it through, and found that he had suffered from a form of persecution complex. The writing was most confused and incoherent, and he had made many wild statements; moreover he had omitted to give any dates, so that only by the color of the ink and the differences in the writing could one tell that it was not all written at one time. Certain sections, however, were not altogether disconnected, and I have copied out a part to serve as a subject for medical research. I have not altered a single illogicality in the diary and have changed only the names, even though the people referred to are all country folk, unknown to the world and of no consequence. As for the title, it was chosen by the diarist himself after his recovery, and I did not change it.

1

Tonight the moon is very bright.

I have not seen it for over thirty years, so today when I saw it I felt in unusually high spirits. I begin to realize that during the past thirty-odd years I have been in the dark; but now I must be extremely careful. Otherwise why should the Zhaos' dog have looked at me twice?

I have reason for my fear.

2

Tonight there is no moon at all, I know that this is a bad omen. This morning when I went out cautiously, Mr. Zhao had a strange look in his eyes, as if he were afraid of me, as if he wanted to murder me. There were seven or eight others who discussed me in a whisper. And they were afraid of my seeing them. So, indeed, were all the people I passed. The fiercest among them grinned at me, whereupon I shivered from head to foot, knowing that their preparations were complete.

I was not afraid, however, but continued on my way. A group of children in front were also discussing me, while their faces too were ghastly pale. I wondered what grudge these children could have against me to make them behave like this. I could not help calling out, "Tell me!" But then they ran away.

I wonder what grudge Mr. Zhao has against me, what grudge the people on the road have against me. I can think of nothing except that twenty years ago I trod on Mr. Gu Jiu's[1] old ledgers, and Mr. Gu was most displeased. Although Mr. Zhao does not know him, he must have heard talk of this and decided to avenge him, thus he is conspiring against me with the people on the road. But then what of the children? At that time they were not yet born, so why should they eye me so strangely today, as if they were afraid of me, as if they wanted to murder me? This really frightens me, it is so bewildering and upsetting.

I know. They must have learned this from their parents!

3

I can't sleep at night. Everything requires careful consideration if one is to understand it.

Those people, some of whom have been pilloried by the magistrate, slapped in the face by the local gentry, had their wives taken away by bailiffs or their parents driven to suicide by creditors, never looked as frightened and as fierce then as they did yesterday.

---

1. The characters *Gu jiu* mean "old." This refers to the age-old history of feudalism in China.

The most extraordinary thing was that woman on the street yesterday who was spanking her son. "Little devil!" she cried. "I'm so angry I could eat you!" Yet all the time it was me she was looking at. I gave a start, unable to hide my alarm. Then all those long-toothed people with livid faces began to hoot with laughter. Old Chen hurried forward and dragged me home.

He dragged me home. The folk at home all pretended not to know me; they had the same look in their eyes as all the others. When I went into the study, they locked me in as if cooping up a chicken or a duck. This incident left me even more bewildered.

A few days ago a tenant of ours from Wolf Cub Village came to report the failure of the crops and told my elder brother that a notorious character in their village had been beaten to death; then some people had taken out his heart and liver, fried them in oil, and eaten them as a means of increasing their courage. When I interrupted, the tenant and my brother both stared at me. Only today have I realized that they had exactly the same look in their eyes as those people outside.

Just to think of it sets me shivering from the crown of my head to the soles of my feet.

They eat human beings, so they may eat me.

I see that the woman's "eat you," the laughter of those long-toothed people with livid faces, and the tenant's story the other day are obviously secret signs. I realize all the poison in their speech, all the daggers in their laughter. Their teeth are white and glistening: they use these teeth to eat men.

Evidently, although I am not a bad man, ever since I trod on Mr. Gu's ledgers it has been touch-and-go with me. They seem to have secrets that I cannot guess, and once they are angry they will call anyone a bad character. I remember when my elder brother taught me to write compositions, no matter how good a man was, if I produced arguments to the contrary he would mark that passage to show his approval; while if I excused evildoers he would say, "Good for you, that shows originality." How can I possibly guess their secret thoughts—especially when they are ready to eat people?

Everything requires careful consideration if one is to understand it. In ancient times, as I recollect, people often ate human beings, but I am rather hazy about it. I tried to look this up, but my history has no chronology and scrawled all over each page are the words "Confucian Virtue and Morality." Since I could not sleep anyway, I read intently half the night until I began to see words between the lines. The whole book was filled with the two words—"Eat people."

All these words written in the book, all the words spoken by our tenant, eye me quizzically with an enigmatic smile.

I too am a man, and they want to eat me!

4

In the morning I sat quietly for some time. Old Chen brought in lunch: one bowl of vegetables, one bowl of steamed fish. The eyes of the fish were white and hard, and its mouth was open just like those people who want to eat human beings. After a few mouthfuls I could not tell whether the slippery morsels were fish or human flesh, so I brought it all up.

I said, "Old Chen, tell my brother that I feel quite suffocated and want to have a stroll in the garden." Old Chen said nothing but went out, and presently he came back and opened the gate.

I did not move, but watched to see how they would treat me, feeling certain that they would not let me go. Sure enough! My elder brother came slowly out, leading an old man. There was a murderous gleam in his eyes, and fearing that I would see it he lowered his head, stealing side glances at me from behind his glasses.

"You seem very well today," said my brother.

"Yes," said I.

"I have invited Mr. He here today to examine you."

"All right," I replied. Actually I knew quite well that this old man was the executioner in disguise! Feeling my pulse was simply a pretext for him to see how fat I was, for this would entitle him to a share of my flesh. Still, I was not afraid. Although I do not eat men my courage is greater than theirs. I held out my two fists to see what he would do. The old man sat down, closed his eyes, fumbled for some time, remained motionless for a while, then opened his shifty eyes and said, "Don't let your imagination run away with you. Rest quietly for a few days, and you will be better."

Don't let your imagination run away with you! Rest quietly for a few days! By fattening me of course they'll have more to eat. But what good will it do me? How can it be "better"? The whole lot of them wanting to eat people yet stealthily trying to keep up appearances, not daring to do it outright, was really enough to make me die of laughter. I couldn't help it, I nearly split my sides, I was so amused. I knew that this laughter voiced courage and integrity. Both the old man and my brother turned pale, awed by my courage and integrity.

But my courage just makes them all the more eager to eat me, to acquire some of my courage for themselves. The old man went out of the gate, but before he had gone far he said to my brother in a low voice, "To be eaten at once!" My brother nodded. So you are in it too! This stupendous discovery, though it came as a shock, is no more than I might expect: the accomplice in eating me is my elder brother!

The eater of human flesh is my elder brother!

I am the younger brother of an eater of human flesh!

I, who will be eaten by others, am the younger brother of an eater of human flesh!

5

These few days I have been thinking again: suppose that old man were not an executioner in disguise, but a real doctor; he would be nonetheless an eater of human flesh. That book on herbs by his predecessor Li Shizhen[2] states explicitly that men's flesh can be boiled and eaten; how then can he still deny that he eats men?

As for my elder brother, I have also good reason to suspect him. When he was teaching me, he told me himself, "People exchange their sons to eat."[3] And once in discussing a bad man he said that not only did the fellow deserve to be killed, he should "have his flesh eaten and his hide slept on." I was still young at the time, and for quite a while my heart beat faster. That story our tenant from Wolf Cub Village told the other day about eating a man's heart and liver didn't surprise him at all—he kept nodding his head. He is evidently just as cruel as before. Since it is possible to "exchange sons to eat," then anything can be exchanged, anyone can be eaten. In the past I simply listened to his explanations and let it go at that; now I know that when he gave me these explanations, not only was there human fat at the corner of his lips, but his whole heart was set on eating men.

6

Pitch-dark. I don't know whether it is day or night. The Zhaos' dog has started barking again.

The fierceness of a lion, the timidity of a rabbit, the craftiness of a fox. . . .

7

I know their way: they are not prepared to kill outright, nor would they dare, for fear of the consequences. Instead they have banded together and set traps everywhere, to force me to kill myself. The behavior of the men and women in the street a few days ago and my elder brother's attitude these last few days make it quite obvious. What they like best is for a man to take off his belt and hang himself from a beam, for then they can enjoy their hearts' desire without being blamed for murder. Naturally that delights them and sets them roaring with laughter. On the other hand, if a man is frightened or worried to death, though that makes him rather thin, they still nod in approval.

---

2. Famous pharmacologist (1518–1593). It is not stated in his *Compendium of Materia Medica* that human flesh could be used as a medicine; this was one of the delusions of the madman.

3. The ancient historical record *Zuo zhuan* states that during a siege in 488 B.C. the besieged were so famished that they "exchanged their sons to eat."

They only eat dead flesh! I remember reading somewhere of a hideous beast with an ugly look in its eye called "hyena," which often eats dead flesh. Even the largest bones it crunches into fragments and swallows; the mere thought of this makes your hair stand on end. Hyenas are related to wolves, wolves belong to the canine species. The other day the Zhaos' dog eyed me several times: it is obviously in the plot too as their accomplice. The old man's eyes were cast down, but that did not deceive me.

The most deplorable is my elder brother. He's a man too, so why isn't he afraid, why is he plotting with others to eat me? Does force of habit blind a man to what's wrong? Or is he so heartless that he will knowingly commit a crime?

8

In cursing man-eaters, I shall start with my brother. In dissuading man-eaters, I shall start with him too.

Actually such arguments should have convinced them long ago. . . .

Suddenly someone came in. He was only about twenty years old and I did not see his features very clearly. His face was wreathed in smiles, but when he nodded to me his smile didn't seem genuine. I asked him, "Is it right to eat human beings?"

Still smiling, he replied, "When there is no famine how can one eat human beings?"

I realized at once he was one of them; but still I summoned up courage to repeat my question:

"Is it right?"

"What makes you ask such a thing? You really are . . . fond of a joke. . . . It is very fine today."

"It is fine, and the moon is very bright. But I want to ask you: Is it right?"

He looked disconcerted and muttered, "No. . . ."

"No? Then why do they still do it?"

"What are you talking about?"

"What am I talking about? They are eating men now in Wolf Cub Village, and you can see it written all over the books, in fresh red ink."

His expression changed. He grew ghastly pale. "It may be so," he said, staring at me. "That's the way it's always been. . . . "

"Does that make it right?"

"I refuse to discuss it with you. Anyway, you shouldn't talk about it. It's wrong for anyone to talk about it."

I leaped up and opened my eyes wide, but the man had vanished. I was soaked with sweat. He was much younger than my elder brother, but even so he was in it. He must have been taught by his parents. And I am afraid he has already taught his son; that is why even the children look at me so fiercely.

9

Wanting to eat men, at the same time afraid of being eaten themselves, they all eye each other with the deepest suspicion. . . .

How comfortable life would be for them if they could rid themselves of such obsessions and go to work, walk, eat, and sleep at ease. They have only this one step to take. Yet fathers and sons, husbands and wives, brothers, friends, teachers and students, sworn enemies, and even strangers, have all joined in this conspiracy, discouraging and preventing each other from taking this step.

10

Early this morning I went to find my elder brother. He was standing outside the hall door looking at the sky when I walked up behind him, standing between him and the door, and addressed him with exceptional poise and politeness:

"Brother, I have something to say to you."

"Go ahead then." He turned quickly toward me, nodding.

"It's nothing much, but I find it hard to say. Brother, probably all primitive people ate a little human flesh to begin with. Later, because their views altered, some of them stopped and tried so hard to do what was right that they changed into men, into real men. But some are still eating people—just like reptiles. Some have changed into fish, birds, monkeys, and finally men; but those who make no effort to do what's right are still reptiles. When those who eat men compare themselves with those who don't, how ashamed they must be. Probably much more ashamed than the reptiles are before monkeys.

"In ancient times Yi Ya boiled his son for Jie and Zhou to eat;[4] that is the old story. But actually since the creation of heaven and earth by Pan Gu[5] men have been eating each other, from the time of Yi Ya's son to the time of Xu Xilin,[6] and from the time of Xu Xilin down to the man caught in Wolf Cub Village. Last year they executed a criminal in the city, and a consumptive soaked a piece of bread in his blood and sucked it.

"They want to eat me, and of course you can do nothing about it single-handed; but why must you join them? As man-eaters they are capable of anything. If they eat me, they can eat you as well; members of the same group can still eat each other. But if you will just change your ways, change right away, then everyone will have peace. Although this has been going on since time

---

4. Yi Ya, a favorite of Duke Huan of Qi in the seventh century B.C., was a good cook and sycophant. When the duke remarked that he had never tasted the flesh of children, Yi Ya cooked his own son for him to eat. Jie and Zhou were kings of earlier periods. This misstatement is presented as a sign of mental derangement.

5. A mythological figure.

6. A revolutionary executed in 1907 for assassinating a Qing official. His heart and liver were eaten.

immemorial, today we could make a special effort to do what is right, and say this can't be done! I'm sure you can say that, Brother. The other day when the tenant wanted the rent reduced, you said it couldn't be done."

At first he only smiled cynically, then a murderous gleam came into his eyes, and when I spoke of their secret he turned pale. Outside the gate quite a crowd had gathered, among them Mr. Zhao and his dog, all craning their necks to peer in. I could not see all their faces. Some of them seemed to be masked; others were the old lot, long-toothed with livid faces, concealing their laughter. I knew they were one gang, all eaters of human flesh. But I also knew that they did not all think alike by any means. Some of them thought that since it had always been so, men should be eaten. Others knew they shouldn't eat men but still wanted to, and were afraid people might discover their secret; so although what I said made them angry they still smiled their cynical, tight-lipped smiles.

Suddenly my brother's face darkened.

"Clear off, the whole lot of you!" he roared. "What's the point of looking at a madman?"

Then I realized part of their cunning. They would never be willing to change their stand, and their plans were all laid: they had labeled me a madman. In future, when I was eaten, not only would there be no trouble but people would probably be grateful to them. When our tenant spoke of the villagers eating a bad character, it was exactly the same device. This is their old trick.

Old Chen came in too in a towering temper. But they could not stop my mouth. I had to warn those people:

"You should change, change from the bottom of your hearts. You must realize that there will be no place for man-eaters in the world in future.

"If you don't change, you may all be eaten by each other. However many of you there are, you will be wiped out by the real men, just as wolves are killed by hunters—just like reptiles!"

Old Chen drove everybody away. My brother had disappeared. Old Chen advised me to go back to my room. It was pitch-dark in there. The beams and rafters shook above my head. After shaking for a while they grew bigger and bigger. They piled on top of me.

The weight was so great, I couldn't move. They meant that I should die. However, knowing that the weight was false, I struggled out, dripping with sweat. But I had to warn them:

"You must change at once, change from the bottom of your hearts! You must know that there'll be no place for man-eaters in future. . . ."

11

The sun has stopped shining, the door is never opened. Just two meals day after day.

Picking up my chopsticks, I thought of my elder brother. I know now how my little sister died: it was all through him. My sister was only five at the time.

I can still remember how sweet she looked, poor thing. Mother wept as if she would never stop, but he begged her not to cry, probably because he had eaten our sister himself and so this weeping made him rather ashamed. If he had any sense of shame. . . .

My sister was eaten by my brother, but I don't know whether Mother realized it or not.

I think Mother must have known, but when she wept she didn't say so outright, probably because she also thought it proper. I remember when I was four or five, sitting in the cool of the hall, my brother told me that if a man's parents were ill he should cut off a piece of his flesh and boil it for them, if he wanted to be considered a good son;[7] and Mother didn't contradict him. If one piece could be eaten, obviously so could the whole. And yet just to think of the weeping then still makes my heart bleed; that is the extraordinary thing about it!

12

I can't bear to think of it.

It has only just dawned on me that all these years I have been living in a place where for four thousand years human flesh has been eaten. My brother had just taken over the charge of the house when our sister died, and he may well have used her flesh in our food, making us eat it unwittingly.

I may have eaten several pieces of my sister's flesh unwittingly, and now it is my turn. . . .

How can a man like myself, after four thousand years of man-eating history—even though I knew nothing about it at first—ever hope to face real men?

13

Perhaps there are still children who haven't eaten men?

Save the children. . . .

1918

7. The doctrine of filial piety used by the feudal ruling class to poison the people preached that a son should, if necessary, cut off his own flesh to feed his parents.

KONG YIJI

Translated by Yang Xianyi and Gladys Yang

The layout of Luzhen's taverns is unique. In each, facing you as you enter, is a bar in the shape of a carpenter's square where hot water is kept ready for warming rice wine. When men come off work at midday and in the evening they spend four coppers on a bowl of wine—or so they did twenty years ago; now it costs ten—and drink this warm, standing by the bar, taking it easy. Another copper will buy a plate of salted bamboo shoots or peas flavored with aniseed to go with the wine, while a dozen will buy a meat dish; but most of the customers here belong to the short-coated class, few of whom can afford this. As for those in long gowns, they go into the inner room to order wine and dishes and sit drinking at their leisure.

At the age of twelve I started work as a pot-boy in Prosperity Tavern at the edge of town. The boss put me to work in the outer room, saying that I looked too much of a fool to serve long-gowned customers. The short-coated customers there were easier to deal with, it is true, but among them were quite a few persnickety ones who insisted on watching for themselves while the yellow wine was ladled from the keg, looked for water at the bottom of the wine pot, and personally inspected the pot's immersion into the hot water. Under such strict surveillance, diluting the wine was very hard indeed. Thus it did not take my boss many days to decide that this job too was beyond me. Luckily I had been recommended by somebody influential, so he could not sack me. Instead I was transferred to the dull task of simply warming wine.

After that I stood all day behind the bar attending to my duties. Although I gave satisfaction at this post, I found it somewhat boring and monotonous. Our boss was a grim-faced man, nor were the customers much more pleasant, which made the atmosphere a gloomy one. The only times when there was any laughter were when Kong Yiji came to the tavern. That is why I remember him.

Kong Yiji was the only long-gowned customer who used to drink his wine standing. A big, pallid man whose wrinkled face often bore scars, he had a large, unkempt, and grizzled beard. And although he wore a long gown it was dirty and tattered. It had not by the look of it been washed or mended for ten years or more. He used so many archaisms in his speech that half of it was barely intelligible. And as his surname was Kong, he was given the nickname Kong Yiji from *kong, yi, ji,* the first three characters in the old-fashioned children's copy book. Whenever he came in, everyone there would look at him and chuckle. And someone was sure to call out:

"Kong Yiji! What are those fresh scars on your face?"

Ignoring this, he would lay nine coppers on the bar and order two bowls of heated wine with a dish of aniseed-peas. Then someone else would bawl:

"You must have been stealing again!"

"Why sully a man's good name for no reason at all?" Kong Yiji would ask, raising his eyebrows.

"Good name? Why, the day before yesterday you were trussed up and beaten for stealing books from the He family. I saw you!"

At that Kong Yiji would flush, the veins on his forehead standing out as he protested, "Taking books can't be counted as stealing. . . . Taking books . . . for a scholar . . . can't be counted as stealing." Then followed such quotations from the classics as "A gentleman keeps his integrity even in poverty," together with a spate of archaisms that soon had everybody roaring with laughter, enlivening the whole tavern.

From the gossip that I heard, it seemed that Kong Yiji had studied the classics but never passed the official examinations and, not knowing any way to make a living, he had grown steadily poorer until he was almost reduced to beggary. Luckily he was a good calligrapher and could find enough copying work to fill his rice bowl. But unfortunately he had his failings too: laziness and a love of tippling. So after a few days he would disappear, taking with him books, paper, brushes, and inkstone. And after this had happened several times, people stopped employing him as a copyist. Then all he could do was resort to occasional pilfering. In our tavern, though, he was a model customer who never failed to pay up. Sometimes, it is true, when he had no ready money, his name would be chalked up on our tally-board; but in less than a month he invariably settled the bill, and the name Kong Yiji would be wiped off the board again.

After Kong Yiji had drunk half a bowl of wine, his flushed cheeks would stop burning. But then someone would ask:

"Kong Yiji, can you really read?"

When he glanced back as if such a question were not worth answering, they would continue, "How is it you never passed even the lowest official examination?"

At once a gray tinge would overspread Kong Yiji's dejected, discomfited face, and he would mumble more of those unintelligible archaisms. Then everyone there would laugh heartily again, enlivening the whole tavern.

At such times I could join in the laughter with no danger of a dressing-down from my boss. In fact he always put such questions to Kong Yiji himself, to raise a laugh. Knowing that it was no use talking to the men, Kong Yiji would chat with us boys. Once he asked me:

"Have you had any schooling?"

When I nodded curtly he said, "Well then, I'll test you. How do you write the *hui*[1] in aniseed-peas?"

Who did this beggar think he was, testing me! I turned away and ignored him. After waiting for some time he said earnestly:

"You can't write it, eh? I'll show you. Mind you remember. You ought to remember such characters, because you'll need them to write up your accounts when you have a shop of your own."

It seemed to me that I was still very far from having a shop of my own; in addition to which, our boss never entered aniseed-peas in his account book. Half amused and half exasperated, I drawled, "I don't need you to show me. Isn't it the *hui* written with the element for grass?"

Kong Yiji's face lit up. Tapping two long fingernails on the bar, he nodded. "Quite correct!" he said. "There are four different ways of writing *hui*. Do you know them?"

But my patience exhausted, I scowled and moved away. Kong Yiji had dipped his finger in wine to trace the characters on the bar. When he saw my utter indifference his face fell and he sighed.

Sometimes children in the neighborhood, hearing laughter, came in to join in the fun and surrounded Kong Yiji. Then he would give them aniseed-peas, one apiece. After eating the peas the children would still hang round, their eyes fixed on the dish. Growing flustered, he would cover it with his hand and, bending forward from the waist, would say, "There aren't many left, not many at all." Straightening up to look at the peas again, he would shake his head and reiterate, "Not many, I do assure you. Not many, nay, not many at all." Then the children would scamper off, shouting with laughter.

That was how Kong Yiji contributed to our enjoyment, but we got along all right without him too.

One day, shortly before the Midautumn Festival, I think it was, my boss, who was slowly making out his accounts, took down the tally-board. "Kong Yiji

---

1. A Chinese character meaning "aniseed."

hasn't shown up for a long time," he remarked suddenly. "He still owes nineteen coppers." That made me realize how long it was since we had seen him.

"How could he?" rejoined one of the customers. "His legs were broken in that last beating up."

"Ah!" said my boss.

"He'd been stealing again. This time he was fool enough to steal from Mr. Ding, the provincial-grade scholar. As if anybody could get away with that!"

"So what happened?"

"What happened? First he wrote a confession, then he was beaten. The beating lasted nearly all night, and they broke both his legs."

"And then?"

"Well, his legs were broken."

"Yes, but after?"

"After? . . . Who knows? He may be dead."

My boss asked no further questions but went on slowly making up his accounts.

After the Midautumn Festival the wind grew daily colder as winter approached, and even though I spent all my time by the stove, I had to wear a padded jacket. One afternoon, when the tavern was deserted, as I sat with my eyes closed I heard the words:

"Warm a bowl of wine."

It was said in a low but familiar voice. I opened my eyes. There was no one to be seen. I stood up to look out. There below the bar, facing the door, sat Kong Yiji. His face was thin and grimy—he looked a wreck. He had on a ragged lined jacket and was squatting cross-legged on a mat, which was attached to his shoulders by a straw rope. When he saw me he repeated:

"Warm a bowl of wine."

At this point my boss leaned over the bar to ask, "Is that Kong Yiji? You still owe nineteen coppers."

"That . . . I'll settle next time." He looked up dejectedly. "Here's cash. Give me some good wine."

My boss, just as in the past, chuckled and said:

"Kong Yiji, you've been stealing again!"

But instead of a stout denial, the answer simply was:

"Don't joke with me."

"Joke? How did your legs get broken if you hadn't been stealing?"

"I fell," whispered Kong Yiji. "Broke them in a fall." His eyes pleaded with the boss to let the matter drop. By now several people had gathered round, and they all laughed with the boss. I warmed the wine, carried it over, and set it on the threshold. He produced four coppers from his ragged coat pocket, and as he placed them in my hand I saw that his own hands were covered with mud—he must have crawled there on them. Presently he finished the wine and, to the accompaniment of taunts and laughter, slowly pushed himself off with his hands.

A long time went by after that without our seeing Kong Yiji again. At the end of the year, when the boss took down the tally-board, he said, "Kong Yiji still owes nineteen coppers." At the Dragon Boat Festival the next year he said the same thing again. But when the Midautumn Festival arrived he was silent on the subject, and another New Year came round without our seeing any more of Kong Yiji.

Nor have I ever seen him since—no doubt Kong Yiji really is dead.

1919

Ye Shaojun (1894–1988)

A POSTHUMOUS SON

Translated by Bonnie S. McDougall

"Variety is the spice of life. When you're tired of salted food you should have something sweet." This was Mr. Wenqing's reply to his wife's charge that he shouldn't look down on his daughters or see their presence as the result of deliberate mischief-making; she said that there was no great difference between girls and boys—both were children and equally precious. "You see, when the first one arrived and they said it was a girl, naturally we were delighted. She was our own flesh and blood blended into one, a jewel that we had made between the two of us."

His wife looked at him fondly, his words reviving memories of former happier days.

"When the second one also turned out to be a girl, it still didn't matter. With only two years between them, we could dress them up like two flowers, they'd be so cute it'd make people green with envy. And then when we grow old, we'd have two daughters by our side, so that we wouldn't get lonely; we'd go out for walks in the park, one daughter supporting you, the other looking after me; and when it gets cold in winter, one daughter will stoke the fire while the other pours the wine. It would be very cozy and agreeable."

At this she visualized herself as a fortunate, venerable old lady.

"But the third one was also a girl!" Mr. Wenqing's voice became rather less mild. "This was getting a bit irritating. We're not gardeners, what can we do with all these flowers, even if they do look pretty; and as far as keeping us company in our old age is concerned, we don't need that many! And then the fourth one was also a girl! I can't help feeling that there must be something wrong with the way your body works, if it can only produce girls and nothing else. What's the point in producing the same thing time after time when what we need is some variety? Don't you know that you can get beriberi if you just eat rice all the time?"

"I think there will be some variety this time," she said warmly, swallowing the spittle in her mouth; the assumed indifference she had just shown at having produced a whole family of girls had now evaporated. "This time it's completely different from the way it was before. Before, my belly stuck out in a point, and now, look, it's as round as a bun. The last four times my complexion was usually good, but look how yellow I am now. If it's different on the outside it must be different inside too." As she spoke her smiling eyes glanced down at the swollen belly beneath her clothes.

"You may be right; after all, it is a different shape." Mr. Wenqing scrutinized her abdomen. "In that case I'll go and get two jars of vintage Shaoxing and two hams, and when our son's born we can celebrate together over a good meal. You can let yourself go a little."

"Really?" Her pleasure, however, was not in the thought of the wine or ham.

"Of course. You know, the birth of a son is a pretty important business." Mr. Wenqing smiled as he gazed indulgently at his wife.

The two jars of vintage Shaoxing and the two hams having duly been purchased, they were laid out in the bedroom as a kind of guarantee of obedience, or a pre-order voucher for a male child.

Their relatives and neighbors believed the story about her belly looking different, and unanimously declared that the new arrival would certainly be a son and heir; and since a late-born son was much more precious than the son of a first or second pregnancy, the number of celebratory red-dyed eggs to be distributed should be four times as many as usual.

"It doesn't look very likely," said the expectant mother, modestly receiving these congratulatory attentions. Inside, however, she was calculating just how many red eggs should be prepared.

When Mr. Wenqing came into the bedroom and saw the Shaoxing wine jars with their gaily painted scenes from opera, his heart would leap for joy. Sometimes, patting her shoulder affectionately, he would say, "You will prove yourself this time, I know you will. Look, I have a reward for you. How about if I take you on a trip to West Lake next spring?"

But the fifth was also a girl.

The mother cried for two whole days and nights, and it was ten days before she was able to produce a thin trickle of milk for the baby, which had up till then been fed on powdered milk.

Mr. Wenqing was deeply angry, but there was nothing he could do. Moving the two jars of vintage Shaoxing and the two hams out of the bedroom, he recruited some friends to finish them off over a few melancholy meals.

"Only girls, never anything else! You can't blame me. I've been as patient as any man could be, I've got no choice but to get another woman." When Mr. Wenqing had raised this possibility before it had always been by way of a joke—he had never sounded as stern as this before. His wife knew that this time, unlike on previous occasions, he had come to a decision. Conscious that her failure to prove herself deprived her of any right to protest, she could only plead with him to reconsider. "If you must have another woman I won't stand in your way. But please, give me one more chance; the sixth may turn out to be a boy. If it's a girl, then you can find someone else." And with this she burst into tears again.

Mr. Wenqing looked at her briefly and said in disgust, "Since you put it that way, I'll wait one more time and then that's it."

The baby's milk supply gradually dried up and she had to be switched back to the powdered milk again. But the change in diet upset her and she wailed continually, her tiny mouth stretched wide open. Within a few days her chubby little face had become very thin until there seemed to be nothing left but a layer of yellow wrinkled skin.

This was a sign that her mother was pregnant again. On previous occasions it had not happened that the babies had got so thin when they were weaned, so that this time represented a distinct change. Then it occurred to the mother that since five was a prime number, it was only reasonable to expect that a new pattern would begin with the number six. Later she noticed that her belly protruded even more roundly than before, without any kind of peak whatsoever, and also that her complexion was more faded than ever before, and turning up her eyelids you couldn't see even a speck of red. She therefore concluded that the last time had only been an omen of change, and that the real change would actually take place this time. So she informed her husband in high spirits that she was seventy to eighty percent confident of success this time.

"I wish you were much more confident than that, more like ninety percent, a hundred percent, a hundred and ten percent, a hundred and twenty percent even." Mr. Wenqing, of course, also entertained urgent hopes for this time. "I'll go and get some Shaoxing wine and ham again. But this time make sure you do the right thing, and you'll earn your reward."

And once more two jars of vintage Shaoxing and two hams were brought into the bedroom.

However, according to public opinion, the outlook was anything but optimistic. To her face, her relatives and friends firmly asserted that it would definitely be a boy this time, and brought forward further strong reasons why this should be so. But behind her back they confided in each other their certainty that it would be another girl, each advancing a different reason for her opinion. Fragments of their gossiping reached the expectant mother, sometimes together with a glimpse of scornfully pursed lips that seemed to say, "Fancy her thinking she's going to have a son!" Then she began to panic—her confidence deserted her and she was left with nothing. As she thought of the ever-approaching date of her confinement, she grew even more fearful than a criminal awaiting execution.

On the day when her delivery was due, Mr. Wenqing waited for news outside her bedroom, occasionally lifting a corner of the door curtain to peek inside. The groans of the mother in labor and the continual murmur of the women in attendance were things he had become well accustomed to, and he was quite oblivious of them. His whole attention was concentrated on one thing only, the all-important report that would follow the baby's first cry.

The woman in labor suddenly gave a loud shriek. There was a slight stir within the bedroom, followed by a mysterious silence. Holding his breath from the suspense, his ear glued to the curtain, Mr. Wenqing stood transfixed awaiting the verdict of fate.

"Wah—" The sound of the baby's first cry was followed by another faint stir. Mr. Wenqing's heart pounded violently.

"It's a dear little girl," said the midwife, in an artificially cheerful tone of voice. "Plump and pretty, a dear, sweet little girl."

"Ooh," the women in attendance responded mechanically.

"Oh—" wailed the mother, bursting into tears of shock and dismay.

Mr. Wenqing suddenly felt suffocated, as if something were choking him, while his legs, acting of their own volition, carried him out of the room.

The Shaoxing wine and the ham from the bedroom were naturally put to the same purpose again of relieving the gloom, being slowly consumed by Mr. Wenqing in the company of a few friends.

"There's no question about it now. I must have another woman." He spoke as if issuing an order, in a way which brooked no discussion.

Tears streaming down her face, the poor mother stuffed her far from full breast into the baby's little mouth. "Please, I beg you, just one more time!" She gazed straight up at him with a woebegone, pleading expression on her tear-swollen face.

"Huh! What's the use of waiting? You'll never do any different! You keep telling me to wait, wait, wait. Don't you know that age doesn't wait for anyone?" In his mid-thirties, the hair at his temples was already streaked with white and several teeth had worked loose. As he spoke these words, a mournful feeling gripped his heart.

Listening to him, she wept more bitterly. It was as if she found herself on top of a cliff facing the sea, and nothing lay before her eyes but a vast expanse of sea and sky. This vast expanse offered her no refuge—how could she go on living? Nevertheless she did not give way to despair, since she retained her faith in her child-bearing capacity. Once more she pleaded with him, "Please wait one more time, just this once! If there's no change this time, I won't stand in your way any longer. I don't want to make things worse for either of us."

Mr. Wenqing looked at the unhappy tears dripping down on the baby's little cheeks and remembered how over the last eight or nine years the two of them had offered each other mutual consolation and support over their lack of an heir. He realized that she too deserved pity. She had aged more than he, her forehead was deeply lined and she had just enough hair to form a bun the size of a duck's egg at the nape of her neck. So he replied with a downcast air, "All right, then, I'll do as you say."

The following year, she entered her seventh pregnancy. Calculating that the shape of the womb was different from before and believing that this time there would certainly be a change, she reenacted line by line the scenario of her last two pregnancies, in an even more zealous way. Mr. Wenqing again fetched Shaoxing wine and ham, and with renewed hope and encouragement, he too reenacted his old lines, with redoubled zeal. They were both so worked up that it seemed as if they were climbing a mountain toward a goal that must needs be won at all costs, where one slip of the foot would send them crashing down, risking total destruction.

However, fate is preordained, and this couple was destined to fall heavily once more—the seventh arrival was another girl!

There was no alternative for her now but to stifle her tears and assume her bitter maternal duties. When the concubine entered the household, overcome with resentment she hid in her room and refused to come out and receive her as the senior wife. But when the concubine entered the bridal chamber opposite, she tiptoed to the doorway and stole a glance outside.

The newcomer was from the countryside, and the lake-blue lined jacket showed off her swarthy complexion. She had a round face, broad cheeks, and large bold eyes. As she passed through the doorway her most prominent feature from the back was a pair of large fat buttocks, which shifted from side to side with every step.

"She should be good for plenty of sons and grandsons," thought the first wife, her understandable jealousy not unmixed with a certain relief.

Matters proceeded smoothly and the concubine became pregnant within six months of entering the household. This was a promising beginning, far different from the senior wife's sowlike immediate conceptions, and provoked a general consensus of public opinion in her favor.

"Country girl she may be, but she's got good luck on her side. There's every chance it's a boy, you know, and what a future she's got ahead of her!"

"The first wife specialized in girls, but this one'll start off with a boy right away. Heaven works in funny ways."

"Wenqing's getting on for forty; it's only proper he should have a son."

"It's really the first wife's fault, she couldn't produce a boy. Now the junior wife's the one with the big belly, of course the pattern will change . . . "

Listening to these remarks, Mr. Wenqing redoubled his attentions to his junior wife. He bought rare drugs for preventing miscarriages for her to take, and did not let her do anything that was in the least bit strenuous; and whenever his various daughters made a racket playing around anywhere near her he always yelled at them to stop, in case their antics might irritate her nerves.

All this of course troubled the first wife deeply. Not even in her first pregnancy, let alone her sixth or seventh, had he shown such careful consideration toward her. In this troubled state she fell pregnant for the eighth time.

"Another girl, for sure." The onlookers passed the word around with a sneer.

Mr. Wenqing took for granted that the child she was carrying was a girl, and did not bother to buy the Shaoxing wine and ham for her reward. All his efforts went into preparing a splendid feast for when his junior wife gave birth to a son, where she would take the place of honor before all the guests.

The elaborate arrangements and preparations that had been made for the senior wife's first confinement were now being put into effect again for the junior wife. The activity was accompanied by the eager anticipation of the relatives and neighbors, and the most enthusiastic of all was Mr. Wenqing, who seemed half intoxicated with joy.

And what do you think happened? Alas, she gave birth to a girl. The same as the first wife!

Mr. Wenqing's grief took a new turn. He began to suspect his own body—perhaps the male seed had already disappeared without trace. Wasn't it more hopeless than ever? On the verge of middle age and still no prospect of an heir in sight, what could keep him going now? Along life's highway a poisoned arrow of tradition had cruelly pierced his heart; the gray hairs gradually spread from the sides to the top of his head, and deep lines were etched along his cheeks.

One evening when he was returning from a friend's place after a game of mahjong, to his surprise he was greeted by two or three of his daughters with cries of "Papa, Papa, Mamma's had a baby."

"Huh," he answered coldly, thinking that it had been an easy delivery this time—they popped out with the ease of long experience.

"It's a baby brother, it's a baby brother, ha, ha, ha." The little girls announced in unison their extraordinary news.

"Ah!" Rushing headlong into the bedroom, he saw the newly born infant in the hands of a servant, while a burst of "Congratulations, a son and heir, congratulations," resounded in his ears, leaving him momentarily speechless.

He looked closely at the baby. Its head was covered with very fine soft hair, and the skin around its nose and tightly closed eyes was red and shiny, just like a newly born puppy. Presently, "Wah—" its adorable little mouth opened wide. He patted the baby on the head, and turning round to look at the new mother on the bed, he found her gazing at him, a tear glittering in the corner of each eye. Her strangely piercing gaze seemed to penetrate his very soul and deeply moved him. He rushed to her bedside and said tenderly, "You're worn out."

The new mother said nothing. Her eyes closed, squeezing out the tears that trickled down her dry, sallow cheeks; a trembling hand reached out and gripped Mr. Wenqing's hand, tightly, something that had never happened before.

The senior wife's dignity was from this point on restored, and all were unanimous in her praise. "Fortune's caught up with her now," they agreed. She herself was very clear that now she was fully entitled to make demands.

"You wanted a son, and now you have one, what do you want a concubine for? Sell her off!"

"Isn't that a little unnecessary?" Mr. Wenqing retained some fondness for her.

"What do you mean unnecessary? Didn't you say in the first place that it was because you didn't have a son? You should be ashamed of yourself! That wasn't the real reason after all." Then turning to the newly born baby, she burst into tears, "You poor little thing, you poor little thing."

"What are you crying for? All right, we'll sell her then. But what about the child?"

"Surely you don't expect me to take care of someone else's brat when I've got my hands full as it is. Let her take it with her, of course."

"But supposing it isn't convenient?"

"There's always the orphanage."

There was nothing further for Mr. Wenqing but to do as instructed. The junior wife was sold to a small merchant, a longtime widower, as his second wife. The child was given in adoption to a family in the front lane, to a couple who had waited in vain for more than ten years for a child of their own and who were now able to taste the joys of parenthood for the first time.

The new baby's name was Ah Jian (Strong-boy), chosen in the hope that this scion of their house would grow big and strong. Since his mother's milk seemed insufficient to keep up his strength, and she herself was hardly fit for much exertion, they departed from their usual practice and hired a wet nurse. They tried out first one and then another, and finally settled on the fourth. She was a fine strong country lass about twenty-two or twenty-three, who had left her own child of less than a month in someone else's care and come into town especially in order to take up this job. The baby clothes that had been passed down from daughter to daughter in turn were of course hardly suitable for their only son, and so from swaddling clothes to outerwear everything was new.

A rather large number of guests turned up at the feast to mark the baby's third day, since even people who were barely nodding acquaintances had been invited. "Man proposes, God disposes." This banquet Mr. Wenqing had actually prepared in honor of his junior wife. Nor had the women dreamt that such a thing would happen. But now, everything had turned out other than had been expected.

When the guests had arrived and the feasting began, Mr. Wenqing came out with the baby boy in his arms. Kissing him on his little brow, he lifted him up and turned around, saying, "Look at all your uncles and granddads." A self-satisfied smile reached across his face from ear to ear.

The guests looked at the plump little child, who was dressed in a red embroidered jacket and pants. His face was lightly dusted with powder, and a dab of rouge had been placed between his eyebrows. In due appreciation of his charms, they chorused, "What a fine child!"

Some of the guests further reasoned that this was a just reward for the accumulated virtues of both Wenqing himself and his ancestors, since to have a son in middle age was no small matter.

Mr. Wenqing, of course, made a modest reply. "You're too kind, I'm afraid this has nothing to do with any merit of mine. It's through Heaven's grace that we have the child; you might say Heaven placed it in our unworthy hands. Ha, ha, ha!" His wrinkled cheeks glowed with a rich red light.

"A toast! Our heartiest congratulations!" Each wine cup was raised high in the air.

"No, please allow me. I propose a toast to all of you." Holding the baby in one arm, Mr. Wenqing took up a cup from an empty place at the table, filled it to the brim and emptied it in one gulp. "Your health!"

Strong-boy's bringing up proceeded smoothly. By the end of his first year he could already understand what people were saying, and he gurgled for joy when they played with him. His constant baby talk, while still incoherent, was nonetheless richly expressive, and if he were put on the ground and given a hand, his little legs would pump up and down in a valiant attempt to walk. His parents idolized him and felt that life was perfect. The girls surrounded him with cries of "Baby brother" and treated him like a little prince.

However, in early summer when the weather was changing, Strong-boy fell sick. Initially it did not seem serious, merely a touch of diarrhea. But afterward he went off his milk and suddenly lost weight and became feverish. This of course caused immeasurable alarm to his parents. One doctor was not enough, so they called in a second opinion. At the same time they also engaged an astrologer to exorcise any evil spirits. The doctors' advice was actually misleading. They said he was suffering from indigestion and when his digestive powers were restored he would be all right. As the days passed, the child became more and more distressed, and his once lively eyes became fixed and dull. From time to time a dreadful thought, too awful to be said aloud even to each other, would flash across his parents' minds—"Could it happen?" However hard they tried to suppress it, it would soon recur—"Could it happen?"

Sure enough, on a day when evil spirits ruled, the child's illness took a critical turn. He didn't cry or toss around but just lay there gasping for breath. He stayed like this for seven or eight hours before his breathing ceased altogether. His eyes were still opened wide, the rigid pupils staring up at the grief-stricken parents.

You can easily imagine how his parents mourned and wept.

One dark evening about a week later, the news suddenly spread that there was a corpse in the small river on the west side of town, of a man in his early forties dressed in a scholar's gown and jacket. When the servant in Mr. Wenqing's household heard this, his heart missed a beat and he rushed to the spot. The dead body had already been fished out and was lying across a stone on the riverbank. "My god, it's our master!"

That evening, Mr. Wenqing had been drinking with friends at a wine shop. According to those friends, there had been nothing unusual about his manner at that time. He had declared philosophically, "Life is but a dream, what does it matter whether you have sons or not?" Nor had he drunk much, barely a catty of wine. It was really a puzzle how he could have fallen into the river on his way back.

This even more tragic turn of events, contrary to what might have been expected, seemed actually to mitigate his wife's not inconsiderable sorrow. Presenting an unusually cheerful face to the world, she frequently declared, "I've found out I'm pregnant again, and my belly's exactly the same shape it was last time. I'm certain it must be a boy. I'm going to love him more than ever, because he'll be a posthumous child."

This posthumous son was slow in arriving, but she did not fret. On the third anniversary of Mr. Wenqing's death, she still presented the same cheerful face, declaring, "It's the same as last time exactly. I'm certain it's a boy. He's my own precious heart, my posthumous son!" And she would stroke her belly, which did not protrude at all.

It was around this time that quite a few people were coming to discuss matches for the two eldest daughters.

1926

Yu Dafu (1896–1945)

SINKING

Translated by Joseph S. M. Lau and C. T. Hsia

1

Lately he had been feeling pitifully lonesome.

His emotional precocity had placed him at constant odds with his fellow men, and inevitably the wall separating him from them had gradually grown thicker and thicker.

The weather had been cooling off day by day, and it had been almost two weeks since his school started.

It was September 22d that day. The sky was one patch of cloudless blue; the bright sun, timeless and eternal, was still making its daily circuit on its familiar track. A gentle breeze from the south, fragrant as nectar, brushed against his face. Amid the half-ripened rice fields or on the meandering highways of the countryside he was seen strolling with a pocket edition of Wordsworth. On this great plain not a single soul was near, but then a dog's barking was heard, softened and rendered melodious by distance. He lifted his eyes from the book and, glancing in the direction of the barking, saw a cluster of trees and a few houses. The tiles on their roofs glittered like fish scales, and above them floated a thin layer of mist like a dancing ribbon of gossamer. "*Oh, you serene gossamer!*

you beautiful gossamer!"[1] he exclaimed, and for reasons unknown even to himself his eyes were suddenly filled with tears.

After watching the scene absently for a while, he caught from behind him a whiff suggestive of violets. A little herbaceous plant, rustling in the breeze, had sent forth this scent and broken his dreamy spell. He turned around: the plant was still quivering, and the gentle breeze dense with the fragrance of violets blew on his pallid face. In this crisp, early autumn weather, in this bright and pellucid *ether*, his body felt soothed and languid as if under a mild intoxication. He felt as if he were sleeping in the lap of a kind mother, or being transported to the Peach Blossom Spring in a dream,[2] or else reclining his head on the knees of his beloved for an afternoon nap on the coast of southern Europe.

Looking around, he felt that every tree and every plant was smiling at him. Turning his gaze to the azure sky, he felt that Nature herself, timeless and eternal, was nodding to him in greeting. And after staring at the sky fixedly for a while, he seemed to see a group of little winged angels, with bows and arrows on their shoulders, dancing up in the air. He was overjoyed and could not help soliloquizing:

"This, then, is your refuge. When all the philistines envy you, sneer at you, and treat you like a fool, only Nature, only this eternally bright sun and azure sky, this late summer breeze, this early autumn air still remains your friend, still remains your mother and your beloved. With this, you have no further need to join the world of the shallow and flippant. You might as well spend the rest of your life in this simple countryside, in the bosom of Nature."

Talking in this fashion, he began to pity himself, as if a thousand sorrows and grievances finding no immediate expression were weighing upon his heart. He redirected his tearful eyes to the book:

> Behold her, single in the field,
>   You solitary Highland Lass!
> Reaping and singing by herself;
>   Stop here, or gently pass!
> Alone she cuts and binds the grain,
> And sings a melancholy strain;
> O listen! for the Vale profound
> Is overflowing with the sound.

After reading through the first stanza, for no apparent reason he turned the page and started on the third:

---

1. Italicized common words, phrases, and sentences in this translation appear in Western languages in the original.

2. An utopia depicted by the poet Tao Qian (365–427) in his poem "Peach Blossom Spring" and its more famous preface.

Will no one tell me what she sings?
  Perhaps the plaintive numbers flow
For old, unhappy, far-off things,
  And battles long ago:
Or is it some more humble lay,
Familiar matter of today?
Some natural sorrow, loss, or pain,
That has been, and may be again?

It had been his recent habit to read out of sequence. With books over a few hundred pages, it was only natural that he seldom had the patience to finish them. But even with the slender volumes like Emerson's *Nature* or Thoreau's *Excursions*, he never bothered to read them from beginning to end at one sitting. Most of the time, when he picked up a book, he would be so moved by its opening lines or first two pages that he literally wanted to swallow the whole volume. But after three or four pages, he would want to savor it slowly and would say to himself: "I mustn't gulp down such a marvelous book at one sitting. Instead, I should chew it over a period of time. For my enthusiasm for the book will be gone the moment I am through with it. So will my expectation and dreams, and won't that be a crime?"

Every time he closed a book, he made up similar excuses for himself. The real reason was that he had already grown a little tired of it. However, a few days or even a few hours later he would pick up another book and begin to read it with the same kind of enthusiasm. And naturally the one that had touched him so much a few hours or days earlier would now be forgotten.

He raised his voice and read aloud once more these two stanzas of Wordsworth. Suddenly it occurred to him that he should render "The Solitary Reaper" in Chinese.[3]

After orally translating these two stanzas in one breath, he suddenly felt that he had done something silly and started to reproach himself: "What kind of a translation is that? Isn't it as insipid as the hymns sung in the church? English poetry is English poetry and Chinese poetry is Chinese poetry; why bother to translate?"

After saying this, unwittingly he smiled a little. Somewhat to his surprise, as he looked around him, the sun was already on its way down. On the western horizon across the great plain floated a tall mountain wrapped in its mists, which, saturated with the setting sun, showed a color neither quite purple nor quite red.

While he was standing there in a daze, a cough from behind his back signaled the arrival of a peasant. He turned around and immediately assumed a melancholy expression, as if afraid to show his smile before strangers.

---

3. Yu Dafu's translation of the two stanzas is omitted here.

2

His melancholy was getting worse with time.

To him the school textbooks were as insipid-tasting as wax, dull and lifeless. On sunny days he would take along a favorite work of literature and escape to a secluded place on the mountain or by the sea to relish to the full the joy of solitude. When all was silent about him at a place where sky and water met, he would now regard the plants, insects, and fish around him and now gaze at the white clouds and blue sky and feel as if he were a sage or hermit who had proudly detached himself from the world. Sometimes, when he ran into a peasant in the mountain, he would imagine himself Zarathustra and would repeat Zarathustra's sayings before the peasant. His *megalomania,* in exact proportion to his *hypochondria,* was thus intensified each day. Small wonder that, in such a mood, he didn't feel like going to school and applying himself to the mechanical work. Sometimes he would skip classes for four or five days in a row.

And when he was in school he always had the feeling that everyone was staring at him. He made every effort to dodge his fellow students, but wherever he went, he just couldn't shake off that uncomfortable suspicion that their malevolent gazes were still fixed on him.

When he attended classes, even though he was in the midst of all his classmates, he always felt lonely, and the kind of solitude he felt in a press of people was more unbearable by far than the kind he experienced when alone. Looking around, he always found his fellow students engrossed in the instructor's lecture; only he, despite his physical presence in the classroom, was wandering far and wide in a state of reverie.

At long last the bell rang. After the instructor had left, all his classmates were as lively and high-spirited as swallows newly returned in spring—chatting, joking, and laughing. Only he kept his brows knit and uttered not a sound, as if his tongue were tethered to a thousand-ton rock. He would have liked to chat with his fellow students but, perhaps discouraged by his sorrowful countenance, they all shunned his company and went their own ways in pursuit of pleasure. For this reason, his resentment toward them intensified.

"They are all Japanese, all my enemies. I'll have my revenge one day; I'll get even with them."

He would take comfort in this thought whenever he felt miserable. But in a better mood, he would reproach himself: "They are Japanese, and of course they don't have any sympathy for you. It's because you want their sympathy that you have grown to hate them. Isn't this your own mistake?"

Among his more sympathetic fellow students some did approach him, intending to start a conversation. But although he was very grateful and would have liked to open his heart to them, in the end he wouldn't say anything. As a result, even they respected his wishes and kept away from him.

Whenever his Japanese schoolmates laughed and joked in his presence, his face would redden because he thought the laughter and jokes were at his expense. He would also flush if, while conversing, one of these students glanced at him. Thus, the distance between him and his schoolmates became greater each day. They all thought him a loner and avoided his presence.

One day after school he was walking back to his inn, satchel in hand. Alongside him were three Japanese students heading in the same direction. Just as he was about to reach the inn, there suddenly appeared before him two girl students in red skirts. His breathing quickened, for girl students were a rare sight in this rural area. As the two girls tried to get by, the three Japanese boys accosted them: "Where are you going?"

Coquettishly the two girls answered, "Don't know, don't know."

The three students all laughed, pleased with themselves. He alone hurried back to his inn, as if he had done the accosting. Once in his room, he dropped his satchel on the tatami floor and lay down for a rest (the Japanese sit as well as sleep on the tatami). His heart was still beating wildly. Placing one hand underneath his head and another on his chest, he cursed himself:

"*You coward fellow, you are too coward!* If you are so shy, what's there for you to regret? If you now regret your cowardice, why didn't you summon up enough courage to talk to the girls? *Oh coward, coward!*"

Suddenly he remembered their eyes, their bright and lively eyes. They had really seemed to register a note of happy surprise on seeing him. Second thoughts on the matter, however, prompted him to cry out:

"Oh, you fool! Even if they seemed interested, what are they to you? Isn't it quite clear that their ogling was intended for the three Japanese? Oh, the girls must have known! They must have known that I am a 'Chinaman'; otherwise why didn't they even look at me once? Revenge! Revenge! I must seek revenge against their insult."

At this point in his monologue, a few icy teardrops rolled down his burning cheeks. He was in the utmost agony. That night, he put down in his diary:

"Why did I come to Japan? Why did I come here to pursue my studies? Since you have come, is it a wonder that the Japanese treat you with contempt? China, O my China! Why don't you grow rich and strong? I cannot bear your shame in silence any longer!

"Isn't the scenery in China as beautiful? Aren't the girls in China as pretty? Then why did I come to this island country in the eastern seas?

"And even if I accept the fact that I am here, there is no reason why I should have entered this cursed 'high school.'[4] Those who have returned to China after studying only five months here, aren't they now enjoying their success and

---

4. A Japanese "high school" of the early modern period provided an education equivalent to the last two years of an American high school and the first two years of college.

prosperity? How can I bear the five or six years that still lie ahead of me? And how can I be sure that, even if I managed to finish my long years of studies despite the thousand vexations and hardships, I would be in any way better off than those so-called returned students who came here simply for fun?

"One may live to a hundred, but his youth lasts only seven or eight years. What a pity that I should have to spend these purest and most beautiful seven or eight years in this unfeeling island country. And, alas, I am already twenty-one!

"Dead as dried wood at twenty-one!

"Dead as cold ashes at twenty-one!

"Far better for me to turn into some kind of mineral, for it's unlikely that I will ever bloom.

"I want neither knowledge nor fame. All I want is a 'heart' that can understand and comfort me, a warm and passionate heart and the sympathy that it generates and the love born of that sympathy!

"What I want is love.

"If there were one beautiful woman who understood my suffering, I would be willing to die for her.

"If there were one woman who could love me sincerely, I would also be willing to die for her, be she beautiful or ugly.

"For what I want is love from the opposite sex.

"O ye Heavens above, I want neither knowledge nor fame nor useless lucre. I shall be wholly content if you can grant me an Eve from the Garden of Eden, allowing me to possess her body and soul."

3

His home was in a small town on the Fuchun River, about eighty or ninety *li* from Hangzhou. The river originates in Anhui and wanders through the length of Zhejiang. Because it traverses a long tract of variegated landscape, a poet of the Tang dynasty wrote in admiration that "the whole river looks like a painting." When he was fourteen, he had asked one of his teachers to write down this line of four characters for him and had pasted it on the wall of his study. His study was not a big one, but since through its small window he could view the river in its ever-changing guises, rain and shine, morning and evening, spring and autumn, it had been to him as good as Prince Teng's tall pavilion.[5] And in this small study he had spent more than ten years before coming with his elder brother to Japan for study.

When he was three his father had passed away, leaving the family in severe poverty. His elder brother, however, managed to graduate from W. University

5. Celebrated in the Tang poet Wang Bo's lyrical prose composition "The Pavilion of Prince Teng."

in Japan, and upon his return to Beijing, he earned the *jinshi*[6] degree and was appointed to a position in the Ministry of Justice. But in less than two years the Republican revolution started in Wuchang. He himself had by then finished grade school and was changing from one middle school to another. All his family reproved him for his restlessness and lack of perseverance. In his own view, however, he was different from other students and ought not to have studied the same prescribed courses through the same sequence of grades. Thus, in less than half a year, he transferred from the middle school in the city K. to one in H. where, unfortunately, he stayed less than three months owing to the outbreak of the revolution. Deprived of his schooling in the city H., he could only return to his own little study.

In the spring of the following year he was enrolled in the preparatory class for H. College on the outskirts of Hangzhou. He was then seventeen. Founded by the American Presbyterian Church, the college was notorious for its despotic administration and the minimal freedom it allowed its students. On Wednesday evenings they were required to attend vespers. On Sundays they were not allowed to go out or to read secular books—they could only pray, sing psalms, or read the Old and New Testaments. They were also required to attend chapel every morning from nine to nine twenty: the delinquent student would get demerits and lower grades. It was only natural that, as a lover of freedom, he chafed under such superstitious restrictions, fond as he was of the beautiful scenery around the campus. He had not yet been there half a year when a cook in the employ of the college, counting on the president's backing, went so far as to beat up students. Some of his more indignant schoolmates went to the president to complain, only to be told that they were in the wrong. Finding this and similar injustices altogether intolerable, he quit the school and returned to his own little study. It was then early June.

He had been home for more than three months when the autumn winds reached the Fuchun River and the leaves of the trees on its banks were about to fall. Then he took a junk down the river to go to Hangzhou where, he understood, the W. Middle School at the Stone Arch was then recruiting transfer students. He went to see the principal, Mr. M., and his wife and told them of his experience at H. College. Mr. M. allowed him to enroll in the senior class.

It turned out, however, that this W. Middle School was also church-supported and that this Mr. M. was also a muddleheaded American missionary. And academically this school was not even comparable to the preparatory class at H. College. After a quarrel with the academic dean, a contemptible character and a graduate of H. College as well, he left W. Middle School in the spring.

---

6. Refers to a successful candidate in the civil service examination system before the founding of the Republic of China. A *jinshi* is one who has passed the examination held in the imperial capital.

Since there was no other school in Hangzhou to his liking, he made no plans to be admitted elsewhere.

It was also at this time that his elder brother was forced to resign his position in Beijing. Being an upright man of strict probity and better educated than most of his colleagues in the ministry, he had invited their fear and envy. One day a personal friend of a certain vice-minister asked for a post and he stubbornly refused to give him one; as a result, that vice-minister disagreed with him on certain matters, and in a few days he resigned his post to serve in the Judicial Yuan. His second elder brother was at that time an army officer stationed in Shaoxing. He was steeped in the habits of the military and therefore loved to squander money and associate with young gallants. Because these three brothers happened at the same time to be not doing too well, the idlers in their hometown began to speculate whether their misfortune was of a geomantic nature.

After he had returned home, he shut himself in his study all day and sought guidance and companionship in the library of his grandfather, father, and elder brother. The number of poems he wrote in his diary began to grow. On occasions he also wrote stories in an ornate style featuring himself as a romantic knight-errant and the two daughters of the widow next door as children of nobility. Naturally the scenic descriptions in these stories were simply idyllic pictures of his hometown. Sometimes, when the mood struck him, he would translate his own stories into some foreign language, employing the simple vocabulary at his command. In a word, he was more and more enveloped in a world of fantasy, and it was probably during this time that the seeds of his *hypochondria* were sown.

He stayed at home for six months. In the middle of July, however, he got a letter from his elder brother saying: "The Judicial Yuan has recently decided to send me to Japan to study its judicial system. My acceptance has already been forwarded to the minister and a formal appointment is expected in a few days. I will, however, go home first and stay for a while before leaving for Japan. Since I don't think idling at home will do you any good, this time I shall take you with me to Japan." This letter made him long for his brother's return, though he did not arrive from Beijing with his wife until the latter part of September. After a month's stay, they sailed with him for Japan.

Though he was not yet awakened from his *dreams of the romantic age*, upon his arrival in Tokyo, he nevertheless managed to pass the entrance examination for Tokyo's First High School after half a year. He would be in his nineteenth year in the fall.

When the First High School was about to open, his elder brother received word from the ministry that he should return. Thus his brother left him in the care of a Japanese family and a few days later returned with his wife and newborn daughter.

The First High School had set up a preparatory program especially for Chinese students so that upon completing that program in a year they could enroll along with the Japanese students in regular courses of study in the high school of their choice. When he first got into the program, his intended major was literature. Later, however, when he was about to complete the course, he changed to medicine, mainly under pressure from his brother but also because he didn't care much either way.

After completing his preparatory studies, he requested that he be sent to the high school in N. City, partly because he heard it was the newest such school in Japan and partly because N. City was noted for its beautiful women.

4

In the evening of August 29, in the twentieth year of his life, he took a night train all by himself from Tokyo's central station to N. City.

It was probably the third or fourth day of the seventh month in the old calendar. A sky the color of indigo velvet was studded with stars. The crescent moon, hooked in the western corner of the sky, looked like the untinted eyebrow of a celestial maiden. Sitting by the window in a third-class coach, he silently counted the lights in the houses outside. As the train steadily surged ahead through the black mists of the night, the lights of the great metropolis got dimmer and dimmer until they disappeared from his ken. Suddenly his heart was overtaken by a thousand melancholy thoughts, and his eyes were again moist with warm tears. "*Sentimental, too sentimental!*" he exclaimed. Then, drying his tears, he felt like mocking himself:

"You don't have a single sweetheart, brother, or close friend in Tokyo—so for whom are you shedding your tears? Perhaps grieving for your past life, or feeling sad because you have lived there for the last two years? But haven't you been saying you don't care for Tokyo?

"Oh, but how can one help being attached to a place even after living there for only one year?"

> The orioles know me well because I have long lived here;
> When I am getting ready to leave, they keep crying, four or five sad notes at a time.[7]

Then his rambling thoughts turned to the first Puritans embarking for America: "I imagine that those cross-bearing expatriates were no less grief-stricken than I am now when sailing off the coast of their old country."

The train had now passed Yokohama, and his emotions began to quiet down. After collecting himself for a while, he placed a postcard on top of a volume of Heine's poetry and with a pencil composed a poem intended for a friend in Tokyo:

---

7. A couplet from a quatrain by the Tang poet Rong Yu, entitled "Bidding Goodbye to the Pavilion on the Lake on the Occasion of Moving My Home." The translators are indebted to Professor Chiang Yee for this identification.

The crescent barely rising above the willows,
I again left home for a distant horizon,
First pausing in a roadside tavern crowded with revelers,
Then taking off in a carriage as the streetlights receded.
A youth inured to partings and sorrows has few tears to shed;
The luggage from a poor home consists only of old books.
At night the reeds find their roots stirred by autumn waters—
May you get my message at South Bank!

Then after resting for a while, he read some of Heine's poetry under a dim lightbulb:

Lebet wohl, ihr glatten Säle,
Glatte Herren, glatte Frauen!
Auf die Berge will ich steigen,
Lachend auf euch niederschauen![8]

But with the monotonous sound of the wheels pounding against his eardrums, in less than thirty minutes he was transported into a land of dreams. At five o'clock dawn began to break. Peering through the window, he was able to discern a thread of blue making its way out of the nocturnal darkness. He then stuck his head out the window and saw a picturesque scene wrapped in haze. "So it's going to be another day of nice autumn weather," he thought. "How fortunate I am!"

An hour later the train arrived at N. City's railroad station. Alighting from the train, he saw at the station a Japanese youth wearing a cap marked by two white stripes and knew him for a student of the high school. He walked toward him and, lifting his cap slightly, asked, "How do I find the X. High School?" The student answered, "Let's go there together." So with the student he left the station and took a trolley in front of its entrance.

The morning was still young, and shops in N. City were not yet open. After passing through several desolate streets, they got off in front of the Crane Dance Park.

"Is the school far from here?" he asked.

"About two *li*."

---

8. "You polished halls, polished men. / Polished women—to all adieu! / I'm off to climb in the mountains, / And smiling to look down on you!" These lines form the last stanza of the Prologue to Heine's "Harzreise" (Travels through the Harz Mountains). See Heinrich Heine, *Werke*, ed. Martin Greiner (Cologne and Berlin: Kiepenheuer & Witsch, 1962), pp. 767–824. The poem is a satire in the form of a travel diary written in late 1824, criticizing the superficial policy of polite society, which Heine's narrator longs to abandon for the simple life in the mountains. The translators are grateful to William Nienhauser for translating this poem.

The sun had risen by the time they were walking the narrow path between the rice fields after crossing the park, but the dewdrops were still on the rice stalks, bright as pearls. Across the fields in front were clusters of trees shading some scattered farmhouses. Two or three chimneys rising above these structures seemed to float in the early morning air, and bluish smoke emanating from them curled in the sky like incense. He knew that the farmers were preparing breakfast.

He inquired at an inn close to the school and was informed that the few pieces of luggage sent out the previous week had already arrived. The innkeeper, used to Chinese lodgers, gave him a hearty welcome. After unpacking, he had the feeling that the days ahead promised much joy and pleasure.

But all his hopes for the future were mocked by reality that very evening. His hometown, however small, was a busy little town, and while he had often felt lonely amid large throngs in Tokyo, nevertheless the kind of city life there was not too different from what he had been accustomed to since childhood. Now this inn, situated in the countryside of N. City, was far too isolated. To the left of its front door was a narrow path cutting across the rice fields; only a square pond to the west of the inn provided some diversity to the scene. Since school had not yet begun, students had not yet returned, and thus he was the only guest in this spacious hostel. It was still not too unbearable in the day, but that evening, when he pushed open the window to look out, everywhere was pitch darkness. For the countryside of N. City was a large plain, with nothing to obstruct one's view. A few lights were visible in the distance, now bright and now dim, lending to the view a spectral quality. Up above the ceiling he could hear the scampering rats fighting for food, while outside the window several *wutong* trees would rustle whenever there was a breeze. Because his room was on the second floor, the rattle of the leaves sounded so close that he was frightened almost to the point of tears. He had never felt a stronger nostalgia than on that evening.

He got to know more people after school started, and his extremely sensitive nature also became adapted to the pastoral environment. In less than three months he had become Nature's child, no longer separable from the pleasures of the countryside.

His school was located on the outskirts of N. City, which, as has already been mentioned, were nothing but open fields offering an unobstructed vision of broad horizons. At that time Japan was not so industrialized or populous as it is now. Hence this large area of open space around the school, diversified only by clumps of trees and little knolls and mounds. Except for a few stationery shops and restaurants serving the needs of the students, there were no stores in the neighborhood. A few inns, however, dotted the cultivated fields in this mainly unfilled wilderness. After supper he would put on his black serge cloak and, a favorite book in hand, take a walk in the lingering glow of the setting sun. Most probably it was during these *idyllic wanderings* that he developed his passion for nature.

So at a time when competition was not as keen as today and leisure was as plentiful as in the Middle Ages, he spent half a year of dreamlike existence in a quiet retreat, simple in its manners and uncontaminated by the presence of philistines. These happy days and months seemed to go by in a flash.

The weather was now getting milder, and the grass was turning green under the influence of warm breezes. The young shoots in the wheat fields near the inn were growing taller inch by inch. With all nature responding to the call of spring, he too felt more keenly the urge implanted in him by the progenitors of the human race. Unflaggingly, he would sin every morning underneath his quilt.

He was ordinarily a very self-respecting and clean person, but when evil thoughts seized hold of him, numbing his intellect and paralyzing his conscience, he was no longer able to observe the admonition that "one must not harm one's body under any circumstances, since it is inherited from one's parents."[9] Every time he sinned he felt bitter remorse and vowed not to transgress again. But, almost without exception, the same visions appeared before him vividly, at the same time the next morning. All those descendants of Eve he would normally meet in the course of the day came to seduce him in all their nakedness, and the figure of a middle-aged *madam* appeared to him even more tempting than that of a virgin. Inevitably, after a hard struggle, he succumbed to temptation. Thus once, twice, and this practice became a habit. Quite often, after abusing himself, he would go to the library to look up medical references on the subject. They all said without exception that this practice was most harmful to one's health. After that his fear increased.

One day he learned somewhere in a book that Gogol, the founder of modern Russian literature, had also suffered from this sickness and was not able to cure himself to the day of his death. This discovery comforted him somewhat, if only because no less a man than the author of *Dead Souls* was his fellow sinner. But this form of self-deception could do little to remove the worry in his heart.

Since he was very much concerned about his health, he now took a bath and had milk and several raw eggs every day. But he couldn't help feeling ashamed of himself when taking his bath or having his milk and eggs: all this was clear evidence of his sin.

He felt that his health was declining day by day and his memory weakening. He became shy and especially uncomfortable in the presence of women. He grew to loathe textbooks and turned increasingly to French naturalistic novels as well as a few Chinese novels noted for their pornography. These he now read and reread so many times that he could almost recite them from memory.

On the infrequent occasions when he turned out a good poem he became overjoyed, believing that his brain had not yet been damaged. He would then swear to himself: "My brain is all right, since I can still compose such a good

---

9. From *The Book on Filial Piety* (*Xiaojing*), an early Confucian classic.

poem: I mustn't do that sort of thing again. The past I can no longer help, but I shall control myself in the future. If I don't sin again, my brain will be in good shape." But when that critical moment came each morning, he again forgot his own words.

On every Thursday and Friday or on the twenty-sixth and twenty-seventh of each month he abandoned himself to this pleasure without a qualm, for he thought that he would be able to stop by next Monday or next month. Sometimes when he happened to have a haircut or a bath on a Saturday evening or the evening of the last day of the month, he would take that as a sign of his reformation. But only a few days later he would have to resume his diet of milk and eggs.

Hardly a day passed in which he was not troubled by his own fears as well as by his sense of guilt, and his hypochondria worsened. He remained in such a condition for about two months, and then the summer vacation began. However, he suffered even worse during the two-month vacation than before: for by the time school resumed, his cheekbones had become more prominent, the bluish-gray circles around his eyes even bigger, and his once-bright pupils as expressionless as those of a dead fish.

5

Again it was fall. The big blue firmament seemed to be suspended higher and higher each day. The rice fields around his inn had now turned the color of gold. When the chilly winds of morning or evening cut into his skin like a dagger, he knew that bright autumn days were not far behind.

The week before, he had taken along a volume of Wordsworth and strolled on the paths in the fields for a whole afternoon. From that day on he had not been able to free himself from the spell of his cyclic hypochondria. Moreover, the two girl students he had met a few days before stayed in his memory and he couldn't help blushing whenever he recalled that encounter.

Recently, wherever he went, he was uneasy. At school he had the feeling that his Japanese classmates were avoiding him. And he no longer wanted to visit his Chinese classmates simply because after each such visit his heart felt all the more empty. Those Chinese friends of his, hard as they tried, still couldn't understand his state of mind. Before each visit he expected to win their sympathy, but as it happened, no sooner had they exchanged a few words than he began to regret his visit. There was one, however, whose conversation he enjoyed, and sometimes he told him all about his private and public life. On his way home, however, he always regretted having talked so much and ended up in a worse state of self-reproach than before. For this reason a rumor circulated among his Chinese friends that he was mentally ill. When the rumor reached him, he wanted as much to avenge himself on these few Chinese friends as on his Japanese schoolmates. He was finally so alienated from the Chinese that he wouldn't even greet them when he met them in the street or on the campus. Naturally he didn't attend any of the meetings for Chinese students, so that he and they became virtual enemies.

Among these Chinese students there was one eccentric. Probably because there was something reprehensible about his marriage, he seemed to take particular delight in malicious gossip—partly as a means of covering up his own immoral conduct. And it was none other than this eccentric who had spread the rumor that he was mentally ill.

His loneliness became most intolerable after he had cut himself off from all social contacts. Fortunately, the innkeeper's daughter held some attraction for him, for otherwise he could really have committed suicide. She was just seventeen and had an oblong face and big eyes. Whenever she smiled, she showed two dimples and one gold tooth, and quite often she put a smile on her face, confident of its charm.

Although he was very fond of her, when she came in to make his bed or deliver his meals he always put on an air of aloofness. And however badly he wanted to talk to her, he never did because he could hardly breathe in front of her. To avoid this insufferable agony, he had lately tried to leave his room as soon as she entered it. But the more he tried to avoid her, the more he longed for her.

One Saturday evening all the other students in the inn had gone to N. City to amuse themselves. For economic reasons he didn't go there. He returned to his room following a brief after-dinner stroll around the pond on the west side. But it was difficult for him to stay by himself on the deserted second floor, and soon he got impatient and wanted to go out again. To leave the place, however, meant passing the door of the innkeeper's own room, which was situated right by the main entrance, and he remembered when he returned that the innkeeper and his daughter were just having dinner. At this thought he no longer had the desire to go out again, since seeing her would mean another torturing experience.

Instead, he took out a novel by George Gissing and started to read; but before he had finished three or four pages, he heard, in the dead silence, the splashing of water. He held his breath and listened for a while, and soon he started panting, and his face turned red. After some moments of hesitation, he pushed open the door quietly and, taking off his slippers, went down the stairs stealthily. With equal caution he pushed open the door to the toilet and stood by its glass window to peer into the bathroom (the bathroom was adjacent to the toilet; through the glass window one could see the goings-on in the bathroom). At first he thought he would be content with just a glance. But what he saw in the next room kept him completely nailed down.

Those snow-white breasts! Those voluptuous thighs! And that curvaceous figure!

Holding his breath, he took another close look at the girl and a muscle in his face began to twitch. Finally he became so overwrought that his forehead hit the windowpane. The naked Eve then asked across the steam, "Who is it?" Without making a sound, he hurriedly left the toilet and rushed upstairs.

Back in his room he felt his face burning and his mouth parched. To punish himself, he kept slapping his own face while taking out the bedding to get ready for sleep. But he could hardly fall asleep. After tossing and turning under the quilt for a while, he strained his ears and concentrated all his attention on the movements downstairs. The splashing had stopped, and he heard the bathroom door open. And judging by the sound of her footsteps, he was positive she was coming upstairs. Immediately he buried his head beneath the quilt and listened to the whisper of his inner voice: "She's already outside the door." He felt as if all his blood were rushing to his head. Certainly he was now in a state of unusual excitement, compounded of fear, shame, and joy, but if someone had asked him at that moment, he would have denied that he was filled with joy.

Holding his breath, he strained his ears and listened—all was quiet on the other side of the door. He coughed deliberately—still no response. But just as he was getting puzzled, he heard her voice downstairs talking with her father. Hard as he tried (he was so tense that his palms were soaked in sweat), he still couldn't make out anything she was saying. Presently her father roared with laughter. Burying his head under the quilt, he said through clenched teeth, "So she's told him! She's told him!"

He didn't get a wink of sleep that night. Early the next morning he stole downstairs to make a quick toilet and rushed out of the inn. It was not yet time for the innkeeper and his daughter to get up.

The sun was rising, but the dew-drenched dust on the road had not yet dried. Without knowing exactly where to go, he headed east and before long saw a peasant pushing a vegetable cart coming his way. "Good morning," the peasant greeted him as their shoulders brushed. This took him by surprise, and immediately his emaciated face flushed red. He wondered, "So he also knows my secret?"

After walking hurriedly with no sense of direction for a long while, he turned his head and saw that he was already a great distance from his school. The sun had now risen. He wanted to determine the time but could not do so, since he had forgotten to take his silver pocket watch along. Judging by the position of the sun, it was probably about nine o'clock. He was hungry, but unwilling to go back and face the innkeeper and his daughter, though all he had on him was twelve cents, hardly enough for a decent snack. Finally he bought from a village grocery store twelve cents' worth of food, intending to eat it in a nook, unseen by others.

He kept walking until he reached a crossroads. There were very few pedestrians on the side path running from north to south. Since the south side sloped downward, flanked by two precipices, he knew that the path had been dug out of a hill. Thus the crossroads was the tip of the hill, while the main path on which he had been walking was its ridge and the intersecting side path sloped in two directions, following the hill's contour. He paused at the crossroads for a while and then came upon a large plain that he knew would lead to the city.

Across the plain was a dense grove where, he thought, the A. Shinto Temple was located. When he had reached the end of the path, he saw that there stood upon its left bank a parapet encircling a few cottages. Above the door of one of these cottages hung a tablet inscribed with three Chinese characters, *xiang xue hai* (sea of fragrant snow).[10] He walked up a few steps to the entrance of the parapet and with one push opened both sides of the door. Stepping casually inside, he found a winding path leading uphill flanked by a great many old *mei* trees and knew for sure that this was a *mei* grove. He walked up the northern slope along this winding path until he reached the hilltop, where he saw stretching before him a plateau of great scenic beauty. From the foot of the hill to the plateau, the whole grove covering the surface of the slope was most tastefully planned.

West of the plateau was the precipice, which faced another across the gulf, and down below was the narrow pathway he had just traversed. Aligned on the edge of this precipice were a two-story house and several cottages. Since all their doors and windows were tightly shut, he knew that they were restaurants and taverns, open only during the season of the *mei* blossoms. In front of the two-story house was a lawn with a ring of white rocks at its center, and inside the ring an old *mei* tree crouched on its gnarled trunk. At the outer edge of the lawn marking the beginning of the southern slope stood a stone tablet recording the history of the grove. He sat on the grass in front of the tablet and started eating the food he had bought in the grocery store.

He sat on the lawn for a while even after he had finished breakfast. There were no human voices; only from the trees in the farther distance came the occasional chirping of birds. Gazing at the azure sky, he felt that everything around him—the trees and houses, the lawn and birds—was being equally nourished by Nature, under the benign influence of the sun. In face of all this, his memory of last night's sin vanished like a boat sailing beyond the outer rim of the sea.

From the plateau to the end of the downhill slope there were many little winding paths. He got up and walked randomly among these until he came to a cottage situated midway down the slope, surrounded by *mei* trees. Nearby on the east side was an ancient well covered with a heap of pine needles. He turned the handle of the pump several times trying to draw some water, but the machine only creaked and no water came up. He thought, "Probably this grove is open only during the flowering season. No wonder there's no one around." Then he murmured as another thought flashed upon him, "Since the grove is unoccupied, why don't I go and ask the owner if I could lodge here for a while?"

10. A traditional metaphor for a grove of *mei* or Japanese apricot trees.

This decided, he rushed downhill to look for the owner. As he came near the entrance, he ran into a peasant around fifty years of age coming into the grove. He apologized and then inquired, "Do you know who owns this place?"

"It's under my management."

"Where do you live?"

"Over there." The peasant pointed to a little house on the west side of the main path. Following his direction, he saw the house on the far end of the western precipice and nodded to acknowledge its existence. Then he asked, "Can you rent me that two-story house inside the grove?"

"Sure. But are you by yourself?"

"Yes."

"Then you might as well save yourself the trouble."

"Why?"

"Because I have had student tenants before, and they hardly stayed more than ten days before they moved out, probably because they couldn't stand the solitude."

"I'm quite different from the others. I won't mind the solitude as long as you agree to rent the place to me."

"I can't think of any reason why not. When do you want to move in?"

"How about this afternoon?"

"It's all right with me."

"Then may I trouble you to clean it up before I move in?"

"Certainly, certainly. Good-bye!"

"Good-bye."

6

After he had moved to the *mei* grove, his *hypochondria* took a different turn.

Over some trivial matters he had started a quarrel with his elder brother, which prompted him to mail to Beijing a long, long letter severing ties of kinship. But after that letter was sent, he mused for many an hour in front of his house. He thought he was the most miserable man in the world. Actually, he was the one to blame for this fraternal split, but precisely because a quarrel of this sort is usually more bitter than a quarrel among friends, he hated his brother like a viper or scorpion. When he was humiliated, he would reason thus: "If even my own brother could be so unkind to me, how can I blame others?" After reaching this conclusion, he would review all the unkind things that he imagined his brother had done to him and declare that his brother was bad and he himself was good. He would then itemize his own virtues and list all his past wrongs and sufferings in an exaggerated fashion. When he had proved to his own satisfaction that he was indeed the most miserable of all men, his tears would course down like a waterfall. A soft voice would seem to be speaking to him from the sky: "Oh, so it's you who are crying. It's really a shame that such a kindhearted person as you should be so maltreated by the world.

But let it be, since it has been decreed by Heaven, and you'd better stop crying, since it won't do your health any good." When he heard this voice, he would feel greatly relieved: there seemed to be infinite sweetness in chewing the cud of bitter sorrow.

As a means of retaliation, he gave up his study of medicine and switched to literature, intending this change of major to be a declaration of war, since it was his brother who had urged him to study medicine. Also, changing his major would delay his graduation for a year, which meant shortening his life by one year, and the sooner he died, the easier it would be to maintain a lifelong enmity toward his brother. For he was quite afraid that he would be reconciled with his brother in a year or two, and he changed his major to help strengthen his sense of enmity.

The weather had gradually turned colder. It had been a month since he moved up the hill. In the past few days dark clouds had hung heavily in the somber sky, and when the frosty northern winds came, the leaves on the *mei* trees would begin to fall.

Upon moving to his retreat, he had sold some old books to buy cooking utensils and had made his own meals for nearly a month. Now that it was getting chillier, he gave up cooking and ate at the grove keeper's house down the hill. Like a retired monk idling in a temple, he had nothing to do but to blame others and reproach himself.

One morning he got up very early. Pushing open the window facing the east, he saw a few curls of red cloud floating on the far horizon. The sky directly above was a patch of reddish silver-gray. Because it had drizzled the day before, he found the rising sun all the more lovely. He went down the slope and fetched water from the ancient well. After washing his face and hands with the water, he felt full of energy and ran upstairs for a volume of Huang Zhongze's[11] poetry. He kept pacing along the winding paths in the grove as he chanted the poetry. Soon the sun was up in the sky.

Looking southward from the plateau, he could see, at the foot of the hill, a large plain checkered with rice fields. The unharvested grain, ripened to a yellowish gold, gave a most brilliant reflection of the morning sun against the background of a violet sky. The scene reminded him of a rural painting by Millet. Faced with this magnificence of Nature, he felt like an early Christian of Jesus' time and could not help laughing at his own pettiness:

"Forgive, forgive! I have forgiven all ye who have wronged me. Come ye all and make peace with me!"

As he was contemplating—with a book of poems in hand and tears in eyes—the beauty of the autumnal scene and thus getting lost in thought, all of a sudden he heard two whispering voices close by him:

---

11. The famous Qing poet (1749–1783) is the hero of Yu Dafu's story "Colored Rock Cliff."

"You have to come tonight!" It was clearly a man's voice.

"I want to very much, but I'm afraid . . . "

It was a girl's seductive voice, and he felt instantly electrified, as if his circulation had stopped. Looking around, he found himself standing by a growth of tall reeds. He was on its right and the couple was probably on its left, completely oblivious of his existence.

"You are so kind. Do come tonight, because so far we haven't . . . in bed," the man continued.

" . . . "

He heard the noise made by their sucking lips, and immediately he prostrated himself on the ground, as stealthily as a wild dog with a stolen morsel in its mouth. "Oh, shame, shame!" he cursed himself severely in his heart. "How can you be so depraved!" Nevertheless, he was all ears, listening to what they were doing and saying.

The crunching of fallen leaves on the ground.

The noise of undressing.

The man's rapid panting.

The sucking of lips.

And the woman pleading in half-audible, broken tones: "Please . . . please . . . please hurry . . . otherwise we . . . we will be seen . . . "

Instantly his complexion turned ash-gray, his eyes reddened with fire, and his upper teeth clattered against his lower. He could hardly get up, let alone run away from the scene. He was transfixed in agony.

He waited there until the couple had left before he went back to his bedroom upstairs like a drenched dog and covered himself up with a quilt.

7

Without bothering with lunch, he slept until four o'clock—until the whole area was suffused with the late afternoon sun. In the distance a thin veil of smoke was seen floating leisurely on top of the trees across the plain. Hurriedly he ran downhill to get on the road and headed south for no apparent reason. He eventually crossed the plain to arrive at the trolley stop in front of the A. Temple. A trolley came by just then and he boarded it, without knowing why he should be taking the trolley or where he was going.

After running for fifteen or sixteen minutes, the trolley stopped and the operator asked him to change cars. So he took another trolley. Twenty or thirty minutes later it reached its last stop, and so he got off. He found himself standing by a harbor.

In front of him was the sea, lazing in the afternoon sun, smiling. Across the sea to the south was the silhouette of a mountain floating hazily in translucent air. To the west was a long dike, stretching to the middle of the bay. A lighthouse stood beyond the dike like a giant. A few tethered boats and sampans were moving slightly, while a number of buoys farther out in the bay shone red on the water. The wind carried from a distance broken snatches of a conversation, but he was unable to tell what it was about or where it came from.

After pacing aimlessly for a while on the bank, he suddenly heard something that sounded like chimes. He went over and saw that the musical signal was designed to attract customers to the ferry. Soon a steamboat came by from the opposite side. Following a middle-aged worker, he too boarded the ferry.

No sooner had he landed on the eastern bank than he found himself in front of a villa. The door was wide open, showing a courtyard neatly decorated with a lawn, flowering plants, and miniature hills made of rocks. Without finding out the identity of the place, he simply walked in and was immediately greeted by a very sweet feminine voice: "Please come in."

Taken by surprise, he stood there in a daze and thought, "This is probably some kind of restaurant, but I have heard a place like this cannot be without prostitutes."

At the thought of this he became invigorated, as if drenched by a bucketful of cold water. But he soon changed color because he didn't know what to do with himself, whether to advance or retreat. It was a pity that he had the lust of an ape and the timidity of a rabbit, which accounted for his present quandary.

"Come in. Please do come in." That seductive voice called from the hall again, accompanied by giggles.

"You devils! You think I am too timid to come in?" he said to himself in anger, his face burning hot. Stamping his feet lightly, he advanced, gnashing his teeth and clenching his fists, as if preparing to declare war on these young waitresses. But hard as he tried, he couldn't possibly erase the flushes of red and blue on his face nor compose its twitching muscles. So when he came near these girls, he almost cried like a child.

"Please come upstairs!"

"Please come upstairs!"

Bracing himself, he followed a waitress of around seventeen or eighteen upstairs and felt somewhat calmer. A few steps on the second floor and he came into a dark corridor; immediately his nostrils were assaulted by a strange mixture of the perfume of face powder and hair tonic and the special kind of bodily fragrance that distinguished Japanese women. He felt dizzy and sparks floated before his eyes, which made him reel. After steadying himself, he saw emerging from the darkness in front of him the oblong, powdered face of a woman who asked him with a smile:

"Would you like to have a place by the sea? Or did you have a special place in mind?"

He felt the woman's warm breath upon his face and he inhaled deeply without being aware of what he was doing. But as soon as he became conscious of his action, his face reddened. With great effort he mumbled an answer:

"I'll take a room facing the sea."

After taking him to a small room by the sea, the waitress asked what kind of food he would like, and he answered:

"Just bring a few dishes of what you have ready."

"Want some wine?"

"Yes."

After the waitress had left, he stood up and pushed open the paper windows to let in some fresh air, for the room was stuffy and her perfumed presence lingered on, suffocating him.

The bay was calm. A light breeze passed by and the surface of the sea was wrinkled into a series of waves that, under the reflection of the setting sun, glinted like the scales of a golden fish.

After watching the scene from the window for a while, he was moved to whisper a line of poetry:

"The setting sun has crimsoned my seaside chamber."[12]

Looking westward, he saw that the sun was now only about ten feet from the horizon. But however beautiful the scene, his thoughts were still with the waitress—the fragrance emanating from her mouth, hair, face, and body. After repeated attempts to engage his mind elsewhere, he resigned himself to the fact that in his present mood he was obsessed with flesh rather than poetry.

Before long the waitress brought in his food and wine. She squatted by him and served him most attentively. He wanted to look closely at her and confide in her all his troubles. But in reality he didn't even dare look her in the eye, much less talk to her. And so, like a mute, all he did was look furtively at her delicate, white hands resting upon her knees and that portion of a pink petticoat not covered by her kimono.

For Japanese women wear a short petticoat instead of drawers. On the outside they wear a buttonless, long-sleeved kimono with a band about fourteen inches wide around the waist fastened into a square bundle on the back. Because of this costume, with every step they take, the kimono is flung open to reveal the pink petticoat inside and a glimpse of plump thighs. This is the special charm of Japanese women to which he paid most attention whenever he saw them on the street. It was because of this habit too that he called himself a beast, a sneaky dog, and a despicable coward.

It was specifically the corner of the waitress's petticoat that was perturbing him now. The more he wanted to talk to her, the more tongue-tied he became. His embarrassment was apparently making the waitress a little impatient, for she asked, "Where are you from?"

At this, his pallid face reddened again; he stammered and stammered but couldn't give a forthright answer. He was once again standing on the guillotine. For the Japanese look down upon Chinese just as we look down upon pigs and

12. Most probably this line of verse is Yu Dafu's own composition.

dogs. They call us Shinajin, "Chinamen," a term more derogatory than "knave" in Chinese. And now he had to confess before this pretty young girl that he was a Shinajin.

"O China, my China, why don't you grow strong!"

His body was trembling convulsively and tears were again about to roll down.

Seeing him in such agitation, the waitress thought it would be best to leave him to drink alone, so that he could compose himself. So she said:

"You have almost finished this bottle. I'll get you another one."

In a while he heard the waitress coming upstairs. He thought she was coming back to him, and so he changed his sitting position and adjusted his clothes. But he was deceived, for she was only taking some other guests to the room next to his.

Soon he heard the guests flirting with the waitress, who said coquettishly, "Please behave. We have a guest in the next room." This infuriated him, and he cursed them silently:

"Bastards! Pigs! How dare you bully me like this? Revenge! Revenge! I'll revenge myself on you! Can there be any true-hearted girl in the world? You faithless waitress, how dare you desert me like this? Oh, let it be, let it be, for from now on I shall care nothing about women, absolutely nothing. I will love nothing but my country, and let my country be my love."

He had an impulse to go home and apply himself to study. At the same time, however, he was envious of those bastards next door, and there was still a secret corner in his heart that expected the waitress's return.

Finally, he suppressed his anger and silently downed a few cups of wine, which made him feel warm all over. He got up and opened some more windows to cool himself, and saw that the sun was now going down. Then he drank a few more cups and watched the gradual blurring of the seascape. The shadow cast by the lighthouse on the dike was getting longer and longer, and a descending fog began to blend the sky and the sea. But behind this hazy veil the setting sun lingered on the horizon, as if reluctant to say good-bye. After watching this view for a while, he felt inexplicably merry and burst out laughing. He rubbed his burning cheeks, muttering, "Yes, I'm drunk. I'm drunk."

The waitress finally came in. Seeing him flushing and laughing idiotically in front of the windows, she asked:

"With the windows wide open, aren't you afraid of the cold?"

"I'm not cold, not cold at all. Who can afford to miss this beautiful sunset?"

"You're indeed a poet. Here is your wine."

"Poet? Yes, I'm a poet. Bring me a brush and some paper and I'll write a poem for you."

After the waitress had left, he was surprised at himself and thought, "How have I become so bold all of a sudden?"

He became even merrier after emptying more cups of the newly warmed wine and broke into another round of loud laughter. In the next room those bastards were singing Japanese songs aloud, and so he also raised his voice and chanted:

> Drunk, I tap the railing and feel the chillier because of the wine;
> Rivers and lakes again turn bleak in the death of winter.
> The mad poet with his profound pity for the parrot
> Was spared through death—his bones buried in the Central Province;
> The further ignominy of another talented youth
> Exiled to Chang'an with the title of grand tutor.
> It's not too hard to try to repay a life-saving meal
> With a thousand pieces of gold,
> But how many could pass through the capital
> Without heaving five long sighs?
> Looking homeward across the misted sea,
> I too weep for my beloved country.[13]

8

When he woke up, he found himself lying underneath a red satin quilt scented with a strange perfume. The room was not large, but it was no longer the same room he had occupied in the late afternoon. A ten-watt bulb suspended from the ceiling gave a dim light. A teapot and two cups were placed beside his pillow. After helping himself to two or three cups of tea, he got up and walked unsteadily to the door. As he was opening it, the same waitress who had taken care of him in the afternoon came in to greet him: "Hey, there! Are you all right now?"

---

13. Like the earlier poem intended for a friend in Tokyo, this poem is Yu Dafu's own composition in the eight-line, seven-character *lüshi* style. The editors have expanded its second and third couplets into eight lines (lines 3–10) because otherwise these highly allusive couplets would not have made much sense to the general reader. The "mad poet" of line 3 is Ni Heng, a precocious and utterly proud scholar of the Later Han dynasty who once wrote a *fu* poem on the parrot, indirectly comparing himself to this bird of supernal intelligence forced to live in captivity. At the age of twenty-six he was executed by Huang Zu, governor of Jiangxia (Central Province), one of the several patrons he had offended with his rude arrogance. "Another talented youth," in line 5, refers to Jia Yi, a Former Han writer of greater fame. His hopes for a political career were dashed when he was assigned, or rather banished, to the state of Changsha to serve as its king's tutor. A few years later he died heartbroken at the age of thirty-three. Han Xin, a prominent general under the founding emperor of the Former Han dynasty, was befriended in his youth by a washerwoman who repeatedly gave him meals when he had nothing to eat. After he had achieved fame, he sought her out and gave her "a thousand pieces of gold" (line 8). Liang Hong, a recluse of the Later Han, once passed through the national capital and composed a "Song of Five Sighs," each of its five lines ending with the exclamatory word *yi* (alas!). Emperor Suzong was highly displeased, and Liang Hong had to change his name and live in hiding.

He nodded and answered with a smile, "Yes. Where is the toilet?"

"I'll show you."

He followed her and again passed through the corridor, but it was now lit up and from far and near came singing and laughter and the sound of the *samisen*. All this helped him to recall what had happened this afternoon, especially what he had said to the waitress when in a drunken state. His face flushed again.

Returning from the toilet, he asked the waitress, "Is this quilt yours?"

"Yes," she answered with a smile.

"What time is it now?"

"It's probably eight forty or eight fifty."

"Would you please give me the check?"

"Yes, sir."

After he had paid the bill, tremblingly he handed the waitress a banknote, but she said, "No, thanks. I don't need it."

He knew she was offended by the small tip. Again red with embarrassment, he searched his pocket and found one remaining note. He gave it to her, saying, "I hope you won't scorn this paltry sum. Please take it."

His hand trembled more violently this time, and even his voice quivered. Seeing him in this state, the waitress accepted the money and said in a low voice, "Thank you." He ran straight downstairs, put on his shoes, and went outside.

The night air was very cold. It was probably the eighth or ninth of the lunar month, and the half moon hung high in the left corner of the grayish-blue sky, accompanied by a few lone stars.

He took a walk by the seashore. From afar the lights on the fishermen's boats seemed to be beckoning him, like the will-o'-the-wisp, and the waves under the silvery moonlight seemed to be winking at him like the eyes of mountain spirits.[14] Suddenly he had an inexplicable urge to drown himself in the sea.

He felt in his pocket and found that he didn't even have money for the trolley fare. Reflecting upon what he had done today, he couldn't help cursing himself:

"How could I have gone to such a place? I really have become a most degraded person. But it's too late for regrets. I may as well end my life here, since I'll probably never get the kind of love I want. And what would life be without love? Isn't it as dead as ashes? Ah, this dreary life, how dull and dry! Everyone in this world hates me, mistreats me—even my own brother is trying to push me off the edge of this world. How can I make a living? And why should I stay on in this world of suffering?"

---

14. In using the term *shangui* (mountain spirits), the author must be alluding to the female deity of identical name celebrated in one of the "Nine Songs" (*Jiuge*). See David Hawkes, trans., *Ch'u Tz'u: The Songs of the South* (Boston: Beacon Press, 1962), p. 43.

This thought gave him pause, and tears began to roll down his face, which was now as pallid as a dead man's. He didn't even bother to wipe away the tears, which glistened on his moon-blanched face like the morning dew on the leaves. With anguish he turned his head to look at the elongated shadow of his thin body.

"My poor shadow! You have followed me for twenty-one years, and now this sea is going to bury you. Though my body has been insulted and injured, I should not have let you grow so thin and frail. O shadow, my shadow, please forgive me!"

He looked toward the west. The light on the lighthouse was doing its job, now beaming red and now green. When the green beam reached down, there would immediately appear on the sea an illuminated path of light blue. Again looking up, he saw a bright star trembling in the farthest reaches of the western horizon.

"Underneath that shaky star lies my country, my birthplace, where I have spent eighteen years of my life. But alas, my homeland, I shall see you no more!"

Such were his despondent, self-pitying thoughts as he walked back and forth along the shore. After a while, he paused to look again at that bright star in the western sky, and tears poured down like a shower. The view around him began to blur. Drying his tears, he stood still and uttered a long sigh. Then he said, between pauses:

"O China, my China, you are the cause of my death! . . . I wish you could become rich and strong soon! . . . Many, many of your children are still suffering."

1921

Mao Dun (1896–1981)

SPRING SILKWORMS

Translated by Sidney Shapiro

1

Old Tong Bao sat on a rock beside the road that skirted the canal, his long-stemmed pipe lying on the ground next to him. Though it was only a few days after the Qingming Festival[1] the April sun was already very strong. It scorched Old Tong Bao's spine like a basin of fire. Straining down the road, the men towing the fast junk wore only thin tunics, open in front. They were bent far forward, pulling, pulling, pulling, great beads of sweat dripping from their brows.

The sight of others toiling strenuously made Old Tong Bao feel even warmer; he began to itch. He was still wearing the tattered padded jacket in which he had passed the winter. His unlined jacket had not yet been redeemed from the pawnshop. Who would have believed it could get so hot right after Qingming?

Even the weather's not what it used to be. Old Tong Bao said to himself, and spat emphatically.

Before him, the water of the canal was green and shiny. Occasional passing boats broke the mirror-smooth surface into ripples and eddies, turning the reflection of the earthen bank and the long line of mulberry trees flanking it into

---

1. A spring festival roughly equivalent to Easter time, around April 5, at which the Chinese worship at the graves of their ancestors. It is also known as "Tomb-sweeping Day."

a dancing gray blur. But not for long! Gradually the trees reappeared, twisting and weaving drunkenly. Another few minutes, and they were again standing still, reflected as clearly as before. On the gnarled fists of the mulberry branches, little fingers of tender green buds were already bursting forth. Crowded close together, the trees along the canal seemed to march endlessly into the distance. The unplanted fields as yet were only cracked clods of dry earth; the mulberry trees reigned supreme here this time of the year! Behind Old Tong Bao's back was another great stretch of mulberry trees, squat, silent. The little buds seemed to be growing bigger every second in the hot sunlight.

Not far from where Old Tong Bao was sitting, a gray two-story building crouched beside the road. That was the silk filature, where the delicate fibers were removed from the cocoons. Two weeks ago it was occupied by troops; a few short trenches still scarred the fields around it. Everyone had said that the Japanese soldiers were attacking in this direction. The rich people in the market town had all run away. Now the troops were gone, and the silk filature stood empty and locked as before. There would be no noise and excitement in it again until cocoon-selling time.

Old Tong Bao had heard Young Master Chen—son of the Master Chen who lived in town—say that Shanghai was seething with unrest, that all the silk weaving factories had closed their doors, that the silk filatures here probably wouldn't open either. But he couldn't believe it. He had been through many periods of turmoil and strife in his sixty years, yet he had never seen a time when the shiny green mulberry leaves had been allowed to wither on the branches and become fodder for sheep. Of course, if the silkworm eggs shouldn't ripen, that would be different. Such matters were all in the hands of the Old Lord of the Sky. Who could foretell His will?

"Only just after Qingming and so hot already!" marveled Old Tong Bao, gazing at the small green mulberry leaves. He was happy as well as surprised. He could remember only one year when it was too hot for padded clothes at Qingming. He was in his twenties then, and the silkworm eggs had hatched "200 percent"! That was the year he got married. His family was flourishing in those days. His father was like an experienced plow ox—there was nothing he didn't understand, nothing he wasn't willing to try. Even his old grandfather—the one who had started the family on the road to prosperity—seemed to be growing more hearty with age, in spite of the hard time he was said to have had during the years he was a prisoner of the Long Hairs.[2]

---

2. In the mid-nineteenth century, China's oppressed peasants rose against their feudal Manchu rulers in one of the longest (1851–1864) and most bitter revolutions in history. Known as the Taiping Revolution, it was defeated only with the assistance of the interventionist forces of England, France, and the United States of America. The Manchus hated and feared the "Long Hairs," as they slanderously called the Taiping Army men, and fabricated all sorts of lies about them in a vain attempt to discredit them with the people. Old Tong Bao, although steadily

Old Master Chen was still alive then. His son, the present Master Chen, hadn't begun smoking opium yet, and the House of Chen hadn't become the bad lot it was today. Moreover, even though the House of Chen was the rich gentry and his own family only ordinary tillers of the land. Old Tong Bao had felt that the destinies of the two families were linked together. Years ago, Long Hairs campaigning through the countryside had captured Tong Bao's grandfather and Old Master Chen and kept them working as prisoners for nearly seven years in the same camp. They had escaped together, taking a lot of the Long Hairs' gold with them—people still talk about it to this day. What's more, at the same time Old Master Chen's silk trade began to prosper, the cocoon raising of Tong Bao's family grew successful too. Within ten years Grandfather had earned enough to buy three acres of rice paddy and two acres of mulberry grove, and build a modest house. Tong Bao's family was the envy of the people of East Village, just as the House of Chen ranked among the first families in the market town.

But afterward both families had declined. Today, Old Tong Bao had no land of his own; in fact he was over three hundred silver dollars in debt. The House of Chen was finished too. People said the spirit of the dead Long Hairs had sued the Chens in the underworld, and because the King of Hell had decreed that the Chens repay the fortune they had amassed on the stolen gold, the family had gone down financially very quickly. Old Tong Bao was rather inclined to believe this. If it hadn't been for the influence of devils, why would a decent fellow like Master Chen have taken to smoking opium?

What Old Tong Bao could never understand was why the fall of the House of Chen should affect his own family. They certainly hadn't kept any of the Long Hairs' gold. True, his father had related that when Grandfather was escaping from the Long Hairs' camp he had run into a young Long Hair on patrol and had to kill him. What else could he have done? It was fate! Still, from Tong Bao's earliest recollections, his family had prayed and offered sacrifices to appease the soul of the departed young Long Hair time and time again. That little wronged spirit should have left the netherworld and been reborn long ago by now! Although Old Tong Bao couldn't recall what sort of man his grandfather was, he knew his father had been hardworking and honest—he had seen that with his own eyes. Old Tong Bao himself was a respectable person; both A Si, his elder son, and his daughter-in-law were industrious and frugal. Only his younger son, A Duo, was inclined to be a little flighty. But youngsters were all like that. There was nothing really bad about the boy.

Old Tong Bao raised his wrinkled face, scorched by years of hot sun to the color of dark parchment. He gazed bitterly at the canal before him, at the boats on

---

deteriorating economically, is typical of the rich peasants. Like others of his class, he felt and thought the same as the feudal landlord rulers.

its waters, at the mulberry trees along its banks. All were approximately the same as they had been when he was twenty. But the world had changed. His family now often had to make their meals of pumpkin instead of rice. He was over three hundred silver dollars in debt.

Toot! Toot-toot-toot . . .

Far up the bend in the canal a boat whistle broke the silence. There was a silk filature over there too. He could see vaguely the neat lines of stones embedded as a reinforcement in the canal bank. A small oil-burning riverboat came puffing up pompously from beyond the silk filature, tugging three larger craft in its wake. Immediately the peaceful water was agitated with waves rolling toward the banks on both sides of the canal. A peasant, poling a tiny boat, hastened to shore and clutched a clump of reeds growing in the shallows. The waves tossed him and his little craft up and down like a seesaw. The peaceful green countryside was filled with the chugging of the boat engine and the stink of its exhaust.

Hatred burned in Old Tong Bao's eyes. He watched the riverboat approach, he watched it sail past, and glared after it until it went tooting around another bend and disappeared from sight. He had always abominated the foreign devils' contraptions. He himself had never met a foreign devil, but his father had given him a description of one Old Master Chen had seen—red eyebrows, green eyes, and a stiff-legged walk! Old Master Chen had hated the foreign devils too. "The foreign devils have swindled our money away," he used to say. Old Tong Bao was only eight or nine the last time he saw Old Master Chen. All he remembered about him now were things he had heard from others. But whenever Old Tong Bao thought of that remark—"The foreign devils have swindled our money away"—he could almost picture Old Master Chen, stroking his beard and wagging his head.

How the foreign devils had accomplished this, Old Tong Bao wasn't too clear. He was sure, however, that Old Master Chen was right. Some things he himself had seen quite plainly. From the time foreign goods—cambric, cloth, oil—appeared in the market town, from the time foreign riverboats increased on the canal, what he produced brought a lower price on the market every day, while what he had to buy became more and more expensive. That was why the property his father left him had shrunk until it finally vanished completely; and now he was in debt. It was not without reason that Old Tong Bao hated the foreign devils!

In the village, his attitude toward foreigners was well known. Five years before, in 1927, someone had told him: "The new Guomindang government says it wants to throw out the foreign devils." Old Tong Bao didn't believe it. He had heard those young propaganda speechmakers the Guomindang sent when he went into the market town. Though they cried, "Throw out the foreign devils," they were dressed in Western-style clothing. His guess was that they were secretly in league with the foreign devils, that they had been purposely sent to delude the countryfolk! Sure enough, the Guomindang dropped the slogan not long after, and prices and taxes rose steadily. Old Tong Bao was firmly convinced that all this had occurred as part of a government conspiracy with the foreign devils.

Last year something had happened that made him almost sick with fury: only the cocoons spun by the foreign-strain silkworms could be sold at a decent price. Buyers paid ten dollars more per load for them than they did for the local variety. Usually on good terms with his daughter-in-law, Old Tong Bao had quarreled with her because of this. She had wanted to raise only foreign silkworms, and Old Tong Bao's younger son, A Duo, had agreed with her. Though the boy didn't say much, in his heart he certainly had also favored this course. Events had proved they were right, and they wouldn't let Old Tong Bao forget it. This year, he had to compromise. Of the five trays they would raise, only four would be silkworms of the local variety; one tray would contain foreign silkworms.

"The world's going from bad to worse! In another couple of years they'll even be wanting foreign mulberry trees! It's enough to take all the joy out of life!"

Old Tong Bao picked up his long pipe and rapped it angrily against a clod of dry earth. The sun was directly overhead now, foreshortening his shadow until it looked like a piece of charcoal. Still in his padded jacket, he was bathed in heat. He unfastened the jacket and swung its opened edges back and forth a few times to fan himself. Then he stood up and started for home.

Behind the row of mulberry trees were paddy fields. Most of them were as yet only neatly ploughed furrows of upturned earth clods, dried and cracked by the hot sun. Here and there, the early crops were coming up. In one field, the golden blossoms of rapeseed plants emitted a heady fragrance. And that group of houses way over there, that was the village where three generations of Old Tong Bao's family were living. Above the houses, white smoke from many kitchen stoves was curling lazily upward into the sky.

After crossing through the mulberry grove, Old Tong Bao walked along the raised path between the paddy fields, then turned and looked again at that row of trees bursting with tender green buds. A twelve-year-old boy came bounding along from the other end of the fields, calling as he ran:

"Grandpa! Ma's waiting for you to come home and eat!"

It was Little Bao, Old Tong Bao's grandson.

"Coming!" the old man responded, still gazing at the mulberries. Only twice in his life had he seen these fingerlike buds appear on the branches so soon after Qingming. His family would probably have a fine crop of silkworms this year. Five trays of eggs would hatch out a huge number of silkworms. If only they didn't have another bad market like last year, perhaps they could pay off part of their debt.

Little Bao stood beside his grandfather. The child too looked at the soft green on the gnarled fist branches. Jumping happily, he clapped his hands and chanted:

Green, tender leaves at Qingming;
the girls who tend silkworms
clap hands at the sight!

The old man's wrinkled face broke into a smile. He thought it was a good omen for the little boy to respond like this on seeing the first buds of the year. He rubbed his hand affectionately over the child's shaven pate. In Old Tong Bao's heart, numbed wooden by a lifetime of poverty and hardship, suddenly hope began to stir again.

2

The weather remained warm. The rays of the sun forced open the tender, fingerlike little buds. They had already grown to the size of a small hand. Around Old Tong Bao's village, the mulberry trees seemed to respond especially well. From a distance they gave the appearance of a low gray picket fence on top of which a long swath of brocade had been spread. Bit by bit, day by day, hope grew in the hearts of the villagers. The unspoken mobilization order for the silkworm campaign reached everywhere and everyone. Silkworm-rearing equipment that had been laid away for a year was again brought out to be scrubbed and mended. Beside the little stream which ran through the village, women and children, with much laughter and calling back and forth, washed the implements.

None of these women or children looked really healthy. Since the coming of spring, they had been eating only half their fill; their clothes were old and worn. As a matter of fact, they weren't much better off than beggars. Yet all were in quite good spirits, sustained by enormous patience and grand illusions. Burdened though they were by daily mounting debts, they had only one thought in their heads—if we get a good crop of silkworms everything will be all right! . . . They could already visualize how, in a month, the shiny green leaves would be converted into snow-white cocoons, the cocoons exchanged for clinking silver dollars. Although their stomachs were growling with hunger, they couldn't refrain from smiling at this happy prospect.

Old Tong Bao's daughter-in-law was among the women by the stream. With the help of her twelve-year-old son, Little Bao, she had already finished washing the family's large trays of woven bamboo strips. Seated on a stone beside the stream, she wiped her perspiring face with the edge of her tunic. A twenty-year-old girl, working with other women on the opposite side of the stream, hailed her.

"Are you raising foreign silkworms this year too?"

It was Sixth Treasure, sister of young Fuqing, the neighbor who lived across the stream.

The thick eyebrows of Old Tong Bao's daughter-in-law at once contracted. Her voice sounded as if she had just been waiting for a chance to let off steam.

"Don't ask me; what the old man says, goes!" she shouted. "He's dead set against it, won't let us raise more than one batch of foreign breed! The old fool only has to hear the word *foreign* to send him up in the air! He'll take dollars made of foreign silver, though; those are the only 'foreign' things he likes!"

The women on the other side of the stream laughed. From the threshing ground behind them a strapping young man approached. He reached the stream and crossed over on the four logs that served as a bridge. Seeing him, his sister-in-law dropped her tirade and called in a high voice:

"A Duo, will you help me carry these trays? They're as heavy as dead dogs when they're wet!"

Without a word, A Duo lifted the six big trays and set them, dripping, on his head. Balancing them in place, he walked off, swinging his hands in a swimming motion. When in a good mood, A Duo refused nobody. If any of the village women asked him to carry something heavy or fish something out of the stream, he was usually quite willing. But today he probably was a little grumpy, and so he walked empty-handed with only six trays on his head. The sight of him, looking as if he were wearing six layers of wide straw hats, his waist twisting at each step in imitation of the ladies of the town, sent the women into peals of laughter. Lotus, wife of Old Tong Bao's nearest neighbor, called with a giggle:

"Hey, A Duo, come back here. Carry a few trays for me too!"

A Duo grinned. "Not unless you call me a sweet name!" He continued walking. An instant later he had reached the porch of his house and set down the trays out of the sun.

"Will 'kid brother' do?" demanded Lotus, laughing boisterously. She had a remarkably clean white complexion, but her face was very flat. When she laughed, all that could be seen was a big open mouth and two tiny slits of eyes. Originally a maid in a house in town, she had been married off to Old Tong Bao's neighbor—a prematurely aged man who walked around with a sour expression and never said a word all day. That was less than six months ago, but her love affairs and escapades already were the talk of the village.

"Shameless hussy!" came a contemptuous female voice from across the stream.

Lotus's piggy eyes immediately widened. "Who said that?" she demanded angrily. "If you've got the brass to call me names, let's see you try it to my face! Come out into the open!"

"Think you can handle me? I'm talking about a shameless, man-crazy baggage! If the shoe fits, wear it!" retorted Sixth Treasure, for it was she who had spoken. She too was famous in the village, but as a mischievous, lively young woman.

The two began splashing water at each other from opposite banks of the stream. Girls who enjoyed a row took sides and joined the battle, while the children whooped with laughter. Old Tong Bao's daughter-in-law was more decorous. She picked up her remaining trays, called to Little Bao, and returned home. A Duo watched from the porch, grinning. He knew why Sixth Treasure and Lotus were quarreling. It did his heart good to hear that sharp-tongued Sixth Treasure get told off in public.

Old Tong Bao came out of the house with a wooden tray-stand on his shoulder. Some of the legs of the uprights had been eaten by termites, and he wanted to repair them. At the sight of A Duo standing there laughing at the women, Old Tong Bao's face lengthened. The boy hadn't much sense of propriety, he well knew. What disturbed him particularly was the way A Duo and Lotus were always talking and laughing together. "That bitch is an evil spirit. Fooling with her will bring ruin on our house," he had often warned his younger son.

"A Duo!" he now barked angrily. "Enjoying the scenery? Your brother's in back mending equipment. Go and give him a hand!" His inflamed eyes bored into A Duo, never leaving the boy until he disappeared into the house. Only then did Old Tong Bao start work on the tray-stand. After examining it carefully, he slowly began his repairs. Years ago. Old Tong Bao had worked for a time as a carpenter. But he was old now; his fingers had lost their strength. A few minutes' work and he was breathing hard. He raised his head and looked into the house. Five squares of cloth to which sticky silkworm eggs adhered hung from a horizontal bamboo pole.

His daughter-in-law, A Si's wife, was at the other end of the porch, pasting paper on big trays of woven bamboo strips. Last year, to economize a bit, they had bought and used old newspaper. Old Tong Bao still maintained that was why the eggs had hatched poorly—it was unlucky to use paper with writing on it for such a prosaic purpose. Writing meant scholarship, and scholarship had to be respected. This year the whole family had skipped a meal and, with the money saved, purchased special "tray pasting paper." A Si's wife pasted the tough, gosling-yellow sheets smooth and flat; on every tray she also affixed three little colored paper pictures bought at the same time. One was the "Platter of Plenty"; the other two showed a militant figure on horseback, pennant in hand. He, according to local belief, was the "Guardian of Silkworm Hatching."

"I was only able to buy twenty loads of mulberry leaves with that thirty silver dollars I borrowed on your father's guarantee," Old Tong Bao said to his daughter-in-law. He was still panting from his exertions with the tray-stand. "Our rice will be finished by the day after tomorrow. What are we going to do?"

Thanks to her father's influence with his boss and his willingness to guarantee repayment of the loan, Old Tong Bao was able to borrow money at a low rate of interest—only 25 percent a month! Both the principal and interest had to be repaid by the end of the silkworm season.

A Si's wife finished pasting a tray and placed it in the sun. "You've spent it all on leaves," she said angrily. "We'll have a lot of leaves left over, just like last year!"

"Full of lucky words, aren't you?" demanded the old man sarcastically. "I suppose every year'll be like last year? We can't get more than a dozen or so loads of leaves from our own trees. With five sets of grubs to feed, that won't be nearly enough."

"Oh, of course, you're never wrong!" she replied hotly. "All I know is with rice we can eat, without it we'll go hungry!" His stubborn refusal to raise any foreign silkworms last year had left them with only the unsalable local breed. As a result, she was often contrary with him.

The old man's face turned purple with rage. After this, neither would speak to the other.

But hatching time was drawing closer every day. The little village's two dozen families were thrown into a state of great tension, great determination, great struggle. With it all, they were possessed of a great hope, a hope that could almost make them forget their hungry bellies.

Old Tong Bao's family, borrowing a little here, getting a little credit there, somehow managed to get by. Nor did the other families eat any better: there wasn't one with a spare bag of rice. Although they had harvested a good crop the previous year, landlords, creditors, taxes, levies, one after another, had cleaned the peasants out long ago. Now all their hopes were pinned on the spring silkworms. The repayment date of every loan they made was set up for the "end of the silkworm season."

With high hopes and considerable fear, like soldiers going into hand-to-hand combat, they prepared for the silkworm campaign!

"Grain Rain"[3] day—bringing gentle drizzles—was not far off. Almost imperceptibly, the silkworm eggs of the two dozen village families began to show faint tinges of green. Women, when they met on the public threshing ground, would speak to one another agitatedly in tones that were anxious yet joyful.

"Over at Sixth Treasure's place, they're almost ready to incubate their eggs!"

"Lotus says her family is going to start incubating tomorrow. So soon!"

"Huang 'the Priest' has made a divination. He predicts that this spring mulberry leaves will go to four dollars a load!"

Old Tong Bao's daughter-in-law examined their five sets of eggs. They looked bad. The tiny seedlike eggs were still pitch black, without even a hint of green. Her husband, A Si, took them into the light to peer at them carefully. Even so, he could find hardly any ripening eggs. She was very worried.

"You incubate them anyhow. Maybe this variety is a little slow," her husband forced himself to say consolingly.

Her lips pressed tight, she made no reply.

Old Tong Bao's wrinkled face sagged with dejection. Though he said nothing, he thought their prospects were dim.

The next day, A Si's wife again examined the eggs. Ha! Quite a few were turning green, and a very shiny green at that! Immediately, she told her husband, told Old Tong Bao, A Duo . . . she even told her son Little Bao. Now

---

3. Falls on April 20 or 21.

the incubating process could begin! She held the five pieces of cloth to which the eggs adhered against her bare bosom. As if cuddling a nursing infant, she sat absolutely quiet, not daring to stir. At night, she took the five sets to bed with her. Her husband was routed out, and had to share A Duo's bed. The tiny silkworm eggs were very scratchy against her flesh. She felt happy and a little frightened, like the first time she was pregnant and the baby moved inside her. Exactly the same sensation!

Uneasy but eager, the whole family waited for the eggs to hatch. A Duo was the only exception. "We're sure going to hatch a good crop," he said, "but anyone who thinks we're going to get rich in this life is out of his head." Though the old man swore A Duo's big mouth would ruin their luck, the boy stuck to his guns.

A clean, dry shed for the growing grubs was all prepared. The second day of incubation, Old Tong Bao smeared a garlic with earth and placed it at the foot of the wall inside the shed. If, in a few days, the garlic put out many sprouts, it meant the eggs would hatch well. He did this every year, but this year he was more reverential than usual, and his hands trembled. Last year's divination had proved all too accurate. He didn't dare to think about that now.

Every family in the village was busy incubating. For the time being there were few women's footprints on the threshing ground or the banks of the little stream. An unofficial "martial law" had been imposed. Even peasants normally on very good terms stopped visiting one another. For a guest to come and frighten away the spirits of the ripening eggs—that would be no laughing matter! At most, people exchanged a few words in low tones when they met, then quickly separated. This was the "sacred" season!

Old Tong Bao's family was on pins and needles. In the five sets of eggs a few grubs had begun wriggling. It was exactly one day before Grain Rain. A Si's wife had calculated that most of the eggs wouldn't hatch until after that day. Before or after Grain Rain was all right, but for eggs to hatch on the day itself was considered highly unlucky. Incubation was no longer necessary, and the eggs were carefully placed in the special shed. Old Tong Bao stole a glance at his garlic at the foot of the wall. His heart dropped. There were still only the same two small green shoots the garlic had originally! He didn't dare to look any closer. He prayed silently that by noon the day after tomorrow the garlic would have many, many more shoots.

At last hatching day arrived. A Si's wife set a pot of rice on to boil and nervously watched for the time when the steam from it would rise straight up. Old Tong Bao lit the incense and candles he had bought in anticipation of this event. Devoutly, he placed them before the idol of the Kitchen God. His two sons went into the fields to pick wildflowers. Little Bao chopped a lamp wick into fine pieces and crushed the wildflowers the men brought back. Everything was ready. The sun was entering its zenith; steam from the rice pot puffed straight upward. A Si's wife immediately leaped to her feet, stuck a "sacred" paper flower and a pair of goose feathers into the knot of hair at the back of her head, and went to the shed. Old Tong Bao carried a wooden scale-pole; A Si followed with the chopped lamp wick and the crushed wildflowers. Daughter-in-law uncovered the cloth pieces to which the grubs adhered, and sprinkled them with the bits of wick and flowers A Si was holding. Then she took the wooden scale-pole from Old Tong Bao and hung the cloth pieces over it. She next removed the pair of goose feathers from her hair. Moving them lightly across the cloth, she brushed the grubs, together with the crushed lamp wick and wildflowers, onto a large tray. One set, two sets . . . the last set contained the foreign breed. The grubs from this cloth were brushed onto a separate tray. Finally, she removed the "sacred" paper flower from her hair and pinned it, with the goose feathers, against the side of the tray.

A solemn ceremony! One that had been handed down through the ages! Like warriors taking an oath before going into battle! Old Tong Bao and family now had ahead of them a month of fierce combat, with no rest day or night, against bad weather, bad luck, and anything else that might come along!

The grubs, wriggling in the trays, looked very healthy. They were all the proper black color. Old Tong Bao and his daughter-in-law were able to relax a little. But when the old man secretly took another look at his garlic, he turned pale! It had grown only four measly shoots. Ah! Would this year be like last year all over again?

3

The fateful garlic proved to be not so psychic after all. The silkworms of Old Tong Bao's family grew and thrived! Though it rained continuously during the grubs' first and second molting, and the weather was a bit colder than at Qingming, the "little darlings" were extremely robust.

The silkworms of the other families in the village were not doing so badly either. A tense kind of joy pervaded the countryside. Even the small stream seemed to be gurgling with bright laughter. Lotus's family was the sole exception. They were only raising one set of grubs, but by the third molting their silkworms weighed less than twenty catties. Just before the fourth, people saw Lotus's husband walk to the stream and dump out his trays. That dour, old-looking man had bad luck written all over him.

Because of this dreadful event, the village women put Lotus's family strictly off-limits. They made wide detours so as not to pass her door. If they saw her or her taciturn husband, no matter how far away, they made haste to go in the opposite direction. They feared that even one look at Lotus or her spouse, the briefest conversation, would contaminate them with the unfortunate couple's bad luck!

Old Tong Bao strictly forbade A Duo to talk to Lotus. "If I catch you gabbing with that baggage again, I'll disown you!" he threatened in a loud, angry voice, standing outside on the porch to make sure Lotus could hear him.

Little Bao was also warned not to play in front of Lotus's door, and not to speak to anyone in her family.

The old man harped at A Duo morning, noon, and night, but the boy turned a deaf ear to his father's grumbling. In his heart, he laughed at it. Of the whole family, A Duo alone didn't place much stock in taboos and superstitions. He didn't talk with Lotus, however. He was much too busy for that.

By the fourth molting, their silkworms weighed three hundred catties. Every member of Old Tong Bao's family, including twelve-year-old Little Bao, worked for two days and two nights without sleeping a wink. The silkworms were unusually sturdy. Only twice in his sixty years had Old Tong Bao ever seen the like. Once was the year he married; once when his first son was born.

The first day after the fourth molting, the "little darlings" ate seven loads of leaves. They were now a bright green, thick and healthy. Old Tong Bao and his family, on the contrary, were much thinner, their eyes bloodshot from lack of sleep.

No one could guess how much the "little darlings" would eat before they spun their cocoons. Old Tong Bao discussed the question of buying more leaves with A Si.

"Master Chen won't lend us any more. Shall we try your father-in-law's boss again?"

"We've still got ten loads coming. That's enough for one more day," replied A Si. He could barely hold himself erect. His eyelids weighed a thousand catties. They kept wanting to close.

"One more day? You're dreaming!" snapped the old man impatiently. "Not counting tomorrow, they still have to eat three more days. We'll need another thirty loads! Thirty loads, I say!"

Loud voices were heard outside on the threshing ground. A Duo had arrived with men delivering five loads of mulberry branches. Everyone went out to strip the leaves. A Si's wife hurried from the shed. Across the stream, Sixth Treasure and her family were raising only a small crop of silkworms; having spare time, she came over to help. Bright stars filled the sky. There was a slight wind. All up and down the village, gay shouts and laughter rang in the night.

"The price of leaves is rising fast!" a coarse voice cried. "This afternoon, they were getting four dollars a load in the market town!"

Old Tong Bao was very upset. At four dollars a load, thirty loads would come to a hundred and twenty dollars. Where could he raise so much money?! But then he figured—he was sure to gather over five hundred catties of cocoons. Even at fifty dollars a hundred, they'd sell for two hundred and fifty dollars. Feeling a bit consoled, he heard a small voice from among the leaf-strippers.

"They say the folks east of here aren't doing so well with their silkworms. There won't be any reason for the price of leaves to go much higher."

Old Tong Bao recognized the speaker as Sixth Treasure, and he relaxed still further.

The girl and A Duo were standing beside a large basket, stripping leaves. In the dim starlight, they worked quite close to each other, partly hidden by the pile of mulberry branches before them. Suddenly Sixth Treasure felt someone pinch her thigh. She knew well enough who it was, and she suppressed a giggle. But when, a moment later, a hand brushed against her breasts, she jumped; a little shriek escaped her.

"Ai-ya!"

"What's wrong?" demanded A Si's wife, working on the other side of the basket.

Sixth Treasure's face flamed scarlet. She shot a glance at A Duo, then quickly lowered her head and resumed stripping leaves. "Nothing," she replied. "I think a caterpillar bit me!"

A Duo bit his lips to keep from laughing aloud. He had been half starved the past two weeks and had slept little. But in spite of having lost a lot of weight, he was in high spirits. While he never suffered from any of Old Tong Bao's gloom, neither did he believe that one good crop, whether of silkworms or of rice, would enable them to wipe out their debt and own their own land again. He knew that they would never get out from under merely by relying on hard work, even if they broke their backs trying. Nevertheless, he worked with a will. He enjoyed work, just as he enjoyed fooling around with Sixth Treasure.

The next morning, Old Tong Bao went into town to borrow money for more leaves. Before leaving home, he had talked the matter over with his daughter-in-law. They had decided to mortgage their grove of mulberries that produced fifteen loads of leaves a year as security for the loan. The grove was the last piece of property the family owned.

By the time the old man ordered another thirty loads and the first ten were delivered, the sturdy "little darlings" had gone hungry for half an hour. Putting forth their pointed little mouths, they swayed from side to side, searching for food. His daughter-in-law's heart had ached to see them. When the leaves were finally spread on the trays, the silkworm shed at once resounded with a sibilant crunching, so noisy it drowned out conversation. In a very short while, the trays were again empty of leaves. Another thick layer was piled on. Just keeping the silkworms supplied with leaves, Old Tong Bao and his family were so busy they could barely catch their breath. But this was the final crisis. In two more days the "little darlings" would spin their cocoons. People were putting every bit of their remaining strength into this last desperate struggle.

Though he had gone without sleep for three whole days, A Duo didn't appear particularly tired. He agreed to watch the shed alone that night until dawn to permit the others to get some rest. There was a bright moon, and the weather was a trifle cold. A Duo crouched beside a small fire he had built in the shed. At about eleven, he gave the silkworms their second feeding, then returned to squat by the fire. He could hear the loud rustle of the "little darlings" crunching through the leaves. His eyes closed. Suddenly he heard the door squeak, and his eyelids flew open. He peered into the darkness for a moment, then shut his eyes again. His ears were still hissing with the rustle of the leaves. The next thing he knew, his head had struck against his knees. Waking with a start, he heard the door screen bang and thought he saw a moving shadow. A Duo leaped up and rushed outside. In the moonlight, he saw someone crossing the threshing ground toward the stream. He caught up in a flash, seized and flung the intruder to the ground. A Duo was sure he had nabbed a thief.

"A Duo, kill me if you want to, but don't give me away!"

The voice made A Duo's hair stand on end. He could see in the moonlight that queer, flat, white face and those round little piggy eyes fixed upon him. But of menace, the piggy eyes had none. A Duo snorted.

"What were you after?"

"A few of your family's 'little darlings'!"

"What did you do with them?"

"Threw them in the stream!"

A Duo's face darkened. He knew that in this way she was trying to put a curse on the lot. "You're pure poison! We never did anything to hurt you."

"Never did anything? Oh, yes, you did! Yes, you did! Our silkworm eggs didn't hatch well, but we didn't harm anybody. You were all so smart! You shunned me like a leper. No matter how far away I was, if you saw me you turned your heads. You acted as if I wasn't even human!"

She got to her feet, the agonized expression on her face terrible to see. A Duo stared at her. "I'm not going to beat you," he said finally. "Go on your way!"

Without giving her another glance, he trotted back to the shed. He was wide awake now. Lotus had only taken a handful, and the remaining "little darlings" were all in good condition. It didn't occur to him to either hate or pity Lotus, but the last thing she had said remained in his mind. It seemed to him there was something eternally wrong in the scheme of human relations; but he couldn't put his finger on what it was exactly, nor did he know why it should be. In a little while, he forgot about this too. The lusty silkworms were eating and eating, yet, as if by some magic, never full!

But when, at sunrise, A Si's wife went to draw water at the stream, she met Sixth Treasure. The girl's expression was serious.

"I saw that slut leaving your place shortly before midnight," she whispered. "A Duo was right behind her. They stood here and talked for a long time! Your family ought to look after things better than that!"

The color drained from the face of A Si's wife. Without a word, she carried her water bucket back to the house. First she told her husband about it, then she told Old Tong Bao. It was a fine state of affairs when a baggage like that could sneak into people's silkworm sheds! Old Tong Bao stamped with rage. He immediately summoned A Duo. But the boy denied the whole story; he said Sixth Treasure was dreaming. The old man then went to question Sixth Treasure. She insisted she had seen everything with her own eyes. The old man didn't know what to believe. He returned home and looked at the "little darlings." They were as sturdy as ever, not a sickly one in the lot.

But the joy that Old Tong Bao and his family had been feeling was dampened. They knew Sixth Treasure's words couldn't be entirely without foundation. Their only hope was that A Duo and that hussy had played their little games on the porch rather than in the shed!

Old Tong Bao recalled gloomily that the garlic had only put forth three or four shoots. He thought the future looked dark.

Hadn't there been times before when the silkworms ate great quantities of leaves and seemed to be growing well, yet dried up and died just when they were ready to spin their cocoons? Yes, often! But Old Tong Bao didn't dare let himself think of such a possibility. To entertain a thought like that, even in the most secret recesses of the mind, would only be inviting bad luck!

4

The "little darlings" began spinning their cocoons, but Old Tong Bao's family was still in a sweat. Both their money and their energy were completely spent. They still had nothing to show for it; there was no guarantee of their earning any return. Nevertheless, they continued working at top speed. Beneath the racks on which the cocoons were being spun, fires had to be kept going to supply warmth. Old Tong Bao and A Si, his elder son, their backs bent, slowly squatted first on this side and then on that. Hearing the small rustlings of the spinning silkworms, they wanted to smile, and if the sounds stopped for a moment, their hearts stopped too. Yet, worried as they were, they didn't dare disturb the silkworms by looking inside. When the silkworms squirted fluid[4] in their faces as they peered up from beneath the racks, they were quite happy in spite of the momentary discomfort. The bigger the shower, the better they liked it.

A Duo had already peeked several times. Little Bao had caught him at it and demanded to know what was going on. A Duo made an ugly face at the child, but did not reply.

After three days of "spinning," the fires were extinguished. A Si's wife could restrain herself no longer. She stole a look, her heart beating fast. Inside, all was as white as snow. The brush that had been put in for the silkworms to spin on was completely covered over with cocoons. A Si's wife had never seen so successful a "flowering"!

The whole family was wreathed in smiles. They were on solid ground at last! The "little darlings" had proved they had a conscience; they hadn't consumed those mulberry leaves, at four dollars a load, in vain. The family could reap its reward for a month of hunger and sleepless nights. The Old Lord of the Sky had eyes!

Throughout the village, there were many similar scenes of rejoicing. The Silkworm Goddess had been beneficent to the tiny village this year. Most of

---

4. The emission of the fluid means the silkworm is about to spin its cocoon.

the two dozen families garnered good crops of cocoons from their silkworms. The harvest of Old Tong Bao's family was well above average.

Again women and children crowded the threshing ground and the banks of the little stream. All were much thinner than the previous month, with eyes sunk in their sockets, throats rasping and hoarse. But everyone was excited, happy. As they chattered about the struggle of the past month, visions of piles of bright silver dollars shimmered before their eyes. Cheerful thoughts filled their minds—they would get their summer clothes out of the pawnshop; at Summer Festival[5] perhaps they could eat a fat, golden fish . . .

They talked too of the farce enacted by Lotus and A Duo a few nights before. Sixth Treasure announced to everyone she met, "That Lotus has no shame at all. She delivered herself right to his door!" Men who heard her laughed coarsely. Women muttered a prayer and called Lotus bad names. They said Old Tong Bao's family could consider itself lucky that a curse hadn't fallen on them. The gods were merciful!

Family after family was able to report a good harvest of cocoons. People visited one another to view the shining white gossamer. The father of Old Tong Bao's daughter-in-law came from town with his little son. They brought gifts of sweets and fruits and a salted fish. Little Bao was happy as a puppy frolicking in the snow.

The elderly visitor sat with Old Tong Bao beneath a willow beside the stream. He had the reputation in town of a "man who knew how to enjoy life." From hours of listening to the professional storytellers in front of the temple, he had learned by heart many of the classic tales of ancient times. He was a great one for idle chatter, and often would say anything that came into his head. Old Tong Bao therefore didn't take him very seriously when he leaned close and queried softly:

"Are you selling your cocoons, or will you spin the silk yourself at home?"

"Selling them, of course," Old Tong Bao replied casually.

The elderly visitor slapped his thigh and sighed, then rose abruptly and pointed at the silk filature rearing up behind the row of mulberries, now quite bald of leaves.

"Tong Bao," he said, "the cocoons are being gathered, but the doors of the silk filatures are shut as tight as ever! They're not buying this year! Ah, all the world is in turmoil! The silk houses are not going to open, I tell you!"

Old Tong Bao couldn't help smiling. He wouldn't believe it. How could he possibly believe it? There were dozens of silk filatures in this part of the country. Surely they couldn't all shut down? What's more, he had heard that they had made a deal with the Japanese; the Chinese soldiers who had been billeted in the silk houses had long since departed.

---

5. May 5 in the Western calendar. Here Mao Dun probably meant *duanwu jie* or Dragon Boat Festival, which falls on May 5 of the lunar calendar.

Changing the subject, the visitor related the latest town gossip, salting it freely with classical aphorisms and quotations from the ancient stories. Finally he got around to the thirty silver dollars borrowed through him as middleman. He said his boss was anxious to be repaid.

Old Tong Bao became uneasy after all. When his visitor had departed, he hurried from the village down the highway to look at the two nearest silk filatures. Their doors were indeed shut; not a soul was in sight. Business was in full swing this time last year, with whole rows of dark, gleaming scales in operation.

He felt a little panicky as he returned home. But when he saw those snowy cocoons, thick and hard, pleasure made him smile. What beauties! No one wants them? Impossible. He still had to hurry and finish gathering the cocoons; he hadn't thanked the gods properly yet. Gradually, he forgot about the silk houses.

But in the village, the atmosphere was changing day by day. People who had just begun to laugh were now all frowns. News was reaching them from town that none of the neighboring silk filatures was opening its doors. It was the same with the houses along the highway. Last year at this time, buyers of cocoons were streaming in and out of the village. This year there wasn't a sign of even half a one. In their place came dunning creditors and government tax collectors who promptly froze up if you asked them to take cocoons in payment.

Swearing, curses, disappointed sighs! With such a fine crop of cocoons the villagers had never dreamed that their lot would be even worse than usual! It was as if hailstones had dropped out of a clear sky. People like Old Tong Bao, whose crop was especially good, took it hardest of all.

"What is the world coming to?" He beat his breast and stamped his feet in helpless frustration.

But the villagers had to think of something. The cocoons would spoil if kept too long. They either had to sell them or remove the silk themselves. Several families had already brought out and repaired silk reels they hadn't used for years. They would first remove the silk from the cocoons and then see about the next step. Old Tong Bao wanted to do the same.

"We don't sell our cocoons; we'll spin the silk ourselves!" said the old man. "Nobody ever heard of selling cocoons until the foreign devils' companies started the thing!"

A Si's wife was the first to object. "We've got over five hundred catties of cocoons here," she retorted. "Where are you going to get enough reels?"

She was right. Five hundred catties was no small amount. They'd never get finished spinning the silk themselves. Hire outside help? That meant spending money. A Si agreed with his wife. A Duo blamed his father for planning incorrectly.

"If you listened to me, we'd have raised only one tray of foreign breed and no locals. Then the fifteen loads of leaves from our own mulberry trees would have been enough, and we wouldn't have had to borrow!"

Old Tong Bao was so angry he couldn't speak.

At last a ray of hope appeared. Huang the Priest had heard somewhere that a silk house below the city of Wuxi was doing business as usual. Actually an ordinary peasant, Huang was nicknamed "The Priest" because of the learned airs he affected and his interest in Taoist "magic." Old Tong Bao always got along with him fine. After learning the details from him, Old Tong Bao conferred with his elder son A Si about going to Wuxi.

"It's about two hundred and seventy *li* by water, six days for the round trip," ranted the old man. "Son-of-a-bitch! It's a goddamn expedition! But what else can we do? We can't eat the cocoons, and our creditors are pressing hard!"

A Si agreed. They borrowed a small boat and bought a few yards of matting to cover the cargo. It was decided that A Duo should go along. Taking advantage of the good weather, the cocoon-selling "expeditionary force" set out.

Five days later, the men returned—but not with an empty hold. They still had one basket of cocoons. The silk filature, which they reached after a journey of two hundred and seventy *li* by water, offered extremely harsh terms—only thirty-five dollars a load for foreign breed, twenty for local; thin cocoons not wanted at any price. Although their cocoons were all first class, the people at the silk filature house picked and chose only enough to fill one basket; the rest were rejected. Old Tong Bao and his sons received a hundred and ten dollars for the sale, ten of which had to be spent on travel expenses. The hundred dollars remaining was not even enough to pay back what they had borrowed for that last thirty loads of mulberry leaves! On the return trip, Old Tong Bao became ill with rage. His sons carried him into the house.

A Si's wife had no choice but to take the ninety odd catties they had brought back and reel the silk from the cocoons herself. She borrowed a few reels from Sixth Treasure's family and worked for six days. All their rice was gone now. A Si took the silk into town, but no one would buy it. Even the pawnshop didn't want it. Only after much pleading was he able to persuade the pawnbroker to take it in exchange for a load of rice they had pawned before Qingming.

That's the way it happened. Because they raised a crop of spring silkworms, the people in Old Tong Bao's village got deeper into debt. Old Tong Bao's family raised five trays and gathered a splendid harvest of cocoons. Yet they ended up owing another thirty silver dollars and losing their mortgaged mulberry trees—to say nothing of suffering a month of hunger and sleepless nights in vain!

1932

Lao She (1899–1966)

AN OLD AND ESTABLISHED NAME

Translated by William A. Lyell

After Manager Qian left, Xin Dezhi—the senior apprentice who now had quite a hand in the operation of the Fortune Silk Store—went for several days without eating a decent meal. Manager Qian had been universally recognized as a skilled old hand in the silk business just as the Fortune Silk Store was universally recognized as an old and established name. Xin Dezhi had been trained for the business under the hands of Manager Qian. However, it wasn't solely personal feeling that made Xin Dezhi take it so hard when Manager Qian left, nor was his agitation due to any personal ambition that might have been stimulated by the vague possibility that he himself might become the new manager. He really couldn't put his finger on the reason for all the anxiety that he felt; it was as though Manager Qian had taken away with him something or other that would be forever difficult to recover.

When Manager Zhou arrived to take things over, Xin Dezhi realized that his anxiety had not been unfounded. Previously he had only felt *sorrow* at the departure of the old manager, but now he felt downright *fury* at the arrival of the new one. Manager Zhou was a hustler. The Fortune Silk Store—an old and established name of years standing!—now demeaned itself into employing every kind of trick to rope in customers. Xin Dezhi's mouth hung so far open in dismay that his face began to look like a dumpling that had split apart while boiling. An old hand, an old and established name, old rules—all had vanished along with Manager Qian, perhaps never to return again. Manager Qian had been very honest and gentlemanly, so much so, in fact, that the Fortune Silk

Store lost money. The owners, for their part, weren't all that impressed by Manager Qian's upright demeanor; they were only concerned with having dividends to split up at the end of the year. Hence, they had let him go.

For as long as anyone could remember, the Fortune Silk Store had maintained an air of cultured elegance—a simple sign with the name of the store in black characters against a gold background, green fittings in the shop itself, a black counter with blue cloth cover, large square stools sheathed in blue woolen cloth, and fresh flowers always set out on the tea table. For as long as anyone could remember, except for hanging out four lanterns with big red tassels upon the occasion of the Lantern Festival, the Fortune Silk Store had never exhibited a trace of that vulgar ostentation so prevalent among ordinary merchants. For as long as anyone could remember, the Fortune had never engaged in such base practices as haggling with customers, letting the customer pay to the nearest dollar, pasting advertisements all over the place, or running two-week sales. What the Fortune Silk Store sold was its old and established name. For as long as anyone could remember, the Fortune had never set free cigarettes out on the counter as a come-on to customers; nor had any of the apprentices in the shop ever spoken in loud tones; the only sound in the store had been the gentle gurgle of the manager's water pipe intermingled with his occasional coughing.

As soon as Manager Zhou walked through the door, Xin Dezhi saw only too clearly that these precedents, as well as many other old and valuable customs, were all going to come to an end. There was something improper about the new manager's eyes. He never lowered his eyelids, but rather swept the whole world with his vision as if he were searching out a thief. Manager Qian, on the other hand, had always sat on a stool with his eyes closed, and yet if any of the apprentices did the slightest thing wrong, he knew about it immediately.

Just as Xin Dezhi had feared, within a few days Manager Zhou had transformed the Fortune into something akin to a carnival sideshow. In front of the main entrance the new manager set up a garish sign bearing the words GIANT SALE. Each word was five feet square! Then he installed two bright gaslights whose flames lit up faces in such a way as to turn them green. As if all this weren't enough, he had a drum and bugle set up by the main entrance, which made a din from dawn until the third watch at night. Four apprentices in red hats stood at the door and roamed up and down the sidewalk passing out handbills to anyone who came within their reach.

But Manager Zhou still wasn't satisfied. He appointed two clerks to the specific task of providing customers with cigarettes and tea; even someone who was buying only half a foot of plain cloth would be dragged to the back counter and given a cigarette. Soldiers, street-cleaners, and waitresses stood about firing up their tobacco until the shop was so smoked up that it looked like a Buddhist temple lost in incense fumes. Manager Zhou even went a step further; if a customer bought one foot of material, he'd give him an extra one free and throw in a foreign doll for the kids. And now all the apprentices were expected to joke and make small talk with the customers. If the customer wanted something that the store didn't have, then the apprentice wasn't to tell him right out that the store didn't have it, but was rather expected to drag out something else and force the customer to take a look at it. Any order over ten dollars would be delivered by one of the apprentices, and Manager Zhou bought two broken-down bicycles for that purpose.

Xin Dezhi longed to find some place where he could have a good cry. In fifteen or sixteen years of faithful service he had never even imagined (much less expected to see) the Fortune Silk Store coming to such a pass. How could he look people in the face? In the past who on the whole street had not held the Fortune Silk Store in great respect? When an apprentice hung out the lantern which served as the store's sign at night, even the policemen on the beat would treat him with special regard. And remember that year when the soldiers came! To be sure, during the pillaging, the Fortune had been cleaned out just like the other stores, but the doors and the signs saying *We Never Go Back on Our Prices* had not been torn away, as had been the case with some of the neighboring shops. Yes, that golden plaque bearing the inscription *Fortune Silk Store* had a certain awe-inspiring dignity about it.

Xin Dezhi had already lived in the city now for twenty-some years and fifteen or sixteen of them had been spent in the Fortune. In fact, it was his second home. His way of speaking, his very cough, and the style of his long blue gown had all been given to him by the Fortune Silk Store. The store had given him his personal pride and he, in turn, was proud of the store. Whenever he went out to collect bills, people would invite him in for a cup of tea. For although the store was a business, it treated its steady customers as friends. Often Manager Qian would even participate in the weddings and funerals of his regular customers. The Fortune Silk Store was a business conducted with "gentlemanly style." The more prestigious people in the neighborhood could often be found sitting and chatting on the bench in front of the main entrance. Whenever there were parades or any lively doings on the streets, the women in his customers' families would contact Manager Qian and he would arrange good seats at his store from which they could observe all of the excitement. This past glorious history of the shop was ever in Xin Dezhi's heart. And now?

It wasn't that he didn't know that the times had changed. For instance, a number of old and established shops on both sides of the Fortune had already tossed their rules to the winds (the newer shops were not worth worrying about because they had never had any traditions to begin with). He realized all this. But it was precisely because the Fortune had remained doggedly faithful to its traditions that he loved it all the more, was all the more proud of it. It was as though the Fortune Silk Store were the only bolt of real silk in a pile of synthetics. If even the Fortune hit the skids, then the world would surely come to an end. Damn! He had to admit it—now the Fortune was just like all the others, if not worse.

In the past, his favorite object of contempt had always been the Village Silk Shop across the street. The manager over there was always shuffling around with a cigarette dangling from lips that occasionally opened wide enough to reveal gold-capped front teeth. The manager's wife was forever carrying little children on her back, in her arms, and seemingly even in her pockets. She scurried in and out of the shop all day clucking and cackling in a southern dialect so that Xin Dezhi couldn't make out what she was jabbering about. When the couple had a good spat, they always picked the shop to have it in; when they beat the children or breast-fed a baby, they always picked the shop to do it in. You couldn't tell whether they were doing business or putting on a circus over there. However, one thing was certain: the manager's wife had her breasts forever on display in the shop with a baby or two hanging from them. He had no idea as to where in the world they had dug up the clerks that worked there. They all wore shoddy shoes, but for the most part dressed in silk. Some of them had Sun-Brand Headache Salve plastered conspicuously on their temples; some had their hair so slicked down that the tops of their heads looked like the bottoms of large lacquerware spoons; and some of them wore gold-rimmed glasses. Besides all these specifics, the place had a generally contemptible air about it: they had GIANT SALES from one end of the year to the other; they always had gaudy gaslights hung out in front of the store; and they were forever playing a phonograph full blast in order to attract business. Whenever a customer bought two dollars' worth of goods, the manager would, with his own hands, offer him a sweet sesame cake; if the customer didn't accept it, he might even shove it right into his mouth. Nothing in the shop had a fixed price and the rate of exchange that was given for foreign currency often fluctuated. Xin Dezhi had never deigned to look directly at the three words on the shop's sign; moreover, he had never gone over there to buy anything. He had never imagined that such a business firm could even exist on this earth, much less have the nerve to be located right across the street from the Fortune Silk Store! But strange to say, the Village Silk Shop had prospered, while the Fortune had gone downhill day after day. He hadn't been able to figure out what the reason was. It certainly couldn't be that there was an inexorable law that required that a business be run completely divorced from any code of ethics before it could make money. If this were really the case, then why should stores bother to train apprentices? Couldn't any old lout do business just as long as he were alive and kicking? It couldn't be this way! It just couldn't! At least he had always been sure that the Fortune would never be like that.

How could he have foreseen that after Manager Zhou's arrival, his beloved Fortune would also hang out gaslights so that its lights combined with those of the Village Silk Shop lit up more than half the block? Yes, they were two of a kind now! The Fortune and the Village a pair!—he must be dreaming! But it wasn't a dream and even Xin Dezhi had to learn to do things in Manager Zhou's way. He had to chitchat with the customers, offer them cigarettes, and then inveigle them into going to the back counter for a cup of tea. He was forced to haul out ersatz goods and pass them off as genuine; he had to learn to wait until a customer became insistent before giving him an honest length of material. He had to learn tricks to be employed in measuring the cloth—he was even expected to use his finger on the sly to pinch back a bit of the cloth before cutting it! How much more could he take?

But most of the apprentices seemed happy with doing things the new way. If a woman came in, it was all they could do to keep themselves from completely surrounding her; they just itched to haul out every piece of goods in the store for her inspection. Even if she bought only two feet of dust-cloth it was all they could do to keep themselves from escorting her home. The manager loved this kind of thing. He wanted to see the clerks turn head over heels and do acrobatics when the customers came in; he would have liked it even better if they had been able to fly around the customers in midair.

Manager Zhou and the boss of the Village Silk Shop became fast friends. Sometimes the two of them would even make up a foursome with the people from the Heaven Silk Store and have a round of mahjong. The Heaven was another silk store on the same street that had been in business now for four or five years. In times gone by, Manager Qian had always ignored the Heaven; hence the Heaven had made it a point to go into direct competition with the Fortune and even boasted that they wouldn't be satisfied until they had put it out of business. Manager Qian had never picked up the gauntlet, but occasionally he used to observe: "We do business on our old and established name." The Heaven was the kind of store that had a Giant Anniversary Sale three hundred and sixty-five days a year. And now even the people from the Heaven were coming over to play mahjong! When they did, Xin Dezhi, of course, utterly ignored them.

Whenever he had a little spare time, he would sit behind the counter and stare vacantly at the racks of materials. Originally all the goods on the racks had been covered up with white cloth. Now, ceiling to floor, all the rolls of material were exposed to full view in all their varied colors so that they might serve as an attraction to the customers. It was such a dazzling sight that it made one's eyes blur just to look at it. In his heart, Xin Dezhi knew that the Fortune Silk Store had already ceased to exist. And yet, after the first business third[1] had passed, he could not help but admire Manager Zhou. Because when it came time to balance the books, although Zhou hadn't made a great deal of money, yet he hadn't lost any either. He had pulled the Fortune out of the red. Manager Zhou smiled at everyone and explained: "You have to bear in mind that this is only my first third. I still have a lot of plans up my sleeve for the future that I

1. "Third" because books were balanced three times a year: at the Dragon Boat Festival (fifth day of the fifth lunar month); at the Midautumn Festival (fifteenth day of the eighth lunar month); and at New Year's.

haven't even tried yet. Furthermore, think of my initial outlay in advertising displays and gas lights. All of that took money, you know. So . . . " (Whenever he felt full of himself in conversation, he'd take a *so* . . . and tack it on the end of whatever he was saying.) "Later on we won't even have to use those advertising displays. We'll have newer and more economical ways of making ourselves known. Then there'll be a profit to show. So. . . . " Xin Dezhi could plainly see that there was no turning back for Manager Zhou. The world had really changed. After all. Manager Zhou was on very good terms with people from the Heaven and the Village, and both of those businesses had prospered.

Just after the books were balanced, there was a great deal of commotion in town about searching out and boycotting Japanese goods. And yet, as if possessed, Manager Zhou started laying in all the Japanese goods he could get his hands on, and even though student investigating teams were already on the streets, he displayed Japanese goods right out in the open. Then he issued an order: "When a customer comes in, show him the Japanese goods first. None of the other places dare to sell them, so we might as well make hay while the sun shines. If a farmer comes in, tell him straight out that it is Japanese cloth; they'll buy it anyway. But if someone from the city comes in, then say it's German material."

When the investigating students arrived, Manager Zhou's face butterflied into smiles as he offered them cigarettes and tea. "The Fortune Silk Store swears by its good name that it will not sell Japanese goods. Look over there, gentlemen. Those goods by the door are German materials along with some local products. Inside the store we have nothing but Chinese silks and satins. Our branch store in the south sends them up to us."

The students began to eye some of the printed materials with suspicion. Manager Zhou smiled and shouted, "Bring me that piece of leftover Japanese material that we have in back." When the cloth had been brought to him, he grabbed the leader of the investigating students by the sleeve and said, "Sir, I swear that this is the only piece of Japanese goods that we have left. It's the same material that the shirt you're wearing is made from. So . . . " He turned his head around and ordered, "All right, let's throw this piece of Japanese material out into the street." The leader of the investigating students looked at his own shirt and, not daring to raise his head, led the rest of the students out the door.

Manager Zhou made quite a bit of money from these Japanese materials, which could at any time turn into German, Chinese, or English goods. If a customer who knew his materials threw a piece of goods right down on the floor in front of Manager Zhou's face, the latter would issue an order to one of the apprentices: "Bring out the *real* Western goods. Can't you tell we have an intelligent man here who knows his materials?" Then he'd say to the customer: "You know what you want. You wouldn't take that even if I gave it to you free! So . . . " Thus he'd tie up another sale. By the time that the whole transaction was completed, it would be all the customer could do to tear himself away from the congenial company of Manager Zhou. Xin Dezhi came to the realization that if you plan to make money in business, you have to be a combination magician and burlesque comedian. Manager Zhou was really something, all right. And yet, Xin Dezhi didn't feel like working at the Fortune anymore. For the more he came to admire Manager Zhou, the worse he felt. Lately even his food all seemed to go down the wrong way. If he were ever again to enjoy a good night's sleep, he would have to leave his beloved Fortune Silk Store.

But before he had found a good position someplace else, Manager Zhou left. The Heaven Silk Store had need of just such talents, and Manager Zhou himself was anxious to make the change: he felt that the stick-in-the-mud traditions of the Fortune were so deeply rooted that he would never really be able to display his talents fully here.

When Xin Dezhi saw Manager Zhou off, it was as though he were seeing away a great burden that had been pressing on his heart. On the basis of his fifteen or sixteen years of service, Xin Dezhi felt that he had the right to talk things over with the owners of the store, although he could not be sure that his words would carry any real weight. However, he did know which of them were basically conservative and had a good idea as to how to influence them. He began to propagandize for Manager Qian's return and even got Qian's old friends to help. He didn't say that everything that Manager Qian had done was right, but would merely observe that each of the two managers had his good points and that these points ought to be combined harmoniously. One could not rigidly stick to old customs, but neither would it do to change too radically. An old and established name was worth preserving, but new business methods ought also be studied and applied. One ought to lay equal emphasis upon preserving the name *and* making a profit—he knew that this line of argument would be potent in persuading the owners.

But in his heart of hearts, he really had something quite different in mind. He hoped that when Manager Qian returned, everything that had been lost would come back with him and the Fortune Silk Store would once again be the *old* Fortune Silk Store; otherwise, as far as he was concerned, it would be nothing. He had it all figured out: they would get rid of the gaslights, the drum and bugle, the advertisements, handbills, and cigarettes; they would cut down on personnel as much as possible, and thus possibly save quite a bit on operating expenses. Moreover, without advertising the fact, they would sell low, use a long foot in measuring, and stock honest-to-goodness materials. Could the customers all be such asses that they wouldn't see the advantages of doing business at the Fortune?

And in the end Manager Qian actually did return. Now the only gaslights left on the street were those of the Village Silk Shop. The Fortune had recovered its former air of austere simplicity—although, in order to welcome Manager Qian back, they had gone so far as to hang out four lanterns decorated with tassels.

The day that the Fortune put out its lanterns of welcome, two camels appeared before the door of the Heaven Silk Store. The camels' bodies were completely draped in satin sash, and flashing, colored electric lights were installed on the humps. On both sides of the camels, stands were set up to sell chances at ten cents each. Whenever at least ten people had bought tickets, a drawing would be held. If lucky, one had hopes of winning a fashionable piece of silk. With this sort of thing going on the area around the Heaven Silk Store soon became something of a country fair, so crowded you could scarcely budge in the press. Because, you see, it *was* true that every once in a while somebody really *did* emerge from the crowd, all smiles, with a piece of fashionable silk tucked under his arm.

Once again the bench in front of the Fortune was covered with a piece of blue woolen cloth. Once again Manager Qian sat within the shop, eyelids drooping. Once again the clerks sat quietly behind the counters. Some of them toyed quietly with the beads of an abacus; others yawned leisurely. Xin Dezhi didn't say anything, but in his heart he was really worried. Sometimes it would seem ages and ages before a single customer appeared. Occasionally someone would glance in from the outside as if he were about to enter, but then he would glance at the small golden plaque and head over in the direction of the Heaven Silk Store. Sometimes a customer would actually come in and look at materials, but upon discovering that one couldn't bargain over the price, would walk out again empty-handed. There were still a few of the old reliables who came regularly to buy a little something or other, but sometimes they merely stopped by to have a chat with Manager Qian. They'd usually sigh a bit over the poverty of the times, have a few cups of tea, and then leave without buying anything. Xin Dezhi loved to listen to them talk, for it would remind him of the good times the store had once known in the past. But even he knew that the past cannot be easily recovered. The Heaven Silk Store was the only one on the whole street that was really doing any business.

At the end of a season, the Fortune had to cut back again on personnel. With tears in his eyes, Xin Dezhi told Manager Qian: "I can do five clerks' work all by myself. What's there to worry about?" Manager Qian took courage and chimed in: "What do we have to be afraid of?" And that night Xin Dezhi slept a very sweet sleep, fully prepared to do the work of five clerks on the very next day.

Yet after a year, the Fortune Silk Store was bought out by the Heaven.

1936

Shen Congwen (1902–1988)

XIAOXIAO

Translated by Eugene Chen Eoyang

Just about every day around the twelfth month,[1] the folks at home seem to be blowing the bamboo pipes for a wedding.

Following the pipes a gaily decked bridal palanquin appears, gliding forward on the shoulders of two bearers. The girl is shut up tight inside, and even though she is wearing a festive gown of greens and reds, something she doesn't get to wear every day—she can't help sobbing to herself. For, in her heart, a young woman knows that becoming a bride and leaving her mother to become, in time, someone else's mother, means having to face a host of new and unexpected problems. It's almost like entering a trance, to sleep in the same bed with someone you hardly know in order to carry on the ancestral line. Naturally, it is somewhat frightening to think of these things, so if one is inclined to cry in such a circumstance—as so many before have cried—is it any wonder?

There are, of course, some who don't cry. Xiaoxiao did not cry when she got married. She had been orphaned, and had been sent to an uncle on a farm to be brought up. All day long, carrying a small, wide-brimmed bamboo hat, she had to look for dog droppings by the side of the road and in the gullies. For her, marriage meant simply a transfer from one family to another. So, when

---

1. References to "months" in this story allude to the lunar calendar; when the term is converted into months in the solar calendar, the name of the month—December, January, etc.—will be given. The twelfth month is roughly February.

the day came, all she could do was to laugh about it, with no sense of shame or fear. She was scarcely aware of what she was getting into: all she knew was that she was to become someone's new daughter-in-law.

Xiaoxiao was eleven when she married, and Little Husband was hardly two years old—almost ten years younger, and not long ago suckling at his mother's breast. When she entered the household she called him "Sonny," according to local custom. Her daily chore was to take "Sonny" to play under the willow tree in front of the house or by the stream; when he was hungry, to give him something to eat; when he fussed, to soothe him; to pluck pumpkin blossoms and dog-grass to crown Little Husband with, or to soothe him with kisses and sweet nothings: "Sonny, now there, hush, there, there." And with that she would kiss the grimy little face: the boy would break out in smiles. In good spirits again, the child would act up once more, and with his tiny fingers, he would paw at Xiaoxiao's hair—the brown hair that was untidy and unkempt most of the time. Sometimes, when he had pulled too hard at her braid, the knot of red wool would come loose, and she would have to cuff him a few times: naturally he bawled. Xiaoxiao, now on the verge of tears herself, would point to the boy's tear-drenched face and say: "Now, now, you naughty thing, you'd better quit that."

Through fair and foul, every day she carried her "husband," doing this and that around the house, wherever her services were needed. On occasion she would go down to the stream to wash out clothes, to rinse out the diapers, but she found time to pick out colorful striped snails to amuse the boy with as he sat nearby. When she went to sleep she would dream dreams that a girl her age dreams; she dreamt that she found a cache of copper coins at the back gate, or some other place, and that she had good things to eat; she dreamt that she was climbing a tree; she dreamt she was a fish, floating freely in the water; she dreamt she was so light and lithe that she flew up clear to the stars, where there was no one, but all she could see was a flash of white and of gold, and she cried aloud for her mother—whereupon she woke up, her heart still thumping. The people next door would scold her: "You silly thing! What were you thinking of?

> Those who do nothing at all but play
> Wind up with bad dreams at end of day."

When she heard this, Xiaoxiao made no response, but merely giggled to herself, thinking of the good dreams that her husband's crying sometimes interrupted. He would sleep by his mother's side, so that it would be easier for her to breast-feed him, but there were times when he had too much milk or was colicky. Then he would wake up in the middle of the night crying, and Xiaoxiao would have to get up and take him to the bathroom. This happened often. Her husband cried so much, her mother-in-law didn't know what to do with him, so Xiaoxiao had to crawl out of bed bleary-eyed and tiptoe in—brushing the cobwebs out of her sleepy eyes—to take the boy in her arms, and distract him with the lamp or the twinkling of the stars. If that didn't work, she'd peck and whistle, make faces for the child, blather on like a baby—"hey, hey, look—look at the cat"—until her husband broke out in a smile. They would play like this for a bit, and then he would feel drowsy and close his eyes. When he was asleep, she'd put him back to bed, watching over him awhile, and, hearing in the distance the insistent sound of a cock crowing, she couldn't help knowing about what time it was when she huddled back in her tiny bed. At daybreak, though she had had a sleepless night, she would flick her eyes open and shut to see the yellow-and-purple sunflowers outdoors shifting forms before her very eyes: that was a real treat.

When Xiaoxiao was married off, to become the "little wife" of a pint-sized little child, she wasn't any the worse for wear; one look at her figure was proof enough of that. She was like an unnoticed sapling at a corner of the garden, sprouting forth big leaves and branches after days of wind and rain. This little girl—as if unmindful of her tiny husband—grew bigger day by day.

To speak of summer nights is to dream. People seek the cool of the evening after summer heat: they sit in the middle of the courtyard, waving their rush-fans, looking up at the stars in the sky or the fireflies in the corners, listening to the "Weaver Maid" crickets—on the roofs of the pumpkin-sheds—clicking away interminably on their "looms." The sounds from near and far are intertwined like the sound of rain, and when the hay-scented wind falls full on the face, that is a time when people are of a mind to tell jokes.

Xiaoxiao grew very tall, and she would often climb the sloping sides of the haystack, carrying in her arms her already sleeping husband, softly singing self-improvised folk melodies. The more she sang, the drowsier she felt—until she too was almost asleep.

In the middle of the courtyard, her in-laws, the grandparents, and two farm-hands sat at random on small wooden stools.

By Grandfather's side there was a tobacco-coil, whose embers glowed in the dark. This coil, made of mugwort, had the effect of repelling long-legged mosquitoes. It was wound around at Grandfather's feet like a black snake. From time to time. Grandfather would pick it up and wave it about.

Thinking about the day in the fields. Grandfather said: "Say, I heard that Old Qin said that, day before yesterday, there were a few coeds passing through town."

Everyone roared with laughter.

And what was behind the laughter? Everyone had the impression that coeds didn't wear braids; wearing the hair in the form of a sparrow's tail made them look like nuns, and yet somehow not like nuns. They wore their clothes in the manner of foreigners, yet they didn't look like foreigners. They ate, behaved in such a way . . . well, in a word, everything seemed out of place with them, and the slightest mention of coeds was cause enough for laughter.

Xiaoxiao didn't understand much of what was going on, and so she didn't laugh at all. Grandfather spoke again. He said:

"Xiaoxiao, when you grow up, you'll be a coed too." At this, everyone laughed once more.

Now, Xiaoxiao was not stupid when it came to people, and she figured this wasn't flattering to her, so she said:

"Grandpa, I won't become a coed."

"But you look like a coed. It won't do if you don't become one."

"No, I certainly won't."

The bystanders mined this for a laugh and egged her on:

"Xiaoxiao, what Grandpa says is right. It's not right if you don't become a coed."

Xiaoxiao was flustered and didn't know what was going on.

"All right, if I have to, I have to." Actually, Xiaoxiao had no idea what was wrong with being a coed.

The whole idea of coeds would always be thought of as queer in these parts. Every year, come June, when the start of the so-called "summer vacation" had finally arrived, they would come in small groups from some outlandish metropolis, and, looking for some remote retreat, they would pass through the village. In the eyes of the local people, it was almost as if these people had dropped down from an altogether different world, dressed in the most bizarre ways, their behavior even more improbable. On the days these coeds passed through, the whole village would come up with joke after joke.

Grandpapa was an old-timer from the region, and, because he was thinking about the carryings-on of the coeds he knew in the big city, he thought it was funny to urge Xiaoxiao to become one. As soon as he made the crack, he couldn't help laughing, but he also had in mind the way Xiaoxiao felt, and so the joke wasn't totally innocuous.

The coeds that Grandfather knew were of a type: they wore clothes without regard to the weather; they ate whether they were hungry or full; they didn't go to sleep until late at night; during the day they worked at nothing at all, but sang and played ball or read books from abroad. They knew how to spend money: with what they spent in a year, you could buy at least sixteen water buffaloes. In the capital cities of the provinces, whenever they wanted to go anywhere, they'd never dream of walking, but would climb instead into a big "box," which took them everywhere. In the cities there were all sorts of "boxes," big and small, all motorized. At school, boys and girls go to class together, and, when they get acquainted, the girls sleep overnight with the boys, with no thought of a go-between or a matchmaker, or even a dowry. This is what they call being "free." They sometimes serve as district officials and bring families to their posts; their husbands are called "Masters" still and their children "Little Master." They don't tend cattle themselves, but they'll drink cow's milk and sheep's milk like little calves and little lambs; the milk they buy is canned.

When they have nothing better to do, they go to a theater, which is built like a huge temple, and take from their pockets a silver dollar (a dollar of their money can buy five setting hens hereabouts). With this they purchase a piece of paper in the form of a ticket, which they take inside, so that they can sit down and watch foreigners performing shadow-plays. When offended, they won't curse at you or cry. By the time they are twenty-four, some still won't marry, while others at thirty or forty still have the cheek to contemplate marriage. They are not afraid of men, thinking men can't wrong them, for if they do, they take the men to court and insist that the magistrate fine them. Sometimes they spend the fine themselves, and sometimes they share it with the magistrate. Of course, they don't wash clothes or cook meals, and they certainly don't raise hogs and feed hens; when they have children they hire a servant to look after them for only five or ten dollars a month so that they can spend all day going to the theater and playing cards, or reading all those good-for-nothing books.

In a word, everything about them is weird, totally different from the lives of farmers, and some of their goings-on are not to be believed. When Xiaoxiao heard her grandfather saying all this, which explained everything, she felt vague stirrings of unrest, and took to imagining herself as a "coed." Would she behave like the "coeds" Grandfather talked about? In any case, there was nothing frightful about these "coeds," and so these notions began to occupy this simple girl's thoughts for the first time.

Because of the picture that Grandfather had painted of the "coed," Xiaoxiao giggled to herself for some time. But when she had collected herself, she said:

"Grandpa, when the 'coeds' come tomorrow, please tell me. I want a look."

"Watch out, or they'll make a maidservant out of you!"

"I'm not afraid of them."

"Oh, but they read all those foreign books, recite scripture, and you're still not afraid of them?"

"They can recite the 'Bodhisattva Guanyin Dispels Disaster' sutra or 'The Curse of the Monkey Sun' for all I care. I'm not afraid."

"They'll bite people, like the officials; they only eat simple folk; they munch even the bones and don't spit up the remains. Are you sure you're not scared?"

Xiaoxiao replied firmly: "No, I'm not scared."

At the time, Xiaoxiao was carrying her husband, who, apparently for no reason, broke out of a sound sleep crying. Daughter-in-law used the tones of a mother and, half in reassurance, half in remonstrance, said:

"Sonny, Sonny, you mustn't cry, the voracious coeds are coming!"

Her husband continued to cry, and there was no choice but to stand up and walk him about. Xiaoxiao carried him off, leaving Grandfather, who went on talking about other things.

From that moment on, Xiaoxiao remembered what "coed" meant. When she dreamt, she would often dream about being a coed, about being one of them. It was as if she too had sat in one of those motorized boxes, though she felt they didn't go much faster than she did. In her dream, the box seemed to resemble a granary, and there were ash-gray mice with little red, piggy eyes, darting all over the place, sometimes squirming through the cracks, their slimy tails sticking out behind them.

With this development, it was only natural that Grandfather would stop calling her "little maidservant" or "Xiaoxiao" and would call her "little coed." When it caught her off guard, Xiaoxiao would turn around involuntarily.

In the country, one day is like any other day in the world: they change only with the season. People waste each day as it comes, in the same way that Xiaoxiao and her kind hang on to each day; each gets his share, everything is as it should be. A lot of city sophisticates while away their summers in soft silk, indulging in good food and drink, not to mention other pleasures. For Xiaoxiao and her family, however, summer means hard work, producing ten catties or more of fine hemp and twenty or thirty wagonloads of melons a day.

The little daughter-in-law Xiaoxiao, on a summer day, must tend to her husband as well as spin four catties of hemp. By August, when the farmhands harvest the melons, she would enjoy seeing piled high in rows on the ground the dust-covered pumpkin melons, each as big as a pot. The time had come to collect the harvest, and now the courtyard was filled with great big red and brown leaves, blown from the branches of the trees in the grove behind the house. Xiaoxiao stood by the melons, and she was working a large leaf into a hat for her husband to play with.

There was a farmhand called Motley Mutt,[2] about twenty years old, who took Xiaoxiao's husband to the date tree for some dates: one whack with a bamboo stick, and the ground would be covered with dates.

"Brother Motley Mutt, no more, please. Too much and you won't be able to eat them all."

Despite this warning, he didn't budge. It was as if, on account of the little husband's yen for dates, Motley Mutt wouldn't listen. So, Xiaoxiao warned her little husband:

"Sonny, Sonny, come over here, don't take any more. You'll get a bellyache from eating all that raw fruit!"

Her husband obeyed. Grabbing an armful of dates, he came over to Xiaoxiao, and offered her some.

"Sis, eat. Here's a big one."

"No, I won't eat it."

"Come on, just one."

She had her hands full: how could she stop to eat one? She was busily putting the hat together, and wished she had some help.

"Sonny, why don't you put a date in my mouth?"

---

2. *Huagou*, literally "piebald dog." The phrase is both appellation and description.

Her husband did as he was told, and when he did he thought it was fun and came out with a laugh.

She wanted him to drop the dates so that he could help her hold the hat together while she added a few more leaves.

Her husband did as he was bidden, but he couldn't sit still, all the while singing and humming. The child was always like a cat, prone to mischief when in a good mood.

"Sonny, what song are you singing there?"

"Motley Mutt taught me this mountain song."

"Sing it properly so that I can follow."

Husband held on to the brim of the hat, and sang what he could remember of the song.

> Clouds rise in the skies, clouds become flowers;
> Among the cornstalks, plant beans for ruth;
> The beans will undermine the stalks of corn,
> And young maidens choke off flowering youth.
> Clouds rise in the skies, one after another
> In the ground, graves are dug, grave upon grave;
> Fair maids wash bowls, bowl after bowl,
> And in their beds serve knave after knave.

The meaning of the song was lost on husband, and when he finished, he asked her if she liked it. Xiaoxiao said she did, asking where it came from, and even though she knew that Motley Mutt had taught him the song, she still wanted him to tell her.

"Motley Mutt—he taught me. He knows lots of songs, but I . . . gotta grow up before he'll sing them."

When she realized that Motley Mutt could sing, Xiaoxiao said: "Brother Motley Mutt, Brother Motley Mutt, won't you sing a proper song for me?"

But that Motley Mutt, his face was as coarse as his heart; he had a touch of the vulgar about him, and, knowing that Xiaoxiao wanted a song, and sensing that she was about at the age to understand, he sang for her the ballad of the ten-year-old bride married to the one-year-old groom. The story says that as the wife is older, she can stray a bit because the husband is still an infant, not yet weaned, so leave him to suckle at his mother's breasts. Of course, Little Husband understood nothing at all of this song; Xiaoxiao, on the other hand, had but an inkling. When she had heard it, Xiaoxiao put on airs, as if to indicate she understood it all. Affecting outrage, she said to Motley Mutt:

"Brother Motley Mutt, you stop that! That song's not nice."

But Brother Motley Mutt took exception: "But it is a nice song."

"Oh, no it isn't. It isn't a nice song."

Motley Mutt rarely said much: he had sung his song; if he had offended anyone, he wouldn't sing again, that's all. He could see that she understood a little of what he sang, and he was afraid that she would tell on him to Grandfather; then he'd really be in for it, so he changed the subject to coeds. He asked Xiaoxiao if she had ever seen coeds exercising in public and singing Western songs.

If Motley hadn't brought this up, Xiaoxiao would have long ago forgotten all about coeds. But now that he mentioned it, she was curious to know if he had seen any lately. She was dying to see them.

While he was moving the melons from the shed to a corner of the courtyard wall, Motley told her stories about coeds singing foreign songs—all of which he had originally heard from Grandfather. To her face, he boasted of having seen four coeds on the main road, each with a flag in her hands, marching down the road perspiring and singing away just like soldiers on parade. It goes without saying that all this was some nonsense he had cooked up. But the stories inflamed Xiaoxiao's imagination. And all because Motley characterized them as instances of "freedom."

Motley was one of those clownish, leering, earthy types. When he heard Xiaoxiao say (with a measure of admiration): "My, Brother Motley, but you have big arms," he would say: "Oh, but that's not all that's big!"

"You've got such a large build."

"I'm big all over."

Xiaoxiao didn't understand this at all; she just thought he was being silly, and so she laughed.

After Xiaoxiao had left, carrying her husband off, a fellow who picked melons with Motley, and who had the nickname "Mumbles" (he was not much given to talk),[3] spoke out on this occasion for once.

"Motley, you're really awful. She's a twelve-year-old virgin, and she's still got twelve years before her wedding!"

Without so much as a word. Motley went up to the farmhand, slapped him, and then walked to the date tree to pick up the fruit that had dropped off.

By the time of the autumn melons harvest, one could reckon a full year and a half that Xiaoxiao had been with her husband.

The days passed—days of frost and snow, sunny days, and rainy days—and everyone said how grown-up Xiaoxiao was. Heaven kept watch over her; she drank cold water, ate coarse gruel, and was never sick the year round; she grew and blossomed. Although Grandmama became something of a nemesis, and tried to keep her from growing up too fast, Xiaoxiao flourished in the clean country air, undaunted by any trial or ordeal.

When Xiaoxiao was fourteen, she had the figure of an adult, but her heart was still as blithe and as unschooled as that of a child.

When one is bigger, one gets a heavier burden of household chores. Besides twisting hemp, spinning thread, washing, looking after her husband, she had

---

3. *Yaba*, literally "mute"; a derisive appellation, referring to his customary inarticulateness.

odd jobs like getting feed for the pigs or working at the mill, flossing silk, and weaving. She was expected to learn everything. It was understood that anyone who could make an extra effort would fit in a few chores to be done in their own quarters: the coarse hemp and spun silk that Xiaoxiao had gathered in two or three years were enough to keep her busy for three months at the crude shuttle in her room.

Her husband had long ago been weaned. Mother-in-law had a new son, and so her five-year-old—Xiaoxiao's husband—became Xiaoxiao's sole charge. Whatever happened, wherever she went, her husband followed her around. Husband was a little afraid of her in some ways, as if she were his mother, and so he behaved himself. All in all, they got along pretty well.

Gradually, as the locality became more progressive, Grandfather would change his jokes to: "Xiaoxiao, for the sake of freedom, you ought to cut off your braids." By this time Xiaoxiao had heard this joke; one summer she had seen her first coed. Although she didn't take Grandfather's ribbing too seriously, she would nevertheless (whenever she would pass by a pond after he made his crack) absentmindedly hold up her braid by the tip to see how good she would look without a braid, and how she would feel about it.

To gather feed grass for the pigs, Xiaoxiao would take her husband up on the dark slope of Snail Mountain.

The child did not know any better, and so whenever he heard singing, he would break into song. And no sooner did he open his mouth than Motley would appear.

Motley began to harbor new thoughts about Xiaoxiao, which she gradually became aware of and that made her nervous. But Motley was a man, with all the wiles and the ways of a man, strong of build, and nimble-footed, who could divert and charm a girl. While he ingratiated himself with Xiaoxiao's husband, he found ways of sidling up to Xiaoxiao and of disarming her suspicions about him.

But what is a man compared to a mountain? With trees everywhere, Xiaoxiao would be hard to locate. So whenever he wanted to find Xiaoxiao, Motley would stand on a rise and sing in order to get a response from Little Husband at Xiaoxiao's side. As soon as Little Husband sang, Motley, after running over hill and dale, would appear face-to-face before Xiaoxiao.

When the little child saw Motley, he felt nothing but delight. He wanted Motley to make insect figures from grass, or to carve out a flute for him from bamboo, but Motley always came up with a way to send him off to find the necessary materials so that he could sit by Xiaoxiao and sing for her those songs that would bring her guard down and produce a blush on her cheeks. At times, she was worried that something might happen, and she wouldn't let her husband go off; at other times it seemed better to send the boy-husband off, so that he wouldn't see what Motley was up to. Finally, one day, she let Motley sing his way into her heart, and he made a woman of her.

At the time, Little Husband had run down the mountain to pick berries, and Motley sang many songs which he performed for Xiaoxiao:

> Pretty maid, an uphill path leads to your door;
> If others have walked a little, I've walked more.
> My well-made sandals are worn out, walked to shreds;
> If not for you, my pretty, then who for?

When he finished, he said to Xiaoxiao: "I haven't slept a wink because of you." He swore up and down that he would tell no one. When she heard this, Xiaoxiao was bewildered: she couldn't help looking at his brawny arms, and she couldn't help hearing the last thing he said. Even when he went to the outhouse, he would sing for her. She was disconcerted. But she asked him to swear before Heaven, and after he swore—which seemed a good enough guarantee—she abandoned herself to him. When Little Husband came back, his hand had been stung by a furry insect, and it was swelling up: he ran to Xiaoxiao. She pinched his hand, blew on the sting, and sucked on it to reduce the swelling. She remembered her thoughtless behavior of a moment ago, and she was dimly aware that she had done something not quite right.

When Motley took her, it was May, when the wheat was brown; by July, the plums had ripened—how fond she was of plums! She felt a change in her body, so when she bumped into Motley on the mountain, she told him about her situation, and asked what she should do.

They talked and talked, but Motley had not the faintest idea of what to do. Although he had sworn before the very heavens, he still had no idea. He was, after all, big in physique but small in courage. A big physique gets you into trouble easily, but small courage puts you at a loss as to how to work your way out.

After a while, Xiaoxiao would finger her snakelike black braid, and, thinking of life in the city, she said:

"Brother Motley, why don't we go where we can be free in the city and find work there? What do you say?"

"That won't do. There's nothing for us there."

"My stomach is getting bigger. That won't do either."

"Let's find some medicine: there's a doctor who sells the stuff in the market."

"You'd better find something quick. I think—"

"It's no use running to 'freedom' in the city. Only strangers there. There are rules even for begging your bread; you can't go about it as you please."

"You're really worthless, and you've been awful to me. Oh, I wish I were dead."

"I swore never to betray you."

"Who cares about betrayal; what I need is your help. Take this living thing out of my belly right away! I'm frightened."

Motley said no more, and after a little while he left. In time, Little Husband came by from a spot where he was gathering red fruit. When he saw Xiaoxiao sitting all alone in the grass, her eyes red from crying, Little Husband began to wonder. After a while he asked:

"Sis, what's the matter?"

"It's nothing. I've got a cobweb in my eye. It smarts."

"Let me blow it away."

"No, don't bother."

"Hey, look at what I've got."

He took out of his pocket little shells and pebbles he had snatched from the nearby brook. Xiaoxiao looked at them, her eyes brimming, and managed a laugh: "Sonny, we get along so well. Please don't tell anyone else I've been crying. They might get upset." And indeed, no one in the family got wind of it.

Half a month went by, and Motley, taking all his belongings with him, left without so much as a word. Grandfather asked Mumbles (who roomed with Motley) whether he knew why Motley had left. Had he merely drifted off into the hills, or had he enlisted in the army? Mumbles shook his head and said that Motley still owed him two hundred dollars; he had gone with not so much as a note when he left. He was certainly a no-good. Mumbles spoke his mind, but gave no indication where Motley might have gone. So the whole family buzzed about it the whole day, talking about this departure until nightfall. But, after all, the farmhand had not stolen anything and had not absconded with anything; so after a while, everyone forgot all about him.

Xiaoxiao, however, was no better off. It would have been nice if she could have forgotten Motley, but her stomach kept on getting bigger and bigger, and something inside began to move. She felt a sense of panic, and she spent one restless night after another.

She became more and more irritable; only her husband was aware of that, because she was now always harsher on him.

Of course, her husband was at her side all the time. She wasn't even very sure what she was thinking herself. On occasion she thought to herself: what if I were to die? Then everything would be all right. But then, why should I have to die? She wanted to enjoy life, to live on.

Whenever anyone in the family mentioned—even in passing—her husband, or babies, or Motley, she felt as if a blow had struck her hard on the chest.

Around October she was worried that more and more people would know. One day, she took her husband to a temple, and, making private vows, she swallowed a mouthful of incense-ashes. But as she was swallowing, her husband saw her and asked what she was doing. She told him this was good for a bellyache. Of course she had to lie. Though she implored the Bodhisattvas to help her, the Bodhisattvas did not see it her way; the child in her grew and grew just as before.

She went out of her way to drink cold water from the stream, and when her husband asked her about it, she said that she was merely thirsty.

Everything she could think of she tried, but nothing could divest her of the awful burden which she carried within. Only her husband knew about her swelling stomach; he did not dare let on to his mother and father. Because of the disparity in their ages and their years together, her husband regarded her with love mixed with fear, deeper even than his feeling for his own parents.

She remember the oath that Motley swore, as well as what happened besides. It was now autumn, and the caterpillars were changing into chrysalises of various kinds and colors all around the house. Her husband, as if deliberately taunting her, would bring up the incident when he had been stung by the furry insect—that brought up unpleasant memories. Ever since that day, she had hated caterpillars, and whenever she saw one she had to step on it.

One day, word spread that the coeds were back again. When Xiaoxiao heard this, her eyes stared out unseeing, as if in a daze, her gaze fixed on the eastern horizon for some time.

She thought, well, Motley ran away, I can run away too. So she collected a few things, bent on joining the coeds on their way to the big city in search of freedom. But before she could make her move, she was discovered. To the people of the farm this was a grave offense, and so they tied her hands, put her away in a shed, and gave her nothing to eat for a whole day.

When they looked into the causes for her thwarted attempt at escape, they realized that Xiaoxiao, who in ten years was to bear a son for her husband to continue the family line, now carried a child conceived with another. This produced a scandal that shook the household, and the peace and tranquillity in the compound were totally disrupted. There were angry outbursts, there were tears, there were scoldings: each one had his own complaint to make. Hanging, drowning, swallowing poison, all these the long-suffering Xiaoxiao had considered desultorily, but in the end she was too young and still wanted to hold on to life, and so she did nothing. When Grandfather realized the way things were, he hit upon a shrewd plan. He had Xiaoxiao locked up in a room with two people to stand guard; he would call in her family to ask them whether they would recommend that she be drowned, or that she be sold. If it was a matter of saving face, they would recommend drowning; if they couldn't bear to let her die, they would sell her. But Xiaoxiao had only the uncle, who worked on a nearby farm. When he was called, he thought at first he was being invited to a party; only afterward did he realize that the honor of the family was at stake, and this put the honest and well-intentioned fellow at a loss as to what to do.

With Xiaoxiao's belly as proof, there was nothing anyone could say. By rights, she should have been drowned, but only heads of families who have read their Confucius would do such a stupid thing to save the family's honor. This uncle, however, hadn't read Confucius: he couldn't bear to sacrifice Xiaoxiao, and so he chose the alternative of marrying her off to someone else.

This also seemed a punishment, and a natural one at that. It was normal for the husband's family to be considered the injured party, and restitution was to be made from the proceeds of the second marriage. The uncle explained all this carefully to Xiaoxiao, and then was just about to go. Xiaoxiao clung to his robe and would not let him leave, sobbing quietly. The uncle just shook his head, and, without saying a word, left.

At the time, no reputable family wanted Xiaoxiao; if she was to be sent away, someone would have to claim her, and so for the moment she continued to stay at the home of her husband. Once this matter had been settled, no one, as a rule, made any more fuss about it. There was nothing to do but wait, and everyone was totally at ease about the matter. At first, Little Husband was not allowed in Xiaoxiao's company, but after a while they saw each other as before, laughing and playing like brother and sister.

Little Husband understood that Xiaoxiao was pregnant; he also understood that, in her condition, Xiaoxiao should be married off to someone living far away. But he didn't want Xiaoxiao to be sent away, and Xiaoxiao for her part didn't want to go either. Everyone was in a quandary as to what to do, though the force of custom and circumstance dictated what had to be done, and there were no two ways about it. Lately, if one asked who was making up the rules and the customs, whether the patriarch or matriarch, no one could rightly say.

They waited for a prospective husband: November came with still no one in sight. It was decided that Xiaoxiao might as well stay on for the New Year.

In the second month of the new year, she came to term, and gave birth to a son, big-eyed, with a large round head, a sturdy build, and a lusty voice. Everyone took good care of both mother and son; the customary steamed chicken and rice wine were served to the new mother to build up her strength, and ritual paper money was burned to propitiate the gods. Everyone took to the baby boy.

Now that it turned out that the child was a boy, Xiaoxiao didn't have to be married off after all.

When, years later, the wedding ceremony for Xiaoxiao and her husband took place, her son was already ten years old. He could do half a man's work, he could look after the cows and cut the grass—a regular farmhand who could help with the chores. He took to calling Xiaoxiao's husband Uncle: Uncle would answer, with never a cross word.

The son was called "Herdboy." At the age of eleven, he was betrothed to a girl six years older. Since she was already of age, she could lend a helping hand and be very useful to the family. When the time for the bamboo wedding pipes to be sounded at the front door came, the bride inside the sedan chair sobbed pitiably. The grandfather and the great-grandfather were both beside themselves.

On this day, Xiaoxiao had lately given birth (the child was already three months old), and when she carried her newborn babe, watching the commotion and the festivities by the fence under the elm, she was taken back ten years, when she was carrying her husband. Now her own baby was fussing, so she sang in low tones, trying to soothe him:

"Now, there, there, look! The pretty wedding-sedan is coming this way. Look at the bride's lovely gown! How beautiful she looks! Hush! Hush! Don't act up now. Behave yourself or Mommy will get angry. Look, look! The coeds are here too! One day, when you grow up, we'll get you a coed for a wife."

1929

Ling Shuhua (1904–1990)

THE NIGHT OF MIDAUTUMN FESTIVAL

Translated by Nathan K. Mao

On the night of the Midautumn Festival, the moon had just risen gracefully above the rooftops; in the clear sky no trace of a cloud could be seen. The roofs and the courtyards seemed to be sheeted in hoarfrost, and the trees and the shrubbery, far and near, covered with thin sleet. From time to time the smoke of incense swirled and the scent of fruits and delicacies emanated from the reception room.

Jingren had just paid his respects to his ancestors.[1] Still wearing an outer jacket and a skull cap,[2] he paced the reception room and smilingly watched his wife put away articles of worship as she gave orders to the cook: "Later, when you serve dinner, no need to heat the fish again; add some cooking wine to the chestnut chicken and stew it again; also add some sugar to the vegetable dish and stew it some more. The 'Together Duck' is a little tough. Simmer it some more."

"That's right, simmer the 'Together Duck' some more. Could we also add some slices of bamboo shoots to it?" Jingren asked his wife, walking up to her. From his beaming face he was quite pleased with her arrangements.

"All right, add some bamboo shoots; fish out the ham bones; make sure the soup doesn't get too greasy."

1. Presumably before a small wooden tablet inscribed with ancestors' names.

2. Traditional Chinese costume worn on formal occasions. The jacket has wide sleeves.

The cook received her orders and left the room, her arms full of bowls.

Jingren sat in a big chair and took off his cap. As he relaxed against the chair's arm, he closed his eyes momentarily. The dress she had on this evening, he realized, was the same one she had worn on the third day of their honeymoon in the spring. It was made of bluish-green silk, with embroidered golden green floral sprigs on its shoulders, sleeves, and hem. Because she had been quite active during the day, she didn't look as pale as usual; her cheeks were lovely, rosy through her light rouge. She was exceptionally beautiful this evening, he thought; if he were a European or an American, he would, at this moment, passionately hug and kiss her. But the Chinese usually do not indulge in such open demonstrations of affection between husband and wife.

"What do you want to drink, rice wine[3] or grape wine?" she asked, walking up to him with a pleasant smile.

In a euphoric mood, he didn't quite hear what she had asked. But vaguely aware that she must be referring to either food or drink, he replied: "Whatever you like."

"I know nothing about drinks. Let's invite someone to drink with you. How does that sound?"

"Tonight, I just want to drink with you and no one else." With his eyes half closed, he smiled, hinting that she should sit by him.

"I get tipsy with two little cups. But you, even ten cups don't affect you." She had taken his hint and sat on a chair to the left of him. Her roundish chin, accentuated by affectionate dimples, appeared especially charming.

Unable to restrain himself, he held her hand, smiled, and said: "I want you to get drunk. This is the first Midautumn we've spent together. It's a festival of family union, and people should be together. Pity that Mother isn't here. She'd enjoy the dishes you cook." Reminded of the loneliness that his mother and sister in the country must be feeling on this festival day, he felt a little downcast. "Mother used to say that if the family stayed together for the Midautumn dinner, they wouldn't be separated for a year. Let's step outside and have a look at the moon before we eat." Together he and his wife went into the courtyard.

At dinner, the second dish had just been served; his wife was still sipping her first cup of wine, and he was about to toast her when Old Dong the doorkeeper rushed in. "Sir, telephone from Mason Lane. The doctor said that your foster sister is failing fast, and they want you there immediately."

"Which doctor said that?" His face turning pale, Jingren rose from the table.

"They didn't say which doctor. They hung up right away; they probably used someone else's phone." Old Dong left the room.

"Why is Foster Sister failing so fast? Didn't Dr. Wang say the other day that she could be cured? I didn't think it was so critical," the wife commented, a touch of frost moving over her face.

---

3. *Huadiao*, a type of rice wine produced in Zhejiang Province.

"I'd better get a good doctor or two to look at her. It's a pity her parents-in-law are too stingy to spend money on her treatment," he said, getting up from the table and preparing to leave.

Although his wife was disconcerted, she was unwilling to see him leave right away, for the "Together Duck" had not been served. If they didn't eat it, she reasoned, the "Together Dinner" would not be complete and might portend some catastrophe. So she quickly pulled him down, saying: "Have some rice before you go. You must eat the rice tonight."

Very much aggrieved, Jingren remembered the way his foster sister had looked the last time he saw her. Her thin face was ashen, and her listless and teary eyes had stared fixedly at the top of the bed-net. Though he was in no mood to eat, he nonetheless realized that he must eat the Midautumn dinner. So he yelled: "Bring the rice. Get the rickshaw ready. I'll leave presently."

A servant brought the rice. Quickly he mixed it with some fish broth and swallowed it down in a hurry.

"Where's the duck? Master is almost done with his dinner." The wife became impatient, worried about his leaving without eating the duck.

When the duck was served, he was already rinsing his mouth and hastily putting on his outer jacket. Quite displeased, she looked at him piteously and the rosy hue on her cheeks faded as she said: "Eat a piece of this 'Together Duck' before you go. How can you not eat a piece on this festival day?" She chose a fat piece and put it on his small serving plate.

"No time to eat. She's dying and waiting for me. How can I eat any more?"

Her feelings were hurt. Still afraid that not eating the "Together Duck" would bring misfortune, she pleaded with him in a whisper: "If you don't eat the 'Together Duck,' it will bring bad luck. Jingren, you must eat this piece."

Jingren felt he must eat. So he sat down and put the piece into his mouth. It was extremely greasy; he spat it out and hurriedly swallowed a mouthful of rice. He rinsed his mouth again and sipped a mouthful of tea.

He walked to the hall outside. "Is the rickshaw ready?"

"It's been ready for some time. They called again and urged you to hurry. They said your foster sister wanted to speak with you."

"Tell them I'm on my way." He stepped quickly into the rickshaw, and the puller dashed away.

It was nearly midnight. The moon hung in the middle of the sky; its clear, faint light shone on the windows and made everything look dismal. Sitting by a window in the bedroom, the wife was wrapped in thought. As her thoughts turned to the evening's dinner, she shivered, as if the demon of bad fortune were pushing around that small piece of uneaten duck and deliberating on what to do with Jingren.

She seemed lost in a dark, dim forest, engulfed in terror, chill, and worry. She prayed for a man to console her, to take her hand and take her out of there. She thought that if she could only hold quietly to a dear one's hand—of course, the first person that came to mind was Jingren—she'd be free of her worries and fears.

Good. Jingren was home. She hurried into the courtyard to greet him. "How was it? Nothing serious, I hope."

Ashen, his eyes red-rimmed, he ran into the reception room and flopped on the guest couch, speaking huskily: "Why do you ask? If I had been there five minutes sooner, I'd have seen her before she died. All because you insisted on my eating that bowl of rice, I was delayed for ten minutes. It's such a pity that in this capital she had only her foster brother, yet she couldn't see him before she died. . . . Her death is so sad." His voice was hoarse. It was as if he saw his newly dead sister again—her emaciated face, her dim and tear-filled eyes, her disheveled hair, her body covered by a white bedsheet with yellow paper money[4] strewn over it, and a lone pair of flickering candles on the floor, between which was a cluster of burning incense sticks. The more he thought about her, the sadder he became. He heaved a long sigh.

"Ai, we really didn't do right by her. It's bad enough that she was widowed a year after she was married, not to mention that she didn't have any children; she couldn't even see her only foster brother before she died. It's all because you forced me to eat that bowl of rice. Zhang Ma said that she asked people to look for me just moments before she died. Ai, I didn't do right by her."

To begin with, she regarded death as a taboo subject on a festive day like this. As Jingren continued to berate her, she became somewhat piqued. Nevertheless she restrained herself, saying merely: "Don't keep blaming me. It's better not to see a dead person on a festival day."

The word "better" unexpectedly provoked him. Strongly resentful of her air of impatience he said indignantly: "I never thought a young woman like you could be so cold-hearted. She died all alone, yet you say it was better not to see her. What's 'better' about it?" His grief had turned to anger. For the first time since his marriage, he felt his wife was wrong. After saying this, he stretched out his foot and violently kicked his shoe upward. The heavy shoe accidentally knocked a vase from a small tea table and shattered it into many pieces.

Dumbfounded by his show of temper, the wife had been considering a rebuttal to air her grievances; then, when she saw how he knocked over the vase—another bad omen—instantly, grief and anger took complete control of her. "What's the matter with you? Are you determined to give me a hard time tonight?" she cried. "On this festival day you were unwilling to eat your rice and now you broke the vase. What future is there for us? I might as well—"

She was crying, her tears soaking her white muslin handkerchief. Haltingly she went on: "What does it matter what I said? It's a festival day and you're deliberately picking on me."

4. Paper money for the dead to use in the nether world.

As his wife used a fresh handkerchief to wipe off her tears, he noticed how unsightly her swollen nose was. How her lips, which he had considered pretty, looked purplish without the lipstick, dark and contorted from crying. He also noticed how slanted her plain eyes really were, a flaw he had failed to notice before because he was in love with her. Suddenly he remembered what his mother used to say: "Slanted-eyed women are the most difficult to handle." This was the first time in his married life that he had become aware of her ugliness.

"Who's giving you a hard time? Damn it, I can't reason with women." In a state of despair and melancholy he walked into the courtyard and gazed at the round bright moon, which seemed to be snickering at him. Unconsciously he heaved a long sigh. After pacing around the courtyard a few times, he felt the cold dew dampening his lined jacket and headed toward the bedroom.

His wife was still sobbing. Showing no patience with her, he crawled into bed.

All night long sleep evaded him. He stole a glance at his wife and noted that her lips were green and her eyes swollen from crying. He felt sorry for her, yet he hated her. He decided not to speak to her. It was nearly dawn. Watching her resting on the tiny couch, he fell asleep.

No sooner had he fallen asleep than his foster sister appeared in a dream, wearing the same clothes she had seven years ago when they lived in the same house in the country. As she smiled and beckoned him, he awoke with a start. His mind replayed the scene where she sat on his bed and cared for him in his mother's place during a bout of malaria. He was averse to taking quinine pills, which he considered unsanitary; and she, with tears brimming in her eyes, had fed him sugar water and coaxed him into taking them. As he drank the last mouthful, his lips accidentally brushed against her smooth, scented hand. Instantly feeling an indescribable, sweet sensation, he sniffed hungrily at her hand. She reddened, and he smiled and lay down again. From that time on, she looked a little embarrassed when she saw him, but she also seemed more concerned about him. She had been promised in marriage to a Feng family when she was still a child. When she married into that family the following year, she was grief-stricken, and he shared her grief. Within a year she was widowed. For five years he hadn't seen her, until last spring in the capital. As he reminisced to this point, unknowingly he again sighed.

"I didn't do right by her! I wasn't there when she died. Will she forgive me?" He crawled out of bed. The white light of dawn slid across the window curtain; it was six thirty in the morning.

He was rather sulky, vexed by his quarrel with his wife the night before. When he saw her cover her eyes with her sleeves in her sleep, he felt sorry for her, but he was also convinced that he had been in the right. He walked to the tiny couch and started a conversation. "Go sleep in the bed. How can you sleep here?"

His wife was silent. He stepped out of the bedroom, hurriedly put on his clothes, and left for his foster sister's home to make the funeral arrangements.

It was ten in the evening when he completed all the arrangements for burial clothes and coffin. Since the Feng family couldn't spend much, and since he felt his sister deserved a decent burial, he spent more than two hundred dollars from the profits he made in his own shop on the funeral. For the coffin alone, he deposited more than a hundred and sixty dollars as down payment; still the man in the coffin shop made clear that the coffin was not of the best quality.

Home in his courtyard, he muttered, "At least I've done my best," as he felt the empty wallet in his pocket.

His wife's hair was uncombed, her eyes puffed, and she seemed oblivious to the world around her. Leaning on a bedpost, she was talking to her personal maid.[5] When he entered the room, they immediately stopped talking.

Trying to make conversation, he sat down on a chair and sighed: "Well, I'm finally done with the funeral arrangements."

"Have you had dinner, sir?" the servant asked, offering him a cup of tea.

"Well, more or less. I couldn't really eat while I was busy making funeral arrangements. Have you all eaten?"

"We waited until nine thirty. Missy had only a tiny morsel," the servant replied. After a short pause, she went on: "Did you see the two bills on the desk, sir? They said you promised to settle the accounts today."

"Damn! I forgot that the money I spent today was to pay those bills. What do I do?" Jingren twisted a short strand of hair on his forehead, looking a little worried. Turning to his wife, he asked: "Have you spent the hundred dollars I gave you two days ago? Let's use that money to pay the bills."

"Didn't I show you an account of how I spent the money yesterday? You didn't look at it yesterday, and now you demand the money. I've never wasted a penny of yours. I don't have a foster brother to give me money or worry about me."

With a bellyful of grievances, the wife had been waiting for this chance to express them. She became garrulous.

"My God, you're strange. What evil spirit's possessed you these last two days? All you want to do is argue with me. What kind of talk is that, a foster brother giving you money to spend? She's dead now; stop saying such nasty things. I really have to get away from you."

"I knew a long time ago that you didn't care for me. I'd better go back to my mother's. Why do you have to pick on me? You embarrassed me on the festival day. What did I ever do to deserve that?" Still sobbing, she yelled, "Yang Ma, pack up; we're going to my mother's. My family can afford to feed one extra mouth. I'm not—" Weeping, she stood up and began to pack.

---

5. A maid who had been with her before her marriage; probably someone who had taken care of her since childhood.

That evening, the wife tearfully returned to her mother's and stayed there for three days. Jingren's friends urged him to bring her home. Still feeling upset, however, he did not go. Every evening he and a few acquaintances, whom he normally didn't often see, visited pleasure haunts, went to the Beijing opera, and followed fashionable ladies in the streets; sometimes he had simple dinners in small restaurants and drank *baigar* wine,[6] and when he was drunk, he shouted bravos at entertainers in opera houses and frequently got home at one or two o'clock in the morning.

A month went by. Jingren's mother-in-law had heard a great deal about Jingren's escapades and became worried for her daughter. On the day of the Double Ninth Festival,[7] she brought her daughter back to him. Though husband and wife no longer quarreled, there had been erected between them a chilly stone tablet on which was inscribed: "You are mere dinner partners who share the same quilt."

By now Jingren was familiar enough with the pleasure dens. In the spring of the second year, he upgraded his dissipation by becoming a regular patron of an establishment in Stone Alley. By the Midautumn Festival of the second year, he had sold his grocery store and used half the money to pay off debts at the Bao Cheng Jewelers and Lao Jiefu Silk and Brocade Shop for two of the establishment's girls.

In the second month of the second year, his wife miscarried a seven-month-old boy with handsome features. The miscarriage was caused by her frequent bouts of anger during pregnancy, which in turn had damaged the embryo, the doctor said. Because of this, the wife lay sick for three months, growing haggard in appearance. She had aged considerably. Jingren was often not at home, and he slowly realized that she was very ugly. When spoken to, he would seldom bother to respond to her.

In the third year, Jingren's mother came from the country to visit him. She saw how addicted Jingren was to pleasure, how the family's grocery store was gone and the deed of the remaining paper shop was mortgaged, though he still ran the business. When her son would not listen to her, she blamed her daughter-in-law's stupidity. Had her daughter-in-law attended to his needs properly, she reasoned, her son would not have squandered the family fortune. Hence, every day she cast unpleasant looks at her daughter-in-law from morning to night.

On the night of the third Midautumn Festival, the wife hid in the kitchen, silently wiping her tears and watching the hearth fire. She dared not cry out loud. The same evening, Jingren suddenly remembered the death of his foster sister three years before. To his mother he blamed his wife for everything. And

6. A type of liquor made from sorghum.

7. Also known as Chongyang Festival; takes place on the ninth day of the ninth month by the Chinese calendar. This day is traditionally celebrated by climbing mountains.

since the foster sister had always been a favorite of hers, the mother, after hearing the story, scolded the wife severely.

Toward the end of the eighth month, Jingren's wife miscarried another boy at six months. Because the boy's nose was not fully formed, and he had only one ear and a few fingers, everyone called it a freak. The doctor, upon examining it, said that the deformities were caused by syphilis.

On Midautumn Festival of the fourth year, Jingren's reception room was full of spiderwebs. When the moon climbed up over the roof ridges, one could see shadows of dark bats flying and fluttering their wings under the moon. From a small room by the kitchen came the voices of two women. One was Jingren's wife, the other probably her mother.

"Ai, do you have to move out the day after tomorrow?"

"Of course, without delay. We were supposed to hand over the house tomorrow. Fortunately, when I begged them they allowed me to stay here for one extra day."

"Are you certain that Jingren won't come to get you?"

"No, he won't. Last night Second Master Wang told me that he's moved to the *sanbuguan* area."[8]

"Ai, who would have thought that the family could fall to such a sad state!"

"No, I guess no one could. But, Mother, this is probably my fate." She blew her nose and sobbed: "On the first Midautumn Festival after my marriage, he and I quarreled. He had a piece of 'Together Duck,' which he spat out. At the time I was rather uneasy about it. Later, when his shoe knocked over an offering vase,[9] I knew for sure it was a bad omen."

"It's the will of Heaven. Who can avoid these catastrophes? I think you'd better be more cheerful, try to be good, and wait for your next life."

After the old woman had said all this, she coughed a few times and started to blow her nose.

It was after two in the morning; the weak oil lamp in the tiny room was near death, and darkness blackened the paper windows. There were still two or three moths ramming themselves against the windows. A little later the light died; moths fell into the chill frost, turned dewy white, and went out to meet their Creator. Heavy breathing, mingled with intermittent *aiyo aiyo* sounds, emanated from the tiny room. The noises of moths plunging against the windows still lingered.

As usual, the moon slowly spread a thin layer of cold frost on the courtyard and covered the treetops in the forest with silvery sleet. Fatigued, the bats went into hiding. In the moonlight, the spiderweb along the big pillar, blown by a gentle breeze, reflected a faint silken ray.

1928

---

8. An area beyond the jurisdiction of the French, Japanese, or Chinese authorities, located between the French and Japanese Concessions in Tianjin.

9. A vase used in religious ceremonies honoring departed ancestors.

Lai He (1894–1943)

THE STEELYARD

Translated by Howard Goldblatt

The residents of Weili Village, south of town, were mostly hardworking, resilient, peaceful, law-abiding farmers. Extreme poverty was the lot of all but the few rich and powerful families who were in charge of governmental business, plus some of their subordinates.

Qin Decan was born into a family that was the poorest of the poor and lost his father soon after he was born. As a tenant farmer, his father had worked a few acres of land, but when he died he left behind only a wretched widow and her son. If the landlord had charitably let them continue working the tiny plot of land, they could have hired a day laborer and managed to eke out a marginal living. But what rich individual would willingly let others share in their profits? If they did, they wouldn't be rich, and that is not what rich people are all about. And so, for the sake of a few additional pecks of grain income, the landlord turned the land over to someone else. The money his father had earned from his own blood and sweat went right back into the ground with him, removing any hope for the survival of the mother and son he had left behind.

Seeing how helpless and alone they were, their neighbors took pity on them, and some of the older ones, in particular, knew they needed to come up with something, since starvation was no laughing matter. What they settled on was a plan to find the widow a new husband. Stepfathers, almost by definition, tend not to open their hearts to the sons who come with a marriage, and Decan's stepfather treated his mother as little more than an instrument to use as he pleased. And so, not only did Decan's life not improve, he actually suffered more verbal and physical abuse than ever, and the relationship between his mother and his stepfather suffered because of it.

Fortunately for him, his mother was able to tolerate backbreaking work and had a talent for getting by. She made their own straw sandals and she raised chickens, ducks, and a pig; through diligence and hard work, she made sure their lives were tolerably human. After struggling to see Decan into his ninth year, his mother sent him out to tend oxen and work in the field for another family. By this time, his stepfather played virtually no role in the life of the family, and mother and son had to fend for themselves to keep the demons of cold and hunger at bay.

The year Decan turned sixteen, his mother had him quit his job and return home to till a few acres of rented land, a difficult proposition at the time, thanks to the highly profitable sugar company. Having been ill treated and exploited by the company, the farmers refused to plant sugarcane, so the company increased the payouts to landowners, who were unconcerned about the farmers' suffering so long as they themselves benefited. As a result, most of the land was grabbed up by the sugar company. A few kindhearted landowners were willing to rent to tenant farmers, but they demanded the same amount of grain as the company did. So Decan was unable to rent any land, and his mother did not want him to work for the company, which would have treated him like a beast of burden. He had no choice but to stay home and wait to be hired to do odd jobs. Strong and hardworking, he managed to be hired out every day. Compared with the work he'd done as a long-term hired hand, the new jobs were easier and brought in more money. Meanwhile, his mother scrimped and saved and, gradually, they put aside a bit of money. Three years passed quickly, and when Decan turned eighteen, the only thing on his mother's mind was his marriage. The money she had struggled to save was enough for him to marry a farmer's daughter from the same village. Fortunately for the newly married Decan, his wife joined him in the fields and worked as hard as a man. The harvest that year was a good one, which made life relatively easy.

During Decan's twentieth year, his mother gained a grandson, bringing a smile to her face and keeping it there, even though she was beginning to show her age. The joy and consolation she felt gradually put her mind at ease, for she had fulfilled her responsibilities as a mother. But twenty years of hardship had taken its toll on her body. And, with a lessening of her sense of responsibility, she let herself relax, thus giving the demon of illness a chance to invade. After lying in bed a few days, she left this world with a contented, happy smile on her face. By then, Decan's stepfather was a father in name only, and now that his mother had passed away, they had nothing more to do with one another.

Poor Decan, his loving mother had taken his happiness along with her.

A daughter arrived the following year. With his mother now gone, his wife had to manage all the household chores, and the children made it impossible for her to go out to work alongside him. Their income thus cut in half, Decan was forced to work doubly hard. Toiling that way for another four years weakened his body and planted the seeds of illness. At the beginning of the harvest season, he contracted malaria and was laid up for four or five days. After a visit to a Western doctor, which cost more than two yuan, he felt better, although his arms and legs weren't nearly as strong as before. But this was a busy time and Decan was a hardworking man; so rather than stay in bed, he dragged his weakened body out to the field. By the time he got home that night, he was not feeling well. At midnight the malaria returned and laid him up in bed again the next day. This time he chose not to see a Western doctor, calculating that his earnings for three days' work weren't enough for one dose of medicine. Where was he going to come up with that much money? But he had to do something about the malaria, so he boiled some herbs that cost nothing or took some Chinese medicine that cost next to nothing. The remedies were not totally ineffectual, but he suffered a bout of malaria every two or three days. It took several months before the malaria stopped recurring, but by then his stomach was bloated. Some said it was caused by too many herbs; others said it was called "swelling of the spleen," and was a side effect from having taken Western medicine. What caused it did not matter to Decan; what worried him was that it kept him from his work.

When Decan was sick, his wife had no choice but go out to work, leaving the children at home, whose cries echoed Decan's moans. They ate one, or at most, two meals a day; although they never reached the point of starvation, all of them, particularly the children, were undernourished. Luckily, his wife did not bear another child.

It was the end of that year before Decan was finally able to do some light work. The last sixteenth-day celebration of the year drew near, but he still could not find a suitable job. When New Year's arrived, everything would come to a complete halt and he would have even less chance of finding work. That made it necessary to save enough food for the first two weeks of the new year. All this worried Decan to the point of panic.

In the end, he heard that selling vegetables in town was a decent way to make a living, so he figured that would suit him. He had no start-up money and, as a naturally shy person, could not bring himself to borrow money from anyone. So, left with no alternative, he asked his wife to pay a visit to her family.

Naturally, a farmer's wife could not have come from a wealthy family, so they dared not expect much help. Fortunately, her sister-in-law was nice enough to take out her only ornament—a gold hairpin—and tell her to pawn it for a little capital to launch Decan's business. This solution posed risks, but it was the only one they had.

One morning, Decan came home with vegetables he had bought and intended to sell in town after breakfast. It was then that his wife realized he lacked a "steelyard." "Now what?" Decan thought. "Steelyards are government monopolies and they don't come cheap. Where am I supposed to get the money?" His wife then went over and borrowed a steelyard from a neighbor, a kind person who lent them one that looked relatively new. The police harassed ordinary people in order to improve their own performance record; the more criminal activities they discovered, the faster they were promoted. They were forever persecuting people who had no recourse or ability to complain for a variety of trumped-up offenses: transportation bans, road laws, food and drink regulations, travel rules, and measurement standards. Every aspect of daily life fell within the scope and restrictions of the law. Decan's wife had borrowed a new steelyard to avoid falling afoul of the law.

Business wasn't bad on the first day and by closing time, he had taken in more than one yuan. First he bought some rice to prepare for the coming year. A few days later he had enough rice and he thought, "This has been a bad year, so the first thing I need to do next year is buy a new Goddess of Mercy poster for the living room altar, then we should change the couplets on the door. I'll also need to buy other necessities, such as the gold and silver spirit paper, incense, and candles." Several more days passed and business remained good; wanting to make some New Year's sticky rice cakes, he bought the rice and sugar.

His wife, unable to hold back, counseled him: "Save the rest of the money so we can redeem that hairpin. Isn't that more important?"

"You're right," Decan said. "I haven't forgotten. It's just that it is only the twenty-fifth. I'm confident I can earn the money and, even if I can't, we still have the seed money. No matter what, we'd have to pay at least one month's interest."

One evening, on his way home after the market had closed, he thought about the children. As a father, he would feel regret over not meeting his responsibilities if he couldn't give them some new clothes for the coming year. A comfortable life was out of the question, but he could at least give them a bit of happiness. So he spent all the money he had made over the past few days, earmarked for the interest payment, on a few yards of patterned fabric.

Then one day just before noon, a patrolman walked by his stand; his gaze fell on Decan's vegetables. Decan asked solicitously, "What would you like, Your Honor?"

"Your vegetables are fresher than most," the policeman said.

"Yes," Decan replied. "Nothing but the best for you city folk."

"How much is the cauliflower?" the policeman asked.

"Your Honor needn't ask the price. Just having you appreciate my goods is an honor." Decan picked out a few good stalks and tied them with straw before respectfully offering them to the policeman.

"No, weigh them first," the policeman replied, refusing the gift.

The simple and unsuspecting Decan put the cauliflower stalks on his steelyard and said, "Your Honor, you're so nice. It's only one catty and fourteen ounces." Asking for something to be weighed normally indicated a sale, a transaction involving money, neither a bribe nor a gift.

"Is that right?" the policeman asked.

"Yes, it's actually two catties, but since it's for Your Honor . . . " Decan said in his normal business tone, indicating that it was not to be a gift.

"Your steelyard must be off. If it's two catties, then it's two catties. Why the shortage?" The expression on the policeman's face changed.

"No, this one's almost new." Decan nodded, unflustered.

"Hand it over." The policeman turned angry.

"The marks are still clear as can be." Decan calmly offered up the steelyard with both hands.

The policeman held it up and, after a cursory examination, said, "This is worthless. I'm taking you to the police station!"

"Why? Can't I have it repaired?" Decan asked.

"Are you refusing to go?" the policeman roared angrily. "You won't go, you swine?" With a grunt the policeman snapped the steelyard in two and tossed it away. He then removed a notepad from his breast pocket and took down Decan's name and address before heading indignantly back to the station house.

Crushed by this unexpected humiliation, Decan stood dazed by his stand, as fury and outrage welled up inside. Some passersby came up to him after the policeman was out of earshot. An older man said, "Damned fool. How can you expect to do business here if you don't even know the rules of the marketplace? When you told him the weight, were you really thinking of taking his money?"

"Do you mean to tell me we should give our goods away?" Decan asked resentfully.

"Ai! You have no idea how mean he can be. Just wait till you taste his herbal paste [torture]," the old-timer said with a mocking laugh.

"What? Are you saying that his official position gives him the right to humiliate and terrorize people at will?" Decan exclaimed.

"We've got a tough guy here!" someone said. After voicing their opinions, the crowd dispersed.

Decan returned home. Having no appetite, he sat there quiet and glum, telling his wife what had happened that day only after she'd asked several times.

"Don't worry," she said. "We'll use what you made over the past few days to buy a new steelyard for our neighbor, and we'll still have enough left to redeem the hairpin. Go get some rest and stay home tomorrow. We have most of what we need for New Year's. I'm afraid that we've tangled with the government because of the rotten luck we've had this year. Maybe our luck will change next year."

Decan took a day off and everything seemed fine. The day after that was New Year's Eve, which meant one last day to do business that year, so he decided to take the vegetables into town at the crack of dawn. It was still dark, but the noise of shoppers resounded in the morning mist, creating a forlorn reminder of the passage of time and man's brief stay on earth.

When daybreak finally arrived, most of the goods at various stalls were nearly gone. Some people had already picked up their baskets and poles to go home, where they would gather with their families for the New Year's Eve dinner as a reward for a year's hard work and to enjoy a happy family life.

Decan ran into the policeman again.

"Where were you yesterday, you swine?" the policeman asked.

"What? You have no cause to talk to me like that," Decan replied.

"Swine, come with me to the station house," the policeman said.

"I'll go if you want me to. But why call people 'swine'?" Decan asked.

The policeman glared at him and dragged him off to the station house.

"Are you Qin Decan?" the judge asked from his bench.

"Yes, I am, Your Honor," Decan answered, as he knelt before the judge.

"Have you been guilty of an offense?" the judge asked.

"Your humble subject has lived more than thirty years and has never committed a single offense," Decan said.

"I don't care about what happened before, but this time you've violated the weights and measures regulations," said the judge.

"That's wrong," Decan said.

"What? Are you saying it didn't happen?"

"I've been falsely accused."

"But a policeman's report cannot be wrong."

"The accusation is false."

"Since you've broken the law, I can't let you go. But I'll only fine you three yuan. You should consider that a special favor."

"But I don't have the money."

"No money? Then you'll have to do three days' jail time. Now, do you have the money or don't you?"

"No!" In Decan's mind, three days in jail over the holiday was nothing compared to the loss of three yuan.

His wife had planned to redeem the hairpin at the pawnshop after finishing the laundry, but heard the bad news before she left the house. Who could she turn to? she wondered. Who would come to her aid at a time like this? She could think of no one and no way out of her quandary, and sadness overcame her. Staying home and weeping was the only way she could lessen the pain in her heart. Eventually, a comforting neighbor urged her to take the redemption money to the station house to find out what this was all about.

The mere sight of a policeman scares the wits out of country folk, so it is easy to imagine the terror a woman who had seen little of the world felt about going to the station house. She had barely stepped in the door when a policeman asked gruffly, "What do you want?" sending her reeling back out the door. Fortunately, a fourteen-year-old janitor came out to see what was going on and she begged him to look into the matter for her. Still imbued with the innocence of youth, the janitor had yet to learn how to mistreat people. He offered to take the three yuan inside and pay the fine.

"How did I get released so quickly?" Decan wondered aloud as he emerged from the station house and saw his wife standing there.

"What are you doing here?" he asked.

"I . . . I heard you'd been arrested," she said, nearly choking on the words.

"It wasn't a serious offense, certainly nothing I'd lose my head over," Decan said unhappily.

The market was closed by the time they were out on the street; firecrackers sending off the old year exploded all around them.

"Did you redeem the hairpin?" Decan asked his wife.

"I heard the news before I left the house, so I rushed over to the station house and paid the three yuan fine. Now we don't have enough," she said.

"Oh." Decan gave voice to his resignation as he took out the three yuan he'd earned earlier that day.

"I'll take the baskets and carry the pole home. The pawnshop will probably close soon, so hurry over and redeem the hairpin."

After the "reunion meal," the children, hoping to get up early for the arrival of the New Year, went to bed to dream their happy dreams. Decan paced back and forth, oblivious to his wife's urgings to go to bed. He was in the grip of an inexplicable sadness. Between sighs, he mumbled, "What has the world come to when a man is treated like a swine, when life is more miserable than death?" He recalled the contented look on his mother's face just before she died. Finally, he saw the light.

On New Year's Day, a clamor of screams, wails, and sobs erupted at Decan's house. Later someone was heard to say, "Is that all there is?"

"That's all, just some gold spirit paper for the dead."

Around that time, a rumor spread through the market that a policeman on night patrol had been killed on his route.

It has been a long time since I witnessed this tragedy. Each time I tried to put it down on paper, I couldn't do it, for the memory always filled me with sorrow. Recently, having read Anatole France's "Crainquebille," I realized that such incidents did not occur only in undeveloped countries; in fact, they occur wherever tyranny reigns supreme. And so, I finally put aside my concerns over a crude style and wrote it down for the approval or rejection of readers.

1926

Ba Jin (1904–2005)

DOG

Translated by Lance Halvorsen

1

I don't know how old I am or what my name is. I'm like a stone that was cast into this world one day and came alive. I have no idea who my parents are. I'm like a lost object that no one ever bothered to come looking for. I have a squat, skinny body, yellow skin, black hair, black eyes, and a flat nose. I'm just one in the multitude and am destined to go on living among them.

Every person has a childhood, but mine was different from other people's. I've never known what it feels like to be warm, well fed, or loved. All I've known is cold and hunger.

One day—I can't remember exactly when—a tall, thin, wrinkled old man standing before me said earnestly, "A boy your age should be in school. Getting a good education is the most important thing in life."

After that, I forgot my cold and hunger and began a search. I looked everywhere. I found grand and imposing buildings as well as plain and simple ones. People told me they were all schools. Head held high, I walked through the gates because I remembered that getting an education is the most important thing in life.

Whether the building was simple or ornate, whether the face I met at the gate was friendly or menacing, invariably I was greeted by, "Get lost! You don't belong here!" The words lashed at me like a whip, until my body burned. I lowered my head and left, but the sound of laughter from children inside rang in my ears. For the first time I began to wonder if I really was a human being at all.

My doubts grew stronger every day. I didn't want to think about it, but a voice in my head kept asking, "Are you really human?"

Inside the abandoned temple stood a statue of the temple god. Gods can do anything, I thought to myself. Since there was no curtain to cover the shrine, the god's dignified image was fully exposed. Even though the gold had peeled off his body, and one of his hands was missing, he was still a god. I knelt in front of the crumbling altar and prayed, "Holy One, please give me a sign. Am I really a human being?"

He didn't answer my prayer. He didn't even give me a sign in my dreams. But in the end, I solved the problem myself. I reasoned, "How could I possibly be a person the way I am? Isn't that an insult to the sanctity of the word itself?" After that I understood that I could not possibly be a person, and the kind of life I had been living suddenly made sense to me. I begged for scraps like a dog because I wasn't human. I was a dog, or something like it.

A thought occurred to me one day: "Since I'm an object, I should be able to sell myself. I can't live a decent life, so I might as well sell myself to someone who will take care of me. I would be his beast of burden if he took me into his household." After I had made up my mind, I stuck a sign on my back to show that I was for sale. I walked slowly through the street markets with my head held high for the sake of prospective buyers. I didn't want to set a price. I would serve anyone as faithfully as a dog so long as he took me in and gave me a few bones to gnaw on.

But not a single person showed any interest in me from sunrise to sunset—nothing but faces twisted with sinister laughter, and a few children who played with the sign on my back.

I was exhausted and hungry. I had no choice but to go back to the dilapidated temple. At the side of the road, I picked up a discarded bun. It was hard and covered with dirt, but I managed to force it down. That made me happy, since it proved that my stomach could handle anything, just like a dog.

The temple was deserted. It occurred to me that my inability to sell myself proved that I was totally useless, worse than not being human. I began to cry, then realized that while human tears were precious, the tears of a useless object were worthless.

I knelt in front of the altar table and cried. I wanted to cry it all out, not so much because I still had tears left, but because tears were all I had. After crying my eyes out in the temple, I ran over to wail at the gate of a lordly mansion. Cold and hungry, I hid in a corner of the wall in front of the gate. I cried in order to swallow my tears; that way the sound of my sobs would drown out the rumblings in my stomach.

A young man dressed in a handsome Western suit emerged. He didn't pay any attention to me. A middle-aged man in an elegant long robe entered. He didn't even look in my direction. A number of people passed by me without noticing I was there.

Finally a tall, robust young man came out. Walking up to me, he cursed, "Beat it! This is no place for you to be crying!"

His words resounded like a clap of brain-numbing thunder. He kicked me as he would kick a dog. I stopped crying. Burying my head in my hands, I stole away without a word because I had nothing to say. When I got back to the temple, I laid down on the ground, exhausted, and howled like a wounded dog. The temple god lowered his eyes and caressed my battered body with his gaze.

My tears were gone. Filled with gratitude, I knelt in front of the altar and pleaded, "I'm not a person, but since I've been fated to live in the world, I might as well go on living. Since I was born like a lost object, parentless and alone, I beg you, Holy One, to be my surrogate father. No one else in the world cares for someone like me."

Though the Holy One didn't reply, he didn't refuse my request. For this reason, I believed I had a father in the just and upright temple god with one missing hand.

2

I went out to beg for bones as usual, but returned to the temple as soon as I had a little something to fill my stomach, because now I had a father at home, just like other people. It was true that my home was a dilapidated temple, my father a god who had never spoken a word to comfort me, but he was the only one in the whole world who wouldn't leave me. He was my family.

Time passed quickly amid cold and hunger. Strange urges began to take root inside me. I wasn't human, that much I knew. But in spite of that, human desires were growing within me. I hungered to live like other people, to eat good food, live in a grand house, wear beautiful clothes, and enjoy warm blankets.

"These are human desires. You're not a human being. What makes you think you can have these things?" I warned myself when I felt these futile desires welling up inside me. But human desires continued to assault my doglike body. I knew that this would lead to disaster, yet I had no way of stopping it.

The goods displayed in store windows along the streets became strangely alluring to me. One day I sighted a pair of beautiful legs walking along the sidewalk. No, they weren't walking exactly; they seemed to be dancing down the street. Anyway, they blocked my vision like two big round pillars. At times they also appeared entwined on the seat of a rickshaw.

Whenever I saw those legs in the distance, I found myself walking toward them. But no sooner would my gaze fall upon them than my mind would caution, "Watch out. You're not a person." At that my courage would evaporate.

One day I saw a white puppy lying next to that pair of legs. His face was snuggled up close, and he even jumped up on top of them. This gave me hope, because it showed that getting close to those legs was not only for human beings. Even dogs were allowed such intimacy. With that in mind, I ran toward that lovely pair of legs, but before I could get too close, a hand reached out from nowhere and grabbed me.

"This will make you see the light!" Those were the only words I heard after I was thrown to the ground. I was dizzy; my brain was seething. I saw stars and passed out.

I was on all fours. All around me were jeering faces. The legs had vanished. The derisive laughter slashed at my ears. I covered them and ran away.

Only then did I fully understand my situation. In the past, I had been content to live like a dog, or something akin to it. Now I realized I had overestimated myself.

I returned to the temple with a sinking heart and sat under the altar, lost in thought. I had a vision of that white puppy snuggling up against those beautiful legs. I saw his comfortable life in a mansion with good food and warm blankets, smothered with tender loving caresses. Jealousy snaked into my heart. I crawled on the ground, rolling my head around, wagging my hindquarters in the air, and barking. I was trying my best to see if I could pass for a dog.

My barks sounded pretty close to the real thing. I thought I could pass for a dog this time. I was overjoyed. I kept crawling around and around on the ground.

But after a while, my feet needed to straighten up and my hands could no longer crawl. Heartbreaking disappointment forced me to face the fact that I wasn't even good enough to be a dog. I lay on the floor again and moaned in despair.

With tears in my eyes, I knelt in front of the altar and pleaded, "Holy One, as my father, please turn me into a dog, like that little white puppy."

No response.

Every day I crawled around and barked, but wasn't lucky enough to turn into a dog.

3

My skin was yellow, my hair and eyes black, my nose flat, and my body squat and skinny. But there were people in the world with fair skin, blond hair, green eyes, big noses, and tall, strong bodies. One, two, three of them, walking briskly down the street or on the sidewalk, proudly holding their heads high and looking all around. They were boisterously singing, yelling, and laughing, as if they had the busy street all to themselves. Other people walked past them timidly or stayed out of their way.

I made a discovery. I realized that what we call people are divided into different categories. It came as a bit of a surprise that there was another kind of person even more honorable than the kind I normally saw. They wore white caps and white uniforms with blue trim, and their collars were wide open, revealing hairy chests. Two, three, four at a time, I often came across these more honorable people on the street. If they were not laughing, singing, or shouting, they were beating pedestrians with liquor bottles, or caressing women's faces in public. Sometimes I saw them sitting in rickshaws with those beautiful legs resting on their laps. They spoke in a language that was beyond me.

People kept a respectful distance from them. I didn't dare get close to them, because they were more honorable than other people. I could only look at them from a distance and secretly worship them. I wished them well. I felt blessed that this kind of honorable person existed in the world. Because of them, I forgot my own misery.

I worshiped them in secret, offering them my blessing, and I often reminded myself not to get too close so as not to defile them. But one time, I did get too close to them.

One day toward evening, I was too tired and hungry to go on walking. I sat down against a wall by the roadside, rubbing my bare feet, which were caked with blood and dirt. Hunger pangs stabbed my heart. My vision became blurry. Everything around me went out of focus. I didn't even notice the Honorable Person walk past. When I finally saw him, I tried to get up and run away, but it was too late.

A pointed shoe kicked my left arm. My arm felt as if it had been sliced in half, hurting so much that I fell down and rolled uncontrollably on the ground.

"Dog!" I heard the Honorable Person spit that word at me.

While I was rubbing my bruises, I mumbled the word "dog" over and over.

I finally made it back to the temple, where I swallowed my pain and crawled around on the ground. I rolled my head, wagged my hindquarters, and barked. I really felt like a dog. I was so happy, I laughed until tears rolled down my cheeks. This time I realized that I really had become a dog.

I knelt before the altar to express my gratitude. "Holy One, my father, I don't know how to thank you. I am a dog now, because that Honorable Person, a man above men, has deigned to call me a dog."

The Holy One didn't comment.

I crawled around and around on the ground and barked, just like a dog.

4

I encountered those legs again. They were slowly walking toward me, and by their side was the white puppy. I could hardly control myself long enough to wait for them to walk over to me. My heart was filled with happiness because now I was a dog, too.

The sound of leather shoes came closer. The puppy barked. Suddenly, it attacked me, pouncing on me and tearing at my tattered clothes. I got down on the ground and wrestled with it. It bit me, and I bit it back.

"You dog! Get off him!" Immediately following that clear, crisp command came a kick to my head from that beautiful leg. I held on to the dog and rolled on the ground. Noise from all directions dinned in my ears. Hands were pulling at me, hitting me, but I held on to the little white dog with all my might.

5

I found myself in a dark cave when I regained my senses. No one was around. The air was stuffy, and breathing became increasingly difficult. I didn't know where I was, but I knew it certainly wasn't a dog's den. I wanted to crawl around and bark like a dog, but I ached all over, and was tied up with a rope so I couldn't move.

My thoughts returned to the dilapidated temple where my surrogate father, the god with one missing hand, was sitting abandoned in his niche. He was waiting for me. I had to go back. No matter what, I had to return to that temple. And no matter how much I ached, I was still a dog. I wanted to bark and bite, to bite through the rope and run back to my abandoned temple.

1931

Shi Zhecun (1905–2003)

ONE EVENING IN THE RAINY SEASON

Translated by Gregory B. Lee

It was the rainy season, and once again the rain was pouring down. I wasn't at all bothered by the rain; what really bothered me were the passing cars whose wheels as they sped by splattered muddy water over my trousers, and sometimes even left me savoring a mouthful of the wonderful stuff.

When things weren't too busy at the office, I'd often stare out of the window at the rain falling against the pale sky, and tell my colleagues how I loathed the wheels of those cars. There's no point in trying to economize when it's pouring rain; you could take the bus, travel in comfort, they'd urge me kindly. But I didn't deign to heed their well-intentioned words, since it was nothing to do with economizing. I just liked putting up my umbrella and returning home amid the pitter-patter of the rain. My home was very close to the company's offices, so there was no need to take the trolley bus at the end of the working day. And there was another reason why I didn't like taking the bus when it rained. I've never had a raincoat and in rainy weather it's usual for everyone to wear a raincoat, and on such narrow buses with the people brushing past each other they are all covered in water, and I, despite my quality umbrella, would inevitably arrive home drenched.

Besides, especially when night was about to fall and the streetlights came on, walking along the sidewalk with a momentarily free and easy mind observing the city in the rain might be muddy and messy but could after all be taken as a personal pleasure. The precise contours of people and traffic, coming and going in the misty drizzle, would all vanish, the broad avenues would reflect the numerous yellow lights, and now and again green and red traffic lights would glisten in the pedestrians' eyes. When it rained hard, the sound of people talking nearby, even when it was loud, seemed to hang in the air.

People often take such behavior as an illustration of how frugal my way of life is, but they don't understand that I draw a great deal of pleasure from it, even if the wheels of the passing cars do splatter mud all over me; and I certainly wouldn't give up the habit just for that. Yes, a habit, what's wrong in calling it a habit? It's already been going on for three or four years now. Every so often, I'll think that I really should buy a raincoat so that I can take the bus on rainy days, and even when walking avoid having my clothes splattered with muddy water, but so far it's simply remained one of those things I ought to get around to one day.

During the recent days of continuous heavy rain, I as usual went off to work in the morning clutching my umbrella, and in the afternoon returned home clutching it. It was the same every day.

Yesterday afternoon, lots of things really piled up at work. When four o'clock came around, I saw that it was still raining hard outside, so I stayed on alone in the office, thinking I might as well get a few more bits of work out of the way, and save having an even larger pile to do the following day, while at the same time put off going out into the rain until it had died down. In the end, I hung around until six o'clock, by which time the rain had long since stopped.

When I got outside, although the street was already all lit up, the sky itself had in the meantime brightened up. Trailing my umbrella, and avoiding the dripping eaves, I strolled along from the southern end of Jiangxi Road to Sichuan Road Bridge, which in the end took me almost half an hour. It was six twenty-five by the big post office clock. Before I'd actually started across the bridge, the sky had grown dark again, but I hadn't noticed since I knew nightfall was approaching. As soon as I stepped onto the bridge, the black clouds unleashed a sudden downpour, which resulted in a resounding pitter-patter of rain. Looking down on the confusion of the pedestrians scurrying for shelter on North Sichuan Road and both sides of Suzhou Creek, I even felt a slight anxiety in my own mind. What were they so worried about? Surely they knew this was simply rain, and presented no danger to their lives. So why were they so urgently trying to hide? Maybe they were frightened of getting their clothes wet, but I could clearly see even those clutching umbrellas and clad in raincoats quicken their pace. I felt that at the very least this was some sort of unwitting chaos. But, if I hadn't felt that I was taking a leisurely stroll in the rain, I too might have dashed madly off the bridge. That's what I was thinking as I opened up my umbrella, without even noticing I'd already crossed the Tiantong Road intersection. It was also raining torrentially down on the main road. It was quite a sight. Apart from a few cars, which, breaching the rain one after another as if boring through it, sped by as normal, there was no traffic, no trolley buses or rickshaws to be seen. I wondered where they'd all taken refuge. As for people, there were almost none moving about, but under the shopfront awnings and shelters you could see little groups of them both with and without umbrellas, with and without raincoats, all huddled together staring out disdainfully at the rain in the face of which they were helpless. For what kind of weather they'd bought their rainwear, I didn't know. As for me, I was already approaching Wenjianshi Road. I wasn't at all put out. I had a good umbrella, and my face couldn't possibly be wet by the rain, and although my feet felt a bit damp, it would merely mean putting on a dry pair of socks when I got home.

As I walked along, I surveyed North Sichuan Road in the rain and had a vague feeling that it was rather poetic, but this "feeling" was certainly no substantial kind of thought; apart from an "I should make a turn here," there was no conscious thought in my mind at all. Stepping off the sidewalk and looking around I saw there was no traffic about, and I had just decided to cross over and turn down Wenjianshi Road when a trolley bus I hadn't seen coming stopped right in front of me. I stopped and stepped back onto the sidewalk and stood next to a telegraph pole waiting for the bus to go. Although I could in fact have happily crossed the street while the bus was stationary, I didn't do so. I've lived in Shanghai a long time and know the traffic regulations. Why didn't I walk to the other side of the street at the moment I could have crossed? I didn't know why.

I counted the passengers descending from the first-class compartment of the bus. Why didn't I count the ones getting off in third class? It was no conscious choice on my part; the first-class seats were at the front of the bus, the passengers getting off were right in front of me, so I could see them very clearly. The first passenger was a Russian wearing a red raincoat, the next one was a middle-aged Japanese woman who hurriedly got off the bus, opened up the plain Oriental umbrella she held in her hand, and, concealing her head in mouselike fashion, rounded the front of the bus and turned into Wenjianshi Road. I recognized her; she ran a fruit shop. The third and fourth looked like merchants of our own from Ningbo. They both wore green rubber Chinese raincoats. The fifth, and in fact the last, passenger to get off was a young woman. She wasn't carrying an umbrella, nor was she wearing a raincoat. It seemed she'd boarded the trolley bus after the rain had stopped, and on arriving at her destination unfortunately found it to be raining hard like this. I surmised that she'd boarded the bus a long way away. She must have got on at least a few stops beyond Carter Road. She got off the bus. She looked trim and slender, but since she had her shoulders covered, it wasn't until she stepped awkwardly onto the sidewalk that I started to notice how beautiful she was. There are many facets to beauty. Granted, a pretty face is important, but what also count are a graceful bearing, a well-proportioned figure, and a pleasant way of expressing oneself or at least one that isn't annoying. And this woman in the rain, I felt, would meet such criteria completely.

She looked up and down the street, then went to the corner and looked down Wenjianshi Road. I knew she was urgently looking for a rickshaw to hail. But I could see, following her glance, that there was no sign of a rickshaw, and the rain was still falling heavily. She turned around, revealing a vexed look on her face, and, knitting her delicate eyebrows, she took shelter under the awning of a furniture shop. I also retreated under the awning, even though the trolley bus had already left. The road was clear, and I could easily have crossed the street. But why didn't I cross over, and continue on my way home? Was it because I felt regretful at the thought of leaving this young woman? Certainly not. I was totally unaware of any such feeling. Yet neither was it anything to do with having a wife at home waiting for me to come home and eat with her in the lamplight. At that moment all thought that I already had a wife had slipped from my mind. Before me was standing a beautiful companion, and one in the midst of difficulty; lonely, standing and staring blankly into the incessant rain. It was quite simply for these reasons that involuntarily I edged up to her side.

Although we were standing under the awning, and although there were no large drops of water coming down from it, we were hit by the cool drizzle when the wind blew. I had an umbrella, and like a brave, medieval warrior I could have used my umbrella as a shield, warding off the attacking spears of the rain, but instead the top half of the young woman's body was periodically drenched. Her thin black silk dress was little use against the rain and merely emphasized her soft, shapely arms. She repeatedly turned and stood sideways to avoid the drizzle attacking her breasts. But, I wondered, didn't it matter then that her arms and shoulders were exposed to the rainwater, letting her dress cling to her skin?

On clear days, the main roads were clogged with rickshaws touting for business, but now that they were needed, there were none to be found. I thought about how poor the rickshaw pullers were at plying their trade. Perhaps it was because there were too many people wanting to hire a rickshaw; demand was outstripping supply, so that even on a bustling thoroughfare such as this, there was not a trace of a rickshaw to be found. Or perhaps all the rickshawmen were themselves sheltering from the rain. In rain as heavy as this, were the rickshaw pullers not entitled to seek shelter themselves? Until now the availability of rickshaws had never been of concern to me, and yet here I was suddenly pondering the question. Besides, I was even thinking what a detestable bunch the rickshawmen were. Why don't you pull your rickshaws by and accept this fare? Here's this pretty young woman, in discomfort and standing in the rain just waiting for any one of you to pass by.

But however much I reflected along these lines, it didn't produce the slightest sign of a rickshaw. Now it was truly getting dark. Across the street a few men, who had been sheltering in the shop doorways and who were only wearing shirts, had grown impatient and decided to brave the rain; risking being drenched from head to toe, they made a dash for it. I saw that the young woman's long eyebrows had knitted yet more tightly; her eyes shone bright, as though she were very anxious. The gaze of her saddened eyes met mine. From her eyes I could tell she was astonished by me. Why do you keep standing there? You have an umbrella, and a pair of leather shoes. Who are you waiting for? In rain like this, who might you be waiting for on the street? How could eyes boring through me like that not harbor some ill intent? From the way she shifted that inquisitorial gaze from me to the darkened sky, I surmised she had certainly entertained these thoughts.

Yes, I had an umbrella. What is more, it was big enough for two. I cannot understand why this realization hadn't come to me sooner. But now that it had, what would it have me do? I could use my umbrella to protect her from this excessive rain. I could go with her a short way in order to find a rickshaw. If it wasn't far I could see her home. If it was far, well, so what? Ought I to cross this divide and make clear my good intentions? But might she not have some other sort of misgivings about my intentions? Perhaps she might misread me, like I had just guessed she had, and then turn me down. But then would she really prefer to stay here in the wind and rain, on this chilly evening street, standing on her own until who knows when? Not a bit of it! The rain would soon have stopped. It had already been raining without letting up for . . . how long? In this rain I'd completely forgotten time flowing by. I took out my watch. Seven thirty-four. Over an hour now. Surely the rain couldn't go on falling like this forever? Look at the road unable to rid itself of the flow, gutters already past containing the rainwater. How much water had already collected in them, whipping up eddies on the surface, and how long before it would inundate the sidewalk? Impossible. It certainly couldn't rain that long. In a while she could surely be on her way. Even if the rain didn't stop, it was likely a rickshaw would pass by, and she would surely take it, whatever fare was demanded. So, should I leave then? Yes, I should. So why didn't I?

Ten minutes went by like this. I still hadn't left. The rain didn't stop and there was not a hint of a rickshaw. She continued to stand there as anxious as before. With cruel curiosity, I wanted to see how she would finally extricate herself from such difficulties. Yet seeing her in such desperate straits, I was divided between impulses of compassion and indifference.

Again she was watching me with astonishment.

Suddenly, I realized why; how could I not have realized just now? She seemed to be waiting for me to present her with my umbrella, and see her home. No, not necessarily see her home, just see her to where she was going. You have an umbrella, but you just stand there. You want to share your umbrella and shelter me from the rain, so what are you waiting for? her eyes said to me.

I blushed but didn't bow my head in shame, turn on my heels, or walk away.

Replying to a young woman's gaze with a blush of shyness was something that hadn't occurred often since my marriage. I immediately felt odd about it. How could I account for this? I couldn't! But immediately a sort of masculinist sentiment welled up inside me; I wanted revenge. Putting it like that makes it seem rather forceful, but at the very least I wanted to subdue the urgent press of her mind on me.

Eventually I moved closer to the young woman and sheltered her with one half of my umbrella.

"Miss, I'm afraid there won't be any rickshaws for a while. If you don't object, I could accompany you on your way. I have an umbrella."

I wanted to say "see you home," but it immediately occurred to me that she wasn't necessarily on her way home, so I resorted to this ambiguous way of phrasing it. While saying my piece, I tried to adopt as nonchalant an air as I could muster, but she could surely see that concealed behind this unconvincingly calm attitude lay a rapidly beating pulse.

For some time she stared at me with a hint of a smile on her lips. She was weighing up the motivation behind my offer. Shanghai is not a friendly place, and people are not trusting in their relations with one another! Perhaps she was putting off her decision. Would the rain really not stop in a short while? Would a rickshaw really not come by? How about accepting his offer of the umbrella just for the time being? Perhaps on turning the corner there'd be a rickshaw, perhaps I should just let him see me to where I'm going. Was there any harm in that? . . . There wasn't. But if I bump into anyone I know, won't they be suspicious? . . . Then again, it's really getting late, and the rain doesn't seem to be letting up.

Then she nodded; a very slight nod.

"Thank you." A soft Suzhou lilt wafted from between her crimson lips.

Turning into the western end of Wenjianshi Road, as the rain pitter-pattered onto the umbrella, with a young woman at my side, I began to wonder at this chance encounter. How could things have come to this? Who was she, this woman walking beside me, letting me shelter her with my umbrella? Aside from with my wife, over the past few years I hadn't done anything like this. I turned my head and glanced over my shoulder. In a shop there were people taking a break from work who were staring at me, or rather at us. Through the mist of the rain, I could see the suspicious expressions on their faces. I started with fright. What if there was someone who knew me? Or could there be someone who knew her? . . . I glanced back at her. She was just lowering her head and carefully picking out her steps as she went. My nose had just brushed her hair, and it smelled so good. No matter which of us was recognized, if they saw us walking together like this, what would they think? . . . I lowered the umbrella slightly so as to hide the upper part of our faces. Unless people intentionally bent down, they wouldn't be able to see our faces. She seemed to approve of this move.

At first I walked on her left side, with my right hand holding up the umbrella. To give her extra shelter from the rain, my arm was stuck right up in the air. I started to feel my arm aching, yet didn't consider it a hardship. I looked at her sideways, detesting the umbrella handle that obstructed my line of view. In profile, she didn't look as pretty as she did from the front. However, I made a new discovery from this perspective: she reminded me very much of someone I knew. But who? I searched and searched my memory, she seemed very reminiscent . . . someone who almost every day came to mind, a girl I knew, with a physique similar to this person I was walking next to right now, with the same kind of face, but now why for the life of me could I not remember? . . . Ah, yes! Now I had it! How was it possible that I couldn't recall her! My very first girlfriend, my schoolmate, and neighbor. Judging from her profile, wasn't she just like her? We hadn't seen one another for years. The last time we were together she was still only fourteen. It must be one, two, . . . oh, seven years ago now. I'd married. I hadn't seen her again. She must have grown even prettier. . . . But it wasn't as if I hadn't seen her grow up; when I pictured her in my mind, she didn't keep the posture and appearance of a fourteen-year-old. Frequently in dreams, when asleep or in daydreams, I'd see her grow up. I myself had constructed her as a beautiful twenty-year-old poised young woman with an attractive voice and carriage. Often when I happened to be feeling sad, in my imagination she'd be a married woman, or even a young mother.

But what was it about her that resembled her so? Her looks still had a lingering air of a fourteen-year-old. Could it really be her? Why should she come to Shanghai? It was her! Was it possible for there to be two people on earth who looked so alike? Had she recognized me or not . . . I should ask her.

"Would I be right in thinking you're from Suzhou?"

"Yes."

It was definitely her. What an unheard-of chance! When did she come to Shanghai? Had her family moved to Shanghai? Or was it, as I feared, that she'd married someone in Shanghai? Surely she'd already forgotten me, otherwise she couldn't allow me to be with her like this. . . . Perhaps I'd changed so much that she couldn't recognize me; a good few years had gone by. . . . But did she know I was married? If she didn't know, and now she recognized me, what could I do? Ought I to tell her? And if it was necessary to tell her, how would I go about it?

I happened to glance to the side of the street where there was a woman leaning on a shop counter. She looked at me with melancholy eyes, or perhaps she was looking at her. Suddenly it seemed that I'd stumbled across my wife. What was she doing here? I was confused.

Where were we walking? I looked about assiduously. A small food market. She was probably getting close to where she was going. I shouldn't lose this chance. I wanted to know a little more about her, but should we resume an already interrupted friendship? Yes, as long as it was just friendship. Or would it not be better to let her go on thinking that I was merely a well-intentioned stranger wanting to help out a young woman? I started to hesitate. What should I do for the best?

I still needed to know where she was headed. She wasn't necessarily on her way home. Home. If it was her parents' home she was headed for there'd be no problem; I could go in, just like when we were kids. But if it were her own home? Why didn't I just ask her if she was married. . . . Perhaps it wasn't even her home, but rather her lover's home. I imagined a cultured young gentleman. I began to have regrets. Why was I feeling so happy today, when I had a wife at home anxiously waiting for me, while here I was minding other people's business? At last there were rickshaws plying North Sichuan Road. If I hadn't been accompanying her like this with my umbrella, surely she would have long since hired one. If I hadn't felt it inappropriate to speak out, I would long since have turned around and walked away, leaving her standing in the rain.

So why not ask one more question?

"Might I ask your name?"

"Liu."

Liu? It must be false. She'd already recognized me, she surely knew everything about me, she was kidding me. She didn't want to know me anymore, and she wasn't interested in renewing our friendship. Women! . . . Why had she changed her name? . . . Perhaps it was her husband's name. Liu . . . but what was her first name?

This little monologue of thoughts didn't take up much time at all. They just quickly danced across my mind in the few moments it took to cross the street with this bewitching young woman. I'd seldom taken my eyes off her, so I hadn't realized that the rain had now let up. There were more people coming and going in front of us now, and it seemed there were a few rickshaws to be seen about. Why didn't she hail one? Perhaps she was getting close to her destination. Could it be that she really had recognized me, but not daring to say, had deliberately extended our walk together? The gust of a breeze caught the hem of her skirt and lifted it behind her. She turned her face to avoid the wind and closed her eyes in a coy yet sweet manner. It was a very poetic pose that recalled a Japanese painting by Harunobu Suzuki entitled "Visiting a Beautiful Lady at the Palace in Evening Rain." She carries a lantern, sheltered from the wind and drizzle by a torn umbrella. Passing at night before the earth god's shrine, clothes and lantern swept up by the wind, she turns aside to avoid the force of wind and rain; it had a rather unconventional feel. Now I noticed that she too had that sort of style. As for me, perhaps I passed for her husband or boyfriend in the eyes of passersby. I was quite proud that people might make such an assumption. Yes, when I considered that she had indeed been my first love, my childhood girlfriend, I was as happy as if their assumption really were the case. And I could tell that the scent wafted from her temples by the wind was the same as the perfume my wife used. . . . And then I thought of that old line of poetry, "Holding up a bamboo umbrella I accompany an elegant beauty," and found it fitted today's chance encounter quite nicely. Suzuki's famous painting once more came to mind. But the beautiful woman depicted by Suzuki didn't resemble her at all, rather it was my wife's lips that resembled the lips of the woman in the painting. Taking another look at her, it was odd, but I now felt that this definitely was not the childhood girlfriend that just now I'd mistaken her for. This was a totally unrelated young woman. The eyebrows and forehead, the nose and cheekbones, even taking into account the intervening years, bore not the slightest likeness. And I particularly disliked her lips, which seen in profile seemed a little too thick.

I suddenly felt quite at ease; even my breathing was more relaxed. Half consciously, half unconsciously holding the umbrella for her, apart from gradually sensing my arm ache more and more, I felt nothing. It was as if the form of the young woman beside me had already been released from the confines of my mind. Only now did I realize night had fallen completely, and the sound of rain was no longer to be heard on the umbrella.

"Thank you, I can make my own way now. The rain's stopped." She chirped into my ear, suddenly startling me, and I closed up the umbrella. A beam of light from a streetlamp shone onto her face, which seemed an orange color. Was she almost there, yet unwilling for me to see her all the way, and so now was taking advantage of the rain's having stopped to get rid of me? Couldn't I think of a way to see where she was eventually going?

"It's no trouble; if you've no objection, I'll see you all the way there."

"There's really no need, I can manage by myself, don't bother coming any farther. It's already very late. So sorry to have kept you."

Evidently she didn't want me to see her all the way there. But what if the rain started up again? . . . I resented the unsympathetic weather. Why couldn't it continue raining for half an hour? Yes, just another half an hour would have done it. For a moment, I could see in her gaze—while waiting for my response—a particular sort of correctness, and I felt an icy chill, as though the wind had blown through the rain into my shoulders. I was about to respond, but she was no longer waiting for a response.

"Thank you. Please go back. Good-bye. . . . " she said faintly and walked away without turning around again. I stood in the middle of the road watching her back, and soon after she disappeared into the night. I kept standing there, right until a rickshaw puller touted for my custom.

In the rickshaw it was as though I were flying in a dream one would forget immediately upon waking. It was as though something remained unfinished, as though there were a burden on my mind, but I was only vaguely aware of it. Several times I thought about putting up the umbrella but immediately laughed off this unconscious thought. Moreover, it wasn't raining, it had cleared completely, and in the sky one could make out a few scattered stars.

I got out of the rickshaw and knocked on the door.

"Who is it?"

It was the voice of the young woman I'd accompanied under the umbrella! I was bemused, how did she come to be in my house? . . . The door opened. The hall was brightly lit, and the person who stood out against the light beside the half-opened front door was not that young woman at all. Rather, in the opaque light I recognized the woman who had been leaning on the shop counter and eyeing enviously both me and the young woman I'd been walking with. I entered feeling lost and confused. Under the lamplight, I found it very strange that now I could no longer find anything in my wife's features resembling the unreal image of that woman.

My wife asked me what had made me so late. I said I'd run into a friend and stopped off for tea and cakes at Sullivan's. Since we'd waited for the rain to stop, we'd sat there a long time. In an effort to lend credence to this lie, I ate very little for supper.

1929

Zhang Tianyi (1906–1985)

MIDAUTUMN FESTIVAL

Translated by Ronald Miao

The wine and dishes were already neatly arranged on the table.

Kui Daniang[1] shifted a chair slightly. In an earnest voice she called to the guest: "Third Uncle, please sit over here!"

Third Uncle crinkled his thin, jaundiced face into a smile. His tongue flickered over parched lips, but his body betrayed not the slightest movement. He merely cast a wistful glance at Kui Daye.[2]

Kui Daye had no intention of sitting down to the feast. He was strenuously lecturing on ingratitude:

"I don't get it . . . I really don't! The human mind these days is really odd! It used to be that tenant farmers acted like tenant farmers. They showed respect for the landlord . . . didn't dare fart! At New Year's they'd send over chicken and meats . . . at least there they showed proper manners! But look at how they treat us now! Here we're celebrating our festival and they don't give a damn! Very few send gifts, and only a few come to pay their respects. None of them stop to think where their food comes from!"

"Yes . . . yes . . . " Third Uncle stared foolishly at his host and gave a faint nod. Kui sighed and stood up, his short, dwarfish body like an upright jar. Third

---

1. Title for the wife in the household.

2. Literally "Great Master," the head of the household. Here used as a proper noun.

Uncle felt a little easier. His sight remained riveted on his host, as if to draw him to the table.

The eight-year-old young master of the house allowed his body to lean forward. Surreptitiously, his eyes swept over the plates of food. Kui Daye, however, paid no heed to any of this. He continued to tell everyone just how strange the world had become. Leaning his face toward Third Uncle, he compared the world to a house: the walls were collapsing yet there was no one to make repairs.

"It's really outrageous. When a house leaks, for example . . . By the way, Third Uncle, when you first built your house, why didn't you open more windows to the south?"

Third Uncle couldn't imagine why anyone would ask such a question. He ventured: "What? Yes, of course." Now this house had originally belonged to Third Uncle. He then mortgaged it to Kui for one hundred dollars. When the time came he was unable to redeem it, and so it reverted officially to his younger sister's husband. The incident was eight years in the past.

Third Uncle was the kind of person who had no interest in things of the past; right now he gazed expectantly at what they were going to eat. His empty stomach rumbled. He hadn't the slightest idea of how to respond to Kui Daye's question. Luckily, the latter dropped the subject. After some further grumbling, he concluded:

"I don't mind telling you, Third Uncle, that there are a lot of things that I don't find pleasing!"

"Yes, yes." Third Uncle's dry, wrinkled face smiled politely as he sighed in sympathy. At that, Kui shifted his round body near the table.

"Well, at last," Third Uncle thought, drawing a deep breath. His little nephew lunged forward, quickly seizing a chair. The boy's eyes were fixed on the food; his hands gripped the edges of the table. Third Uncle also considered sitting down. His eyes grew larger, his knees shook slightly. As the steamy aroma rose to his nostrils, saliva suddenly formed under his tongue.

Kui Daniang stared at him apprehensively. Although she addressed him as Uncle, he was, in fact, a first cousin on her father's side. Now she was afraid that her family might lose face before her husband. She was convinced that when a man was poor he would show it in unbecoming speech and expressions. "Ah, why did you squander a whole family fortune in the first place?" she complained silently.

This Third Uncle had now become a pathetic bachelor, taking temporary quarters upstairs in the eastern part of the city temple. He muddled through his days, sometimes eating and sometimes not. Most people spent Midautumn Festival with their families, but he was an old man all by himself. For seven or eight years he had received no word from his only son, who was off somewhere. Taking pity on him, Kui Daniang took the matter up with her husband. In a manner that was half politeness and half condescension, they had invited Third Uncle to spend the Midautumn Festival with them. Now the woman glanced at her husband, taking note of his attitude by observing his facial expression. Suddenly, with quick steps, he rushed to the child and raised one palm. *Slap!*

"This little devil! So big, and so stupid! Grown-ups haven't come to the table and there you are! Will you starve if you wait a little longer? You, you!"

Slap! Slap!

Third Uncle, the guest, quickly composed himself and stood still. Stealthily he retreated a few steps as if he had no intention of ever sitting down. As he did so, he swallowed back the saliva that had seeped through his lips.

"Such a big boy, and still no manners!" Kui Daniang knit her brows. She dragged the little boy off and at the same time said to her husband, "Really, why make such a fuss? Couldn't we have a peaceful dinner?"

"What? What did you say?"

Third Uncle started to fidget, occasionally shifting his body and waving his right hand in an empty gesture. He wanted to put in a word, but he didn't dare. With a wry face and an imploring look, all he could do was mumble: "Oh, well . . ."

The sky just then grew as overcast as Kui Daye's face. Ash-colored clouds drifted from east to west. The withered leaves in the courtyard, swept up by the wind, were rustling impatiently.

Third Uncle shivered. His spine felt as if glued to a cold plate of steel. After taking a quick look at what was laid on the table, he felt an uncontrollable, crazy urge—he wanted very much to take the pot of warm wine and in one gulp to pour it down his throat.

Kui Daye was jumping heatedly up and down, as if he wanted to match heights with Third Uncle. His eyes bulged, and a hail of words poured fast and furious from his mouth.

"Bastard! Bastard! These are terrible times, terrible. What a fine son you've raised! And people say I'm lucky to have two sons. Just look at our eldest. Look how he treats me! Others remember that Midautumn is a time of reunion. Our eldest doesn't even come home!" His wife interrupted gently: "His school doesn't let out for the holidays. Why blame him?"

"Why not blame him? He's the one who wanted to enter that damn school in the first place!"

Third Uncle sat down on a chair. His whole body grew lax. Suddenly he felt his stomach contract tightly; then he felt it gradually expand. The dishes of food had ceased to give off steam. Only a gust of air would waft a rich, oily aroma to him. Eyes half closed, he drew in a deep breath: his intestines began to tremble. Suddenly he felt as if some painful event of his life had gripped him, and all he wanted to do was to burst into a loud wail.

The boy had long since controlled his sobs. He clung to his mother's side, chewing on his index finger. Not once did his eyes leave the table. He seemed unaware that he was the cause of his father's furious outburst. Others too would find it hard to believe that Kui was really angry at his son. Clearly, Kui Daye's remarks had now taken a new turn. He began to mutter about things that he was in the habit of repeating every day.

"I work like an ox all year round to earn forty or fifty piculs of grain from rented land. And what do you know, I'm treated just like an ox or a horse! Of course I make money for you people to enjoy. But you at least should show a little conscience." As soon as his eyes fell on Third Uncle, the latter would give a start. Third Uncle straightened up, offering him a quick "Yes, yes."

The host folded his hands behind him and paced back and forth. There was a rasping noise from his mouth, like the sound of wind cutting through withered trees. "The world has changed completely!" With such earnest words did old Kui warn his family. "If we go on like this, the end will surely come . . . the grain harvest is never enough . . . there is never enough money . . . and man's heart is wicked." At that, he sighed.

The guest, feeling as if he had been unjustly wronged, asked himself: "Why does he choose to complain just before a meal?" As for Kui Daniang, she behaved as if she hadn't heard a thing. She stared at the floor and from time to time her eyebrows arched slightly. Everything had become very still; even Third Uncle's faint breathing could be heard clearly. Slowly she raised her eyes and observed him: the jutting bones in that miserable face caused her to shudder. Her husband tugged his own sleeves and said loudly:

"Other people have relatives, and they rely on their relatives for help. Me? Every relative uses my money and sponges off me. I really don't understand it. I really don't!" He glanced at Third Uncle, who snorted gently.

"Sponge off him?" Third Uncle thought to himself, confused. He recalled that old Kui had never given him anything. On the contrary, when *he* still had property he had been generous: without a thought he had given away a bamboo-covered hillside to his sister's husband. Since youth he and Kui had been schoolmates and good friends. He had acted as the marriage go-between for Kui and his sister. But now he said nothing. His lips quivered slightly as his gaze reverted to the table. Again he felt his stomach tighten.

Kui sighed, grumbling over the misery of his lot. People did everything to use him and eat off him. And who knew whether someone hadn't already made off with his money to act the stupid philanthropist! "No matter how you look at it, I've been taken advantage of. Isn't that nice?"

"Now you're exaggerating!" his wife cut in finally. In the same breath she asked: "Which relative has 'sponged' off you? Who's taken your money to act the foolish philanthropist? Really, you're getting upset over nothing!"

"What? What?" Whenever his wife interrupted him he would resort to such a trick. Unable to go on, he would jump up and smack the tea table.

Third Uncle lifted a hand painfully, as if he wanted to sneeze but couldn't. "Well, in fact . . . " His mind went blank. His tongue was numb.

Kui apparently wanted to continue. He waved his fists in the air, his mouth open. But as he was about to speak his tenant farmer Foolhardy hurried in. His large buck teeth flashed in a grin; his hands were clutching a capon. Angry that his speech had been interrupted, Kui glared at the intruder. "It's really good of you to remember that today is Midautumn Festival!" he blurted out.

"What can we do? Right now, we, well, you know very well, Kui Daye, not only are we on the point of starving; worse still, we're up to our necks in debt!"

Third Uncle wanted to stand up, but he sank down again. His body felt like wax exposed to the scorching summer heat. Yet his fingertips grew cold. Sweat gathered in his palms. For the life of him he couldn't see why he had been invited to spend this holiday—it must be a trap! His stomach tightened. Bubbles of saliva filled his mouth; secretly he swallowed. With a shaking hand he clutched at his throat. The room seemed to revolve, yet there was Kui firmly planted on the ground and about to shout something. "That son of a bitch!" Third Uncle thought. In his bewilderment, he saw Kui take up a steelyard to weigh the capon. A flurry of ear-piercing cries filled the room.

"Not even three catties! Not even three!" There followed shouts of "sponging!" "I'm just an ox, a horse!" "Everybody takes my money—no conscience!"

Third Uncle opened his mouth as if to speak, but something seemed to be stuck in his throat. The smile suddenly disappeared from Foolhardy's face. With a strained expression he asked:

"What are you talking about? When have we ever taken your money? Sure, we've borrowed money from you, at eight percent interest. We're even mortgaged to you. But when in God's name have we ever sponged off you?" Discretion was not one of this farmer's virtues.

Third Uncle's body was visibly shaken, as though something tightly fastened had been suddenly released. He couldn't help feeling a sense of relief: the pleasure was like draining a glass of good wine. He blinked, and then took a long look at the coarse face of the tenant farmer. But in spite of himself, he felt a chill creep down his spine, and in a flash he had returned to his senses. The corner of his mouth curled into two folds. Half in contempt, half in anger he blurted out between his teeth:

"How dare you! How can you treat your landlord like this?" Even though he was poor and starving, he had still been a member of an honored and respected family. He still wore the long gray gown befitting a gentleman, even if he didn't have a short jacket underneath.

The volume of Kui's voice overwhelmed his words. Kui was jumping about with the steelyard in his hand, as if he wanted somehow to strike Foolhardy's head. From his lips poured a volley of bitter curses, but not to the extent of demeaning a man of his status. After hopping about for a while, he finally hoisted the steelyard and aimed at his target.

The young master cried out in fright. Kui Daniang ran over to restrain her husband. At the same time, she looked imploringly at Third Uncle. Although he tried his best to stand up, his thighs collapsed under him. Again he struggled to rise, but his legs gave no support. He swooned and quickly leaned against the incense table. The flames from the two red candles danced. "Ah-h-h . . . " came his hoarse voice. His vision blurred.

Completely losing control of his temper, Foolhardy seized the steelyard in one hand. Spitting flecks of saliva he shouted: "Well said! Well said—the money you've earned! Whore mothers! Money *you've* earned." It seemed now that they would fight it out.

Third Uncle huddled against the incense table, not daring to move. Eyes half shut, his mind revolved in a daze. Foolhardy's coarse voice swelled and stuck in his ears.

"I won't rent your land! I quit! Send a middleman over and give me back my rent!" So shouting, he grabbed the capon and marched off.

"What? That idiot's taking his gift back?"

Kui Daniang for the moment would rather go against her husband than let Foolhardy go. "Don't go! Don't leave! Everything can be settled. Kui Daye always gets riled, don't you know that by now?" Then, anxiously to Third Uncle: "Reason with him!"

The dazed guest awoke with a violent start. For the sake of his sister and her husband he had to think of something, of course. Like a little boy first learning to walk, he threw caution to the winds and bounded to the door.

"Hey, hey, you there! . . . He won't listen, he's gone! Oh, no!" His hands gripped the door as if he felt suddenly nauseous. Up and down heaved his thin, flat chest as he gasped for breath. Sweat on his face gathered and dripped from the end of his chin.

Kui's anger had again shifted its target. His squat, bucketlike legs jumped and stamped. His right fist alternately pounded the tea table and his own chest.

"I just don't understand it! I just don't! My relatives and friends know only how to take advantage of me. When there's food, they come running. When there's a problem, they fold their hands and look on. Such wonderful relatives—wonderful!"

Third Uncle clenched his teeth. He could not stop their chattering. He shot a glance full of hatred at his sister's husband. Still, Third Uncle said nothing. He didn't want to talk back. Only the relatives of this house had anything to do with him; if they cut him off, it would end his sole chance at a livelihood! His only hope of existence was for this household to take pity on him. Leaning motionless against the lintel, he let his legs tremble.

Kui Daye continued to stare at him. Not for a second did his mouth stop moving. Like some creature with inborn docility, Third Uncle never once answered back. Besides, in view of the trouble that Foolhardy had just stirred up, if he did make any complaint he would appear to be siding with the tenant farmer. Thus he blinked his quivering eyelids and looked away.

The dinner table seemed to jump. In a bowl of stewed pork in the right-hand corner, a cube of fatty meat jiggled, as if it possessed some inner resilience; it threatened to leap out of the dish at any time. The wine pot tottered. Third Uncle thought he spied something spilling out of the mouth of the pot. His lips turned pale. In the meantime, Kui's harangue went on in fitful bursts.

"Spongers! . . . Fine relatives! . . . Just want to eat and drink—wonderful, wonderful!"

But now these sounds gradually receded for Third Uncle. He seemed to be hearing them from the other side of a city wall. In a few moments even these faint sounds could no longer be heard.

Kui Daniang sighed. She was afraid that her husband would say something even more unpleasant to a member of her family. Gently she prodded Third Uncle. "You'd better go home now."

Third Uncle swayed a few steps. The courtyard began to roll and pitch like a ship, ever faster and harder. In a moment even the sky was overturned. His legs no longer supported him. He tripped and fell fainting to the ground.

The withered leaves in the courtyard made a swishing sound; listening to them was like hearing wine being poured into a cup.

1936

Ding Ling (1907–1986)

WHEN I WAS IN XIA VILLAGE

Translated by Gary J. Bjorge

Because of the turmoil in the Political Department, Comrade Mo Yu decided to send me to stay temporarily in a neighboring village. Actually, I was already completely well, but the opportunity to rest for a while in a quiet environment and arrange my notes from the past three months did have its attractions. So I agreed to spend two weeks in Xia Village, a place about ten miles from the Political Department.

A female comrade from the Propaganda Department, who was apparently on a work assignment, went with me. Since she wasn't a person who enjoyed conversation, however, the journey was rather lonely. Also, because her feet had once been bound and my own spirits were low, we traveled slowly. We set out in the morning, but it was nearly sunset by the time we reached our destination.

The village looked much like any other from a distance, but I knew it contained a very beautiful Catholic church that had escaped destruction and a small grove of pine trees. The place where I would be staying was in the midst of these trees, which clung to the hillside. From that spot it would be possible to look straight across to the church. By now I could see orderly rows of cave dwellings and the green trees above them. I felt content with the village.

My traveling companion had given me the impression that the village was very busy, but when we entered it, not even a single child or dog was to be seen. The only movement was dry leaves twirling about lightly in the wind. They would fly a short distance, then drop to earth again.

"This used to be an elementary school, but last year the Jap devils destroyed it. Look at those steps over there. That used to be a big classroom," my companion, Agui, told me. She was somewhat excited now, not so reserved as she had been during the day. Pointing to a large empty courtyard, she continued: "A year and a half ago, this area was full of life. Every evening after supper, the comrades gathered here to play soccer or basketball." Becoming more agitated, she asked, "Why isn't anyone here? Should we go to the assembly hall or head up the hill? We don't know where they've taken our luggage either. We have to straighten that out first."

On the wall next to the gate of the village assembly hall, many white paper slips had been pasted. They read "Office of the [Communist Party] Association," "Xia Village Branch of the [Communist Party] Association," and so on.[1] But when we went inside, we couldn't find a soul. It was completely quiet, with only a few tables set about. We were both standing there dumbly when suddenly a man rushed in. He looked at us for a moment, seemed about to ask us something, but swallowed his words and prepared to dash away. We called to him to stop, however, and made him answer our questions.

"The people of the village? They've all gone to the west entrance. Baggage? Hmm. Yes, there was baggage. It was carried up the hill some time ago to Liu Erma's home." As he talked, he sized us up.

Learning that he was a member of the Peasant's Salvation Association, we asked him to accompany us up the hill and also asked him to deliver a note to one of the local comrades. He agreed to take the note, but he wouldn't go with us. He seemed impatient and ran off by himself.

The street too was very quiet. The doors of several shops were closed. Others were still open, exposing pitch-black interiors. We still couldn't find anyone. Fortunately, Agui was familiar with the village and led me up the hill. It was already dark. The winter sun sets very quickly.

The hill was not high, and a large number of stone cave dwellings were scattered here and there from the bottom to the top. In a few places, people were standing out in front peering into the distance. Agui knew very well that we had not yet reached our destination, but whenever we met someone she asked, "Is this the way to Liu Erma's house?" "How far is it to Liu Erma's house?" "Could you please tell me the way to Liu Erma's house?" Or, she would ask, "Did you notice any baggage being sent to Liu Erma's house? Is Liu Erma home?"

The answers we received always satisfied us, and this continued right up to the most distant and highest house, which was the Liu family's. Two small dogs were the first to greet us. Then a woman came out and asked who we were. As soon as they heard it was me, two more women came out. Holding a lantern,

---

1. Bracketed items were given as [XX] in the original, a form of self-censorship during that period.

they escorted us into the courtyard and then into a cave on the side toward the east. The cave was virtually empty. On the *kang* under the window were piled my bedroll, my small leather carrying case, and Agui's quilt.

Some of the people there knew Agui. They took her hand and asked her many questions, and after a while they led her out, leaving me alone in the room. I arranged my bed and was about to lie down when suddenly they all crowded back in again. One of Liu Erma's daughters-in-law was carrying a bowl of noodles. Agui, Liu Erma, and a young girl were holding bowls, chopsticks, and a dish of onions and pepper. The young girl also brought in a brazier of burning coal.

Attentively, they urged me to eat some noodles and touched my hands and arms. Liu Erma and her daughter-in-law also sat down on the *kang*. There was an air of mystery about them as they continued the conversation interrupted by their entry into the room.

At first I thought I had caused their amazement, but gradually I realized that this wasn't the case. They were interested in only one thing—the topic of their conversation. Since all I heard were a few fragmentary sentences, I couldn't understand what they were talking about. This was especially true of what Liu Erma said because she frequently lowered her voice, as if afraid that someone might overhear her. Agui had changed completely. She now appeared quite capable and was very talkative. She listened closely to what the others were saying and seemed able to grasp the essence of their words. The daughter-in-law and the young girl said little. At times they added a word or two, but for the most part they just listened intently to what Agui and Liu Erma were saying. They seemed afraid to miss a single word.

Suddenly the courtyard was filled with noise. A large number of people had rushed in, and they all seemed to be talking at once. Liu Erma and the others climbed nervously off the *kang* and hurried outside. Without thinking, I followed along behind them to see what was happening.

By this time the courtyard was in complete darkness. Two red paper lanterns bobbed and weaved above the crowd. I worked my way into the throng and looked around. I couldn't see anything. The others also were squeezing in for no apparent reason. They seemed to want to say more, but they did not. I heard only simple exchanges that confused me even more.

"Yuwa, are you here too?"

"Have you seen her yet?"

"Yes, I've seen her. I was a little afraid."

"What is there to be afraid of? She's just a human being, and prettier than ever too."

At first I was sure that they were talking about a new bride, but people said that wasn't so. Then I thought there was a prisoner present, but that was wrong too. I followed the crowd to the doorway of the central cave, but all there was to see was more people packed tightly together. Thick smoke obscured my vision, so I had no choice but to back away. Others were also leaving by now, and the courtyard was much less crowded.

Since I couldn't sleep, I set about rearranging my carrying case by the lantern light. I paged through several notebooks, looked at photographs, and sharpened some pencils. I was obviously tired, but I also felt the kind of excitement that comes just before a new life begins. I prepared a time schedule for myself and was determined to adhere to it, beginning the very next day.

At that moment there was a man's voice at the door. "Are you asleep, comrade?" Before I could reply, the fellow entered the room. He was about twenty years old, a rather refined-looking country youth. "I received Director Mo's letter some time ago," he said. "This area is relatively quiet. Don't worry about a thing. That's my job. If you need something, don't hesitate to ask Liu Erma. Director Mo said you wanted to stay here for two weeks. Fine. If you enjoy your visit, we'd be happy to have you stay longer. I live in a neighboring cave, just below these. If you need me, just send someone to find me."

He declined to come upon the *kang*, and since there was no bench on the floor to sit on, I jumped down and said, "Ah! You must be Comrade Ma. Did you receive the note I sent you? Please sit down and talk for a while."

I knew that he held a position of some responsibility in the village. As a student he had not yet finished junior high school.

"They tell me you've written a lot of books," he responded. "It's too bad we haven't seen a single one." As he spoke he looked at my open carrying case that was lying on the *kang*. Our conversation turned to the subject of the local level of study. Then he said, "After you've rested for a few days, we'll definitely invite you to give a talk. It can be to a mass meeting or to a training class. In any case, you'll certainly be able to help us. Our most difficult task here is 'cultural recreation.'"

I had seen many young men like him at the Front. When I first met them, I was always amazed. I felt that these youth, who were somewhat remote from me, were really changing fast. Changing the subject, I asked him, "What was going on just now?"

"Zhenzhen, the daughter of Liu Dama, has returned," he answered. "I never thought she could be so great." I immediately sensed a joyful, radiant twinkle in his eyes. As I was about to ask another question, he added, "She's come back from the Japanese area. She's been working there for over a year."

"Oh my!" I gasped.

He was about to tell me more when someone outside called for him. All he could say was that he'd be sure to have Zhenzhen call on me the next day. As if to provoke my interest further, he added that Zhenzhen must certainly have a lot of material for stories.

It was very late when Agui came back. She lay down on the *kang* but could not sleep. She tossed and turned and sighed continuously. I was very tired, but I still wished that she would tell me something about the events of the evening.

"No, comrade," she said. "I can't talk about it now. I'm too upset. I'll tell you tomorrow. Ahh . . . How miserable it is to be a woman." After this she covered her head with her quilt and lay completely still, no longer sighing. I didn't know when she finally fell asleep.

Early the next morning I stepped outside for a stroll, and before I knew it I had walked down to the village. I went into a general store to rest and buy red dates for Liu Erma to put in the rice porridge. As soon as the owner learned that I was living with Liu Erma, his small eyes narrowed and he asked me in a low, excited voice, "Did you get a look at her niece? I hear her disease has even taken her nose. That's because she was abused by the Jap devils." Turning his head, he called to his wife, who was standing in the inner doorway, "She has nerve, coming home! It's revenge against her father, Liu Fusheng."

"That girl was always frivolous. You saw the way she used to roam around the streets. Wasn't she Xia Dabao's old flame? If he hadn't been poor, wouldn't she have married him a long time ago?" As she finished speaking, the old woman lifted her skirts and came into the store.

The owner turned his face back toward me and said, "There are so many rumors." His eyes stopped blinking and his expression became very serious. "It's said that she has slept with at least a hundred men. Humph! I've heard that she even became the wife of a Japanese officer. Such a shameful woman should not be allowed to return."

Not wanting to argue with him, I held back my anger and left. I didn't look back, but I felt that he had again narrowed his small eyes and was feeling smug as he watched me walk away. As I neared the corner by the Catholic church, I overheard a conversation by two women who were drawing water at the well. One said, "She sought out Father Lu and told him she definitely wanted to be a nun. When Father Lu asked her for a reason, she didn't say a word, just cried. Who knows what she did there? Now she's worse than a prostitute . . . "

"Yesterday they told me she walks with a limp. Achh! How can she face people?"

"Someone said she's even wearing a gold ring that a Jap devil gave her!"

"I understand she's been as far away as Datong and has seen many things. She can even speak Japanese."

My walk was making me unhappy, so I returned home. Since Agui had already gone out, I sat alone in my room and read a small pamphlet. After a while, I raised my eyes and noticed two large baskets for storing grain sitting near a wall. They must have had a long history, because they were as black as the wall itself. Opening the movable portion of the paper window, I peered out at the gray sky. The weather had changed completely from what it had been when I arrived the day before. The hard ground of the courtyard had been swept clean, and at the far edge a tree with a few withered branches stood out starkly against the leaden sky. There wasn't a single person to be seen.

I opened my carrying case, took out pen and paper, and wrote two letters. I wondered why Agui had not yet returned. I had forgotten that she had work to do. I was somehow thinking that she had come to be my companion. The days of winter are very short, but right then I was feeling that they were even longer than summer days.

Some time later, the young girl who had been in my room the night before came out into the courtyard. I immediately jumped down off the *kang*, stepped out the door, and called to her, but she just looked at me and smiled before rushing into another cave. I walked around the courtyard twice and then stopped to watch a hawk fly into the grove of trees by the church. The courtyard there had many large trees. I started walking again and, on the right side of the courtyard, picked up the sound of a woman crying. She was trying to stop, frequently blowing her nose.

I tried hard to control myself. I thought about why I was here and about all my plans. I had to rest and live according to the time schedule I had made. I returned to my room, but I couldn't sleep and had no interest in writing in my notebook.

Fortunately, a short while later Liu Erma came to see me. The young girl was with her, and her daughter-in-law arrived soon after. The three of them climbed up on the *kang* and took seats around the small brazier. The young girl looked closely at my things, which were laid out on the little square *kang* table.

"At that time no one could take care of anyone else," Liu Erma said, talking about the Japanese attack on Xia Village a year and a half before. "Those of us who lived on the hilltop were luckier. We could run away quickly. Many who lived in the village could not escape. Apparently it was all fate. Just then, on that day, our family's Zhenzhen had run over to the Catholic church. Only later did we learn that her unhappiness about what was happening had caused her to go to talk to the foreign priest about becoming a nun. Her father was in the midst of negotiating a marriage for her with the young proprietor of a rice store in Xiliu Village. He was almost thirty, a widower, and his family was well respected. We all said he would be a good match, but Zhenzhen said no and broke into tears before her father. In other matters, her father had always deferred to her wishes, but in this case the old man was adamant. He had no son and had always wanted to betroth his daughter to a good man. Who would have thought that Zhenzhen would turn around in anger and run off to the Catholic church? It was at that moment that the Japs caught her. How could her mother and father help grieving?"

"Was that her mother crying?"

"Yes."

"And your niece?"

"Well, she's really just a child. When she came back yesterday, she cried for a long time, but today she went to the assembly in high spirits. She's only eighteen."

"I heard she was the wife of a Japanese. Is that true?"

"It's hard to say. We haven't been able to find out for sure. There are many rumors, of course. She's contracted a disease, but how could anyone keep clean in such a place? The possibility of her marrying the merchant seems to be over. Who would want a woman who was abused by the Jap devils? She definitely has the disease. Last night she said so herself. This time she's changed a lot. When she talks about those devils, she shows no more emotion than if she were talking about an ordinary meal at home. She's only eighteen, but she has no sense of embarrassment at all."

"Xia Dabao came again today," the daughter-in-law said quietly, her questioning eyes fixed on Erma.

"Who is Xia Dabao?" I asked.

"He's a young man who works in the village flour mill," replied Liu Erma. "When he was young, he and Zhenzhen were classmates for a year. They liked each other very much, but his family was poor, even poorer than ours. He didn't dare do anything, but our Zhenzhen was head over heels in love with him and kept clinging to him. Then she was upset when he didn't respond. Isn't it because of him that she wanted to be a nun? After Zhenzhen fell into the hands of the Jap devils, he often came to see her parents. At first just the sight of him made Zhenzhen's father angry. At times he cursed him, but Xia Dabao would say nothing. After a scolding he would leave and then come back another day. Dabao is really a good boy. Now he's even a squad leader in the self-defense corps. Today he came once again, apparently to talk with Zhenzhen's mother about marrying Zhenzhen. All I could hear was her crying. Later he left in tears himself."

"Does he know about your niece's situation?"

"How could he help knowing? There is no one in this village who doesn't know everything. They all know more than we do ourselves."

"Mother, everyone says that Xia Dabao is foolish," the young girl interjected.

"Humph! The boy has a good conscience. I approve of this match. Since the Jap devils came, who has any money? Judging from the words of Zhenzhen's parents, I think they approve too. If not him, who? Even without mentioning her disease, her reputation is enough to deter anyone."

"He was the one wearing the dark blue jacket and the copper-colored felt hat with the turned-up brim," the young girl said. Her eyes were sparkling with curiosity, and she seemed to understand this matter very well.

His figure began to take shape in my memory. When I went out for my walk earlier that morning, I had seen an alert, honest-looking young man who fit this description. He had been standing outside my courtyard, but had not shown any intention of coming in. On my way home, I had seen him again, this time emerging from the pine woods beyond the cave dwellings. I had thought he was someone from my courtyard, or from a neighboring one, and hadn't paid much attention to him. As I recalled him now, I felt that he was a rather capable man, not a bad young man at all.

I now feared that my plan for rest and recuperation could not be realized. Why were my thoughts so confused? I wasn't particularly anxious to meet anybody, and yet my mind still couldn't rest. Agui had come in during the conversation, and now she seemed to sense my feelings. As she went out with the others, she gave me a knowing smile. I understood her meaning and busied myself with arranging the *kang*. My bedroll, the lamp, and the fire all seemed much brighter. I had just placed the teakettle on the fire when Agui returned. Behind her I heard another person.

"We have a guest, comrade!" Agui called. Even before she finished speaking, I heard someone giggling.

Standing in the doorway, I grasped the hands of this person whom I had not seen before. They were burning hot, and I couldn't help being a bit startled. She followed Agui up onto the *kang* and sat down. A single long braid hung down her back.

In the eyes of the new arrival, the cave that depressed me seemed to be something new and fresh. She looked around at everything with an excited glint in her eyes. She sat opposite me, her body tilted back slightly and her hands spread apart on the bedroll for support. She didn't seem to want to say anything. Her eyes finally came to rest on my face.

The shadows lengthened her eyes and made her chin quite pointed. But even though her eyes were in deep shadow, her pupils shone brightly in the light of the lamp and the fire. They were like two open windows in a summer home in the country, clear and clean.

I didn't know how to begin a conversation without touching an open wound and hurting her self-respect. So my first move was to pour her a cup of hot tea.

It was Zhenzhen who spoke first: "Are you a Southerner? I think so. You aren't like the people from this province."

"Have you seen many Southerners?" I asked, thinking it best to talk about what she wanted to talk about.

"No," she said, shaking her head. Her eyes still fixed on me, she added, "I've only seen a few. They always seem a little different. I like you people from the South. Southern women, unlike us, can all read many, many books. I want to study with you. Will you teach me?"

I expressed my willingness to do so, and she quickly continued, "Japanese women also can read a lot of books. All those devil soldiers carried a few well-written letters, some from wives, some from girlfriends. Some were written by girls they didn't even know. They would include a photograph and use syrupy language. I don't know if those girls were sincere or not, but they always made the devils hold their letters to their hearts like precious treasures."

"I understand that you can speak Japanese," I said. "Is that true?"

Her face flushed slightly before she replied, in a very open manner, "I was there for such a long time. I went around and around for over a year. I can speak a fair amount. Being able to understand their language had many advantages."

"Did you go to a lot of different places with them?"

"I wasn't always with the same unit. People think that because I was the wife of a Jap officer I enjoyed luxury. Actually, I've been back here twice before. Altogether, this is my third time. I was ordered to go on this last mission. There was no choice. I was familiar with the area, the work was important, and it was impossible to find anyone else in a short time. I won't be sent back anymore. They're going to treat my disease. That's fine with me because I've missed my dad and mom, and I'm glad to be able to come back to see them. My mother, though, is really hopeless. When I'm not home, she cries. When I'm here, she still cries."

"You must have known many hardships."

"She has endured unthinkable suffering," Agui interrupted, her face twisted in a pained expression. In a voice breaking with emotion, she added, "It's a real tragedy to be a woman, isn't it, Zhenzhen?" She slid over to be next to her.

"Suffering?" Zhenzhen asked, her thoughts apparently far, far away. "Right now I can't say for certain. Some things were hard to endure at the time, but when I recall them now they don't seem like much. Other things were no problem to do when I did them, but when I think about them now I'm very sad. More than a year . . . It's all past. Since I came back this time, a great many people have looked at me strangely. As far as the people of this village are concerned, I'm an outsider. Some are very friendly to me. Others avoid me. The members of my family are just the same. They all like to steal looks at me. Nobody treats me the way they used to. Have I changed? I've thought about this a great deal, and I don't think I've changed at all. If I have changed, maybe it's that my heart has become somewhat harder. But could anyone spend time in such a place and not become hardhearted? People have no choice. They're forced to be like that!"

There was no outward sign of her disease. Her complexion was ruddy. Her voice was clear. She showed no signs in inhibition or rudeness. She did not exaggerate. She gave the impression that she had never had any complaints or sad thoughts. Finally, I could restrain myself no longer and asked her about her disease.

"People are always like that, even if they find themselves in worse situations. They brace themselves and see it through. Can you just give up and die? Later, after I made contact with our own people, I became less afraid. As I watched the Jap devils suffer defeat in battle and the guerrillas take action on all sides as a result of the tricks I was playing, I felt better by the day. I felt that even though my life was hard, I could still manage. Somehow I had to find a way to survive, and if at all possible, to live a life that was meaningful. That's why I'm pleased that they intend to treat my disease. It will be better to be cured. Actually, these past few days I haven't felt too bad. On the way home, I stayed in Zhangjiayi for two days and was given two shots and some medicine to take orally. The worst time was in the fall. I was told that my insides were rotting away, and then, because of some important information and the fact that no one could be found to take my place, I had to go back. That night I walked alone in the dark for ten miles. Every single step was painful. My mind was filled with the desire to sit down and rest. If the work hadn't been so important, I definitely wouldn't have gone back. But I had to. Ahh! I was afraid I might be recognized by the Jap devils, and I was also worried about missing my rendezvous. After it was over, I slept for a full week before I could pull myself together. It really isn't all that easy to die, is it?"

Without waiting for me to respond, she continued on with her story. At times she stopped talking and looked at us. Perhaps she was searching for reactions on our faces. Or maybe she was only thinking of something else. I could see that Agui was more troubled than Zhenzhen. For the most part she sat in silence, and when she did speak, it was only for a sentence or two. Her words gave voice to a limitless sympathy for Zhenzhen, but her expression when silent revealed even more clearly how moved she was by what Zhenzhen was saying. Her soul was being crushed. She herself was feeling the suffering that Zhenzhen had known before.

It was my impression that Zhenzhen had no intention whatever of trying to elicit sympathy from others. Even as others took upon themselves part of the misfortune that she had suffered, she seemed unaware of it. But that very fact made others feel even more sympathetic. It would have been better if, instead of listening to her recount the events of this period with a calmness that almost made you think she was talking about someone else, you could have heard her cry. Probably you would have cried with her, but you would have felt better.

After a while Agui began to cry, and Zhenzhen turned to comfort her. There were many things that I had wanted to discuss with Zhenzhen, but I couldn't bring myself to say anything. I wished to remain silent. After Zhenzhen left, I forced myself to read by the lamp for an hour. Not once did I look at Agui or ask her a question, even though she was lying very close to me, even though she tossed and turned and sighed all the time, unable to fall asleep.

After this Zhenzhen came to talk with me every day. She did not talk about herself alone. She very often showed great curiosity about many aspects of my life that were beyond her own experiences. At times, when my words were far removed from her life, it was obvious that she was struggling to understand, but nevertheless she listened intently. The two of us also took walks together down to the village. The youths were very good to her. Naturally, they were all activists. People like the owner of the general store, however, always gave us cold, steely stares. They disliked and despised Zhenzhen. They even treated me as someone not of their kind. This was especially true of the women, who, all because of Zhenzhen, became extremely self-righteous, perceiving themselves as saintly and pure. They were proud of never having been raped.

After Agui left the village, I grew even closer to Zhenzhen. It seemed that neither of us could be without the other. As soon as we were apart, we thought of each other. I like people who are enthusiastic and lively, who can be really happy or sad, and at the same time are straightforward and candid. Zhenzhen was just such a person. Our conversations took up a great deal of time, but I always felt that they were beneficial to my studies and to my personal growth. As the days went by, however, I discovered that Zhenzhen was not being completely open about something. I did not resent this. Moreover, I was determined not to touch upon this secret of hers. All people have things buried deeply in their hearts that they don't want to tell others. This secret was a matter of private emotions. It had nothing to do with other people or with Zhenzhen's own morality.

A few days before my departure, Zhenzhen suddenly began to appear very agitated. Nothing special seemed to have happened, and she showed no desire to talk to me about anything new. Yet she frequently came to my room looking disturbed and restless, and after sitting for a few minutes, she would get up and leave. I knew she had not eaten well for several days and was often passing up meals. I had asked her about her disease and knew that the cause of her uneasiness was not simply physical. Sometimes, after coming to my room, she would make a few disjointed remarks. At other times, she put on an attentive expression, as if asking me to talk. But I could see that her thoughts were elsewhere, on things that she didn't want others to know. She was trying to conceal her emotions by acting as if nothing were wrong.

Twice I saw that capable young man come out of Zhenzhen's home. I had already compared my impression of him with Zhenzhen, and I sympathized with him deeply. Zhenzhen had been abused by many men, and had contracted a stigmatized, hard-to-cure disease, but he still patiently came to see her and still sought the approval of her parents to marry her. He didn't look down on her. He did not fear the derision or the rebukes of others. He must have felt she needed him more than ever. He understood what kind of attitude a man should have toward the woman of his choice at such a time and what his responsibilities were.

But what of Zhenzhen? Although naturally there were many aspects of her emotions and her sorrows that I had not learned during this short period, she had never expressed any hope that a man would marry her or, if you will, comfort her. I thought she had become so hard because she had been hurt so badly. She seemed not to want anything from anyone. It would be good if love, some extraordinarily sympathetic commiseration, could warm her soul. I wanted her to find a place where she could cry this out. I was hoping for a chance to attend a wedding in this family. At the very least, I wanted to hear of an agreement to marry before I left.

"What is Zhenzhen thinking of?" I asked myself. "This can't be delayed indefinitely, and it shouldn't be turned into a big problem."

One day Liu Erma, her daughter-in-law, and her young daughter all came to see me. I was sure they intended to give me a report on something, but when they started to speak, I didn't allow them the opportunity to tell me anything. If my friend wouldn't confide in me, and I wouldn't ask her about it directly, then I felt it would be harmful to her, to myself, and to our friendship to ask others about it.

That same evening at dusk, the courtyard was again filled with people milling about. All the neighbors were there, whispering to one another. Some looked sad, but there were also those who appeared to find it all exciting. The weather was frigid, but curiosity warmed their hearts. In the severe cold, they drew in their shoulders, hunched their backs, thrust their hands into their sleeves, puffed out their breath, and looked at each other as if they were investigating something very interesting.

At first all I heard was the sound of quarreling coming from Liu Dama's dwelling. Then I heard Liu Dama crying. This was followed by the sound of a man crying. As far as I could tell, it was Zhenzhen's father. Next came a crash of dishes breaking. Unable to bear it any longer, I pushed my way through the curious onlookers and rushed inside.

"You've come at just the right time," Liu Erma said as she pulled me inside. "You talk to our Zhenzhen."

Zhenzhen's face was hidden by her long disheveled hair, but two wild eyes could still be seen peering out at the people gathered there. I walked over to her and stood beside her, but she seemed completely oblivious to my presence. Perhaps she took me as one of the enemy and not worth a moment's concern. Her appearance had changed so completely that I could hardly remember the liveliness, the bright pleasantness I had found in her before. She was like a cornered animal. She was like an evening goddess. Whom did she hate? Why was her expression so fierce?

"You're so heartless. You don't think about your mother and father at all. You don't care how much I've suffered because of you in the last year." Liu Dama pounded on the *kang* as she scolded her daughter, tears like raindrops dropping to the *kang* or the floor and flowing down the contours of her face. Several women had surrounded her and were preventing her from coming down off the *kang*. It was frightening to see a person lose her self-respect and allow all her feelings to come out in a blind rage. I thought of telling her that such crying was useless, but at the same time, I realized that nothing I could say now would make any difference.

Zhenzhen's father looked very weak and old. His hands hung down limply. He was sighing deeply. Xia Dabao was seated beside him. There was a helpless look in his eyes as he stared at the old couple.

"You must say something. Don't you feel sorry for your mother?"

"When the end of a road is reached, one must turn. After water has flowed as far as it can, it must change direction. Aren't you going to change at all? Why make yourself suffer?" The women were trying to persuade Zhenzhen with such words.

I could see that this affair could not turn out the way that everyone was hoping. Zhenzhen had shown me much earlier that she didn't want anyone's sympathy. She, in turn, had no sympathy for anyone else. She had made her decision long ago and would not change. If people wanted to call her stubborn, then so be it. With teeth tightly clenched, she looked ready to stand up to all of them.

At last the others agreed to listen to me, and I asked Zhenzhen to come to my room and rest. I told them that everything could be discussed later that night. But when I led Zhenzhen out of the house, she did not follow me to my room. Instead, she ran off up the hillside.

"That girl has big ideas."

"Humph! She looks down on us country folk."

"She's such a cheap little hussy and yet she puts on such airs. Xia Dabao deserves it . . . "

These were some of the comments being made by the crowd in the courtyard. Then, when they realized that there was no longer anything of interest to see, the crowd drifted away.

I hesitated for a while in the courtyard before deciding to go up the hillside myself. On the top of the hill were numerous graves set among the pine trees. Broken stone tablets stood before them. No one was there. Not even the sound of a falling leaf broke the stillness. I ran back and forth calling Zhenzhen's name. What sounded like a response temporarily comforted my loneliness, but in an instant the vast silence of the hills became even deeper. The colors of sunset had completely faded. All around me a thin, smokelike mist rose silently and spread out to the middle slopes of the hills, both nearby and in the distance. I was worried and sat down weakly on a tombstone. Over and over I asked myself, "Should I go on up the hill or wait for her here?" I was hoping that I could relieve Zhenzhen of some of her distress.

At that moment I saw a shadow moving toward me from below. I quickly saw that it was Xia Dabao. I remained silent, hoping that he wouldn't see me and would continue on up the hill, but he came straight at me. At last I felt that I had to greet him and called, "Have you found her? I still haven't seen her."

He walked over to me and sat down on the dry grass. He said nothing, only stared into the distance. I felt a little uneasy. He really was very young. His eyebrows were long and thin. His eyes were quite large, but now they looked dull and lifeless. His small mouth was tightly drawn. Perhaps before it had been appealing, but now it was full of anguish, as if trying to hold in his pain. He had an honest-looking nose, but of what use was it to him now?

"Don't be sad," I said. "Maybe tomorrow everything will be all right. I'll talk to her this evening."

"Tomorrow, tomorrow—she'll always hate me. I know that she hates me." He spoke in a sad low voice that was slightly hoarse.

"No," I replied, searching my memory. "She has never shown me that she hates anyone." This was not a lie.

"She wouldn't tell you. She wouldn't tell anyone. She won't forgive me as long as she lives."

"Why should she hate you?"

"Of course—" he began. Suddenly he turned his face toward me and looked at me intently. "Tell me," he said. "At that time I had nothing. Should I have encouraged her to run away with me? Is all of this my fault? Is it?"

He didn't wait for my answer. As if speaking to himself, he went on, "It is my fault. Could anyone say that I did the right thing? Didn't I bring this harm to her? If I had been as brave as she, she never would have—I know her character. She'll always hate me. Tell me, what should I do? What would she want me to do? How can I make her happy? My life is worthless. Am I of even the slightest use to her? Can you tell me? I simply don't know what I should do. Ahhh! How miserable things are! This is worse than being captured by the Jap devils." Without a break, he continued to mumble on and on.

When I asked him to go back home with me, he stood up and we took several steps together. Then he stopped and said that he had heard a sound coming from the very top of the hill. There was nothing to do but encourage him to go on up, and I watched until he had disappeared into the thick pines. Then I started back. By now it was almost completely dark. It was very late when I went to bed that night, but I still hadn't received any news. I didn't know what had happened to them.

Even before I ate breakfast the next morning, I finished packing my suitcase. Comrade Ma had promised that he would be coming this day to help me move, and I was all prepared to return to the Political Department and then go on to [my next assignment]. The enemy was about to start another "mopping-up campaign," and my health would not permit me to remain in this area. Director Mo had said that the ill definitely had to be moved out first, but I felt uneasy. Should I try to stay? If I did, I could be a burden to others. What about leaving? If I went, would I ever be able to return? As I was sitting on my bedroll pondering these questions, I sensed someone slipping quietly into my room.

With a single thrust of her body, Zhenzhen jumped up onto the *kang* and took a seat opposite me. I could see that her face was slightly swollen, and when I grasped her hands as she spread them over the fire, the heat that had made such an impression on me before once again distressed me. Then and there I realized how serious her disease was.

"Zhenzhen," I said, "I'm about to leave. I don't know when we'll meet again. I hope you'll listen to your mother—"

"I have come to tell you," she interrupted, "that I'll be leaving tomorrow too. I want to leave home as soon as possible."

"Really?" I asked.

"Yes," she said, her face again revealing that special vibrancy. "They've told me to go in for medical treatment."

"Ah," I sighed, thinking that perhaps we could travel together. "Does your mother know?"

"No, she doesn't know yet. But if I say that I'm going for medical treatment and that after my disease is cured I'll come back, she'll be sure to let me go. Just staying at home doesn't have anything to offer, does it?"

At that moment I felt that she had a rare serenity about her. I recalled the words that Xia Dabao had spoken to me the previous evening and asked her directly, "Has the problem of your marriage been resolved?"

"Resolved? Oh, well, it's all the same."

"Did you heed your mother's advice?" I still didn't dare express my hopes for her. I didn't want to think of the image left in my mind by that young man. I was hoping that someday he would be happy.

"Why should I listen to what they say? Did they ever listen to me?"

"Well, are you really angry with them?"

There was no response.

"Well, then, do you really hate Xia Dabao?"

For a long time she did not reply. Then, in a very calm voice, she said, "I can't say that I hate him. I just feel now that I'm someone who's diseased. It's a fact that I was abused by a large number of Jap devils. I don't remember the exact number. In any case, I'm unclean, and with such a black mark I don't expect any good fortune to come my way. I feel that living among strangers and keeping busy would be better than living at home where people know me. Now that they've approved sending me to [Yan'an] for treatment, I've been thinking about staying there and doing some studying. I hear it's a big place with lots of schools and that anyone can attend. It's better for each of us to go our own separate ways than it is to have everyone stay together in one place. I'm doing this for myself, but I'm also doing it for the others. I don't feel that I owe anyone an apology. Neither do I feel especially happy. What I do feel is that after I go to [Yan'an], I'll be in a new situation. I will be able to start life fresh. A person's life is not just for one's father and mother, or even for oneself. Some have called me young, inexperienced, and bad-tempered. I don't dispute it. There are some things that I just have to keep to myself."

I was amazed. Something new was coming out of her. I felt that what she had said was really worth examining. There was nothing for me to do but express approval of her plan.

When I took my departure, Zhenzhen's family was there to see me off. She, however, had gone to the village office. I didn't see Xia Dabao before I left either.

I wasn't sad as I went away. I seemed to see the bright future that Zhenzhen had before her. The next day I would be seeing her again. That had been decided. And we would still be together for some time. As soon as Comrade Ma and I walked out the door of Zhenzhen's home, he told me of her decision and confirmed that what she had told me that morning would quickly come to pass.

1940

Wu Zuxiang (1908–1994)

YOUNG MASTER GETS HIS TONIC

Translated by Cyril Birch

I'm a country boy. My thanks to Yama, Lord of the Underworld, for bringing me into the world in a family that amounted to something, so from the moment I popped forth it was "Young Master" this and "Young Master" that. Sit all day with my hands tucked cozily in my sleeves, I'd still get something nice to eat. Since there was someone else to bother about all those things people have to bother about to stay alive, I was only too happy to escape from that barbarous, boring place and take my station with the smart set. I'm quite a passable individual by this time: nice pale complexion, nice pale hands, stylish dress, stylish conversation too, and not a dance hall or a movie theater that I'm not perfectly at home in.

I was very young when I left home—must be ten years now. We have a lot of land and property back there, which makes it impossible for the family to move out; then there is my mother, a grande dame of the old school, who objects to moving her old bones elsewhere for fear of becoming a "lonely ghost" when she reaches the shades. So she prefers to stay on in the country, never stirring out of the old mansion that has been handed down for two or three centuries, and this is quite a nuisance because I have to make an annual trip home to visit her. Out of regard for my mother's feelings I do go back every year for a short stay. This year the whole region was plagued with bandits, but I still risked it and managed to get home safe and sound under the protection of four stout militiamen my uncle sent to escort me.

From boyhood on I've remained a typical "young master," my delicate constitution a frequent prey to sickness. Once I grew up I developed as well that kind of fashionable sickness that gives you headaches and cold sweats. Then in Shanghai last summer I was out for an airing with Miss Tenderness Lu and got into a bad car smash. I lost a great deal of blood, and though they gave me a blood transfusion my health really suffered. Now I'm thinner than ever. My mother, her maternal instincts undiminished, began prattling away: "Young Master's run down, he needs a tonic."

Now I'm no simpleton, I'm fully aware of the benefits of a tonic. In the city it was the simplest thing in the world to take a tonic. Things like pasteurized milk or even Kepler's Cod Liver Oil and Malt: pleasant-tasting and did you good. But back in the village: hopeless! These country people eat porridge and rice and beyond that they've simply no idea what one might take: where would one find cod liver oil? As for milk, these country cows are like the country people; all they're good for is careering up and down a field, neck hunched, head down, dragging a clumsy plow. How can they compare with city cows that live in luxury just like city people, lying about in sheds with just the right temperature, just the right ventilation, making their milk?

"Guanguan, how would it be if we hire a wet nurse and get some mother's milk for you?" said my mother.

I laughed: a grown man five feet tall, cuddling up to a woman's bosom sucking tit! Nothing wrong with that, mark you: but these country women aren't quite your city girls! All these women can offer you is a weather-beaten brown complexion and a stink of sweat from head to foot. They've no notion of caring for their skin until it's white and soft, and doing it up with perfume and scented powders from Paris ready for you to kiss and fondle!

I frowned and shook my head.

"Why are you shaking your head?"

"I'd be embarrassed."

"What's there to be embarrassed about?" My mother laughed as she corrected my misunderstanding. "Silly boy, we're not going to make you go and suckle for yourself the way you did as a baby. We'll have her squeeze into a cup so you can drink it!"

This clever idea had never occurred to me. I was amazed, and asked: "You mean it's like cow's milk, you can squeeze it out and drink it?"

"Of course! But it's ten times better for you than cow's milk!"

"Let's give it a try, then."

My mother was delighted and sent out word at once. The very next day a wet nurse of around thirty was led in by one of the servants whose nickname was Auntie Iron Plantain. Auntie Plantain came in first, cradling in her arms a little baby boy with a huge plump head; the wet nurse followed. The wet nurse was your standard type of village woman: top-heavy on her thin legs, a tangle of dry-looking hair like a sparrows' nest; tiny feet with swelling arches jammed crookedly into "stub-fronted" clogs; lackluster eyes, snub nose, dun-colored lips crusted with some sort of grayish crud at the corners of her mouth; and with all this, naturally, a dried-up complexion and a rancid sweaty smell. She had on an oversized, tatty old blue cotton jacket, and her big breasts bounced in their hiding place as she waddled forward, up and down in rhythm with every step.

My mother told her to sit down and she did so, blushing. When the maid poured tea she scrambled to her feet again, took the cup in both hands, opened her mouth and murmured with a shy smile, "Too kind of you, miss."

"No need to be formal," said my mother. "Our Young Master—I'm sure Aunt Plantain must have mentioned it—he grew too fast and didn't get enough milk when he was small. He's too frail altogether and we're looking for someone to give a drop of milk for him. You seem like a healthy woman, and well behaved too. I'm very glad. I just wonder if your milk is all right?"

Auntie Iron Plantain slid both hands under the baby's arms and dandled him in the air, then came up to my mother and said in a grating voice like a man's, "Ma'am, don't take any notice of this girl's dirty looks—see what good rich milk she has for babies. Now then, just look at this little turtle's spawn. No more than a few months old and he's a real Li Kui!"[1]

The little beggar clenched a pair of little fists like dumplings and stuffed them into a dimpled mouth with toothless pink gums. Mother pinched his cheek, and the firm, fat, brown flesh quivered and shook. There were more bands of firm fat flesh at his chin and his wrists.

"How many months old?" Mother asked.

The wet nurse had been watching her brat and smiling. When she heard my mother's question she pursed her lips and then said, soft and slow, "Seven months. A year old come September."

"Nothing wrong with your milk, to judge by the baby."

"Unbutton yourself so madam can have a look." Auntie Plantain was only too anxious to please.

I was lying on the couch enjoying a cigarette. The wet nurse turned her dull gaze bashfully in my direction; presumably she felt awkward about unbuttoning in front of me.

"Troublemaking bitch!" said Auntie Iron Plantain. "You think our Young Master's never seen anything like these goddamn gourd-shaped tits of yours before? Nearly thirty, already dropped a couple of little turtles, and still pretending to be godalmighty shy!"

The wet nurse, red-faced, looked timidly across again to where my mother had been sitting, but Mother had already walked over to her. There was nothing for it; shyly she undid her buttons.

---

1. Bandit-hero of *The Water Margin* and other tales, whose build and role correspond roughly to Little John's in the Robin Hood legends.

Her breasts, nipples jutting, really were the size of a pair of giant pumpkins hanging off a trellis. Clusters of dark brown freckles mottled their slopes, and a network of blue veins spread back to her chest like rivers on a map. With the air of a customer carefully discriminating between various wares my mother inspected them closely. She reached out her fingers and gave a little tweak, whereupon a white milk like liquid bean curd came spurting out. Auntie Plantain wetted her finger, tasted it, smacked her lips and said, "Sweet and fresh. No wonder her brat's growing like a little pig! Just taste it and see, ma'am."

"I can see it's good from the color. No need to taste it. Very well, Auntie Plantain, you can settle the payment with her."

Auntie Plantain instructed the wet nurse: "We'll leave it up to you. Just give us a fair price."

"I couldn't say. My mother-in-law said to ask the lady to give what she thinks is right. I know madam wouldn't cheat us."

"Well, that's sensible talk." My mother settled comfortably into a chair. "The usual rate when we hire a wet nurse to live in and look after the baby is three dollars a month. In this case I only want you to come and give a cupful twice a day. Your own little one can suckle as before . . . You needy people, I know how hard things are for you, I'll let you have a dollar fifty a month."

"Just come twice a day and you get a whole silver dollar and a half every month—that's a smart piece of business for you! If only that luckless old man of mine weren't in his coffin, I'd quit service and sit at home making milk to sell and take it easy all my life!"

My mother laughed as Auntie Plantain bellowed away. The wet nurse shyly ran the tip of her tongue around the crusted corners of her mouth, and said with a slow smile: "Madam is a real saint of mercy. Heaven grant the master will rise to the highest office in the land, and we'll all come and share the crumbs from his table. But ma'am, you don't realize, it's not easy for us to get by in times like these. Too many to feed at home, and my father-in-law a cripple and getting on in years; and the little one's daddy . . . "

"Get on with your job and give your milk. When you've done that you can go on with your song of woe!" This was Auntie Plantain, croaking like a frog as she went to fetch a lidded tea bowl.

The wet nurse blushed, hurriedly took the bowl, and began to unfasten again the buttons she had just done up. With her right hand she heaved out her left tit, rolled the nipple in her fingers, and squeezed it at the bowl. I heard a crisp swoosh, and the white milk came jetting out in streams.

I watched, intrigued, from across the room. This wet nurse was as clumsy as any cow, but she was smarter than a cow when all was said and done. When a cow's made its milk it needs someone to come along and squeeze it out to sell, while the cow itself just goes on sticking its head in the manger and chewing its cud. But this cow of a wet nurse had the ability to squeeze it out with her own fingers and then sell it to feed both herself and her family. People are smarter than cows when all's said and done, I said to myself.

"I didn't think to ask: who've you got at home?" my mother said sympathetically.

Auntie Plantain butted in: "I'm sure you'll remember them when I tell you, ma'am. Her father-in-law is that should-have-died-already old Chen with the paralytic leg; her husband's that Young Baldy that gave the blood for the master when he was in the hospital after his accident in Shanghai last year."

"Oh yes, that tenant who used to work the three acres over at Poplar Bank by West Village, and then gave up his rental year before last?"

"That's who it is, that good-for-nothing."

When she mentioned old Cripple Chen and Young Baldy the two of them came back to me. Of all the tenants we had, Cripple Chen was the biggest nuisance. All the rest would make their payments as agreed in good white rice; his alone would turn up in poor-quality grain in baskets of every size and shape. Of his thirty piculs rent a year he'd be short scores of catties that never did reach us. If you pressed him or threatened to rent to someone else, he'd come crawling up like a snail, dragging his bad leg, a mournful expression on that miserable face of his, and start buttering up my mother or my uncle. He could talk your head off: how the rain hadn't fallen right, and how many bugs there'd been; how Poplar Bank was too far from the river, and the land too steep to get water up to it properly; what a world it was, land tax, poll tax, militia assessments, too much to manage; and then himself a cripple and only one son, a man had only one pair of hands, and wages too high for him to afford a laborer. He'd plead with my mother, a drop of coarse gruel for the half-dozen mouths waiting at home, for pity's sake, it would be such a good deed she'd be doing, none greater. My mother is all compassion and he would soon have her all softened up, every time. Until, year before last, a drought interfered with the harvest, and then he came up short fully one half of his rent. My uncle blew up, said he was resisting payment, defying the law, wanted to haul him before the county magistrate and jail him. Every word my uncle said made perfectly good sense: he said we all had the same sky over our heads, we all had to get by with the same sort of harvest conditions. How come every other tenant's fields got even rainfall, water everywhere, it just happens to be your land that misses it? How come no locusts in anyone else's fields, it's just your land they come to? Militia assessments, poll tax, land tax, it's the same for all the other tenants, and they all have to hire laborers to work their land, how come they can manage it and every year it's just you we hear weeping and wailing and bemoaning your fate? My uncle said, it's all right there in the deeds: "so many piculs of good white rice to be delivered annually without fail, regardless of pests, blight, flood, or drought. In the event of nonpayment, delay, or shortfall, fully accept obligation of court process for recovery. . . . " And your own thumb print right there. You must understand the law and not go breaking it, accept your lot and be content. It was cast-iron logic, and for all his cunning, the old cripple could do nothing but stand there staring with his eyes brimming tears, not a word in reply. Then his only hope is to go to my mother, ask her to put in a word for him, don't let them file a complaint with the county magistrate. My mother's the kindest-hearted old lady you'll ever meet. She saw the state he was in and had the idea of laying in a little store of blessing for her descendants, and told my uncle not to prosecute. She said what did a few piculs of rice one way or the other matter to us? Let him off his past debts too, get another tenant in his place and cut free of these tangles and tendrils for the future or we'll just go on to-ing and fro-ing and never get clear.

Cripple Chen's son. Young Baldy, was drifting around Shanghai last year; it was myself that rescued him and brought him back. This was what Auntie Plantain was just referring to:

It was last summer in Shanghai, and I'd just fallen in love with Tenderness Lu. She was a taxi dancer at the Luna Dance Hall, with skin like ivory. Her dark eyes sparkled, full of love and passion. She knew songs in English, and she could write a letter in the new vernacular style. You'd never find anything in the world to compare with that slender, alluring body of hers.

It was one evening, there'd been a tea-dance at the Luna. I was really in the mood and I'd danced a dozen sets in a row with Tenderness. The dance ended but I was still in the swing of it. No more band, so we turned on the phonograph and I got Tenderness Lu to teach me the tango. We went on having fun until nearly dawn. It had been hot as blazes for days, not a breath of air. The thick smoke puffed straight up from the mill chimneys and never stirred, just hung there in a black fog right across the city, made you feel even more like your chest was stuffed with cotton; even electric fans weren't much use. Tenderness Lu couldn't stand the heat any longer and wanted a ride in a motorcar to get some air. We got in the car and I urged the driver to go full speed so that the wind roared and beat all over us. Tenderness Lu snuggled her face against my chest and her hair, with all its fragrance, whipped against my cheek. I was like drunk, like crazy, I thought up something to say to her like in those writers people go for: "I want you and me to die together. If only this car now could be like the ones I've kept seeing in the papers the last day or two, hit a telegraph pole or flip over into the river, and then we'd die holding each other like this, with smiles on our lips, so sudden we'd never feel it. Wouldn't it be wonderful!" I was kidding. I didn't realize it was a prophecy. I don't know whether the driver was drunk or drowsy; he came to a bend of the riverbank and the whole car just overturned and landed in a ditch by the side of the road.

It was a really sad thing to happen: my darling Tenderness Lu had internal injuries. She was bleeding from mouth and nose and died on the way to the hospital. I was unconscious for thirty minutes and more, the back of my head lacerated by shards of glass, and I only came to when they gave me a shot to stimulate my heart. The driver was the only lucky one. He got off light with just a broken right hand. What with the medical costs and the compensation to Tenderness Lu's family, the accident cost us close to ten thousand, and I came in for a lot of grumbling and lecturing from my uncle and my mother.

I'd lost a lot of blood and been very upset. I was really down in body and spirit, and a couple of weeks in the hospital brought hardly any improvement. When my uncle came up from the country with the money, he saw how badly I was hurt and had an anxious talk with the doctor, insisting I be given the best and fastest treatment. It was a foreign doctor and he said I ought to have a blood transfusion. I'd no idea what this blood transfusion thing was supposed to be and didn't want to let them. The foreign doctor was very nice and friendly. He spoke Shanghainese with a thick Foreign Settlement accent: "Blood transfusion very good, very good. Not hurt at all. Just like mosquito bite, nothing more."

"But what kind of medicine is it you inject me with?"

"We use someone else's blood to supplement your own." My uncle, after all, knows more about things than I do.

"Whose blood? You mean you can buy it?"

"What a young innocent, a real young gentleman!" The foreign doctor clapped his hand on my shoulder. "If there's one thing China has plenty of it's paupers. They don't have the ability to earn money for themselves, but their stomachs won't let them off, they have to eat just the same. Either they sell their blood or put up with an empty belly. Haven't you seen them? When you're a little better go look outside the door: those ragamuffins of beggars who line the benches day after day both sides of the hall, they're all here to sell blood."

I laughed for sheer joy. What a wonderful world it is; if you have the money there's nothing you can't buy.

"But this Shanghai's a filthy place," the doctor went on, wrinkling his prominent nose and shaking his head. "Take blood from ten of these deadbeats and you'll find nine of them impure. It's infected, contaminated. No use, no use."

My uncle's got brains, and he's been around; he said this matter wasn't one to be handled any old way. Here in Shanghai every street and alley bristles with VD notices, every sidewalk has its low-class whores, "pheasants." None of these men selling their blood can afford to take a wife; you can imagine what kind of low conduct they get up to. Then, once contaminated blood of that sort is injected into your veins, there's no way of getting it out again. As my uncle was speaking, suddenly a thought struck him, and he told us of a man from our own village he'd come across at North Station yesterday afternoon when he got off the train. This man's blood would surely be more dependable. I asked who it was, and my uncle said it was this Young Baldy, Cripple Chen's son.

"What's a fellow like that doing, trotting up to Shanghai to see the world?"

"What indeed! Tried to bum five dollars from me the moment he saw me. But he's getting what he deserves, this fellow. Told me after we canceled their tenancy last year he couldn't make a living in the village, but he heard from a traveling cloth-peddler about how many mills there were in Shanghai, high wages and the work not too hard. So his eyes sparkle and like an idiot he comes hightailing it to Shanghai with the cloth-peddler. Well, this peddler did help him get a job as a laborer in a mill across the river, wages thirty cents a day. But the bastard was out of luck—five months later the mill shuts down. He said the mill failed, it was losing money, something about competition with the Japanese mills, but how can you believe that sort of crap. Anyway, he'd lost his job, lost touch with his peddler friend, didn't know another soul in Shanghai, and no way to get back to the village. But he's a slick customer, he goes and stands guard outside the North Station every day, on the lookout for someone he knows from the village traveling through."

"Did you give him the money? If you did, he'll have left Shanghai by now."

"Fat lot a youngster like you knows of the ways of the world! It was someone else brought him to Shanghai. Why should I present him with five dollars for no reason at all? And how should I know whether it was a true story he was telling me or a pack of lies?"

I was on edge and pressed my uncle to go hunt him out right away. My uncle told the doctor he could find a reliable donor, someone he knew; was it all right?

"Very good, very good. As it happens the hospital hasn't received any good blood the last couple of days. Bring the man here and I'll examine him, see whether we can use it."

My uncle was gone for a while and when he got back there was Young Baldy Chen with him. I remembered Young Baldy the moment I saw him. Somewhere over thirty, a few straggly hairs the color of straw across his scalp, slant eyes. He had on a dirty white jacket and pants. Bare-chested, feet bare inside a pair of sneakers that gaped open at the toe. He looked a bit thinner than before, but still strong as a water buffalo with his rippling muscles. He came in, greeted me, and stood with his slit eyes taking in everything in the room.

The doctor didn't want him in the sickroom and ordered him straight out for a blood test. When the doctor came back he kept exclaiming, "Jesus Christ," absolutely delighted, congratulated my uncle on his perspicacity, said the man's blood was terrific and exactly the type for me, God was looking after me. But he said I was still too frail to accept too large a transfusion. Three quarters of a pint would be plenty.

The usual price when the hospital bought blood was ten dollars a pint. But it was quite common for a donor to get the feeling that some sick person had a desperate need for his blood, and then he'd hang back to boost the price. Young Baldy was as sly as his father. He'd seen how my uncle had come searching for him at North Station, and heard the doctor say his blood was terrific when he took the test. So now he seized his chance, tried to rip us off by asking my uncle twenty dollars for his three quarters of a pint.

"You scoundrel, you don't realize when people are doing you a good turn?" My uncle got mad at him. "Our Young Master only threw this deal your way because he felt sorry for you, drifting about like this away from the village. And now you try to swindle us! All right, let's see you try! But be careful you don't trip yourself—what do you think all those poor slobs waiting outside the door are there for? Think we can't buy blood anytime we want?"

Young Baldy put his head back and sighed, as if he felt he'd no room to maneuver. He asked me to put in a good word for him, see whether he couldn't give a bit extra. All I wanted was to get my health back and not have to go on cooped up in this hospital that was driving me crazy. I asked my uncle to give him fifteen dollars, since he was a man from our village after all.

The doctor drew the blood (keeping it safe in a bottle that had medicine in it to stop it cooling or clotting), and that evening he gave me my transfusion. It really didn't hurt much. Only, about ten minutes later I started sweating and shivering as if I'd caught malaria; I shook so much the bedsprings were twanging away. I got scared.

"I've been tricked!" I yelled shakily. "The doctor didn't test it properly. Young Baldy's blood is infected, it's got to be!"

The doctor and the nurses explained calmly and quietly that this was the inevitable consequence of a transfusion and that it would clear up in a little while, I lay dozing all night, and next day the fever had subsided, but I still felt achy all over and completely listless.

I stayed three months in the hospital until my health and spirits were completely restored, whereupon my uncle pressured me into going back home for a few months more.

My mother asked sympathetically: "Where is your husband now?"

"He came back from Shanghai last year," the wet nurse replied, changing over to her right breast and continuing to press and squeeze. "But how can people of our sort support a man, ma'am, who has nothing to do all day but eat? His parents were at him all the time. He sat around at home a couple of weeks, then he got together with some of our neighbors and they all went off. They said they were heading for the provincial city to join the army. But they'd no money to get there. Been gone seven or eight months now, not a word, I don't really know where he can be."

"A low-down daddy like that, better off dead for all his brat can expect from him!" This was a bellow from Auntie Plantain as she placed a series of lip-smacking kisses on the kid's face. Then she went on to the kid: "Don't copy that precious pa of yours! When you grow up you want to be a real water buffalo, get on with your job and put up with it, earn some money to look after your ma."

The wet nurse had given a bowlful and was worrying about getting cussed out by her mother-in-law for being home late, so she took her child up in her arms and went straight off. My mother told her to drink a lot of soup. If she drank soup it would be good for her milk. She said too we wouldn't worry about an extra mouth to feed, it was all right for her to come and eat her meals every day at our house. The wet nurse smiled and came out with all kinds of blessings and benedictions.

Auntie Plantain heated up the milk over some boiling water and brought it to me to drink. You don't need to put sugar in mother's milk, it's really sweet;

and there's no unpleasantly strong flavor to it at all. In the city you pay four dollars a month for a pint of regular milk a day, and most of it's watered down with bean juice, it's not a patch on this mother's milk.

I drank a couple of bowls of milk every day. The wet nurse never missed coming twice a day to our house for her midday meal and her supper. She'd eat her meal and then give her milk, and when she'd given her milk she'd hurry off again back home. The milk really was good stuff. After a month or so my appetite had improved by leaps and bounds and my cheeks were fuller and pink with health. I wasn't used to living in a boring, barbaric place like this and thought of taking a trip or two; but there were troubles with bandits all over the county, and although every town and village of any size had raised its own militia, they hadn't been able to root the bandits out and get rid of them completely. Because of this my mother didn't feel comfortable about letting me risk it outside, but said I should use this time to keep on with the milk for another month or two and really get my strength back. And it would be no easy business getting milk if I went away.

Speaking of bandits, the talk has been scarier than ever this last month. A month ago the bandits on Seven Stars Ridge joined forces with another bunch; they've collected over five hundred men and all the guns and ammunition they need. They wrote a letter to the county seat demanding thirty thousand dollars to be handed over in full within a week; otherwise they'd launch an immediate attack on the county town and plunder every village they came to. When word of this got out, the militias in every town and village started pooling their defense plans and posting sentries night and day along all the highways. Anyone whose movements were suspicious was picked up for interrogation.

My uncle is a militia commander and has been at work from morning to night in his headquarters. I've been bored sitting around the house, so every day I've been over there for a chat and to learn what's happening. The best is when they arrest someone whose movements are suspicious and have him up for questioning? That's fun. The headquarters is located in our ancestral shrine in the village. The last couple of days all the commanders have been getting together for a bit of company and to talk things over.

"A comet appeared in the sky in the first half of the year. I knew it was an omen of great disorders." This was one of the militia commanders. "They say these bandits are in touch with the extremists. If we don't find some way to exterminate them pretty soon, we'll have a fine situation when the time comes they start spreading their wings!"

"Perhaps it's our own time of reckoning. Like the ancients said, calamity can't be avoided, everything's a matter of fate. No need to look: just tell me of any village, any town that isn't going downhill from one day to the next? Nine out of ten families too poor to eat, seven or eight out of every ten businesses failing and closing down. If this isn't fate what is it?" An old fellow, stroking his beard: what he said made good sense.

The most novel argument came from a distant cousin of mine who is a partner in a business in the city and just recently came back for a summer break: "Everything around here going downhill from one day to the next has nothing to do with fate. If you ask me, it's because we've been cheated out of all our money by the foreigners. I can remember when we were small, there wasn't a household in the village that didn't spin its own yarn and weave its own cloth. There wasn't a household that didn't light its lamps with bean oil. Or take smoking: you lit your pipe with a flint and a twist of paper. When did you ever see anybody strike a match and light up a cigarette, a Player's or a Capstan Navy Cut? We made our own things for our own use, and the money went back and forth from one hand to the next among ourselves. And nobody had to worry in those days where his next meal was coming from. But then it all changed: you spun your yarn, wove your cloth, no place to sell it. Everybody knows a calico dress or an imported cotton suit is both cheaper and smarter. A bean-oil lamp isn't bright enough, you have to fill up with Mobil kerosene. All these things are foreign invented, foreign manufactured, ways they've thought up to cheat us Chinese out of our money; and once they've made off with your money there's no way to get it back—how are you going to stop the country from getting poorer? And then you talk about fate! And recently worse than ever: your farmer's hard at it year-round, pays his rent, pays his assessments, pays his taxes, and ends up empty-handed for all his efforts; if he wants a bowl of coarse gruel it's no easy thing to come by. When it comes to trade, it's just not possible anymore. Anyone with any money in the countryside is off to the city. Everybody knows the city's where all the fun and excitement are nowadays. Who's going to put up with living in the countryside when he could be riding in cars or watching movies? Just take this cousin of mine here, nothing but Shanghai this, Shanghai that from morning to night, no patience to live at home!"

"Don't drag me into this." I was blushing and laughing. "How about yourself? Don't you prefer living in the city?"

"That's just it!" My cousin went on: "The rich are off to the city to see the world, middle-class people are getting more hard-pressed every day; what's left but a bunch of poverty-stricken beggars? Nothing but what they stand up in, work all day for a mouthful of gruel—what kind of money have they got to buy anything with? You say the businesses shouldn't be closing down. Who are they going to trade with? All right, so the peasants leave the farms, the tradesmen, shopkeepers, assistants, not a scrap of business for any of them in the interior. Let's say they all move into the city. The city's just the same, there's more unemployed in the city even than in the interior. If these people don't turn into robbers and bandits, what else is there? So what's fate got to do with it?"

"You can talk till you're blue in the face, you can't get away from fate," the old man argued. "Otherwise, how is it the foreigners never used to be able to cheat us Chinese out of our money, it's just right now at this moment they can manage it? What's this if it isn't fate?"

"Because it used to be that we Chinese closed our ports and kept ourselves to ourselves, don't you see?" My cousin was a good one in an argument. "Foreigners never used to be allowed into China. Then we were defeated in one war after another, and the foreigners came in, and can't you see how China's gotten poorer from one day to the next ever since?"

"But they say the foreigners are in a hopeless mess as well! Wasn't it in the papers a few days ago, how many million unemployed in America, how many million more in Japan? It's fate and the foreigners can't escape it any more than China can! What I say is, when you get right down to the root of it, it's nothing but fate!"

To tell you the truth, I haven't the slightest interest in this kind of discussion. What I was hoping for was that the militiamen guarding the highway would pick up a few more suspicious characters; I really enjoy watching the interrogations. Like one time, they brought in a troupe of acrobats from Shandong, five of them, two of them girls. The tale was they were expert cat burglars because they could somersault over the highest wall. They were questioned over and over and no one was willing to let them go, but since we couldn't prove they were lookouts for the bandits, we couldn't just execute them on the spot. In the end we had to send them off to the county seat to get rid of them.

Then a thing that really surprised us happened one noontime. That was when a bunch of militiamen from Xue Family Village, ten miles away, suddenly marched in with Young Baldy Chen as their prisoner.

The men carried a message from the guard commander at Xue Village. The message said that this Baldy Chen they'd arrested, not only were his movements suspicious, they'd searched him and found an important communication, sewn into the waistband of his trousers, from the Seven Stars Ridge bandits to the Phoenix Mountain bunch (the gist of it was to set the date for the attack on the county seat), clear proof he was acting as a messenger for the bandits. On examining him they'd discovered he was from our village so they were forwarding him to our village headquarters for disposal of the case.

It gave me a start, I can tell you.

Young Baldy looked better than the last time I saw him, and as soon as he saw my uncle and me he started protesting mightily—he'd never been a bandit, he'd started up as a peddler over at North River. He hadn't been home for a long time and so he'd come back especially to see how things were going, but he'd been arrested for no reason when he got to Xue Village. The trousers weren't his, he'd switched by mistake with somebody else at an inn. If there was a message sewn into the waistband he knew nothing about it. However, the Xue Village men insisted that the road he was on wasn't the one to our village, it was the road to Phoenix Mountain. There was no question but that he was carrying messages for the bandits and no need for further interrogation.

"I always knew you'd come to no good!" my uncle railed at him. "Nothing but sly tricks, you and your old man, when you were tenants on our land; and you tried to swindle us when we were in Shanghai last year! Well, there'll be no end to our problems unless we deal with a scoundrel of your sort properly!"

Everybody was in agreement. You could tell this turtle's-spawn was a real criminal; just look at his slant eyes and his villainous expressions! You had to make an example of him, kill one to warn a hundred, or there was no justice.

They did the job with amazing speed. They tied Baldy's hands behind his back right away and hauled him off to the South Village riverbank. He kept a set face throughout, watching us with his staring eyes, no fear at all; he even asked permission to go back home to see his parents and his wife and kids, but of course he didn't get it.

Because the idea was to set an example, my uncle proposed that he not be shot but beheaded, short and sweet, with a sword. They picked one of the militiamen who was a pork butcher to act as executioner. This fellow had a face that was all black pockmarks. He'd drunk a bellyful of hot sorghum liquor and marched behind Young Baldy with a great old-fashioned saber clutched in his fist; a vicious-looking face with his eyes bloodshot from the drink. But he didn't look as terrifying to me as Young Baldy did. One look at Young Baldy's expression and you couldn't help shivering.

The riverbank was packed.

They marched Young Baldy up to the riverbank; my uncle ordered the executioner to kick him to his knees. But the executioner couldn't manage it with kicking, so he gave him a wild shove with his hand and sent him sprawling among the rocks. Young Baldy wasn't going to give up while he still had breath; he deliberately stuck his head and neck against a big boulder and wouldn't be prized loose from it.

The executioner was helpless, he just stood there with both hands gripping the saber's hilt, he couldn't stop shaking, no way he could bring the saber down. Until my uncle went over and bawled him out furiously: then he hacked away three or four times like splitting firewood, turning the edge of his blade until it looked like a row of fangs.

The onlookers were solemn and silent, except for a few urchins who clapped their hands and yelled.

A few of the hacks had got to Young Baldy. His blood was spattered all over the jumbled rocks. He lay there stiff and motionless, and the executioner staggered off supported by some of the other militiamen, when suddenly the corpse struggled up, raised its arms, and began to scream in a wild shrill voice like some evil demon. Everybody ran off in terror as far as they could get, stumbling and shrieking. My uncle's lips went bloodless, his face turned green, he dragged me away with him and we kept tripping and falling. It was only a handful of the bolder ones among the farmers there who went up and helped him. I was terrified out of my wits and clung to my uncle's hand, wouldn't let go.

"Imagine this fellow joining the bandits!"

"Must be one of those stars of retribution, come down on earth in human form! Way he carried himself, you've got to say he was a real desperado!"

Tongues were wagging all the way back, everybody chipping in. My uncle did nothing but damn the executioner and the militiamen for a pack of shitheads; but after a while he managed to joke out of it: "You wouldn't get a cent for this son-of-a-turtle's blood now, and last year he was asking twenty dollars a pint!"

But when Uncle and I got back to militia headquarters we saw my wet nurse coming out the door, weeping and yelling, her hair streaming: "My husband's no bandit, my husband's no bandit!"

She stood like a crazy woman, head back, mouth wide open, bawling at the top of her voice: "A wrong to blacken Heaven! A wrong to blacken Heaven! We paid our share for this militia, paid our money and then you come killing us! Heaven is dark and blind to my wrong!"[2]

Still yelling, she went waddling off in the direction of the riverbank. A crowd of children and womenfolk followed along behind to see what would happen. Auntie Iron Plantain pushed through them, caught up with her, grabbed hold of the still screaming wet nurse and started berating her in her man's voice that grated like a frog's: "What's wrong with you, woman, your brains full of shit? That man of yours deserved slicing to death—they did him a favor cutting his head off! Why don't you get back and squeeze your milk for our Young Master, instead of wailing your goddamn funeral cries like you'd run up against the Demon Fiveways![3] You . . . "

1932

2. The wet nurse's cry gains an epic dimension by recalling an ancient image of injustice that is often found, for example, in Yuan plays: the magistrate's court trapped beneath an overturned bowl that shuts out the light of Heaven, and with it all justice and human decency.

3. A malevolent spirit in old folk belief who specialized in taking possession of women.

Xiao Hong (1911–1942)

HANDS

Translated by Howard Goldblatt

Never had any of us in the school seen hands the likes of hers before: blue, black, and even showing a touch of purple, the discoloring ran from her fingertips all the way to her wrists.

We called her "The Freak" the first few days she was here. After class we always crowded around her, but not one of us had ever asked her about her hands.

Try though we might, when our teacher took roll call, we just could not keep from bursting out laughing:

"Li Jie!"

"Present."

"Zhang Zhufang!"

"Present."

"Xu Guizhen!"

"Present."

One after another in rapid, orderly fashion, we stood up as our names were called, then sat back down. But when it came Wang Yaming's turn, the process lengthened considerably.

"Hey, Wang Yaming! She's calling your name!" One of us often had to prod her before she finally stood up, her blackened hands hanging stiffly at her sides, her shoulders drooping. Staring at the ceiling, she would answer: "Pre-se-nt!"

No matter how the rest of us laughed at her, she would never lose her composure but merely push her chair back noisily with a solemn air and sit down after what seemed like several moments. Once, at the beginning of English class, our English teacher was laughing so hard she had to remove her glasses and wipe her eyes.

"Next time you need not answer *hay-er*," she commented. "Just say 'present' in Chinese."

We were all laughing and scuffling our feet on the floor. But on the following day in English class, when Wang Yaming's name was called we were once again treated to sounds of "*Hay-er, hay-er.*"

"Have you ever studied English before?" the English teacher asked as she adjusted her glasses slightly.

"You mean the language they speak in England? Sure, I've studied some, from the pockmarked teacher. Let's see, I know that they write with a *pun-sell* or a *pun*, but I never heard *hay-er* before."

"'Here' simply means 'present.' It's pronounced 'here,' 'h-e-r-e.'"

"*She-er, she-er.*" And so she began saying *she-er*. Her quaint pronunciation made everyone in the room laugh so hard we literally shook. All, that is, except Wang Yaming, who sat down very calmly and opened her book with her blackened hands. Then she began reading in a very soft voice: "*Who-at . . . deez . . . ahar . . .*"[1]

During math class she read her formulas the same way she read essays: "$2x + y = \ldots x\ 2 = \ldots$"

At the lunch table, as she reached out to grab a *mantou*[2] with a blackened hand, she was still occupied with her geography lesson: "Mexico produces silver . . . Yunnan . . . hmm, Yunnan produces marble."

At night she hid herself in the bathroom and studied her lessons, and at the crack of dawn she could be found sitting at the foot of the stairs. Wherever there was the slightest glimmer of light, that's where I usually found her. One morning during a heavy snowfall, when the trees outside the window were covered with a velvety layer of white, I thought I spotted someone sleeping on the ledge of the window at the far end of the corridor in our dormitory.

"Who's there? It's so cold there!" The slapping of my shoes on the wooden floor produced a hollow sound. Since it was a Sunday morning, there was a pronounced stillness throughout the school; some of the girls were getting ready to go out, while others were still in bed asleep. Even before I had drawn up next to her I noticed the pages of the open book on her lap turning over in the wind. "Who do we have here? How can anybody be studying so hard on a Sunday!" Just as I was about to wake the girl up a pair of blackened hands suddenly caught my eye. "Wang Yaming! Hey, come on, wake up now!" This was the first time I had ever called her name, and it gave me a strange, awkward feeling.

---

1. "What . . . these . . . are . . . "
2. Chinese steamed bread.

"*Haw-haw* . . . I must have fallen asleep!"

Every time she spoke she prefaced her remarks with a dull-witted laugh.

"*Who-at* . . . *deez* . . . *yoou* . . . *ai*," she began to read before she had even found her place in the book.

"*Who-at* . . . *deez* . . . this English is sure hard. It's nothing like our Chinese characters with radicals and the like. No, all it has is a lot of squiggles, like a bunch of worms crawling around in my brain, getting me more confused all the time, until I can't remember any more. Our English teacher says it isn't hard—not hard, she says. Well, maybe not for the rest of you. But me, I'm stupid; we country folk just aren't as quick-witted as the rest of you. And my father's even worse off than me. He said that when he was young he only learned one character—our name Wang—and he couldn't even remember that one for more than a few minutes. *Yoou* . . . *ai* . . . *yoou* . . . *ah-ar* . . . " Finishing what she had to say, she tacked on a series of unrelated words from her lesson.

The ventilator on the wall whirred in the wind, as snowflakes were blown in through the window, where they stuck and turned into beads of ice. Her eyes were all bloodshot; like her blackened hands, they were greedily striving for a goal that was forever just beyond reach. In the corners of rooms or any place where even a glimmer of light remained, we saw her, looking very much like a mouse gnawing away at something.

The first time her father came to visit her he said she had gained weight: "I'll be damned, you've put on a few pounds. The chow here must be better'n it is at home, ain't that right? You keep working hard! You study here for three years or so, and even though you won't turn into no sage, at least you'll know a little somethin' about the world."

For a solid week after his visit we had a great time mimicking him. The second time he came she asked him for a pair of gloves.

"Here, you can have this pair of mine! Since you're studyin' your lessons so hard, you oughta at least have a pair of gloves. Here, don't you worry none about it. If you want some gloves, then go ahead and wear these. It's comin' on spring now, and I don't go out much anyway. Little Ming, we'll just buy another pair next winter, won't we, Little Ming?" He was standing in the doorway of the reception room bellowing, and a crowd of his daughter's classmates had gathered around him. He continued calling out "Little Ming this" and "Little Ming that," then gave her some news from home: "Third Sister went visitin' over to Second Auntie's and stayed for two or three days! Our little pig has been gettin' a couple extra handfuls of beans every day, and he's so fat now you've never seen the like. His ears are standin' straight up. Your elder sister came home and pickled two more jars of scallions."

He was talking so much he had worked up a sweat, and just then the school principal threaded her way through the crowd of onlookers and walked up to him: "Won't you please come into the reception room and have a seat?"

"No thanks, there's no need for that, that'll just waste everyone's time. Besides, I couldn't if I wanted to; I have to go catch a train back home. All those kids at home, I don't feel right leavin' 'em there." He took his cap off and held it in his hands, then he nodded to the principal. Steam rose from his head as he pushed the door open and strode out, looking as though he had been chased off by the principal. But he stopped in his tracks and turned around, then began removing his gloves.

"Daddy, you keep them. I don't need to wear gloves anyway."

Her father's hands were also discolored, but they were both bigger and blacker than Wang Yaming's.

Later, when we were in the reading room, Wang Yaming asked me: "Tell me, is it true? If someone goes into the reception room to sit and chat, does it cost them anything?"

"Cost anything! For what?"

"Not so loud; if the others hear you, they'll start laughing at me again." She placed the palm of her hand on top of the newspaper I was reading and continued: "My father said so. He said there was a teapot and some cups in the reception room, and that if he went inside the custodian would probably pour tea, and that he would have to pay for it. I said he wasn't expected to, but he wouldn't believe me, and he said that even in a small teahouse, if you went in and just had a cup of water you'd have to pay something. It was even more likely in a school; he said, 'Just think how big a school is!'"

The principal said to her, as she had several times in the past: "Can't you wash those hands of yours clean? Use a little more soap! Wash them good and hard with hot water. During morning calisthenics out on the playground there are several hundred white hands up in the air—all but yours; no, yours are special, very special!" The principal reached out her bloodless, fossil-like transparent fingers and touched Wang Yaming's blackened hands. Holding her breath somewhat fearfully, she looked as though she were reaching out to pick up a dead crow. "They're a lot less stained than they used to be—I can even see the skin on the palms now. They're much better than they were when you first got here—they were like hands of iron then! Are you keeping up with your lessons? I want you to work a little harder, and from now on you don't have to take part in morning calisthenics. Our school wall is low, and there are a lot of foreigners strolling by on spring days who stop to take a look. You can join in again when the discoloring on your hands is all gone!" This lecture by the school principal was to bring an end to her morning calisthenics.

"I already asked my father for a pair of gloves. No one would notice them if I had gloves on, would they?" She opened up her book bag and took out the gloves her father had given her.

The principal laughed so hard at this she fell into a fit of coughing. Her pallid face suddenly reddened. "What possible good would that do? What we want is uniformity, and even if you wore gloves you still wouldn't be like the others."

The snow atop the artificial hill had melted, the bell being rung by the school custodian produced a crisper sound than usual, sprouts began to appear on the willow trees in front of the window, and a layer of steam rose from the playground under the rays of the sun. As morning calisthenics began, the sound of the exercise leader's whistle carried far into the distance; its echo reverberated among the people in the clump of trees outside the windows. We ran and jumped like a flock of noisy birds, intoxicated by the sweet fragrance that drifted over from the new buds on the branches of the trees. Our spirits, which had been imprisoned by the winter weather, were set free anew, like cotton wadding that has just been released.

As the morning calisthenics period was coming to an end we suddenly heard someone calling to us from an upstairs window in a voice that seemed to be floating up to the sky: "Just feel how warm the sun is! Aren't you hot down there? Aren't you . . . "

There standing in the window behind the budding willows was Wang Yaming.

By the time the trees were covered with green leaves and were casting their shade all over the compound, a change had come over Wang Yaming—she had begun to languish and black circles had appeared around her eyes. Her ears seemed less full than before and her strong shoulders began to slump. On one of the rare occasions when I saw her under one of the shade trees I noticed her slightly hollow chest and was reminded of someone suffering from consumption.

"The principal says my schoolwork's lagging behind, and she's right, of course; if it hasn't improved by the end of the year, well . . . *Haw-haw!* Do you think she'll really keep me back a year?" Even though her speech was still punctuated with that *haw-haw*, I could see that she was trying to hide her hands—she kept the left one behind her back, while all I could see of the right one was a lump under the sleeve of her jacket.

We had never seen her cry before, but one gusty day when the branches of the trees outside the windows were bending in the wind, she stood there with her back to the classroom and to the rest of us and wept to the wind outside. This occurred after a group of visitors had departed, and she stood there wiping the tears from her eyes with darkened hands that had already lost a good deal of their color.

"Are you crying? How dare you cry! Why didn't you go away and hide when all the visitors were here? Just look at yourself. You're the only 'special case' in the whole group! Even if I were to forget for the moment those two blue hands of yours, just look at your uniform—it's almost gray! Everybody else has on a blue blouse, but you, you're special. It doesn't look good to have someone wearing clothes so old that the color has faded. We can't let our system of uniforms go out the window because of you alone." With her lips opening and closing, the principal reached out with her pale white fingers and clutched at Wang Yaming's collar. "I told you to go downstairs and not come back up until after the visitors had left! Who told you to stand out there in the corridor? Did you really think they wouldn't see you out there? And to top it all, you had on this pair of oversized gloves."

As she mentioned the word *gloves* the principal kicked the glove that had dropped to the floor with the shiny toe of her patent shoe and said: "I suppose you figured everything would be just fine if you stood out there wearing a pair of gloves, didn't you? What kind of nonsense is that?" She kicked the glove again, but this time, looking at that huge glove, which was large enough for a carter to wear, she couldn't suppress a chuckle.

How Wang Yaming cried that time; she was still weeping even after the sounds of the wind had died down.

She returned to the school after summer vacation. The late summer weather was as cool and brisk as autumn, and the setting sun turned the cobbled road a deep red. We had gathered beneath the crab-apple tree by the school entrance and were eating crab-apples when a horsecart from Mount Lama carrying Wang Yaming rumbled up. In the silence following the arrival of the cart her father began taking her luggage down for her, while she held on to her small wash-basin and a few odds and ends. We didn't immediately make way for her when she reached the step of the gate. Some of us called out to her: "So here you are! You've come back!" Others just stood there gaping at her. As her father followed her up to the steps, the white towel which hung from his waistband flapping to and fro, someone said: "What's this? After spending a summer at home, her hands are as black as they were before. Don't they look like they're made of iron?"

I didn't really pay much attention to her ironlike hands until our post-autumn moving day. Although I was half asleep, I could hear some quarreling in the next room:

"I don't want her. I won't have my bed next to hers!"

"I don't want mine next to hers either."

I tried listening more attentively, but I couldn't hear clearly what was going on. All I could hear was some muffled laughter and an occasional sound of commotion. But going out into the corridor that night to get a drink of water, I saw someone sleeping on one of the benches. I recognized her at once—it was Wang Yaming. Her face was covered with those two blackened hands, and her quilt had slid down so that half was on the ground and the other half barely covered her legs. I thought that she was getting in some studying by the corridor light, but I saw no books beside her. There was only a clutter of personal belongings and odds and ends on the floor all around her.

On the next day the principal, followed closely by Wang Yaming, made her way among the neatly arranged beds, snorting as she did so and testing the freshly tucked bedsheets with her delicate fingers.

"Why, here's a row of seven beds with only eight girls sleeping on them; some of the others have nine girls sleeping in six beds!" As she said this she took one of the quilts and moved it slightly to one side, telling Wang Yaming to place her bedding there.

Wang Yaming opened up her bedding and whistled contentedly as she made up the bed. This was the first time I had ever heard anyone whistle in school. After she made up the bed she sat on it, her mouth open and her chin tilted slightly higher than usual, as though she were calmed by a feeling of repose and a sense of contentment. The principal had already turned and gone downstairs, and was perhaps by then out of the dormitory altogether and on her way home. But the old housemother with lackluster hair kept shuffling back and forth, scraping her shoes on the floor.

"As far as I'm concerned," she said, "this won't do at all. It's unsanitary. Who wants to be with her, with those vermin all over her body?" As she took a few steps toward the corner of the room, she seemed to be staring straight at me. "Take a look at that bedding! Have a sniff at it! You can smell the odor two feet away. Just imagine how ludicrous it is to have to sleep next to her! Who knows, those vermin of hers might hop all over anyone next to her. Look at this, have you ever seen cotton wadding as filthy as that?"

The housemother often told us stories about how she had accompanied her husband overseas to study in Japan, and how she should be considered an overseas student also. When asked by some of the girls: "What did you study?" she would respond: "Why study any particular subject? I picked up some Japanese and noticed some Japanese customs while I was there. Isn't that studying abroad?" Her speech was forever dotted with terms like "unsanitary," "ludicrous," "filthy," and so on, and she always called lice "vermin."

"If someone's filthy the hands show it." When she said the word *filthy* she shrugged her broad shoulders, as though she had been struck by a blast of cold air, then suddenly darted outside.

"This kind of student! Really, the principal shouldn't have . . . " Even after the lights-out bell had sounded the housemother could still be heard talking with some of the girls in the corridor.

On the third night Wang Yaming, bundle in hand and carrying her bedding, was again walking along behind the white-faced principal.

"We don't want her. We already have enough girls here."

They started yelling before the principal had even laid a finger on their bedding, and the same thing happened when she moved on to the next row of beds.

"We're too crowded here already! Do you expect us to take any more? Nine girls on six beds; how are we supposed to take any more?"

"One, two, three, four . . . " the principal counted. "Not enough; you can still add one more. There should be six girls for every four beds, but you only have five. Come on over here, Wang Yaming!"

"No, my sister's coming tomorrow, and we're saving that space for her," one of the girls said as she ran over and held her bedding in place.

Eventually the principal led her over to another dormitory.

"She's got lice. I'm not going to sleep next to her."

"I'm not going to either."

"Wang Yaming's bedding doesn't have a cover and she sleeps right next to the cotton wadding. If you don't believe me, just look for yourself!"

Then they began to joke about it, saying they were all afraid of Wang Yaming's black hands and didn't dare get close to her.

Finally the black-handed girl had to sleep on a bench in the corridor. On mornings when I got up early I met her there rolling up her bedding and carrying it downstairs. Sometimes I ran into her in the basement storage room. Naturally, that was always at nighttime, so when we talked I kept looking at the shadows cast on the wall; the shadows of her hands as she scratched her head were the same color as her black hair.

"Once you get used to it, you can sleep on a bench or even on the floor. After all, sleep is sleep no matter where you lie down, so what's the difference? Studying is what matters. I wonder what sort of grade Mrs. Ma is going to give me in English on our next exam. If I don't score at least sixty I'll be kept back at the end of the year, won't I?"

"Don't worry about that; they won't keep you back just because of one subject," I assured her.

"But Daddy told me I only have three years to graduate in. He said he won't be able to handle the tuition for even one extra semester. But this English language—I just can't get my tongue right for it. *Haw-haw* . . . "

Everyone in the dormitory was disgusted with her, even though she was sleeping in the corridor, because she was always coughing during the night. Another reason was that she had begun to dye her socks and blouses right in the dormitory.

"When clothes get old, if you dye them they're as good as new. Like, if you take a summer uniform and dye it gray, then you can use it as an autumn uniform. You can dye a pair of white socks black, then . . . "

"Why don't you just buy a pair of black socks?" I asked her.

"You mean those sold in the stores? When they dye them they use too much alum, so not only don't they hold up, but they tear as soon as you put them on. It's a lot better to dye them yourself. Socks are so expensive it just won't do to throw them away as soon as they have holes in them."

One Saturday night some of the girls cooked some eggs in a small iron pot, something they did nearly every Saturday, as they wanted to have something special to eat. I saw the eggs they cooked this time when they took them out of the pot. They were black, looking to me as if they had been poisoned or something. The girl who carried the eggs in roared so loudly her glasses nearly fell off: "All right, who did it! Who? Who did this!?"

Wang Yaming looked over at the girl as she squeezed her way through the others into the kitchen. After a few *haw-haw*'s she said: "It was me. I didn't know anyone was going to use this pot, so I dyed two pairs of socks in it. *Haw-haw* . . . I'll go and . . . "

"You'll go and do what?"

"I'll go and wash it."

"You think we'd cook eggs in the same pot you used to dye your stinky old socks! Who wants it?" The iron pot was hurled to the floor, where it clanged in front of us. Scowling, the girl wearing glasses then flung the blackened eggs to the floor as though she were throwing stones.

After everyone else had left the scene, Wang Yaming picked the eggs up off the floor, saying to herself: "Hm! Why throw a perfectly good iron pot away just because I dyed a couple of pairs of socks in it? Besides, how could new socks be 'stinky'?"

On snowy winter nights the path from the school to our dormitories was completely covered by a blanket of snow. We just pushed on ahead as best we could, bumping our way along, and when we ran into a strong wind we either turned around and walked backward or walked sideways against the wind and snow. In the mornings we had to set out again from our dormitories, and in December it got so bad that our feet were numb with the cold, even if we ran. All of this caused a lot of grumbling and complaining, and some of the girls even began calling the principal names for placing the dormitories so far from the school and for making us leave for school before dawn.

Sometimes I met Wang Yaming as I was walking alone. There would be a sparkle to the sky and the distant snow cover as we walked along together, the moon casting our shadows ahead of us. There would be no other people in sight as the wind whistled through the trees by the side of the road and windows creaked and groaned under the driving snow. Our voices had harsh sounds to them as we talked in the sub-zero weather until our lips turned as stiff and numb as our legs and we stopped talking altogether, at which time we could hear only the crunching of the snow beneath our feet. When we rang the bell at the gate our legs were so cold they felt like they were about to fall off, and our knees were about to buckle under us.

One morning—I forget just when it was—I walked out of the dormitory with a novel I wanted to read tucked under my arm, then turned around and pulled the door shut tight behind me. I felt very ill at ease as I looked at the blurred houses off in the distance and heard the sound of the shifting snow behind me; I grew more frightened with every step. The stars gave off only a glimmer of light, and the moon either had already set or was covered by the gray, dirty-looking clouds in the sky. Every step I took seemed to add another step to the distance I had yet to go. I hoped I would meet someone along the way, but dreaded it at the same time; for on a moonless night you could hear the footsteps long before you saw anyone, until the figure suddenly appeared without warning right in front of you.

When I reached the stone steps of the school gate my heart was pounding, and I rang the door bell with a trembling hand. Just then I heard someone on the steps behind me.

"Who is it? Who's there?"

"Me! It's me."

"Were you walking behind me all the time?" It gave me quite a fright, because I hadn't heard any steps but my own on the way over.

"No, I wasn't walking behind you; I've already been here a long time. The custodian won't open the door for me. I don't know how long I've been here shouting for him."

"Didn't you ring the bell?"

"It didn't do any good, *haw-haw*. The custodian turned on the light and came to the door, then he looked out through the window. But he wouldn't open the door for me."

The light inside came on and the door opened noisily, accompanied by some angry scolding: "What's the idea of shouting at the gate at all hours of the night? You're going to wind up at the bottom of the class anyway, so why worry about it?"

"What's going on! What's that you're saying?" Before I had even finished, the custodian's manner changed completely.

"Oh, Miss Xiao, have you been waiting there long?"

Wang Yaming and I walked to the basement together; she was coughing and her face, which had grown pale and wrinkled, shivered for a few moments. With tears induced by the cold wind on her cheeks, she sat down and opened her school book.

"Why wouldn't the custodian open the door for you?" I asked.

"Who knows? He said I was too early. He told me to go on back, saying that he was only following the principal's orders."

"How long were you waiting out there?"

"Not too long. Only a short while . . . a short while. I guess about as long as it takes to eat a meal. *Haw-haw*."

She no longer studied her lessons as she had when she first arrived. Her voice was much softer now and she just muttered to herself. Her swaying shoulders slumped forward and were much narrower than they had been, while her back was no longer straight and her chest had grown hollow. I read my novel, but very softly so as not to disturb her. This was the first time I had been so considerate, and I wondered why it was only the first time. She asked me what novels I had read and whether I knew *The Romance of the Three Kingdoms*. Every once in a while she picked the book up and looked at its cover or flipped through the pages. "You and the others are so smart. You don't even have to look at your lessons and you're still not the least bit worried about exams. But not me. Sometimes I feel like taking a break and reading something else for a change, but that just doesn't work with me."

One Sunday, when the dormitory was deserted, I was reading aloud the passage in Sinclair's *The Jungle* where the young girl laborer Marija had collapsed in the snow. I gazed out at the snow-covered ground outside the window and was moved by the scene. Wang Yaming was standing right behind me, though I was unaware of it.

"Would you lend me one of the books you've already read? This snowy weather depresses me. I don't have any family around here, and there's nothing to shop for out on the street—besides, everything costs money."

"Your father hasn't been to see you for a long time, has he?" I thought she might be feeling a little homesick.

"How could he come? A round trip on the train costs two dollars, and then there'd be nobody at home."

I handed her my copy of *The Jungle,* since I had read it before.

She laughed—"*haw-haw*"—then patted the edge of the bed a couple of times and began examining the cover of the book. After she walked out of the room, I could hear her in the corridor reading the first sentence of the book loudly just as I had been doing.

One day sometime after that—again I forget just when it was, but it must have been another holiday—the dormitory was deserted all day long, right up to the time that moonlight streamed in through the windows, and the whole place was extremely lonely. I heard a rustling sound from the end of the bed, as though someone were there groping around for something. Raising my head to take a look, I noticed Wang Yaming's blackened hands in the moonlight. She was placing the book she had borrowed beside me.

"Did you like it?" I asked her. "How was it?"

At first she didn't answer me; then, covering her face with her hands and trembling, she said: "Fine."

Her voice was quivering. I sat up in bed, but she moved away, her face still buried in hands as black as the hair on her head. The long corridor was completely deserted, and my eyes were fixed on the cracks in the wooden floor, which were illuminated by moonlight.

"Marija is a very real person to me. You don't think she died after she collapsed in the snow, do you? She couldn't have died. Could she? The doctor knew she didn't have any money, though, so he wouldn't treat her . . . *haw-haw.*" Her high-pitched laugh brought tears to her eyes. "I went for a doctor once myself, when my mother was sick, but do you think he would come? First he wanted travel money, but I told him all our money was at home. I begged him to come with me then, because she was in a bad way. Do you think he would agree to come with me? He just stood there in the courtyard and asked me: 'What does your family do? You're dyers, aren't you?' I don't know why, but as soon as I told him we were dyers he turned and walked back inside. I waited for a while, but he didn't come back out, so I knocked on his door again. He said to me through the door: 'I won't be able to take care of your mother, now just go away!' so I went back home." She wiped her eyes again, then continued:

"From then on I had to take care of my two younger brothers and two younger sisters. Daddy used to dye the black and blue things, and my elder sister dyed the red ones. Then in the winter of the year that my elder sister was engaged her future mother-in-law came in from the countryside to stay with us.

The moment she saw my elder sister she cried out: 'My God, those are the hands of a murderess!' After that, Daddy no longer let anyone dye only red things or only blue things. My hands are black, but if you look closely you can see traces of purple; my two younger sisters' hands are the same."

"Aren't your younger sisters in school?"

"No. Later on I'll teach them their lessons. Except that I don't know how well I'm doing myself, and if I don't do well then I won't even be able to face my younger sisters. The most we can earn for dyeing a bolt of cloth is thirty cents. How many bolts do you think we get a month? One article of clothing is a dime—big or small—and nearly everyone sends us overcoats. Take away the cost for fuel and for the dyes, and you can see what I mean. In order to pay my tuition they had to save every penny, even going without salt, so how could I even think of not doing my lessons? How could I?" She reached out and touched the book again.

My gaze was still fixed on the cracks in the floor, thinking to myself that her tears were much nobler than my sympathy.

One morning just before our winter holiday Wang Yaming was occupied with putting her personal belongings in order. Her luggage was already firmly bound, standing at the base of the wall. Not a soul went over to say good-bye to her. As we walked out of the dormitory, one by one, and passed by the bench that had served as Wang Yaming's bed, she smiled at each of us, at the same time casting glances through the window off into the distance. We shuffled along down the corridor, then walked downstairs and across the courtyard. As we reached the gate at the fence, Wang Yaming caught up with us, panting hard through her widely opened mouth.

"Since my father hasn't come yet, I might as well get in another hour's class work. Every hour counts," she announced to everyone present.

She worked up quite a sweat in this final hour of hers. She copied down every single word from the blackboard during the English class into a little notebook. She read them aloud as she did so and even copied down words she already knew as the teacher casually wrote them on the board. During the following hour, in geography class, she very laboriously copied down the maps the teacher had drawn on the board. She acted as though everything that went through her mind on this her final day had taken on great importance, and she was determined to let none of it pass unrecorded.

When class let out I took a look at her notebook, only to discover that she had copied it all down incorrectly. Her English words had either too few or too many letters. She obviously had a very troubled heart.

Her father still hadn't come to fetch her by nightfall, so she spread her bedding out once again on the bench. She had never before gone to bed as early as she did that night, and she slept much more peacefully than usual. Her hair was spread out over the quilt, her shoulders were relaxed, and she breathed deeply; there were no books beside her that night.

The following morning her father came as the sun was fixed atop the trembling snow-laden branches of the trees and birds had just left their nest for the day. He stopped at the head of the stairs, where he removed the pair of coarse felt boots that were hanging over his shoulders, then took a white towel from around his neck and wiped the snow and ice off his beard.

"So you flunked out, did you?" Small beads of water were formed on the stairs as the ice melted.

"No. We haven't even had exams yet. The principal told me I didn't need to take them, since I couldn't pass them anyway."

Her father just stood there at the head of the stairs staring at the wall, and not even the white towel that hung from his waist was moving. Having already carried her luggage out to the head of the stairs, Wang Yaming went back to get her personal things, her washbasin, and some odds and ends. She handed the large pair of gloves back to her father.

"I don't want them, you go ahead and wear them!" With each step in his coarse felt boots, he left a muddy imprint on the wooden floor.

Since it was still early in the morning, few students were there looking on as Wang Yaming put the gloves on with a weak little laugh.

"Put on your felt boots! You've already made a mess of your schooling, now don't go and freeze your feet off too," her father said as he loosened the laces of the boots, which had been tied together.

The boots reached up past her knees. Like a carter, she fastened a white scarf around her head. "I'll be back; I'll take my books home and study hard, then I'll be back. *Haw . . . haw*," she announced to no one in particular. Then as she picked up her belongings she asked her father: "Did you leave the horsecart you hired outside the gate?"

"Horsecart? What horsecart? We're gonna walk to the station. I'll carry the luggage on my back."

Wang Yaming's felt boots made slapping noises as she walked down the stairs. Her father walked ahead of her, gripping her luggage with his discolored hands. Beneath the morning sun long quivering shadows stretched out in front of them as they walked up the steps of the gate. Watched from the window, they seemed as light and airy as their own shadows; I could still see them, but I could no longer hear the sounds of their departure. After passing through the gate they headed off into the distance, in the direction of the hazy morning sun.

The snow looked like shards of broken glass, and the farther the distance, the stronger the reflection grew. I kept looking until the glare from the snowy landscape hurt my eyes.

1936

Zhang Ailing (1921–1995)

SEALED OFF

Translated by Karen Kingsbury

The tramcar driver drove his tram. The tramcar tracks, in the blazing sun, shimmered like two shiny eels crawling out of the water; they stretched and shrank, stretched and shrank, on their onward way—soft and slippery, long old eels, never ending, never ending . . . the driver fixed his eyes on the undulating tracks, and didn't go mad.

If there hadn't been an air raid, if the city hadn't been sealed, the tramcar would have gone on forever. The city was sealed. The alarm-bell rang. Ding-ding-ding-ding, every "ding" a cold little dot, which added up to a line that cut across time and space.

The tramcar ground to a halt, but the people on the street ran: those on the left side of the street ran over to the right, and those on the right ran over to the left. All the shops, in a single sweep, rattled down their metal gates. Matrons tugged madly at the railings. "Let us in for just a while," they cried. "We have children here, and old people!" But the gates stayed tightly shut. Those inside the metal gates and those outside the metal gates stood glaring at each other, fearing one another.

Inside the tram, people were fairly quiet. They had somewhere to sit, and though the place was rather plain, it still was better, for most of them, than what they had at home. Gradually, the street also grew quiet: not that it was a complete silence, but the sound of voices eased into a confused blur, like the soft rustle of a straw-stuffed pillow, heard in a dream. The huge, shambling city sat dozing in the sun, its head resting heavily on people's shoulders, its spittle slowly dripping down their shirts, an inconceivably enormous weight pressing down on everyone. Never before, it seemed, had Shanghai been this quiet—and in the middle of the day! A beggar, taking advantage of the breathless, birdless quiet, lifted up his voice and began to chant: "Good master, good lady, kind sir, kind ma'am, won't you give alms to this poor man? Good master, good lady . . . " But after a short while he stopped, scared silent by the eerie quiet.

Then there was a braver beggar, a man from Shandong, who firmly broke the silence. His voice was round and resonant: "Sad, sad, sad! No money do I have!" An old, old song, sung from one century to the next. The tram driver, who also was from Shandong, succumbed to the sonorous tune. Heaving a long sigh, he folded his arms across his chest, leaned against the tram door, and joined in: "Sad, sad, sad! No money do I have!"

Some of the tram passengers got out. But there was still a little loose, scattered chatter; near the door, a group of office workers was discussing something. One of them, with a quick, ripping sound, shook his fan open and offered his conclusion: "Well, in the end, there's nothing wrong with him—it's just that he doesn't know how to act." From another nose came a short grunt, followed by a cold smile: "Doesn't know how to act? He sure knows how to toady up to the bosses!"

A middle-aged couple who looked very much like brother and sister stood together in the middle of the tram, holding on to the leather straps. "Careful!" the woman suddenly yelped. "Don't get your trousers dirty!" The man flinched, then slowly raised the hand from which a packet of smoked fish dangled. Very cautiously, very gingerly, he held the paper packet, which was brimming with oil, several inches away from his suit pants. His wife did not let up. "Do you know what dry-cleaning costs these days? Or what it costs to get a pair of trousers made?"

Lu Zongzhen, accountant for Huamao Bank, was sitting in the corner. When he saw the smoked fish, he was reminded of the steamed dumplings stuffed with spinach that his wife had asked him to buy at a noodle stand near the bank. Women are always like that. Dumplings bought in the hardest-to-find, most twisty-windy little alleys had to be the best, no matter what. She didn't for a moment think of how it would be for him—neatly dressed in suit and tie, with tortoiseshell eyeglasses and a leather briefcase, then, tucked under his arm, these steaming hot dumplings wrapped in newspaper—how ludicrous! Still, if the city were sealed for a long time, so that his dinner was delayed, then he could at least make do with the dumplings.

He glanced at his watch; only four thirty. Must be the power of suggestion. He felt hungry already. Carefully pulling back a corner of the paper, he took a look inside. Snowy white mounds, breathing soft little whiffs of sesame oil. A piece of newspaper had stuck to the dumplings, and he gravely peeled it off; the ink was printed on the dumplings, with all the writing in reverse, as though it were reflected in a mirror. He peered down and slowly picked the words out: "Obituaries . . . Positions Wanted . . . Stock Market Developments . . . Now

Playing . . . " Normal, useful phrases, but they did look a bit odd on a dumpling. Maybe because eating is such serious business; compared to it, everything else is just a joke. Lu Zongzhen thought it looked funny, but he didn't laugh: he was a very straightforward kind of fellow. After reading the dumplings, he read the newspaper, but when he'd finished half a page of old news, he found that if he turned the page all the dumplings would fall out, and so he had to stop.

While Lu read the paper, others in the tram did likewise. People who had newspapers read them; those without newspapers read receipts, or lists of rules and regulations, or business cards. People who were stuck without a single scrap of printed matter read shop signs along the street. They simply had to fill this terrifying emptiness—otherwise, their brains might start to work. Thinking is a painful business.

Sitting across from Lu Zongzhen was an old man who, with a dull clacking sound, rolled two slippery, glossy walnuts in his palm: a rhythmic little gesture can substitute for thought. The old man had a clean-shaven pate, a reddish yellow complexion, and an oily sheen on his face. When his brows were furrowed, his head looked like a walnut. The thoughts inside were walnut-flavored: smooth and sweet, but in the end, empty-tasting.

To the old man's right sat Wu Cuiyuan, who looked like one of those young Christian wives, though she was still unmarried. Her Chinese gown of white cotton was trimmed with a narrow blue border—the navy blue around the white reminded one of the black borders around an obituary—and she carried a little blue-and-white-checked parasol. Her hairstyle was utterly banal, so as not to attract attention. Actually, she hadn't much reason to fear. She wasn't bad-looking, but hers was an uncertain, unfocused beauty, an afraid-she-had-offended-someone kind of beauty. Her face was bland, slack, lacking definition. Even her own mother couldn't say for certain whether her face was long or round.

At home she was a good daughter, at school she was a good student. After graduating from college, Cuiyuan had become an English instructor at her alma mater. Now, stuck in the air raid, she decided to grade a few papers while she waited. The first one was written by a male student. It railed against the evils of the big city, full of righteous anger, the prose stiff, choppy, ungrammatical. "Painted prostitutes . . . cruising the Cosmo . . . low-class bars and dancing-halls." Cuiyuan paused for a moment, then pulled out her red pencil and gave the paper an "A." Ordinarily, she would have gone right on to the next one, but now, because she had too much time to think, she couldn't help wondering why she had given this student such a high mark. If she hadn't asked herself this question, she could have ignored the whole matter, but once she did ask, her face suffused with red. Suddenly, she understood: it was because this student was the only man who fearlessly and forthrightly said such things to her.

He treated her like an intelligent, sophisticated person; as if she were a man, someone who really understood. He respected her. Cuiyuan always felt that no one at school respected her—from the president on down to the professors, the students, even the janitors. The students' grumbling was especially hard to take: "This place is really falling apart. Getting worse every day. It's bad enough having to learn English from a Chinese, but then to learn it from a Chinese who's never gone abroad . . . " Cuiyuan took abuse at school, took abuse at home. The Wu household was a modern, model household, devout and serious. The family had pushed their daughter to study hard, to climb upward step by step, right to the tip-top . . . A girl in her twenties teaching at a university! It set a record for women's professional achievement. But her parents' enthusiasm began to wear thin and now they wished she hadn't been quite so serious, wished she'd taken more time out from her studies, tried to find herself a rich husband.

She was a good daughter, a good student. All the people in her family were good people; they took baths every day and read the newspaper; when they listened to the wireless, they never tuned into local folk-opera, comic opera, that sort of thing, but listened only to the symphonies of Beethoven and Wagner; they didn't understand what they were listening to, but still they listened. In this world, there are more good people than real people . . . Cuiyuan wasn't very happy.

Life was like the Bible, translated from Hebrew into Greek, from Greek into Latin, from Latin into English, from English into Chinese. When Cuiyuan read it, she translated the standard Chinese into Shanghainese. Gaps were unavoidable.

She put the student's essay down and buried her chin in her hands. The sun burned down on her backbone.

Next to her sat a nanny with a small child lying on her lap. The sole of the child's foot pushed against Cuiyuan's leg. Little red shoes, decorated with tigers, on a soft but tough little foot . . . this at least was real.

A medical student who was also on the tram took out a sketchpad and carefully added the last touches to a diagram of the human skeleton. The other passengers thought he was sketching a portrait of the man who sat dozing across from him. Nothing else was going on, so they started sauntering over, crowding into little clumps of three or four, leaning on each other with their hands behind their backs, gathering around to watch the man sketch from life. The husband who dangled smoked fish from his fingers whispered to his wife: "I can't get used to this cubism, this impressionism, which is so popular these days." "Your pants," she hissed.

The medical student meticulously wrote in the names of every bone, muscle, nerve, and tendon. An office worker hid half his face behind a fan and quietly informed his colleague: "The influence of Chinese painting. Nowadays, writing words in is all the rage in Western painting. Clearly a case of 'Eastern ways spreading Westward.'"

Lu Zongzhen didn't join the crowd, but stayed in his seat. He had decided he was hungry. With everyone gone, he could comfortably munch his spinach-stuffed dumplings. But then he looked up and caught a glimpse, in the third-class car, of a relative, his wife's cousin's son. He detested that Dong Peizhi was a man of humble origins who harbored a great ambition: he sought a fiancée of comfortable means, to serve as a foothold for his climb upward. Lu Zongzhen's eldest daughter had just turned twelve, but already she had caught Peizhi's eye; having made, in his own mind, a pleasing calculation, Peizhi's manner grew ever softer, ever more cunning.

As soon as Lu Zongzhen caught sight of this young man, he was filled with quiet alarm, fearing that if he were seen, Peizhi would take advantage of the opportunity to press forward with his attack. The idea of being stuck in the same car with Dong Peizhi while the city was sealed off was too horrible to contemplate! Lu quickly closed his briefcase and wrapped up his dumplings, then fled, in a great rush, to a seat across the aisle. Now, thank God, he was screened by Wu Cuiyuan, who occupied the seat next to him, and his nephew could not possibly see him.

Cuiyuan turned and gave him a quick look. Oh no! The woman surely thought he was up to no good, changing seats for no reason like that. He recognized the look of a woman being flirted with—she held her face absolutely motionless, no hint of a smile anywhere in her eyes, her mouth, not even in the little hollows beside her nose; yet from some unknown place there was the trembling of a little smile that could break out at any moment. If you think you're simply too adorable, you can't keep from smiling.

Damn! Dong Peizhi had seen him after all, and was coming toward the first-class car, very humble, bowing even at a distance, with his long jowls, shiny red cheeks, and long, gray, monklike gown—a clean, cautious young man, hardworking no matter what the hardship, the very epitome of a good son-in-law. Thinking fast, Zongzhen decided to follow Peizhi's lead and try a bit of artful nonchalance. So he stretched one arm out across the windowsill that ran behind Cuiyuan, soundlessly announcing flirtatious intent. This would not, he knew, scare Peizhi into immediate retreat, because in Peizhi's eyes he already was a dirty old man. The way Peizhi saw it, anyone over thirty was old, and all the old were vile. Having seen his uncle's disgraceful behavior, the young man would feel compelled to tell his wife every little detail—well, angering his wife was just fine with him. Who told her to give him such a nephew, anyway? If she was angry, it served her right.

He didn't care much for this woman sitting next to him. Her arms were fair, all right, but were like squeezed-out toothpaste. Her whole body was like squeezed-out toothpaste, it had no shape.

"When will this air raid ever end?" he said in a low, smiling voice. "It's awful!"

Shocked, Cuiyuan turned her head, only to see that his arm was stretched out behind her. She froze. But come what may, Zongzhen could not let himself pull his arm back. His nephew stood just across the way, watching him with brilliant, glowing eyes, the hint of an understanding smile on his face. If, in the middle of everything, he turned and looked his nephew in the eye, maybe the little no-account would get scared, would lower his eyes, flustered and embarrassed like a sweet young thing; then again, maybe Peizhi would keep staring at him—who could tell?

He gritted his teeth and renewed the attack. "Aren't you bored? We could talk a bit, that can't hurt. Let's . . . let's talk." He couldn't control himself, his voice was plaintive.

Again Cuiyuan was shocked. She turned to look at him. Now he remembered, he had seen her get on the tram—a striking image, but an image concocted by chance, not by any intention of hers. "You know, I saw you get on the tram," he said softly. "Near the front of the car. There's a torn advertisement, and I saw your profile, just a bit of your chin, through the torn spot." It was an ad for Lacova powdered milk that showed a pudgy little child. Beneath the child's ear this woman's chin had suddenly appeared; it was a little spooky, when you thought about it. "Then you looked down to get some change out of your purse, and I saw your eyes, then your brows, then your hair." When you took her features separately, looked at them one by one, you had to admit she had a certain charm.

Cuiyuan smiled. You wouldn't guess that this man could talk so sweetly—you'd think he was the stereotypical respectable businessman. She looked at him again. Under the tip of his nose the cartilage was reddened by the sunlight. Stretching out from his sleeve, and resting on the newspaper, was a warm, tanned hand, one with feeling—a real person! Not too honest, not too bright, but a real person. Suddenly she felt flushed and happy; she turned away with a murmur. "Don't talk like that."

"What?" Zongzhen had already forgotten what he'd said. His eyes were fixed on his nephew's back—the diplomatic young man had decided that three's a crowd, and he didn't want to offend his uncle. They would meet again, anyway, since theirs was a close family, and no knife was sharp enough to sever the ties; and so he returned to the third-class car. Once Peizhi was gone, Zongzhen withdrew his arm; his manner turned respectable. Casting about for a way to make conversation, he glanced at the notebook spread out on her lap. "Shenguang University," he read aloud. "Are you a student there?"

Did he think she was that young? That she was still a student? She laughed, without answering.

"I graduated from Huaqi." He repeated the name. "Huaqi." On her neck was a tiny dark mole, like the imprint of a fingernail. Zongzhen absentmindedly rubbed the fingers of his right hand across the nails of his left. He coughed slightly, then continued: "What department are you in?"

Cuiyuan saw that he had moved his arm and thought that her standoffish manner had wrought this change. She therefore felt she could not refuse to answer. "Literature. And you?"

"Business." Suddenly he felt that their conversation had grown stuffy. "In school I was busy with student activities. Now that I'm out, I'm busy earning a living. So I've never really studied much of anything."

"Is your office very busy?"

"Terribly. In the morning I go to work and in the evening I go home, but I don't know why I do either. I'm not the least bit interested in my job. Sure, it's a way to earn money, but I don't know who I'm earning it for."

"Everyone has family to think of."

"Oh, you don't know . . . my family . . . " A short cough. "We'd better not talk about it."

"Here it comes," thought Cuiyuan. "His wife doesn't understand him. Every married man in the world seems desperately in need of another woman's understanding."

Zongzhen hesitated, then swallowed hard and forced the words out: "My wife—she doesn't understand me at all."

Cuiyuan knitted her brow and looked at him, expressing complete sympathy.

"I really don't understand why I go home every evening. Where is there to go? I have no home, in fact." He removed his glasses, held them up to the light, and wiped the spots off with a handkerchief. Another little cough. "Just keep going, keep getting by, without thinking—above all, don't start thinking!" Cuiyuan always felt that when nearsighted people took their glasses off in front of other people it was a little obscene; improper, somehow, like taking your clothes off in public. Zongzhen continued: "You, you don't know what kind of woman she is."

"Then why did you . . . in the first place?"

"Even then I was against it. My mother arranged the marriage. Of course I wanted to choose for myself, but . . . she used to be very beautiful . . . I was very young . . . young people, you know . . . " Cuiyuan nodded her head.

"Then she changed into this kind of person—even my mother fights with her, and she blames me for having married her! She has such a temper—she hasn't even got a grade-school education."

Cuiyuan couldn't help saying, with a tiny smile, "You seem to take diplomas very seriously. Actually, even if a woman's educated it's all the same." She didn't know why she said this, wounding her own heart.

"Of course, you can laugh, because you're well-educated. You don't know what kind of—" He stopped, breathing hard, and took off the glasses he had just put back on.

"Getting a little carried away?" said Cuiyuan.

Zongzhen gripped his glasses tightly, made a painful gesture with his hands. "You don't know what kind of—"

"I know, I know," Cuiyuan said hurriedly. She knew that if he and his wife didn't get along, the fault could not lie entirely with her. He too was a person of simple intellect. He just wanted a woman who would comfort and forgive him.

The street erupted in noise, as two trucks full of soldiers rumbled by. Cuiyuan and Zongzhen stuck their heads out to see what was going on; to their surprise, their faces came very close together. At close range anyone's face is somehow different, is tension-charged like a close-up on the movie screen. Zongzhen and Cuiyuan suddenly felt they were seeing each other for the first time. To his eyes, her face was the spare, simple peony of a watercolor sketch, and the strands of hair fluttering at her temples were pistils ruffled by a breeze.

He looked at her, and she blushed. When she let him see her blush, he grew visibly happy. Then she blushed even more deeply.

Zongzhen had never thought he could make a woman blush, make her smile, make her hang her head shyly. In this he was a man. Ordinarily, he was an accountant, a father, the head of a household, a tram passenger, a store customer, an insignificant citizen of a big city. But to this woman, this woman who didn't know anything about his life, he was only and entirely a man.

They were in love. He told her all kinds of things: who was on his side at the bank and who secretly opposed him; how his family squabbled; his secret sorrows; his schoolboy dreams . . . unending talk, but she was not put off. Men in love have always liked to talk; women in love, on the other hand, don't want to talk, because they know, without even knowing that they know, that once a man really understands a woman he'll stop loving her.

Zongzhen was sure that Cuiyuan was a lovely woman—pale, wispy, warm, like the breath your mouth exhales in winter. You don't want her, and she quietly drifts away. Being part of you, she understands everything, forgives everything. You tell the truth, and her heart aches for you; you tell a lie, and she smiles as if to say, "Go on with you—what are you saying?"

Zongzhen was quiet for a moment, then said, "I'm thinking of marrying again."

Cuiyuan assumed an air of shocked surprise. "You want a divorce? Well . . . that isn't possible, is it?"

"I can't get a divorce. I have to think of the children's well-being. My oldest daughter is twelve, just passed the entrance exams for middle school, her grades are quite good."

"What," thought Cuiyuan, "what does this have to do with what you just said?" "Oh," she said aloud, her voice cold, "you plan to take a concubine."

"I plan to treat her like a wife," said Zongzhen. "I—I can make things nice for her. I wouldn't do anything to upset her."

"But," said Cuiyuan, "a girl from a good family won't agree to that, will she? So many legal difficulties . . . "

Zongzhen sighed. "Yes, you're right. I can't do it. Shouldn't have mentioned it . . . I'm too old. Thirty-four already."

"Actually," Cuiyuan spoke very slowly, "these days, that isn't considered very old."

Zongzhen was still. Finally he asked, "How old are you?"

Cuiyuan ducked her head. "Twenty-four."

Zongzhen waited awhile, then asked, "Are you a free woman?"

Cuiyuan didn't answer. "You aren't free," said Zongzhen. "But even if you agreed, your family wouldn't, right?"

Cuiyuan pursed her lips. Her family—her prim and proper family—how she hated them all. They had cheated her long enough. They wanted her to find them a wealthy son-in-law. Well, Zongzhen didn't have money, but he did have a wife—that would make them good and angry! It would serve them right!

Little by little, people started getting back on the tram. Perhaps it was rumored out there that "traffic will soon return to normal." The passengers got on and sat down, pressing against Zongzhen and Cuiyuan, forcing them a little closer, then a little closer again.

Zongzhen and Cuiyuan wondered how they could have been so foolish not to have thought of sitting closer before. Zongzhen struggled against his happiness. He turned to her and said, in a voice full of pain, "No, this won't do! I can't let you sacrifice your future! You're a fine person, with such a good education . . . I don't have much money, and don't want to ruin your life!"

Well, of course, it was money again. What he said was true. "It's over," thought Cuiyuan. In the end she'd probably marry, but her husband would never be as dear as this stranger met by chance—this man on the tram in the middle of a sealed-off city . . . it could never be this spontaneous again. Never again . . . oh, this man, he was so stupid! So very stupid! All she wanted was one small part of him, one little part that no one else could want. He was throwing away his own happiness. Such an idiotic waste! She wept, but it wasn't a gentle, maidenly weeping. She practically spit her tears into his face. He was a good person—the world had gained one more good person!

What use would it be to explain things to him? If a woman needs to turn to words to move a man's heart, she is a sad case.

Once Zongzhen got anxious, he couldn't get any words out, and just kept shaking the umbrella she was holding. She ignored him. Then he tugged at her hand. "Hey, there are people here, you know! Don't! Don't get so upset! Wait a bit, and we'll talk it over on the telephone. Give me your number."

Cuiyuan didn't answer. He pressed her. "You have to give me your phone number."

"Seven-five-three-six-nine." Cuiyuan spoke as fast as she could.

"Seven-five-three-six-nine?"

No response. "Seven-five-three-six-nine, seven-five . . . " Mumbling the number over and over, Zongzhen searched his pockets for a pen, but the more frantic he became, the harder it was to find one. Cuiyuan had a red pencil in her bag, but she purposely did not take it out. He ought to remember her telephone number; if he didn't, then he didn't love her, and there was no point in continuing the conversation.

The city started up again. "Ding-ding-ding-ding," every "ding" a cold little dot, which added up to a line that cut across time and space.

A wave of cheers swept across the metropolis. The tram started clanking its way forward. Zongzhen stood up, pushed into the crowd, and disappeared. Cuiyuan turned her head away, as if she didn't care. He was gone. To her, it was as if he were dead.

The tram picked up speed. On the evening street, a tofu-seller had set his shoulder pole down and was holding up a rattle; eyes shut, he shook it back and forth. A big-boned blond woman, straw hat slung across her back, bantered with an Italian sailor. All her teeth showed when she grinned. When Cuiyuan looked at these people, they lived for that one moment. Then the tram clanked onward, and one by one they died away.

Cuiyuan shut her eyes fretfully. If he phoned her, she wouldn't be able to control her voice; it would be filled with emotion, for he was a man who had died, then returned to life.

The lights inside the tram went on; she opened her eyes and saw him sitting in his old seat, looking remote. She trembled with shock—he hadn't gotten off the tram, after all! Then she understood his meaning: everything that had happened while the city was sealed was a non-occurrence. The whole of Shanghai had dozed off, had dreamed an unreasonable dream.

The tramcar driver raised his voice in song: "Sad, sad, sad! No money do I have! Sad, sad, sad—" An old beggar, thoroughly dazed, limped across the street in front of the tram. The driver bellowed at her. "You swine!"

1943

Wu Zhuoliu (1900–1976)

THE DOCTOR'S MOTHER

Translated by Sylvia Li-chun Lin

The backyard gate creaked open and out stepped a dignified old lady who seemed accustomed to a comfortable life. Wearing tiny, pointed shoes, she was followed by a young maid carrying a bamboo basket with three kinds of sacrificial meat, gilded paper, and joss sticks.

An old beggar outside the gate craned his neck to see what was going on inside as he waited for the old lady to emerge. He knew she went to the temple to burn incense on the fifteenth day of each month. But, fearful that his fellow beggars might get wind of it, he took great care to conceal the old lady's monthly visits. Each fifteenth day of the month, he stole over to wait by the back gate, something he had done unfailingly for a decade.

When he spotted the old lady, he went up and greeted her respectfully, as if meeting a real live fairy. White-haired, scruffy, he wore tattered and patched clothes, but his staff had a glossy sheen. As he walked up to the old lady, he pined sadly: "Mrs. Doctor, bestow mercy and compassion!"

Aroused by a sense of pity, the doctor's mother quickly handed the beggar's rice sack to the maid with an order, "Go get two pecks of rice."

But the maid hesitated, which made the doctor's mother anxious. She asked sharply: "What are you afraid of? Xinfa is my son, isn't he? You needn't fear him over such trivial matters. Go get it quickly."

"The mistress is right, but I'm such a coward. I'm frightened out of my wits whenever I see the young master."

Having said her piece, the maid crept back into the kitchen, where she looked to her left and right to make sure no one was around before quickly opening the rice bin and measuring the right amount into the beggar's sack. She then fled the kitchen in a panic; going up to the old lady, she patted herself on the chest, finally calming down. The kitchen was next to Qian Xinfa's room, and he would have given her a good dressing-down had he spotted her measuring out rice. He was ruthless in situations like this, unconcerned about how anyone else might feel.

On one occasion, the maid was measuring rice when Qian Xinfa stormed in. Seized by rage, he bellowed at her: "So you're the culprit! How would the beggar get any rice if you didn't give it to him? If the old mistress says one peck, all you need to give him is one liter."

The maid had no choice but to do as he said and measure out a liter. When the doctor's mother heard why she had done that, she flew into a rage.

"That's ridiculous!"

Grabbing the beggar's staff, she rushed into the house, filled with anger. Qian Xinfa, who had yet to learn that his mother was furious, kept on with his harangue.

"This is ridiculous! A beggar usually merits a cup of rice at most. Who ever heard of giving them a peck or two?"

That set his mother off and, without listening to any more, she struck him with the beggar's staff.

"Xinfa! You received more than three thousand bushels of grain from your tenant farmers, but you're unwilling to give away a single peck. You despise the poor, but you go through all sorts of trouble when a prefectural magistrate or section head drops in. Preparing meat and spirits, you spare nothing to entertain them. You've become a lackey, no longer a man."

As she railed against her son, she raised the staff to strike him again. Startled, everyone in the house begged the old lady to calm down, until she was finally appeased. Angry but not willing to talk back to her, Qian Xinfa could only blame the maid for causing him all this trouble. The poor maid didn't dare disobey the old lady but found it hard to disregard the young master's order. So each month, when the fifteenth arrived, she was invariably seized by a minor panic, as she hurriedly measured out rice for the beggar.

Later, as wartime conditions worsened, food rationing, including rice, took effect. The doctor's mother was forced to stop giving rice and replace it with money. Finally, the maid's monthly dilemma was resolved.

A public health physician on K Street, Qian Xinfa wore his uniform wherever he went, when he was traveling, for major or minor public events, funerals, or house calls. No one in the neighborhood had ever seen him in civilian clothes. His uniform was always neatly pressed, as if he were an official, and he wore it as a sign of his prestige. His medical skills, on the other hand, were mediocre, certainly nothing special, although his name was known far and wide. How had that happened? Because of his ability to trick the honest, simple commoners into believing that his friendliness and kindness toward his patient was genuine. Incapable of seeing the real person, they mistook him for a decent doctor. And so his reputation spread by word of mouth and he grew wealthy. In a mere fourteen or fifteen years, he had accrued more than three thousand bushels of annual grain revenue. Qian Xinfa came from a poor family. During his student days, his uniform had been mended over and over, ridiculed by his classmates as a judo uniform. Patch was sewn over patch until the uniform was so thick it truly did look like a judo uniform. The humiliation angered him beyond words, but he could do nothing but allow himself to be a laughingstock. His father worked hard by day and his mother wove hats by night to pay his tuition and keep him in school. After struggling for five years he finally graduated and married a woman from a wealthy family; her brothers helped him set up a private clinic. For the opening ceremony, his brothers-in-law also helped him by inviting officials, local gentry, merchants, and other powerful dignitaries, who came together for a grand celebration to promote his medical skills. The celebratory gathering helped him garner goodwill from the locals, an unexpected positive result. So he was even more solicitous; his attention to his patients went beyond the usual businesslike manner of other doctors in private practice. He inquired after the patients in great detail and chatted easily with them about things that had nothing to do with their illnesses; but listening to him, the patients were taken by his kind words. When a farmer came, he asked about work in the field; with a merchant, he discussed business. If it was a woman, he said things she wanted to hear.

"Your little gentleman here has such an elegant, refined look, he'll surely be an official when he grows up."

Nothing but flattery.

Sometimes he'd tell a mother sympathetically, "This is a tough illness that could lead to pneumonia. I'd recommend an injection, but it would be quite expensive. What is your opinion, Madam?"

This sweet consultative tone always worked with the country folk, who worried about the severity of their children's illnesses and were won over by his honeyed, soothing words; whatever the expense, they willingly emptied their pockets for the injections.

In addition to this sort of self-promotion, Qian Xinfa always nodded and bowed to people, children as well as adults, when he was on his house calls. If he took a sedan-chair, he climbed down to walk when they reached a steep incline, which won the approval of sedan-chair carriers and the country folk.

During his leisure time at home, he would utilize visiting fortune-tellers and charity workers who came to spread the word. And his self-promotion techniques did not stop here, but even included taking his physician's satchel with him when he was away on personal business. As a result, his prescriptions were in constant demand; his boiled water sold especially well.

What did Qian Xinfa care about most? The balance in his bankbook. His savings went from one thousand to two thousand, then, almost imperceptibly, to three thousand. As the balance increased daily, so did his happiness. He counted the days until his savings would reach ten thousand. After settling on a date, he redoubled his efforts to get patients to opt for injections. Once he reached his goal of ten thousand yen, he bought a plot of land through a middleman. And so it went, year after year, and, before anyone realized it, he had become one of the wealthiest men in the area.

As someone who had gone through tough times as a youngster, Qian Xinfa developed a pathological love for money, which went far beyond the virtue of economizing. His meddling with his mother's rice-giving was a manifestation of his obsession over money. But he was generous in other regards. Such as? Well, he could part with tens of thousands of yen without blinking an eye for matters concerning his reputation and status. These expenditures were made for the sake of his business, a selfish design, pure and simple. But he was praised nonetheless and, gradually, he became a powerful local magnate who assumed most of the local honorary positions, including public health physician, chairman of the Customs Rectification Society, a member of the Coordination Council, and chairman of the local Elders Society. His name appeared on every list of honorary official titles. As a result, he became a leading force on K Street; always the first to follow orders, he gained the trust of the local government, leading the way in implementing the policy of Japanese-only at home and adopting a Japanese name.

But he could never get "the doctor's mother" to follow his lead, no matter how hard he tried.

"Only those who understand and follow the trends can reach the top. Under current circumstances, Mother, why won't you learn to speak Japanese?"

". . ."

"Why don't I get Jinying to teach you?"

"That's ridiculous. How can a daughter-in-law teach her mother-in-law?"

"If you don't want your daughter-in-law to teach you, Mother, I can ask Mr. Chen at the school to be your tutor."

"That's even more ridiculous! Since I'm much older than you, you needn't worry. I'm not long for this world and will soon stop being a bother to you."

Left with no recourse, Qian Xinfa let the matter drop so as not to cause himself any more trouble.

But that was not his only problem. Whenever people came to visit, his mother insisted upon meeting the guests in the living room. Dressed in traditional Taiwanese clothes, she spoke Taiwanese in a loud, shrill voice, like someone just in from the countryside. She never changed her style, even if it was the prefectural magistrate or the head of the neighborhood. When he watched the way she greeted these officials, Qian Xinfa prayed that she would stop talking and go quickly to her room. But unresponsive to his prayers, she would continue her loud conversation in Taiwanese with the guests. Outraged beyond words, he could only suffer in silence. The Qians were a Japanese-only household, and no one was supposed to use Taiwanese. But the doctor's mother did not understand Japanese and had no one to talk to at home, so she took great pleasure in chatting with visitors in the living room. So as not to slight her, the Taiwanese guests spoke with her in Taiwanese, which so delighted her that she was like a child. Japanese visitors were also courteous to the doctor's mother, who, although she did not understand what they said, smiled and returned the courtesy in Taiwanese. Qian Xinfa was pained by the sight of his mother socializing with guests; it upset him terribly, for he was afraid of losing his social status and worried that the officials would think lightly of him. He was also upset by his mother's choice of Taiwanese clothes.

One day Qian Xinfa said to her in front of a guest, "Mother, I have a visitor. Hurry and go inside." Incensed, she yelled back, "What nonsense is this? You have a visitor. You have a visitor. You treat me like a thorn in your side. Go back inside. Where do you expect me to go? Isn't this my house?"

Her scolding so shamed him that his face throbbed redly and had there been a hole nearby, he would have crawled into it. From then on Qian Xinfa no longer dared to make an issue of his mother's presence in the living room. But he remained troubled by the fear that he would lose face and his status in society because of her.

When the Japanese government began promoting the use of Japanese at home, Qian Xinfa tried to deceive himself as well as others and lied to the clerk that his mother knew enough Japanese to socialize, so they passed muster. His family was now classified as a Japanese-only family, which made him feel tremendous pride. He quickly remodeled the house in the Japanese style; the new tatami mats and the sliding paper doors let in so much light that he was praised by those who saw the house. But barely a week had passed before the doctor's mother grew upset over the new Japanese lifestyle. She disliked the miso soup they had for breakfast, forcing herself to swallow it, and she could not tolerate the pain of sitting cross-legged on the Japanese straw mat. At mealtimes she had to bend her stiff legs to sit on the tatami, and the sheer agony and numbness after less than ten minutes made it impossible for her to force anything down her throat; with numbness, she could barely try to stand up.

The doctor's mother was in the habit of taking afternoon naps. But hanging a large mosquito net in a Japanese-style house was difficult, and she had to do it once at midday and again at night, which upset her so much that she nearly burst with anger. This went on until dinner on the ninth day, when the excellent food prolonged mealtime so long that even a massage could not bring circulation back to her feet. Left with no alternative, Qian Xinfa returned the dining room and his mother's room to their original style. He was unhappy, but could do nothing but sigh. Thoughts of his mother always brought with them dark clouds. Hoping to fully implement his ideas, he inevitably ran up against his mother, who refused to budge no matter how sad or put upon he looked. If he insisted on doing things his way, he would be scolded, even beaten, by his mother. Not being able to enlighten her meant not being able to carry out his ideas. But he was not prepared to give up; rather, he did everything possible to keep from lagging behind others. He was among the first to change his name into Japanese. When the Japanese government allowed the Taiwanese to use Japanese names, he eagerly changed his to Kanai Shinsuke and immediately hung a new sign on the door; at the same time, the family began dressing in kimonos. He even discarded his favorite public health physician uniform. Now that he had built a fully Japanese-style house, he was so elated that he wanted to take a picture and asked his mother to put on a kimono for the occasion. But she refused and was finally photographed in her old Taiwanese clothes. The regret Kanai Shinsuke felt was like that of a rock paired with jade on the same shelf, but he dared not say a word, and could only let the anger build up inside. After the pictures were taken, for some unknown reason, the doctor's mother sliced up the kimono prepared for her with a cleaver, shocking those who looked on and assumed that the doctor's mother had gone mad.

"If I kept this thing, I'm afraid someone might put it on me after I die. I could not face our ancestors wearing something like this."

She continued slicing it until it was beyond recognition, and everyone finally understood how she felt; they were touched by her candor.

Only two people in the area responded to the first call to change their names. One was Kanai Shinsuke, the other was Oyama Kinkichi. Oyama was also a man of wealth and power, so the two of them often got together to study styles of Japanese living and embrace the spirit of the Japanese. Oyama did whatever he wanted, since he did not have to worry about parental interference. Observing the speed at which Oyama changed, Kanai grew anxious over the likelihood that he would be left behind, and his thoughts settled on his obstinate mother, which brought him more anguish.

Four or five names appeared on the next government list of name changes, all second-tier families. Kanai Shinsuke frowned when he heard the news; he actually became light-headed, feeling that his self-respect was on the verge of crumbling and his sense of superiority shaken, as if by a strong wind. He quickly phoned his comrade, Oyama Kinkichi, who rushed over to his living room wearing a newly tailored kimono, carrying a persimmon walking stick in hand, and clip-clopping along in a pair of paulownia-wood geta.

"Mr. Oyama, have you read the news?"

"No. Anything interesting today?"

"Singularly outlandish news! Lai Liangma has changed his name. What makes him think he is qualified?"

"Hmph, that's incredible . . . Ah, ah, Xu Faxin, Guan Zhongshan, Lai Liangma . . . scoundrels, all of them. A bunch of monkey-headed, rat-eared creatures who are trying to act human."

Kanai slammed his fist on the table and roared, "They can try all they want, but at home they don't speak only Japanese, they don't have tatami, they don't even bathe in an ofuro."

"Monkeys like them only know to ape humans. They're nothing but phonies."

"Precisely!"

"What was the government thinking?"

They talked on, filled with indignation, and then fell into a prolonged, pained silence. Kanai could do nothing but smoke, releasing sighs with the cigarette smoke. Oyama fidgeted with his walking stick and said in anguished self-mockery, "Let them be." He sighed and changed the subject.

"I bought a new tea chest, made solely from black sandal-wood. I'll bet rural Japanese don't have anything like it."

"I'd like to see it one of these days. I bought a koto, made from a five- or six-hundred-year-old paulownia tree. Guess how much it cost? Twelve hundred."

When he heard this, Oyama went up to look at the koto in the tokonoma, the living room alcove, and plucked a note.

When the current prefectural magistrate was replaced, the new man came to inspect the area. The neighborhood head was away, so his "assistant" gave a report on the area to the new magistrate. After the ceremony, the new magistrate met with the local gentry, including Kanai. Dressed in a new kimono of Oshima pongee, he looked so impressive that no one could tell he was Taiwanese. The new magistrate was quite a talker and chatted freely with them. When the neighborhood assistant introduced the local gentry individually, he unintentionally revealed Kanai Shinsuke's old name. Shinsuke's face throbbed redly. "What a terrible assistant!" he thought to himself. His disgust raged like a stormy sea, but not a single member of the gentry realized what was going through his mind, and it was all he could do to suppress his emotions. Then it occurred to him that he ought to laugh it off, since professionally it would not be to his advantage to argue with the assistant. Having made up his mind, he smiled and feigned a modest attitude as he continued the conversation. The assistant mentioned Kanai's good points, but it was too late to dispel the humiliation the assistant had caused him.

He was even more upset when the third list of name changes was made public. On it were many people, all with lowly backgrounds. He was too incensed for words, like a mute who cannot express his anguish. Shortly after that, the fourth list was published. Too indignant to sit or to stand, he walked out of the house and went straight to Oyama's house. "Oyama kun," he blurted out, "this is absolutely unheard of. I've never seen the likes of it. Even a barber has changed his name." After reading the article in the newspaper Kanai had brought with him, Oyama was speechless. Finally he released a loud sigh. Short-tempered and impatient, Kanai blurted out in Taiwanese, "Even the lowest of the low are changing their names." He believed that changing one's name was a great honor for a Taiwanese, for his family was now on a par with the Japanese.

Once a Taiwanese changed his name, he was just like the Japanese. But now that even barbers, shoe repairmen, and flute entertainers were changing their names, all his efforts vanished like bubbles; he could feel his status sliding into quicksand, with no hope of pulling himself out.

He agonized over this for a long moment before finally saying to Oyama in despair, "Things are going downhill. All the way down. You can't count on anything. If I'd known this earlier . . . " Without realizing it, he had uttered the truth. It felt to him much the same as if a beggar in rags had stormed into a party thrown by the gentry class.

One day at the local elementary school, Kanai Ryokichi and Ishida Saburo were walking so fast they bumped into each other. Ryokichi balled up his fist and slugged Saburo.

"Uppity dumbbell!" Saburo growled. "My family's changed our name too. I'm not afraid of you." He hit back.

"Your name is phony," Ryokichi replied.

Saburo refused to back down. "Yours is the real phony."

They went at each other in a free-for-all.

Since Saburo was stronger, Ryokichi was quickly pinned to the ground, with Saburo straddling him as he punched nonstop. Just then a sixth-grader walked up and shouted, "No fighting at school." The sixth-grader pushed Saburo off Ryokichi, who was by then sobbing. "Bakayaro!" he cursed. "You changed your name without owning an ofuro, so you're a real phony."

"If you're man enough, let's have it."

Their eyes bulging, the two of them exchanged insults. They would have been fighting again if the sixth-grader hadn't already stopped them. Ryokichi, unable to vent his anger, walked off shouting, "My father said a barber belongs to the lowest of the low. You're lowlife, lowly lowlife. Can't get any lower."

Kanai Ryokichi was the son of a public health physician, while Ishida Saburo's father ran a barbershop. They were third-graders at the same school. A few days after the incident, the barber's wife paid a secret visit to the doctor's mother. "Mistress, at school your little grandson calls others 'lowly lowlifes' and says they are phony. My little one feels too ashamed to show his face. Would you please talk to the doctor about this?"

Having softly pleaded with the doctor's mother, the barber's wife left.

After dinner, Kanai Shinsuke's family gathered round him and his wife, as usual, to enjoy each other's company. His oldest son, his daughter, along with his wife, the nurse, and the pharmacist, all took this opportunity to relax. At such times, Kanai Shinsuke proudly lectured them on the spirit of the Japanese: how they washed their faces, drank their tea, walked, and socialized. He then gave meticulous demonstrations to impress upon them what it meant to be Japanese. After that, his wife elaborated upon the beauty of the koto and the difficulty of ikebana, taking the opportunity to boast of her own accomplishments. The pharmacist, a movie fan, often spoke of his love of movies, while Kanai's eldest son, a college graduate who knew a bit of English, often contributed a few unintelligible phrases to the conversation. After everyone else had spoken, his daughter would pick up the koto and send tinkling melodies throughout the house. In the end they'd join in a chorus of Japanese songs, with the nurse singing louder and clearer than anyone else. That's how it went, night after night, without fail.

Only the doctor's mother refused to participate in the entertainment. After dinner, she would go alone to her room, where the mosquitoes would sometimes bite her feet. In the winter, she would sit up in bed against the headboard with a blanket over her legs to stay warm, since there was no brazier in her room. Occasionally she would look in on the entertainment room, but since they were all speaking Japanese, which she could not understand, she found them uninteresting. All she heard was a loud clamor and she had no idea what they were doing—which was why she went to her room after dinner. But not on the night after the visit from the barber's wife. Once everyone had settled in, she roared, "Xinfa, why did you teach Liangji [Ryokichi] to call the barber's family 'lowlifes'?"

Shinsuke hemmed and hawed, making excuses and trying to explain, but his mother shook her head to show she did not believe him, pointing out the fight Ryokichi had had at school as proof. When she'd scolded him enough, she explained some things to him: "You have forgotten your past. Your father was a laborer and a sedan-chair bearer. If you call a barber a lowlife, what would you call a sedan-chair bearer?"

Her forceful words seemed to have an effect on Shinsuke, who murmured his agreement.

But a few days later, he was once again acting like a puppet, manipulated by his old feelings.

On the morning of the fifteenth day, the doctor's mother coughed softly as she made her way to burn incense at the temple. The old beggar was waiting at the back gate, as always, and was shocked when he saw her. Alarmed, he said, "Mistress, you don't look so good. Are you not feeling well?"

Showing no concern, the doctor's mother replied lightly, "It's just old age."

She handed the beggar some money.

The next day she felt indisposed, and then she fell ill. Her condition worsened by the day and, although she felt a little better some of the time, the medicine she was taking could not cure her completely.

The old beggar, who knew nothing of her illness, came to wait by the back gate on the fifteenth of the following month, but no one came out. He grew increasingly anxious as he waited; he tried to look inside, but could not get a sense of what was wrong. It was nearly noon when the maid emerged.

"The doctor's mother isn't feeling well, and just now remembered that today is the fifteenth. She told me to bring this for you."

She turned to leave as soon she'd handed the beggar twenty yen. But when he saw that it was so much more than the usual five yen, he sensed that the doctor's mother was not doing well at all. He pleaded with the maid to let him see the old lady. Feeling sorry for him, the maid sneaked him inside, where he stood respectfully by the head of the bed. When the doctor's mother saw him, she struggled to prop her frail body up into a sitting position.

"I didn't think we'd see each other again. I'm glad you came. Really glad."

She happily invited the beggar to sit. But, conscious of his tattered clothes, the beggar did not want to sit on the glossy, clean stool. He declined several times, but after the doctor's mother's repeated invitations, he had no choice. That put her at ease and she began to chat with him. It was as if she had found someone who truly understood her, and she forgot her troubles. Finally, she said, "Old Brother, I won't be in this world much longer. My only wish is to enjoy one more of those crullers. Then I can die in peace."

Recalling the aroma of the crullers that she had eaten during the hard times, she wanted to taste one once more. But Shinsuke would not buy one, because his was a Japanese-only family that ate miso soup, not crullers.

The next day the beggar bought some crullers and sneaked them into the house. The doctor's mother happily bit into one and chewed it with great pleasure, praising its taste over and over.

"Old Brother, you know that we were once very poor. My husband did manual labor and I wove hats every day till midnight. Sometimes we had nothing to eat but sweet potatoes. But I think I was happier then than now. What's the point of having money? Having a son doesn't guarantee happiness. And a college graduate is useless."

She sighed as she talked, a heartrending sound to the beggar's ears. As the doctor's mother saw the sad second half of her life rushing past her eyes, tears streamed down her face. The beggar tried to comfort her. "Don't be so sad, Mistress. You'll get better."

"Better? No, I won't get better. Besides, what's the point of getting better?"

She muttered to herself as she took out some money from under her pillow for the beggar. After he left, she sent for Shinsuke to instruct him about her funeral.

"I don't know Japanese, so do not hire Japanese monks."

She continued with detailed instructions.

Her condition turned critical on the third day and then she died. But as Shinsuke was the chairman of the Customs Rectification Society, he did not follow her instructions. Instead of hiring Taiwanese monks, he held a Japanese-style funeral. Many people came to pay their respects, including the prefectural magistrate and the neighborhood head; not a single one of the area's powerful individuals was missing. But in spite of the grand spectacle, no one felt the loss of the doctor's mother, not even Shinsuke himself; for him the funeral was business, pure and simple. And yet, there was one person who was truly grief-stricken—the old beggar. He did not dare to get too close on the day of the funeral; instead he lagged behind and wept at the sight of her coffin. From then on, he prepared incense and paper money to burn by her grave on the fifteenth of each month. After burning the incense, he watched the swirling smoke and could not hold back his tears. He would sigh and say, "Ai! Old Mistress, now you're just like me."

1945

PART TWO

Fiction, 1949–1976

Wang Ruowang (1917–2001)

A VISIT TO HIS EXCELLENCY: A FIVE-MINUTE MOVIE

Translated by Hualing Nieh

1

An elderly man who was obviously from the country stopped at the building's entrance. He looked about sixty, and he carried under his arm a straw raincape and on his back a cloth bundle that made him seem humpbacked. He peered at the sign, almost fifteen feet long, above the building's entrance, then turned to detain a man passing by long enough to show him the envelope he carried. "You're at the right place," the man informed him, looking first at the envelope and then at the sign.

Intimidated by the size of the huge building, the old man was at a loss. He placed one foot through the doorway. Nothing terrible happened to him. He walked straight through the door, where he was greeted by a middle-aged man who came out of the doorman's room: "Hey, you. What are you doing?"

"I—I—nothing," the old man told him.

"You know where you are? These are government offices."

"I mean to find my son." The old man produced his envelope.

"Is this your letter of introduction?"

"No," the old man said.

"No visits without a letter of introduction," the doorman said.

"But I've got that there, at least," the old man said, gesturing toward the envelope.

"It's not enough." The doorman shook his head.

Disappointed, the old man made as if to leave, but paused and turned again toward the doorman. "I came from the country, clear from Shandong. That's a long hard trip."

The doorman had another look at the envelope. "Well, we don't have anybody here by this name."

"But the fellow outside just now told me I'd find my boy here. Cao Dingzhong is his name."

The doorman looked suddenly respectful, and a bit incredulous. "You mean the Minister?"

"Name's not the Minister," the old man corrected him. "Name's Cao Dingzhong."

"Well, everybody calls him the Minister. Nobody knows his name. Okay then, here, fill out the visitors' form."

The old man slumped into a chair and looked with some embarrassment at the pen and the registration book. "Well, Comrade," he said, "I can't write, exactly."

"If you don't sign then you can't visit," the doorman said. "The Minister made that rule himself."

Another visitor, a woman in her twenties, came into the building and presented the doorman with her letter of introduction. He pointed with his chin and pursed lips at the registration book. "Sign there." The woman signed, and filled out the form and gave it to him.

"What's your relationship to him?" the doorman asked with suspicion. "You didn't put it down."

The woman was impatient. "What do you mean, relationship? I don't have any relationship to him at all," she said.

"No relationship? Then what do you want to see him for?" The doorman seemed rather concerned.

"Call it comradeship then. It's a business visit," she said a little angrily.

"Then put 'comradeship' on the form, please," the doorman said.

The woman sat down again, and began filling in the blanks. The doorman looked her up and down with interest, and then picked up the phone. "A woman to see the Director."

The old man rose from his chair, looking helpless and anxious.

A man came from the interior of the building, heading for the entrance. "Hey," the doorman called after him. "Didn't you bring back your visitors' form?"

The man fumbled in his pockets with embarrassment. "I'm sorry," he said. "I suppose I left it upstairs."

"Then you'll have to go back and get it, please," the doorman informed him. "It has to be filed."

"Damn it, it's four flights up," the man said. He had no choice but to retrieve his form.

The doorman turned again to the young woman. "Okay, go on up. Don't forget to bring your form with you when you come back down." He turned to address the old man. "Now what are we going to do about you, Old Sir?"

"Please," the old man said. "Fill out the form for me."

The doorman dialed the phone.

In the Minister's office, the secretary answered and said: "What? The Minister? He's in conference. . . . His schedule is full. No visitors. . . . Well, if he has to see the Minister send him to the Director first. . . . What? From the country? Then send him to the People's Reception Room. It's in the Outlying District Administration of the City Government. . . . No, no, I said his schedule *is full*. . . . What do you mean, his father? . . . Okay, I'll tell the Minister."

2

In the reception room, Cao Dingzhong kept his distance from the old man from the country. "Father, I'm so glad you've come."

"It's some job finding this place," the old man said.

Cao surveyed his father, noting the straw raincape. "Why on earth did you bring that thing?"

"To keep dry when it rains," his father said. "I could sleep on it if I had to. Why, in the militia it was the only thing to use. Use it for a sheet and a blanket, both at once."

"But this is the city. It's out of place here." Cao pointed at the cloth bundle his father carried. "And what's this?"

"Treats, for the kids." The old man unwrapped the bundle and displayed a selection of fried cakes and sliced dried potatoes.

Shamefaced, Cao turned to look out the window. He covered the dried potatoes with the cloth they had been wrapped in. "All that way, and you brought these. I don't know if the kids will go for this stuff."

"But this is from home. The kids need to know how things taste back home."

Outside the building, a car drew to a halt. "Take him to my home, will you please?" Cao said to the secretary.

As the old man stepped into the car at the entrance, his straw raincape under his arm, the doorman ran to stop him. "Your form! Your visitors' form!"

The old man considered for a moment. "Well, looks like I didn't bring it back."

"Let him go," Cao said. "I'll make the form out for you."

3

Leaning against the car window, the old man observed the tall buildings with interest as they passed.

"Perky little thing, this car!" he told the secretary.

"Isn't it," the secretary said.

"Runs on the same fuel as a tractor, does it?"

"No," the secretary said. "Cars use gas. Tractors use diesel fuel. It's a little cheaper. A gallon of gas costs about four dollars."

"What's a gallon?" the old man asked.

"Oh, I guess about six bowls of rice would be a gallon of rice," the secretary said.

The driver interrupted. "A gallon takes you about twenty miles."

"Good Lord!" the old man said. "Six bowls of gas costs as much as a bushel of wheat. Stop the car," he told the driver. "Stop! If it takes a bushel of wheat to go twenty miles, I'll get out and use my feet."

The secretary laughed. "This is the city, Old Sir. Your son is the Minister. It's no trouble to anyone if you use up a little gas."

"I've got legs!" the old man said. "Stop this thing and let me use them!"

4

The old man entered the elegant apartment.

The two children, forgetting their toys for the moment, stood at a safe distance and examined the stranger.

The old man sat on the sofa, sinking into it so deeply he feared he could not rise again. He seemed angry. "Everything you touch hereabouts is some kind of a machine," he said. "This thing lacks the firmness of a mud bed."

Lushan, the little boy, was nine years old, and his sister, Qidong, was two years younger. Lushan now donned his grandfather's straw raincape and stood on the bench. "Lookit! Lookit! I'm Monkey![1] I can do somersaults."

Qidong had become very involved in her grandfather's cloth bundle. The old man handed her a piece of fried cake. "There you are," he told both children. "Your father ate this cake all his life. That's why he's big and husky today." He showed them the potato slices. "Can't eat these till they are cooked."

"Ick! Ack! Ugh!" Lushan announced, throwing his cake onto the floor. "It doesn't taste like our kind of cake."

The old man rescued the slice of cake and blew the dust from it. "This boy scorns *cake*? Waste of good food. Even heaven won't forgive this." He was talking to himself.

Cao's wife arrived home and found a country yokel lounging in her living room. She summoned the maid. "Did you admit this old peasant while we were out? What is he doing here?"

---

1. "Monkey" is a character in the classical Chinese novel *Xiyouji* (*Journey to the West*). It deals with the adventures of the Buddhist monk Tripitaka on his way across China to bring Buddhist texts back to India. His companion, Monkey, saved him from many disasters with his magical powers.

"He's the Minister's father," the maid put in hastily. "The Old Sir."

Cao's wife changed color, silent. She took a look at the old man, who was quite embarrassed at being referred to as a peasant. He had wanted to rise and greet her, but had hesitated. Now he stepped up to her. "I think, well, you must be my daughter-in-law."

"I must be," she said. "So sorry we didn't recognize one another. It's understandable, considering we haven't met before. Sit down, won't you?" She turned to catch sight of Qidong nibbling a slice of dried potato, and snatching it from her, examined the item. "What are you doing with this?" she said, giving her a slap. "It's for pigs. Where did you get it?"

"He was wearing Monkey clothes, Ma," Lushan said, pointing at his grandfather.

The old man sat on the sofa looking like a condemned man, his face in his hands.

"How's life in the country?" she asked indifferently.

"Things went bad this year," he said. "Lost the cotton. Lost the peanuts. If things had worked out, I could have brought some peanuts for the kids."

5

Cao Dingzhong had put his father to bed on a spring mattress that quivered each time the old man made the slightest movement. He turned and turned in the bed and could not sleep. "Around here, you even have to *sleep* on a machine." He was talking to himself. "I think I'm not enjoying it." He rose from the bed and located his straw cape. Spreading it on the floor, he lay down on it and slept.

Dawn came and the old man got up from the floor. "Will you look at this floor?" He was talking to himself again. "Smooth as a breadboard."

Lushan pushed the door open and peered in, looking ready for mischief. His expression changed to one of fright, and he retreated stealthily. "Monkey Grandpa was sleeping on the floor!" he reported to his sister.

Their father overheard this, and cuffed his son lightly. "Don't talk about your grandpa that way. He happens to be my father."

"If he's your father, Daddy, then how come he's not the Minister, like you?"

"Not everybody can be a Minister," Cao said.

His wife glanced toward the old man's bedroom. She seemed a bit irritated.

"What's the trouble?" Cao asked.

"It's just not right, having your old man around," she said.

"Why?"

"He's just . . . shabby. He'll give us a bad name, wandering around for everyone to see."

"What do you mean, 'shabby.' That's the way all peasants look. The trouble here is with your attitude. Well, all right. I've got a couple of old uniforms. We'll give them to him and see if we can work a miracle."

6

Cao examined his father before the full-length mirror. In his newly acquired woolen uniform, the old man looked awkward and uncomfortable. His neck was held stiffly and extended, and he could not move a step in the long-legged trousers. Standing before the mirror, he could not help laughing a bit as he twisted his beard with his hand. "How do I look?"

Lushan clapped his hands. "Now Grandpa can be the Minister too!"

Even Cao's wife stood by enjoying the sight, and she smiled, though a bit contemptuously.

Cao instructed his father in how to carry his new uniformed self. "You've got to stand up straight. Otherwise you don't look right in a uniform."

The old man began unbuttoning the uniform. "It's not my style. I don't think I can tolerate it."

"It's fine, it's fine," Cao told him. "In a few days you'll get used to it. Clothes make the man, you know. Look at yourself. In a different outfit, you're a different man." He looked his father over once more. "Now your only problem is your hair. You need a haircut right away."

Cao took a theater ticket from his portfolio. "There's going to be a show tonight, and this is your complimentary ticket. With this uniform you can sit right up front, and won't look the least bit out of place."

"Me too, Daddy, me too!" Lushan shouted.

Cao removed the visor cap from his head and put it on the old man's. "You look ten years younger," he said.

7

Wearing his woolen uniform and visor cap, walking with difficulty, the old man followed his son into a store displaying a selection of raincoats. The salesman showed one to them.

"Try it on, why don't you," Cao said. "It's a cut above that straw cape, don't you think?"

The old man donned the raincoat.

"What's the price?" Cao asked.

"Twenty-five dollars," the salesman told him.

Immediately the old man stripped himself of the raincoat. "No. Let it go."

"But it's a good fit," Cao said. "Twenty-five, that's not too expensive. Let's take it."

"Never. I'll take my old raincape anytime. It only set me back sixty cents. Lord above, this thing costs what five bushels of rice cost. In the country they'll all laugh at me."

"Take it anyway," Cao said.

"Never," the old man said.

8

Following his reformation, the old man seemed a denizen of the city. Burdened with several flat cakes and buns, he approached the apartment building's entrance, but was detained by the armed guard. "Who do you wish to see, please?"

The old man dropped a bun. "Why, I'm staying up here," he said as he tried to collect himself.

"Have you got a pass?"

"I just went out to get some *food*," the old man said.

"I can't let you in without the pass."

"Then just let me go in and get my cape. I'll go home. This is no place for the likes of me."

"You can't go up for any reason without the pass," the guard said coldly.

The old man squatted before the entrance, chewing on one of the buns. A car passed too near, honking loudly.

"You can't sit there. You're going to get yourself run over," the guard said.

With a troubled look the old man moved aside, trying to get out of the traffic. "I'll just wait here for him," he said. "He'll vouch for me when he gets back."

"Who the hell are you talking about?" the guard said.

"My son."

"You mean the Minister?"

"The Minister. If he wasn't the Minister I'd be having no trouble."

"You just came here?"

"I've been here a few days. Staying with them on floor number six."

"Well, then go to the guard's room and fill out a visitors' form."

"That form again! Sweet Lord, I can't go on!"

9

The old man changed back into his country clothes. Under his arm he carried his straw raincape. He stepped languidly out of the apartment building.

"Your visitors' form?" the guard said.

"You go to hell, and don't forget to take your forms. This is a government building. It's not for me. I'm gone." He walked rapidly away, as if departing from the scene of some disaster.

"Your form! Your form!" The guard's stern tones faded behind him.

The old man walked along the street in solitude, a long shadow following behind.

1957

Chen Yingzhen (1936–)

MY KID BROTHER KANGXIONG

Translated by Lucien Miller

When I was a young girl, I kept a diary and wrote letters, but I never thought of writing anything else. Strangely enough, here I am, in the second year of my marriage, taking pen in hand to record some things about my kid brother Kangxiong. Just this week I spent three whole days reading all the volumes of his diary from beginning to end. From Kangxiong's death through the first few months of my marriage, I would weep helplessly whenever I opened the diary. When I glimpsed his crabbed handwriting, I would immediately see a thin, pale youth sitting before my desk, a weary smile on his face. Suddenly I would be filled with a nameless sadness, and would cry and cry, unable to read on.

Two days ago I finally managed to complete the three volumes of the diary without becoming too agitated, most probably because his death has gradually become distant. Also, I've felt an enormous change since getting married, both physically and emotionally, and I don't just mean belonging to a man. All at once I was part of an extraordinarily wealthy family and no longer always hard up and caught short. This sudden Cinderella-like metamorphosis has been too much for me to absorb. In short, what I mean to say is this: in the face of my sumptuous new life, my grief for the one I revered has gradually wasted away.

"Wealth can poison much that is fine and delicate in human nature." This is what Kangxiong says in his diary. And he also observes: "Poverty itself is the greatest evil . . . it inevitably debases and sullies a person to some extent."

Is poverty behind my being depraved and tainted? Well, I don't want to put up any argument at all. I remember that when Kangxiong was alive, he always talked about things I didn't understand or that didn't make sense. But I never argued. Not once. This gives me great comfort now.

A wistful mood has settled on me.

In the winter following Kangxiong's death, I got married. Since the early fall when his grave was dug, an epitaph of disintegration and disillusionment, barely four months had passed. My sudden consent to marry my present husband, a rich man, completely surprised poor Father. This marriage business had been drawn out for nearly half a year, for I had intended that it wear itself out. I was secretly infatuated with a struggling painter who was to graduate from college the next summer, and I was also very much under the influence of my brother Kangxiong. Unaware of what I was doing, I unwittingly assumed his scorn for wealthy persons. Besides, my husband had always been one of those earnestly polite, straitlaced, upper-crust types whose every word is well spoken. Kangxiong and the dear artist I distantly admired were completely different from my husband. Their hair was long and unkempt; they had pallid complexions and puffy red circles under their eyes from bad diets. When they talked, there was an individuality to their speech that made listening to them a delight. Sometimes they would become neurotically depressed and not utter a sound for hours.

Immediately after my brother's sudden death, I was numb. Then came the bitter weeping and paralysis, until finally I felt a cold, clear awakening. It was as if overnight I had become exceptionally enlightened. I adopted the heroic view of the philosopher and said to myself: "From this time forward, may everything die!" I finally felt the truth of my father's words. My brother and the artist I admired from afar, and everything they stood for, were tainted with what my father called "infantilism." Poor Father, a self-educated social critic who had never made a name for himself. It has been six years since he turned to religion. My anarchist brother committed suicide;[1] that dear artist of mine had to quit school when he ran out of money, and ended up selling himself to an advertising agency. And as for me, a simple girl, what could I do? From this time forward, may everything die.

And so, with the heroic resignation of a Faust, I sold myself to wealth. This move rather comforted my poor father, who had lost his son in his old age. He had made every effort to urge me to seriously consider marrying into this wealthy home, because "a person ought to do her utmost to rid herself of the evil ghost of poverty, just as she ought to do everything possible to cast off sin." Apparently, he had another reason besides wealth for urging me to consider the marriage. The other party was from a righteous religious family of good repute; religious compassion had led a rich man to overlook our poverty and bestow

---

1. The author mixes up "anarchist" and "nihilist"; possibly he is attempting to reflect the muddleheaded views of the older sister, but he himself may be confused. Kangxiong is more nihilistic than anarchistic. We gather from his sister that he starts off with an anarchist's aspirations, then despairs, and becomes a nihilist and, finally, a suicide.

his glance upon me, a girl from a humble family. But I didn't think much about such considerations. Maybe what I really wanted to do, in consenting to marry, was to give my poor father a thread of comfort in his old age. He had not been able to escape poverty despite a lifelong trust in hard work and intelligence; his descendants would at last be freed, and all because of a little delicate feminine beauty. He could take consolation in knowing that the seed of his own flesh and blood would henceforth be planted in rich, lovely soil.

In fact, I was harboring the last vestiges of a rebellious consciousness when I put aside my girlish dreams. Just four months after Kangxiong's death I went to my wedding—an irreverent unbeliever standing before the altar and receiving the blessing of the priest. The whole affair gave me a feeling of defiant joy. But of course this joy was accompanied by a deep, hopeless mourning—grief at the loss of girlhood, but also a sad adieu to schools of social thought and modern art which I would never clearly understand. My last act of resistance, however, invigorated me with the faint excitement of revolution, destruction, massacre, and martyrdom. For a simple girl like myself, this was sufficient greatness.

Yet—and it is only now that I have come to understand this—my brother, throughout his eighteen years, never experienced the joy that accompanies action. "Nihilist that I am, I am devoid of that wild life which was Shelley's. Shelley lived in his dreams, but all I can do is mark time like a prophet. How fascinating—a nihilist prophet!" This is how Kangxiong described himself in his diary.

The wearisome watching and waiting which fills the latter half of the three diaries finally came to an end when he took poison. The youthful nihilist waited patiently like a small child, and childlike as well he sipped a dose of potassium cyanide. For me, what is most important about this diary, apart from nostalgia, is that it allowed me to trace the tortuous windings of the brief life of a young nihilist. The first volume describes the miseries of a romantic adolescent: the lack of willpower along with indulgence in masturbation. The first part of the second book explores the concerns of the fledgling nihilist. During this period, Kangxiong set up clinics, schools, and orphanages for the poor in his imaginary utopia. It was after this that he gradually took the road of anarchism and began that waiting which was so inappropriate for one his age.

My admiration for my brother deepened and strengthened as I came closer to the day of his suicide in the diary. It was here that I really perceived his truth. Kangxiong died in a mournful spirit of self-rebuke. In the nihilist's dictionary there is no God, much less any sin. Wasn't he really a nihilist? Wasn't he a Shelley after all?

In the summer of his last year, Kangxiong got a job at a warehouse to save money for the next semester's tuition. He rented space in a bunkhouse for workers near the warehouse. As my brother put it, the woman in charge was "the motherly type." Probably they fell in love—one can guess from the veiled language Kangxiong uses in the diary that he had already lost his virginity—

because he suddenly quit work and moved to a place called Pinyanggang in a neighboring county. I remember that during this brief period he wrote many letters home. He was out of work and could not rent a place to live. Reluctantly, he ended up living in a church. From this point on, there is nothing in the diary but self-incrimination, self-cursing, and self-torture. "I sought a fish and got a snake. I sought food and got a stone."

"I did not expect," he cries out helplessly, "that a person like me, who had pursued nihilism for so long, would end up unable to escape religion's moral law." And he adds, "Above the altar of the church hangs suspended the body of the crucified Jesus on His cross. Standing before this flesh, which never knew an instant of craving desire from birth to death, I see the supreme beauty that my loathsome self does not deserve to enjoy. I know I belong to the devil. I know my fate."

Such was the final trace my brother Kangxiong left of himself. His suicide occurred about half a month later. On the date of his death this aphorism is copied in his diary:

"Nothing is really beautiful but truth."—N. Boileau

I was overwhelmed by a feeling of contempt and a sense of absurdity because of these words, and also something bordering on the kind of joy one feels upon discovering a secret. No one in the world had understood my brother, not even myself; now, at least, I had some idea of Kangxiong's struggle before his death. Even my father could only say that his son's death originated in the madness and death wish of the nihilists of the previous century—and this was the most understanding thing anyone could ever say. The French priest, who stubbornly refused to grant a suicide a Catholic burial, was even more confused.

"I don't understand it," he said. "During his last days, I saw him with my own eyes secretly going into church in the dead of night and praying for a long time on his knees—it makes no sense."

But none of them knew that this young nihilist died because his utopia had fallen to pieces in a wicked world. Jesus, who with so much love and pain forgave the adulterous woman in front of a group of Jews—perhaps this Jesus can also forgive my brother Kangxiong. But in the end Kangxiong could not forgive himself. A newly born lust and passion, along with anarchism and God or Jesus—all these conspired to kill him.

(Because of this I want to sue for justice.)[2]

Kangxiong's funeral was one of the loneliest imaginable. In Pinyanggang we did not have a single relative, not even a distant one. Following behind the

2. Why parentheses? The author has the sister diarist use parentheses from time to time. They indicate a mood change on the diarist's part, or else a point where she comments on what she is saying.

rough wooden casket were only a withered old man and a disheveled young girl. There were no tears. The pitiful procession wound its way through the streets of Pinyanggang and out to the desolate fields beyond the town. After the burial, father and daughter remained sitting face-to-face at the graveside, their forlorn shadows lengthened by the setting sun of an autumn afternoon. The plain was a swath of reed flowers—an endless bloom of cotton-white. Like an arrow, a black crow cut through the ash-gray sky. As I walked out of the cemetery, I turned and stared at my brother Kangxiong's new dwelling place: the freshly turned dirt and the gravestone. How repulsive! Still another black crow, like an arrow, cut through the ash-gray sky.

It was not until my wedding that my feeling of humiliation was eased. The priest and those officiating all wore new vestments, and I was told that the choir was made up of boys especially selected to sing for me. Throughout the entire ritual I held up my head. I had wanted to see what pious people were like, to observe the grand entertainment of the leisure class, to gaze at stained-glass windows, but instead I found myself looking at Jesus suspended from the wooden cross. Though it was a man's naked body, it transcended sexual and physical being. I remembered the preparation of my brother's body for burial. When my father and I had entered Kangxiong's room, his corpse was lying on its back on the edge of the bed. One hand trailed to the floor; the other was placed on his chest. His head was settled comfortably on a large pillow. His face looked pale, yet so lovely and at peace. Smears of bloody sputum that he must have coughed up stained his snow-white shirt. A mere boy, one who had innocently played the role of immoralist in the forbidden garden. In his innocence he had stolen a taste of passion's forbidden fruit, and now he had naively destroyed his life. Now all that had been Kangxiong was obliterated—all except for that breath of innocence anointing his whole body. When I first saw the body of my long-estranged brother, the brother I loved, I cried and threw myself on his cold breast. At the time of the washing of the body, my father was almost useless, so, for the first time since grammar school, I saw the naked body of my eighteen-year-old brother. His torso was pure white like a girl's, his hair full and lovely, his brows finely shaped. His physique was not yet mature.

I seemed to see my brother Kangxiong with his undeveloped body coming down from the cross and smiling warmly at me. Immediately I remembered a letter from him and heard his voice murmuring: "Though I am a nihilist, of course I must come to your wedding, for I love you. I love you deeply, as I love our dead mother."

Instantly my vision blurred with tears, though I remained steadfast. I had to rebel, and rebel like a martyr. A martyr should not cry.

It's been two years now. I've become indolent, affluent, and beautiful. My husband is temperate and polite, and is becoming well known in his church. At morning mass, when he escorts me up the stairs to the entrance of the church, he is especially considerate and gentle. We have reserved seats in the very first pew, but I can never bring myself to look up at that male body hanging from the cross—in some deep recess of my mind, two gaunt torsos become fused into one. To say that this is fear is preferable to saying it is a kind of mourning, isn't it? The grief that moved me to tears has long since abated. This makes me feel sorry. Could it be that wealth really "destroyed" part of my "fine and delicate nature"? Or is it that poverty made me "depraved" and "tainted"? Well, I don't want to argue at all, but I have made every effort to make amends. I've privately helped that poor father of mine financially—he's now teaching philosophy at a second-rate university and studying theology and the classics. And as for my brother Kangxiong, I've been considering taking advantage of the special affection my in-laws have for me. I could get my powerful father-in-law to use his influence in the church so that Kangxiong might have a cross over his grave; I want to make up for the feeling of inferiority and humiliation that is deep within me. But it occurs to me that this wouldn't be something that would please my kid brother. So I've made up my mind to rebuild his gravesite and make it luxurious. Once this wish is fulfilled, I probably can pamper myself in peace and live out an opulent life under the care of a doting husband.

1960

Bai Xianyong (1937–)

WINTER NIGHTS

Translated by John Kwan-Terry and Stephen Lacey

In Taipei, winter nights are usually cold and wet. A chill gust of wind was blowing again this evening and then, without warning, the rain fell, pitter-pattering onto the pavements. The alleys around Wenzhou Street already were under more than an inch of water. Professor Yu Qinlei made his way to the entrance of the alley where he lived, and looked around. On his feet were a pair of wooden clogs, and he held a torn, old-fashioned umbrella made of oil-paper; through the gaping hole the raindrops dribbled down onto his bald head. He was wrapped in his customary thick, padded gown, but even this was no protection against the bone-chilling cold of a Taipei winter night. He hunched his shoulders and shivered.

The alley was shrouded in a hazy gray mist. Not a shadow of a creature could be seen anywhere. The heavy silence was broken only by the sound of the rain that fell like a faint shower of fine-grain sand on the tiled roofs of the low houses that stretched far and near. Professor Yu stood stiffly in the cold rain, his hands propping up the torn umbrella. After a while, he turned around and plodded back to his house in the alley. He was lame in his right leg, and in his clogs he shuffled along very awkwardly, his body jerking to one side at every step.

The house that Professor Yu made his shelter looked exactly the same as the other University quarters in the alley, old buildings that had survived the Japanese occupation. It bore all the scars of long neglect. The eaves, door, and windows were moldering from decay and disrepair. The sitting-room floor was still covered with tatami mats, heavy with years of dampness. They emitted a faint odor of rotting straw that hung in the air at all times of the day. The sitting room itself was simply furnished: a desk, a tea table, a pair of tattered armchairs so worn with age that the cotton padding was hanging out of the burst seams. Books were chaotically strewn about the desk, chairs, and tatami mats. These were books in hard covers once, but the binding had come off some, mold had eaten into others, and many were scattered about like so many disembodied corpses with missing heads and limbs. Incongruously entangled in the confusion were a few storybooks of knight errantry bound in brown paper and rented from neighborhood bookshops. Ever since the day Professor Yu chastised his wife in extreme ill humor, no one had ventured to touch even a single stray page in that pileup in the sitting room. Some time before, his wife had taken his books out to air and lost his notes on Byron's poems, which he had left between the pages of an Oxford edition of the poet's works. He had written these notes when he was teaching at Beijing University more than twenty years ago and they contained the fruits of long study and reflection.

Professor Yu went into the sitting room and dropped onto one of the tattered sofas, panting slightly. He massaged the joints in his wounded leg a few times vigorously with his hands, because whenever the weather turned damp and cold they would start to ache. In the afternoon, just before his wife went to Professor Xiao's next door for a game of mahjong, she had specifically admonished him: "Don't forget! Stick on that plaster from the Yushan Herb Clinic."

"Please be back early this evening, all right?" he had replied solicitously. "Wu Zhuguo is coming."

"What's all the fuss about Wu Zhuguo? Won't you be enough company for him by yourself?" She wrapped up some bank notes in her handkerchief and walked out the front door.

He was holding a copy of the *Central Daily News* in his hands, and had wanted to stop his wife to show her the photo of Wu Zhuguo with the caption: "Professor Wu Zhuguo, world-renowned historian residing in the United States, gave a lecture at the Academia Sinica yesterday. More than one hundred scholars and dignitaries attended." Unfortunately he was not quick enough. His wife had raced out the door before he could get in another word. Mrs. Xiao scheduled mahjong games for Tuesday, Thursday, and Saturday, and his wife never missed a single session. Whenever he would begin to protest, she would seal his mouth with: "Don't spoil the sport, old man. I'm going to win a hundred dollars and stew a chicken for you." He couldn't impose economic sanctions on her, because she invariably came back on the credit side and had her own private hoard to draw on. Earlier he had suggested that they invite Wu Zhuguo over for a family dinner, but as soon as he brought up the subject, he was vetoed.

As her ample broad back stomped out the door, a feeling of helpless resignation suddenly overwhelmed him. If Yaxing were still here, she would help him welcome his guest properly; she would go to the kitchen herself and prepare a whole table of Wu Zhuguo's favorite dishes. He remembered the time they entertained Wu Zhuguo when he was about to leave for the States. They were living in Beiping [Beijing] then. Wu Zhuguo ate and drank till he was quite lit up and red in the ears. It was then he said to Yaxing, "Yaxing, I'll have more of your Beijing duck when I'm back next year." Who could have known that the next year Beijing would fall? So Wu Zhuguo's one trip abroad lasted twenty years.

At Songshan Airport the other day, when Wu Zhuguo finally arrived in Taipei, he was engulfed in such a flood of people—government officials, newspaper reporters, and curious onlookers—that not a shadow could have slipped through. Yu Qinlei saw him, but was elbowed out to the fringe of the crowd and didn't even have a chance to greet him from a distance. Wu Zhuguo was wearing a black woolen overcoat and a pair of silver-rimmed glasses. He had a rich crop of snow-white shiny hair. With pipe in hand, he looked completely poised answering the questions put to him by the reporters. He had mellowed with the passing years; now he carried himself with the eminence and deportment befitting a scholar who inspired immediate respect wherever he went. In the end it was Wu Zhuguo who spotted him in the crowd. He squeezed his way forward and, gripping Yu Qinlei's hand, whispered close to his ear, "Let me come to see you in a couple of days. It's impossible to talk here."

"Qinlei . . . "

Professor Yu got up hastily and limped to the door to welcome the caller. Wu Zhuguo was already walking up the entranceway.

"I had been waiting for you at the alley entrance. I was afraid you couldn't find your way." Professor Yu then knelt down and fumbled in a low cupboard near the doorway. It took him a while to produce a pair of straw slippers, which he gave to Wu Zhuguo to change into; one was so worn that the front section had popped open at the toe.

"The alleys in Taipei are like a labyrinth." Wu Zhuguo smiled. "Even more confusing than the *hutong*[1] of Beijing." His hair was dripping wet, and tiny drops of water had formed a film on his silver spectacles. He took off his overcoat, shook it a few times, and handed it to Professor Yu. He was wearing under the overcoat a jacket of padded silk. As he was sitting down, he pulled out his handkerchief and gave his head and face a brisk rub. When he was finished, his silvery-white hair was all fluffed and disheveled.

"I've been wanting to bring you here myself." Professor Yu took out the thermoflask which was usually reserved for his own use, brewed some Dragon Well tea in it, and placed the glass before Wu Zhuguo; he still remembered that Wu Zhuguo did not drink black tea. "But knowing how busy you must be these few days, I thought I wouldn't go and jostle with the crowd."

"We Chinese do have a weakness for lavish entertainment, don't we?" Wu Zhuguo shook his head gently and smiled. "I've been attending banquets every day for the last few days, and each time it was twelve courses, fifteen courses . . ."

---

1. Traditional term for alleys.

"At this rate, if you stay on longer, you'll eat your way back to your old stomach trouble," Professor Yu said, smiling. He sat down opposite Wu Zhuguo.

"I'll say. It's already been too much for my stomach. Shao Ziqi gave a dinner tonight, and I just couldn't eat anything at all. . . . He told me it's been several years since you last saw each other. The two of you . . . " Wu Zhuguo fixed his gaze on Yu Qinlei, who, passing a hand over his smooth, bald head, heaved a quiet sigh and smiled. "He is a government official now and a busy man. Even if we were to see each other, we wouldn't find anything to talk about. Besides, I'm not good at idle talk, least of all with him. So it might be just as well that we don't run into each other. You remember, don't you, the year all of us joined the Society for the Common Cause? What was the first oath we all took?"

Wu Zhuguo smiled. "Not to join the Government for twenty years."

"And to think that it was Shao Ziqi who led the oath-taking that day! Oh, of course, of course, the twenty years have long expired." Professor Yu and Wu Zhuguo both laughed at the same time. Wu Zhuguo held the glass of green tea in both hands, gently blew aside the tea leaves swimming on the surface, and took a sip. The tea was hot, and the vapor fogged up his spectacles. He took them off and, while cleaning them, squinted as if he were trying to concentrate, then sighed deeply. "Yes. Now I have come back, and most of our old friends in the Society have passed away . . . "

"Jia Yisheng died last month," Professor Yu replied. "It was tragic the way he died."

"I read about it in the papers abroad. They didn't report it in detail though."

"Very tragic . . . " Professor Yu murmured. "I saw him on campus the day before he died. By then, his neck had gone stiff, and his mouth was twisted to one side. He had fallen six months earlier and ruptured an artery. When I saw how terrible he looked, I did my best to persuade him to go home and rest. All he did was force a smile. It was pitiful. I knew, of course, that he was broke and, on top of it all, his wife was in the hospital. That same night he had to teach evening classes. At the school entrance, he slipped into a shallow gutter, and that was the end." Professor Yu threw out both hands and gave a dry laugh. "So Jia Yisheng breathed his last, just like that."

"Really. So that's how," Wu Zhuguo mumbled vaguely.

"I heard that Lu Chong also passed away. Living abroad, you probably know more about this than we do here."

"Yes, and I guessed what was coming long before it happened," Wu Zhuguo sighed. "During the 'Let a Hundred Flowers Bloom' backlash, the students at Beijing University tried to purge him. They accused him of championing Confucianism in his *History of Chinese Philosophy* and forced him to write a confession. How could a man of Lu Chong's temperament take that? So at that point, in front of all the students, he jumped off a building."

"Good! Good for him, I'd say!" Professor Yu suddenly exclaimed and gave his knee two sharp slaps. "What a man. I bow to him. He died a martyr, a 'Confucian man of character'!"

"Still, the irony of life in his case was too cruel, perhaps." Wu Zhuguo shook his head. "For after all, wasn't he one of the big denouncers of Confucius and Company?"

"Precisely," Professor Yu laughed helplessly. "Just take the few of us—Shao Ziqi, Jia Yisheng, Lu Chong, you, me, and that great traitor who was executed, Chen Xiong—what was the resolution we made together when we were at Beida?"[2]

Wu Zhuguo took out his pipe, lit it, inhaled deeply, then blew the smoke out slowly, his mind for the moment lost in thought. Then all of sudden he began shaking his head and laughing to himself. He leaned forward toward Professor Yu and said, "Let me tell you something, Qinlei. Most of the courses I give at universities abroad cover Chinese history only up to the Tang or Song dynasty. I've never offered a course on the Republican era. Last semester, at the University of California, I gave a course on the Tang political system. This was the time when student riots were at their peak in America. Our students were the worst—they burned down classrooms, chased out the Chancellor, and beat up the instructors. I must confess, that sort of stupidity really bothered me. One afternoon, I was lecturing on the civil examination system in the early Tang. Outside the students were scuffling with the police, who were spraying tear gas all over campus. The whole place looked like a madhouse. It was beyond endurance! Just imagine—I was lecturing on seventh-century China. Under those conditions, what interest could that hold for our tousle-haired, barefooted young American kids, only screaming for action? They were sitting in the classroom, but their attention was constantly drawn to the scene outside. I put down my book and announced: "So *this* is what you call a 'student riot,' is it? I have a few things to tell you. More than forty years ago, the students in Beijing started a revolt which was a hundred times more explosive than yours." This seemed to jolt them, all right. They looked incredulous, as if to say, "Chinese students revolting? Don't be ridiculous!" Wu Zhuguo and Professor Yu burst into laughter at the same time. "And so, I explained. 'On May 4, 1919, a bunch of Beijing University students, rising in protest against the Japanese, fought their way into the compound of a treacherous Government official, set fire to his house, and then dragged out the envoy to Japan who was hiding there and gave him the beating of his life.' By this time, the room was dead silent and the students were listening with awed attention. After all, they had been prattling about the war in Vietnam, but they never had enough guts to burn down the Pentagon! Then I went on: 'Later, this group of students, about a thousand of them, were imprisoned in Beida's Law Building.' Seeing that I had their attention, I slowly announced: 'The leader of the group who beat up the envoy is yours truly, standing here in front of you.' The whole room roared with laughter, some of

2. *Beida* is the short form of "Beijing Daxue," i.e., Beijing University.

the students stamping their feet, others clapping. They didn't even hear the sound of the gunfire outside." Professor Yu was shaking with laughter himself, and his bald head was bouncing up and down in response.

"Everybody asked at once how we attacked Zhao's Pavilion.[3] So I told them that we climbed into Cao Rulin's house on each other's shoulders, forming a sort of human pyramid. The first man who jumped over the wall lost his shoes and then, barefooted, ran like mad all over the garden setting fire to everything in sight. 'Where's that student now?' they asked in one voice, and I said, 'He is teaching in a university in Taiwan, teaching Byron.' They doubled up, laughing hysterically."

Professor Yu couldn't help blushing, and his wrinkled face broke into a boyish smile. He sat there grinning with embarrassment and then looked down at his feet. He did not have his slippers on, but was wearing a pair of coarse woolen socks with two large black patches sewn on at the heels. Unconsciously, he brought his feet together and rubbed them against each other several times.

"I told them: 'When we were prisoners in the school building, a lot of college girls came to give us moral support. One of them, the beauty queen from a woman's normal school, and the barefoot arsonist became China's Romeo and Juliet of the moment and got married eventually.'"

"You're pulling my leg, Zhuguo." Professor Yu ran his hand over his bald head. There was a nostalgic expression in his smile. Then, noticing that Wu Zhuguo's tea was getting cold, he got up and limped over to pick up the thermoflask. As he was refilling his friend's glass with boiling water, he retorted, "And why didn't you tell your students who it was that proudly bore a flag that day, and had his glasses broken during a fight with the police?"

"Well," Wu Zhuguo said, somewhat embarrassed, "I did tell them how Jia Yisheng slit his finger and wrote in his own blood 'Qingdao back to China' on the wall, and how Chen Xiong paraded in the streets, dressed in mourning and carrying a funeral scroll with the inscription 'Cao, Lu, Zhang stink.'"

"Jia Yisheng . . . All along, he hoped to achieve something important in life . . . " Professor Yu sat down and drew a long breath.

"Do you know if he finished writing his *History of Chinese Thought*?" Wu Zhuguo asked with concern.

"Actually, I'm in the process of editing his manuscripts. He only got to the Neo-Confucianism of the Song and Ming. But . . . " Professor Yu knitted his brow. "Well, he seemed to have been in a great hurry over the last chapters. His thinking was not as perceptive as before. I haven't been able to find a publisher for his book yet. We even had to pool our resources—a few of us, his old friends—to pay for his funeral."

"Oh?" Wu Zhuguo could not hide his surprise. "Was he really that . . . "

---

3. "Zhao's Pavilion" was the historical name for Cao Rulin's mansion.

The two men sat facing each other and fell silent. Wu Zhuguo slipped his hands into his sleeves while Professor Yu tapped his rheumatic leg absent-mindedly.

"Zhuguo . . . " Yu Qinlei hesitated, then raised his head and looked at his visitor. "There's no question about it, you are the most successful of our group."

"Me? Most successful?" Wu Zhuguo looked up, startled.

"It's true, Zhuguo!" Professor Yu's voice betrayed a note of agitation. "Look at me. What have I accomplished all these years? Absolutely nothing! Every time I picked up the papers and read reports of your performance abroad, I couldn't help feeling mortified . . . yet comforted, too, that there's you at least to vindicate all our lost hopes." As he spoke, he stretched his arm and gave Wu Zhuguo a gentle squeeze on the shoulder.

"Qinlei . . . " Wu Zhuguo blurted out as he tried to free himself from his grasp. Professor Yu found his friend's voice filled with agony. "Don't talk like that, please. You leave me nothing to stand on!"

"How? . . . " Yu Qinlei mumbled confusedly and withdrew his hand.

"Qinlei, let me tell you something, and you'll understand how it felt to be out of the country all these years." Wu Zhuguo put his pipe down on the tea table, took off his silver-rimmed spectacles, and with his other hand kneaded the heavy wrinkles between his eyes. "I know what most people are thinking. They think I am having a good time visiting this country and that, giving lectures here, attending conferences there. Well, last year, I was at a convention of the Oriental History Society in San Francisco. In one session there was an American student freshly graduated from Harvard who read a paper entitled, 'A Re-evaluation of the May Fourth Movement.' From the start this young fellow tore the movement to pieces. He was obviously carried away by his own eloquence. But it was his conclusion. His conclusion! These overzealous young Chinese intellectuals, he said, in an iconoclastic outburst against tradition completely wiped out the Confucian system that had prevailed in China for over two thousand years. They were ignorant of the current condition of their country; they blindly worshiped Western culture, and had an almost superstitious belief in Western democracy and science. This created an unprecedented confusion in the Chinese intellectual climate. That is not all. As the Confucian tradition they attacked cracked up, these young people, who had grown up in a patriarchal system and lacked both independence of inquiry and the willpower to hold their own, found that they were in fact losing their only source of spiritual sustenance, and, gripped by a sense of panic, they began to wander about like lost souls haunted by the specter of a murdered father. They had overthrown Confucius, their spiritual father, and so they had to go through life carrying the burden of their crime. Thus began the long period of their spiritual exile: some threw themselves into totalitarianism; some retreated and took refuge in their tattered tradition; some fled abroad and became wise hermits concerned only with themselves. Thus what started as a revolutionary movement disintegrated and changed its nature. Then he concluded: 'Some Chinese scholars like to compare the May Fourth Movement to a Chinese Renaissance. But I consider it, at best, to be a cultural miscarriage!'

"By the time he finished reading the paper, there was a great deal of excitement in the room, especially among the several Chinese professors and students. Everyone turned to look at me, obviously expecting some sort of rebuttal. But I didn't say a thing, and after a while, quietly left the room."

"But, Zhuguo . . . "

"To tell you the truth, Qinlei, some of the youngster's conclusions wouldn't be difficult to refute. The only thing is . . . " Wu Zhuguo spoke with a lump in his throat. He hesitated a moment, then gave a nervous laugh. "Just think, Qinlei. During all these years of living abroad—they add up to several decades—what have I been really? A plain deserter. And on an occasion like that, how could I have mustered enough self-respect to stand and speak up for the May Fourth Movement? That's why, too, in all my expatriate days, I've never talked about the history of the Republican period. That time at the University of California I saw how excited the students were in the middle of their movement, so I mentioned May Fourth only to humor them—it was no more than a joke. The glories of the past are easy to talk about. I don't have to feel ashamed when I tell my students, 'The Tang dynasty created what must have been the most powerful, and culturally the most brilliant, empire in the world at that period in history.' And I have been making such pronouncements abroad all these years. Sometimes I couldn't help laughing to myself and feeling like one of Emperor Xuan Zong's white-haired court ladies, who just kept telling foreigners the anecdotes of the Tianbao reign."

"But Zhuguo, what about all your writings?" Professor Yu tried to cut him short with a vehement objection.

"Yes, I've written a few books, like *The Power and Office of the Tang Prime Ministers, Frontier Commanders of Late Tang,* and a monograph on *Pear Garden Actors of Emperor Xuan Zong.*[4] Altogether, I must have put on paper several hundred thousand words, but they are just empty words, all of them . . . " Wu Zhuguo was sawing the air with his hands and almost shouting. Then he laughed. "These books are stacked in the library gathering dust. Who will flip through them except perhaps, now and then, a student working on his Ph.D.?"

"Zhuguo, your tea is getting cold. I'll go get you a fresh cup." As Professor Yu stood up, Wu Zhuguo suddenly grabbed his wrist and, looking up at him, said, "Qinlei, I'll tell you this frankly. All that stuff has been written only to fulfill the requirements of the American university system: 'publish or perish.' That's why every couple of years I would squeeze out a book. If I hadn't been required to publish, I would certainly not have written a single word."

---

4. "Pear Garden" is the location in his palace where Emperor Xuan Zong established the well-known operatic company and training institute.

"I'll go make you a fresh cup of tea," Professor Yu repeated vaguely. He noticed that a slight twitching had begun to show on Wu Zhuguo's scholarly looking face. He dragged himself over to a table at one corner of the sitting room, emptied the cold dregs into the spittoon, and made a fresh cup of Dragon Well tea. Then, holding the thermoflask in both hands, he limped slowly back to his seat, betraying signs of great exertion. His right leg was feeling more and more stiff from prolonged sitting, and the numbing pain seemed to come in waves, seeping out from the very marrow of the bones. After he had sat down, he began to knead his leg firmly with one hand.

"You seem to have hurt your leg pretty badly," Wu Zhuguo said. There was a note of concern in his voice as he received the hot tea.

"It's never recovered from that accident. Still, I suppose I'm lucky that I wasn't crippled."

"Have you tried everything you can with the doctors?"

"Don't even mention doctors to me!" Professor Yu shook his hand emphatically. "I stayed five months in Taiwan University Hospital. They operated on me, they gave me electrotherapy, they did this and that to me, and the result was that my leg got steadily worse. Eventually I became paralyzed. Then my wife, in spite of my objections, got—I don't know where—an acupuncturist to treat me. And after a few jabs with some needles, believe it or not, I could walk again!" Yu Qinlei threw his hands up in a gesture of resignation. "We Chinese are a funny lot when it comes to being ill. Sometimes Western treatment just won't work, and we simply have to turn to some secret cure of native therapy, like acupuncture. A few random jabs of the needle sometimes unlock the secret of the trouble." They both shook their heads slowly and smiled. Then Wu Zhuguo stretched out his hand and gave Professor Yu a gentle pat on the troublesome leg, "You don't know, Qinlei. Whenever I thought of you and Jia Yisheng, I couldn't help feeling ashamed of myself. Look what hard lives you lead here, and yet you still stand firm, educating our own young people." As he spoke, his voice began to quiver. He gave his friend another light pat and continued, "Qinlei, it's really not been easy for you."

Professor Yu fixed his gaze on Wu Zhuguo without saying a word. Then he scratched his bald head and broke into a smile. "All my students are girls now. There wasn't a single boy in my courses last semester."

"Well, you're teaching Romantic literature, and girls naturally take to it."

"Yes. There was this girl who asked me, 'Was Byron really that handsome?' And I told her, 'Byron was a cripple. I'm afraid he was worse than me!' There was such a pained expression on her face that I had to comfort her, so I quickly added 'But he did have a ravishingly handsome face.'" Professor Yu and Wu Zhuguo burst out laughing. "In my final exam last semester, I asked them to define Byron's romantic spirit. One girl wrote down an impressive list of Byron's mistresses, including his sister Augusta!"

"Still, I must say, teaching young girls has its rewards. How is your translation of Byron's *Collected Poems* selling? It must be in great demand here."

"I've never finished translating it."

"Oh . . . "

"Actually, only the last few cantos of *Don Juan* remain to be translated. These seven or eight years I haven't written a single word. And even if I had translated the whole of Byron, I'm afraid there wouldn't be many people who would read it now." Professor Yu heaved a sigh and looked directly at Wu Zhuguo. "Zhuguo, all these years, I haven't been doing what you imagined at all. 'Standing firm,' as you put it, has been the last thing in my mind. To tell you the truth, I have spent my time figuring out ways to go abroad . . . "

"Qinlei, you . . . "

"Yes. I've not only wanted to go abroad, I have also tried to grab every opportunity to leave the country. Each year, as soon as I learned about any foreign grants to our Arts Faculty, I was always the first to apply. Five years ago, after a great deal of trouble, I finally got a Ford Foundation fellowship for two years of research at Harvard. I was to be given almost ten thousand U.S. dollars a year. All my travel arrangements and formalities were being taken care of. The day I went to the American Consulate to have my visa signed, the Consul even shook my hand and congratulated me. But—can you imagine—as I was stepping out of the Consulate gates, a Taida[5] student, riding past on his motor scooter, drove straight into me. The next thing I knew, I had a broken leg."

"Oh, Qinlei!" Wu Zhuguo was speechless.

"Anyway, when I was in the hospital, I should have given up the fellowship immediately. Instead, I wrote to Harvard to say that my injuries were only minor, and that I would leave for the States as soon as I was better. But I wound up staying five months, and by the time I came out, Harvard had withdrawn the fellowship. If I had given it up right away, then Jia Yisheng would probably have gotten to go."

"Jia Yisheng?" Wu Zhuguo exclaimed.

"Yes, he had applied for the fellowship as well. That's why when he died I felt so wretched; I felt I'd done him a bad turn. If he had been able to go to America on that fellowship, he wouldn't have died the way he did. When he passed away, I went all over the place to collect contributions for his funeral expenses. His wife, as I told you, was also very sick in the hospital. I wrote to Shao Ziqi, but he didn't come himself. He just dispatched someone with a contribution—and only a thousand Taiwan dollars at that."

"Ah," Wu Zhuguo sighed.

"The fact is, Zhuguo," Professor Yu blushed slightly, then looked directly at his friend, "I needed that fellowship very much myself. When Yaxing passed away, my two sons were still small. Before she died, she made me promise to bring them up properly and to give them the best education possible. When my older son went abroad to study engineering, he was not on any scholarship.

---

5. Short form of "Guoli Taiwan Daxue," i.e., National Taiwan University.

I had to borrow money—and a considerable amount, as it turned out—to finance his studies. I have been repaying it for a number of years, but I'm still in the red. That's why at that time I thought that if I got the fellowship and used it sparingly I would be able to pay off all my debts. How would I know that . . . "

Wu Zhuguo raised his hand and was about to say something, but his lips only moved a little and then he fell silent. After a while, he forced himself to smile, "Yaxing—she was really an unforgettable woman."

Outside, the rain came down more heavily, beating on the rooftop with increasing insistence. The cold crept into the room through every available crack along the door and windows. Suddenly the front door opened and banged shut, and a young man entered through the narrow doorway. He was tall and wore a navy blue plastic raincoat. His jet-black hair glistened with raindrops. He was carrying a pile of books under one arm. He nodded with a smile and continued on his way toward his room.

"Junyan, come meet Uncle Wu," Professor Yu called to the young man. Wu Zhuguo glanced briefly at his fine, handsome face.

"Why, Qinlei, you two . . . " Wu Zhuguo laughed in spite of himself and gestured toward Junyan: "Junyan, if I had seen you first when I came here, I would have thought your father had regained his youth! Qinlei, you know you looked exactly like that when you were at Beida." The three of them burst out laughing.

"Uncle Wu is teaching at the University of California. Didn't you say you would like to study there? Well, here's your chance. You can ask Uncle Wu all about it."

"Uncle Wu, is it easy to get a fellowship in physics at the University of California?" Junyan asked with interest.

"Well . . . " Wu Zhuguo hesitated a moment. "I'm not too up on that. Of course, there is more financial aid in the sciences than in the humanities."

"Is it true that the Physics Department often spends more than half a million dollars on one single experiment?" Junyan's youthful face gleamed with envy.

"America is a very rich country, after all," Wu Zhuguo responded. Junyan stood there for a while, then excused himself. Watching the retreating figure of his son. Professor Yu whispered, "Every young man nowadays dreams of going abroad to study science or engineering."

"Yes, that's the trend, that's the trend."

"We went all out for 'Mr. Science' in our time, didn't we? Now look what science has done—it's almost snatched away our rice bowl!" The two men laughed. Professor Yu stood up to fetch some fresh tea, but Wu Zhuguo stopped him hurriedly and stood up himself.

"I am scheduled to give a lecture early tomorrow morning at the National

Zhengzhi University.[6] I think I ought to be leaving." He hesitated, then resumed in a low voice, "Day after tomorrow, I'm flying to West Germany to attend a conference on Sinology. Please save yourself the trouble of seeing me off. I'll say good-bye here."

Professor Yu handed Wu Zhuguo his overcoat and said apologetically, "Really . . . now you've finally come back, and I haven't even asked you over for dinner. My present wife . . . " Professor Yu mumbled embarrassedly, but Wu Zhuguo interrupted him, "Oh yes, I almost forgot! I haven't met your wife."

"She's next door," Professor Yu squirmed slightly, "playing mahjong."

"Oh, well, then please give her my regards, will you?" Wu Zhuguo walked toward the door as he spoke. Professor Yu slipped on his wooden clogs, took up his tattered umbrella, and followed behind.

"Oh, no, no, don't come out. It's too difficult for you."

"You didn't bring your hat. Let me walk you part of the way." Professor Yu put one arm around Wu Zhuguo's shoulders and held the paper umbrella over his friend's head as they made their way carefully out into the alley. The alley was steeped in darkness, and the rain fell endlessly, a torrential downpour swept furiously about by the wind. Leaning against each other, their feet soaked in pools of water, their backs staggering under the weight of the wind, the two men trudged slowly along, taking one sluggish step at a time. When they were almost at the entrance to the alley, Wu Zhuguo's voice dropped. "Qinlei, I'll probably be coming back in a short while—this time for good."

"You're coming back?"

"I'll be retiring in a year."

"Really?"

"I'm all by myself over there. Yingfen passed away, and it is too difficult to live alone. My stomach is giving me trouble all the time, and then, well, I don't have any children, you see."

"Oh . . . "

"I think the area around Nangang is a good quiet neighborhood. Besides, the Academia Sinica is there, too."

"Yes, Nangang is not a bad place at all to live in."

The rain streamed through the hole in the umbrella and splashed their faces. They hunched their shoulders against the cold. Just then, a taxi approached and Professor Yu raised his hand to signal it. As the driver pushed open the door. Professor Yu extended his hand to Wu Zhuguo to say good-bye. Holding the latter's hand in his, suddenly he said with a quivering voice, "Zhuguo, there's something I haven't been able to bring myself to say all along."

"Yes?"

---

6. National Zhengzhi University is a college in Taiwan supported by the government; *zhengzhi* means "political."

"Do you think you could recommend me . . . I mean, I'd still like to go abroad to teach for a year or two, and if there is a university in the States that happens to have an opening . . . "

"Well, I'm afraid they might be reluctant to hire a Chinese to teach English literature."

"Of course, of course." Professor Yu cleared his throat. "I wouldn't go to America to teach Byron—what I mean is, if there is a school which needs someone to teach Chinese or something like that . . . "

"Oh . . . " Wu Zhuguo hesitated a moment. "Sure, I'll give it a try."

After Wu Zhuguo was seated in the taxi, he reached out his hand and gave him a firm handshake. Professor Yu trudged back home. The bottom of his long gown had become thoroughly soaked by now and clung cold and wet to his legs. His right knee was hurting more than ever. He hobbled into the kitchen, took the Yushan Herb Clinic plaster that was being warmed on the stove, and pressed the steaming hot dressing firmly over his knee. As he entered the sitting room he noticed that the window over his writing desk had been blown open and was flapping noisily in the wind. He hurried over and bolted it. Through the cracks, he could see that the light in his son's room was still on. Junyan was seated at the window, studying with his head bent down low. His son's handsome profile caught Yu Qinlei by surprise. For a split second he thought he was looking at himself when he was a young man. It was so long ago that the memory of what he looked like then had gradually slipped away. He remembered that he was twenty, the same age as Junyan, when he first met Yaxing. They were together in Beihai Park. Yaxing had just emancipated herself by bobbing her hair, and it was blowing loosely in the wind. She was wearing her dark blue college skirt and standing by the lake. Her skirt fluttered in the breeze. The evening clouds, a brilliant red, gathered in the western skies, transforming the surface of the lake into a sea of fire and throwing flickering crimson shadows on Yaxing's face. He had even contributed a poem to *New Tide*. It was written for Yaxing:

As you recline on the emerald waves,
Red clouds in the evening sky
Melt into lotus flowers
That gently lift you up,
To waft freely with the drifting wind.
Xing, Oh Xing,
You are the goddess of the waves . . .

Professor Yu shook his very bald head and smiled shamefacedly. Then he noticed that tiny pools of water had collected on the desk by the window, and that the books strewn over it were sprinkled with raindrops. He swept his sleeve over them with one quick wipe and then picked up a book at random. It was *The Knight-Hermit of Willow Lake*. He sat down on the sofa and leafed through a page or two. But under the dim light his eyes wouldn't stay open, and soon he began to nod and his head slipped forward. Half asleep, he could still hear the sound of mahjong tiles being shuffled and women laughing.

Outside the window icy rain continued to fall, as the night in Taipei deepened into winter.

1970

Huang Chunming (1935–   )

THE FISH

Translated by Howard Goldblatt

"You told me to bring a fish with me the next time I came home, Grandpa. Well, I've brought one—it's a bonito!" Ah-cang shouted happily to himself as he left the little town behind him on his rickety old bicycle.

A twenty-eight-inch bike was not made for a boy as small as Ah-cang, and as he set out he was tempted to stick his right leg through the triangular space below the crossbar. But then he changed his mind, figuring he shouldn't be riding a bike that way anymore. After all, he wasn't a kid any longer.

Perched on the big bike, Ah-cang could not keep his rump from slipping off first one side of the seat and then the other. The cooked bonito, wrapped in a taro leaf and hanging from the handlebars, swayed violently with the motion of the bike. Ah-cang knew that bringing a bonito back to the mountain would make his grandpa and his younger brother and sister very happy. They'd also be surprised to see that he had learned to ride a bicycle. Besides, riding a bike to and from the foot of the mountain at Pitou would save him twelve Taiwan dollars in bus fare. That was why he'd pleaded with the carpenter to lend him the rickety old bike that lay unused in the shed.

Ah-cang pedaled down the road with the single-minded purpose of getting that fish home to his grandfather as quickly as possible; not even the clanking sounds of the old bike disturbed his thoughts. The moment he saw his grandfather, he'd hold the fish up high and say: "Well, what do you say? I've got a pretty good memory, haven't I? I brought a fish home."

"Ah-cang, the next time you come home, try to bring a fish back with you. It's not easy getting saltwater fish up here on the mountain. Bring a big one if you can."

"But I don't know when I'll be able to come home again."

"I'm saying *when* you come home."

"That'll be up to the master."

"I know that! That's why I said to bring a fish back with you *when* you come home."

"*When* I come home? I may not have any money when I come home."

"I mean when you *do* have the money."

"That'll depend on the master too."

"When will he start paying you wages?"

"You should know—you're the one who took me there. Didn't he say I'd have to be an apprentice for three years and four months before I got any pay?"

"That's right. You're there to learn a trade. How long before you can nail a table together all by yourself?"

"Nailing a table together is easy. I learned how to do that a long time ago."

"Then you shouldn't be an apprentice any longer."

"I haven't been there three years and four months yet."

"Oh? How long have you been there?"

"I still have a year and a half to go." Ah-cang sighed. "Sometimes I feel I might spend my whole life there without ever finishing."

The old man quickly chided him: "Hush! Children aren't supposed to sigh!"

"Why not?"

"Because they're not supposed to." He paused for a moment. "It's bad luck. You remember that."

"Grandpa." Ah-cang looked up at the old man.

"Hm?"

"When you're really low, it makes you feel good to sigh."

The old man laughed loudly.

"What're you laughing at?"

"You don't look any older, but you talk like you've grown up a lot."

"I mean it! After I sigh, I always feel really really good."

"Don't walk on that side where the road curves. The day before yesterday one of the shop owners from the foot of the mountain got a little careless while he was coming up to collect some bills and lost his footing there."

"Was he hurt?" Ah-cang craned his neck to look over the side.

"Of course he was hurt. The bamboo down there had just been cut, and each stalk looked like a crow's beak. When he went over the side, he was stuck by pointed bamboo all over. He also broke his leg. Okay, that's enough looking down there. That bend in the road has always been a nasty spot."

"Who owed him money?"

"Who up here on the mountain doesn't owe money to the flatlanders?"

They silently skirted the bend in the road.

"Where are you going?"

"Nowhere. I'll just walk you down the mountain."

"You don't have to. I'll be careful, and I'll remember to bring a fish back with me the next time I come home."

"That's great. But if you can't, don't worry about it. Sometimes when the weather turns bad, the fishermen don't go out to sea, and then you can't get a fish even if you've got the money."

"Then I hope there's no bad weather."

As they approached a narrow stretch of road, the old man let his grandson walk ahead of him; he gazed at the boy from behind and asked: "Is it a rough life?"

"What can I do about it? They make me do just about everything in the master's house, even wash the baby's diapers . . . " The boy began to choke up.

"Then what does the master's wife do?"

The boy just shook his head without saying a word.

"So *that's* the kind of woman she is!" Then the old man comforted the boy by saying: "It doesn't make any difference. You've put up with it so far, haven't you?"

"You told me I had to."

"Then you're doing the right thing. You have to set a good example for your brother and sister."

Ah-cang looked off at nothing in particular on the mountain slope. He saw a herd of goats grazing in the acacia grove.

"How're our goats?"

"Oh, they're just fine."

"We ought to raise a few more."

"That's what I've been thinking."

"Let them hurry up and have some kids."

"That's what I was planning to do."

"After all the time we've been raising goats, we still only have those three."

"That's because they're all males."

"Males are worthless!"

"If they were all females, they'd be just as worthless."

"I figure we should raise a few more goats, then we could swap them for a set of carpenter's tools." Ah-cang casually picked a blade of mugwort from the side of the road.

"Be careful, that can cut your finger." The old man quickly returned to the subject at hand. "Are you ready for a set of carpenter's tools?"

"Sure!" the boy said. "I can do more than make tables—I know how to make wardrobes, doors, beds, and chests, too."

"That's wonderful!" the old man said delightedly. "I'll go ahead and raise a few more goats so you can exchange them for carpenter's tools."

"When?"

"What's your hurry? Grandpa'll take care of it right away. I'll swap two of our male goats for one female with a flatlander, and we can start."

"You'd better hurry, because I'll be a carpenter pretty soon!"

"That's what I mean!" the old man said, then added lovingly: "But you'll have to put up with whatever comes along for the time being. You know that, don't you?"

"I know. I'll have to be patient."

Once they passed the acacia grove, they could see the bus sign off in the distance at Pitou. They fell silent. When they finally reached flat land the old man said: "Do you get enough to eat?"

". . ."

"Do they beat you?"

". . ."

"What's wrong? Why don't you say something?" The boy lowered his head and fought back the tears. "Don't cry. Why would anyone cry when he's about to become a carpenter?"

The boy shook his head as he wiped away the tears. "I'm not crying." But he refused to raise his head.

"Hey, do as Grandpa says and take this sack of sweet potatoes along for your master. Maybe they'll treat you better if you do."

"No."

"Go ahead, take it." The old man slipped the sack of sweet potatoes off his shoulder and set it in front of the boy. "Don't forget to bring the sack back."

"I said no! They'd laugh at me!"

"These are the best sweet potatoes anywhere around here!" The boy looked up at the old man with eyes red from crying and shook his head.

"All right, then!" the old man said angrily. "I'd rather feed them to pigs than give them to anyone who'd touch a single hair on my grandson's head!"

"Grandpa, go on back now."

"All right, after I've rested here a minute. You hurry on down to wait for the bus."

Before the boy had taken more than a few steps, he was called to a halt by the old man.

"Are you sure you don't want to take the sweet potatoes?"

"I'm sure."

"Who knows, they might even buy a fish for you to bring back the next time you come home."

"I told you I'd bring a fish back for you."

"Come over here." The old man took a couple of steps toward the boy. "Your grandpa once carried a heavy load of sweet potatoes to market because he wanted to buy a fish for you kids. Is the bus coming?"

"Not yet."

"Tell me when it is. You know that fish costs more than most foods. That day I walked around and around the fish stalls until the fishmongers finally got tired of calling out to me. But I kept walking, trying to make up my mind. You know why?"

"You were going to steal one?"

"Nonsense!" The old man straightened up. "That's something you must never do. I could never do anything like that. I'd rather starve!" Then he bent over again and explained to the boy: "I did it because fish was so expensive and the fishmongers are all crooks. If they aren't tampering with the scales, they're padding the weight. I didn't know how to figure, and I knew if I just asked them how much the fish sold for, they'd reach in to get a fish and weigh it using wet rush stems. Keep your eye out for the bus. Tell me when it's coming."

"Not yet."

"So I kept walking around the fish stalls looking the fish over and trying to find an honest face among the peddlers. Finally I stopped at a stall where bonitos were sold and pointed to one of them. I repeatedly told the fishmonger to give me an honest weighing and not take advantage of an old man. She told me not to worry, over and over, so I bought a three-catty bonito. But when I weighed it at home I found it was a catty and a half light!" The old man knitted his brows. "I should have been able to buy a three-catty bonito with the money I got for a full load of sweet potatoes . . . "

"The bus is coming! I can hear it."

The old man, having stooped over too long, straightened up with considerable difficulty and looked with the boy off in the direction where the bus would be.

"If you can only hear it, then we've still got time."

"Who knows, maybe it's a Forestry Department truck," the boy said excitedly.

"That's even better. You could hitch a ride." The old man paused. "Let's see now, where was I?"

"You were saying you should have been able to buy a three-catty bonito with the money you got for a full load of sweet potatoes."

"So you *have* been listening to me?"

The boy nodded.

"They robbed me of a load of sweet potatoes. Those people are bandits, pure and simple. I was so upset I fretted over it for days. To tell you the truth, even today I won't go near fish stalls in the marketplace!" He heaved a deep sigh. "Ai! It's not easy for us mountainfolk to eat saltwater fish . . . "

"Here comes the bus."

The old man gazed off, bleary-eyed.

"Over there. See that trail of dust?"

"You're probably right. You go on now. Grandpa'll stay here and rest a moment."

"I'm going now."

"Ah-cang, don't forget . . . "

" . . . to bring a fish back with me," the boy finished the sentence.

They both laughed.

"Grandpa, I didn't forget. I brought a fish back with me—a bonito!" Ah-cang said repeatedly to himself, his happiness tinged with feelings of triumph. As he rode along he envisioned wide-eyed looks on the faces of his brother and sister when they saw the bonito, and he could almost see the tips of his grandfather's trembling chopsticks as they reached out to pick up a morsel of fish. "Grandpa, I'll be a carpenter in two months!"

Clank! "That damned chain!" Ah-cang jumped down off the bike, put the slipped chain back onto the sprocket, then turned a pedal until it was once again engaged. The chain had kept slipping off the sprocket the whole way, so he knew he shouldn't ride too fast—but he invariably forgot. This time, after brushing some of the rust and oil off his hands, he discovered to his horror that the fish had fallen off! All that was left hanging on the handlebars was the now-empty taro leaf. He quickly headed back, and a mile or so down the road he found what he was looking for, though now it was nothing but a squashed imprint on the muddy road. The fish had been run over by a truck.

More than two hours later, as he headed back up the mountain, the crestfallen Ah-cang could cry no longer over this freak accident. Off in the distance he saw his grandfather sitting in the doorway weaving implements out of green bamboo. Lacking the courage to call out "Grandpa," he just quietly walked up to the old man.

The old man jerked his head up. "Hey! When did you get back?"

"Just now," the boy answered as he walked into the house.

The old man laid the things in his hand down, then stood to follow the boy inside. But between the time he started getting to his feet and the time he finally straightened up, he had plenty of time to ask the boy several questions.

"Ah-cang, did you see our goats by the roadside on your way home?" No answer. "They're over there in the couch grass. Your brother and sister are watching them. I managed it for you—you'll have your set of carpenter's tools any day now."

That made Ah-cang feel even worse.

"Ah-cang, did you hear what I said?" the old man asked as he walked into the house. Still no response. "What's wrong with you? You're acting like a bride who hides in the corner the minute she steps into the house." He walked into the bedroom, then into the tool shed, and finally into the kitchen, where he found Ah-cang taking big gulps from the water ladle.

"Ah, here you are! Did you bring a fish home?"

Ah-cang kept drinking.

"The weather's been bad the past few days, so there wouldn't be any fish for sale in the marketplace," the old man said, knowing full well that the weather had been fine. "You can't use our weather here as a gauge—out at sea it's always changing."

Ah-cang purposely got his face all wet so his grandfather wouldn't know he'd been crying. He raised his wet face and said: "They're selling fish."

"Well?"

"I bought one—a bonito."

"Where is it?" The old man searched the kitchen with his eyes.

"I dropped it!"

"Dropped it?"

"Dropped it!" Ah-cang didn't dare look the old man in the eye, so he buried his face in the water ladle again, though he didn't want any more water—he couldn't drink another drop.

"How . . . how could that have happened?" The old man was bewildered. The pain he'd felt that time when he'd been cheated on the weight of the bonito returned.

But Ah-cang, not knowing how the old man felt, argued defensively: "I really did! I'm not lying to you. I hung it on the handlebars of the bike, and it just fell off."

"The bike?"

"That's right. I know how to ride a bike now!" He waited to see if this made his grandfather happy.

"Where's the bike now?"

"I left it in the care of a shop at the foot of the mountain."

"It fell off the handlebars?" The old man spoke every word slowly and clearly.

Ah-cang's disappointment was now complete.

"I really did buy a bonito, but a truck ran over it and squashed it."

"Isn't that the same as not bringing one home?"

"No! I did bring one!" he shouted.

"That's right, you did, but you dropped it. Is that right?"

Ah-cang was angry that his grandfather had taken such a matter-of-fact attitude.

"I really did bring one with me," the boy said angrily.

"I'm aware of that."

"I'm not lying to you! I am *not* lying to you! I swear!" Ah-cang began to cry.

"I know you're not lying to your grandpa. You've never lied to me. It's only that the fish fell on the road," he said in a comforting tone.

"No! You don't believe me! You think I'm lying . . . " Now Ah-cang was sobbing.

"You can bring one home next time. Won't that take care of it?"

"But I already brought one back today!"

"You say you brought a fish with you today, and I believe you, so what are you crying about? You're acting silly."

"But it never got here."

"It fell off and was squashed by a truck, right?"

"No! You don't know! You don't know! You think I'm lying to you . . . "

"Grandpa believes every word you're saying."

"I don't believe you."

"What do you want me to say?" Beginning to lose his patience, the old man spread his hands in a helpless gesture.

"I don't want you to believe me, I don't want you to believe me . . . " Ah-cang shouted as he threw the ladle to the floor, then began to sob again, sounding like a calf.

The old man, finding himself cornered, began to fume. He reached behind the door to pick up his carrying pole, and began hitting out with it. Ah-cang was struck on the shoulder and quickly darted out of the room, the old man right on his heels.

Ah-cang ran through the tea orchard, followed closely by the old man. He then ran over to the bramble patch and quickly threaded his way in to a depth of five or six feet. From there he hopped down onto the road leading home. The old man stopped at the entrance to the bramble patch. Ah-cang turned and saw that the old man had stopped, so he did too. There was by then a considerable distance between them.

The old man stood there gasping, one hand waving the carrying pole, the other resting on a bramble bush.

"Don't you dare enter my door again!" he shouted. "If you do, I'll beat you to within an inch of your life!"

Ah-cang responded in the loudest voice he could manage: "I really did bring a fish back!"

It was then approaching evening, and the mountain was very quiet. The old man and the boy were both startled to hear the crisp echo coming to them from the valley:

" . . . really did bring a fish back!"

1968

Wang Zhenhe (1940–1990)

AN OXCART FOR A DOWRY

Translated by the author and Jon Jackson

There are moments in our life when even Schubert has nothing to say to us.
—*Henry James, The Portrait of a Lady*

The villagers all laughed at Wanfa behind his back. Even right under his nose they curled their lips in contempt, without fear of arousing his anger. It may be that their insolence was due to his near-deafness. But Wanfa was not quite deaf. More often than not, their offensive words came thumping into his ears. To him, this was the truly unfortunate thing.

When Wanfa came home from his carting job he would go to the *ryoriten*[1] for a good meal. He had finally come to own his own ox and cart. With his oxcart he got as much as thirty dollars for a single hauling job. Things were going rather well for him, of late. Compared with the past, one might say the present was quite comfortable for Wanfa. He no longer needed to support his family, so he could spend everything he earned on himself. And this after being released from prison! He had not expected it, certainly. It was strange, was it not?

Whenever there was money in his pocket, he soon found himself sitting in the *ryoriten,* tasting the duck cooked in *danggui*[2] wine. He had never had a chance to taste such good food before. All the villagers laughed at him and teased him unmercifully. And it was worse that his two nearly deaf ears were not quite able to ward off the villagers' scorn completely. Had he been generous

---

1. A Japanese-style restaurant.

2. *Ligusticum acutilobum:* an aromatic herb, the root of which has medicinal uses.

enough to let his ears fail completely, he might have felt less uneasy among the villagers. He might also feel much better now about holding the bottle of beer in his hands, a free beer, given him by that guy named Jian.

No sooner had he taken a seat than the manager rushed over to welcome him with a flood of courteous words, none of which quite reached Wanfa's ears. No, not even a single polite word. It was like watching a silent film: Wanfa saw only the two dry lips of the manager making the open-and-shut motion over and over, with no notion of what was being said. Sometimes the man's mouth moved so slowly he seemed to be yawning; again so rapidly that it was like a hungry dog gnawing at a meatless bone. These incessant lip movements made the manager ridiculous in Wanfa's eyes. Thinking that he had at least found someone that *he* could ridicule, Wanfa felt his spirits lift. As if to whisper a secret, the manager put his mouth right up to Wanfa's ear and shouted what he had said before in a thundering voice issuing quite incongruously from such a tiny, skeletonlike body.

"A plate of fried snails and a bowl of Tainan noodles," Wanfa ordered, his gaze fixed on the keeper's greasy bald head.

"How about drinks? We have some ten-year-old Red Dew wine."

Shaking his head as monotonously as if it were operated by an electric motor, Wanfa pompously set out the bottle of beer given him as compensation by Jian.

Two tables away sat five young villagers. They were having a feast and noisily playing the finger-guessing game. Catching sight of Wanfa, one of them opened his mouth in speech. The other four broke off their game and turned their heads in unison, almost as if they were performing a "Right face!" in response to a drill sergeant, except that their faces all wore a nasty look of contempt and were quite devoid of any military solemnity. Then another villager stood up, his mouth flapping. He had hardly finished when he doubled up with a great roar of laughter that was so contagious the other four also burst into guffaws that had the effect of distorting them from head to toe. One villager, whose head seemed larger than his expanded chest, suddenly extended his hand to silence the others, nervously glancing at Wanfa. The one who had first noticed Wanfa jumped to his feet clutching one ear and exclaimed, "Don't worry! He's stone deaf. Do you think this scandal could ever have taken place otherwise?"

Each word rang against Wanfa's double-locked ears like a brass gong. There was a time once, when he had just been released from prison, that such words would have made him flush with embarrassment. Now, his face would not color at all; it was as if he were beneath this mockery.

The five young men put their heads back together and resumed their wild carousals.

Having opened the beer, Wanfa poured himself a cup. As he was about to drink it, he felt in his throat a surge of nausea, a taste he would find in every cup of Jian's beer.

Yes, it was Jian who had turned his beer to gall.

Perhaps in his former existence Wanfa had been a bad debtor, and that is why he had always been troubled by money matters in this life. He married one Ahao, but instead of his life improving, it got worse and worse. From his father he inherited a small plot of land on which he and his wife tried to plant vegetables and herbs of all sorts, but no vegetables and herbs would grow. One year they cultivated the "pneumonia-cure grass"; the grass grew fast and promised a good harvest. Then, with a storm came a flood that not only washed away all the "pneumonia-cure grass," but alas, even the very soil. Not long after, they were fleeing from bombing raids. Wanfa got an earache at that time. It must have been caused, he said, by some "unclean water" splashing into his ears when he took a bath in a river. He had not gotten immediate treatment, for it was very hard to find a doctor during wartime. Only when the pain became unbearable did he find a doctor—one who specialized in female disorders. The doctor treated Wanfa with his rich knowledge of ovaries and uteruses. The result was a hearing loss of only eighty percent. It was not so bad, technically speaking, but on account of this eighty percent, Wanfa no sooner found a job than he was fired from it. People grew tired rather quickly of having to shout at him as if in argument. They moved from county to county, district to district, until finally they settled in this village. He and his family made their home in a tiny hut near the graveyard, two miles out of town. He was hired by an oxcart owner and was able to barely keep his family from starvation. If only his wife, Ahao, had not been too fond of gambling. Whenever she got up to her ears in debt, she would sell off a daughter, and one by one, all three daughters were sold. For some reason (perhaps to propagate more offspring), she did not sell either of her two sons. Relentlessly, their life retreated toward the primitive state.

By the path leading to the graveyard stood their little hut, low and drooping; it was like a shabby old man who could not walk with his back upright in the frigid air. They were not alone out there. About three yards away was a dilapidated shanty in which some people had once lived. But these people had left the year before for some other place; they were perhaps too frightened by the ghostly atmosphere of the cemetery. Like a resort for spirits and ghosts, the shanty was now completely without living occupants.

Only Wanfa and his family lived by the graveyard now, with only spirits and ghosts for company. So it was natural that Ahao, when she spotted someone moving into the empty shanty, should be so ecstatic and immediately rush to break the hot news to her husband.

"Somebody is moving to that shanty. No need to fear that evil spirits will do us harm at night anymore. We have a neighbor now."

However, this message did not impress Wanfa. Not a bit. Half of his life he had lived in a silent world; to him, neighbors made little impression.

Wanfa took his undershirt down from a bamboo pole and covered his bare chest with it. It was his only undershirt. At night he took it off for washing; by noon the next day it was dry enough to wear outdoors. Once, he had owned another undershirt, for rotation. But his oldest son had "borrowed" it when he had gone to town to look for a job. "To be hard up on the road is worse than hard up at home." So Wanfa, like any father, sacrificed something for his son's sake.

Putting his wide rain hat on his head, Wanfa went straight out to work, with no intention of visiting his new neighbor. Ahao followed him to the door, hands on hips like parentheses to her bamboo-pole figure. "Aren't you going to visit our new neighbor? Maybe you can give him a hand fixing something," said Ahao, her mouth cracking open from ear to ear.

Pretending he had heard nothing, Wanfa sped away without a word.

At dusk he came back. Sitting on the ground in the doorway, he leisurely smoked a cheap cigarette. Still he had no mind to call on his neighbor, although it would only have taken him a minute to go over. This evening Ahao's tone in regard to the new neighbor was not nearly so delightful as it had been that morning. She was complaining now.

"*Gan!*[3] He has no dependents at all. He is all alone and single. He is from Lugang, you know. Talks just like any Lugangnese, like with a heavy cold. So hard to make out his babbling. *Yiniang!*[4] I thought there might be some womenfolk for company."

Puffing on his cigarette, Wanfa did not respond. Presuming he had not heard her, Ahao was prepared to repeat her remarks, moving as near him as possible. But Wanfa declined her efforts, saying, "Don't be repetitious, will you? I am not deaf at all."

"Oh, you're not deaf? Don't make me laugh." Again cracking her face open wide from ear to ear (Ahao could have swallowed Wanfa in one mouthful), she added, "Shame on you. You are like the hog who doesn't know he is filthy."

Neither the next day nor those that followed did Wanfa visit the Lugang man. He was afraid that with his sickened ears he might make a bad impression on the stranger. And he could not understand why the Lugangnese did not drop in to say hello or to borrow a hammer—he simply has to nail something on a wall, having just moved in. As if for fear of the she-ghost, the Lugang man bolted his door very early in the evening. Although he had yet to meet his new neighbor, Wanfa was nonetheless familiar with his neighbor's history—at least elementarily. Day in and day out, Ahao supplied a bundle of information about the Lugangnese for Wanfa's study and research. The man was thirty-five, almost ten years younger than Wanfa, and his last name was Jian. Jian was a clothing peddler. At present, he peddled clothes of all sorts in the village. And he rented the shanty from its owner. Wanfa could see no advantage for Jian in living so near the graveyard. With all the information he had gained from his wife, Wanfa

3. A profanity.

4. A Taiwanese profanity.

began to think that he was already on friendly terms with Jian, though they had yet to meet.

"Does he cook for himself?" asked Wanfa concernedly.

"I didn't pay any attention to that matter," said Ahao with her head turned and her eyes looking sidelong toward Jian's shanty. "Yeah, I think so. Or who would prepare meals for him? *Yiniang!* He both sells clothes and cooks meals single-handedly. He is great, isn't he?"

At last Wanfa and Jian encountered one another.

Watching Jian approach with his mouth opening and shutting repeatedly, Wanfa had no idea whether Jian was munching food or speaking. Like a crane, Jian hopped near him. "Ah, he stinks horribly," muttered Wanfa under his breath. But he did not cover his nose with his hand, out of politeness. Both of Jian's hands rubbed deep in his armpits again and again; it appeared that whole families of ringworms had been living in Jian's underarms for some time without paying rent, and now he was determined to send them packing. The more he rubbed his armpits the worse he stank. Now Jian spoke. Wanfa was not able to follow what he was saying, only catching a string of sounds—ah, ah, ah—as if the man's mouth were plugged with a big piece of steamed bread. However, Wanfa forced himself to smile a broad smile of understanding. Soon he felt that he was unable to close his mouth, having forced so many grins. Occasionally, Wanfa would say something, but each time he spoke Jian would look utterly at a loss. His answer must be beyond the question again. The hell with them ears. The hell with them! All of a sudden he took a dislike to Jian. Ahao came out of the door and waved a needle and thread at the peddler.

"This is Mr. Jian," she said to Wanfa. "He has come to borrow a needle and thread. He said he should have come to see you earlier, but he is just too busy with selling clothes. You know, he has to go out to his business very early in the morning." She raised her voice to top volume, as if speaking to thousands.

Turning to Jian she spoke softly. With a finger pointing to her ear, she shook her head incessantly, and with great exaggeration. Obviously, she was informing Jian of Wanfa's deafness. She must have told him so, otherwise Jian would not bear on his face such a look of amazement, as if he had come across something in the dark that would surely startle the universe. Now he gave a long look at Wanfa, apparently trying to see what had been missing in his face. Wanfa was not embarrassed. In the past he would have been very upset, even irritated at having his shortcomings made public.

"How is your business doing?" asked Wanfa with a forced smile.

"Well, so-so," Ahao repeated Jian's reply in a shout. "Mr. Jian asks what line you are in."

"Oh." Crossing his hands on his chest, Wanfa gave Jian another smile with a hint of self-mockery and answered, "I just move goods with a rented oxcart from one place to another for other people."

"Is it good?" inquired Jian. Like a current of electricity traveling up his spine, Jian's hands dived into his armpits with a violent jerk. He must itch badly. Even his mouth was twisted into an ugly grimace. At any rate, this simple inquiry was heard distinctly by Wanfa, so Ahao's assistance was dispensed with for once.

"Just enough for us to live hand-to-mouth. If I owned an oxcart, I would certainly make more."

Ahao repeated Jian's next question: "How much will an oxcart cost?"

"Well, a used one is around three or four thousand dollars. What are you saying? Me? Purchase a cart? Oh no, where can I raise the money? I'm going to turn fifty; I'm no longer young. Can I not save? Don't you know the old saying: If you have not saved enough by the time you are forty, you will toil and suffer until you breathe your last."

In the wake of this meeting, a congregation of the same sort occurred almost every night at Wanfa's, with Ahao sitting between the two men and serving as a hearing aid. Jian still stank horribly. Still scratching himself in public with an easy conscience. Time and again Jian and Ahao would chat pleasantly together, ignoring the presence of Wanfa altogether. Since Jian had traveled a lot, Ahao would urge him to tell her of the gaiety and pomp of city life, her voice falling into a low and soft whisper. At such times, Wanfa would go to bed with his youngest son, Lao-wu,[5] leaving Jian and Ahao to spin yarns until all hours.

Ahao went over to chatter with Jian quite often now. She also helped him with washing and sewing. By his own account, Jian had lost his parents in childhood and since then had gone a-roving. No one, he often said to Ahao, had ever cared for him as much as Ahao. From time to time he would have Ahao take home all those badly damaged clothes that the customers refused to buy. Thanks to this generosity, Wanfa no longer had to worry about his one and only undershirt drying in time for him to cover his nakedness the next day.

Perhaps in order to express his gratitude, Wanfa began to frequent Jian's shanty. And he was getting more and more used to the heavy odor of Jian's armpits.

Jian's business seemed to be doing very well. He always seemed to need help. He made Ahao fully aware of his new plan. Hardly had she heard the joyous news than she raced home to relate it to Wanfa, in a high-spirited mood.

"I have a piece of exciting news," she said, going near to where Wanfa lay on his mat and touching his shoulder. "I have a piece of exciting news. With his business Jian always has more than he can do. So he asks us a favor: Let our Lao-wu help him sell clothes. Besides providing meals, he will pay our son two hundred dollars a month. *Yiniang!* Where can you expect anything better than this? *Gan!* What you make each month is no more than this. Well, what do you say? Will you accept his offer? Lao-wu is fifteen now; time for him to see the world."

---

5. Literally, "Old-fifth"; one way of referring to the fifth child in a family. Here used as a proper name.

With this additional income they could surely improve their lot. It made no sense at all to turn it down. Wanfa sat up and said, "Tell Mr. Jian to take good care of our Lao-wu." Then he lay down again, a smile of joy shining around the corners of his mouth.

Seating herself on the mat, Ahao said, "When I have Lao-wu's pay in my pocket, I shall buy some piglets to keep. We can feed them with the sweet potatoes we plant on the mountain slope. We won't need to buy fodder and we can save a lot. You must have heard how the price of pork is soaring every day. We will surely make a lot if we keep pigs."

Lao-wu went to help Jian the next day. He and Jian pushed a rickshaw full of clothes of all sorts to the village. Spreading the clothes on the mat near the marketplace, they began their sale. Usually Ahao did not go to the village very often. Now she made a point of accompanying Jian and Lao-wu almost daily. If they were too busy with their selling, she would give them a hand. Sometimes she would bring an armful of taro leaves to sell to the pork-mongers and fish dealers to sack their goods. Once she had sold out and had money in her purse, she would go gambling. No matter how secretly she went to the gambling house, she could not escape the eyes of Jian. Not that she was afraid that Jian might disclose her wrongdoing to Wanfa: with his Lugang accent Jian could never make himself understood by Wanfa. What's more, Jian was no less inveterate a gambler than Ahao. It was not long before the villagers observed Ahao and Jian going together to the gambling house.

And it was not long either before the villagers started passing around a joke, which they all agreed was even funnier than the slapstick of Laurel and Hardy. Oh, would you believe that Jian has started screwing Ahao? Somebody had even watched Ahao and Jian while fervently engaged in love battles in the graveyard, behind the pigpen. . . . By no means would they declare a truce, even when it rained cats and dogs. Would you believe they undressed each other in the pouring rain and struggled in the mud until they had their pleasure? As the saying goes, those who love to wrangle over nothing at all don't give a damn for anything, not even their own life. Those who abandon themselves to pure lust don't worry about falling sick.

"I'm not lying," someone would say, "Ahao is at least ten years older than that peddler. She's old enough to be his mama. Well, I could understand it if Ahao, that old hag, looked like a human being; but then she's ugly as hell, isn't she? She weighs no more than four ounces but has a yap as big as a toilet bowl. And a chest like a washboard! It must be painful to press one's chest against it. I can't imagine what part of that old hag could arouse the lust of that silly Lugangnese." Thus did the villagers amuse themselves with the scandal.

A month and a half had gone by before the well-guarded ears of Wanfa began to hear the gossip clearly. At first, Wanfa was shocked out of his wits, which was not odd at all since he had never met with such a situation before. Then, a kind of excitement began to swell in his breast. More than once he had complained that Ahao's ghastly looks had been the cause of his miserable fate. But now, a much younger man than Ahao was having a love affair with her. From this point of view, it appeared that the ugly looks of Ahao must mean something to a man after all. Then he considered that Jian's behavior with his wife was an insult to his lost virility. All at once he recalled the unpleasant odor of Jian's armpits and worked himself into utter hatred of the man. As his fury mounted, he determined not to let Jian off too easy. But, as the saying goes, "If you want to convict a thief, you must catch him with the loot; if you want to lay a charge against the adulterers, you must catch the two of them in bed." Thus Wanfa said to himself, "All right, Jian, you just wait and see."

At last, he began to think that it must all be his imagination. Yes, he must have heard wrongly, for Ahao and Jian still talked and laughed happily in his presence, entirely without any intention to avoid suspicion. Or . . . might they not be pulling the wool over his eyes just by pretending to get along as usual, as if nothing had happened? If they had stopped seeing each other all of a sudden, wouldn't that have aroused his suspicion? Although he was stormed with question after question, he had yet to make any powerful protest or declaration against Jian. He merely quit calling at the peddler's shanty.

The Lugang man usually closed his business around six in the afternoon. Then he had supper with Lao-wu at a village food stand. When they returned home, Lao-wu would go to sleep in the shanty and Jian would come over to Wanfa's to talk. On the pretext that his hearing had failed, Wanfa seldom said anything to Jian, keeping silent mostly, as if he held a grudge against the Lugang man. Or he just wanted to show Jian that he was not so dumb as to know nothing at all.

In the meantime, the undershirts and the khaki trousers, gifts from Jian, reminded Wanfa of the peddler's generosity toward his family. He hated to be called an ingrate. So on some occasions he would break the ice and respond a little to Jian's conversation. But never more would he allow Ahao and Jian to be alone together. He would stay awake through the night until Jian turned back to his own shanty. Then he would retire with Ahao. He would lay with his hand across her chest, not yearning for love but to prevent her slipping out. "Better late than never." Now he would cart goods one less trip per day in order to return early in the afternoon. He must have been reminded of the story of Pan Jinlian and Wu Dalang.[6] And it might be from this story that he learned to do business less and watch his wife more.

Every night he kept an eye on Ahao and Jian. Every night he watched over them attentively, save one night—a night with a full moon hanging in the sky.

With the first payment of Lao-wu's monthly salary in her pocket, Ahao showed no inclination to buy piglets to raise, as she had suggested. Wanfa was

6. Pan Jinlian, better known to Western readers as Golden Lotus, is a notoriously licentious woman in the two popular Chinese novels *The Water Margin* and *The Golden Lotus*. Wu Dalang is her husband, whom she eventually poisons to death.

lenient enough to let her have her own way, realizing that she neglected her promises on purpose. After deducting cigarette and lunch bills from his own monthly wages, there had been only about two hundred and forty dollars in actual take-home pay. With such sparse wages he and his family had had to live a whole month, so that it was all but impossible for them to have even modestly passable meals. All the year round they had eaten nothing but gruel, with more water than rice, and a few cheap dried turnips. But now with Laowu's income Ahao had made several rich suppers and breakfasts, and Wanfa was so happy for so many days that he dropped the idea of checking Ahao's accounts.

On the night of the full moon, Ahao prepared rice, carp soup, and fried bamboo shoots. Almost in a single breath Wanfa had consumed five bowls of rice with lots of soup and bamboo shoots to go with it. Taken aback by his wolfish appetite, Ahao could not help making a strange sound in her throat—ah, ah, ah, ah, ah—as if she were belching.

Pouring the last spoonful of soup from the small cooking pot into the empty soup bowl, Ahao said with a shrug, "Shame on you, eating like a tiger. Like you haven't eaten anything for ages. Oh, you still want more rice? Eh?"

When Wanfa finally finished, his cheeks were hot and shining, as if from too much wine. "Getting drunk from gorging" seemed to be a truth. Wanfa felt tipsy enough to drop off, though it was still only half past seven. Don't go to sleep! Here comes Jian! Don't go to sleep!

Jian squatted on his haunches opposite Ahao, as if he were going to relieve himself, and started to talk. Silently puffing a cigarette, Wanfa dozed off several times. His cigarette slipped from his fingers and fell to the ground. Ahao leaned over to him, nearly to the point of sucking his ears, and said twice, "Go to sleep, will you? You look exhausted."

With a start, Wanfa opened his eyes and saw, to his great surprise, that Jian was still there. Not gone yet. And he seemed to have no desire to leave soon.

Saying, "Don't stop your conversation," and "Pay me no attention, please," Wanfa bent over and retrieved his cigarette butt. It had gone out long before. He lit it again and resumed puffing. Through a mist of tobacco fumes he watched Ahao and the clothing peddler talking and laughing together affectionately.

The moon was bright and as full as on the first or fifteenth night of the lunar month. Outside the hut there were no chairs. They squatted on their haunches or sat on rocks: it was like enjoying the moonlight at Midautumn Festival. Through the smoke Wanfa saw the two gesticulating with hands and feet, their mouths opening and closing. He did not understand a word they were saying and he was unable to enter their world: he seemed to be listening to a tête-à-tête between a man-spirit and a woman-spirit in a spirit language.

He must have dozed off again.

Getting up, Ahao yelled in his ear: "Go to sleep, will you?" She yelled it twice, as usual. She wore an extremely loose Western dress that was a milky yellow but became rat-gray in the moonlight. Above all, it was made from a foreign material. She had gotten it from a church after she had attended worship and listened to a sermon given by a man with a high nose and blue eyes. She could not remember now the reason why she had gone to the church. Without making any alterations on the skirt, she shortened it by sewing the lower part a few inches up. To the bodice of the dress was attached an ornament that bore a strong resemblance to a double lock with an iron chain. There was another lock with an iron chain on the shirtwaist. These locks and chains gave the impression that they were safeguarding the secret parts of the female.

"Go to sleep," said Ahao. She sat down on a rock again. She resumed her talk with Jian. They were sitting in the doorway with moonlight shining on them.

Yawning, Wanfa went into the house to sleep. His daring to leave the two alone may have been encouraged by the locks and chains embroidered on the dress.

When he awoke, the moon seemed fuller and brighter, almost beaming with smiles. Reaching out his hand to the other end of the mat, Wanfa felt for Ahao. But Ahao was not there. He jumped out of bed as though bitten by a snake. He was out of his sleeping quarters so fast that his cold sweat hardly had time to start. In the dark he kicked over a wooden box, making a noise that would scare any ghost in the graveyard to death. He slapped his forehead with his hand, cursing his clumsiness. They might have heard the noise. They must have. And if they did, what would be the use of his search?

And they had heard him. In the doorway was spread an old tattered mat. The door was open and the moon shone in. Ahao sat on the mat, her face pale in the moonlight, as though it had been drowned for quite some time. Jian sat up too and turned his head toward the noise. There was perspiration glistening on his forehead.

With a sharp, cutting "What are you doing there?" Wanfa came up to them, both his hands made into fists. Like efficient recruits obeying a command, both Ahao and Jian stood up in a split second. They spoke in the same breath, each trying to speak louder and faster than the other, as if it were a recitation contest between grade-school students. But Wanfa could only make out sheer sound, sound, sound. Sweat poured from the body of Jian. His nipples grew firm and readily apparent through the shirt which stuck to his skin. Ahao pushed Jian into a corner, telling him not to speak any more. Perhaps she was unable to bear the sight of his mobilizing his energy so intensely. She took the floor with every word carefully calculated. But all that Wanfa heard was: "We only . . . That's all . . . nothing else . . . Isn't it? Isn't it?" It was to Jian that she directed the "Isn't it? Isn't it?" glancing at him from time to time.

Don't believe her, Wanfa warned himself. He had been married to her for thirty years. What else could there be that he did not know about her? She would talk anyone to death, seeming to be gifted with two ready tongues in her great mouth. She could talk flowers from the sky. Don't believe her. And the locks and chains on her dress seemed to be all gone. Tightly she clutched at the bodice of her dress, as if afraid that the garment would slip down. Don't listen to her! But she kept on talking and talking, her mouth open wide from ear to ear. And she began to use nasty words and dirty phrases. She must have been very upset in her inability to talk Wanfa around.

"*Yiniang!* Did you hear what I said? I talk almost half a day, and you don't even open your mouth to speak. Say something, will you? *Yiniang!* Are you mute, now, as well?"

All of a sudden, Jian stepped forward, bringing an odorous whiff of armpits. His face shone with joy, as though he had thought of a way out of the situation. Patting Ahao's shoulder, he pointed at a corner of the house where the moonlight did not reach. It seemed someone was sleeping there. Ahao's eyes lit up at once. She exchanged a few hurried words with Jian, then went to the corner. Yes, someone was sleeping there. She shook the sleeper awake with both hands.

"Wake up, Lao-wu. Wake up. Wake up and be your Uncle Jian's eyewitness. Wake up, do you hear? *Yiniang!* You dropped dead sleeping or something?"

When Wanfa climbed back into bed, hoping to resume his sleep, Ahao continued her harangue. Her mouth kissed his ears again and again, as if she loved his ears very much: "You're a real brute, without the slightest idea of what common courtesy demands. You should know better than to call a good fellow like Jian to account. You're just impossible. Lao-wu woke up at midnight to go out for a piss and saw some shadowy form moving in the graveyard. He was frightened and began to cry.

"Jian was unable to calm him down, so he brought him over here. And after Lao-wu went to sleep, I asked Jian to sit down for a cup of water, to show my thanks for his kindness. Then you came out with your long, devilish face. Well, the thing is just as simple as that. *Gan*, your imagination has really gone too far. I tell you, everything is as simple as that. You heard Lao-wu's testimony yourself, didn't you? Then you must believe there is nothing between me and Jian; but why were you still angry with Jian? Why? Why?" She repeated these lines over and over, and the more she repeated them, the more furious her tone became.

Wanfa could find no way to escape the harangue; he wished sincerely he could have been as deaf as a stone.

"Who says I got mad at Jian?" he said.

"Then why didn't you say something? Why didn't you say a word? Do you think it was polite to close your mouth like a dead clam, when the situation demanded you say something to ease his nerves? Tell me, are you jealous of Jian? Are you? You can't even get it up, how can you be jealous?"

An awkward silence fell on them.

As if suddenly recalling something quite important, Wanfa broke the silence: "By the way, what happened to those locks and chains on your dress?" He tried his best to make the question sound casual.

Well, she has nothing to say now. Or maybe my ears just failed me again and I didn't hear. Tired, and having a slight headache, Wanfa dropped the idea of pressing his wife for an explanation.

"You're asking about the locks and chains?" said Ahao, purposely talking in a low, inaudible tone. "Jian said they're not nice to look at and he tore them off my dress."

"What did you say?" asked Wanfa. Oh—my ears—my ears always escape the words they should hear distinctly.

"Lost! I said they were lost!" Ahao yelled into his ears. "*Yiniang!* You're deaf enough to be a stone."

Pressing her body against his, Ahao poked him here and there with seducing fingers. She had not been so interested in him since that time he could not get an erection. Wanfa looked out the window. The moon hung in the sky, round and full like the laughing face of an obese girl. He recalled some lyrics of a popular song: "Miss Moon laughs at me because I am a tomfool, even cheated by the wind."[7]

Maybe he was just that tomfool.

As he was on the verge of sleep the scene came back to him of Ahao and Jian sitting on the mat in the doorway. Then the odor of Jian, more irritating than usual, again floated under his nose as he watched again the unlocked parts of Ahao's dress. Maybe Ahao had played him false. Maybe it was sheer imagination. With question after question in his mind, he lay tossing for hours and could find no sleep.

But he was not to be afforded time to get to the bottom of the matter. Only a few days later, the oxcart owner announced that the ox would be let for plowing. Wanfa might as well stay home for a while. At the same time, Jian declared that he must go back to Lugang to visit, then on to Taipei for a new supply of clothes. He said he might be back in a month. Did he really mean to come back? In order to avoid any further venture into troubled waters with Ahao, he might be going for good. But one thing was certain: during his absence Lao-wu would draw no pay and would have to return to live with his parents. This was truly bad news.

Wanfa had no job now. At first, he went to the mountain slope to dig sweet potatoes to sell in the market. With this he could manage to stave off two-thirds of his hunger. When there were no more sweet potatoes, he set out to climb mountain after mountain in search of taro leaves to sell. Although he could only conquer half of his hunger this way, he had to put up with all kinds of ill

7. The song is titled "Wishes in the Springtime." It tells of a girl who, sitting alone in her room as the spring breeze whistles by her face, begins to dream of her love. Then she hears some noise outside. Thinking that it must be her prince charming calling on her, she rushes to open the door. But no one is outside. Looking up, she sees the moon bright and full, as if mocking her for being fooled by the wind, which has caused the door to make the noise.

remarks from the village women who earned their allowances by plucking taro leaves to sell. They complained that Old Deaf Wanfa collected all the taro leaves and left none for them, and because of Old Deaf Wanfa they were bound to have fewer new dresses this year. To hell with that Old Deaf Wanfa!

Then came the day when there were no more taro leaves. And still he had to fill his empty stomach, which was, as the saying goes, "a hole as deep and bottomless as the sea." What could he do? At the end of his rope, he went to help dig graves to get some pennies for food. The job did not come up every day. Not every day did a man die. Sometimes he had to wait two or three days for a corpse. Ah, it was a pity that people were not generous enough to die sooner. And then, even when he was lucky enough to hear of a death, more often than not some fast-leggers had already won the job before him. He came to realize that if he wanted to live on grave digging, he must do something more than just wait. So he changed his waiting policy. Day and night he searched the whole village for a family with dying people. If he found one, he would hasten to apply for a position as the grave digger, or coffin bearer, even though the dying one was not yet deceased. Soon, when he showed up at a dying man's home the door would be slammed in his face. He was looked upon as the fearsome messenger of Death.

To Wanfa, a single day seemed to last a whole year. He could hardly get the upper hand on even a tenth of his formidable hunger.

One day, Ahao thought her oldest son, who was working in town, might do something for them. In hunger she walked four hours on sandy roads to get to town. When she got back, she brought only a catty of pork and fish. Nothing more. Life in town was not easy either.

Someone recommended Ahao to do cooking and cleaning at Dr. Lin's clinic. If she was accepted she could draw, apart from room and board, one hundred dollars per month. On the day of the interview there was not a grain left to stop her hunger. Stealing some sweet potatoes from a farmer's vegetable garden, she put them under heated ashes and baked them. They were her only lunch. Sweet potatoes. Troublemaking sweet potatoes.

When Dr. Lin inquired how many children she had, she volleyed five big, loud farts before she could open her mouth. Her stomach had given her no warning.

Dr. Lin grinned, trying to inject a sense of humor into the situation, and said, "You have five children?"

To her shame, the gas in her stomach started to cannon one after another, consistently and rhythmically. Her chance for the job was gone with her wind.

Wanfa and Ahao often quarreled now. Almost every minute they found themselves engaged in a battle of words. It looked as though they were venting their disappointments in life by offending each other bitterly. Well, for them to shout at each other was not so bad as it sounded. At least it showed they were still alive—they were not yet totally beaten down by poverty. However, they never fought physically. They were both so emaciated that they were all bones and no flesh. Obviously, it would hurt one's hand very much to beat a bony body like theirs. So there was no pleasure to be gained in it.

Then Jian came back after forty days' absence.

"Jian is back!" Unable to hide her secret joy, Ahao stammered out the news. "He has bou-bought so-so many clo-clothes to-to sell. And you know, he-he is e-even fatter." She stopped for a moment, unable to continue.

Then she added, "He wants our Lao-wu to help him tend his business tomorrow. Do you agree to that? Do you?" There was a brightness in her eyes, betraying her joy at Jian's return. "Oh God, I thought he would never come back."

With Lao-wu's income, they might stop their hunger a bit—hunger like an alarm clock out of order, buzzing and crying at any time or place. No, Wanfa warned himself, I must not let her know I am pleased to see Jian back. And I can't let Jian feel he is doing us a favor, either. He was surprised to find himself so calculating all of a sudden. But, after all, he told himself, a poor man is not poor at all in self-respect.

Receiving no reply from Wanfa, Ahao reiterated her question in a voice close to shrieking.

Wanfa ran his fingers through his hair again and again, causing a shower of dandruff on his shoulders. "If you wish Lao-wu to help Jian, go ahead," he replied, in a manner aloof enough to make a person feel cold.

"You don't want Lao-wu to help Jian?"

"Why not?" Even he himself was astonished at the ice-cold tone.

Ahao did not say anything. But as she left she said something quite indecent to Wanfa. Then she was gone like a whiff of wind. Wanfa had not heard distinctly and did not know what rubbish she had said.

When Wanfa returned from a coffin-bearing job that evening, Ahao had already cooked him a pot of rice.

"Did Jian give you rice?" His eyes fixed on the steaming pot, Wanfa suddenly felt unable to bear his hunger any longer.

As soon as the name of Jian was mentioned, Ahao's voice became unnatural, with a lot of "eh" sounds, as if she had taken too much sickly-sweet food and had to clear her throat before she spoke. "Eh . . . you know we've not eaten a bowl of decent rice for years, so, eh . . . I just borrowed some rice from, eh, Jian. Eh . . . "

Wanfa quickly swallowed the saliva that had filled his mouth and seized the opportunity to speak. He would not let Ahao see how hungry he was. "Listen, don't bother Jian anymore with our troubles, understand?"

Ahao did not reply, as though too exasperated to speak.

Thereafter, whenever she mentioned the man from Lugang, her tone would suddenly become serene, somber, and cautious, as though she spoke of some god. The Lugang man had hardly come to call on Wanfa since his return. He must still remember vividly the embarrassment of that night of the full moon. Or perhaps he was only too occupied with his business.

Now that Lao-wú was helping Jian again and bringing home the whole of his pay each month, Wanfa and Ahao began to live more like human beings. Sweet potatoes were growing on the mountain slope again. Taro leaves were green and large everywhere. Wanfa had no need now to go hunting for corpses each day. He had more time to stay at home and keep an eye on Ahao and Jian. He made up his mind to never allow them an opportunity for further physical contact.

Then the situation changed abruptly. The owner of the shanty in which Jian lived wanted it back, so Jian asked if he could move in with Wanfa.

"What do you say to Mr. Jian's proposal?" Sitting between the two men, Ahao relayed what Jian had said, each word circumspectly coined to get the meaning just right, like announcing a communiqué. "If you have any objection, Mr. Jian will find some single room in the village. After all, it is more convenient for him to live in the village. Well, what do you say?"

Jian went on smoking and smoking, not looking at Wanfa. The weather had turned cool and the odor of Jian's armpits, once so familiar to Wanfan's nose, no longer fouled the air. Wanfa had a sudden feeling that he had lost his way in a strange land and was totally bewildered about what to do: the feeling a newcomer usually has when he works his first day in a strange firm.

"I'll think it over."

"You'll think it over? *Yiniang!* What airs are you putting on? Mister, may I tell you one thing? Your affectations make you stink like a poor sick dog all your life." Gritting her teeth, she glared at Wanfa.

Don't talk back to her when she is so inflamed, Wanfa warned himself, or she'll try her best to vomit out something filthy. By giving out a loud "oh" to indicate he had not heard her reproach, Wanfa managed to escape the further resounding tantrum. It was nice to be able to utilize deafness for the best, wasn't it?

"How much will he pay?" Wanfa put his lips to Ahao's ear as soon as Jian had gone.

Jumping up, Ahao exclaimed, "How much do you expect? He will pay four hundred and eighty dollars a month for room and board. You think that's not reasonable? He is used to living here, otherwise he wouldn't even look at your tumbled-down shack. *Yiniang!* The rent for a nice single room in the village is no more than two pecks of rice! So four hundred and eighty dollars is still less than you expect? *Yiniang!* You'll think it over? Think it over? You try to spoil everything nice. You're just a bad hen that lays no eggs but filth. All filth. You good-for-nothing deaf-mute!" She screamed at the top of her lungs. Like a rooster's morning crow, her tirades could be heard clearly for miles.

So Jian moved in, to live and eat with Wanfa and his family under the same roof. At night, Wanfa and Ahao slept in their own quarters, while Jian slept with Lao-wu on the mat in the doorway. Jian's goods were stored in the back of the hut.

Soon a new rumor swept the village: "*Yiniang!* Old Deaf Wanfa and Jian and Ahao, all three of them, sleep together in one bed. You don't believe it? *Yiniang!*"

Unless he could absolutely not help it, Wanfa would not go to the village. The mockery of the villagers and their white eyeballs of disdain made him all the more embarrassed. With four hundred and eighty dollars from Jian, Wanfa and Ahao could buy enough to eat now. Lao-wu's pay was kept in Wanfa's pocket—this was one prerequisite for allowing Jian to share the same roof with him. He no longer needed to go to the village for work. By day, with the help of Ahao, he worked on his sweet potato farm. By night, he devoted mind and might to keeping Ahao out of Jian's reach. He followed her like a shadow everywhere she went. He even trod on her heels when she went out to relieve herself in the cemetery. Naturally, he was polite enough to stand off always when she was defecating.

One night, Ahao got mad at his spying.

"What do you mean by this, *yiniang*, shadowing me all the way here? Want to watch me urinate? I warn you, if you ever come a step closer, I'll piss right in your face!"

The cold war between Wanfa and Jian was hottest at dinnertime. Usually, Wanfa ate in silence while openly watching Jian and Ahao. He ate so soundlessly that he did not seem to chew his food at all. In spite of everything, he would be the last to leave the dining table, so that every tiny contact between Ahao and Jian would not escape his watchful eyes. Occasionally, Ahao and Jian would lower their voices in the middle of their pleasant chatter, so that Wanfa could hardly hear a sound. Then he would cough harshly, in warning. Sometimes, they ignored his warning and kept on whispering with smiles on their faces. Deaf and mute, are they? Wanfa cursed under his breath. They are even blind to my presence. What an insult! I won't stand for it. With a loud crash, he put down his bowl and stalked away in anger. It looked like a hot war was just around the corner.

But in less than twenty-four hours peace was made without a battle. Each time Wanfa got angry and rushed out of the house, he would generally go to the cemetery and unfasten from his belt a long purse from which he would take out all the coins and bills to count. He counted them forward and backward. Ah! Still not enough to buy an oxcart. Still a long way to go. Then he would say to himself: It's not right to be so hard on Jian. After all, he is my god of wealth, and it would be stupid to send this god away. Then he would close one eye to the doings between Jian and Ahao for a few days.

In the old shanty there now dwelt a pickle vendor who seemed to be a relative of the landlord. Day in and day out he dried cabbages, carrots, beans, and whatnot, causing a great influx of flies. He called at Wanfa's when he was free. He always came with a swarm of flies around him. Once he sat down to talk, his little rat's eyes peered eastward and westward, looking for some secret to gossip about in the village. The features of his face were harsh and mean. And he smelled as sour as a pickle. Wanfa did not care for him at all. He remembered the old saying: "He who calls has nothing to offer but trouble." But Jian and the pickle vendor got along quite well; perhaps they liked each other's odor.

One evening, in a cloud of dirty flies, the pickle vendor came to visit. Jian had gone to the river to bathe. Wanfa, still indoors, could tell from the visitor's excessively nasal twang that it was the pickle vendor. Ahao was busy washing dishes in the kitchen. Lao-wu was playing marbles outdoors. Wanfa could not clearly hear what the pickle vendor and Lao-wu were saying. Then the vendor raised his voice to a high pitch, apparently intentionally. "Where's 'Screw-your-mother' off to?"

Wanfa could not hear Lao-wu's reply.

"I mean Jian. Jian, that Jian who screws your mother. Where is that 'Screw-your-mother'?"

"God damn you!" Wanfa shouted, dashing from the hut. He shivered all over with exasperation. Seizing the pickle vendor with one sweep, Wanfa violently beat him, kicked him, beat him, and kicked him. . . . The flies were frightened away in all directions.

When Jian returned from cleansing his body in the river, he found all his belongings—clothes, shoes, socks, cooking utensils, overnight bags—scattered here and there in front of the hut. It looked like there had been a fire and everything in the house had been hastily removed for safety's sake. The Lugang man named Jian had a feeling of being hollowed out.

Wanfa stood at the door. As soon as Jian, bearing a washbasin, approached the door, Wanfa rushed up to him waving his fists menacingly before him.

"*Gan!* Goddammit! Get out of here! *Gan!* Get out! I feed a rat to bite my own sack. *Gan!* You think you can pull the wool over my eyes just because I can't hear very well? *Gan!* You must have swallowed tiger balls! You take advantage of my deafness, huh? Fuck your mother! You think I'm blind? You think I can't see what you're trying to hide? *Gan!* I feed a rat to bite my own sack . . . " Almost every line was punctuated with an abusive word, scaring Jian nearly out of his wits.

Jian borrowed an oxcart and moved his belongings to the village the same night. He dared not give Ahao a farewell glance, let alone say good-bye.

Then the villagers commenced their gossip. They said Jian had refused to give Wanfa money, so Wanfa had got mad and thrown him out the door. Quite a few people came to visit Wanfa with the intention of digging up some dirt. Wanfa disappointed them all, saying his ears were completely out of order.

Again life was hard on Wanfa. Some farmer leased the mountain slope from the Municipal Government, where Wanfa had planted sweet potatoes. The unripe potatoes were dug up. Wanfa received only one hundred dollars for his loss. To dampen his courage even more, Lao-wu fell seriously ill with acute diarrhea. All the coins and bills he had saved to buy an oxcart were spent to save the child. As he paid the bills to the doctor, tears came suddenly to his eyes. He might have been feeling the pain of losing his savings, or he might have been lamenting his ill fate.

At last, his former employer, the oxcart owner, hired him again. But a week later, an accident happened. The ox assigned to Wanfa suddenly went wild and struck down a child, killing it. For this accident, Wanfa was sentenced to quite a long period of imprisonment. Although the oxcart owner was not jailed, he was fined a big sum of money. At the time that he paid the fine, he uttered in agony, "Heavens! Heavens! Heavens!"

In prison, Wanfa worried about Ahao and Lao-wu. He wondered where they would find the money for rice. He could hardly sleep at night, for worry. One day, for no reason at all, he suddenly regretted having driven Jian away. Thereafter, he spent a few moments each day blaming himself for being rude to Jian. Sometimes, he imagined Jian might have come back to room with Ahao in the hut. According to the opinion of his fellow prisoners, a wife had a right to divorce a husband if the husband was in prison. With Jian's help, Ahao might have already divorced him. If so, what could he do about it? He probably could ask for money from them, as his prison mates suggested. It was reasonable to demand money when one submitted one's darling wife to another man. After all, he had paid a considerable dowry when he married Ahao, so it would not be too much for him now to claim some compensation. It's ridiculous that I'm afraid to lose my wife, while I'm unable to keep her. Huh, ridiculous, indeed!

The fact that Ahao had not come to see him lately as often as before led Wanfa to believe that she and Jian were together again. One day she paid a visit and he asked about her life. At first, she evaded the question by talking about something else. After Wanfa kept asking the same question several times, she lowered her head and said, "Jian is back."

She smoothed the edges of her skirt. "Well, we're fortunate to have him to take care of us, aren't we?"

Wanfa did not say anything. In fact, he had nothing to say. He thought of her face blushing red as a peach when she told him. Yes, it's nice to have someone take care of my family while I am in prison.

One the day he was released, Ahao and Lao-wu came to meet him at the prison gate. Lao-wu had on new clothes. Wanfa saw no sign of Jian when he got home. In the evening, Jian came in, bringing two bottles of beer to welcome him home. Jian was talking to him in his heavy Lugang accent. Wanfa could not make out a word he said.

Ahao came in and joined them. "Mr. Jian has bought you an oxcart; from tomorrow on you can earn more with your own oxcart."

"He has bought me an oxcart?" Wanfa was quite astonished. He had dreamed of owning an oxcart all his life, and now the dream had come true. For a moment he was pleased and delighted. Then he felt disgusted with himself. What a disgrace! I exchange my wife for an oxcart. What a disgrace!

But, in the end, he accepted the gift. Reluctantly, of course.

Once a week, Jian sent him into the night with a bottle of beer. With the beer he would go to the *ryoriten* and have a regular feast. He was considerate enough to stay out quite late into the night. Sometimes, when he got back a little too early, he would wait outside the door patiently until Jian had finished and had come out of Ahao's bedroom to sleep on the mat with Lao-wu in the doorway. Then, and only then, would Wanfa enter the house, with a look of aloofness on his face as if he had not seen Jian at all, nor had smelled the unpleasant odor of his armpits.

Only once a week did Jian give Wanfa a bottle of beer. Never more than once a week. This Jian believed in moderation in all things.

Among the villagers, the prevailing axiom was improvised: "You need only a wedding cake to marry a virgin, but an oxcart to marry an old married hag." It spread far and wide and lasted a long time.

The five young villagers finished their revel in the village *ryoriten* and stood up to pay their bill. As they were leaving, the one whose head seemed larger than his expanded chest spat toward Wanfa. The deaf man narrowly dodged the flying gob.

Cup after cup, Wanfa emptied his beer. Thinking it was still too early to go home, he slapped the table and shouted, "Hey, bring me a bowl of duck cooked in *danggui* wine, please."

He did not understand why the five young villagers who had just left had turned back again. They stood outside the door, their eyes flickering toward him. They were talking and laughing; it looked as if they had discovered that Wanfa's ass had grown on his head.

1967

Hua Tong

YAN'AN SEEDS

Translated by Mark Caltonhill

1

The county Party committee meeting on spring plowing had been going on for a full three days. It was pretty intense and I hadn't even had the time to read a newspaper in any depth. I just happened to open a two-day-old paper after dinner when the following headline caught my eye: "Fine Successor to the Poor and Lower-Middle Peasants." I pored over the rest of the article:

> Rosy dawn filled the cold winter sky. The Chunfeng Valley production team from the Red Flag Commune eagerly joined the battle to level mountains and build canals. Among the young lads, a robust young girl also wielded hammer and drill rod to lay blast holes. Her crimson cheeks flushed with perspiration, she worked energetically, sending chips of stone and sparks scattering as her iron hammer struck the steel drill rod. Suddenly someone shouted, "Danger, look out!" The girl looked up to see that a large boulder which had been knocked free by two lads above and to the side of her was about to roll down. A little in front of her, poor peasant Wang Shizhu was squatting down fixing a damaged drill rod. The girl raced over and pushed him aside, and at that moment the rock tumbled down on top of her. . . .
>
> The poor peasant escaped danger, but the girl was seriously injured. This girl, who risked her own life to save someone else, is an educated

youth, come to work in this northern mountain village from her home in Shanghai. Her name is Ji Yanfeng. . . .

"Ji Yanfeng!" I blurted out. Surely she had to be the daughter of my old comrade-in-arms Commissar Ji Zhengming. I pulled open my drawer to reread the letter he'd sent me the month before:

> Zheng Min, my dear war buddy and comrade. Good heavens, twenty years have passed already. I finally heard about you recently from an old colleague while I was attending a meeting in Beijing. He told me that you'd been transferred to a county post. What a coincidence! Three years ago my daughter Yanfeng, the one we called Nannan, who was born amid the artillery fire of the Huaihai campaign,[1] was sent to work in the same county that you're going to. When she was leaving I gave her a present, a present you yourself know well. I wanted her to be just like we were when we went forward from Yan'an, surmounted all obstacles and followed the way guided by Chairman Mao. I haven't received a letter from her in a very long time, so if you come across her, please check on the progress of her re-education for me. . . .

There was no mistake then, this Ji Yanfeng had to be Old Ji's daughter. Just to make sure, I telephoned the Party secretary at Red Flag Commune to inquire.

"Yes, yes, Ji Yanfeng is from our commune. You must have read about her heroic deeds in the paper!" It was evident from his tone at the other end of the telephone that he was proud that his commune had a youth such as this.

"How is she now?" I asked, concerned.

"She's still in the county hospital. I've been to see her and the most serious was the injury to her back. She's almost recovered now and I hear she'll be out of hospital soon."

"Good. You know you ought to make the most of her example and use it to educate the other young people who have come to the countryside."

"Right, we've already drawn up a plan and are preparing a report for the county committee. Secretary Zheng, why don't you drop by one day soon and check up on our preparations for plowing and sowing?"

"Yes, of course, I'll come tomorrow or the day after." I hung up. So that confirmed it, the girl in the report who had stepped forward bravely in a moment of danger was indeed the same Nannan who had once been carried through gunfire in a horse-borne wicker basket.

Meaning to finish the article, I picked up the newspaper again, but my thoughts wandered and the typeset words swam before my eyes, blurring into

---

1. The Huaihai Campaign (6 November 1948–10 January 1949) was the second of three decisive campaigns in the Chinese civil war.

a misty cloud. Once more my ears thundered with the cannon of the Huaihai battlefields as I returned to the moment of Nannan's birth amid the flames of war. . . .

In the autumn of 1948, our unit received orders to join the Huaihai campaign, and we traveled from southern Anhui to the front lines in northern Jiangsu. Comrade Fang Wei, wife of then regiment secretary Ji Zhengming, was unable to join the advance as she was pregnant, and so remained in southern Anhui to continue the political struggle. Our unit had barely arrived in Jiangsu when we heard that Fang Wei had been surrounded by a Nationalist unit of local landlords while carrying out work among the masses in a village. When I related this news to Old Ji he was bending over a map considering strategies. He said, "Oh," and his eyebrows shot up. He got to his feet, and, staring out the window, added, "Sure! That was to be expected. Revolution always requires sacrifice." Then he immersed himself once more in the battle plans.

The Huaihai campaign continued for a full two months. Under the personal command of the Great Leader Chairman Mao we achieved a great victory that astonished not only our own people but also the whole world. After the conclusion of the final battle in the Qinglongji area, I accompanied Old Ji as he hurried back to the unit headquarters before the battlefield had been cleared. Unable to contain his triumphant excitement, he hummed a tune the whole way. As we progressed, however, he noticed something and pulled up suddenly.

Looking ahead to the right, I strained to make out Liu, the division HQ's press correspondent, walking next to a female comrade in civilian clothing who was leading a horse. On one flank the horse carried luggage, on the other a wicker basket.

Taking a closer look at the woman, I shouted in astonishment, "Hey! Isn't that Comrade Fang Wei?" Evidently Old Ji had recognized her before I had. His clenched mouth was trembling slightly.

"Ji, Zheng," a voice called across. It really was Fang Wei. She was thin and sallow, but her face showed her excitement.

Coming face-to-face, Old Ji grasped Fang Wei's hand tightly and, in a voice charged with meaning, said, "So, you didn't make the final sacrifice?"

"It was the local people of the south Anhui base who shielded me! . . . " That was all Fang Wei managed to say in her excitement. Tears glistened in her eyes.

"Commissar Ji," Liu saluted as he explained, "the Division Commander got news of Comrade Fang Wei four days ago and ordered me to bring her back."

"Thank you for your effort." Then pointing at the wicker basket on the horse's back, Ji asked, "What's this?"

"That's your daughter!" Fang Wei replied with more than a little pride.

We both stepped forward to take a look. In the basket a baby was sleeping on a cotton quilt. Her face looked very yellow and she was fast asleep. As Old Ji looked at his newborn daughter his eyes became moist.

"How old is she?"

"Three months."

"Have you given her a name?"

"Only the pet name Nannan."

"Why do you call her Nannan?" Ji asked.

"When I was surrounded, after getting me out of the village quickly, the local people hid me safely in the same gully our unit had been stationed in. After a few days I gave birth to her. As my health was poor, my milk quickly dried up, so both mother and daughter relied on sweet potatoes the villagers gave us and pumpkins left behind by the departing troops. Seeing as she'd eaten *nangua* pumpkins so soon after being born, I called her Nannan!" As she explained, Fang Wei took a paper bag from her pocket. "See, I've even brought back a bag of pumpkin seeds!"

Ji took the paper bag, and looking through those large seeds asked me, "Zheng, do you remember them? These are Yan'an seeds!"

"How could I forget? For us, everything to do with Yan'an is engraved on our minds." Looking at the baby's tiny face down there in the basket I said, "This is also a Yan'an seed."

"That's true. She's also a seed of Yan'an, so she should inherit the revolutionary spirit of Yan'an."

Thinking about it, this is probably the origin of the name she was later given: *Yanfeng*, "the Spirit of Yan'an."

More than twenty years have gone by. From what the older generation went through, to the birth of a new generation; from an impression glimpsed in that horse-borne basket, to today's description in the county newspaper, so much diligent irrigation and cultivation has been needed for the creation, sprouting, and maturing of this Yan'an seed.

I decided to make time the next morning to go to the county hospital and see her.

2

Early the next morning I arrived at the hospital and went to ward four where Yanfeng was staying. I was about to open the door and go in when I saw an old man in his sixties sitting in the corridor outside the ward, beckoning to me. When I went across he asked, "Have you come to see Yanfeng?"

"How did you know, sir?" I couldn't help feeling somewhat surprised.

"You're a reporter, right?"

"How do you know I'm a reporter, sir?"

"I've met a lot of reporters while I've been here, some from the county-newspapers, others from the radio station," the old man said, filling his pipe.

"Ah, so you think I look like one?" I asked with interest.

"I'd say you're pretty much the same, though you're a little older."

I couldn't help smiling. Taking off my cap and scratching my graying hair, I said, "Then I'm an old reporter, eh?"

"Yanfeng is still asleep and she's lost a lot of weight recently. How about letting her rest a while longer?" The old man's tone was filled with fondness.

"Okay, I'll do as you suggest, sir," and I too sat down on the bench. I sized up the old man. He was wearing a sheepskin jacket, had graying hair around his temples and was a picture of health. He had the face of a laboring peasant, one who had known his share of life's hardships. He puffed away at his pipe, a cart whip stuck in his waistband.

"Sir, you are . . . ?"

"My name is Tian. I'm from Yanfeng's team. She's expecting to get out of hospital this afternoon, so I've come to collect her."

"Uncle Tian, as you've said, I'm a reporter, so how about letting me interview you?" I wanted to take this opportunity to have a chat with the old fellow.

He smiled, and drawing on his pipe, replied, "All that I want to say has already been 'investigated' by your fellow journalists. When I came to visit Yanfeng a few days ago I met a reporter wearing glasses who was also on his way to interview Yanfeng. I don't know if he's one of yours. Yanfeng wouldn't talk, so he pestered me. I said he shouldn't just write about her saving someone's life. He should come to Chunfeng Valley and interview lots of people to find out how she'd studied the works of Chairman Mao, how she had faith in what we poor and lower-middle peasants have to say, how she always studied thoroughly and worked vigorously. As the saying goes: 'A pine tree doesn't grow a hundred *zhang* tall in a day.' The seedling that is Yanfeng grew tall in the soil of our Chunfeng Valley."

"You're right there, Uncle Tian." I realized he had quite a sharp mind.

Just then the ward door was pushed open and out ran a round-faced girl with short pigtails.

"Uncle!" she cried, cheerfully rushing toward Old Tian.

"Dear, have you fully recovered?"

"See for yourself, Uncle," and the girl spun around, swinging her arms. "I can still strike thirty hammer blows in one go."

"Don't show off! Whatever you might say, I'm not going to let you go drilling blast holes just yet."

"That can't be right! Haven't you often told me that a good knife mustn't be afraid of being polished and a good martial artist mustn't be afraid of tumbling? If I get all soft after being hit by a rock, would I still have the moral integrity of a peasant?"

"Young woman, don't talk back to me," Old Tian said, raising his pipe and pointing it at the girl.

Listening to this conversation between young and old, I knew that this really was Yanfeng, the same Nannan I'd seen so many years before. Her eyes were just like her father's. Turning her head, she caught sight of me and was slightly taken aback.

"Do you recognize me, Yanfeng?" I inquired, smiling.

"Aiyo!" she cried. "If it isn't Uncle Zheng!" Without waiting for me to reply she spun around and ran back into the ward, returning with a faded army satchel. She took out a red cloth bag which she opened. It contained a mimeographed copy of Chairman Mao's report "On the Chongqing Negotiations."[2] On seeing this booklet my heart immediately warmed, and I watched as she opened it and took out a yellowed photograph.

"Look." She passed me the photograph.

It was of a group of soldiers wearing Eighth Route Army armbands posing in front of Pagoda Hill on the outskirts of Yan'an. Among them were her father, mother, and myself. That had been in 1945, when we all headed south with the army. A reporter from the *Liberation Daily* had taken the photo before we left Yan'an.

"That was twenty-five or -six years ago. We must have been about the same age as you are now. Do I still look the same?"

"Just the same! Otherwise how would I have recognized you straightaway? My father and mother have often spoken of you, Uncle Zheng, but they never knew what had become of you," Yanfeng said excitedly. She then introduced me to Uncle Tian.

I shook his hand, saying, "We're already acquainted!"

Old Tian gave a laugh.

I took the copy of Chairman Mao's report from Yanfeng. Memories surged as I caressed the familiar cover and dog-eared pages.

"Uncle Zheng, this is the present Father gave me when I left for the countryside. I never let it leave my side." She flipped through a few pages as she spoke and took out a flattened red envelope. "Look." She opened it. Inside there were two pumpkin seeds.

"Father kept them for more than twenty years." Yanfeng sat down between Old Tian and myself and explained the origin of this treasured gift.

For me, however, it was unnecessary, as I knew the whole story. Recalling it made me very nostalgic. This had been the most glorious period of my life, an experience that will remain with me as long as I live. . . .

In 1942, during the hardest period of the War of Resistance against the Japanese, I was in Yan'an with Yanfeng's father and mother alongside the Great Leader Chairman Mao. To overcome the extreme difficulties and survive the enemy's blockade, Chairman Mao called on us to set to work ourselves and

2. Mao Zedong's report of 17 October 1945 to a meeting of cadres in Yan'an after his return from negotiating with the KMT in Chongqing. *Selected Works of Mao Tse-tung*, vol. 4 (Beijing Foreign Languages Press, 1960), pp. 53–63.

help develop production. The liberated areas launched into a great production campaign. Though Chairman Mao regularly worked around the clock in his efforts to save the Chinese people from destruction, he still personally engaged in production work. At that time our unit was stationed near the Central Guard Regiment. In the autumn of 1943, comrades in the Guard Regiment sent us a packet of pumpkin seeds, and told us they were seeds from the pumpkins grown personally by Chairman Mao. The following spring we planted them on a mountain slope and tended the pumpkin patch with such special attention that come autumn it produced a large crop of big, round pumpkins. The next year our whole unit dined on these exceptional pumpkins!

In 1945, Yanfeng's parents and I were ready to go south with the army. During his report "On the Chongqing Negotiations" Chairman Mao gave special encouragement to those cadres heading south: "**We communists are like seeds and the people are like the soil. Wherever we go, we must unite with the people, take root and blossom among them.**" Chairman Mao also said, "**Arduous work is like a heavy burden lying in front of us. The question is: do we dare to shoulder the responsibility?**" After that Ji Zhengming always carried this mimeographed copy of Chairman Mao's speech with him in his satchel. We must have studied it together countless times.

We were sad when the time came for us to leave Yan'an, and each of us decided to take a little something to remember it by. As he wrapped up a bundle of pumpkin seeds Old Ji said, "Chairman Mao instructed us to take root and blossom among the people like seeds, so I'm taking a packet of Yan'an seeds which were personally cultivated by Chairman Mao."

Later on, after we arrived in southern Anhui to carry out guerrilla warfare, we planted the seeds on a hillside. In the autumn of 1948, with the pumpkins still unharvested, the unit moved out to join the Huaihai campaign. Subsequently the pumpkins became Yanfeng's mother's food.

As I looked over this mimeographed work of Chairman Mao, the seeds and the photograph, I came to a deep appreciation of the emotions underlying my old comrade's attempt to instruct his daughter.

"Yanfeng, your father's presents are charged with meaning," I told her, wrapping up the pamphlet, photo and seeds.

"That's true. Father hoped I'd be a seed of the revolution!" Yanfeng replied solemnly.

"Well, this young girl hasn't failed to live up to her father's hopes. She's toughened up pretty well. At the branch plenary session last month she was unanimously accepted into the Party. As the one who proposed her, I'm happy too," Uncle Tian told me in a loud voice.

As I looked at her face, pale from her period of hospitalization, for some reason the image of that tiny yellow face in the basket on the horse flashed through my mind. . . . How quickly time goes by!

3

A whip crack resounded across the open countryside. A rubber-tired cart drawn by two mules and a horse was speeding along the main road that ran between the county town and the Red Flag Commune.

It was that same afternoon. Uncle Tian was driving the cart, taking Yanfeng back to Chunfeng Valley. I'd decided to hitch a ride to Red Flag Commune so that I could continue my chat with Yanfeng.

"Secretary Zheng, you'll be bounced to death riding in my cart," Old Tian laughed as he wielded the whip.

"There's nothing wrong with a bit of a bouncing. A whole day spent sitting in a chair softens the bones and makes a person spineless. You just keep the horse spurred on and I'll make sure I've got a tight hold," I shouted back.

Yanfeng's face took on a ruddy glow in the sunshine. I was genuinely happy to see my old comrade's child all grown up.

"Yanfeng, what's the most important thing you've learned during these years in the country?" I asked.

"The most important? I'd need a while to think about that." Looking at the back of Old Tian, she added, "For instance, I've learned so much from Uncle Tian! So far you only know about me saving someone. You don't yet know of Uncle Tian's life-saving deed."

The horse's hooves beat their rhythm on the road, the cart rocked gently as Yanfeng, staring forward, drifted into recollection.

"Three years ago, when Father presented me with these precious gifts, I felt I was a Yan'an seed that was sure to blossom into a revolutionary flower. I arrived in Chunfeng Valley in high spirits with my fellow Red Guards. That first evening I talked to my comrades-in-arms and our host, Uncle Tian, about the presents from Father. At work I always wanted the dirty and strenuous duties, to make myself stand out from others. But before long I became downhearted. This was partly due to exhaustion. Each evening my back and legs ached and I just lay on my *kang* unable to move. But it was also because when I'd arrived here everything had been new, whereas by now, the sun rose every morning from a spur of the eastern hill and set behind the western hills; inside the compound were thatched buildings and earthen *kangs*, while outside the village was a vast range of rocky mountains. Life seemed so monotonous. It became worse after a fellow named Du returned to the village from somewhere else. He was particularly fond of approaching young people. He would say, 'Urban Youth coming to the countryside is a good thing,' but privately he expressed his 'concern' to us: 'Your coming to the countryside is good, but a decade of study shouldn't be wasted! It would be a great pity if you had to spend a whole lifetime digging clods of earth!'

"His words struck a chord with me; at school I'd had the highest grades, yet here they were meaningless. There wasn't even a tractor, just hoes and sickles.

This situation made me more and more downcast, which, of course, was impossible to hide from Uncle Tian.

"One evening I was selecting maize seeds under a lamp with Uncle Tian. Picking up a plump seed, he asked, 'Yanfeng, what do you think of this seed?'

"'This one is really fine; it's sure to grow into a strong seedling,' I replied.

"'That's not absolutely certain,' he told me. 'For sure having a good seed is an important element, but if you were to plant it in a flower pot or in a warm cellar then it wouldn't grow well. What's more, once the seedling emerges you have to defend it against insects, hoe weeds, irrigate, and spread manure; it also has to survive the wind and rain. Otherwise it won't be able to produce a stalk, blossom, or bear seeds. You see it has to undergo many toils and struggles.' Uncle gave me a significant look, emphasizing the word 'struggles.' I carefully considered his words, realizing they contained pearls of wisdom.

"Seeing me fall silent, Uncle went on to ask, 'Now that you've been here a couple of months, what do you think of our little village?'

"'I've been everywhere. Even the hills around the village are very familiar to me now,' I answered.

"'That's true, it's a small place, all pretty much the same. It only takes a few days for the newness to wear off. I've spent over sixty years in this mountain valley, I know every tree on every hillside. Nevertheless I still find Chunfeng Valley a nice place to be.' Uncle paused to take another look at me. I looked down, picking out the seeds one by one.

"'Yanfeng, what do you think of this old communist?' Uncle asked me.

"'You've been in the Party longer than I've been alive and you've remained steadfastly revolutionary all these years. Everyone in the village respects you. Is there really any need to ask?'

"'You're wrong, this Party member hasn't done anything worthwhile. I haven't contributed a thing to our nation!' Uncle intentionally let out a long sigh.

"'What?' I asked incredulously.

"'I haven't studied and can't read. I'm fit for nothing but tilling the soil.'

"'Tilling the soil, producing food for the nation. Isn't that making a contribution? Agriculture is the foundation, without peasants where would we be?' I asked earnestly.

"'But people say that spending one's whole life digging clods of earth means you're no good!'

"'That's the attitude of the exploiting class!' I said.

"'Hm! So you mean that sort of thinking is wrong?' Uncle asked rhetorically. 'Think about it. I've tilled the soil my whole life in this mountain valley. But now we don't labor for a landlord like in the past, now we work to fill our own bellies. As a Party member I have to think what's the best way to assist the revolution and build socialism! What can I give the people of the world? How should one fight for communism? What you just said has given me peace of mind. This old fellow doesn't care so much about how long he has left to live,

I must just work all out for the realization of communist ideals in this mountain valley. Fighting for communism in our poor mountain valley requires even greater effort.'

"I finally understood that Uncle had spoken as he did to instruct me and tears filled my eyes.

"'Uncle!' I looked up and cried out emotionally.

"Uncle spoke with sincere concern, 'Child, I know that your morale has been low recently. Remember when you first arrived, how you told me about your father's gifts? There's no way you can let the older revolutionary generation down. Haven't you inherited the revolutionary spirit of Yan'an? Aren't you forever reading the piece by Chairman Mao that your father gave you, repeatedly studying his guidance that **"we communists are like seeds"**? Hasn't your seed taken root here in Chunfeng Valley? Yanfeng, I've seen that fellow Du always sidling up to you youngsters. He's up to no good. Have you analyzed this according to the viewpoints of class and class struggle as instructed by Chairman Mao? You mustn't forget class struggle!'

"Uncle Tian's words tugged away at my heart. Tears welled in my eyes. 'Uncle, I was wrong. . . . ' I let everything spill out, about what I'd been feeling, and what Du had said. The next day Uncle Tian reported the situation with Du to the Party branch, and following a commune investigation it turned out that the fellow had a case history as a counter-revolutionary and was a bad element. With extreme anger I took the lead in speaking out at his mass criticism meeting. Later Uncle Tian told me, 'Yanfeng, now you really think like one of us poor and lower-middle peasants, and speak like us!'

"It was at that moment that I made up my mind to dedicate my whole life to the struggle for this mountain valley.

"Gradually I went up in the village's estimation. Though I said, 'I still have a long way to go,' in my heart I felt 'things are about right.' It was at this time that Uncle Tian once again taught me an unforgettable lesson through his actions.

"That was the winter before last. Uncle Tian had taken a group of youngsters, including myself and Zhang Xiaoxia, to a depression behind the mountain to cut earth for making adobe blocks. We worked all morning, digging out more than a dozen cartloads of earth. The more we dug, the deeper the hole on the hillside became. Xiaoxia and I were totally engrossed in the job of digging. Uncle reminded us, 'Beware of cave-ins, and don't dig into the hillside.' Before his words had even reached us I saw a huge crack appear in the earth above Xiaoxia's head, which then sank downward. I screamed in surprise but just stood and stared, dumbstruck, while Uncle Tian rushed down and pushed Xiaoxia free, supporting the sagging earth with his back and shouting, 'Hurry! Quick, get out!' As he spoke the earth collapsed. Fortunately the layer of soil wasn't too thick, but even so Uncle Tian's back was injured.

"I replayed this heartrending scene over and over again in my mind. The one step that Uncle Tian had taken had left me far behind! It was no ordinary distance, but a gap in perception of the world. . . .

"Uncle Zheng, you see, over the last three years, during the unfolding of this struggle, it has been Uncle Tian who has guided me through. It really has been a case of working steadily and making step-by-step progress."

"No, your summary is incomplete." Uncle Tian, who had remained silent until now, turned his head around to interrupt Yanfeng. "As I see it, the reason for your progress at Chunfeng Valley is not only because you have studied Chairman Mao's works but also because you worked hard at doing what he says. Not only did you feel close to us poor and lower-middle peasants, but you also set your heart on studying our ways. As for this old fellow, the most I can hope to do is to pour a bowl of water over such a seed as you push forth your shoots."

Yanfeng's reminiscences and Uncle Tian's additional comments made me think about many issues. I reckoned that many lessons could be learned from the story of Yanfeng's growing up. . . .

Uncle Tian cracked the whip and the cart sped forward. Yanfeng, "The Spirit of Yan'an," sat in the cart and looked at the distant mountains, her body bathed in the brilliant sunshine of early spring. . . .

1971

Li Ang (1952–)

CURVACEOUS DOLLS

Translated by Howard Goldblatt

She had yearned for a doll—a curvaceous doll—ever since she was a little girl. But because her mother had died and her father, a poor man, hadn't even considered it, she never got one. Back then she had stood behind a wall every day secretly watching a girl who lived in the neighborhood carrying a doll in her arms. The way the girl left her doll lying around surprised and confused her; if she had a doll of her own, she reasoned dimly, she would treat it lovingly, never letting it out of her sight.

One night as she lay in bed clutching the sheet to her chest, obsessed with the idea of a doll, she figured out a way to get one that she could hug as tightly as she wished. After digging out some old clothes, she twisted them into a bundle, then cinched it up with some string about a quarter of the way down. She now had her very first doll.

The ridicule this first doll brought down upon her was something she would never forget. She recalled it years later as she lay in the warmth and comfort of her husband's embrace. She sobbed until he gently turned her face toward him and said in a relaxed tone of voice that was forced and revealed a hint of impatience:

"It's that rag doll again, isn't it!"

Just when it had become the "rag doll" she couldn't recall with certainty, but it must have been when she told him about it. One night, not terribly late, he lay beside her after they had finished, still somewhat breathless, while she lay staring at the moon's rays streaming in through the open window and casting a fine net of light at the foot of the bed. She had a sudden impulse to reveal everything, to tell him about her first doll; and so she told him, haltingly, blushing with embarrassment, how she had made it, how she had embraced it at night in bed, and how, even though her playmates ridiculed her, she had refused to give it up. When she finished, he laughed.

"Your very own rag doll!"

Maybe that wasn't the first time anyone had called it a "rag doll," but he had certainly used the word that night, and his laughter had hurt her deeply. She failed to see the humor in it, and telling him had not been easy. He could be pretty inconsiderate sometimes.

She never mentioned the doll again, probably because of his mocking laughter, and from that night on she began sleeping with her back to him, unable to bear facing his broad, hairy chest. Although it was the same chest that had once brought her solace and warmth, she now found it repulsive. It seemed to be missing something, although she couldn't say just what that something was.

Later on, her nightly dreams were invaded by many peculiar transparent objects floating randomly in a vast grayness, totally divorced from reality yet invested with a powerful life force. She seldom recalled such dreams, and even when she knew she had been dreaming, they vanished when she awoke.

It was a familiar feeling, the realization that she had obtained something without knowing what it was, and it worried her and drove her to tears. She often wept as she lay in her husband's arms, and he invariably blamed the rag doll. But it's not the rag doll! she felt like shouting. The rag doll had disappeared that night, never to return. But she couldn't tell him, maybe to avoid a lot of meaningless explanations.

The dreams continued, troubling her more than ever. She would sit quietly for hours trying to figure out what the floating objects were, but with no success. Occasionally she felt she was getting close, but in the end the answers always eluded her. Her preoccupation took its toll on her husband; after being casually rebuffed in bed a few times, he grew impatient, and when he realized that things were not going to get better, he decided to take her to see a doctor. By now she was fed up with his bossiness and the protector's role on which he prided himself, but her dreams had such a strong grip on her that she finally gave in.

On the way, the oppressive closeness inside the bus made her regret going. She had no desire to open up to a doctor, nor did she think a doctor was the answer. As she looked over at her husband, a single glance from him convinced her that it would be useless to argue. Slowly she turned away.

Someone brushed against her. Glancing up, she saw a pair of full breasts, whose drooping outline she could make out under the woman's blouse. Her interest aroused, she began to paint a series of mental pictures, imagining the breasts as having nipples like overripe strawberries oozing liquid, as though waiting for the greedy mouth of a child. Suddenly she felt a powerful urge to lean up against those full breasts, which were sure to be warm and comforting, and could offer her the sanctuary she needed. She closed her eyes and recalled the time she had seen a child playing with its mother's breasts. If only she could be those hands, enjoying the innocent pleasure of fondling a mother's soft, smooth breasts. Her palms were sweaty, and she wondered what her hands might do if she kept this up much longer.

Feeling a strong arm around her shoulders, she opened her eyes and found herself looking into the anxious face of her husband.

"You're so pale," he said.

She never learned how she had been taken off the bus, recalling only the extraordinary comfort and warmth of her husband's arm. She leaned up against him in the taxi all the way home, gradually reacquainting herself with his muscular chest. But she couldn't stop thinking about those breasts, so soft and smooth, there for her to play with. If only her husband could grow breasts like that on his chest, with drooping nipples for her to suck on! In a flash she realized what was missing from his chest—of course, a pair of breasts to lean on and provide her with sanctuary.

Later on, to her amazement, the objects in her dreams began to coalesce. Those unreal and disorderly, bright yet transparent objects took on concrete form with curves and twists: two oversized, swollen objects like resplendent, drooping breasts; beneath the translucent surface she could see thick flowing milk. It's a woman's body, a curvaceous woman's body! she wanted to shout as the astonishing realization set in.

When she awoke, she experienced an unprecedented warmth that spread slowly from her breasts to the rest of her body, as though she were being baptized by the endless flow of her own milk as it coursed placidly through her body. Overwhelmed by such bountiful pleasure, she began to moan.

When she opened her eyes and glanced around her she saw that her husband was sound asleep. In the still of the night the moon's rays swayed silently on the floor beneath the window like a pool of spilled mother's milk. She began to think of her second doll, the one made of clay. Since her first doll was called the rag doll, this one turned out to be known as the clay doll.

The idea of making a clay doll occurred to her one day when she had felt a sudden desire to hold the neighbor girl's doll. She had approached her, not knowing how to make her desire known, and after they had stared at each other for a few moments, she reached out and tugged at the doll's arm. The other girl yanked it back and pushed her so hard she fell down. Her cries brought the girl's mother out of the house; the mother had picked her up gently and cradled her against her breasts to comfort her.

She had never touched anything so soft and comfortable before. She didn't know what those things were called, but she was instinctively drawn to them and wanted to touch them. After that, she lost interest in her rag doll, since it lacked those protruding, springy objects on its chest and could no longer afford her any solace. She thought about her mother. It was the first time in years that she had truly missed her mother, who had left no impression on her otherwise, but whose bosom must have offered safety, warmth, and a place to rest.

The feeling returned: she longed to tell her husband about her clay doll, but then she recalled how he had laughed before, a humiliating laugh without a trace of sympathy, the sound coming from the depths of his broad chest, ugly and filled with evil. As she turned slightly to look at her sleeping husband, from whom she felt alienated and distant, a vague yet profound loneliness came over her, and she desperately missed her clay doll.

It had been raining then, and the water was streaming down the sides of a mound of clay near where she lived. She regularly went there with the other children to make clay dolls, but hers were always different from theirs. She molded small lumps of clay onto their chests, then worked them into mounds that jutted out. Most of the time she rubbed their bodies with water until they took on a silky, bronze sheen, glistening like gold. She fondled them, wishing that someday she could rub real skin as soft and glowing as that.

In fact, her husband's skin, which also had a bronze sheen, was as lustrous as that of her clay dolls. When she reached out to caress his body, her hand recoiled slightly when she touched his hairy chest, and she wished fervently that a pair of soft breasts were growing there instead! Moved by a strange impulse, she unbuttoned her pajama top and exposed her breasts, full like a married woman's, and let them rest on her husband's chest, praying with unprecedented devotion that her breasts could be transplanted onto his body.

The weight of her heavy breasts on his chest woke him, and with an apologetic look in his eyes, he embraced her tightly.

Whenever she did something like this she had no desire to explain herself, so he would just look at her apologetically and she would calmly accept what he did. But each time his chest touched her breasts, she felt a strange uneasiness, and a peculiar shudder, tinged with revulsion, welled up from the hidden depths of her body. At times like this she felt that the man on top of her was nothing but an onerous burden, and she was reminded of old cows in her hometown, which stumbled along pulling their heavy carts, swaying helplessly back and forth.

She couldn't imagine that she would ever be like an old cow, wearily and dispiritedly bearing a heavy burden that could never be abandoned. Her husband's body had become a pile of bones and rotting flesh that made a mockery of his robust health, although it was slightly warm and exuded an animal stench. It was an instrument of torture that made her feel like she had been thrown into a wholesale meat market.

She began to experience a mild terror: the concept of "husband" had never seemed so distant and fragmented. Before they were married, she had often stroked his shoulders through his shirt with something approaching reverence. Though powerful, they retained some of the modesty and stiffness characteristic of virgin men. They could be called a young man's shoulders, not those of a grown man; yet despite the stiffness, the masculine smoothness of his well-developed muscles intoxicated her. After they were married, whenever she stroked his shoulders she noticed how all the roughness and sharp edges had disappeared; his shoulders had become a soft place where all her cares and doubts melted away. She then sank into a new kind of indulgence, a feeling of nearly total security that became purely physical.

Her mild terror helped her renew her love for her husband's body, and although she was partially successful in this regard, she knew that this renewal would not last for long and that someday a new weariness would set in to make him repulsive again. The only foolproof way to avoid that was for him to grow a pair of breasts to restore the novelty and security she needed so desperately.

The following days were spent in constant prayer and anticipation of the time when breasts would grow on her husband's chest, there to await the hungry mouth of a child.

How she wished she could be that child's mouth, sucking contentedly on her mother's breasts just as she had once rubbed her lips against the breasts of her clay doll, a form of pleasure so satisfying it made her tremble. She still remembered the times she had hidden in an underground air-raid shelter and covered her clay doll's lustrous skin with kisses. She was like a mole wallowing in the pleasure of living in an underground burrow that never sees the light of day. She derived more gratification from this activity than any father, any neighbor girl's doll, or any neighbor girl's mother could ever have provided.

One question remained unanswered: had there been a struggle the first time she kissed the clay doll? She recalled the time she had raised one of her clay dolls to her lips, then flung it to the floor and shattered it, leaving only the two bumps that had been on the chest looking up at her haughtily.

But she never had to worry about being discovered in her underground shelter; she felt safe in that dark, empty space deep underground. Besides, kissing her clay doll like that was perfectly proper; there was nothing to be ashamed of.

How she wished that her home had a cellar, a room unknown to anyone else, or some dark place where she could hide. But there was none—the place was neat, the waxed floors shone, and there were no out-of-the-way corners. She was suddenly gripped by an extraordinary longing for her hometown, where the vast open country and sugarcane patches provided an infinite number of hiding places where no one could ever find her. She missed it so badly and so often that the thought brought tears to her eyes.

She finally decided to tell her husband that she had to go back home. He lay there holding his head in his hands, frowning.

"I can't for the life of me figure out where you get such ideas. Didn't you say you'd never go back to that godforsaken home of yours, no matter what?" he said contemptuously.

"That was before. Things were different then," she said earnestly, ignoring the impatience in his voice. "Now all I want is to go home, really, I just want to go home."

"Why?"

"No reason."

"Do you think you can?"

"I don't know," she answered, suddenly losing interest and feeling that defending herself was both meaningless and futile. It was all so ridiculous that she turned away.

"Are you angry?" He gently put his arm around her.

"Not at all," she said.

She was genuinely not angry. She let him draw her close, but when her back touched his flat chest, the image of those vast sugarcane patches flashed before her, until the bed seemed surrounded by them, as far as the eye could see. "He has to grow a pair of breasts, he just has to!" she thought to herself, in fact, said it very softly, although he was so intent upon unbuttoning her pajama top that he failed to notice.

As in the past, his hands made her feel unclean. She had always believed, although somewhat vaguely, that the hands fondling her breasts ought to be her own and not his. The weak light in the room barely illuminated the outline of his hands, which she allowed to continue fondling her breasts. It was funny that she was aware of his hands only when they were in bed together.

But it hadn't always been like that when she first met him. His hands had represented success and achievement; like his chest, they had brought her contentment and security. Then once they were married, his hands had brought her unimaginable pleasure. And now all she could think of was how to escape them. The foolishness of it all made her laugh.

She knew that this was inevitable, that all she could do was pray for him to grow a pair of breasts. For the sake of domestic tranquillity and happiness, she had to pray with increased devotion.

From the beginning she knew that in a unique situation like this, simply kneeling in prayer was hopeless. A more primitive kind of supplication was called for, a thoroughly liberating form of prayer. And so, after her husband left for work in the morning, she locked herself in the bedroom and pulled down the shades, stood in front of the full-length mirror and slowly undressed herself. As she looked at her reflection in the slightly clouded mirror she fantasized that she was being undressed by an unknown force. She knelt naked on the cold hardwood floor, which was warmed by no living creature, put her palms together in front of her, and began to pray. Invoking the names of all the gods she had ever heard of, she prayed that a pair of breasts like her own would grow on her husband's chest. She even prayed for her own breasts to be transplanted onto his body. If the gods would only answer her prayers, she was willing to pay any price.

She derived immense pleasure from her prayers, and wherever her limbs touched the icy floor she got a tingling sensation like a mild electric shock. She looked forward to these sensations, for they made her feel more clean and pure than when she lay in bed with her husband, their limbs entwined. She began to pray in different postures, sometimes that of a snake wriggling on the floor, at other times a pregnant spider, but always praying for the same thing.

Her husband remained ignorant of what was going on, so everything proceeded smoothly, except that now a strange creature began to creep into her prayers; at first it was only a pair of eyes, two long ovals, their color the dense, pale green of autumn leaves that have withered and fallen. In the dim light of the room they gazed fixedly at every part of her naked body with absolute composure and familiarity. She took no notice and remained on the floor, where she laid bare her womanly limbs. Those eyes, expressionless and filled with a peculiar incomprehension, watched her, but since the creature's very existence was dubious, it had no effect on the fervor of her performance. She embraced the icy floor and kissed it with the vague sense that she was embracing a lover sculpted out of marble.

The pale-green eyes continued to keep watch, although now they were filled with cruelty and the destructive lust of a wild animal. At some point she discovered with alarm that she had fallen under the spell of the frightful sexual passion in those eyes, which she now believed belonged to a half-man, half-animal shepherd spirit sent down by the gods in answer to her prayers; moved to the point that she felt compelled to offer up her body in exchange for what she sought, she opened up her limbs to receive that mysterious man-beast. Under the gaze of those eyes, she lay back and exposed herself to their enshrouding vision. She had completed a new rite of baptism.

This may have been the moment she had been waiting for all along, for it surpassed her marble lover and her obsession with the hoped-for breasts on her husband's chest. She was rocked and pounded by the waves of a profound, unfathomable happiness, which also turned the pale-green eyes into a placid lake, on the surface of which they rose and fell in a regular cadence. Her happiness was compressed into a single drop of water, which fell without warning into the pale-green lake and spread out until every atom of her being had taken on a pale-green cast. After that she felt herself reemerging whole from the bottom of the lake. When she reached the surface she discovered that she was a pale-green mermaid with hair like dried seaweed blown about by the pale-green winds. The water of the pale-green lake suddenly and swiftly receded, as darkness fell over everything and blotted out the pale-green eyes.

When she regained consciousness her first thought was that she had been defiled. Emerging from the chaotic spell of sexual passion, she slowly opened her eyes and was struck by the knowledge that her body, which she had always thought of as incomparably alluring, was in fact just another body; for the first time in a long while she realized that she was merely a woman, no different from any other woman, with neither more or fewer womanly attributes. She lay on the floor, sobbing heavily and recalling the breasts she had hoped would appear on her husband's chest. An inexplicable sadness made her sob even more pitifully. She was living in a dream, an illusion containing vast, hazy, transparent, and mysterious things, with no way to bring them all together. She knew there was no way, even though she had tried before, and even though she once believed she had succeeded; there was no way, she knew that, no way she could ever bring them all together.

She stopped sobbing. Numbly, vacantly, and reluctantly she got to her feet and slowly, aimlessly got dressed, as she knew she must.

She lay there, her arm gently wrapped around her husband's neck as he slept on his side. She felt safe, for the darkness around her was free of all objects; it revealed nothing but its own sweet self—boundless, profound, and bottomless. She gazed at her husband's dark, contented eyes and smiled. She had known that sort of happiness before, and was consoled by the knowledge that it would soon be hers again. Feeling like a wandering child returning to its mother's warm embrace, she believed that any child who had come home was entitled to return to its mother's breast. Gladdened by the thought of the pleasure awaiting her and her husband, she continued to smile.

She couldn't say how long the smile remained on her face, but it must have been a very long time. Since emerging from the vast emptiness of her dream, she had begun to love her husband's flat, manly chest with an uncustomary enthusiasm. She gave herself over to enjoying it and caring for it tenderly, for now she was relieved of her burden of uncleanliness and evil. When her husband perceived this change in her attitude, he started to treat her with increased tenderness. And in order to assure her husband of her purity and rebirth, she began to want a child.

Her image of the child was indistinct. She had always avoided thinking of children, for they reminded her of her own childhood and caused her to experience overwhelming waves of pain. But in order to prove her ability as a mother and show that she no longer required a pair of mother's breasts for herself, she needed a child, whose only qualification was that it be a child, with no special talents nor any particular appearance; as long as it had a mouth to suck on her breasts and two tiny hands to fondle them, that was enough for her. Her only requirement for a child was that it be a child.

She told her husband of her decision. As he lay beside her he heard her out, then laughed derisively.

"You sure have some strange ideas!" he said.

His remark amused her. She could—in fact, she should—have a child. Which meant that *he* was the strange one. She realized for the first time that her husband could be unreasonable and think illogically. The idealized vision of her husband, who had always been the epitome of correctness and reason, began to dissolve, and she knew she could now forget all that she had done and achieve the kind of stability her husband knew; all she needed now was to await the birth of her child.

Her husband did not share her enthusiasm, and was, in fact, decidedly cool to the idea. But she took no notice, intoxicated with the happy prospect of becoming a mother. She enjoyed standing naked on the icy bathroom floor and playing with her swelling, full breasts, pretending that it was her child's hands fondling the objects that represented absolute security—its mother's breasts. Her pleasure brought her fantasies that the tiny hands of the child were actually her own and that the mother, mysterious yet great, was actually an endless plain whose protruding breasts were a pair of mountains poised there for her to lay her head upon and rest for as long as she wanted.

Oh, how she yearned for rest; she was so weary she felt like lying down and never getting up again. Although the nightmares no longer disturbed her in their many forms, they still made indirect appearances. Late one night her husband shook her awake while she was crying and screaming in her sleep; her cheeks were wet with tears as he took her gently into his arms and comforted her. Deeply touched, she decided to reveal everything to him. More than anything else she wanted peace, complete and unconditional. So in a low voice she began to tell him about her clay doll, how she had made it and how she had played with its symbolic breasts. When she finished, he looked at her for a moment with extraordinary calmness, then reached out and held her icy, sweaty, trembling hands tightly in his warm grip.

A great weariness spread slowly throughout her body, and she closed her eyes from exhaustion. Her husband's attitude took her by surprise, for she had expected the same mocking laughter as before. But all he did was look at her with a strange expression on his face, a mixture of indifference and loathing, as though he were observing a crippled animal. She felt the urge to cry, but knew that the tears would not come; she felt like someone who had done a very foolish thing.

Maybe she had actually been hoping for her husband to react by mocking her again, for she remembered how he had laughed so cruelly when she told him about the rag doll; the rag doll had suddenly vanished from her dreams, and for the first time in her life she had known peace of mind. Now she was hoping he would laugh like that again to rid her of the clay doll, like amputating an unwanted limb to regain one's health.

She rolled over on her side, turning her back to the awkward look frozen on her husband's face, then closed her eyes and waited wearily for sleep to come.

In the haziness of her dream she was running on a broad plain, devoid of trees and shrubs, an unbroken stretch of flat grassland. She was running in search of far-off solace when she spotted two mountains rising before her—two full, rounded mounds standing erect in the distance. She ran toward them, for she knew that the solace she sought could be found there. But whenever she felt she had drawn near to them, they faded beyond her reach, even though she kept running.

She awoke and saw the moonlight at the foot of the bed, looking like a pool of mother's milk, and her heart was moved in a peculiar way. She yearned for those mountainlike breasts, and as her eyes began to fill with tears, she clutched a corner of the comforter and cried bitterly.

Suddenly, through her tears she saw something stirring in the surrounding darkness, rocking restlessly in the motion of her tears. Then, slowly it became visible in the form of a flickering thin ray of pale-green light. She sat up in alarm, shutting her eyes tightly and squeezing the tears out and down her cheeks, cold, as though she had just emerged from underwater. Then she opened her eyes again, and there lurking in the darkness were those eyes again, pale-green, cunningly long slits that were laughing with self-assured mockery. Oh, no! she wanted to shout, but she couldn't move. They stared at each other in the two-dimensional darkness, although she was sure that the eyes were slowly drawing closer to her. The pale greenness was growing crueler and becoming an approaching presence of overwhelming power. There was no way she could back off, nowhere for her to turn, and nothing with which she could ward off the attack. And all this time her husband slept soundly beside her.

She had no idea how long the confrontation lasted. The pale-green eyes stood their ground as they kept watch over her, sometimes revolving around her. The milky light of the moon grew denser, slowly creeping farther into the room. During one of the pale-green eyes' circuits around her, something else was revealed in the moonlight—the tail of an animal, covered with long, silky black hairs, suspended lightly and noiselessly in the air. She knew what to do: she reached over to the table lamp beside the bed. The pale-green eyes did not stir; they kept watching her, smiling with consummate evil, as though they were looking at her with a slight cock of the head. She touched the light switch with her finger, but she knew she lacked the courage to press it.

The pale-green eyes knew it too, and willfully remained where they were, watching her calmly with a mocking viciousness. All she had to do was press the light switch to win the battle, but she knew she couldn't do it, she simply couldn't. The pale-green eyes also sensed that the game was over. They blinked several times, then started to retreat. And as they gazed into her eyes for the last time, there was an unmistakable hint that they would be back, that she could never escape them—for her there would be no escape.

From then on she often awoke from disturbing dreams late at night, only to discover those pale-green eyes keeping watch over her quietly from afar or floating past her; they seemed to add to her sinful mission, and every time they appeared, her past reappeared before her with a stabbing pain. Needing a liberating force, she began to wish even more fervently for a child.

She sought the sucking mouth of a child, for she knew that the only time the pale-green eyes would not appear was when a mouth was vigorously sucking at her breasts. She wanted the consoling feeling of rebirth that comes with a child's greedy mouth chewing on her nipples, knowing that it would be more wonderful than her husband's light, playful nibbling during their lovemaking. She wanted a child, one that could show the pale-green eyes that she had become a mother. In order to achieve her goal, she felt a need to turn to a supernatural power for help, and that was when she thought of her wooden doll.

She no longer derived any stimulation from stroking her husband's body or from the imaginary breasts that once preoccupied her. The chest that had filled her with such longing was now nothing more than a mass of muscle, flat and completely ordinary. As she recalled the breasts she had once hoped to find on his chest, she was struck by how comical and meaningless it had all been. She knew that no one could help her, that she had to find her own way out.

She had searched, ardently and with an ambition rooted in confidence, for a pair of breasts that belonged to her alone, not distant and unattainable like those on the neighbor girl's mother. Finally, in an abandoned military bunker, she had found a wooden figurine of a naked woman with pointed breasts, two even, curvaceous mounds on the doll's upper torso. This was the first time she had truly appreciated the form of those breasts she loved so dearly. Her clay doll's chest had been adorned only with shapeless bumps. As she fondled the exquisitely proportioned curves of the wooden doll she felt a heightened sense of beauty and a reluctance to stop.

Standing in front of the full-length mirror bare to the waist, she examined her own full breasts, finding them so alluring that she had a sudden yearning for them. Crossing her arms, she fondled them until they ached. She longed for them, she longed for those soft and lovely, yet dark and shadowy lines, she longed to rest her head on them, she longed to chew on those delightful nipples. She bent her head down toward them, only to discover that they were forever beyond her reach.

She would never forget the first time her lips had touched the nipples of the wooden doll and how much pleasure that had brought her. Those tiny nipples seemed to exist only for her to suck on, and since she could fit an entire breast into her mouth, she could thus possess it completely. She prayed to the wooden doll for a pair of real nipples to suck on or for a tiny child's mouth to replace her own and suck on her breasts.

She wanted a mouth that was devoid of sexual passion, and her husband did not fit the bill. So when the pale-green eyes reappeared late one night, she climbed gently out of bed and began deftly unbuttoning her pajama top. As they watched her, the pale-green eyes appeared puzzled for the first time. She unfastened her bra and began to fondle her breasts. The pale-green eyes, quickly falling under her spell, moved toward her. Two long, gleaming fangs shone through the darkness. The taste of imminent victory was wonderfully sweet to her.

As the pale-green eyes drew near, the gleaming fangs grew brighter. She dropped her hands to her sides, exposing her breasts to the approaching eyes. She imagined those fangs biting on her nipples and bringing her the same pleasure as a child's tiny sucking mouth. Overcome by this exquisite pleasure, she began to moan.

The pale-green eyes were startled out of their trance. They quickly recovered their mocking attitude and retreated nimbly after a long stare that betrayed the remnants of sexual passion.

She believed that the pale-green eyes, with their primitive lust, were capable of bringing her happiness and release. She craved them, and in order to have them she had to do as they dictated. The vast sugarcane fields of her hometown spread out around her in all directions, layer upon layer, dark and unfathomable.

She knew that there would be countless pale-green eyes staring at her in the heart of the sugarcane fields, that there would be countless tails stroking her limbs, that there would be white feathers filling her vagina, and there would be gleaming white fangs biting down on her nipples. But it was a sweet, dark place, boundless and eternally dark, a place where she could hide. She longed for all of this, she longed to possess it all, and nothing else mattered. She yearned for her hometown and for the sugarcane fields where she could hide. She shook her husband awake.

"I want to go back," she said with uncharacteristic agitation. "I want to go home."

The sleepiness in her husband's eyes was quickly replaced by a totally wakeful coldness. "Why?"

"Just because."

"You have to give me a reason."

"You wouldn't understand."

"Is it because of those damned dolls of yours?" he asked in an intentionally mocking tone.

"Since you already know, yes, that's it."

Her frigid indifference enraged him.

"Haven't you had enough?" he said angrily. "I forbid you to go."

"Do you think I really *want* to go back? I'm telling you, I have no choice, there's nothing I can do. I have to return."

She shut her eyes slowly, wishing she hadn't brought up the subject in the first place. Dimly she sensed that somewhere in the illusory, distant dreamscape the little girl's mother's breasts had exploded for some unknown reason, and a thick white liquid began to seep slowly out of them like spreading claws, snaking its way toward her. In her bewilderment, her first thought was to run away, but she discovered that she was easily drawn toward the thick white liquid, which was trying to detach her limbs from her body and suck them up into its cavernous mouth. Her feet were frozen to the spot. The meandering liquid drew closer and closer to her, until it was at her feet. It began to creep up her body, and she could feel the snakelike clamminess and springy round objects wriggling on her skin, as though two dead breasts were rubbing up against her. The liquid climbed higher and higher, until it reached her lips, and just as it was about to enter her mouth, it suddenly coiled itself tightly around her like a snake. The feelings of suffocation and pain she experienced were eclipsed by an immense sense of joy.

She knew that the stream of white liquid would never enter her mouth, and that she would always be searching and waiting. Yet she wanted to seize it, for she believed that it offered her the only hope of attaining a kind of solace, a truth that would allow her to offer up everything in tribute. In the dim light, she set off on a search, not concerned that her husband might oppose her, for she was convinced that this was her only way out.

When she opened her eyes he was gazing at her, his eyes filled with remorse.

"Work hard at it, no matter how long it takes, and someday it will happen to you."

"Maybe," she thought, "but not if I go about it your way. I have to do it my own way." But that was a long way off. She leaned gently against his chest, recalling a naked mannequin she had once seen in a display window. "I'll possess her someday, and maybe I'll call her my wax doll!" she said to herself softly.

1969

PART THREE

Fiction Since 1976

Liu Yichang (1918–)

WRONG NUMBER

Translated by Michael S. Duke

Chen Xi was lying in bed staring at the ceiling when the telephone rang. It was Wu Lichang. She invited him to go to the five-thirty movie at the Lee Theater. His spirits were instantly buoyed up and he shaved, combed his hair, and changed clothes with alacrity. As he was changing clothes, he softly whistled the currently popular tune "A Courageous Chinese." Examining himself in the mirror after dressing, he decided that he really must buy himself a famous-brand shirt. He loved Lichang and Lichang loved him. As soon as he could find a job, they could go to the Marriage Bureau and register. He had just returned from America, and, although he had his degree, he still had to rely on luck to find a job. If his luck was good he would find a job very quickly, but if his luck was bad he might have to wait for some time. He had already sent out seven or eight letters in answer to job advertisements; some replies should be coming in this week. It was on this account that he had been staying at home for the past few days waiting for phone calls from those companies and not going out unless absolutely necessary. But since Lichang had called to invite him out to a movie, he definitely had to go. It was already four-fifty; he had to step on it to get to the Lee Theater on time. If he was late, Lichang would be angry. And so he went forth with long strides, opened the front door, pulled back the steel grating, stepped outside, turned around, closed the front door, locked the steel grating, got into the elevator, went downstairs, left the building, and strode off in the direction of the bus stop with a feeling of breezy relaxation. Just as he reached the bus stop, a bus came speeding along, swerved out of control, careened up onto the bus stop, ran into Chen Xi, an old woman, and a little girl, and crushed them into bloody pulp.

Chen Xi was lying in bed staring at the ceiling when the telephone rang. It was Wu Lichang. She invited him to go to the five-thirty movie at the Lee Theater. His spirits were instantly buoyed up and he shaved, combed his hair, and changed clothes with alacrity. As he was changing clothes, he softly whistled the currently popular tune "A Courageous Chinese." Examining himself in the mirror after dressing, he decided that he really must buy himself a famous-brand shirt. He loved Lichang and Lichang loved him. As soon as he could find a job, they could go to the Marriage Bureau and register. He had just returned from America, and although he had his degree, he still had to rely on luck to find a job. If his luck was good he would find a job very quickly, but if his luck was bad he might have to wait for some time. He had already sent out seven or eight letters in answer to job advertisements; some replies should be coming in this week. It was on this account that he had been staying at home for the past few days waiting for phone calls from those companies and not going out unless absolutely necessary. But since Lichang had called to invite him out to a movie, he definitely had to go. It was already four-fifty; he had to step on it to get to the Lee Theater on time. If he was late, Lichang would be angry. And so he went forth with long strides, opened the front door, and . . .

The telephone rang again.

Thinking it was one of those companies calling, he turned around quickly and ran over to answer it.

"Hello!"

A woman's voice came through the receiver:

"Is Uncle there?"

"Who?"

"Uncle."

"There's no Uncle here."

"Is Auntie there, then?"

"What number are you calling . . . ?"

"Three nine five seven . . . "

"You trying to call Kowloon?"

"Right."

"You got the wrong number! This is Hong Kong."

Indignantly slamming down the receiver, he went out with long strides, pulled open the steel grating, stepped outside, turned around, closed the front door, locked the steel grating, got into the elevator, went downstairs, left the building, and strode off in the direction of the bus stop with a feeling of breezy relaxation. When he was about fifty yards from the bus stop, he saw a bus come speeding along, swerve wildly out of control, careen up onto the bus stop, run into an old woman and a little girl, and crush them into bloody pulp.[1]

1983

1. Author's note: This story was written on April 22, 1983; that day the papers reported a fatal bus accident in Taikoshing.

Wang Zengqi (1920–1998)

A TAIL

Translated by Howard Goldblatt

Old Huang, our personnel consultant, was an interesting fellow. The position of personnel consultant did not exist at the factory until he assumed it. He'd worked in personnel so long he knew pretty much everything there was to know about the employees. But over the last couple of years, as age began to overtake him, his health started to fail, and he was always complaining about aches and pains and rising blood pressure. So he asked to become a consultant, and since most of his consultations came in the area of personnel matters, everyone called him the personnel consultant. Although it started out as a nickname, it had a decidedly formal ring to it. He never missed a meeting concerning personnel matters if he could help it. Sometimes at these meetings he spoke up, sometimes he didn't. Some of the people liked what he had to say, some didn't. He was an eclectic reader and an inveterate storyteller. Sometimes he'd tell one of his stories right in the middle of a very serious meeting. This is one of them.

An engineer named Lin was slated to become chief engineer at the factory, but the leaders were anything but unanimous in their decision. Some approved the promotion, some opposed it, and even after a series of meetings the issue remained unresolved. The opinions of those who approved should be obvious, while those of the opposition can be summarized as follows:

1. Bad background: he came from a capitalist family;
2. Unclear social connections: he had a relative living outside the country—a cousin in Taiwan;

3. He was suspected by some of having had rightist tendencies during the Anti-Rightist campaign;
4. He didn't get along particularly well with the masses—his ideas were sometimes too penetrating.

The strongest opposition came from a personnel-section chief by the name of Dong. This particular fellow was very excitable, and every time the issue arose, he made the same unreasonable comment over and over again as his face turned bright red: "An intellectual! Ptui! An intellectual!"

The personnel consultant listened to him each and every time without taking a stand one way or the other. One day the party secretary asked, "What's your opinion, Huang?" Huang answered in measured tones, "Let me tell you a story—

"Once upon a time there was a man named Aizi. One day Aizi was on a boat that docked alongside a riverbank. In the middle of the night he heard the sound of crying down in the water. He listened carefully. A group of water denizens were crying. 'Why are you crying?' Aizi asked them. 'The Dragon King has given an order,' they said, 'that all animals with tails will be killed. We're crying because we all have tails.' Aizi was greatly moved by their plight. He looked down at each of them and noticed that there was a frog among them. It, too, was crying. Aizi was puzzled. 'Why are you crying?' he asked the frog. 'You don't have a tail.' The frog looked up and said, 'I'm afraid he'll dig up my past as a tadpole!'"

1983

SMALL-HANDS CHEN

Translated by Howard Goldblatt

In the old days there were never very many obstetricians where I come from. Most of the people hired midwives when it was time to have their babies, and each family used the same midwife every time one of their babies was due. The "little gentlemen" and "little ladies" born to Eldest Mistress, Second Eldest Mistress, Third Eldest Mistress, and however many others there were in the family would all have been delivered by the same midwife. Certainly it would never do to have a stranger in the house at a time like this. The regular midwife knew her families so well—including which of the old maidservants could be counted on to assist her—that there was no need to go looking for a special "waistholder." Not only that, most of the people had a superstitious belief that everything would be fine as long as their "lucky" midwife was in attendance. Since these midwives offered up prayers to the Matriarch of Sons and burned incense every day, what respectable family would ever think of asking a male doctor to deliver one of their babies?

The real doctors in our region were all men—except for the daughter of Pock-Faced Li, that is. Having taken over for her father, she was the only woman doctor in town. But she was a specialist in internal medicine, not someone trained to deliver babies, and besides, she was an old maid. Certainly no self-respecting male who planned on going into medicine would ever become an obstetrician. The men all shunned it as a disgraceful calling with no future. That isn't to say there were no exceptions. Small-Hands Chen, as a matter of fact, was a renowned male obstetrician.

Small-Hands Chen's reputation rested on the fact that his hands were so small—smaller than those of a woman, not to mention softer and more delicate. Specializing in difficult deliveries, he was particularly adept at sideways births and breech births (naturally, he was aided in his efforts by medications and medical equipment). People said his hands were so small and his movements so precise that he was able to lessen his patients' labor pains a great deal. No upper-class family would ever have considered engaging him except under the most extreme circumstances. But, since middle- and lower-class families were encumbered with far fewer taboos, whenever one of their women was having a difficult labor, the midwife would acknowledge her inadequate skills and recommend, "You'd better go get Small-Hands Chen."

Naturally, Small-Hands Chen had a large following, but he was still known everywhere as Small-Hands Chen.

In the business of delivering a baby there can be no delay, for two lives hang in the balance. Small-Hands Chen had a horse, a pure white steed the color of snow, that was born to run. People who knew horses said that this animal exhibited the high-stepping gait known as "pheasant willow"—fast, sure-footed, and straight. There are so many lakes and rivers in our region that horses were a rarity. So whenever armies with mounted troops came through the area, the inhabitants all flocked to the banks of the canal to look at and marvel over the "cavalry." Since Small-Hands Chen was often seen riding his white horse across the countryside on his way somewhere to deliver a baby, the people began to lump him and his horse together: White-Horse Small-Hands Chen, they said.

Other doctors, internists and surgeons alike, all looked down on Small-Hands Chen, saying that instead of being a real doctor, he was nothing more than a male midwife. But this didn't bother Small-Hands Chen, who would leap onto his white horse and be off like the wind whenever anyone requested his services. The moment a woman in labor heard the comforting sound of the bells on his horse's bridle, her moaning stopped. A while (sometimes a long while) after he had dismounted and gone into the delivery room, the cry of a newborn baby would signal another successful delivery. Small-Hands Chen, his face bathed in sweat, would emerge from the room and greet the head of the household respectfully: "Congratulations! Mother and child are doing fine." The father, his face wreathed in smiles, would hand over the red envelope in which he had placed the fee, which Small-Hands Chen would stuff into his pocket without looking inside. Then he would go wash his hands, drink a glass of hot tea, and say, "I hope I haven't offended you," before walking outside, mounting his horse, and riding off, the bridle bells jangling noisily.

A lot of people owed their very existence to Small-Hands Chen.

One year the Allied Forces came. For several years that place of ours was the scene of constant warfare between two opposing forces—the National Revolutionary Army, which we called the "Government Forces," and the troops under the command of Sun Chuanfang, who referred to himself as "Commandant of the Allied Forces of Five Provinces." These Allied Forces made their headquarters in the local Buddhist monastery, which housed an entire regiment. The commandant's wife (she might have been his real wife, but she also might have been his concubine) was in labor, but the baby would not come. Several midwives had been summoned, but they were powerless to help this woman who was screaming like a pig in a slaughterhouse, so the commandant finally sent for Small-Hands Chen.

When Small-Hands Chen entered the monastery, the commandant was pacing back and forth in front of the delivery room. He welcomed Small-Hands Chen by saying, "I'm placing both lives in your hands, sir. If you don't save them, I'll have your head! Now you may go in."

The woman had rolls of fat, making Small-Hands Chen's work particularly difficult. But his efforts paid off, and the baby was born, even though delivering the fat woman's child had exhausted him. Almost totally spent, he stumbled out of the delivery room and made his sign of respect to the regiment commandant.

"Congratulations, Commandant, it's a boy. You have a son."

"I've put you to a great deal of trouble," the commandant said with a broad smile on his face. "This way, please."

Food and drink had been set up for him, with the commandant's adjutant serving as host. After Small-Hands Chen had finished two cups of wine, the commandant handed him twenty gold pieces.

"This is for you. I hope it's not too little."

"You are too generous, much too generous."

Having drunk the wine and pocketed his twenty gold pieces, Small-Hands Chen rose to take his leave. "I hope I haven't offended you."

"You can find your own way out, I trust."

Small-Hands Chen walked out of the monastery and mounted his horse. The commandant, who was standing behind him, took out his pistol and shot him dead.

"I couldn't let him get away with putting his filthy hands all over my woman. Her body belongs to one man, and that's me. Who does he think he is, trying to do me like that. Fuck him!"

The regiment commandant was feeling greatly wronged.

1983

Wang Meng (1934–)

TALES OF NEW CATHAY

Translated by Howard Goldblatt

DISPUTATIASIS

A physician I know told me of an encounter he had had at his clinic with a sufferer of disputatiasis.

"Please be seated," he had said to the patient.

"Why should I be seated?" the patient snapped back. "You're not trying to deprive me of my right to *not* be seated, are you?"

There was nothing the physician could do but pour a glass of water and say, "Here, have some water."

"Now that's the sort of crap you hear from people who only see one side of an issue. Not all water is drinkable. If, for example, you had mixed cyanide in with this water, it sure wouldn't be drinkable."

"I didn't put any poison into this water," the physician replied. "Not to worry."

"Who said you put any poison in it?" the patient demanded. "Are you intimating that I've falsely accused you of trying to poison me? Are you hinting that you're about to be formally charged by the Public Prosecutor's office for trying to poison me? I never said you were trying to poison me, You're the one who said that I said you're trying to poison me. That sort of poisonous slander is *worse* than trying to poison me."

The physician, sensing that defending himself would be useless, heaved a sigh and changed the subject: "Nice weather we're having, eh?"

"What a stupid thing to say!" the patient snarled. "Just because we're having nice weather here doesn't mean that they're having nice weather everywhere else in the world, you know. Take the North Pole, for instance. They're having rotten weather there at this very moment, what with strong winds, nights that are twenty-four hours long, icebergs crashing into each other . . . "

His patience exhausted, the physician cut him off abruptly: "This is *not* the North Pole!"

"That doesn't give you the right to deny the existence of the North Pole," the patient shot back. "If you do that, you're guilty of distorting the facts and covering up the truth to serve your own purposes."

"You'd better leave," the physician said.

"Where do you get off ordering me to leave?" the patient demanded. "This is a medical clinic, not a public security office. You don't have the authority to detain me, and you can't execute me."

. . . Following a thorough investigation, it was determined that the patient had participated in the collective writing clinic organized at Beijing universities during the Cultural Revolution and was thought to be showing residual effects of his training.

THE UPHOLDER OF UNITY

Unity Ai noiselessly entered Old Wang's house, where he said to Old Wang in a hushed voice, "Don't pay any attention to him, Old Wang. A man of greatness has to be magnanimous. A sensible fellow like you shouldn't let it get to him."

Old Wang had no idea what this was all about. He blinked once or twice, but since he was just then making some furniture, he went back to work without responding to whatever it was Unity Ai was saying.

"Actually, you've known all along. You're not one to get all caught up in petty things. You're at a different level altogether."

Old Wang lowered his head as he cleaned up his plane.

Unity Ai bent over and moved up closer: "You know that Old Zhou said you're wearing a phony nose."

Old Wang's only response was a sort of grunt.

Unity Ai put his face up even closer, until Old Wang could feel his hot breath on his ear. "Old Zhou said that you found the nose you're wearing in the garbage bin by his house, and that you used pigskin paste to stick it on your face."

Old Wang looked up.

"Old Zhou also said that you sold your real nose to smugglers so you wouldn't have to pay any tax."

Old Wang frowned.

Unity Ai said, "Don't be angry, now, don't be angry. Everyone knows that you've got a first-rate nose, a real treasure, an original, and all his comments prove is that he's a know-nothing. You're not one to get all caught up in petty things, not you . . . "

Old Wang lowered his head again as he tried to figure out what was going on. "I wonder what's on Old Zhou's mind that would make him go around saying bad things about me."

As he was leaving. Unity Ai made sure that he got his point across: "Unity is all-important. Yes sir, unity is all-important."

Unity Ai took his leave of Old Wang and went looking for Old Zhou in his role as the "upholder of unity."

LITTLE LITTLE LITTLE LITTLE LITTLE . . .

The local drama in "H" Province has declined in recent years. Here's the reason why:

About a hundred years ago a truly gifted performer appeared on the scene, an actress whose stage name was Fragrant-and-Red. She had mastered every aspect of her art—song, gesture, monologue, acrobatics—and was all the rage for quite a while. But the years took their toll on Fragrant-and-Red, who eventually was no longer able to perform. By then the people's choice had become Fragrant-and-Red's favorite disciple, Little Fragrant-and-Red. Not only was Little Fragrant-and-Red a carbon copy of her mentor where theatrical skills were concerned but she looked exactly like her, enjoyed the very same things, and displayed identical idiosyncrasies. Fragrant-and-Red had an oval face, so did Little Fragrant-and-Red; Fragrant-and-Red smoked a water pipe, so did Little Fragrant-and-Red; Fragrant-and-Red had a mole beneath her left eye, so did Little Fragrant-and-Red; and so on and so forth. As the years overtook Little Fragrant-and-Red, domination of the stage passed to Little Little Fragrant-and-Red. Currently, the mainstay of the "H" dramatic stage is Little Little Little Little Fragrant-and-Red.

Based upon the principles of calculus, if this "Littling" process continues unimpeded, we will soon reach zero.

RIGHT TO THE HEART OF THE MATTER

A meeting to discuss cold drinks for summertime was held in a place called "M."

MA put forward his proposal to raise the quality level of osmanthus-flavored sour-plum nectar, and voiced his opinions on the issue of beverage production facilities in general.

MB made a recommendation regarding the opening up of additional sources of cold milk and liquid yogurt.

MC advocated an energetic expansion of the production and supply of bottled beer, ale, and light beer.

MD made known his ideas regarding the production of top-grade soft drinks.

ME demanded the return of the traditional thirst-slaking dried fruit from North China.

MX stood up, pounded the table, raised his index finger, and sounded a warning: "Gentlemen, friends, since we are discussing the issue of beverages, we mustn't forget for a single moment man's most basic, his principal, his most essential, his most important beverage, the one that can never be overlooked: not beer, not fruit juice, not yogurt, and not soft drinks, but H_2O—that's water! Talking about beverages and ignoring water is a perfect example of reversing the relationship between principal and subordinate, which can only lead to chaos. At this rate, before long the people will be drinking urine, lime wash, maybe even lubricating oil. Why? Because they will have forgotten that water is *the* source, that water is at the heart of all things, that they must hold on to water at all costs! If we can tolerate this sort of trend, then what's left for us *not* to tolerate?"

All the others, from MA to ME, gazed at each other in blank dismay, not knowing what to do now.

MF was the first to respond to the challenge. "I'm in total agreement with MX's point of view," he shouted, "and I want to go even further by stating that it's not enough just to drink water, that in order to ensure its survival, mankind must also eat! Whether it's flour or rice, vegetables or seafood, makes no difference at all, as long as we eat. Just ponder for a minute the serious consequences of drinking water and not eating! Therefore, of primary . . . "

MA was clearly getting worked up. He unbuttoned his shirt to expose his chest, shouting as he did so: "I want to solemnly declare that I have never opposed the eating of food or the drinking of water, not in the past, not now, and certainly not tomorrow, or the day after, or the day after that. . . . " His declaration thus completed, he took a biscuit out of his pocket, poured himself a glass of cool water, and began eating and drinking right there in front of the others.

MB entered the fray at that moment, calling the others to account: "I want you all to take note that it's not nearly enough just to eat food and drink water. We must also wear clothing! Clothing is necessary to keep us warm *and* to keep our bodies concealed from view. Without clothing we would be no better than beasts!" And the debate goes on.

1982

Chen Ruoxi (1938–)

THE TUNNEL

Translated by Chi-Chen Wang

Early in July Nanjing launched a "Good Men, Good Deeds" movement and Master Hong, a retired worker, was selected by his neighborhood committee as a "Good Man" and given the additional designation of "model old man." Master Hong had mixed feelings about the honor that had come to him: he felt much like a man chewing on a raw olive and finding it refreshing but also somewhat astringent in taste.

The fact was that Master Hong did not feel old.

He was sixty-four and had been retired from the electron tube factory three years, but people in the dormitory continued to address him as Master Hong[1] or simply Old Master out of affection for him. He could see in the mirror that his temples had turned white, but his salt-and-pepper hair was thick and healthy and felt firm to the touch, and his short beard gave him an appearance of power and virility. His flesh was firm and his face remarkably free from wrinkles, though somewhat flawed by age spots. His eyes, however, were always bloodshot from long years of working under strong, harsh light in the factory and had a tendency to become watery under strain. This more than anything else betrayed

---

1. *Shifu* (Master), a term applied to cooks, barbers, carpenters, and skilled craftsmen generally, who are "masters" only to their apprentices and are so addressed by others out of courtesy.

his age. Otherwise, he was healthy and strong of limb, and proud of the fact that he could walk four or five *li* without stopping to rest.

Master Hong did not want to retire so early and had several times requested permission to keep on working—but to no avail, because this was the stated policy of the government.

In the matter of retirement, there was a great difference between factory and intellectual workers. According to his oldest son, who taught at the university, many old professors requested permission to retire but were not allowed to do so. These included doddering old men who were virtually invalids. But the university authorities would not let them go, saying that the central government wished to "protect" the old intellectuals.

Master Hong could not understand this policy of the government. With the retirement of the old professors, the young ones would have a chance for advancement. It would also save money for the government since their pension would be only 70 percent of their regular salary. It didn't make any sense to him to force this kind of "protection" on the intellectuals.

"The general retirement age of 60 for men and 55 for women cannot be applied to the intellectuals at the present," his son explained to him. "If it were, all professors of 60 and over would retire en masse! It would not only be detrimental to culture and learning but also to our national prestige. Don't you realize that foreign visitors always ask to see these professors and that they serve an important United Front[2] purpose?"

Master Hong could not quite follow his son's reasoning, but he accepted it on faith. Was he not a professor at the University and a fully accredited member of the Communist Party? How could he be wrong?

He would like to have worked a few more years, not because his income would be reduced by 30 percent if he retired but because he wanted to have something to do. But the workforce at the factory was fixed, and its regulations required prompt retirement when a worker reached the mandatory age except under special circumstances. As a matter of fact, he should have retired in 1968, but because of the disruptions during the Cultural Revolution, he had been kept on for another year so that he might train a batch of new workers. So he did not retire until 1969.

Time weighed heavily on his hands the first year. He did not know what to do with his hands, so long used to holding an electric welding gun. He would have liked to be helpful around the house, but there was nothing for him to do. After his younger son's marriage, he had moved into his older son's dor-

---

2. *Tongzhan*, abbreviation of *Tongyi zhanxian* (United Front), a Communist slogan dating from the early days of the anti-Japanese War in the 1930s. It represents the policy of "uniting" with any non-communist or foreign ally against a common enemy. In recent years, the term is also applied to getting Taiwan to unite with the "Motherland."

mitory in the University and lived with him and his wife. His daughter-in-law did not work because she had had tuberculosis and was not strong. However, she was a good housekeeper and managed everything well. His grandchildren were then in kindergarten, and he got to see them only mornings and evenings. His son and daughter-in-law were very thoughtful of him. He had worked all his life and deserved all the leisure and comforts in his old age. So they treated him as if he were the lord of the manor and would not let him lift a finger.

Thus Master Hong had nothing to do except go out for a stroll on days when the weather was fine. He never went to school, but during the first few years after his wife's death he joined a reading class and learned enough characters to enable him to write simple reports on his work and to read the newspaper with good comprehension. But he was not interested in the newspapers. They were hard on the eyes and their subject matter was dull and of no interest to him. He never learned to smoke and rarely touched any wine. By his example neither of his sons acquired these habits. His older son had thoughtfully provided him with a bottle of grape wine, but it was no fun drinking alone and he did not indulge in it except to take a few sips on cold nights before going to bed. He could do some carpentering and masonry work and used to fix the leaky roof and collapsed wall of his own adobe house. But even that occupation was denied him now because the dormitory rooms were kept in good repair.

Luckily there was an unprecedented activity during those two years in organizing old and young, along with housewives, into neighborhood committees. A committee was set up in the dormitory affiliated with the larger neighborhood committee. Master Hong's family was recognized as a distinguished one. Having been a worker all his life, he was considered a man of superior background—that is to say, one "gravely wronged" and therefore an "implacable enemy of the exploiting class." By virtue of the fact that his younger son was an officer in the Liberation Army, his family became at the same time an "army household," to say nothing of the fact that his older son was a member of the Party and the younger one was going through his probationary period as a Party member. Thus his family became a truly "red" one. It was inevitable that he should be recruited for the dormitory committee and soon elected to the neighborhood committee, to play an important part in the work of fighting the class enemies and investigating men of questionable backgrounds. In the purification campaigns of '68, several old men were ferreted out for investigation, and quite a stir was created. When the time came for making a final disposition of the cases,. Master Hong was invited to help. Since he had nothing to do with his time, he never missed a meeting and was always eager to do whatever chores he was assigned. He discovered that his words actually carried weight in deciding the political fate of those under investigation; he exulted in his work. He no longer regarded it as a way of passing the time but felt that he was doing something for the Revolution. He became absorbed in the work and put all his heart in it.

It was during this time that he first heard the name of Li Mei.[3]

At one point the neighborhood committee was deliberating whether or not to brand a certain old man as a bad element. The man in question not only had a complex background but kept bad company. At one time he was a good friend of Li Mei's husband, who was said to be a drunkard. During the Great Leap Forward, he had cursed the Communist Party and Mao Zedong, and defied authority. He even assaulted some Party cadre, for which he was finally sent to prison. To dissociate herself from such a man, Li Mei asked for a divorce. After it was granted she lived with her little daughter and made a living by babysitting, cooking and washing for people in the neighborhood. The old man under investigation had pestered Li Mei with his attentions, and it was said that she had driven him away with a carrying pole. Members of the committee all took the position that Li Mei must have encouraged the man in some way. Master Hong was inclined to go along with others, and so decided that Li Mei could not have been blameless since her husband was a counterrevolutionary, though no one could put a finger on just what she had done.

It was not until the winter of 1970, when in response to Mao Zedong's directive, Nanjing, like all large cities in China, began a mad rush to dig air-raid tunnels, that Master Hong first met Li Mei.

As it was with all past directives "from the highest level," the latest decree galvanized everybody into action—in government organizations, schools, factories, and residential neighborhoods. The main tunnels were to be deep enough to afford protection against atomic bombs and wide enough for buses to drive through. They were supposed to be spacious enough to accommodate shops and hospitals, and the network was to cover the entire city so that within fifteen minutes of an air-raid warning the entire population of the city would be able to move underground. The city government decreed that each unit was to be responsible for the section of the tunnel in its locality and to begin work immediately without preliminary surveys or blueprints.

There were three entrances to the tunnel planned for the dormitory area where Master Hong lived, one of which was near a locust tree not far from his apartment. Since most of the teachers in the university had been sent to the northern part of the province for re-education in the May 7th school for cadres, the responsibility for digging tunnels fell upon their families, and Master Hong was drafted to direct the work. The older men and women being too frail for any heavy work, the actual digging was done by the housewives.

Master Hong had lost his wife more than ten years before and rarely came into contact with members of the opposite sex. Now thrown together with a

---

3. Mei, literally "younger sister," is sometimes used as a girl's name for want of a better word or adopted by women who work as domestic help.

crowd of women, he felt strange and not a little thrilled when he happened to come into physical contact with them in the narrow tunnel. Because of his age, the women did not feel constrained to be reticent. While they labored, they kept up a stream of gossip as if he weren't there at all. One of them was quiet, a middle-aged matron who worked harder than anyone else, wielding her pick with abandon. Being a worker himself, Master Hong appreciated her zeal and wondered who she was.

One day she arrived at work before anyone else and he summoned up enough courage to ask her name.

"My surname is Li; I am called Li Mei." She gave him a modest smile with the answer.

So she was the divorced woman! Master Hong was surprised but there was not the slightest trace of distaste in his feeling toward her.

"How does it happen that you have come to work in our section of the tunnel?"

"I do odd jobs for Professor Sun. His loved one[4] is in poor health and can't do heavy work. I am here to take her place."

Li Mei's voice was soft and low and very pleasant to the ear. Master Hong's wife had had a shrill voice and when excited she had sounded as if she were quarreling. His daughter-in-law's voice was hoarse and always sounded as if she were short of breath. Li Mei was different. She spoke in a low voice as if whispering into his ears, and yet every word she spoke came to him like the clear notes of a bell. He could not hear enough of it and regretted that he had not heard it before. For the first time in his life, he became aware that a woman's voice could actually be enchanting.

That night his mind was full of Li Mei as he rested his weary bones in his bed. Her face was already familiar to him. The image now had a name and was endowed with sound; it began to perform like a motion picture before his eyes.

Li Mei's face reminded him of the goddess Guanyin, whose image he had seen years ago in the country. It was roundish, with arched eyebrows, and full of infinite sweetness and compassion for the sufferings of mankind. The physical exertions gave her complexion a healthy glow which overshadowed the wrinkles that were brought on by her smiles and made them seem like added ornaments to her charm. Her eyes were small, as was her nose; but her lips were full and purplish-red like ripe mulberries. Such thick lips would have seemed ugly on other women, but on Li Mei they suggested a "happy destiny." It seemed to him unjust that, with such a physiognomy, she should suffer virtual widowhood. She wore a padded coat and trousers, so Master Hong could not tell whether she was fat or thin, but he judged from the fullness of her face that

---

4. "Loved one" refers to one's husband or wife in the People's Republic.

she could not be too thin. His late wife had been comfortably plump, and he had always liked women that way. It gives one such a soft, warm feeling.

With this thought, Master Hong forgot about his aching bones. He turned over, put his arms around the pillow, buried his face in it and in his heart called out the name Li Mei.

From then on Master Hong took advantage of every opportunity to be near her. She lived in a lane nearby, and once he went to her place on the pretext of notifying her of a meeting. To avoid gossip he stood at the door and called to her. Though he did not go in when she opened the door, he had a good look inside her house.

It reminded him of his own old home. Like hers, it was in a dingy lane, a two-room house constructed of wood with plastered earthen walls and tamped earth floor. The difference was that while his became very messy after his wife died, Li Mei's was kept neat and clean. The unpainted table and stools were well scrubbed and shiny and the dirt floor swept. The only decoration on the wall was a portrait of Mao Zedong. He saw her daughter too, bent over the table doing her lessons. She was a little over ten and looked somewhat like her mother. It was an ordinary enough house, but with Li Mei smiling and standing in the doorway, it acquired an air of simple dignity. He was so absorbed in what he saw that he would have forgotten his errand if Li Mei had not reminded him of it.

It was probably because of his lack of education that he could not appreciate the strategic significance of "deep tunnels," Master Hong had always admitted to himself. If he had his way, he would simply spread a quilt under the table and curl up under it instead of crawling into the tunnel in the event the Soviets dropped their hydrogen bombs. But he was very grateful indeed that Mao Zedong's sudden inspiration should have made it possible for him to meet Li Mei. He would speak to her whenever he could do so without attracting attention, and he was always alert to keep her out of the way of falling earth or a carelessly swung pick. Li Mei appreciated his thoughtfulness and cast him grateful glances.

In the spring of the following year, the tunnels had reached quite a depth and were to be joined very soon. Electric lights were installed, and because the air was stagnant and the danger of falling earth was ever present, the workers were divided into two-hour shifts and the night shift abolished. Once he followed Li Mei into the tunnel and heard the sound of crumbling earth just as she lifted her pick. He sprang forward and pulled her back, with the result that they both fell to the ground. She wasn't hit by the falling earth, but she was much moved by Master Hong's selflessness in risking his own life to save her. Her eyes were filled with tears as she was helped out of the tunnel.

Just about this time tunnel construction was suddenly stopped in Nanjing. It happened that a professor of civil engineering was home on furlough from farm labor and noticed a slight tilt in his dormitory building and that the sinking was due to tunnel work. He reported the risks involved, and the school authorities had no choice but to stop the digging. This and similar incidents were brought to the attention of the city government. In the southern part of the city an entire building actually collapsed. The tunnels should have been propped up with beams or shored up with concrete after they reached a certain depth, but because of shortages of construction materials the higher echelon of the government had done nothing except to exhort the people to promote the revolution by practicing economy. The result was collapsed houses and loss of lives. When the city government realized that it was impossible to realize Mao Zedong's pipe dream with the resources available, it did what the authorities in Beijing had done: it finished in style a few sections of the tunnel in areas frequented by foreign visitors and abandoned the rest.

Though Master Hong was pleased that the government had at last abandoned this senseless undertaking, he was distressed also because it deprived him of the opportunity to be near Li Mei. The day became as monotonous and boring as when he first retired. The only time when life had any meaning for him was when he caught glimpses of Li Mei as she went from one family to another to do their washing and cooking. He discovered that his days were made or spoiled by whether or not he managed to catch sight of her. He missed above all her enchanting voice, for in dreams people spoke without sound and he always woke up disappointed at not having heard her speak. He also cursed himself for making a fool of himself over a woman at his age, and a grandfather too. But that did no good. If anything, he seemed to think about her all the more.

Winter came, with its predictable storms and snow; his daughter-in-law took care to keep him indoors as much as possible for fear that he would suffer exposure. Confined to his room and gazing through the window at the overcast sky, he felt all the more restless. When he did venture out to attend meetings of the neighborhood committee he made it a point to go by way of Li Mei's home, keeping his eyes fixed on her door as he passed the modest little earthen house as though hoping to catch something. Once it happened that Li Mei was emerging from the house to fetch coal just as he walked by. Their two pairs of eyes met and lingered momentarily, and he paused to exchange a few words with her before resuming his steps. For the rest of the way his heart leaped with joy and he found himself all but humming a tune.

As the lunar New Year approached and everyone was making preparations for celebrating the festival, Master Hong wanted to buy something to give Li Mei but was afraid to let his daughter-in-law know. He waited until the day before New Year's Eve, when he finally went out of his way after visiting an old fellow worker and knocked on Li Mei's door.

Li Mei's eyes brightened when she saw who it was, and she asked him in without a word. Master Hong took from the inner pocket of his padded jacket two ten-yuan notes and held it out to her rather timidly, saying, "This is for you to buy some holiday present for the little sister."

Li Mei stepped back and would not take it, her round face reddened in confusion.

Master Hong was never eloquent. Now he stood openmouthed and did not know what to say. Then taking Li Mei's hand, he pressed it to his heart and said, "It comes from here."

After staring at him for a moment, Li Mei freed her hand and with both her hands she lifted his and touched her thick, hot lips against it.

Master Hong slept beautifully that night, fondling the hand which Li Mei had kissed. On New Year's Eve, he reverted to the old custom of giving his grandchildren good luck money, which had been condemned by the Red Guards. Thus amid occasional reports of firecrackers, he sent off another year. He had not been so happy for a long time and felt more than ten years younger.

Shortly after the Spring Festival, the university sent Master Hong's son to Shenyang on a "learning" mission, and Master Hong immediately took upon himself the responsibility of the family's morning shopping. He knew that Li Mei shopped for her employers on her way to work, so he waited for her and walked to the market with her.

Li Mei being a good listener, Master Hong gradually unburdened to her all that was on his mind. He talked about his grandchildren, of his younger son in Qinghai, even of his dead wife. He told her how fond he was of her and how he was afraid that she considered him too old for her. Then Li Mei would comfort and encourage him, assuring him that he looked as strong as when he first moved into the dormitory. This made him feel more than ever that he was not old after all.

He became more and more fond of Li Mei. She was a woman of few words, but she had a good heart and always meant what she said. She did have an opportunity to marry again, but she loved her daughter dearly and did not want to risk marrying someone who might not be kind to her. So she chose to remain unmarried and earn her living by doing odd jobs.

Master Hong should have been content with the knowledge that Li Mei was well disposed toward him, but man has a way of courting unhappiness. After a while he began to wonder if she was being nice to other men and to recall the things that had been said about her when he first heard her name. Was there anything between her and that old man under investigation? He was troubled by these thoughts and suspicions.

When Li Mei saw that he doubted her, she was distressed and once burst into tears, saying, "Lao Hong, do you want me to tear out my heart and show it to you?"

He was touched and at the same time ashamed of himself for being jealous like a young man.

"Don't cry, Li Mei," he said to her, taking her hand and squeezing it. "It is only that I—I love you so much."

His cheeks grew hot to the ears as he uttered the word which belongs to the vocabulary of the young. He never imagined that at his age he would be capable of saying such a thing.

Hearing this, Li Mei threw away all restraint, drew close to him and rested her face on his shoulder.

"Lao Hong, if you do not dislike me and would have me, I would like to throw in my lot with you."

Dislike her? Willing to have her? What absurd talk was this? Master Hong almost shouted right there on the street.

"Li Mei-mei." He was so excited that he stuttered. "For a long time, I have wanted to marry you."

This happened that autumn, a few days before his son returned from Shenyang.

But things will come out. His meetings with Li Mei were observed and talked about, and eventually reached the ears of his daughter-in-law. He had no inkling that she knew, for she never said anything to him. But on the evening of his son's return, the young couple whispered to each other all night. He could not make out what they said but concluded that it was only natural that they should have so much to say to each other after many months' absence. He did not realize what had happened until the following day, when they began to reproach him none too subtly.

First his son spoke of his mother, who had been dead for fourteen years, how capable she was, how delicious her dumplings were, how thrifty and industrious she was, all for the sake of her husband and her children. Then the daughter-in-law took over and brought up the name of Li Mei, recounted and embroidered upon the rumors about her.

"You can't expect very much of a divorced woman," was her rather arbitrary conclusion. "Otherwise she would have remarried long before this. What could she be waiting for?"

"She asked for a divorce only after the man she married became a counterrevolutionary," Master Hong protested.

"Perhaps she was an opportunist," his son chimed in. "She might have divorced him only to show that she was a good revolutionary. Who knows what was actually on her mind?"

"You are quite right," the daughter-in-law agreed. "She is a 100 percent opportunist. The reason she has remained unmarried so long is because she is waiting for someone with an unimpeachable background that she could lean upon. She is only dreaming; no Party member or cadre would have a woman like her, who will only be a drag on him."

The old man had never expected such violent objection from his son and daughter-in-law. They had anticipated him and virtually vetoed him before he had a chance to speak. He was crushed and spoke no more. He realized that he was no match for his son, a high-level intellectual and a member of the Party. He had no chance against him even without any help from his wife.

What he objected to was the toadyism of the rank and file of the Communist Party such as his son. It seemed so unjust to him that they should be ever-ready to accommodate themselves to Party politics while showing no sympathy whatever for an unfortunate and helpless woman like Li Mei. Moreover, the New Marriage Laws were drawn up by the Communist Party. For a time after the Liberation, the people were encouraged to break their old bonds and to form new, revolutionary ties; yet now his son, a Party member, did not want to be contaminated by a divorced woman. But when he thought more about the matter, he realized that this double standard was typical of the Communists. His son did not invent it and could not be blamed for it. Both Mao Zedong and Liu Shaoqi divorced their wives and remarried. Yet they would not permit the people to allude to it, under the penalty of being charged with slandering the leaders and engaging in counterrevolutionary activity. They did not put much stock in their own marriage and divorce laws.

Not long afterward he got a letter from his younger son in Qinghai, expressing concern for his welfare and his desire to have his father come and live with him. His son also said something about how gossip is to be feared and how it might adversely affect the brilliant career that his older brother had before him and jeopardize his own chances of full membership in the Party. After reading the letter Master Hong realized he had utterly no chance, with everyone in the family against him. He wanted to cry out in protest but felt a lump in his throat; he had to swallow his unhappiness, his feeling of having been misused.

That an old man who entertains the idea of becoming a bridegroom again should be subjected to criticism is more or less to be expected. In this respect the New Society was still very tradition-bound; it gave no thought to the loneliness of the old and their needs. For the sake of Li Mei's happiness and his own, he was willing to brave public prejudice, but there was no way for him to cast off the fetters formed by his own flesh and blood. His children were still young when his wife died. For their sake he had remained a widower, because he was afraid that the woman he married might not be a good stepmother to them. Now that they had both achieved a degree of respectability, it was only natural they did not want anyone to intrude and muddy up clear waters. He had sacrificed his own happiness for theirs when he was still in his prime. There didn't seem to be any valid reason why he should not make a sacrifice of himself again for their sake. He sighed.

He could appreciate his daughter-in-law's point of view too. Of his retirement pay of 56 yuan a month, he kept only ten for himself and turned over the rest to her. His son earned 54 yuan a month. Even with these two incomes, it took careful management to keep their household of five in a modest degree of comfort. If he were to marry again, the greatest blow would fall on the daughter-in-law. It would be much harder for her to make ends meet, and quite impossible to maintain their accustomed standard of living. The violence of her feelings against Li Mei was only a reflection of her panic.

Thus Master Hong's idea of remarrying died in the womb. His son took back the chore of shopping, and he was deprived of the opportunity to meet Li Mei. He was in fact ashamed of meeting her. In his chance encounters with her in the dormitory, she looked subdued but uncomplaining, as if she understood the position he was in. He wished he could rush up to her, hold her in his arms and have a good cry.

That winter was unusually cold. Master Hong curled up in his room like a frozen snake, numb to all feelings. He lost interest in everything, and barely managed to attend to the work of the neighborhood committee, which he did without his former zeal. His only diversion was the delight he took in his two grandsons; still, lying awake in the middle of the night, he couldn't help the cold loneliness weighing heavily on him. When it snowed he would stand there, hands in his sleeves, and gaze dumbly at the blank whiteness of the world on the other side of the windowpane. His glance would come to rest across the way on the entrance of the abandoned tunnel near the locust tree. Through prolonged neglect, the tunnel had collected rainwater and become a garbage dump; now the snow covered it all, leaving only traces of a tunnel mouth like some animal trap. The sight of this recalled to his mind the times when he and Li Mei were laboring shoulder to shoulder, digging and shoveling earth. Then he would be all tensed up and restless, walking round and round in his room like a man lost in a maze. He wanted to forget Li Mei, but he found that it was impossible.

Another Lunar New Year was soon at hand. The people were as usual exhorted to practice thrift and simplicity and celebrate the Spring Festival in a revolutionized way, and as usual every family did everything it could to buy up what was desired. One day in the afternoon Master Hong decided to go downtown and buy some presents for his grandchildren.

Li Mei happened to be on a shopping expedition also, and the two ran into each other at the New Street Plaza. They were so happy to see each other after such a long absence that they grinned at each other and forgot for the moment their disappointment and heartaches. The department store was crowded. Li Mei led him in and out of the milling throngs, going from counter to counter, making suggestions and selections for him. No long-married couple could have been more thoughtful and understanding of each other than they. Before they parted, he invited her to see the model film *Harbor* with him on the Feast of Lanterns, agreeing to meet in front of the movie theater.

After that they began to meet regularly every two or three weeks at the movies. Since there were not many motion pictures available, they soon saw them all, each many times over, until they could re-create everything with their eyes closed. But there was no place else to go. In the theater. Master Hong would take Li Mei's hand as soon as the lights were turned out, place it on his knees and caress it. Only at such times did Li Mei's hands, swollen from long immersion in soapy water, receive any tender attention. Sometimes he would put her hand against his chest so that she could feel his wild heartbeats which restored youth had excited. Only then were they able to close their eyes and luxuriate in the feeling of oneness of body and soul brought on by the touch of flesh against flesh.

A change came over Master Hong. He enjoyed his food and slept well and a smile always played around the corners of his mouth. The beard he had neglected all winter now received meticulous attention. This caused his daughter-in-law to look on with a frown. He kept more of his pension for his own use. His daughter-in-law was naturally suspicious but pretended that she noticed nothing and said nothing about it to her husband. She preferred to see him happy than to have him mope around, as he had lately, when hardly a word was exchanged between father and son.

He also took a renewed interest in the affairs of the neighborhood. He read the newspaper, studied Mao Zedong's writings, organized campaigns for "Remembering Bitterness," and took the lead in street cleaning and other public works. It was no wonder, then, that he should be first to be honored when the movement for good men and good deeds was launched that summer, and the old men and old ladies were called upon to emulate and learn from him. And it was no wonder that he should be dubbed a "model old man," since just then "model plays" were monopolizing the Chinese stage.

There was a heat wave of more than ten days' duration in July. It was so humid that the stone slabs under people's eaves were covered with condensation. On the day agreed upon Master Hong was already waiting in front of the movie theater, though its doors had not yet been opened for the three o'clock show.

Presently Li Mei came, greeting him with a smile the minute she saw him from the distance. She wore a colorful blouse with short sleeves, a black silk skirt and a pair of black plastic sandals. Because of her work, Li Mei had always worn long trousers. Wishing to see her dressed like the women in the dormitory, Master Hong had bought her a piece of silk, and was pleased to see her wearing the skirt she had made out of the material.

Li Mei felt shy like a young girl when she came up to him. Having never been exposed to the sun, her unclad legs were white and smooth like radishes that had just been washed and taken out of the water. Master Hong stared at them awhile and then feasted his eyes on her bare arms, round and smooth like lotus roots. He could hardly take his eyes off her.

"Let's skip the movie today," he suddenly said to Li Mei.

"Where could we go?"

That was a problem. Looking around, he saw a hotel opposite the theater, but without a letter of introduction from the unit where he worked there was no chance of getting a room. He wanted to be alone with Li Mei, but big as Nanjing was, it afforded no trysting place.

He decided to go as far as he could.

"Let us go to the Zhongshan Mausoleum. Today is Monday. It shouldn't be crowded."

Li Mei agreed, and they went on the No. 9 bus.

Though the area was not as crowded as on holidays, visitors were gathered everywhere in groups of twos and threes busily engaged in conversation. It was quiet only in comparison with such thoroughfares as the New Street Plaza. Master Hong had no mind for the scenery; all he was interested in was to find a secluded spot where he could be alone with Li Mei. Halfway up the flight of stairs leading up to the mausoleum itself, he turned off and led Li Mei through an orchard and into the woods.

After stumbling around for a while without knowing where they were, they came to an ancient pine with exposed roots that could serve for seats.

"Lao Hong, let's rest for a while and catch our breath."

Li Mei solicitously helped him to sit down on the root and then took out a handkerchief and wiped the sweat off his brow.

He had not done any climbing for a long time and was therefore a little out of breath. He soon recovered his breath but Li Mei kept on wiping him off around the neck, her lotus-root-like arm swinging before him. He suddenly seized it, brought it up to his mouth and bit it gently with his teeth, whereupon Li Mei fell into his arms and sat down on his lap.

Master Hong held her tightly and pressed her soft body against his chest as if trying to quiet his beating heart with her weight. Then, noticing her white legs, he freed one hand to rub against them.

Just then they heard someone's laughter.

Li Mei jumped up with a start, her face red like cockscomb.

The laughter came from a young couple sitting under a tree not far from where they were. They were stealing glances at Li Mei and Master Hong; the young woman was trying to brush back her hair with her hands and blushing with some embarrassment.

Master Hong stood up and, taking Li Mei by the hand, walked farther on. The sun was quite low now, casting long shadows of the tree and of the closely entwined figures of the lovers.

The trees thinned out and disclosed the entrance of a tunnel. This tunnel was an impressive one. The entrance was plastered with cement and had an iron gate, which happened to be open. It was dark and quiet inside. Here at last was a spot where they could be alone. Master Hong took Li Mei's hand and walked into the tunnel with her.

They walked on hand in hand, leaning upon each other. The tunnel echoed their footsteps but they did not hear it: they could only hear the voice of their own hearts responding to each other.

At six o'clock sharp a keeper of the park came and locked the gate. It was opened one day a week to air out the tunnel and keep it dry. Another week would pass before it was to be opened again.[5]

1978

5. When this story first appeared in the Literary Supplement of the *United Daily News*, Taipei, November 11, 1977, it had a different ending, translated by Mr. Wang as follows:

At six o'clock a park keeper came and locked the iron gate.

A week later, the keeper again came, according to regulations, to open the gate to air the tunnel out and keep it dry.

When the gate was opened, the keeper discovered two corpses right inside, that of a woman curled up against that of a man. On the cement wall near the gate were scrawled two irregular lines of writing in blood:

We love each other

We are not suicides

In the book *Laoren* (Old Man), published by Linking Co., Taipei, April 1978, the present version is given. The author noted in her preface that she made the change on the advice of a friend, who thought the ending a "superfluous touch." She explained that the Chinese Communists condemn suicide as an act of "rejection of the people" and that their fear of the consequences of such an act was what originally motivated her to end the story of Master Hong and Li Mei the way she did. She agreed, however, that their story is sad enough without the addition of this grim commentary.

Xi Xi (1938–)

A WOMAN LIKE ME

Translated by Howard Goldblatt

A woman like me is actually unsuitable for any man's love. So the fact that the emotional involvement between Xia and me has reached this point fills even me with wonder. I feel that the blame for my having fallen into this trap, from which there is no escape, rests solely with Fate, which has played a cruel trick on me. I am totally powerless to resist Fate. I've heard others say that when you truly like someone, what may be nothing more than an innocent smile directed your way as you sit quietly in a corner can cause your very soul to take wing. That's exactly how I feel about Xia. So when he asked me: Do you like me? I expressed my feelings toward him without holding back a thing. I'm a person who has no concept of self-protection, and my words and deeds will always conspire to make me a laughingstock in the eyes of others. Sitting in a coffee shop with Xia, I had the appearance of a happy person, but my heart was filled with a hidden sorrow; I was so terribly unhappy because I knew where Fate was about to take me, and now the fault would be mine alone. I made a mistake at the very beginning by agreeing to accompany Xia on a trip to visit a schoolmate he hadn't seen for a long time, then later on, by not declining any of his invitations to go to the movies. It's too late for regret now, and, besides, the difference between regretting and not regretting is too slight to be important, since at this very moment I am sitting in the corner of a coffee shop waiting for him. I agreed to show him where I work, and that will be the final chapter. I had already been out of school for a long time when I first met Xia, so when he asked me if I had a job, I told him that I had been working for several years.

What sort of job do you have?

He asked.

I'm a cosmetician.

I said.

Oh, a cosmetician.

He remarked.

But your face is so natural.

He said.

He said that he didn't like women who used cosmetics and preferred the natural look. I think that the reason his attention had been drawn to my face, on which I never use makeup, was not my response to his question but because my face is paler than most people's. My hands too. Both my hands and my face are paler than most people's because of my job. I knew that as soon as I divulged my occupation to him, he would jump to the same erroneous conclusion that all my former friends had. He has already assumed that my job is to beautify the appearance of girls in general, such as adding just the right touch of color to the face of a bride-to-be on her wedding day. And so when I told him that there were no days off in my job, that I was often busy Sundays, he was more convinced than ever that his assumption was correct. There were always so many brides on Sundays and holidays. But making brides-to-be beautiful is not what I do; my job is to apply the final cosmetic touches to people whose lives have already come to an end, to make them appear gentle and at peace during their final moments before leaving the world of man. In days past I had brought up the subject of my occupation to friends, and I always immediately corrected their momentary misconception, so that they would know exactly what sort of person I am. But all my honesty ever brought me was the loss of virtually all my friends. I frightened them all off; it was as though the me who was sitting across from them drinking coffee was actually the ghost of their own inner fears. And I never blamed them, for we all have an inborn, primitive timidity where the unknown mysteries of life are concerned. The main reason I didn't give a fuller answer to Xia's question was my concern that the truth would frighten him; I could no longer allow my unusual occupation to unsettle the friends around me, something for which I could never forgive myself. The other reason was my natural inability to express what I think and feel, which, over a long period of time, has led to my habit of being uncommunicative.

But your face is so natural.

He said.

When Xia said that, I knew that it was a bad omen for the emotional road he and I were taking; but at that moment he was so happy—happy because I was a woman who didn't use makeup on herself. Yet my heart was filled with sadness.

I don't know who will someday be applying makeup to my face—will it be Aunt Yifen? Aunt Yifen and I have one hope in common: that in our lifetimes we will never have to make up the face of a loved one. I don't know why, after the appearance of this unlucky omen, I continued going on the pleasure excursions with Xia, but maybe, since I'm only human, I lack self-control and merely go where Fate takes me, one ordained step after another. I have no logical explanation for my behavior, and I think that this might just be what humans are all about: much of our behavior is inexplicable, even to ourselves.

Can I come and see you work?

Xia asked.

That shouldn't be a problem.

I said.

Will they mind?

He asked.

I don't imagine any of them will.

I said.

The reason Xia asked if he could see how I worked was that every Sunday morning I have to go to my workplace, and on those days he never has anything else to do. He offered to walk me to work, and since he'd be there already, he might as well hang around and take a look. He said he wanted to look at the brides-to-be and their maids of honor and all the hustle and bustle; he also wanted to watch me as I made the pretty ones prettier or the unattractive ones plain. I agreed without a second's thought. I knew that Fate had already led me up to the starting line and what was about to happen was a foregone conclusion. So here I am, sitting in a small coffee shop waiting for Xia, and from here we'll go together to my workplace. As soon as we get there he'll understand everything. Xia will know then that the perfume he thought I was wearing for him actually serves to mask the smell of formaldehyde on my body. He'll also know then that the reason I wear white so often is not a conscious effort to produce an appearance of purity but merely as a convenience in going to and coming from work. The strange medicinal odor that clings to my body has already penetrated my bones, and all of my attempts to wash it off have failed. Eventually, I gave up trying and even got to the point where I no longer even notice the smell. Xia knows nothing of all this, and he even once commented to me: That's a very unusual perfume you wear. But everything will soon become crystal clear. I've always been a technician who can fashion elegant hairdos and tie a bow tie with the very best. But so what? Look at these hands of mine; how many haircuts and trims have they completed on people who could no longer speak, and how many bow ties have they tied around the necks of totally solemn people? Would Xia allow me to cut his hair with them? Would he allow me to tie his tie carefully for him? In the eyes of others, these soft, warm hands have become cold; in the eyes of others, these hands, which were made to cradle a newborn infant, have already become the hands for touching the white bones of skeletons.

There may have been many reasons why Aunt Yifen passed her skills on to me and they can be clearly perceived through her normal daily remarks. Sure, with these skills, no one would ever have to worry about being out of work and would be assured of a good living. So how can a woman like me, with little schooling and not much knowledge, compete with others in this greed-consumed, dog-eat-dog world? Aunt Yifen was willing to pass the consummate knowledge of this life work on to me solely because I was her niece. She had never let anyone watch her when she was working until the day she took me on as her apprentice, when she kept me by her side instructing me in every detail, until I lost my fear of being alone with the cold, naked corpses. I even learned how to sew up the sundered bodies and split skulls as though they were nothing more than theatrical costumes. I lost my parents when I was very young and was reared by Aunt Yifen. The strange thing is that I began to resemble her more and more, even becoming as taciturn as she, as pale of hand and face as she, and as slow in my movements as she. There were times when I couldn't shake my doubts that instead of being me, I had become another Aunt Yifen; the two of us were, in fact, one person—I had become a continuation of Aunt Yifen.

From today on, you'll not have to worry about your livelihood.

Aunt Yifen had said.

And you'll never have to rely upon anyone else to get through life, like other women do.

She had said.

I really didn't understand what she had meant by that. I couldn't figure out why I wouldn't have to worry about my livelihood if I learned what she had to teach me, or why I wouldn't have to rely upon anyone else to get through life, like other women do. Was it possible that no other profession in the world could free me from worrying about my livelihood or let me avoid having to rely upon others to get through life? But I was only a woman with little knowledge, so of course I would not be able to compete with other women. Therefore, it was strictly for my own good that Aunt Yifen had taken such pains to pass her special skills on to me. Actually, there is not a single person in this city who doesn't need help from someone in our profession. No matter who they are—rich or poor, high or low—once Fate has brought them to us, we are their final consolation; it is we who will give them a calm, good-natured appearance and make them seem incomparably gentle. Both Aunt Yifen and I have our individual hopes, but in addition to these, we share the common hope that in our lifetimes we will never have to make up the face of a loved one. That's why I was so sorrowful last week: I had a nagging feeling that something terrible had happened, and that it had happened to my own younger brother. From what I heard, my younger brother had met a young woman whose appearance and temperament made her the envy of all, a woman of talent and beauty. They were so happy together, and to me it was a stroke of joyous good fortune. But the happiness was all too short-lived, for I soon learned that—for no apparent reason—that delightful young woman had married a man she didn't love. Why is it that two people who are in love cannot marry but wind up spending the rest of their lives as the bitter victims of unrequited love? My younger brother changed into a different person; he even said to me: I don't want to live anymore. I didn't know what to do. Would I someday be making up the face of my own younger brother?

I don't want to live anymore.

My younger brother had said.

I couldn't understand how things could have reached that stage. Neither could my younger brother. If she had merely said: I don't like you anymore. He would have had nothing more to say. But the two of them were clearly in love. It was not to pay a debt of gratitude, nor was it due to economic hardships, so could it be that in this modern, civilized society of ours there are still parents who arrange their daughters' marriages? A lifetime covers many long years; why must one bow to Fate? Ai, I only hope that during my lifetime I will never have to make up the face of a loved one. But who can say for sure? When Aunt Yifen formally took me on as an apprentice and began passing her consummate skills on to me, she said: You must follow my wishes in one respect before I will take you on as my apprentice. I didn't know why she was being so solemn about it. But she continued with extreme seriousness: When it is my turn to lie down, you must personally make up my face; you are not to permit any stranger to so much as touch my body. I didn't feel that this would present any problems, but I was surprised by her inflexibility in the matter. Take me, for example: when it is my turn to lie down, what will the body I leave behind have to do with me? But that was Aunt Yifen's one and only personal wish, and it is up to me to help her fulfill it, if I am still around when that day comes. On this long road of life, Aunt Yifen and I are alike in that we harbor no grandiose wishes; Aunt Yifen hopes that I will be her cosmetician, and I only hope to use my talents to create the "most perfectly serene cadaver," one that will be gentler and calmer than all others, just as though death were truly the most beautiful sleep of all. Actually, even if I am successful, it will be nothing more than a game to kill a little time amid the boredom of life; isn't the entirety of human existence meaningless anyway? All my efforts constitute nothing more than an exercise in futility; if I someday manage to create the "most perfectly serene cadaver," will I gain any rewards from it? The dead know nothing, and my efforts will surely go unnoticed by the family of the deceased. Clearly, I will not hold an exhibition to display to the public my cosmetic skills and innovations. Even less likely is the prospect that anyone will debate, compare, analyze, or hold a forum to discuss my cosmetic job on the deceased; and even if they did, so what? It would cause as much of a stir as the buzzing of insects. My work is purely and simply a game played for the benefit of myself in my workroom. Why then have I bothered to form this hope in the first place? More than likely to provide a stimulus for me to go on working, because mine is a lonely profession: no peers, no audience, and, naturally, no applause. When I'm working, I can only hear the faint sound of my own breathing; in a room filled with supine bodies—male and female—I alone am breathing softly. It's gotten to the point where I imagine I can hear the sounds of my own heart grieving and sighing, and when the hearts of others cease producing sounds of lament, the sounds of my own heart intensify.

Yesterday I decided to do the cosmetic work on a young couple who had died in a love-inspired suicide pact, and as I gazed into the sleeping face of the young man, I realized that this was my chance to create the "most perfectly serene cadaver." His eyes were closed, his lips were pressed lightly together, and there was a pale scar on his left temple. He truly looked as though he were only sleeping very peacefully. In all my years of working on thousands of faces, many of which had fretful, distressed looks on them, the majority appearing quite hideous, I had done what I felt was most appropriate to improve their looks, using needle and thread or makeup to give them an appearance of unlimited gentleness. But words cannot describe the peaceful look on the face of the boy I saw yesterday, and I wondered if his suicide should be viewed as an act of joy. But then I felt that I was being deceived by appearances, and I believed instead that his had been an act of extreme weakness; I knew that, considering my position, I should have nothing to do with anyone who lacked the courage to resist the forces of Fate. So not only did I abandon all thoughts of using him to create the "most perfectly serene cadaver," I refused to even work on him, turning both him and the girl who had joined him in stupidly resigning themselves to Fate's whims over to Aunt Yifen to let her carefully repair the cheeks that had been scalded by the force of the powerful poison they had ingested.

Everyone is familiar with Aunt Yifen's past, because there are some around who personally witnessed it. Aunt Yifen was still young at the time, and she not only liked to sing as she worked but she talked to the cadavers who lay in front of her, as though they were her friends. It wasn't until later that she became so uncommunicative. Aunt Yifen was in the habit of telling her sleeping friends everything that was in her head—she never kept a diary—letting her monologues stand as a daily record of her life. The people who slept in her presence were mankind's finest audience: they listened to her voluble outpourings for the longest time, yet her secrets were always completely safe with them. She told them how she had met a young man and how they had shared the happiness of all young lovers whenever they were together, even though there were times when they had occasional ups and downs. In those days Aunt Yifen went to a school of cosmetics once a week, rain or shine, fifty weeks a year, to learn new techniques, until she had mastered all that the instructors could teach her. But even when the school informed her that there was nothing left for her to study, she persisted in asking if there weren't some new techniques that they could pass on to her. Her interest in cosmetology was that keen, almost as though it were inborn, and her friends were sure that someday she would open a grand salon somewhere. But no, she merely applied this knowledge of hers to the bodies of the people who slept in front of her. Her young lover knew nothing of any of this, for he was convinced that physical beauty was a natural desire of all girls, and that this particular one was simply fonder of cosmetics than most. That is, until that fateful day when she brought him along and showed him where she worked, pointing out the bodies that lay in the room and telling him that although hers was a lonely profession, in a place like this, one encountered no worldly bickerings, and that no petty jealousies, hatreds, or disputes over personal fame or gain existed; when these people entered the world of darkness, peace and gentleness settled over each and every one of them. He was shocked beyond belief; never in his wildest dreams had he thought that she could be a woman like this, one engaged in this sort of occupation. He had loved her, had been willing to do anything for her, vowing that he would never leave her, no matter what, and that they would grow old together, their mutual love enduring until death. But his courage failed him, his nerve abandoned him there among the bodies of people who could no longer speak and who had lost the ability to breathe. He let out a loud yell, turned on his heel and ran, flinging open every door that stood in his way. Many people saw him in a state of complete shock as he fled down the street. Aunt Yifen never saw him again. People sometimes overheard her talking to her silent friends in her workroom: Didn't he say he loved me? Didn't he say he would never leave me? What was it that suddenly frightened him so? Later on, Aunt Yifen grew more and more uncommunicative. Maybe she had already said everything she wanted to say, or maybe since her silent friends already knew all about her, there was no need to say anything more—there truly are many things that never need to be spoken. When Aunt Yifen was teaching me her consummate skills, she told me what had happened. It was I whom she had chosen as her apprentice, not my younger brother, and although there were other factors involved, the major reason had been that I was not a timid person.

Are you afraid?

She asked.

Not at all.

I said.

Are you timid?

She asked.

Not at all.

I said.

Aunt Yifen selected me as her successor because I was not afraid. She had a premonition that my fate would be the same as hers, and neither of us could explain how we grew to be so much alike, although it may have had its origins in the fact that neither of us was afraid. There was no fear in either one of us. When Aunt Yifen was telling me about what had happened to her, she said: I will always believe that there have to be others somewhere who are like us, people who are unafraid. This was before she had become so uncommunicative; she told me to stand by her side and watch how she reddened lips that had already become rigid, and how she worked gently on a pair of long-staring eyes until she had coaxed them into restful sleep. At that time she still talked now and then to her sleeping friends: And you, why were you afraid? Why do people who are falling in love have so little faith in love? Why do they not have courage in their love? Among Aunt Yifen's sleeping friends were many who had been timid and cowardly, and they were even quieter than the others. She knew certain things about her sleeping friends, and sometimes, as she powdered the face of a girl with bangs on her forehead, she would say to me: Ai! Ai! What a weak girl she was. She gave up the man she loved just so she could be considered a filial daughter. Aunt Yifen knew that this girl over here had placed herself into Fate's hands, of her own accord, out of a sense of gratitude, while that one over there had done the same by meekly accepting her lot. She talked about them not as though they had been living, feeling, thinking human beings, but merely pieces of merchandise.

What a horrible job!

My friends said.

Making up the faces of dead people! My God!

My friends said.

I wasn't the least bit afraid, but my friends were. They disliked my eyes because I often used them to look into the eyes of the dead, and they disliked my hands because I often used them to touch the hands of the dead. At first it was just dislike, but it gradually evolved into fear, pure and simple; not only that, the dislike and fear that at first involved only my eyes and hands later on included everything about me. I watched every one of them drift away from me, like wild animals before a forest fire or farmers before a swarm of locusts. Why are you afraid? I asked them. It's a job that someone has to do. Is it that I'm not good enough at what I do, or that I'm not professional enough? But I gradually grew to accept my situation—I got used to being lonely. So many people search for jobs that promise sweetness and warmth, wanting their lives to be filled with flowers and stars. But how does a life of flowers and stars give one the chance to take firm strides in life? I have virtually no friends left today; a touch of my hands reminds them of a deep and distant land of ice and cold, while a look into my eyes produces innumerable images of silent floating spirits, and so they have become afraid. There is nothing that can make them look back, not even the possibility that there is warmth in my hands, that my eyes can shed tears, or that I am warmhearted. And so I began to be more and more like Aunt Yifen, my only remaining friends being the bodies of the deceased lying in front of me. I surprised myself by breaking the silence around me as I said to them: Have I told you that tomorrow I'm going to bring someone named Xia here to meet you? He asked me if you would object, and I told him you wouldn't. Was I right in saying that? So tomorrow Xia will be here, and I think I know how it's all going to end, because my fate and Aunt Yifen's are one and the same. I expect to see Xia as his very soul will take wing the moment he steps foot in here. Ai! We cause each other's souls to take wing, but in different ways. I will not be startled by what happens, because the outcome has already been made clear to me by a variety of omens. Xia once said to me: Your face is so natural. Yes, my face is natural, and a natural face lacks the power to remove someone else's fear of things.

I once entertained the thought of changing my occupation; is it possible that I am incapable of doing the kinds of work that other women do? Granted that I'm not qualified to be a teacher, a nurse, or a secretary or clerk in an office building, but does that mean I can't work as a saleswoman in a shop, or sell bakery products, or even be a maid in someone's home? A woman like me needs only a roof over her head and three square meals a day, so there must be some place I could fit in. Honestly speaking, with my skills I could easily find work as a cosmetician for brides-to-be, but the very thought that lips I was applying color to could open to reveal a smile stops me cold. What would be going through my mind at a time like that? Too many memories keep me from working at that occupation, which is so similar to the one I have now. I wonder, if I did change jobs, would the color return to my pale face and hands? Would the smell of formaldehyde that has penetrated to my very bones completely disappear? And what about the job I have now, should I keep Xia completely in the dark about it? Hiding the past from a loved one is dishonest, even though there are countless girls in the world who will do anything to cover up their loss of chastity and the authentic number of years they have lived. But I find people like that despicable. I would have to tell Xia that for a long time I had done cosmetic work on the sleeping bodies of the deceased. Then he would know and would have to acknowledge what sort of woman I am. He'd know that the unusual odor on my body is not perfume but formaldehyde, and that the reason I wear white so often is not symbolic of purity but a means of making it more convenient for going to and coming from work. But all of this is as significant as a few drops of water in a vast ocean. Once Xia learns that my hands often touch the bodies of the deceased, will he still be willing to hold my hand as we cross a fast-flowing stream? Will he let me cut his hair for him, or tie his tie? Will he be able to bear my gazing intently at him? Will he be able to lie down in my presence without fear? I think he will be afraid, extremely afraid, and like all my friends, his initial shock will turn into dislike and then fear, and he will turn away from me. Aunt Yifen once said: There can be no fear where love is concerned. But I know that although what many people call love is unyielding and indomitable on the surface, it is actually extraordinarily fragile and pliable; puffed-up courage is really nothing but a layer of sugar-coating. Aunt Yifen said to me: Maybe Xia is not a timid person. That's one of the reasons why I never went into detail with him about my occupation. Naturally, another reason was that I'm not very good at expressing myself, and maybe I'd botch what I wanted to say, or I'd distort what I hoped to express to him by choosing the wrong place or time or mood. My not making it clear to Xia that it is not brides-to-be whom I make up is, in actuality, a sort of test: I want to observe his reaction when he sees the subjects I work on. If he is afraid, then he'll just have to be afraid. If he turns and flees, then I'll just tell my sleeping friends: Nothing really ever happened at all.

Can I see how you work?

He asked.

That shouldn't be a problem.

I said.

So here I am, sitting in the corner of a coffee shop waiting for Xia to arrive.

I spent some of this time carefully thinking things over: Maybe I'm not being fair to Xia by doing it this way. If he feels frightened by the work I do, is that his fault? Why should he be more courageous than the others? Why does there have to be any relationship between a fear of the dead and timidity where love is concerned? The two may be totally unrelated. My parents died while I was still young, and I was reared by Aunt Yifen. Both my younger brother and I were orphans. I don't know very much about my parents, and the few things I have learned were told to me later by Aunt Yifen. I remember her telling me that my father was a cosmetician for the deceased before he married my mother. When they were making their plans to get married, he asked her: Are you afraid? No, I'm not, she said. I believe that the reason I'm not afraid is that I take after my mother—her blood flows in my veins. Aunt Yifen said to me that my mother lives on in her memory because of what she had once said: I'm not afraid, and love is the reason. Perhaps that's why my mother lives on in my memory too, however faintly, even though I can no longer recall what she looked or sounded like. But I believe that just because she was my mother and that she said that love had kept her from being afraid does not mean that I have the right to demand the same attitude of everyone else. Maybe I ought to be hardest on myself for accepting my fate from the time I was a child and for making this occupation that others find so hard to accept my life's work. Men everywhere like women who are gentle, warm, and sweet, and such women are expected to work at jobs that are intimate, graceful, and elegant. But my job is cold and ghostly dark, and I'm sure that my entire body has long been tainted by that sort of shadowy cast. Why would a man who exists in a world of brightness want to be friendly with a woman surrounded by darkness? When he lies down beside her, could he avoid thinking that this is a person who regularly comes into contact with cadavers, and that when her hands brush up against his skin, would that remind him that these are hands that for a long time have rubbed the hands of the dead? Ai! Ai! A woman like me is actually unsuitable for any man's love. I think that I myself am to blame for all that has happened, so why don't I just get up and leave and return to my workplace; I have never known anyone by the name of Xia, and he will forget that he once had such a woman for a friend, a cosmetician who made up the faces of brides-to-be. But it's probably too late for that now. I see him there through the window, crossing the street and walking this way. What's that in his hand? What a large bouquet of flowers! What's the occasion? Is it someone's birthday? I see him enter the coffee shop; he spots me sitting in this shadowy corner. The sun is shining brightly outside, and he has brought some of it in with him, for the sun's rays are reflected off of his white shirt. He is just like his name, Xia—eternal summer.

Hey, happy Sunday!

He says.

These flowers are for you.

He says.

He is so happy. He sits down and has a cup of coffee. We have had so many happy days together. But what is happiness, after all? Happiness is fleeting. There is such sadness in my heart. From here it is only a walk of three hundred paces before we arrive at my workplace. After that the same thing will happen that happened years ago. A man will come flying through that door as though his very soul had taken leave of him, and he will be followed by the eyes of the curious until he disappears from view. Aunt Yifen said: Maybe somewhere there is a man of true courage who is unafraid. But I know that this is just an assumption, and when I saw Xia crossing the street heading this way, a huge bouquet of flowers in his hand, I already knew, for this was truly a bad omen. Ai! Ai! A woman like me is actually unsuitable for any man's love; perhaps I should say to my sleeping friends: Aren't we all the same, you and I? The decades fly by in the blink of an eye, and no matter what the reason, there's no need for anyone to shock anyone else out of their senses. The bouquet of flowers Xia brought into the coffee shop with him is so very, very beautiful; he is happy, but I am laden with grief. He doesn't know that in our profession flowers symbolize eternal parting.

1984

Yuan Qiongqiong (1950–)

TALES OF TAIPEI

Translated by Howard Goldblatt

A LOVER'S EAR

He noticed that she carried an ear pick in her purse. She told him that her ears itched from time to time, and she carried it with her so she could clean them whenever she felt like it.

He asked if she would mind cleaning his ears for him. They also itched from time to time.

They had strong feelings for each other by then, and had already done lots of things. Cleaning one another's ears had not been one of them.

In fact, she had used her ear pick only on herself, never to clean anyone else's ears. She had felt that cleaning someone else's ears was the height of intimacy—except, of course, when it was done professionally. Her mother had been the only other person ever to clean her ears. It seemed to her that if a relationship was lacking in passion or in trust, there was little chance that one person would clean the other's ears.

She giggled nervously. "Now?" she asked.

They had agreed to meet somewhere else this time, an open, well-lighted place with lots of people, someplace public. She had insisted on it. She had told him she didn't want to go to his place or to her place this time. There was so much passion in their relationship at that point that whenever they were alone they fell immediately into each other's arms. That left them no time to do anything else.

He smiled back and took her hand. Holding it tightly, he looked her in the eye and said softly and a little conspiratorially: "Yes, now." The same tone of voice he used when he wanted to do *it.* He would say: "I'm putting it in."

For some strange reason she blushed. Two women at the next table were talking about a man. No more than three paces separated the tables, so every word they said came through as clear as a bell.

He was sitting across from her, but it was a small table. She told him to lay his head down on the table, right side facing up. His head was so large it took up nearly half the tabletop. That made it easy for her. She could see all the way down into his ear canal. He had fleshy ears and a wide opening to his ear canal. Strange how you could know everything about someone you were in love with, how you could see their most private parts, yet surprisingly never really notice their ears. Since the light was fairly weak, everything looked a little fuzzy. She asked if she was hurting him. "No," he said.

When she had finished with the right ear, he turned his head to the other side. Neither spoke while she was cleaning his ear, so they could hear every word spoken at the next table. One of the women was saying to the other: "What in the world could have happened? With all that love, I just don't understand it." They were discussing a relationship that had gone sour for no apparent reason. She was concentrating so hard on cleaning his left ear that her eyes began to blur; just then her hand slipped. "Ouch!" he complained tenderly, as though the pain itself were an expression of love. "Oops," she blurted out. "I'm sorry." Drops of blood oozed from the inside wall of his ear. She didn't have the nerve to tell him. "I'm not going to do it anymore," was all she said.

He sat up and felt around in his ear with his pinky, his eyes narrowing as he savored the feeling. Then he gave her a wicked little look and said: "That was sort of like putting it in, wasn't it?"

They broke up not long after that.

Their breakup was accompanied by a very unpleasant scene. It took her a long, long time to get over her feelings of loathing for him and pity for herself. Her only reaction to the news that he had gotten married was indifference—not a trace of emotion. He had become totally irrelevant to her life.

From now on, she reflected, his wife can clean his ears for him.

Inexplicably, this thought saddened her—she suddenly felt very, very sad.

EMPTY SEAT

He heard somebody sobbing.

It was the woman sitting next to him.

At first he hadn't noticed. He'd simply spotted the empty seat when he boarded the bus and sat down in it. But once he was settled in he heard a strange sound like an imperfection in a machine wheel. Click click click click, rhythmic, constant. Hard to tell what it was, what with the bus noises and all, but after a while he identified it. The woman next to him was sobbing.

He turned just enough to sneak a look. She wasn't trying to cause a scene or anything, since she had buried her face in her hands to stifle the sound. But she couldn't hide the depth of her sorrow, no matter what she did. Her shoulders were heaving, yet the way she was being bounced around by the bus made it look kind of silly.

What in the world could cause such unhappiness?

He faced forward and instinctively leaned away from the woman. He didn't want people to think he had anything to do with her. But he had to hold on to the seat in front to keep his balance, and even then he rocked a little.

He glanced at his fellow passengers. A college boy in the aisle nearby was staring at him, but looked away when he realized he was being watched. Too obvious. No doubt what *he* was thinking.

He glared, wanting to catch his eye one more time to let him know he had absolutely nothing to do with the woman. But the college boy not only looked away nonchalantly, he even turned his back on him.

No one else paid him any attention.

She kept sobbing. Impossible to tell how long she'd been at it, but she'd begun long before he sat down. If anything it was worse now, and louder. The other passengers would have to be deaf not to hear it.

Some were already glancing his way.

The person in the seat in front turned to look, then quickly faced front again without showing any emotion.

He crinkled his brow to show how disgusted he was, yet even that didn't prove he had nothing to do with the woman. A couple of indecisive seconds later he slid over until he was more off the seat than on.

She was still sobbing. Nearly in convulsions by now. Why did she have to cry on a bus, of all places? He looked at her again. She was pouring her grief into her hands. You'd think she was the only person on the bus.

He returned one of the passengers' stares. The man shrank back. But he wasn't the only one. Strange how they were more interested in him than in her. He wasn't crying, why gawk at him?

Of course! He should have known there was something peculiar about an empty seat on a crowded bus. No wonder.

With a show of insouciance he got up and mingled with the passengers in the aisle, stopping in front of the college boy, who smiled, as if to say, I know what you mean. Of course! The college boy had vacated the seat before he got on.

The bus pulled up to a stop. He and the college boy watched one of the new passengers take the seat.

CAT

"My cat, if I'm around, so is he. I have only him, and he has only me."

That's the way she always talked, her voice low, with a lethargic drawl and an affected languor. Even with his back to her he could easily picture her expression: head raised, face framed in black shoulder-length hair, eyelids drooping slightly. She was saying, "All by myself . . . live in such . . . a big house. Except for . . . my cat, that is." Soft and purry. She breathed a long sigh. "Ah, my Blue."

Her cat was always called "Blue." Who knows which generation of Blue this was. He had once been so captivated by the throaty, clipped way she spoke that his heart nearly melted. The man talking to her now was more or less the same: guarded, respectful, in a husky voice he felt made him dignified. "Me, I've never liked cats. They're . . . too much like women."

"Oh?" She responded, teasing, surprised, the sound trailing off into the air. "Me, too?"

He didn't have the patience to listen anymore, so he walked over to a corner of the room, keeping his back to her until he got there. When he turned around, she looked just as he had pictured her. Still beautiful, the petite, slim figure of a classic fragile beauty. She was having a one-woman art show, and everyone knew that her physical beauty was half the reason her paintings were causing such a sensation.

The man was young, no more than twenty-five. Young and innocent. He probably knew nothing about cats and nothing about women.

They had lived together for a while. Never much of a pet fancier, he had somehow gotten along with Blue just fine. It was a plump, furry little thing, so in the winter he'd put it on his lap to stay warm. Eventually Blue came to like him so much she got jealous. She had said the cat acted as though it were his.

She turned around while she was talking and spotted him. Fixing her eyes on him from way across the room, she smiled fetchingly. Up to her old tricks. He was unhappy with himself for still finding her irresistible. She walked up and said, "You never come . . . my house." That same old seductive purr. "All alone. Still." A string of high-pitched titters followed.

Instead of responding, he just smiled politely. A moment later he asked, "How's Blue?"

"Ah." Her eyes brightened. "This time, it's . . . Siamese. Really blue. Its eyes."

She truly seemed to have forgotten. How strange.

He could never forget. When he came home that day, Blue was lying dead on his table, a wire coiled three times around its neck. No one would ever believe that those hands gesturing in front of him, so tiny, so delicate, held such strength.

"I see!" He was at a loss for words.

She was calmly talking about her current cat. He observed the artless, contented look on her face.

He guessed he didn't understand women either.

NOT SEEN

Drenched when he walked into the house, he left a trail of water all the way to the kitchen as he went looking for Mama. She wasn't there, so he went into the bathroom to shower off. He had just come back from swimming.

He looked at himself in the bathroom mirror. His freckles were nearly popping out, and his hair looked like a clump of kelp stacked up on his head. His face was white as a ghost, all except for his lips, which were purple. As he stared at his reflection he had the strange sensation that he was gazing at the face of a drowned person. The skin seemed gray, sort of translucent—almost metallic. Maybe it was all a result of psychological, not physiological, factors—in a word, fright.

He had come very close to drowning in the swimming pool.

He had only recently learned how to swim, and today was his first venture out to the deep end. The first two laps, using the Australian crawl, went off without a hitch. It was about six o'clock in the evening, and though there was still plenty of light, the sun's rays were getting weak. The pool was crowded. Off to his left a young fellow was teaching his girlfriend how to swim, while to the right of him a kid was floating on his back, paddling back and forth along the edge of the pool. Three lifeguards sat up in their chairs; people poolside were talking among themselves. The shallow end was packed, mainly with families—parents and their children. Most of the people at the deep end were swimming alone, like him.

The buoyant water gently supported him as he held on to the trough at the edge of the pool. He felt very relaxed, and his success the first two times had filled him with confidence. He started his kick, took a breath, and put his head under the water. Then he began his stroke.

He could no longer recall what happened then—how the situation could have changed so fast puzzled him. All he knew was that suddenly he needed air, but he didn't know how to float to the surface or sink to the bottom where he could push off—all around him nothing but water, like a wall enclosing him within, no matter where he turned. It was a pliant, flowing wall: it yielded when he struck it with his hand or foot, yet it was still there in front of him. He kicked frantically—nothing but water. It assailed his nose and his mouth—he swallowed some.

He opened his eyes. The water was transparent, with a trace of blue. He didn't know which way was up. Thrusting his arms above his head to claw at the water, when he sensed he had broken the surface he yelled HELP! but the sound died on his lips as he slipped below the surface again, leaving a trail of bubbles.

Was this how he was going to die? He was surprised to note how clear his head was at that moment. Glug glug, he swallowed more water. It was all so incredible: the kid floating on his back, the lifeguards, the fellow who had brought his girlfriend to the pool—they were all so near, could they possibly not see him? He was suspended in the water right in front of them, his eyes wide open. His thrashing caused tiny waves on the surface of the water in front of him, a little like floating gossamer. Was this how he was going to die? It seemed so strange, so very strange. He was sinking to the bottom—he swallowed more water. Everyone said drowning was a fast way to go—it only took a few moments. He suddenly regretted not having worn his waterproof watch. But what if he had? What was he going to do, time himself?

He sank slowly to the bottom.

When he touched the bottom his swimming ability was restored immediately. He pushed off with his legs and shot upward; as he broke the surface he gulped down the dry air. He was alive.

He looked at his face in the bathroom mirror. A while ago, while he was drowning, he hadn't been afraid—the thought hadn't occurred to him. But now he was quaking with fright. He had come that close to dying; it would have been so easy.

He heard a door open—it must be Mama. He heard it slam shut. Then the stern voice of his mother: "Now look what you've done!"

Tap tap tap, her footsteps stopped at the bathroom door. "When are you going to grow up? Do you know how much water you've tracked into the house?" Really loud. Normally she'd have jerked the door open and given him hell. Except that now he was seventeen—a seventeen-year-old son in the bathroom. Four or five years earlier, she wouldn't have thought twice about opening the door, but now he was, after all, seventeen.

"Ma." He called out. His heart was filled with the unspeakable terror of someone who has been snatched from the jaws of death; he was afraid—truly, desperately afraid.

At the instant he broke the surface he discovered that the world hadn't changed one bit. The lifeguards were still sitting in their chairs, the people poolside were still talking, the fellow off to his left was hugging his girlfriend—whatever he was teaching her made her giggle. The kid to the right of him was still paddling back and forth on his back, slowly, peacefully. The sun was weak, the sky was bright, the surface of the white water that seemed blue was smooth except for the occasional ripple caused by swimmers.

No one had so much as noticed him.

So close, right in front of their eyes, and not one of them had so much as noticed him.

He opened the bathroom door. "Ma."

Mama said: "You may be a big boy now, but all you know how to do is get into trouble." She glared at him, disgusted. "Look at that hideous face of yours!"

A scene from the past flashed into his mind: he'd never learned how to ride a bike because he'd fallen on his first try and Mama had said that was it.

He swallowed. If he told her what had just happened he'd probably never swim again.

Mama slammed the bathroom door behind her, but not before one final comment: "I wonder if you'll ever grow up."

He turned back and looked in the mirror again.

With anxiety creeping into his heart, he thought back to the peaceful, happy scene at the pool: parents swimming with their children, the warm rays of the sun, the balmy breezes. He had been fighting for his very life, and no one had seen him.

What did he have to do to be seen?

As he reflected on the incident at the pool he was suddenly struck by the realization that Mama was like all the others—she didn't see him either. Just because he was right in front of her didn't mean she saw him.

What did he have to do to be seen?

Drown, maybe.

1988

Li Rui (1950–)

ELECTING A THIEF

Translated by Jeffrey C. Kinkley

"So elect already!"

The head of the production team banged a rock down onto the mill roller like a gavel, then hoisted his leg up in the air and landed it smack on the millstone in a most imposing manner.

It was stifling, hot enough to addle the brain. The faces of the villagers under the old sandalwood tree went blank one after another. They stood there glued to their places, silent as posts. The team head had become angry.

"Fuck your forebears! You think I'm bullying you even now? We give you self-determination, and you still won't make your move, so what then? Are you gonna make me do even your democracy for you? His Honor the Lord High Magistrate in the city doesn't make such a big deal of things. Elect! If you don't elect a grain thief this very day, there'll be no threshing, which means no wheat harvest this year. Come New Year's you'll just have to fill up on coarse cornmeal cakes! Come on, hurry up about it, everybody pick whoever he wants, but no talking allowed!"

Still no one spoke or gave any hint of what he thought. It really wasn't as easy as all that.

The team leader had been on sentry duty last night. When he checked first thing this morning after awakening, one sack of grain from the wheat harvest was missing. He called in the team accountant and the man in charge of the storehouse; one sack missing it was. The team head began cursing people's ancestors. He swore he'd nab the culprit and bring him to justice. They investigated up and down, but there was only one clue—one sack of wheat was missing. Everybody put their heads together. First, it couldn't have been stolen by one of the women, for none of them could have shouldered the 50-kilo-plus load. Second, it couldn't have been one of the six sissy students from Beijing, because they all lived together in the newly built dormitory.[1] They had no place to hide it. Third, it couldn't have been the team head, for he'd been on sentry duty all night. It had to have been done by a thief. But a thief was in it for himself; he wouldn't have the courage to give himself up, the bastard. There was nothing you could do about someone who was not only despicable but sneaky. Yet the more people grew philosophical about it, the more the team head cursed out their ancestors. He took it as a serious insult. The grain thief had specially picked that night not on account of the wheat but to get at him, the team leader. He was so angry he couldn't see straight. He saw the word *thief* written on every villager's forehead. In a fit he assembled them all together. He'd mobilize the masses to conduct an election and solve the case. There was no suffrage for women, so they clasped their babies in their arms and squeezed into a corner to watch the excitement. Students didn't vote, either. After preparing the paper and pens, they just waited for someone to make up his mind, then come on up and lean over to whisper the name in their ears. Then they'd make up the ballot—just writing down the name of the person voted for.

But it was just too hot, brain-addling hot, so hot that the men waiting in the shade couldn't concentrate. Seeing that he couldn't curse them into action, the team head relaxed his taut face:

"Don't be afraid. This is a democratic election, you can pick anyone you please. Elect whoever looks like he might have stolen the wheat." Then he beat his breast: "Pick me for all I care! The one you elect won't necessarily be the thief. What we're going for is a clue. Come on, cast your vote, we'll start with you."

The team head poked his finger at the man nearest the millwheel. He kept pointing until the man had to react. So the first gap appeared in the passel of men all glued together, then a second, and then a third. A magpie alighted on the sandalwood tree and started chirping excitedly, as if it, too, wanted to fly down and cast a ballot.

The voters were very serious about it. One by one they came up and whispered into the students' ears, then returned to where they were, still wearing a very grave expression. The election went forward very smoothly. Fourteen bal-

1. At the end of the Cultural Revolution in the late 1960s, millions of youths upon finishing middle school were sent from the city to settle in the countryside. This Maoist policy was designed to make urban youth learn about the peasant revolution. The youths gradually made their way back to the cities beginning in the mid-1970s. The story describes a situation in the early 1970s, when rural cadres had tremendous control over peasant livelihood because of their connections with the state machinery.

lots were cast; no one gave up his right to vote. All smiles, the students handed the ballots over to the team head. He suddenly frowned.

"All right, you sons of bitches. Is this how low you think of me? Have I been working for you all these years for nothing? You all elected me. If I really wanted the wheat, would I have stolen it from the threshing yard? Sons of bitches, I've been with you all these years without really knowing you. I . . . I fuck all your ancestors! Every one of them! I quit. Whoever wants this lousy job can have it. Come the end of the year, whoever thinks he's up to it can go to the commune and plead for your emergency loan and relief grain. You think you can fart it out of them? We'll see if you get a cent. Sons of bitches, you can fill your bellies with the northern wind for all I care!"

Washing his hands of the matter, the team head withdrew from the polls and stomped off.

The dazed electors were still stuck together.

"Fuck him and his, who would have thought we'd be so unanimous, gosh!"

Somebody or other who couldn't stand the tension sniggered. Suddenly the ground beneath the old sandalwood tree shook with laughter. Menfolk and womenfolk laughed till they were crying, till they had stomach cramps and couldn't walk straight. You would have thought the wheatfield had been hit by a whirlwind.

When they'd had their fill of laughter, some began to worry.

"If he really has quit, then from now on there'll be no one to call us to work and assign tasks. If we mess up, the wheat harvest really will be delayed."

"A man can't walk without his head, and a bird won't fly without a leader. Can the village do without a head man, without someone to manage it?"

Quite out of their depth, the students said, "If he's really gone, we'll pick another leader!"

"Who'll we pick? You? Will you be able to bring us back relief loans and relief grain at the end of the year?"

The villagers under the old sandalwood woke up from their previous mirth; how could they joke about the wheat in front of them, their subsidies at the end of the year, their food, their clothing, their very lives? They'd gotten a bit slaphappy just now. Their smiling faces were blank again, and now with some lines of worry. From the women's corner came a jabber of complaints.

"You've ruined everything. You've got him mad, so what are you to do now?"

"Whoever causes the problem has to solve it. So why don't you fellows be the team leader?"

"Just a sack of wheat—if it's already lost or eaten then it's too late to do anything about it—was it worth offending him?"

It was stifling, hot enough to addle the brain. Aware that they'd brought on a disaster, the menfolk sheepishly grinned toothy white smiles, but this couldn't hide their rising fear. Nobody could think of how to put an end to this today. With the team leader gone, there was suddenly a space beneath the old sandalwood that couldn't be filled. Under the merciless sun the villagers' fear began to produce resentment.

"The thief, that bastard, if he wanted to steal it, all right, but did he really have to wait until the night the team head was on duty?"

"The son of a bitch did this purposely to ruin us—catch him and don't show him any mercy!"

"I hope that wheat rots out his gut, dissolves it into little pieces."

"Let's get the second-generation turtle-spawn bastard and pulverize him!"

"Search for the grain! We'll go door-to-door and just see if we don't find that wheat!"

And yet, however agitated they became, however full of righteous indignation, the team leader who'd abandoned his flock did not return. Without him, they could only worry in the shade of the sandalwood tree.

"Let's pick a person to go to his house," someone proposed.

But who would go?

Their indignation cooling off, the crowd congealed again—everybody had had a hand in provoking this calamity, so who deserved now to bear the burden all by himself? And what response could he expect? He'd better prepare his last eighteen generations of ancestors for this, at least.

"This concerns all of us, so let's everybody go."

The crowd began to stir. At this point someone decided, "Women in front—they're good with words—their small talk and making-up will keep anyone from losing face."

"Right, women go first."

The villagers' shiny-black faces were offset by toothy white smiles again. The huddled crowd finally set off. Following the cloud of dust they shook off from their behinds, the whole village, women in front and men bringing up the rear, straggled from under the sandalwood into the scorching sunlight. In the twinkling of an eye, there was nothing left but an empty patch of shade and a few bewildered students.

An audacious rooster self-confidently hopped up onto the millstone and pecked some old grains of rice and flour from the cracks. Then, cocking up his magnificent comb and raising his head, he began to crow, as if he had the place all to himself. By bearing and manner, he was every inch a leader.

1986

Can Xue (1953–)

HUT ON THE MOUNTAIN

Translated by Ronald R. Janssen and Jian Zhang

On the bleak and barren mountain behind our house stood a wooden hut.

Day after day I busied myself by tidying up my desk drawers. When I wasn't doing that I would sit in the armchair, my hands on my knees, listening to the tumultuous sounds of the north wind whipping against the fir-bark roof of the hut and the howling of the wolves echoing in the valleys.

"Huh, you'll never get done with those drawers," said Mother, forcing a smile. "Not in your lifetime."

"There's something wrong with everyone's ears," I said with suppressed annoyance. "There are so many thieves wandering about our house in the moonlight, when I turn on the light I can see countless tiny holes poked by fingers in the window screens. In the next room, Father and you snore terribly, rattling the utensils in the kitchen cabinet. Then I kick about in my bed, turn my swollen head on the pillow and hear the man locked up in the hut banging furiously against the door. This goes on till daybreak."

"You give me a terrible start," Mother said, "every time you come into my room looking for things." She fixed her eyes on me as she backed toward the door. I saw the flesh of one of her cheeks contort ridiculously.

One day I decided to go up to the mountain to find out what on earth was the trouble. As soon as the wind let up, I began to climb. I climbed and climbed for a long time. The sunshine made me dizzy. Tiny white flames were flickering among the pebbles. I wandered about, coughing all the time. The salty sweat from my forehead was streaming into my eyes. I couldn't see or hear anything.

When I reached home, I stood outside the door for a while and saw that the person reflected in the mirror had mud on her shoes and dark purple pouches under her eyes.

"It's some disease," I heard them snickering in the dark.

When my eyes became adapted to the darkness inside, they'd hidden themselves—laughing in their hiding places. I discovered they had made a mess of my desk drawers while I was out. A few dead moths and dragonflies were scattered on the floor—they knew only too well that these were treasures to me.

"They sorted the things in the drawers for you," Little Sister told me, "when you were out." She stared at me, her left eye turning green.

"I hear wolves howling." I deliberately tried to scare her. "They keep running around the house. Sometimes they poke their heads in through the cracks in the door. These things always happen after dusk. You get so scared in your dreams that cold sweat drips from the soles of your feet. Everyone in this house sweats this way in his sleep. You have only to see how damp the quilts are."

I felt upset because some of the things in my desk drawers were missing. Keeping her eyes on the floor, Mother pretended she knew nothing about it. But I had a feeling she was glaring ferociously at the back of my head, since the spot would become numb and swollen whenever she did that. I also knew they had buried a box with my chess set by the well behind the house. They had done it many times, but each time I would dig the chess set out. When I dug for it, they would turn on the light and poke their heads out the window. In the face of my defiance they always tried to remain calm.

"Up there on the mountain," I told them at mealtime, "there is a hut."

They all lowered their heads, drinking soup noisily. Probably no one heard me.

"Lots of big rats were running wildly in the wind," I raised my voice and put down the chopsticks. "Rocks were rolling down the mountain and crashing into the back of our house. And you were so scared cold sweat dripped from your soles. Don't you remember? You only have to look at your quilts. Whenever the weather's fine, you're airing the quilts; the clothesline out there is always strung with them."

Father stole a glance at me with one eye, which, I noticed, was the all-too-familiar eye of a wolf. So that was it! At night he became one of the wolves running around the house, howling and wailing mournfully.

"White lights are swaying back and forth everywhere." I clutched Mother's shoulder with one hand. "Everything is so glaring that my eyes blear from the pain. You simply can't see a thing. But as soon as I return to my room, sit down in my armchair, and put my hands on my knees, I can see the fir-bark roof clearly. The image seems very close. In fact, every one of us must have seen it. Really, there's somebody squatting inside. He's got two big purple pouches under his eyes, too, because he stays up all night."

Father said, "Every time you dig by the well and hit stone with a screeching sound, you make Mother and me feel as if we were hanging in midair. We shudder at the sound and kick with bare feet but can't reach the ground." To avoid my eyes, he turned his face toward the window, the panes of which were thickly specked with fly droppings.

"At the bottom of the well," he went on, "there's a pair of scissors which I dropped some time ago. In my dreams I always make up my mind to fish them out. But as soon as I wake, I realize I've made a mistake. In fact, no scissors have ever fallen into the well. Your mother says positively that I've made a mistake. But I will not give up. It always steals into my mind again. Sometimes while I'm in bed, I am suddenly seized with regret: the scissors lie rusting at the bottom of the well, why shouldn't I go fish them out? I've been troubled by this for dozens of years. See my wrinkles? My face seems to have become furrowed. Once I actually went to the well and tried to lower a bucket into it. But the rope was thick and slippery. Suddenly my hands lost their grip and the bucket flopped with a loud boom, breaking into pieces in the well. I rushed back to the house, looked into the mirror, and saw the hair on my left temple had turned completely white."

"How that north wind pierces!" I hunched my shoulders. My face turned black and blue with cold. "Bits of ice are forming in my stomach. When I sit down in my armchair I can hear them clinking away."

I had been intending to give my desk drawers a cleaning, but Mother was always stealthily making trouble. She'd walk to and fro in the next room, stamping, stamping, to my great distraction. I tried to ignore it, so I got a pack of cards and played, murmuring "one, two, three, four, five. . . . "

The pacing stopped all of a sudden and Mother poked her small dark green face into the room and mumbled, "I had a very obscene dream. Even now my back is dripping cold sweat."

"And your soles, too," I added. "Everyone's soles drip cold sweat. You aired your quilt again yesterday. It's usual enough."

Little Sister sneaked in and told me that Mother had been thinking of breaking my arms because I was driving her crazy by opening and shutting the drawers. She was so tortured by the sound that every time she heard it, she'd soak her head in cold water until she caught a bad cold.

"This didn't happen by chance." Sister's stares were always so pointed that tiny pink measles broke out on my neck. "For example, I've heard Father talking about the scissors for perhaps twenty years. Everything has its own cause from way back. Everything."

So I oiled the sides of the drawers. And by opening and shutting them carefully, I managed to make no noise at all. I repeated this experiment for many days and the pacing in the next room ceased. She was fooled. This proves you can get away with anything as long as you take a little precaution. I was very excited over my success and worked hard all night. I was about to finish tidying my drawers when the light suddenly went out. I heard Mother's sneering laugh in the next room.

"That light from your room glares so that it makes all my blood vessels throb and throb, as though some drums were beating inside. Look," she said, pointing to her temple, where the blood vessels bulged like fat earthworms. "I'd rather get scurvy. There are throbbings throughout my body day and night. You have no idea how I'm suffering. Because of this ailment, your father once thought of committing suicide." She put her fat hand on my shoulder, an icy hand dripping with water.

Someone was making trouble by the well. I heard him letting the bucket down and drawing it up, again and again; the bucket hit against the wall of the well—boom, boom, boom. At dawn, he dropped the bucket with a loud bang and ran away. I opened the door of the next room and saw Father sleeping with his vein-ridged hand clutching the bedside, groaning in agony. Mother was beating the floor here and there with a broom; her hair was disheveled. At the moment of daybreak, she told me, a huge swarm of hideous beetles flew in through the window. They bumped against the walls and flopped onto the floor, which now was scattered with their remains. She got up to tidy the room, and as she was putting her feet into her slippers, a hidden bug bit her toe. Now her whole leg was swollen like a thick lead pipe.

"He," Mother said, pointing to Father, who was sleeping stuporously, "is dreaming it is he who is bitten."

"In the little hut on the mountain, someone is groaning, too. The black wind is blowing, carrying grape leaves along with it."

"Do you hear?" In the faint light of morning. Mother put her ear against the floor, listening with attention. "These bugs hurt themselves in their fall and passed out. They charged into the room earlier, at the moment of daybreak."

I did go up to the mountain that day, I remember. At first I was sitting in the cane chair, my hands on my knees. Then I opened the door and walked into the white light. I climbed up the mountain, seeing nothing but the white pebbles glowing with flames.

There were no grapevines, nor any hut.

1985

Gao Xingjian (1940–   )

THE ACCIDENT

Translated by Mabel Lee

It happened like this . . .

A gust of wind swept up a pile of dirt from the roadwork outside Xinhua Bookshop on the other side of the road, swirled it up in an arc, then dumped it everywhere. The dust has just settled. It is five o'clock in the afternoon, right after the fourth beep has sounded on the radio in the radio repair shop in Desheng Avenue. It isn't the dust storm season and the weather is only starting to turn warm. Some cyclists are still wearing short gray cotton coats, although on the pavements there are already young women in pale blue spring clothes. There are endless streams of cyclists and pedestrians, but it isn't at a time when everyone is finishing work and traffic congestion is at its worst. However, inevitably there are people who are finishing work early, as inevitably there are people on work leave, so there are busy and idle people coming and going on the street. At this time of day it's always like this. The buses aren't too crowded even if all the seats have been taken and some people are standing, holding on to the handrail as they look out of the windows.

A bicycle fitted with an extra wheel for a baby buggy with a red-and-blue-checkered cloth shade is crossing diagonally from the other side of the road, and a man is riding it. Coming from the opposite direction is a two-carriage electric trolley bus that is going quite fast, but not too fast. It is clearly going more slowly than the small pale-green sedan car about to overtake the bicycle, but neither is necessarily exceeding the city speed limit. The man on the bicycle arches his back, pedaling hard, and the little green car overtakes him on the other side. On this side, the trolley bus is heading toward him. The man hesitates but doesn't brake, and the bicycle with the buggy unhurriedly continues to cross diagonally. The trolley bus sounds the horn but doesn't reduce its speed. As the man crosses the white line in the middle of the road, the dust from the gust of wind has already settled, so his vision isn't obscured. Unblinkingly, he looks up; about forty, he is not a young man, and his hat, tilted slightly to the back of his head, shows that he is balding. He must be able to see the trolley bus coming toward him, and hear the horn. He hesitates again, seems to brake, although not hard, and the bicycle with the buggy clumsily continues crossing the road diagonally. The trolley bus is now close and the horn is sounding nonstop. However, the bicycle keeps going, as before. Sitting in the buggy under the shade is a child with rosy cheeks, barely three or four years old. Suddenly there is the screech of brakes and the horn sounds louder and louder as the trolley bus fast approaches. The bicycle's front wheel continues heading diagonally toward the bus, slowly, as the horn grows louder and the screeching of the brakes turns shrill. The bus has reduced its speed, but the front of the bus keeps moving ominously forward, closing in like a wall. The bus and the bicycle are about to collide and a woman on the pavement on this side of the road starts screaming. Pedestrians and cyclists alike all look on, but no one seems capable of moving. As the front wheel of the bicycle passes the front of the bus, the man starts pedaling hard, maybe he will just make it, but he reaches forward to touch the red-and-blue-checkered shade, as if he is trying to push it down. As his hand touches the shade, the buggy flies off, bouncing on the single wheel. The man's legs are caught as he throws up his arms and falls backward off the bicycle. In the clamor of the horn and brakes and women screaming, before onlookers have time to gasp, the man is instantly crushed under the wheels. The bicycle he was riding, completely twisted, is thrown ten or so feet along the road.

The pedestrians on both sides of the road are aghast and cyclists get off their bicycles. It is quiet all around, and only the gentle singing from the radio repair shop can be heard:

You may remember
Our meeting in the mist, under the broken bridge . . .

It is probably a record of some post–Deng Lijun singer from Hong Kong. Front wheels in a pool of blood, the bus comes to a halt. Blood on the front of the bus is dripping back down onto the body. The first to approach the body is the bus driver, who has opened the door and jumped down. Next, people from both sides of the road also come running, while others surround the overturned buggy, which has rolled into the gutter. A middle-aged woman takes the child from the buggy, shakes it, and examines it all over.

"Is it dead?"

"It's dead!"

"Is it dead?"

Talk in low voices all around. The child, drained of color, has its eyes shut tight, and blue veins can be seen through the child's soft skin. But there is no sign of external injury.

"Don't let him get away!"

"Hurry, call the police!"

"Don't move anything! Don't go over there. Leave everything as it is!"

A crowd several layers deep has surrounded the front of the bus. Only one person is curious enough to lift the twisted wreck of the bicycle. The bell rings as he puts it back down.

"I clearly sounded the horn and braked! Everyone saw it; he was intent on getting himself killed by charging into the bus—how can you blame me?" It is the strained voice of the driver trying to explain, but no one takes any notice.

"You can all be witnesses. All of you saw it!"

"Move aside! Move aside—move aside, all of you!" A policeman with a big hat emerges from the crowd.

"We've got to hurry to save the child's life! Quick, stop a car and get the child to a hospital!" It is a man's voice.

A young man in a coffee-colored leather jacket runs to the line in the middle of the road, waving an arm. A small Toyota sedan sounds its horn nonstop to make its way through the pedestrians who have spilled onto the roadway. Next, one of those 130 light trucks comes along, and it stops. Inside the windows of the bus involved in the accident, passengers are bickering with the conductress. Another trolley bus pulls up behind. The doors of the one in front open and the passengers surge out, blocking the trolley bus that has just arrived. There is a loud clamor of voices.

I will never, never be able to forget . . .

The singing on the stereo is drowned out.

Blood is still dripping, and there is a stench of blood in the air.

"*Waaa* . . . " The child's repressed wailing finally breaks out.

"It's a good sign!"

"It's still alive!"

There are sighs of happy relief. As the wailing grows louder, people also come back to life: it is as if they have been liberated. They then all rush to join the crowd surrounding the body.

Screaming sirens. A police car with flashing blue lights on the roof has arrived, and the crowd parts as four policemen quickly get out. Two of them are wielding batons, and people stand back immediately.

Traffic has come to a standstill and long queues of vehicles are waiting at both ends of the street. Honking horns have replaced the din of voices. One of the policemen goes to the middle of the road and waves his white-gloved hands to direct the traffic.

The police summon the conductress from the second trolley bus. She tries at first to make excuses, then reluctantly takes the child from the middle-aged woman and gets into the 130 light truck. A white glove signals. The truck drives off, taking with it the child's shrill screams and wailing.

As the police wielding batons shout at them, the onlookers move back to form a rectangle that includes the twisted wreck of the bicycle.

What is happening to the driver can now be seen from this side of the road. He is wiping off the sweat with his cotton cap. A policeman is questioning him. He takes out his driver's license in its red plastic folder, and the policeman confiscates it. He immediately protests.

"Why are you making excuses? If you've run over the man, then you've run over him!" A youth pushing a bicycle yells out.

The conductress wearing sleeve protectors comes out of the bus and rebukes the youth. "He was trying to get himself killed. The horn was sounding and the bus had braked, yet the man wouldn't give way. He just went under the bus."

"The man was in the middle of the road and had a child with him. It was broad daylight, so he must have seen him!" someone in the crowd says angrily.

"What does it matter to drivers like him if they run over someone? He won't have to pay for it with his life." This is said with derision.

"What a tragedy. If he didn't have the child with him, he would have got across long ago!"

"Is there any hope for the man?"

"His brain came out?"

"I just heard this *plop*—"

"You heard it?"

"Yes, it went *plop*—"

"Stop all this talk!"

"Ai, life's like that, a person can die just like that . . . "

"He's crying."

"Who?"

"The driver."

The driver, sitting on his haunches with his head down, has covered his eyes with his cap.

"He didn't do it deliberately . . . "

"If this had happened to anyone, they would . . . "

"The man had a child with him? What happened to the child? What happened to the child?" someone who has just arrived asks.

"The child wasn't hurt, it was very lucky."

"Luckily the child was saved."

"The man was killed!"

"Were they father and child?"

"Why did he have to hook a buggy to his bicycle? It's hard enough not to have an accident even with just one person on a bicycle."

"And he'd just picked up the child from kindergarten to take home."

"Kindergartens are hopeless; they won't let you leave children for a whole day!"

"You're lucky if you can get into one."

"What's there to look at! From now on, if you run without looking across the road—"

A big hand drags away a child who is trying to squeeze between people in the crowd.

The Hong Kong star has stopped singing. People are crowded on the steps of the radio repair shop.

Red lights flashing, the ambulance has arrived. As medical personnel in white carry the body to the ambulance, the people in doorways of all the shops stand on their toes. The fat cook wearing an apron from a small eatery nearby has also come out to watch.

"What happened? Was there an accident? Was someone killed?"

"It was father and son, one of them is dead."

"Which of them died?"

"The old man!"

"What about the son?"

"Unhurt."

"That's shocking! Why didn't he pull his father out of the way?"

"It was the father who had pushed his son out of the way!"

"Each generation is getting worse, the man was wasting his time bringing up the son!"

"If you don't know what happened, then don't crap on."

"Who's crapping on?"

"I wasn't trying to start an argument with you."

"The child was carried away."

"Was there a small child as well?"

Others have just arrived.

"Do you mind not shoving?"

"Did I shove you?"

"What's there to look at? Move on! Everyone move on!"

On the outer fringes of the crowd people are being arrested. Traffic security personnel with red armbands have arrived and they are more savage than the police.

The driver, who is pushed into the police car, turns and tries to struggle, but the door shuts. People start to walk away and others get on their bicycles and leave. The onlookers thin out, but people keep arriving, stopping their bicycles or coming down off the pavement. The second trolley bus leads a long line of sedans, vans, jeeps, and big limousines slowly past the buggy with the torn red-and-blue-checkered shade in the gutter on this side of the road. Most of the people standing on shop steps have either gone inside or left, and the long stream of cars has passed. At the center of what has become a small crowd in the middle of the road, two policemen are taking measurements with a tape measure, while another makes notes in a little notebook. The blood under the wheels of the bus has begun to congeal and is turning black. In the trolley bus with its doors open, the conductress sits by a window staring blankly across to this side of the street. On the other side of the street, the faces in the windows of an approaching trolley bus look out and some people even poke their heads out. People have finished work: it is peak traffic time, and there are even more pedestrians and people riding bicycles. However, shouts from the police and traffic security personnel stop people from going to the middle of the road.

"Was there an accident?"

"Was someone killed?"

"Must have been—look at all that blood."

"The day before, there was an accident on Jiankang Road. A sixteen-year-old was taken to the hospital, but they couldn't save him. They said he was an only son."

"Nowadays, whose family doesn't have only one son?"

"Ai, how will the parents survive?"

"If traffic management isn't improved, there'll be more accidents!"

"Every day after school, I worry until my Jiming gets home . . . "

"It's easier for you with your son—daughters are more worry to parents."

"Look, look, they're taking photographs."

"Did he deliberately run over the man?"

"Who knows?"

"It couldn't have been attached, otherwise it would have been hit for sure."

"I was just passing by."

"Some drivers drive like maniacs, and aggressively. If you don't get out of the way, they certainly won't make way for you!"

"There are people who work off their frustrations by killing people, so anyone could be a victim."

"It's hard to guard against such occurrences. It's all decided by fate. In my old village there was a carpenter. He was good at his trade but he liked to drink. Once he was building someone a house and, on his way home at night, rotten drunk, he tripped and cracked his head open on a sharp rock . . . "

"For some reason, the past couple of days my eyelid has been twitching."

"Which one?"

"When you're walking you shouldn't be so engrossed in thought all the time. Quite a few times I've seen you . . . "

"Nothing's ever happened."

"If something had, it'd be too late and I wouldn't be able to bear it."

"Stop it! People are looking at us . . . "

The lovers look at one another and, holding each other's hands even more tightly, walk off.

They finish taking photographs of the scene of the accident, and the policeman with the tape measure takes a shovelful of dirt and spreads it over the blood. The wind has died down completely and it is getting dark. The conductress sitting by the window of the trolley bus has put on the lights and is counting the takings from the tickets. A policeman carries the wreckage of the bicycle on his shoulder to the car. Two men with red armbands get the buggy from the gutter, put it into the car, and leave with the policemen.

It is time for dinner. The conductress is left standing at the door of the trolley bus and looks around impatiently while waiting for the depot to send a driver. Passersby only occasionally glance at the empty bus stopped for some reason in the middle of the road. It is dark and no one notices the blood covered with dirt in front of the bus that can no longer be seen.

Afterward, the streetlights come on and at some time the empty bus has driven off. Cars speed endlessly on the road again, and it is as if nothing has happened. By around midnight hardly anyone is about. A street-washing truck slowly approaches from the intersection some way off where traffic lights flash from time to time next to an iron railing with a blue poster. There is a row of words in white: FOR YOUR OWN SAFETY AND THAT OF OTHERS, PLEASE OBSERVE TRAFFIC RULES. At the spot where the accident had occurred, the truck slows down and, turning on its high-speed sprinkler jets, flushes clean any remaining traces of blood.

The road cleaners don't necessarily know that a few hours ago an accident had occurred and that the unfortunate victim had died right here. But who is the deceased? In this city of several million, only the man's family and some close friends would know him. And if the dead man wasn't carrying identification papers, right now they might not even know about the accident. The man probably was the child's father, and when the child calms down, it will probably be able to say the father's name. In that case, the man must have a wife. He was doing what the child's mother should have been doing, so he was a good father and a good husband. As he loved his child, presumably he also loved his wife, but did his wife love him? If she loved him, why wasn't she able to carry out her duties as his wife? Maybe he had a miserable life, otherwise why was he so distracted? Could it have been a personal failing and he was always indecisive? Maybe something was troubling him, something he couldn't resolve, and he was destined not to escape this even greater misfortune. However, he wouldn't have encountered this disaster if he had set out a little later or a little earlier. Or, if after picking up the child he had pedaled faster or slower, or if the woman at the kindergarten had spoken longer to him about his child, or if on the way a friend had stopped him to talk. It was unavoidable. He didn't have some terminal illness but was just waiting to die. Death is inescapable for everyone, but premature death can be avoided. So if he hadn't died in the accident, how would he have died? Traffic accidents in this city are inevitable; there are no cities free of traffic accidents. In every city there is inevitably this probability, even if the daily average is one in a million, and in a big city of this size there will always be someone encountering this sort of misfortune. He was one such unfortunate person. Didn't he have a premonition before it happened? When he finally encountered this misfortune what did he think? Probably he didn't have time to think, didn't have time to comprehend the great misfortune that was about to befall him. For him, there could be no greater misfortune than this. Even if he was that one in a million, like a grain of sand, before dying he had clearly thought of the child. Supposing it was his child, wasn't it noble of him to sacrifice himself? Maybe it was not purely noble but to a certain extent instinctual, the instinct of being a father. People only talk about a mother's instinct, but there are some mothers who abandon their babies. To have sacrificed himself for the child was indeed noble, but this sacrifice was entirely avoidable: if he had set out a little later or earlier, if at the time he had not been preoccupied, and if he were more resolute by nature, or even if he were more agile in his movements. The sum total of all these factors hastened his death, so this misfortune was inevitable. I have been discussing philosophy again, but life is not philosophy, even if philosophy can derive from knowledge of life. And there is no need to turn life's traffic accidents into statistics, because that's a job for the traffic department or the public security department. Of course a traffic accident can serve as an item for a newspaper. And it can serve as the raw material for literature when it is supplemented by the imagination and written up as a moving narrative: this would then be creation. However, what is related here is simply the process of this traffic accident itself, a traffic accident that occurred at five o'clock, in the central section of Desheng Avenue in front of the radio repair shop.

1985

Han Shaogong (1953–)

THE LEADER'S DEMISE

Translated by Thomas Moran

From the time he heard that the leader really had expired, Changke lived in fear and grief. He got the news while on his way to the butcher's to pick up a cut of pork. He was immediately so overcome with sorrow that there was no way he could treat himself to meat, and there was no way he could have the tailor over to make that new clothing, as he had planned. Of course, Changke's right to grieve was slightly suspect in that his old man had never been in the Red Army or the Peasants' Association, and no aunt or sister-in-law of his had ever been violated by the Jap devils. People were always telling stories about that sort of thing at meetings to—as they said—"recall the sufferings of the old society." More importantly, though, as a boy Changke had actually gone and enrolled in a Western-style school, he had eaten solid red rice rather than gruel, and he had worn both shoes and socks. Later, when he was teaching in the County Town, Changke had stolen some food from the school cafeteria, and for that he was fired and sent back to his village in disgrace. Changke could hardly bear to think back on those stains on his record. The more he thought about them, the more he believed that he had let the leader down. How, then, could he now pull a long face and stare at the ground in a daze like everybody else?

Changke was afraid of being noticed, but he was also afraid of not being noticed. If his conscience were clear, then he had no reason to hide. Inwardly, he envied the village women. Women cried easily. His neighbor from up the street, Benshan, had a daughter-in-law who could dampen both sleeves with tears if so much as a chicken died. Whenever any family from one of the surrounding villages held a funeral, somebody would be sure to wrap up a gift for Benshan's daughter-in-law and request that she spring into action alongside the bereaved family in mourning. Without this woman and her ability to weep at the drop of a hat in her captivating, undulating, sustained musical tones, the rites would just not be proper, and if the rites were not proper, then what face would be left to the host? But Benshan's daughter-in-law was illiterate, and none too bright to boot. Sometimes she cried things into a real muddle. She would cry the Chens into the Lis, or a grandson into a son. Recently, at a big meeting to denounce some landlord who had killed himself in an effort to cheat justice, Benshan's daughter-in-law, not hearing clearly who it was who had died, undid the front flap of her jacket, fished around for something, and then started mopping up tears and snivel by the handful. Mingxi, the brigade Party branch secretary, listened to her for a while, growing more and more annoyed, until finally he reached out and slapped the silly woman.

No one in the village sang anymore. Everyone appeared to be quite sad. The villagers watched one another carefully, and they all walked around as if on eggshells. Nobody seemed to know just how to hold their mouths, or noses, or chins. At one point, a child watched as someone stepped right in the pile of shit he had just deposited, and he started laughing and clapping his hands. Immediately several adults swarmed over the boy in a panic. They covered his mouth and spanked him. No one was permitted to laugh until after the state funeral; that was Uncle Mingxi's proclamation. Changke quietly counted the days and watched cautiously as the time slipped by. He was particularly afraid that ants might crawl down his neck. If things went badly, he would be unable to stand the tickling, and he would break out in laughter, which would make him a reactionary. Changke could see that many of his fellow villagers were distraught, but as for himself, no matter how he furrowed his brow, or wrinkled his nose, or blinked his dry eyes, he could not squeeze out a single tear. But in his anxiety he did work up a good sweat. And then he stood around in a draft and caught cold. He did not dare go to see the local doctor, of course. With the recent demise of the leader, how could Changke run off to the doctor for a prescription of herbal medicine for some minor complaint? He tried hard to grieve; he walked slowly and deliberately, and he spoke in a heavy, halting voice. When carrying the manure bucket up to the collective greenfeed plot to fertilize the crops, Changke seemed so crushed by sorrow that he could barely breathe, and his sorrow appeared somehow to have its source in the very plants that were sprouting in the garden. Every chirp from a bird rent his heart. A great man had passed away; the sun and the moon were without light. Changke truly lacked the courage to go on living. He truly lacked the courage to go on spreading manure over the garden.

Changke figured to have the most book learning of any of the village literati, and he often composed slogans for the banners that were displayed during celebrations and such. Mingxi now came to tell Changke to write a few elegiac couplets and fix up the mourning hall.

Changke was so busy grieving that he did not come around right away to what Mingxi was saying. He responded with a very quiet "Mm." His voice was almost inaudible.

"Did you hear me?" Mingxi was a bit deaf.

"Yes!" Flustered, Changke roused himself with a start. "What should I write?"

"That's up to you!"

"Will we use the usual place for the celebration?"

Even before he had finished speaking, Changke was beside himself with terror. Ai-ya-ya! How had he managed with one slip of the tongue to turn "memorial" into "celebration"? In the swiftly passing instant of that swiftly passing twinkling of an eye, Changke realized that he should correct himself, but his tongue had gone as rigid as a foot, and he could not stop it before it had cleanly booted the reactionary words right out.

"No. No. I meant celebration, not memorial . . . " Changke corrected himself hastily. But as he did, once again he turned pale with fright. Wasn't that still wrong? He wanted to bite his tongue and so make it stop, but his mouth was not obeying any orders at all. In hurried excitement, his monstrous slander rushed on to its last word—"service!" There was silence. Changke had finished what he had to say.

Changke's head spun.

"What did you say?" Mingxi furrowed his brow and stared at Changke.

Changke noticed that Mingxi was watching him. He watched Mingxi watch him watch Mingxi. He watched Mingxi watch him watch Mingxi watch him. Changke also noticed that two women were sitting by the pond at a spot not too far away pounding their laundry. They were not looking Changke's way, but they would have been perfectly able to hear what he had said.

"Hey, you got any matches?" Mingxi took a match, lit his cigarette and walked away. The rifle slung across his back swayed back and forth. Ever since the death of the leader, Mingxi had maintained a posture of combat readiness. He kept a vigilant eye on the airplanes that occasionally flew overhead, just in case one of them might drop the bomb that would start World War III. Although Mingxi's old, rust-scored Japanese rifle did not have a single bullet, it was nevertheless a clear and stern warning to all who were just pretending to grieve.

All day Changke had his heart in his mouth. The village dogs started barking, and he thought it was the county public security bureau come to arrest him. Only later did he discover that it was just an itinerant peddler arriving in the village. Out in the clearing where the villagers spread grain to dry, a couple of people were twisting straw into rope, and Changke assumed that they were getting ready to tie him up. Later he found out that they needed the rope to lasso a cow. Clang! A deafening noise sounded behind Changke's back. He was so frightened he wet his pants, but then nothing happened. Nervously, he looked back. It turned out to be neither the muzzle of Mingxi's rifle barrel nor the revolutionary masses with their enraged, threatening eyes, but just a piglet, assiduously rooting around in the mud. Apparently it had knocked over a hoe, which had fallen against the trough, flipping it upside down. All the blood in Changke's body surged straight to his forehead, and the veins in his neck bulged. Changke was infuriated, and he slashed violently at the pig with a pair of scissors. The pig stared at Changke in stupefaction for a moment. It stood stoically, as if completely unafraid of death, while a row of bloody bubbles formed on its back. Next there was a piercing wail as the pig charged to meet danger head on. Its damp snout glanced off Changke's face and its little hooves scrambled over his shoulders. Changke was now even angrier. He dove under a table in an effort to grab the pig's tail but missed. He chased it outside to the bank of the pond, where he stabbed it in the leg with the scissors. The owner of the pig and Changke then got into a huge argument and cursed each other in horribly venomous and obscene language that had to do with ancestors and ancestors' ancestors and other terribly distant people like that. The folks in the crowd that had gathered to watch were puzzled. Such ferociousness was rarely seen from Changke.

Mingxi had gone to meet with the higher-ups and did not see any of this. When he came back to the village, the Party branch secretary's eyes were red and his voice was hoarse; evidently he had had another cry while at the meeting, which caused Changke to feel once again ashamed and frightened. Mingxi called the villagers together in front of the kiln shack to announce the latest news. Fortunately, for the time being at least, Mingxi did not divulge Changke's reactionary speech and did not say that the fighting in World War III had reached the border. All he said was that because the leader had once been to their village during the revolution, therefore on the day of the state funeral everyone was to burn commemorative incense, and the higher-ups were to send people down to take some television pictures. Changke knew that these days it was not proper to talk about burning commemorative incense, and that it was "shoot some television footage" not "take some television pictures," but he absolutely did not dare correct Mingxi. Mingxi also said that on the day of the service the villagers were to have a really good, heartfelt cry. The woman from Benshan's household cried the best, but unfortunately she was pregnant. It would be too embarrassing to have her on television, and they would do without her. This meant that Changlan's family, Dehu's family, and Sangui's family all had to do a little preparation. They all came from dirt-poor backgrounds. Under the puppet regime they had no padded pants to wear in the cold weather and didn't even know whether money was round or square. They had plenty to cry about.

Changke stared at the pitch-black mouth of the rifle muzzle at the secretary's side. His heart began to beat violently as he waited for Mingxi to single him out with his next sentence.

"That's it." Mingxi did not so much as glance at Changke before adjourning the meeting. "Don't walk off with any bricks!" Mingxi knew there were a few people who often sneaked home with the bricks they sat on during meetings.

This was a little odd. Was Mingxi waiting until Changke had finished writing the couplets before punishing him? Or had he not heard Changke's indiscreet remark in the first place?

"I told you not to take any bricks!" Mingxi shouted in Changke's direction. Changke looked down. In his hand there was indeed a brick. Ai-ya-ya! Changke would never dare steal so much as a blade of grass from the collective. But now the more he did not want to do a thing the more likely he was to do it. It was as if his head were full of shit. He hastened to put the brick back in its place. Then he pulled himself together, looked, and discovered that he had, in fact, put the brick back in its place. Thus reassured, Changke finally walked away.

In a village of short people, Changke was the only tall one. Naturally, it took more than the usual amount of cloth to make clothing for him. Moreover, when he stood up in a crowd he was always a head above everybody else, so that his neck was exposed to chilly breezes from all around, which gave him a vague sense of danger. He knew that when the day of the memorial service came around, no matter how he bent his back and ducked his head it would be no use. It would be impossible for other people not to see him. What would he do if, in that critical moment of all critical moments, his damn eyeballs still would not squeeze out any tears? A television shoot was no joking matter. They used electricity, and there was nothing that could top electricity. Mingxi had bad eyesight and would not be able to see him that well, but what if the men from the county public security bureau singled him out? Everybody else was crying, so why wasn't he? When a difficult birth had put his wife's life in danger, had he cried? He had. When his nephew had drowned in an accident while rafting logs down the river, had he cried? He had. That was all very clear.

Changke realized that he really was reactionary.

His mouth suddenly went dry, and a kind of ferocious aridity seemed to climb up from the soles of his feet and spread quickly through his entire body. It steamed away all his blood, and scorched his organs and entrails and even his eyes. His eyeballs hurt, and his eyelids scraped over them every time he blinked, which seemed to make a scratching sound. It felt as if his throat was so parched that it had split into a network of fissures, and air seemed to be whooshing through the cracks. Only once before had he experienced this sort of horrible dryness, and that was when he heard the news that he was fired from his job. He was done for. Changke was convinced that when the time came he would be unable to cry, and besides that, neither Mingxi nor the two women beating their laundry could possibly have failed to hear his slip of the tongue. There was ample proof of his guilt. Then again, his life to date could not be called short. In his previous existence he had simply not accumulated enough virtue, and if he were now done for, then it was of no more consequence than the death of a dog. Since he could not cry, then he should either go to prison or take a bullet. It was just too bad about his old lady and his gang of kids. The youngest, who had a big nose just like Changke, had just been weaned and was always looking all around. If the old man were heartless enough to leave them all in the lurch, how were they going to survive? All this was on Changke's mind as he took his place in the crowd at the memorial service. He gazed at his old lady's stooped back and at the familiar mole at the base of her neck. He looked at the delicate little child in the bamboo basket on her back. The boy recognized his father and started to bounce up and down in the basket. The sun was very intense. The heads and shoulders of the people in the crowd baked in the terrible heat. Gadflies flitted about restlessly in the fierce sunlight.

Earlier, before setting out from home, Changke had filled the water vat, seen to it that the wood box was sufficiently loaded with firewood, and paid back his neighbors one by one for all the kerosene and dried sweet potatoes he had borrowed. He settled all accounts that had to be settled. Now he brushed another gadfly from his son's boil. Changke imagined that this would be the last time he would drive gadflies away from his son's body; he imagined that this would be the last time he would touch his son's skin. But his son seemed to like gadflies. The boy chewed on his fingers, drooled, and laughed.

Before anybody was ready for it, firecrackers went off with a boom. The unexpected, ferocious explosion shook them all to their very bones, loosening their joints and leaving them with an empty, floating feeling throughout their entire bodies. The crows in the old scholartrees started suddenly into flight, and their flapping shadows banged down on the heads and backs of the people in the crowd.

Changke's son began to cry. Changke's nose started to tingle and something warm crawled up out of his eyes. Changke was the first adult at the memorial service to cry. This was very important.

Let us look closely to see what was going on at the service during those moments when Changke thought he was bidding farewell to the world. This was an important day because two officials from the county had come along to the village with the television crew. The presence of outsiders shouldering weird machinery had given rise to a confused nervousness among the villagers. They claimed that the chickens were hiding in their coops and that the dogs had run up into the hills and wouldn't come down. One young fellow was actually unable to hoist an eighty-pound sack of grain onto his shoulders like he usually could. Earlier, when Uncle Yuhuai went to light the firecrackers, he had broken a dozen or so matches without getting one to light. Mingxi had to help him out with his cigarette lighter. Of even more urgency, not only was Benshan's daughter-in-law too frightened to cry, but all the others listed in the plan as principal mourners started to behave like criminals as soon as they got to the ceremony. They all looked at one another in panic. Everyone who got in front of the camera immediately looked somehow sneaky. It was as if the unfamiliar camera lenses were actually gun barrels; whoever they pointed at moved to one side or ducked behind somebody else. This turned out to be very effective for chasing away the children who had gathered around in curiosity. They had made a mess of the ranks of the mourners, and the vehement reprimands of the adults proved useless. Mingxi's brass whistle and rifle were of no use either. There was really nothing that could be done until Mingxi asked one of the reporters to raise his camera and wipe them all out. The kids were stampeded—without any actual firing of guns or cannon—and took cover a long way off.

Mingxi arrived at the head of his family, each of whom, like Mingxi himself, wore a sackcloth hood. It was not until one of the outsiders told him that it was not the fashion in the new society to wear sackcloth in mourning that Mingxi unhappily took his headdress off and gave it to someone to use as a seat cushion. The venerable old secretary had been in the Red Army's 16th Regiment. Once, while on maneuvers, he had become separated from his unit and had gotten lost after being tricked down a side road by a ghost, and that was the only reason he had not been along on the Long March (there were also those who said that Mingxi had deserted). Mingxi's ears had been blasted half deaf by German bombs; he had attended meetings at the county seat; he had seen the world.

Mingxi told the villagers to relax. "Being on TV doesn't harm your skin and can't steal away your soul. It's no big deal. When we were making revolution with the leader back in the old days, we weren't even afraid of German and American artillery! Hmph! And now you mean to say you're afraid of being on TV?"

Mingxi started his speech amid the heavy smell of sulfur from the firecrackers. First he bowed three times toward the picture of the leader, lifting the two muddy spots and wisps of grass on his rear end high in the air each time. He cleared his throat. He was fairly satisfied with the grandeur and pageantry of the ceremony. He said that the day was going pretty well. The great leader had passed away, and the poor and lower-middle peasants had come together to burn commemorative incense and set off firecrackers. They had really created a pestilential mood. Uh-huh, a pestilential mood. A reporter at Mingxi's side panicked. He tugged on Mingxi's sleeve. "Don't say 'pestilential mood.' That expression's no good." Mingxi blinked. "What's wrong with a terrific expression like that?"

Mingxi had heard that when talking about pictures of the leader or about his written works one could not say "buy" but had to say "invite" and so forth, but he had never heard that there was anything wrong with the expression "pestilential mood."

For the moment, Mingxi swallowed his skepticism. He glared down at a gadfly on the edge of the table, and then he went on with his talk. His speech took him from fighting local tyrants with the 16th Regiment all the way up through the planting of late-ripening rice, the stockpiling of fertilizer, and the harvesting of autumn yams. He counted all the blessings that the leader had brought to his impoverished people. "Just take my family. These days I've got two big cabinets, two beds with carved decorations, sixteen chairs, a sewing machine, and two cigarette lighters. I've got one and my boy Qingqiang has one!" He looked all around to see who was as yet not cowed by his and his son's cigarette lighters. "And my political standing is a lot higher than before. I'm the Party branch secretary, no need to mention that, of course. Qingqiang and his wife are both state cadres, and my eldest daughter is . . . great-grandmother Shazhi." Mingxi meant that his daughter had participated in an amateur theater group and had had the honor of playing the older female lead in the model opera *Shajiabang*. Mingxi did not, of course, leave out the final member of the family: "My old lady is . . . " He paused before finally finding a word that could be used in the new society and that was both dignified and not too far from the facts. "A woman, uh-huh, a woman."

Someone in the crowd could not keep from laughing.

"Who dares laugh!" Mingxi's eyes snapped open in hopes of finding the enemy agent who was disrupting the memorial service. But his eyesight wasn't too good, and search as he might, all he could see was rows of incomparably solemn faces. But the atmosphere had been wrecked. No matter how patiently he tried to get the crowd worked up, Mingxi was unable to dispel his audience's nervousness. Mingxi himself noticed that his talk had grown somewhat chaotic, and he couldn't help but hold a silent grudge against those outsiders who hadn't let him wear the sackcloth. It was that unexpected blow that had upset his mood. Really, what was improper about wearing sackcloth in mourning? Once again he stared angrily at the gadfly on the edge of the table.

It was then that there was a faint commotion in the crowd. Mingxi followed the gaze of the people at his side and saw, sticking up a head taller than anybody else, Changke, his face all twisted from crying.

The sound of crying is contagious. As soon as Changke started to cry, his wife and children started weeping along with him, and then two women standing nearby buried their faces and started to sob, and that dragged tears from Mingxi. Mingxi wailed with feeling and, completely forgetting the program for the memorial service, yelled, "Comrade Changke, come up and talk. Come up onto the podium and talk!" Then he announced to the crowd, "Changke is an honest man, a good man. Same with his uncle. When he sold you bean curd he always gave you good weight." In the moment, Mingxi seemed to remember all the good points of Changke's family.

Changke was pushed and pulled up to the podium. He didn't know who the people were who shook his hand, but they squeezed so hard that as he stood on the podium his nose tingled more than ever. He started crying, really crying. Only now did he finally believe what had happened. He had been rescued from a desperate situation. He was pleasantly surprised and actually did feel like crying over the happy turn of events. Mingxi had just called him comrade, which was to say that the secretary did not consider him to be a bad fellow, which was to say that the secretary was not going to fuss about his indiscreet remark, or had not even heard it. This was also to say that instead of going to prison, he could eat, sleep, feed his pigs, and read the papers with his mind at ease. All of this was very clear and had taken place before he had time to think about it. It had really happened. This was the first time he had been looked up to by so many people, or had his hand shaken by so many people, so how could he not cry? At first Changke had merely been rejoicing at his good fortune, but now his heart was full of warmth.

We must in all seriousness explain that Changke's hand was fully deserving of being clasped by so many other hands, soft and calloused alike. He was loyal to the leader. As the village schoolmaster he honored the leader's teachings and served the people. Almost every day he had to cross two big mountains on trips to three different villages to teach his students. It even fell to Changke to undo the knots on the children's drawstrings so they could relieve themselves. One stormy night his lantern had been blown out and he nearly fell off a cliff to be dashed against the rocks below. He groped his way through the cogon grass on the pitch-black mountain slope, and it wasn't until dawn that he arrived home, soaked and covered in mud. But had he complained to anyone? Another time Changke noticed that many of the children could not afford to buy textbooks, so he took them out to cut firewood to sell to raise money. But Changke stumbled into a wasps' nest. He made the children run away, but he was stung so badly by the enveloping black mass of wasps that he almost passed out. The blood rushed to his head, which turned red and swelled up to the size of a washbowl. This scared the village children so badly that they hid from Changke. But had he complained to anyone?

Changke burst out with the kind of piercing wail that sometimes a man just can't hold in. It bore right up people's nostrils and drove right into the backs of their heads, and with that the memorial service was pushed toward its climax.

Changke had a few tearful words to say. He called on the leader not to go and asked him for guidance. He said he planned to sell some grain after the fall harvest for traveling expenses so he could go call on the great leader and so on. But the crowd didn't pay much attention to what he was saying.

The day's memorial service was successful and moving. Those in attendance cried until they could barely stand. Even the television reporters were wiping away tears and blowing their noses, and one of them collapsed with sunstroke. Bystanders came to his assistance; they took off his shirt and, as practice dictated in such cases, repeatedly pinched and poked him in the back, raising long lines of purple-black bruises that stuck up like leeches. The villagers' souls had been cleansed. They were much more amiable now; when they crowded round to watch the reporter get first aid, nobody pushed anybody else and they all made way for one another. And when they went down to the fields to haul manure they all fought to carry the heaviest basket.

Then while spreading the manure they cursed the Japanese and other such enemies, and their enemies' ancestors as well. They reminisced about the leader and expressed regret that when the Red Army was in their village it had eaten only sweet potatoes and not meat. In regard to the questions as to whether the leader had been treated for sunstroke or not and as to whether the leader had ridden a white horse or a black horse, they argued for a long time.

It seemed to Changke that the number of smiling faces around him had increased. The manner in which the others now treated him was at least a little different from before. When they took down the podium, each of the villagers carried his own door planks home, but Changke couldn't lift his by himself. Right away somebody came over to lend a hand. When Changke's bamboo hat disappeared, Uncle Yuhuai went right away to help him look for it. Yuhuai discovered that his son had the hat, but the child had already sat on it and crushed it. Right away Yuhuai rapped the child on the head twice with his knuckles, which stunned the boy so badly that he covered his head in silence for a long time before he finally started to cry. Actually, Yuhuai had absolutely no need to be so upright in this case. Changke would have been satisfied if Yuhuai would simply pay his children's tuition on time and stop stealing chilies and gourds from Changke's yard. Flustered, Changke bowed repeatedly to Yuhuai.

One cannot be sure exactly when it started, but down by the pond rumors began to circulate. Changke had appeared on television for longer than anybody else, and it was said that perhaps this meant he was to be made a state cadre once again. If he became a cadre, then of course he would be put in charge of the grain and oil supply station—that was the conclusion reached by the women of the village while they did their laundry. Changke laughed, waved his hands in protest, and said this was nonsense, utter nonsense. No such thing was going to happen. Since when did he have that kind of luck? All that had happened was that he had accepted an invitation to go up to the county seat to attend a meeting to discuss the leader's glorious achievements and talk about what he had learned from studying the leader's works. Of course, he couldn't help but cry his eyes out again. And, therefore, other county-level conference organizers invited him to come to their meetings. Changke did an increasingly wonderful job of grieving. For example, he too now began his talks with the old society and enumerated all the suffering he had endured (Changke was vague about the exact nature of that suffering). Of course, the most important thing Changke had to talk about was his loyalty to the leader. When he got stung by the wasps his face swelled up to the size of a washbowl and he couldn't eat a thing for three days and three nights (recently two days and two nights had begun to appear in his memory as three days and three nights). But had his revolutionary conviction wavered? No. Had he taken into account his own safety and personal benefit? Once again, no (Changke had begun to make use of this sort of rhetorical self-questioning, which the younger generation seemed to like). Every evening, deep into the night, Changke sat by his lantern diligently studying the writings of the leader. He almost read himself blind. Every time he got to this point in his talk Changke got a lump in his throat, his hands went cold from nervousness and excitement, and he could not go on. Changke himself knew that there was no need to get this worked up. If he got too excited it would affect his speech adversely, and that would cause the conference hosts to get up to pour water for him and pass him handkerchiefs, which was embarrassing. But there was nothing he could do. Ever since the day of the state funeral, for reasons Changke didn't understand, he could pump out tears more quickly than Benshan's daughter-in-law. As soon as somebody mentioned the leader, or as soon as he heard the national anthem or something like that, Changke would be overcome by emotion and his nose would tingle. He was completely unable to keep his nose under control and he could not calm the solemn emotions that welled up in his chest. Every time this happened he gazed up at the sky while turbid tears swirled and pooled in his eyes. His lips trembled as he did his best just to bear it, and bear it, and bear it.

Below the podium, naturally, there would be nary a peep. Next would come the faint sound of sobbing or a sudden explosion of slogans, like "Study the admirable example of comrade Changke!" and things of that sort. The sound would come lapping forward in waves.

The slogans only made Changke cry even harder, which brought the conference hosts forward in greater numbers to add water to his glass or pass him more handkerchiefs.

Changke became an extremely busy person. He was away a lot, and his family vegetable plot went to seed. He often dropped by Mingxi's house to pick up notices that summoned him to meetings. Under a rather uncertain status he even attended one or two meetings for cadres only. In the past, Changke rarely had the opportunity to visit Mingxi's house. Just passing by his door usually made Changke's knees a little weak. Now he discovered that the rooms on the other side of this particular threshold were actually quite ordinary. He discovered that the netting over Mingxi's carved beds was black and torn; he discovered that a bucket was hung from the ceiling beam in Mingxi's place, and there was a swallow's nest up there too; he discovered that Mingxi's pigs never fattened up and were always fighting with one another to get to the trough; he discovered that the earthenware jar that Mingxi's family used to steep tea was chipped. Changke gradually came to find fault with this formerly unfamiliar world. Mingxi passed the water pipe to him and asked him to sit down. He sat, of course. Changke loved the leader, and so, of course, if he felt like sitting, he sat. Mingxi objected that plain water was flavorless, and he ordered his daughter to boil a pot and mix in some fried beans and grated ginger. At that moment, Changke discovered that there was a spot of swallow shit behind Mingxi's ear, and he said, "So, you didn't wash your face today, did you, sir? You have some swallow shit on your ear, you know." And then Changke actually stuck out his hand and took a couple of swipes across the secretary's bare head. Changke was not reactionary in the least these days, and therefore, if he felt like touching somebody else's head he could go ahead and touch somebody else's head. There was nothing to be afraid of.

Changke let go a wanton sneeze and its echo lingered in the air.

After quite a few years had passed, Mingxi died. They easily could have carried him off to the hospital, but Mingxi could not bear the thought of having unmarried, pretty young girls order him to drop his pants for shots, and so he refused to go and he died at home. When he was on his last breath, Mingxi grasped Changke's hand and stared into his eyes for a long time, as if he had something to say. But phlegm stopped up his throat and he never did say anything. What was he about to say? This became an eternal riddle.

Changke chewed the question over for quite a while. What did Mingxi want to say? Because he couldn't figure it out, Changke's hair turned much whiter in no time at all.

1992

Chen Cun (1954–)

A STORY

Translated by Robert Joe Cutter

1

When Zhang San was little, he was a fine son. Even at six he used to go out with his mother to cut straw to sell, and by the time he was eight he knew how to light the coal stove and cook. His father ran off with some slut when Zhang San was five. He asked his mother what a "slut" was, and she told him a slut was garbage. Garbage was something Zhang San knew very well, for there was a garbage bin just outside their door. What he couldn't figure out was why his father had run off with garbage instead of some decent person.

With his father gone, it was much harder to get by. He was always hungry. His mother wouldn't even let him buy a new pencil until his old one was down to half an inch. When the school had its spring outing, Zhang San had but two filled buns to take. He couldn't remember when he'd seen a movie. The school waived his tuition, but wasn't able to drop his fees.

The more he thought about his father, the more he hated him. He had looked forward to his father's returning and the two of them walking together in front of his friends, to his father bringing him lots of fish and meat and candy. But when it didn't happen, his heart was even more consumed by hatred, and he swore that after he grew up he'd take the bum and knock him into a garbage can. Sad to say, there wasn't much to eat, and Zhang San always grew very slowly. When he pushed up his sleeves, his stringy arms were unsightly.

His mother sold straw for a living, and every day she walked to the outskirts of town to cut a bit. She sold blood when they were really hard up. Once she fainted beside a field. Zhang San wanted to quit school on several occasions and cut straw instead, but his mother slapped that idea out of his head. And once when he stole a scrumptious bear claw from a large bakery, she boxed his ears even harder. She was skinny and weak, but every slap was harder than the last.

As he recalled, it was probably when he was in second grade that an "uncle" from the country started coming to the house all the time. This uncle always brought some dried broad beans, corn, and red beans and would stay a night or two before leaving. Zhang San could tell that his mother wanted the uncle to come.

Before he started school, Zhang San slept with his mother. She fanned him in the summer, and he kept her feet warm in the winter. He often played on her tummy and liked holding her dried-up breasts in his mouth. She always held him in those days and patted his back. Later, after he started school, she wouldn't let him sleep with her anymore, and she always sent him out to play for a while when she took a bath. He resisted, but it was no use. In time he got used to sleeping on the plank bed. When it was too hot to sleep, he lay there by himself catching and squashing bedbugs.

The first time the uncle came from the country, he slept on Zhang San's plank bed. Afterward, he slept with Zhang San's mother, and Zhang San was alone once again.

In time Zhang San learned that the uncle had a wife and three kids in the country. He made a fuss about wanting to go back with the uncle to play and to catch some crickets to bring back for cricket fights. But the uncle would never take him. His mother told him never to talk to anyone about this uncle.

Whenever the uncle came, his mother's bed always shook like mad far into the night. Three generations had already used that bed, and it didn't seem strong enough. When they got too loud, Zhang San would wake up and silently watch them wrestle around.

By and by Zhang San's mother found a temporary job, and he was able to eat his fill, even if the food wasn't very good. Occasionally, the uncle would also take him to see a movie. Anytime kids bullied him, Zhang San threatened to have this uncle beat them up, for he was very strong. At some point, they all started to laugh at him. Echoing the adults, they said his mother was a slut, was shacking up, was shameless. Zhang San immediately thought of his father and the slut who seduced him into running off. Afterward, he never again mentioned the uncle and ignored him when he saw him.

Later, the uncle suddenly stopped coming, and Zhang San couldn't help asking his mother why. She told him he had gotten tangled in weeds and drowned while netting shrimp. Tears welled up in her eyes.

Zhang San felt the house was as still as if it were empty.

2

Even though life was hard, the days passed very quickly. Zhang San grew up to be a skinny little adult.

First thing after they began organizing revolutionary brigades, Zhang San took off to get even with his father.

His father was living in a third-floor garret in a new-style neighborhood. There was no denying that he had in the past served for several days in the puppet police. Taking along some comrades-in-arms, Zhang San went there, and he gave the slut a slap as soon as he was inside the main entrance. He and his father encountered one another beneath the garret's sloped ceiling. His father was pitiful, not at all as he remembered. With twenty years of resentment concentrated in his fists, he hit him so hard that the old man was bleeding from his nose and mouth. Zhang San wanted very much to pummel him some more, but didn't. His father sat in the corner and kept wiping the blood with his hand until his whole face was smeared blood red.

Zhang San and his comrades confiscated everything in the house.

He hated those new clothes, the nice furniture, and especially the toys. In his eyes, his father's house was wealthy beyond belief. He recalled having eaten chaff and wild greens, recalled his mother's "uncle" from the country. Again and again he kicked his father, kicked him until his own eyes were brimming with tears.

Thereafter, Zhang San steeled his heart against any sympathy for the rich. He was obsessed with confiscating the property of capitalists and that of the families of overseas Chinese. The more expensive the clothes he ripped apart, the more anger he worked off. He smashed gas stoves, pissed on pianos, polished his shoes on curtains, and only stopped short of setting everything on fire.

He took any expensive food he confiscated home with him, but his mother was too frightened to enjoy it. She wanted him to know his place: "Good repays good, evil repays evil." "Revolutionaries have always wound up dead."

Zhang San thought his mother was incredibly stupid. She had suffered her whole life and still imagined there was some kind of reward for goodness. Now retribution was his. He had food and clothes, and no one dared to lord it over him. There had never been such a sweet life. To be a revolutionary was nothing, Zhang San knew. As long as you didn't rebel against Chairman Mao, other revolutionary acts were not only justified, they were a downright service. He actually pitied his mother a little, the slavish mentality that would have her starve rather than rebel.

He really was different since the revolution, Zhang San thought. In the old days he'd doze off at work, but once the revolution began, he could go all night without shutting his eyes. Maybe it had to do with food; maybe once he had enough to eat, he didn't need as much sleep anymore. With the revolution, he was no longer like some old fogy—he had even begun to sing and to dance the dance of allegiance. He had even developed a revolutionary's temper. And Shanghai was suddenly better. Every single street meant something to him.

His mother died on the First of October, National Day. She was returning home all right from work at the factory, but as soon as she stepped off the streetcar, she was unable to move. She ought to have been off for the holiday, but no, she wanted to go get in some overtime. And now she was gone for good.

For days after, Zhang San felt a wave of grief whenever he thought of her. In her whole miserable life she hadn't had a single day of happiness, no one had rewarded her kindness, and then she just dropped dead in her tracks. Thinking about it made him so full of hatred that he wanted to beat the hell out of his father again.

But with his mother dead, Zhang San began to feel differently. After a few days he realized that he no longer had any cares. He was a bachelor, and it wouldn't matter even if he were killed.

3

The headquarters of Zhang San's revolutionary brigade was in a Western-style house quite some distance from the factory. The house had belonged to the capitalist who had owned the factory. The night they confiscated the capitalist's property, he and his wife had killed themselves to escape punishment. The capitalist was survived by a mistress and his two daughters, who tucked their tails between their legs and moved out to the garage. The revolutionary brigade ordered the mistress to clean the whole house from top to bottom bright and early every morning and to rinse out the thermos bottles. She was as conscientious as could be and came whenever called.

By now Zhang San had become a little more worldly. He could light the gas and turn on a television, and he no longer crapped or peed in the bathtub. He had discovered that toilets were better, better than either commodes or latrines. That house of his father's hadn't been so hot. Again he thought of his mother. She dumped a lifetime of chamber pots and to the day she died never once sat on a real toilet. She lit a lifetime of coal stoves and never once struck a match to light gas and heat a bowl of rice porridge. But as time went by, Zhang San got used to things and seldom made these associations anymore. After all, she was dead, and there was no point.

Zhang San officially lived in the Western-style house from the time his mother died. It was better designed and much more comfortable. His room on the second floor had a balcony and faced south. It had been the bedroom of the capitalist. When he opened the French doors, he could see the flowers and lawn in the garden and the roofs of other Western-style houses. The bedroom had a fireplace. Zhang San lit it once, even though the weather wasn't cold, and roasted himself till he was sweating all over. He ran down to the garden several times to watch the smoke coming out of the chimney. When it gets cold, he thought, I'll have a fire every day and won't get chilblains on my hands and feet anymore. That fucking capitalist had it pretty good.

What a waste my life would have been if I hadn't become a revolutionary!

4

Zhang San's meals were sent over from the factory most of the time, and he ate while playing chess with his comrades-in-arms. The late capitalist's mistress cooked when the factory was closed. Zhang San initially was afraid that she would poison him, so he always made her taste the food. At first she didn't know what was going on. She thought he was afraid to eat the food because it wasn't cooked right. Once she caught on, she'd look contemptuously at Zhang San and icily eat three big bites, one right after the other. After a time, they dispensed with this procedure. She was a much better cook than his mother had been, and the food was delicious.

The capitalist's name had been Zhang, and the mistress's name was Zhang, too—Zhang Yujuan, which was slightly awkward to pronounce. Since the two girls were not her daughters, they called her auntie rather than mom. The three of them seemed more like sisters. After moving into the garage, the so-called "mother and daughters" still didn't have a day's peace. There was no one to keep them in line after the old capitalist died. The revolutionaries were too preoccupied with the important business of revolution to deal with their squabbles. Normally, they'd keep their voices down when they quarreled. But when they had a big fight, they really gave each other hell. After dinner Zhang San often strolled over to the garage door, picking his teeth and enjoying their rows. But if they heard footsteps, they'd stop fighting immediately and grow as quiet as if they had seen a ghost.

When Zhang San was alone and feeling bored in the evening, he looked through the Chinese and foreign movie magazines piled in the closet. They were all back issues, but they were new to Zhang San. The girls in them were absolutely beautiful, beautiful and lewd. Zhang San stroked their thighs and nestled his face against their faces, against their breasts, against their legs.

After looking at the magazines until he felt horny, he'd dial a phone number at random. If a woman answered, he'd blurt out something obscene. The woman was always momentarily stunned, then she'd swear at him and quickly slam down the receiver. But Zhang San was getting sharper. He knew that if the caller didn't hang up, the connection wasn't broken. So he waited patiently until the woman picked up the receiver again, then he'd suddenly let out an eerie laugh. He always felt better after making these calls. The revolutionary brigade stressed class struggle all day long. It was too much for his brain, and if he didn't relax somehow, he was going to go nuts. Besides, he had never made any sense of the goings-on of the top brass. Making the phone calls was something he could do on his own, something he could do without reading the press.

Just once Zhang San had the wind taken out of his sails. Not only did the woman not hang up, she swore at him loudly. "You little prick! I could be your grandmother. What gall! You fuzz-faced . . . "

Zhang San quickly hung up the phone.

5

Zhang San had by now eaten chicken, duck, and fish to his heart's content. He had drunk *maotai* and Western booze. He had used scented imported soap. Such things were no longer oddities to him.

What Zhang San wanted was a woman.

No matter how good-looking the women in the magazines, they were still only photographs; no matter how great the women on the phone sounded, he still couldn't see them. Zhang San craved a flesh-and-blood woman.

In the second year of his traineeship, he had found a girlfriend at the factory, but you've got to spend a little when you've got a girl, and Zhang San didn't have any money to spend. Pretty soon they broke up. But he had had a little bit of experience. He had two nights of love with Ms. Hua from the factory. When the Great Cultural Revolution began, Ms. Hua was sent back to the countryside with her fugitive landlord husband, and their romance came to an end. Those two nights taught Zhang San a lot. The days and nights that followed were all the more difficult.

Zhang San had set his eye on the capitalist's elder daughter. She was naturally attractive and had developed a good figure. Zhang San often went downstairs and found some excuse to drop in on Zhang Yujuan and sit in the garage for a while. As soon as he entered, the women all became extremely subdued and left this worker awkwardly trying to make conversation by himself. It was especially hard because he wanted to come across with the imposing air of a revolutionary *and* to affect the thoughtfulness of a lover.

The elder sister's name was Anna; the younger one was called Lisa.

From the balcony Zhang San saw Anna standing in the garden one day leaning against a tree and looking depressed. He rushed downstairs. After Zhang convinced Anna to make a clean break with her suicidal parents, he solemnly stated that she could henceforth bathe in the bathroom and, unlike the others, needn't keep to the tiny room where water had to be carried in and out. When Anna heard this, she went around the tree without a word to get away from Zhang San. He stood by the tree for a long time. He had no idea how to please her.

Anna never did come to use Zhang San's bathtub.

Zhang San finally understood. Though in terms of class he was a leader and Anna was scum, psychologically speaking, things were far different. As soon as he opened his mouth, he had felt inferior and simply given this rotten daughter of a capitalist a good laugh at his expense. It was like that time he stole the bear claw.

He hated his ineptitude.

Zhang San sighed. It was inborn, and there was no way to change it. Fuck it!

6

The revolution was still going great. But there was a lot of bitterness among the workers. They resorted to violence against one another and fought more zealously than they did against class enemies.

Zhang San was involved in violence on two occasions. Once was when he went to attack the headquarters of an opposing faction. Unfortunately, word leaked out, so they didn't get to beat up anyone, just smash some stuff. The second time was when the other guys came after them. Zhang San was so frightened that he fled onto the roof and hid behind the chimney until daylight. After it got light, the opposition withdrew. Zhang San was just working the numbness out of his legs and getting ready to come down when Anna discovered him. Talk about humiliating! He didn't set foot in the garden for a week.

Luckily, before long a new directive came down. The two rival camps were united and placed under the leadership of a factory headquarters command, so such horrifying incidents wouldn't happen again. If he were beaten to death or killed in a fall from the roof before the revolution succeeded and before he had a chance to enjoy fully his good fortune, wouldn't he be worse off than the capitalist?

Zhang San felt deeply that life was precious. "Dare to climb a mountain of swords, dare to dive into a sea of fire!" sounded great, but that was it. Bluster didn't count for shit. The more a guy was afraid of death, the more the bluster. He'd shoot off his mouth in and out of meetings. They'd talk it over, then forget about it. The proletarian revolutionary faction wanted to stay alive, too.

When he was about to fall asleep, Zhang San liked to fantasize how Anna would come to him and ask him to give her a good screw. He would then screw her again and again. Zhang San knew perfectly well that he was fooling himself, but imagining it made him feel a little better.

As a kind of a hobby, Zhang San often went round to the bamboo pole where they dried their clothes and stood there a moment. He could tell which panties were Anna's. After fondling them with his fingers for a time, he would go away in agony. His hands would be wet, moist with the water from the panties. As he rubbed his thumb over his fingers, he could feel the water dry a bit. But once, Anna caught him in the act. He awkwardly pulled his hand away, coughed a few times, and spat.

From then on the two girls quit drying their underwear outside.

From then on Zhang San was out of a hobby.

Zhang San had already thumbed those magazines to pieces. He could recite what was in them in detail with his eyes closed. When he had been a kid in school, memorization was what he was worst at. He never dreamed he'd memorize these magazines without even trying. It was sure a lot less effort than memorizing the "Three Essays by Chairman Mao."

Zhang San was miserable. He felt things were worse even than during the years when he didn't have enough to eat. These days he never got to see the women in the factory anymore. He longed to defile these rotten little bitches savagely, just as he'd once pissed all over those pianos.

7

At headquarters, Zhang San was the number three man. Number One's mind was set on the city, and he seldom came back. Number Two was the office manager of the original plant of the newly merged factory and was responsible for production. Only Zhang San, whose name meant Zhang Number Three, attended to revolutionary business. Thus, he was actually Zhang Yi, or Zhang Number One, and much sought after.

The capitalist's mistress still had to come and clean every day, and one day each week she cooked for Zhang San. When he was fed up with the food at the factory, he'd have her work an extra day. She was already quite proficient at cleaning house, and she could fill two thermos bottles with a pot of hot water and scarcely splatter a drop. Although he hadn't seen her speak yet, she often had a smile on her face. He noticed that she was actually still pretty young and, when she smiled, only a little less attractive than the girls in the magazines. At nearly forty she had a complexion so fair and smooth she looked good enough to eat.

One rainy morning, Zhang San stepped in front of Zhang Yujuan. She was so startled she dropped her broom. Zhang San kicked it aside and pushed her into the bedroom that had once been hers but was now his own.

She didn't cry out.

After her initial paralysis, she resisted. Seeing that he couldn't deal with her peacefully, Zhang San raised his hand and slapped her. He knew she hated and despised him. In the past, he hadn't even thought he was good enough to speak to her. But now was now. She was much more docile after being struck. Crying, she put up only token resistance. Later on, she no longer cried. She neither resisted nor catered to his desires. She just closed her eyes tightly and let him have his way.

Rain pounded on the window and on the balcony, and it splashed into the room. The garden was a lush green.

Zhang Yujuan lay with her back to him and pulled the blanket up snugly about her. Zhang San contentedly smoked a cigarette. Now his score with the capitalists was finally settled in full.

"Turn your back." She finally spoke.

Zhang San didn't understand why.

"I want to get up."

Zhang San thought this was hilarious. Not only had he had sex with her, he had had sex with her in every possible way. And now she wanted him to turn his back so she could get up and get dressed. It didn't make sense. He reached out and touched her face and found that it was wet.

He didn't let her get up.

8

From then on, Zhang San's revolutionary zeal abated considerably. To his way of thinking, he'd gotten tangled up with a snake in the guise of a beautiful woman. Such a creature was really dangerous. He thought the old saying "It's hard for a brave man to stand up to a beautiful woman" was right on. He felt inwardly pleased over being such a brave man.

After that wet and drizzly morning, it was taken for granted. Zhang San guessed correctly that she wouldn't dare report him. She could never stand up to a charge of seducing and corrupting a revolutionary. Zhang Yujuan still came every day to clean up and still cooked for him. And she did not sprinkle his food with heaps of salt or add poison. Gradually, she quit offering even token resistance, and gradually she reminded Zhang San of Ms. Hua. But she never spent the night upstairs, no matter how much he pressed her.

Zhang San had thought his score with the capitalists had been settled in full, but he found that was far from the case. The capitalist had been properly married and had not been afraid of what people would say about his having a mistress. But Zhang San was like a dog stealing food. At night they were so close it was hard to tell them apart, but by day he had to put on a stern expression. As the days went by, some affection developed between them, even though they weren't from the same class. All Zhang San could get for her was a bit of scented soap from the sealed-up confiscated goods. She took it and held it to her nose, smelling it again and again, but he never saw her use it.

Zhang San didn't want her to have to get up so early every morning. It would do for the rooms to be cleaned every three days. Sometimes he even did a little straightening up himself. He couldn't help recalling his "uncle," so he took a little money from the revolutionary brigade's office funds and gave it to Zhang Yujuan. She was afraid to take it and looked at it as though it were on fire. Zhang San told her it was his wages and had nothing to do with his being a revolutionary. She accepted it. When she took the money, she inexplicably shed a tear.

Zhang San gave no thought to the days ahead. Even people with big names were at risk. What did a poor stiff like him have to think about? Fate would bring what it would bring. He had food, clothing, a girl, and pals. Nothing else mattered.

But Zhang San gradually drifted apart from his pals. He didn't have time to suck up to anyone, and he wasn't inclined to let anyone suck up to him. The boozing all day and bullshitting all night of the old days lost interest for him. He only wanted to have the house to himself and then to send word for Zhang Yujuan. It was tough.

After they had become accustomed to their relationship, in bed one day Zhang San pressed her to tell him about when she was together with the capitalist. When she didn't speak, Zhang San beat her out of hatred and jealousy. She knew she couldn't bear it, so she hemmed and hawed and told him a few kinky details. One by one Zhang San did those same things to her. He had Zhang Yujuan give him a bath, and he sat on the toilet and watched her bathe. He watched her for a long time, but couldn't see the point to it. The techniques that old bastard had thought up were disagreeable and sloppy.

Zhang Yujuan's pale face actually took on a little color. Somewhat unexpectedly, she told Zhang San a little about her domestic matters. The two so-called daughters were getting harder and harder to handle. They'd fight over a bit of food or over a little hot water and were making life miserable. Whenever she'd bring this up, Zhang San would encourage her, saying that things would slowly get better. Just what would get better, or how, he didn't know.

"Can the future really be better than the past?" she asked.

When Zhang San heard this, his heart sank. What she longed for was a change back to the old days. Only then did Zhang San understand that if she had her way, he couldn't have his. Even though by some strange turn of events they had come to share a bed and make small talk, their lots in life differed.

When he thought more about it, her life hadn't exactly been a bed of roses, either. Being a mistress had given her a bad reputation. And being "married" to that old guy twenty years her senior certainly couldn't have been as pleasant as being with Zhang San. The old man was no match for her in bed. Even Zhang San felt it was a little difficult. Perhaps all she was thinking about were some trivialities.

"Actually, the past wasn't so great." She sighed as she spoke. She thought of the suicide pact her "husband" had made with his real wife.

Zhang San loved hearing this.

9

Zhang San wasn't stupid. He could see that Zhang Yujuan liked him. This was apparent from the dishes she served and her manner in bed. She was staying in the house with him longer and longer. He thought he loved her, too. If he weren't the number three man, he would just marry her without further ado. But if he weren't a revolutionary, could he have her? His class standpoint was not firm enough, and class standpoint was nothing to joke about. Although he'd never run into trouble, he'd seen plenty who had. Whether to marry her or not could wait. Wasn't being married just sleeping together?

But Zhang San in fact very much did have a class standpoint of his own. Though the old capitalist had been thoroughly destroyed, his ghost was still lurking about. Whether Zhang San despised him or imitated him, he never could transcend him. And the longer this went on, the more it could be seen in everything he did.

Zhang San knew he was far from a match for Zhang Yujuan. Even if she had been only a mistress, her every move showed she was from an important family. Through determined effort Zhang San taught himself to have some style, even learning to turn his back when she was getting dressed or getting out of bed. But what he got for his efforts was an unemotional "You're really lecherous."

He would never in his life have imagined it. Had he been even more lecherous, he could not have outdone that old bastard. The old man's virility had been failing, but he had a whole bag of lecherous tricks. As he listened to Zhang Yujuan speak in an irritated and snotty tone, he knew he didn't have the makings for this.

Zhang San hated the hell out of that old bastard. The old capitalist had died long ago and been burned to ashes. Not even the ashes were left. Even if Zhang San did want to beat him, to kill him, to devour him, there was nothing left to lay his hands on or sink his teeth into. He vented his anger on Zhang Yujuan. They were of the same sort. However you put it, they were of the same family. He wanted to make her just as dirty as he himself was, as devoid of any fucking upbringing.

He thundered obscenity after obscenity at her. She half closed her eyes, her face full of disdain and indifference. Zhang San slapped her and demanded that she pay attention. She coolly replied that she was listening.

"What did I just say, then?"

Zhang San pressed her to repeat the obscenities. He knew this was what she hated most. She could surrender her body, but she wouldn't surrender her nauseating airs. When she wouldn't speak, he hit her, then used all sorts of gentle guile and cruel torments. He couldn't stand her poise.

After he was done hitting her, he felt a little sorry. He had been too rough. After all, the woman did have feelings. But when he thought about how she absolutely refused to utter a single obscenity even though he beat her, he was filled with hate.

"Are you going to say it or not?"

There was no sound.

"Yes or no?"

He grabbed her hair with one hand and started beating her hysterically. Zhang San was insane and didn't care if he beat her to death.

"I'll say it . . . "

"Say it!"

"I'm—"

"Say it!"

"I'm a cunt . . . " After she got this much out, she was choking with tears. "I'm a cunt, a stinking cunt!" She was screaming.

Zhang San hugged her tightly. He kissed and stroked her desperately. She just cried and took no notice.

Zhang San got off of the bed and sat on the floor watching her white body shudder. He had just taken two drags of his cigarette when he suddenly began to cry. He cried his heart out.

That night it also rained.

10

After that night, Zhang Yujuan lost hope. She lost her smile and the color to her face and hardly spoke at all. When she had to talk, it was in a very low voice. She spoke quickly and tersely.

When Zhang San tried to play up to her, she ignored him. Even when he risked stealing a piece of confiscated jewelry for her, not only did she not take it, she didn't so much as raise her eyelids. When Zhang San wanted her in bed, she'd get in bed, woodenly, and never say a thing. Afterward, she'd get dressed and go downstairs. If Zhang San wouldn't let her go, she wouldn't go. But eventually Zhang San would be frightened that her "daughters" would see what was going on, so he would send her back. She'd go away without speaking, looking apathetic.

Zhang San knew he'd screwed things up, and that they could never go back to the way they had been in the past. It was wrong to beat her and would have been wrong not to beat her. Confronted with this wooden Zhang Yujuan, Zhang San several times felt a total lack of interest and shooed her away.

She was nothing but the mistress of a shriveled old man, yet she had actually looked down on Zhang San while sleeping with him. He ground his teeth with hatred. He decided that he'd gotten a bad deal. Backgrounds aside, she was over ten years his senior. And regardless of how fine and fair her face, she was still used goods. After all the trouble and worry, he had only managed to get her kind of "cunt" and had been so taken in that he wanted to marry her. Really fucking dumb!

Once he'd calmed down, he could view Zhang Yujuan through different eyes. He discovered she wasn't so great. Her man had been hounded to death, yet she enthusiastically started sleeping with the enemy. How could such a woman be any good? And even though she had slept with him, she still pretended to be decent and wouldn't say "cunt." She never was willing to say it, and had shown a lot of spunk after all. But she couldn't take the beating and, so, sullied herself. Since they were both tainted now, there was no longer anything infatuating about her. Zhang San quit playing up to her. She still cleaned house and cooked, and when he wanted to go to bed with her, he didn't give a damn if she was silent or not.

He got by just fine.

There was only one trouble. One day just as they were doing it, Anna came straight upstairs and called at Zhang San's bedroom door for her auntie to come home. She said Lisa had a fever. She seemed to know all about what was going on.

Zhang San was at a bit of a loss.

He wasn't afraid of Anna's reporting him. She could have done that long ago, and there was no need to let him know that she was the one who had found out. Maybe she was only giving him a kind of warning, blowing off some steam? Anna only called twice at the door, then went away, but it seemed like a long time to Zhang San.

Ever since things had turned chilly with Zhang Yujuan, Zhang San had again begun to notice Anna. Her youth and good looks aside, Anna was untouched. This was very important. Zhang San had his pride. Besides, she was the capitalist's daughter. If you were going to defile a girl, it ought to be one like Anna.

Now, Zhang San had really learned a few things from Zhang Yujuan and was much more articulate. Once he had an outlet for his sexual urges, he no longer needed to sneak around feeling bras and panties. In order to make it easier to speak to Anna, Zhang San volunteered to be leader of the propaganda team at her school. She was one of the graduating students and would have to ask things of him.

In the still of the night, when he wasn't busy with revolutionary work, Zhang San examined his conscience, scrutinizing himself over and over. He recalled his yearning for affection as a youth. He'd had a lot of bad luck. First he'd lost his "virginity" to Ms. Hua in the factory, now he'd been bewitched by this "cunt." At this point he wanted to make a clean break with Zhang Yujuan, then pursue Anna sincerely and wholeheartedly. He'd walk through fire and water for her. After several attempts, he realized this wasn't going to work and grew discouraged. Anna was not about to respect him. If this was how it was even when he had power and influence, he wouldn't have a prayer should he someday lose that power and influence.

Taking advantage of Zhang Yujuan's absence, Zhang San went to see Anna one day. She called him Mr. Zhang, invited him to sit down, and poured him some tea. He watched her closely as she poured. She was striking from any angle. He was aroused as he looked at her.

He congenially asked her what she wanted to do after she graduated. Anna unequivocally replied, "Shanghai. Industry and Mining." Zhang San laughed. He approved of her choice. Workers were the preeminent social class, and to desire to be a worker was politically correct. "But . . . " Zhang San drank some tea. It was tasty. He didn't complete the sentence.

Anna refilled his cup.

Zhang San suddenly grasped her hand and kept her from pulling it back. She turned her head away. Zhang San stood up and hugged her to him. The thermos crashed to the floor, scalding their feet. Although Zhang San was only slightly burned, it hurt enough that he had to abort his attempt to tell her how he felt. He limped gingerly back to the house and called for a car to take them to the hospital.

His comrades-in-arms surrounded the doctor and made him admit Zhang San to the hospital. When the doctor tried to argue with them, they almost beat him up. Zhang San stopped them and said it wasn't necessary. He asked the doctor if Anna's burns were severe and asked him to show a little revolutionary humanitarianism. If she needed to stay in the hospital, admit her. The doctor said he would consider it. Anna didn't want to.

Zhang Yujuan hurried to the hospital. One look told her what had transpired.

They rode home in the same car.

11

The factory doctor came over every day to change Zhang San's dressings. Zhang San had him take the opportunity to treat Anna as well. The doctor readily agreed.

Zhang San didn't mind much about his own injury. He thought, This was just the price you paid for love. He limped downstairs to see Anna. She was sitting up in bed making a little dog out of nylon yarn. Zhang Yujuan was sitting next to the bed.

He asked solicitously how she was doing.

"Fine, thanks," she replied.

"Would you like to go to the hospital to be examined? I've got a car. It's no problem."

"No, thanks anyway."

Zhang San made a fuss over how realistic the dog she was making was and asked her to make him one for his key ring when she had time. She didn't reply.

The scene of Anna turning her head away from him, her soft hand in his palm, was etched in Zhang San's mind. A girl can't help being a little shy, he told himself. If it hadn't been for that thermos, he might already have gotten what he was after.

He directed his attention to finding Anna home alone. But for some strange reason, Zhang Yujuan seldom went out. She sent Lisa running after things. The three of them seemed not to quarrel anymore. Yet they weren't affectionate either, but rather spiritless. You could listen at their door for a long time without hearing a single sentence spoken.

Finally, he got his chance. Zhang Yujuan was summoned by the neighborhood committee for admonishment. Zhang San put on a clean shirt, shaved, combed his hair, and went downstairs pretending that he was going for a stroll. He slipped into the garage.

He said nothing, but went straight over to take hold of the small hand he had dreamt about so often. But it rapidly avoided his and left him clutching at air. Zhang San simply pushed her back and kissed her excitedly. Anna covered up to get away.

"Mr. Zhang!"

When he heard the shout, Zhang San let go. Turning his head, he saw Zhang Yujuan standing at the door. He left without a word.

So, this hussy of a mistress was going to make mischief. Zhang San hated her so much he could have skinned her alive. Early the next day, he waited at the top of the stairs, and when she came up carrying her broom, he grabbed her and pushed her into the bedroom.

"Cunt, stay out of my business!"

"I won't let you touch my daughter."

"Your daughter?"

Her expression was extremely menacing. After she spoke, she tried to leave, but Zhang San raised his hand, causing her to fall onto the bed. Before Zhang San could follow, she climbed out the other side. He was not about to let her off the hook now. He wanted to blow off some steam on her, to humiliate her, to let her know she was nothing but a bitch.

Zhang Yujuan ran out onto the balcony. "If you come any closer, I'll jump!"

Zhang San had lost.

Once a loser, always a loser.

Because of the good word put in beforehand by Zhang San, Anna was assigned to the factory she wanted in Shanghai. The day after she reported for work, and before Zhang San had a chance to offer his congratulations, Zhang Yujuan turned him in. She told the whole story of her relationship with Zhang San, but she didn't mention Anna. She said that she was giving herself up to the revolutionary masses and that she was asking for Chairman Mao to punish her.

She was beaten till her nose was bruised and her eyes swollen, and she got a slight concussion. Here the punishment fit the crime. But Zhang San was excused from his post on the revolutionary committee. Thanks to a directive from above calling for "protecting old revolutionaries," no further inquiries were made. Zhang San moved out of the Western-style house and returned to his own place. Only after his fall did he know how many people had been waiting for him to step aside. They sucked up to others, and took advantage of the situation to kick him while he was down. Nowadays, he was just a registered member of a revolutionary brigade. Though the entire country was red and the revolution was at its zenith, Zhang San still felt disappointed.

He firmly believed that had it not been for that rotten woman, Anna would have fallen for him. A girl like her either didn't fall in love or, if she did, was very passionate. He was now a middle-aged man, he sadly reflected, who was over the hill and who had honestly never once been in love. Even if he became the commander of a revolutionary brigade, the best he could do was simply to marry a female worker. He had risked his life in rebellion only to have it all ruined by the mistress of a capitalist. How could he get it off his mind?

12

Zhang San was locked up for several months at the time of the hunt for Cultural Revolution activists. In the end he was dealt with leniently, exempted from prosecution, and let go. Back home he helped out around the house and played with his two-year-old son. If the factory distributed some Western-style clothes or some pressed duck, he was as happy as anyone. His wife was a good manager and very resourceful. They bought a fourteen-inch Goldstar color TV and watched it every night. It was still the same old house, but it had been whitewashed and painted and was nicer than before. The blood from the squashed bedbugs was gone. The bed that had shaken so hard it woke him up had been replaced, as had the rest of the furniture. Come to think of it, life was much better than before. But he still felt a little depressed.

He inquired discreetly about events at capitalist Zhang's old house. Anna had married the son of a company boss and was living there. Lisa had gone to study in the U.S. He heard she had married an American imperialist. On the way home from work, he once ran into Zhang Yujuan. Her skin was as fair as ever and seemed to have lost none of its tone. She'd probably had a face-lift. She recognized him too. She gave him an indifferent glance and then went on.

Considering all that had happened, Zhang San thought to himself that despite the troubles he had afterward, being a revolutionary had been worth it. He would never again experience such status or enjoy so many blessings. That woman may have ruined things for him, but in the final analysis she had fallen for him. If someone with her looks and upbringing could fall for him, then he had done all right at love.

When they learned that his father had implemented Party policy and been given back some money, Zhang San's wife made him go apologize for the sake of the inheritance. Zhang San thought about his mother and the days when there was nothing to eat and flatly refused. But his wife always had a way to make him give in—she nagged him day and night. Zhang San couldn't stand it, so he had no choice but to take along a present and go with his wife and son to capitulate. The slut was long gone, and as soon as his new stepmother saw them she snickered and went out. The old man held his grandson and spoke only to him. Zhang San felt thoroughly rebuffed.

Time is on the side of the determined. After they had been to see him four or five times, the old man's face gradually relaxed. But the old lady, whom Zhang San's wife called a slutty witch, was even less inclined to speak civilly to them.

One day as he was squatting on the latrine, Zhang San let his mind wander. Inheritance, status, romance, feelings of gratitude and resentment—all essentially were meaningless. You do what you must. Given the chance to be a revolutionary again, he suspected he wouldn't bother. As he thought about all that he had experienced, it was like a dream, like a big Technicolor lie. When his son grew up and he told him, he'd never ever believe it.

Here Zhang San shook his head. He dropped his toilet paper into the latrine, slapped his legs, which were numb from squatting, walked out of the privy fastening his pants, and headed back to work at the shop.

1986

Liu Heng (1954–   )

DOGSHIT FOOD

Translated by Deirdre Sabina Knight

The events described in the following story probably took place during the Great Leap Forward (1958), when the peasants, after being instructed in the virtues of self-reliance, were urged to engage in an all-out effort to increase production. The campaign turned out to be a disaster and was abandoned in 1959.

Many years later, when the villagers tried to recall how Yang Tiankuan had left Flood Water Valley that morning, they didn't know how to begin. They could only remember one thing, though they had no idea if it had any particular significance.

"He was carrying a hundred kilograms of millet."

This insipid phrase had been repeated in the village for more than thirty years. It was insipid because the days ahead of Yang Tiankuan after that morning turned out to be anything but insipid.

Yang Tiankuan waded lightly through the fog. He had a straw basket over his shoulder; the sack inside was bulging with grain. As they were shrouded in the morning fog, the villagers suspected that his basket was empty. But the fact was that for the last few days he had been borrowing grain from various families, hemming and hawing about what he planned to do with it. Maybe that is why he was able to run so swiftly.

But the people only repeated, "He was carrying a hundred kilograms of millet." The comment cut deeply into the ego of this sex-starved bachelor.

Yang Tiankuan carried the grain on his back like a donkey to the appointed place, his self-respect compromised. Panting, his eyes went white and he could no longer speak. He was in a daze when a man approached him and asked, "New grain?"

Yang Tiankuan nodded, wiping his sweaty face with a towel. The man had a squat mule behind him. Without bothering to gauge the weight, he lifted the sack onto his shoulder and swung it over the mule's saddle.

"Okay, it's a deal. You can rest up a bit now."

Then the man laughed and led his mule away. Someone emerged from behind the mule, standing there watching Yang, who took a quick glance but didn't dare to look closer. He felt like dismembering the man who had just left, but didn't have the strength.

He heaved a long sigh, which was to become his habit and for which he would occasionally be mocked later.

What an ugly monster! A hundred kilograms of millet in trade for a giant goiter? Was she worth it? He mulled it over and concluded that she probably was. After all, the woman was his now. He led her down the road, preoccupied with what he would do with her on the *kang*. Things happened faster than he expected; the woman had set his passions afire.

"How did you get that goiter?" He started a conversation only after they had left the back streets of Clear Water Town.

"I've had it since I was little."

"Your man sold you because he couldn't stand the sight of . . . "

"I've been sold six times. If you decide to sell me, it'll be seven. Are you going to? If you are, you might as well do it here and save the trouble of making the round-trip. This town has a market. Do you want to sell me or not?"

"No, no . . . " The woman talked so fast that Tiankuan had to compose himself before deciding. "I'm not selling you."

"That's good, since you might be crushed to death carrying a hundred kilograms of millet back to the mountains." Laughing, the woman took off in front of him. The goiter above her shoulder swayed back and forth, but Tiankuan no longer paid any attention to it. His gaze was fixed on her buttocks, fat as a horse's, and her yamlike feet scurrying along the mountain road.

"Will the goiter get in the way of having babies?" Tiankuan appeared a bit worried.

"Get in the way of what? It isn't growing on my crotch." The woman's words had a coquettish air that roused Tiankuan's ardor. "Whatever you want, I'll make it, believe it or not."

"Okay, okay!"

The woman went down the mound to piss. But after squatting down, she didn't get back up. She let Tiankuan carry her into the bushes where they finished their business amid moans and screams. By the time they entered the village, Tiankuan no longer felt ashamed of his wife's goiter. On the contrary, he now cherished it like a precious part of his own body.

All this happened not long after the Communists parceled out the land. Since Yang Tiankuan's household had increased, his acreage no longer sufficed. So the village assigned him another two acres of carrot plots. The land was fertile, but far from the road. It hadn't been planted in years, not since the Japanese guerrilla invasion, when the farmers burned the crops to keep the Japanese from getting at them. Rather dull by nature, Tiankuan didn't even complain when he was given land no one else wanted. He just swallowed the injustice. But not his woman. She climbed on top of the pigsty to curse loudly, and even though her curses appeared to be directed at the pigs, the real message was lost on no one. The village cadres were so frightened by her, they dared not show their faces.

"Hey, you pig! What were you in your previous existence? You must have sinned and bullied my man in your former life. Well, you sure are a beautiful sight now! What are you snorting at? Watch me take a shit and feed it to you. You putrid guts . . . "

The villagers knew that Tiankuan had married an extremely ugly woman with a goiter, but were surprised to learn that she was a foulmouthed demon as well. No one dared to cross her. Even Tiankuan was afraid of her. The more she cried, the shinier her goiter became, expanding into a huge balloon. Tiankuan felt dwarfed in her presence, wondering if he was really a man, since she was so much more aggressive than he.

He went to the stove and ladled out some water. Timidly he reasoned with her. "You must be tired. That should do it. Come down and have a drink."

"Don't you have any balls? You probably can't even squeeze out a drop of urine or a single fart! I'll get down if you take my place, climb up here and give those fucking bastards hell for me."

Tiankuan helped her into the house, burdened with worries. This sharp-tongued woman promised only hard days ahead. Still, she was his woman, able-bodied and vigorous, as good in bed as she was skilled in the field. Wasn't that the kind of woman he had wanted?

The woman proved to be not only capable but hardworking. She took a hoe and some food straight to Hulun mound to build a grass hut. She worked for five days and five nights straight without going home. During the day the couple would work bare-chested, turning over black soil. At night they'd couple in the grassy brush, their naked legs entangled. In three days Tiankuan was worn out, but his wife showed no sign of exhaustion. After work she would let her husband rest in the hut to nourish his male essence, while she went home to fetch baskets of yam shoots. Back at the mound she would cut them into equal pieces, mix them with grass ashes, and plant them in the spongy soil, carefully spacing them two hands apart. The woman was a skilled farmer.

That fall Tiankuan and his woman harvested more yams than they could eat. Since his cousin Yang Tiande had a large family with four children and a very poor crop that year, Tiankuan wanted to help him.

"Bullshit! In times of plenty you forget about hunger. You may not worry about the future, but I'm scared of starving. If he wants to eat, let him grow his own food."

To prevent him from giving away their yams, she dug a cellar behind the hut and piled the yellow-skinned yams up as carefully as if they were eggs. Then she sealed up the cellar.

Her deeds were as abusive as her foul tongue. Tiankuan was embarrassed to raise his head in front of his fellow villagers, but he knew in his heart that his wife treated him well. This knowledge assured him that they would survive all hardships.

In due course they became parents. After their first child came, it seemed as if the woman had opened her gate: a crying, hungry baby would come into the world as soon as her legs were parted. Until the age of forty, there was hardly a moment when she wasn't nursing a little cub whose yellow mouth sucked at her small turnip-like breasts. Once the baby drank its fill it would chew on her goiter with its baby teeth, smearing her neck with saliva and mucus. There was always plenty of milk. On hot summer days, Tiankuan would squat under the northern eaves to eat while she sat by the kitchen door, a baby playing with her breasts. A little squeeze sent a white stream straight into Tiankuan's bowl. When, in frolicking moods, they turned to tease each other, a stream of milk from her breast would smack Tiankuan right in the eye. He took great pride in this special skill of hers.

But the woman was not a bottomless udder, and the children would not be babies forever. The couple had to eat and the children had to be fed. They had to find enough food to fill eight mouths, big and small. When Tiankuan first became a father, he had plenty of fun with his children. But now that he was a father of six, he realized that he and his wife were digging a deep pit. Each child was a black hole.

They saw the corn porridge in their pot begin to get thin when their third child was born. And it never got thicker after that. By the time the fourth child could hold a bowl and use chopsticks, the porridge started to look green. Meal after meal they had to add leaves to make enough.

But the children all had good hearty names associated with food. Their eldest son was Buckwheat. Next came a whole line of daughters: Soybean, Little Pea, Red Bean, and Mung Bean. The baby was another boy. They called him Millet. Two boys with beans and pea in between made for a prosperous family. But once they all lay down, there was just a line of empty stomachs. Tiankuan and his wife could do nothing but sigh.

The children had well-trained tongues, long and skillful. After every meal Mother would examine their bowls, and whoever left crumbs would not get away without a scolding and a beating.

"What are you, short-tongued? Lick it clean."

She'd beat the back of their heads until tears ran down their cheeks. Tongues hanging out over their chins, they'd squeeze their little faces into their bowls as hard as they could. This was the task the children learned earliest and most earnestly. If they came at the right moment, visitors could see all eight faces of Tiankuan's household submerged behind their bowls. The chorus of licking and slurping against the rough surface of the pottery was enough to make a person jump with fright.

After dark, when a person's figure could no longer be seen, Tiankuan would go out under the stars to visit his neighbors. He'd carry a little bag, shamefaced and frightened, as if he were holding out his own heart. When he came across people unwilling to lend him food, he wished he could shrivel up and squirm into his little worn bag. The inhabitants of Flood Water Valley were mostly good people. Few had refused to lend Tiankuan food. Tiande was an exception.

"If you want food, send your goiter hag here."

A harsh retort from his cousin forced Tiankuan to realize that the ill feelings generated by the yam incident of so many years back still lingered. He could only leave. When he reported this to his wife she cursed. "Are you two really from the same grandfather? Fuck that bastard!"

As if this weren't enough, she stomped over to Tiande's garden and picked a pumpkin she had earlier set her eyes on and boiled it with salt. By the time Tiande discovered the empty vine in his garden, and was cursing up and down, Tiankuan's children were already shitting pumpkin seeds.

The household lived on like this.

The woman's surname was Cao. No one knew her given name. She told people it was Apricot, but no one took her seriously. The barren lands in the Western Water region grew no apricot trees. Apricots were grown only in Flood Water Valley. Apricot was the name she picked after her marriage. But since no one found her deserving of such a name, they didn't use it. She was referred to only by what grew on her neck: Goiter.

Her Western Water accent was rapid-fire and prickly. When she spoke fast she sounded like a mating rooster, full of *cluck cluck guk guk* cocklike hot air. People thought her mouth was fit only for cursing. And could she ever curse! When she was at it, obscene words would pour out in a stream. In one fell swoop, she seemed to have transformed herself into a man, even more daring and resourceful than most men in her ability to humiliate her opponents and all their female kin, dead or alive.

In these parts men beat their wives as often as they eat. But the woman named Cao seemed to have castrated her man. She'd pull Tiankuan's ears and swing him around the yard. This was a custom of the Western Water region. No one dared get near her, considering her a Western Water tigress.

The year Red Bean was born the Production Brigade's canteen went out of business, and famine struck the region. Even the sight of bark on trees made the people's eyes light up. And a handful of grass would literally make their mouths water. One day a platoon of soldiers doing maneuvers passed the hill near their house. Goiter, taking month-old Red Bean along, followed them and returned with a basketful of steamy dung from the cannon-carrying mules. When Tiankuan saw it baking in the sun, he thought it was ordinary shit and carried it over to the pigsty. When Goiter found out what had happened, she sprang out of her room and gave him two slaps across the face.

"Are you blind? You couldn't stand the sight of their shit, while I had to put up with their farts? Now see if you can shit something we can put in the pot and boil!"

The children watched their father reel from the slaps. He had to struggle to regain his balance. Neighbors craned their necks over the fence to watch, laugh, and sigh. If she wasn't a tigress, what was she? But then they saw her take a sieve and head toward the river.

Now that the mule dung was mixed with the stench of the sty, she had to rinse it with extra care. After the grass roots and the dregs were washed away, some whole or broken corn kernels remained. These golden nuggets of grain looked like shining stars in a pot of boiled apricot leaves. While they were savoring these tiny grains, the family must have been feeling the digestive movements of the mules' intestines. But they seemed to be content with what they got. As Tiankuan was stroking his cheek with his chopsticks, he had to admit that his woman was really something. What could his neighbors do but hold their tongues? One virtue redeemed many vices. No one could say that this woman was completely rotten.

No graves had been dug that year in Tiankuan's family plot, thanks partly to sheer luck and partly to this foulmouthed and evil-hearted woman.

Their days were certainly full of hardship, but no one seemed to have any sympathy for this woman. She could work alongside any man, although it depended on where she was working. If the task at hand were for her own family, she would turn the millstone herself, stamping around as forcefully as a blindfolded beast of burden. She could even swing her children as they held on to the secondary mill shafts. Tiankuan would have to stop to rest six times when carrying firewood from Windy Fire Valley; she needed to rest only twice. And the bundle of firewood she carried was big enough to hide half a fence behind it. Rain or shine, she made fifteen trips a day, at dawn and at dusk, to fetch water. Five trips were for her own family's water vat, the rest for families whose fathers or sons were either martyrs or currently in the military. She didn't do it out of kindness; she wanted to add four extra work points toward her daily credits.

But once she found herself in the field she was a different person. When it was time to work, her muscles and energy began to sag, turning her into a pile of lazy flesh. In the time fellow workers could hoe two rows of cornstalks, she would stitch half a shoe sole, hiding in the shade of the stalks. Her hoe never touched the soil. When they went far off to collect hemp for rope, men would carry eighty bundles, and women would carry fifty. But she, like a dainty damsel, would carry under one arm a single bundle no thicker than the handle of a pickax.

"Are you telling me your goiter grows down to your ass? Can't you carry anything on your back?" The team leader gave her a piece of his mind.

"I can't put anything on my back because your dick is stuck between my legs."

"I see your basket has something in it."

"If my basket were empty, wouldn't my children, your six little ancestors, starve? Oh, of course, they are Tiankuan's children. You wouldn't dare pick on your own."

She laughed with such abandon that the team leader was at a loss for words, and only raised his eyebrows. Her basket was half filled with freshly watered hemp shoots, green and fragrant, all ready to be thrown into a pot and cooked. When at noon her fellow workers took a break, she used the time to comb the hilltop looking for hemp shoots. This kind of wild vegetation was rare in the hills near the village. What could the team leader say? He could neither chastise nor condone her. He could only leave her alone.

But that wasn't the only trick she pulled. She also sewed special pockets in her clothes. When she got home from work, she would fumble around and always manage to pull out something: baby cobs of corn, a few ears of grain, pears or plums. It became her daily habit, and she collected quite a handsome harvest. No one could catch her, however, because they couldn't figure out where the pockets were. Some suspected that she hid the stuff in her crotch. But it was hard to prove, for even though she was an ugly old hag, that part of her body was no place to conduct a search. Or it may have been that no one was really interested in catching her. Tiankuan might not know the details behind these stolen harvests, but he knew that from the beginning his wife's problem was her filthy mouth. After their children were born and they were always hungry, her bad habits extended from her mouth to her hands. He couldn't stop her, because he was not her match, verbally or physically. Besides, her abilities had proven to be valuable in raising a herd of hungry children.

Her claws went wild and spread in all directions.

The neighbors had built a trellis along the courtyard wall to grow bottle gourds. A sheath of tender, juicy leaves sprang up, and several white flowers reached over the wall. Mung Bean and Millet stretched their little hands up to pick the flowers.

"Don't break them. Let them grow." Goiter had her own plan. Once the flowers withered, from the stalks hung some fist-sized gourds, swollen up like big balloons. The woman next door was no slouch either. Waiting until Goiter was at work, she took the opportunity to sneak over and used a basket made from chaste-tree twigs to scoop up the gourds. This would prevent the vine from drooping. Besides, it would let Goiter know who was the owner of these gourds. Goiter behaved as if nothing had happened. When the neighbor peeped through the fence to see her reaction, she did her best not to reveal a trace of her intentions.

When the gourds were grown. Goiter estimated that, mixed with two eggplants, they would provide enough food for a whole day. Quick as the north wind, she reaped a hefty harvest. The gourds were duly cooked. Goiter was excoriated. Her neighbor's children took the lead, straddling the fence to shout, "You fucking mother of a thief!" After the urchins had their say, Goiter charged forth majestically. She didn't curse anyone. She just berated the gourds, calling them names in such a roundabout way that they became metaphors for bewitching women who climb over fences to seduce the innocent.

"My darling gourd meat, you were born to be fucked over. You should remember this tomorrow. If you are going to look so sexy, stay in your own yard. Let your own kind have fun with you."

Angry shouts from the neighbor were thus silenced. She was so humiliated that the only strength she could muster was used to pull up the plants. She tore the trellis to pieces. Those who had been bested by Goiter often wondered if the slut from the Western Water region was a human being. Even Tiankuan thought his wife was probably possessed.

That year's crop was sparse once again. And little Millet was already seven. Goiter's days of being possessed seemed endless.

Tiankuan turned fifty, though he couldn't figure out how he'd managed to live this long, nor what kind of guts filled his belly. He was as lively as a tree stump. Lying on his brick *kang*, he couldn't help recalling that day in his youth when he carried the hundred kilograms of grain on his back. He'd sniffle with sadness. Grief swelled in his chest, and he sighed repeatedly.

"What are you sighing about? The first day you saw me you started sighing. Now we've spent half our lives together. Have I ever mistreated you?"

"Never, never."

Husband and wife covered themselves with a ragged cotton quilt. There wasn't any activity other than an occasional exchange of words. In the past Tiankuan would respond to the slightest hint of flirtation by rolling on top of his woman until they were both bathed in sweat. But he wouldn't be able to do it anymore. Tiankuan didn't even want to look at his wife's behind. Besides, the children slept with them, and Buckwheat and Soybean were old enough to know what their parents' panting meant.

The last time they did it was in the garden, behind the cucumber trellis, under the moonlight. They were rocking back and forth in the heat of passion when suddenly she asked, "What are we going to eat tomorrow?"

Taken aback, Tiankuan asked himself, "What are we going to eat?" then pulled up his pants in despair and squatted down. At that moment the connection between what they had been doing and what they were going to eat finally dawned on him. Following this train of thought, he was able to capture some hazy images of a time prior to the incident with the hundred kilograms of grain. His faceless ancestors faintly came into view, copulating and eating, with one nagging at the other, "What are we going to eat tomorrow?"

"What *are* we going to eat tomorrow?" he asked Goiter. Her rough skin shone white and smooth in the moonlight, but he'd lost interest.

"Wheat bran."

"Where did you find it?"

"In the saddle shed. Little Pea has a quick eye. She has gotten clever."

"There are some rat holes in the field behind the warehouse. I bet you could find some real provisions there."

Tiankuan concentrated on the arrangement of the rat holes. From that time on he was devoid of any sexual desire, and rubbing flesh with his woman had become a thing of the past. Goiter also came to terms with reality. She no longer reached out for him when they were lying on the *kang*.

What to eat? He thought hard every day about the same old question that had occupied his ancestors for generations.

His wife began to look gaunt. If she was once a tigress, she was now a sick one, weighed down with anxiety and sadness. Her goiter grew wrinkled, no longer a shiny pink air balloon. It no longer puffed up when she cursed people.

Tiankuan thought to himself idly: Haven't I worried enough? He looked at the six children with their hungry faces. They had all developed a habit of licking their runny noses with their tongues. His heart blazed up in anger.

He felt like beating the brains out of something.

The year Mung Bean dropped out of school and Millet began, life in Flood Water Valley wasn't too bad. New babies were born into the world one after another, and the average land per person went from nine-tenths of an acre down to seven. Nonetheless, the food rations were still adequate. Each household got a book of food coupons for twenty kilograms of grain per person. If not enough, they could go to the grain co-op and buy more. As the summer grain was still growing green in the fields, people were already shuffling back and forth carrying empty sacks or sacks full of grain along the mountain roads.

One morning after Goiter had carried eight buckets of water, leaving seven buckets to be fetched that evening, she fed the chickens, the pigs, and her family and left with the food coupons under her arm. Those who saw her leave the village thought that she looked quite benign. Only later did they realize that a kind look on an evil person was no good omen.

People crowded around the counter outside the grain co-op. But despite their jostling, they didn't look hungry. Goiter grasped her empty sack, only to discover that her coupons and money were missing. A hot-tempered woman all her life, she let out a long screech. She fell on the ground, spitting foam. All the people buying and selling grain surrounded her to watch the funny goiter rolling up and down on her breasts. They craned their necks like chickens and their eyes bulged out like crows'. A man from the grain store, unable to get through the crowd, began ceremoniously quoting from Chairman Mao's little red book, reminding them that though they came from all corners of the earth, they were gathered here for a common purpose. What he really meant was that he wanted to get through the crowd to help. At that time, quoting from Mao's sayings was both fashionable and effective. The people quickly parted to make way for him. He took a good look at the woman before fetching a teakettle from behind the counter. After gargling some water to clear his throat, he spat it into her face. He repeated this several times. Her mouth ceased to twitch, though her eyes remained glassy.

"Which village are you from?"

"Lost."

"What's your name?"

"Lost."

"What did you lose?"

"Lost, lost . . . lost . . . "

Goiter was hysterical. Those surrounding her grew even more interested. Her rescuer doubled his efforts to show off. He grabbed her head and, with all his strength, rubbed his finger on the acupuncture point of her upper lip, summoning her: "No, you won't lose it. Come back! Wake up!" Struggling madly and screaming "Motherfucker!" Goiter crept up and fought her way out of the crowd.

She cried until she was limp. Tough as nails her whole life, it surprised even her that she had shed so many tears. She retraced her steps twice, leaving no stone unturned along the ten-mile mountain road. She even went into the bushes and stripped, turning over every patch and pocket of her clothing in hopes of finding her lost coupons and money. She didn't get home until the moon had appeared in the sky. Under a lantern Tiankuan was smoking a long bamboo pipe. On the table next to the *kang* a bowl of rice porridge had been left out for her. She stared at the bowl of rice porridge as if in a trance.

"Mother, eat some porridge." Millet leapt over and pulled at her.

"I'm not eating. I won't eat anymore . . . " She sounded like a little cat.

Tiankuan knew at once that something bad must have happened. As he questioned her, the fire in his heart surged. His palms trembled so violently he didn't know what to do with them. His wife's sudden weakness made his courage swell. It's really something when a puny dick suddenly acquires balls.

"You thief!"

He yelled and smashed the bowl of porridge on the floor.

"You scum!"

In all his life he had never felt such gratification.

"So you lost the grain, eh? We'll have to use you for food. I'll have to eat you!"

As he spoke, he lost control of his hand. He lunged at her and slapped her face madly, striking her head and her goiter to his heart's content. The villagers squatted outside in the darkness to listen, understanding that Tiankuan had finally regained his manhood by overturning the tyranny of his wife. Half her life she'd paraded her skill at scrounging neighbors' food. Now she'd mysteriously lost her own grain. Such was the retribution visited upon the woman from the Western Water region. The villagers seemed to share the sentiment that Tiankuan should beat her to death.

As he was beating her, a wail froze his hand in midair.

"Heaven, let whoever stole my grain coupons return them to my family. My grain . . . "

Her wailing was like the refrain of a song. She sang it over and over again. The moonlight made her goiter shine like a white ball, lighting up the darkness. Tiankuan blew his nose, lit a lantern, and carried it outside.

In the middle of the night some villagers, unable to sleep, overheard Goiter fetching water from the spring, her pale feet slapping on the stone platform. They also heard the sound of the garlic smasher, very crisp, as though some nutshells were being broken. Then came silence.

While Tiankuan was crawling around the mountain roads waving his lantern back and forth in search of the coupons, his wife swallowed bitter apricot kernels and lay on a mat. There were quite a few stars in the sky, blinking and looking down upon them with icy stares.

When his lantern died down, Tiankuan returned home. He could hear pitiful crying from two miles away. The sobs came from his nest of children. He was met in the noisy courtyard by his little girls.

"Father, come look at Mother *quick*!"

He was frightened. Nearly collapsing, he slowly made his way to the edge of the *kang*. The old hag's ugly face was all twisted. She was still breathing, but the sound of her gasping chilled his bones. He took the bowl Millet was holding. Inside the crude china he felt some shards of broken apricot kernel. Only then did he remember how she'd not eaten anything all day. She no longer wanted to worry about eating, so she'd gone and eaten this. Since one would never go hungry again after eating this, he wanted to follow suit.

At dawn a wooden stretcher left the village. Some young men in the neighborhood helped carry it; Goiter slept high on top, her waxen face shining bright. Buckwheat led the way, and Tiankuan followed, accompanied by his cousin Tiande. In the morning fog the procession slowly moved downhill. As he trudged along, Tiankuan had the illusion that he'd returned to that morning nearly twenty years ago, except that the weight of the hundred kilograms of grain he imagined he was carrying was about to crush him into a thin cake of bones.

Buckwheat called to him, "Father, Mother's talking!"

They steadily lowered the stretcher, and Tiankuan put his ear up close to her. He gently pushed aside the goiter to get nearer to her mouth.

"Dogshit . . . "

After a moment of silence, she spit out another word.

"Food . . . "

Tiankuan nodded his head in agreement, mournfully, and stroked his wife's hair for the last time.

As the stretcher was about to float out of the valley. Buckwheat replaced Tiande's son so he could relieve himself. The boy went behind a big rock to piss. Then he let out a terrible scream as though his dick had been bitten by a snake. Tiankuan ran over and spotted a small bandana bound up with a rubber band. It was lying under a rock, covered by a few blades of grass and looking like a piece of gray mortar. A couple of feet away were two sections of not-quite-fresh green human shit. Tiankuan could guess why it was green, but felt utterly confused, looking around aimlessly like a fool. His complexion was ashen.

If human shit could petrify, it would expose the folly of future archaeologists. They would sink into the labyrinth of history, tangled up in enigmas related to questions of time and race.

Tiande's son didn't realize that his aunt had drawn her last breath. Anxious to impress her with his find, he showed her the recovered bandana. "Auntie, look. Heaven has returned your coupons."

The woman's eyes stayed open, and her large lips were parted. The goiter shone yellow, as if she were taken aback by being suddenly forced to confront her misery.

"Auntie, look. Look!"

"Shut your trap!"

Tiankuan roared at his nephew, and Buckwheat began to cry. Tiande gave his son a kick. When he had made sure that Tiankuan's wife was no longer breathing, he ran over and gave his son another kick. Tiankuan began to cry. He took the bandana from his nephew and pulled a hemp sack out from under his wife's body. There was no longer any need to go to the clinic, but food had to be purchased. So while the rest of the procession carried his wife back, he went to the co-op. For the time being the couple was parted, one already stiff and the other still moving.

Tiankuan returned with a sack of grain, just enough to cook a meal for the villagers attending the funeral. His children also forced their way into the crowd to grab some food, devouring it voraciously. Their mother's death served them after all.

"But what will we eat tomorrow?"

Tiankuan was now left alone to ponder the bitter question the couple had always faced together. Only now did he fully understand how difficult it is to be a woman. At night he'd roll his naked body over restlessly. The empty spot beneath the quilt made his heart ache. Then he'd remember the crisp sound of her vulgar language.

"Dogshit . . . food."

His virtuous wife was gone.

With the departure of the tigress from Flood Water Valley, life grew quieter and lonelier. Without the rhythms of her cursing like a mating rooster, the days passed uneventfully. Freed of their mother's abuse, life for the children turned out to be happier. Times had certainly changed. Each child's belly grew to twice its previous size, but for the most part they were kept fed.

Yang Tiankuan is now over sixty years old, still as gentle and benign as ever. He speaks with the soft voice of a woman. Never in his life has he shown off his manly power. Perhaps he tried once, but that once cost his wife's life. On his way to work in the fields leased to the peasants, he often makes a detour to visit the graveyard, carefully weeding out the wild grass on the mound. He is full of remorse.

The children feel no debt to their mother. They seem to have forgotten her completely. Looking back dispassionately, one might be convinced that she was simply an incomprehensible person. When Millet was a senior in high school, he once flipped through a medical book in which he discovered that a goiter is some kind of enlargement of the thyroid gland. Only at that moment did his mother, with her hanging ball of flesh, appear in his mind. Although it was but a flash, he felt a touch of nostalgia, which is an indication of pious feelings.

Now that Buckwheat, Soybean, and Little Pea have children of their own, they never let them play with bitter apricot kernels. Obviously, they still remember something of their mother.

The older generation, however, loves to tell the story of Goiter. They invariably begin: "He was carrying a hundred kilograms of grain." The stress is always on the word *grain*, emphasizing that it wasn't dirt or stone or firewood, but "grain," which is food, what people have craved and fought over for generations.

Apricot Cao had come for it and had died over it. She was deeply in love with it.

"Dogshit . . . food."

How could this phrase be called cursing? It was plainly affectionate. Was she cursing? Who was she cursing? This you would have to ask Tiankuan, who is taking a stroll around her grave. Perhaps the old man knows the secret.

1986

Mo Yan (1955–)

IRON CHILD

Translated by Howard Goldblatt

During the Great Leap Forward smelting campaign, the government mobilized 200,000 laborers to build an eighty-*li* rail line; it was completed in two and a half months. The upper terminus linked with the Jiaoji trunk line at Gaomi Station; the lower terminus was located amid dozens of acres of Northeast Gaomi Township bush land.

Only four or five years old at the time, we were housed in a nursery school thrown up beside the public canteen. Consisting of a row of five rammed-earth buildings with thatched roofs, it was surrounded by saplings some two meters tall, all strung together by heavy wire. Powerful dogs couldn't have bounded over it, let alone children like us. Our fathers, mothers, and older siblings—in fact, anyone who could handle a hoe or a shovel—were conscripted into the labor brigades. They ate and slept at the construction site, and we hadn't seen any of them for a very long time. Three skeletal old women were in charge of our "nursery school" confinement. Since all three had hawklike noses and sunken eyes, to us they looked like crones. Each day they prepared three cauldrons of porridge with wild greens: one in the morning, another at noon, and a third in the evening. We wolfed it down until our bellies were tight as little drums. Then after the meal we went up to the fence to gaze at the scenery outside. New branches of willow and poplar sprang from the fence. Some, those with no green leaves, were already rotting away; if they weren't removed, they sprouted yellow wood-ear fungi or little white mushrooms.

Yes, after each meal we went up to the fence to gaze at the scenery outside, feasting on the little mushrooms as we watched out-of-town laborers walk up and down the nearby road. They were grubby and listless, their hair a mess. As we searched for relatives among these laborers, tears in our eyes, we asked:

"Good uncle, have you seen my daddy?"

"Good uncle, have you seen my mommy?"

"Have you seen my brother?"

"Have you seen my sister?"

Some of them ignored us, as if they were deaf. Others cocked their heads and cast a fleeting glance, then shook their heads. But some ripped into us savagely:

"Wriggle your little ass out of here, you son of a bitch!"

The three old women just sat in the doorways and paid no attention to us. The two-meter fence was too tall for us to climb over, and the spaces between the saplings were too narrow for us to wriggle through.

From our vantage point behind the fence we saw an earthen dragon rise up out of the distant field and watched hordes of people scramble busily up and down the earthen dragon, like ants swarming over a hill. The laborers who passed in front of our fence said that was the roadbed for the rail line. Our kinfolk were a part of that human ant colony. From time to time people would suddenly stick thousands of red flags into the dragon; at other times they would suddenly insert thousands of white flags. But most of the time there were no flags. Some time later, a great many shiny objects appeared on top of the dragon. The passing laborers told us those were the steel rails.

One day, a sandy-haired young man came walking down the road. He was so tall we felt he could touch our fence by simply stretching out one of his long arms. When we asked about our relatives, he surprised us by walking up to the fence, squatting down, and cheerfully rubbing our noses, poking our bellies, and pinching our little peckers. He was the first person who had answered our calls. With a big smile he asked:

"What's your daddy's name?"

"Wang Fugui."

"Ah, Wang Fugui," he replied, rubbing his chin. "I know Wang Fugui."

"Do you know when he'll come get me?"

"He won't be coming. The other day, he was crushed while carrying steel rails."

"Wah . . . " One of the kids began to bawl.

"Have you seen my mommy?"

"What's your mommy's name?"

"Wan Xiuling."

"Ah, Wan Xiuling," he replied, rubbing his chin. "I know Wan Xiuling."

"Do you know when she'll come get me?"

"She won't be coming. The other day, she was crushed while carrying railroad ties."

"Wah . . . " Another of the kids began to bawl.

. . .

Before long, we were all bawling. The sandy-haired young man stood up and walked off whistling.

We cried from noon until sunset. We were still crying when the old women called us to dinner. "What are you crying about?" they snarled. "If you don't stop, we'll throw you into Dead Man's Pit."

We had no idea where Dead Man's Pit was, but we knew it had to be a horrible place. We stopped crying.

The next day, we were back at the fence gazing at the scenery on the other side. At midmorning, several laborers rushed up to us carrying a door on which a bloody person was laid out. We couldn't tell if it was a man or a woman, but we could see *and* hear the blood dripping off the edge of the door and splattering on the ground.

One of the kids started crying, and in no time we were all crying, as if the person lying on the door were *my* relative.

After finishing our noon porridge, we went back to the fence, where we spotted the sandy-haired young man walking toward us in the custody of two swarthy, husky men armed with rifles. His hands were tied behind his back; his nose and eyes were bruised and swollen; his lips were bleeding. As he passed in front of us, he turned and gave us a wink, as if he couldn't have been happier.

We called out to him as one, but one of the guards jabbed him in the ribs with his rifle and shouted: "Get moving!"

On yet another morning, while we were leaning against the fence, we saw that the distant railway bed was suddenly alive with red flags, and we heard the clang of gongs and the beating of drums. All those people were shouting joyously for some reason. At lunchtime the old women gave each of us an egg and said: "Children, the rail line has been completed. The first train is due today. That means your daddies and mommies will be coming to get you. We've carried out our responsibility to look after you. These eggs are in celebration of the completion of the railway."

We were ecstatic. Our kinfolk weren't dead, after all. The sandy-haired young man had lied to us. No wonder they'd trussed him up and dragged him away.

Eggs were such a rare treat that the old women had to show us how to peel them first. Clumsily we peeled away the shells, only to find feathery little chicks inside. They chirped when we bit into them, and they bled. When we stopped eating, the old women took switches to us and demanded that we keep eating. We did.

When we were sprawled against the fence the next day, we saw even more red flags on the rail line. Later that afternoon, people on both sides of the tracks began to whoop and holler as a giant object with thick smoke belching out of its head appeared. It was long and black and very big; it howled as it approached from the southwest. It was faster than a horse. It was the fastest thing we'd ever seen. We felt the earth move under our feet, and we were scared. Then we saw several women dressed all in white appear out of nowhere, clapping loudly and announcing:

"The train's coming! The train's here!"

The rumbling train headed off to the northeast, and we watched it until its tail end had disappeared from view.

After the train passed through, as promised, adults began showing up to pick up their children. Mutt was taken away, and so were Lamb, Pillar, and Beans, until I was the only one left.

The three old women led me out beyond the fence and said: "Go home!"

I'd long forgotten where I lived, and tearfully begged one of the old women to take me home. But she shoved me to one side, turned and ran back inside, closing the gate behind her. Then she secured it with a big, shiny brass lock. I stood outside the fence crying, screaming, and begging, but they ignored me. Through a crack in the fence, I watched the three identical old women set up a little pot in the yard, light some kindling under it, and pour in some light green oil. As the kindling crackled and flames licked upward, the oil began to foam. When the foam dissipated, white smoke rose from the edges of the pot. The old women cracked some eggs open and flipped the feathery little chicks into the pot with makeshift chopsticks. They sizzled and rolled around in the hot oil, releasing the fragrance of cooked meat. The old women then picked the cooked chicks out of the oil, blew on them a time or two, and flipped them into their mouths. Their cheeks puffed out—first one side, then the other—and their lips smacked noisily. Tears flowed from their eyes, which were shut the whole time. They wouldn't open the gate, no matter how I cried or screamed. Soon my tears dried up and my voice failed me. I noticed a puddle of muddy water at the foot of an oily black tree. I went over to quench my thirst. But just as I was about to drink, I spotted a yellow toad beside the puddle. I also spotted a black snake with white dots running on its back. The toad and snake were locked in a fight. I was scared, but I was also very thirsty. So, holding my fear in check, I knelt down and scooped some water up with my hands. It dripped through my fingers. The snake had the toad's leg in its mouth, and a white liquid was oozing from the toad's head. The water was brackish, and slightly nauseating. I stood up, but didn't know where to go. I needed to cry, and so I did. But no tears came.

I saw trees, water, yellow toads, black snakes, fighting, fear, thirst, kneeling, cupping water, rank water, nausea. I cried, no tears . . . Hey, what are you crying for, is your daddy dead? Is your mommy dead? Is everyone in your family dead? I turned my head. I saw the kid who asked me the questions. I saw that he was my height. I saw that he wasn't wearing any clothes. I saw that his skin was rusty. It seemed to me that he was an iron child. I saw that his eyes were black. And I saw that he was a boy, just like me.

He said, What are you crying for, Woody? I said, I'm not made of wood. He said, I'm going to call you Woody, anyhow. He said, Woody come play with me over there on the railroad. He said there were lots of good things over there to look at, to eat, and to play with.

I told him a snake was about to swallow a toad. He said, Let it, don't bother it, snakes can suck out a kid's marrow.

He led me off in the direction of the railroad. It seemed so close, but we couldn't reach it. We walked and walked, looked and looked, but the railroad was as far away as ever, as if all the time we were walking, it was too. It took some doing, but we finally made it. By then my feet were killing me. I asked him his name. He said, My name is whatever you want it to be. I said, You look like a piece of rusty iron. He said, If you say I'm iron, then that's what I am. I said, Iron Child. He grunted a reply and laughed. I followed Iron Child up onto the railroad tracks. The roadbed was very steep. I saw that the rails were like two long serpents that had crawled over from what must have been somewhere very far away. I imagined that if I stepped on one of them, it would start to wriggle, and that it would wrap its headless wooden tail around my legs. I stepped on one cautiously. The iron was cold, but it didn't wriggle and it didn't swish its tail.

I saw that the sun was about to set behind the mountain. It was very big and very red. A flock of white birds landed next to some water. I heard an eerie screech. Iron Child said that a train was coming. I saw that the iron wheels were red, and that iron arms were turning them. It felt to me as if the air rushing beneath the wheels could suck a person in. Iron Child waved to the train, as if it were his friend.

Hunger began to gnaw at me that night. Iron Child picked up a rusty iron bar and told me to eat it. I said, I'm a human, so how can I eat iron? Iron Child asked why a human can't eat iron. I'm a human and I can eat it. Just watch if you don't believe me. I watched as he put the iron bar up to his mouth and—*chomp chomp*—began to eat. Apparently, the iron bar was crisp and crunchy, and, by the looks of it, very tasty. I began to drool. I asked him where he'd learned to eat iron, and he said, Since when do you have to learn *how* to eat iron? I said I couldn't do it. And he asked me why not. Try it if you don't believe me. He held out the uneaten half of the steel bar and said, Try it. I said I was afraid I'd break my teeth. He said, Why? He said, There's nothing harder than people's teeth, and if you try it, you'll see what I mean. I took the iron bar hesitantly, put it up to my mouth, and licked it to see how it tasted it. It was salty, sour, and rank, sort of like preserved fish. Take a bite, he said. I tried biting off a chunk and, to my surprise, succeeded with hardly any effort. As I began to chew, the flavor filled my mouth, tasting better and better until, before I knew it, I had greedily finished off the whole thing. Well? I wasn't lying, was I? No, you weren't, I said. You're a good kid, teaching me how to eat iron like that. I won't need to drink broth with greens anymore. He said, Anybody can eat iron, but people don't know that. I said, If they did, they wouldn't have to plant crops anymore, would they? He said, Do you think smelting iron is easier than planting crops? In fact, it's harder. Be sure you don't tell people how delicious iron is, because if they find out, they'll all start eating it, and there won't be any left for you and me. How come you let me in on this secret? I asked him. He said, I wanted to find a friend, since eating iron alone is no fun.

I followed him along the rails heading northeast. Now that I knew how to eat iron, I was no longer afraid of the rails. I muttered to myself, Iron rails, iron rails, don't get cocky, because if you do, I'll eat you up. Now that I'd finished off half an iron bar, I was no longer hungry, and my legs felt strong. Iron Child and I each walked down one of the rails. We walked so fast that in no time we reached a spot where the sky had turned red. Seven or eight huge ovens were spewing flames into the air, and I could smell the fresh, tantalizing aroma of iron. He said, Up ahead there is where they smelt iron and steel. Who knows, maybe that's where your daddy and mommy are. I said, I don't care if they're there or not.

We walked and walked until the railway came to an abrupt end. We were surrounded by head-high weeds that were home to heaps of rusty scrap iron and steel. Several crushed trains lay on their sides in the weeds, their scrap iron and steel cargo spilled on the ground beside them. Walking on a bit farther, we ran across crowds of people squatting down and eating amid the iron and steel. Flames from the smelting ovens turned their faces bright red. It was mealtime. What were they eating? Meaty dumplings and sweet potatoes with eggs. The food must have been delicious, the way their cheeks were all puffed out, as if they had the mumps. But to me the stench of those meaty dumplings and sweet potatoes and eggs was worse than dog shit, and it made me so sick to my stomach I had to run downwind to avoid it. Just then a man and a woman in the crowd stood up and shouted:

"Gousheng!"

They scared me at first. But then I recognized them as my daddy and mommy. They came stumbling toward me, and it suddenly dawned on me what horrifying people they were, at least as horrifying as the three old women at the "nursery school." I could smell the stench on their bodies, worse than dog shit. So when they reached out to grab me, I turned and ran away. They took out after me. I didn't dare turn my head to look back, but I could feel their fingers each time they touched my scalp. And that's when I heard my good friend, Iron Child, yell at me from somewhere in front:

"Woody, Woody, head for the scrap iron heap!"

I watched as his dark red body flashed for an instant in the scrap iron heap, and then vanished from sight. I ran into the heap, stepping on woks, hoes, plows, rifles, cannons, and other things as I climbed to the top. Iron Child waved to me from inside a drainpipe. With a quick hunch of my shoulders, I scrambled inside. It was black as night, and I was surrounded by the fragrance of rust. I couldn't see a thing, but I felt an icy hand grab hold of my hand, and I knew it was Iron Child. He whispered:

"Don't be afraid. Follow me. They can't see us in here."

So I crawled along behind him. I had no idea where the pipe, with all its twists and turns, led to, so I kept crawling until I saw a light up ahead. I followed Iron Child out of the pipe and onto the treads of an abandoned tank; from there we crawled up to the turret. White five-pointed stars had been painted on the turret, from which the rusted, pitted barrel of a cannon protruded, pointing up at an angle. Iron Child said he wanted to crawl into the turret, but the hatch was rusted shut. Iron Child said:

"Let's bite off the screws."

Still on our hands and knees, we circled the hatch, biting off all the rusty screws, quickly chewing them up, until we'd broken through. We tossed the hatch away. The turret was made of soft metal, sort of like overripe peaches. Once we were inside, we settled into the soft, spongy iron seats. Iron Child showed me a tiny opening, through which I could see my parents. They were crawling over a distant heap of scrap iron, tossing objects around and making loud clanging noises that blended with their tearful shouts:

"Gousheng, Gousheng, my son, come out, come out and have some meaty dumplings and sweet potatoes and eggs . . . "

They looked like strangers to me, and when I heard them trying to tempt me with meaty dumplings and sweet potatoes and eggs, I sneered contemptuously.

Finally they gave up looking for me and headed back.

After crawling out of the turret, we straddled the barrel of the cannon, a great vantage point to watch the flames leaping out of ovens, some near and some far, and all the people scurrying around them. Picking up iron woks, with a One—Two—Three, they tossed them into the air and then watched them as they broke apart when they hit the ground. They then smashed them to pieces with sledgehammers. The sweet aroma of burned iron filings drifted over to us; my stomach started to rumble. Apparently sensing what was on my mind, Iron Child said:

"Come on, Woody, let's get one of those woks. Iron woks are delicious."

We sneaked into the glow, where we selected a great big wok, picked it up, and ran off with it, shocking the men who saw us so badly they dropped their hammers. Some even took off running.

"Iron demons," they shouted as they ran. "The iron demons have come!"

By that time we'd made it to the top of a heap of scrap iron and had begun breaking the wok into edible pieces. It was much tastier than the iron bar.

As we were feasting on our iron wok, we saw a man with a gimpy leg and a holstered revolver on his hip limp over and smack the men who were shouting "iron demons."

"Bastards," he cursed them. "Your damned rumors are creating a disturbance! A fox can turn into a demon, and so can a tree. But whoever heard of iron turning into demons?"

The men replied as if with one voice:

"We're not lying, Political Instructor. We were smashing up some iron woks when a pair of iron kids, covered with rust, came rushing out of the shadows, snatched one of the woks, and ran off with it. They simply vanished."

"Where did they run off to?" the gimpy man asked.

"The scrap iron heap," the men answered.

"You fucking rumormongers!" the gimpy man said. "How could there be kids in this desolate spot?"

"That's why we were scared."

The gimpy man drew his pistol and fired three shots into the scrap iron heap—*clang clang clang*. Golden sparks flew from the scrap iron.

Iron Child said:

"Woody, let's take his gun away from him and eat it, what do you say?"

I said:

"What if we can't get it away from him?"

Iron Child said:

"Wait here. I'll go get it."

Iron Child climbed lightly down off the scrap heap and crawled on his belly through the weeds. The people out in the light couldn't see him, but I could. When I saw him crawl up behind the gimpy man, I picked up a piece of iron plate and banged it against the wok.

"Hear that?" the men shouted. "The iron demons are over there!"

Just as the gimpy man raised his pistol to fire, Iron Child jumped up and snatched it out of his hand.

The men shouted:

"An iron demon!"

The gimpy man fell down on his backside.

"Help!" he screamed. "Catch that spy—"

Pistol in hand, Iron Child crawled up next to me.

"Well?" he said.

I told him how great he was, which made him very happy. He bit off the barrel and handed it to me.

"Eat," he said.

I took a bite. It tasted like gunpowder. I spit it out and complained:

"It tastes terrible. It's no good."

He bit off a chunk above the handle to taste it.

"You're right," he said, "it's no good. I'm going to toss it back to him."

He flung the pistol down at the feet of the gimpy man.

I flung the partially eaten barrel at the same spot.

The gimpy man picked up the two pieces of his pistol, gaped at them, and started to howl. He tossed the things away and hobbled off as fast he could go. From where we sat on the scrap heap we had a big laugh over the funny way he ran.

Late that night a narrow beam of light pierced the darkness off to the southwest, accompanied by a loud chugging noise. Another train was coming.

We watched as it steamed up to the end of the tracks, where it plowed into another train already there. The cars of the train accordioned into one another, noisily dumping the iron they were hauling onto the side of the tracks.

There would be no more trains after that. I asked if there were any parts of the train that were tasty. He said the wheels were the best. So we started eating one of them, but stopped when we were halfway through it.

We also went down to the smelting ovens to find some newly smelted iron, but none of it tasted as good as the rusty iron we were used to.

We slept on the scrap iron heap during the day, then made life difficult for the smelters at night, sending them scurrying off in fear.

One night, we went out to frighten the men who were smashing woks. Spotting a rusty red wok in the flames of one of the ovens, we ran over. But we no sooner got our hands on it than we heard a loud *whoosh* as a rope net dropped over us.

We attacked the net with our teeth, but no matter how hard we tried, we couldn't bite through the rope.

"We caught them," they cried out ecstatically. "We caught them!"

Soon afterward, they scraped our rusty bodies with sandpaper. It hurt, it hurt like hell!

1993

Zhu Tianwen (1956–)

FIN DE SIÈCLE SPLENDOR

Translated by Eva Hung

This is Taipei's unique city skyline. Mia often stands on her ninth-floor terrace, observing the skies. And when she is in the right mood, she lights some sandalwood in her flat.

The roofs are covered with illegal structures built with corrugated iron; the thousands of structures extend like an ocean of trees to where the sun sets and where the sun rises. We need lightweight building material, Duan, Mia's lover, had once said. Duan used lightweight perforated tin plate to solve the problem of sun glare from skylights and French windows in some villas. On Mia's sun terrace there is also one such awning, where all sorts of dried flowers are hanging upside down.

Mia is a fervent believer in the sense of smell; her life is dependent on memories evoked by different smells. The fragrance of the sandalwood brings her back to the spring fashion show of 1989, when she was drowned in chiffon, georgette, crepe, sari tied, wound, wrapped, and hanging in the sweeping Indian trend. In such a perfect collection the Sikh turban was of course a must. To complement this collection the decor was of the style that dominated Viennese architecture and paintings at the end of the last century. Kamali, with his heavy use of beads and sequins, was the leading figure.

Mia is also dependent on memories evoked by color. For instance, she has always been looking for a particular shade of purple. She cannot remember when or where she has seen it, but she is absolutely certain that if she were to come across it again it would not get away; of course everything loaded onto that shade of purple would reappear, too. However, compared with smell, color is much slower. Smell, being shapeless and intangible, is sharp and accurate.

The structures of corrugated iron bear witness to the fact that Taiwan is fighting for space with earth itself. Of course we can also see in this our predecessors' solution to the problem of heat and leaking related to flat roofs: they invented this semi-outdoor space. Our predecessors' accumulated life experience has given us a building style that copes well with Taiwan's climate: lightweight. It is different from the West and again different from Japan; light in form, in space, and in visuality, it provides a breathing space for the crowded, sunbaked cities of Taiwan. According to I. M. Pei, style emerges from problem solving. If Pei had not had a group of technicians to help him solve the problems, the glass on his pyramid at the Louvre would not have had that glittering transparency, said Duan.

These words of Duan's were mixed with the scent of peppermint in herb tea. They were chatting under the awning, and she went in and out to make tea.

The fresh taste of peppermint herb tea recalls for her the pale seaside colors of the 1990 summer show. Those were not the colorful prints of the Caribbean, but of the North Pole shores. Several icebergs from Greenland floating in the misty North Pole seas; every breath was ice-cold. All was snow-white, with hints of green or traces of emerald. The details were a continuation of the 1989 autumn/winter trend—lace was given new life with mesh patterns or braided with motifs of fish fins and shells.

When Mia and Duan are not talking, they watch the metamorphosis of the city skyline in the sunsetlike impressionist painters. Just as Monet, that great master who captured time on canvas recorded, with clocklike precision, the shimmering lights on the river at Giverny on a single day, they too are entranced by the subtle changes in their surroundings caused by the shifting hours. Prawn-red, salmon-red, linen-yellow, and reed-yellow; the sky turns from peach to emerald. Before the curtain falls it suddenly lights a huge fire on the horizon, torching the metropolis. They indulge themselves aesthetically, so much so that either their energy is exhausted in the process or their spirit shattered by the overwhelming spectacle, and very often they do not even do what lovers are supposed to do.

This is what Mia wants; this is the lifestyle she has chosen. In the beginning this was not what she wanted, but finally it became her only choice.

Her girlfriends—Ann, Joey, Wanyu, Baby, Christine, and Ge; at twenty-five she is the oldest. Ann with her beautiful suntan is always trying to make herself a shade tanner, so that she will really stand out in psychedelic red, green, and yellow. Ann does not need men; Ann says she has her vibrator. And so Ann has chosen as her lover a forty-two-year-old married man with a successful career. Married, so that he would not bother her. Ann is busy as a beautician, and even when she has time, she only sees him if she feels like it. As for the young bachelors, deficient in both money and patience, Ann has absolutely no interest in them.

Because of her profession Ann exudes a cold smell of scrub creams. Actually it's a cold fragrance reduced to a very low temperature and pressed into a thin blade—that's Ann.

In Japanese there is a shade of gray called "romantic gray." A fifty-year-old man with a full head of soft black hair, white at the temples, arousing in a young girl the dream of romance—the gray of life, of experience. Mia had come out of childhood very early. Nevertheless, she was attracted to Duan by his "romantic gray," and by his smell—it was the smell of sunlight unique to Duan.

In those days, Mia had seen clothes hung out to dry on bamboo poles stuck between a willow tree and a wall. Those were the days before fabric softeners. After a whole day in the sun, the clothes became hard and rough. When she put them on, the distinct difference between cloth and flesh reminded her of the existence of her clean body. Mother folded the family's clothes up for easy storage; women's clothes had to be put under the men's, just as she insisted that men's clothes had to be hung in front of the women's. Mia fought openly against this taboo; her young mind wanted to see whether this would bring a natural disaster. After the willow tree had been cut down and the land repossessed by the government for public housing, her elder sisters got married and her mother grew old. All this became gentle memory, with the smell of clothes washed in White Orchid powdered detergent and baked in the July sun.

The smell of a husband. Mixed with the smell of aftershave and cigarettes, that's Duan. A husband provides security. Although Mia can support herself and does not have to take any money from Duan, when Duan takes her out of the city for a pleasure trip, he gives her a wad of notes with which she pays their expenses throughout the journey; there is always some left, which Duan tells her to keep. Mia is happy with the way he spends money, treating her like his wife, not his lover.

How the times have changed! Even Comme des Garçons has made a clean break with the asexual look that made her name and has joined the camp of sheer femininity. Layers of thin gauze and an irregular cut emphasize a gentle softness. The wind of change had come much earlier, in early 1987, when the fallen angel Gallianno returned to purity. A collection of pre-Chanel suits for the Nineteenth-Century New Woman, and for the evening low-cut, tight-fitting dresses with crinoline, and the colonial white beloved by royal families, all came onto the stage.

Ge has discarded her three-piece suits with heavy shoulder pads. The career women's stiff outfit is just like a housewife's apron; wearing it constantly equals giving up your rights as a woman. Ge dons the body-hugging fifties style: narrow-waisted, three-quarter sleeves. In the flash of a second it dawned on her: Why not? She fully intends to take advantage of the fact that she is a woman, and the more feminine a woman is the more she can get out of men. Ge has learned to camouflage her vicious designs with a low profile, and since then success has come with much less effort on her part.

The hang of the fabric has taken over from clear-cut lines; silk is in, linen out. Washable silk and sand-washed silk have brought the fabric to the modern age. Rayon is made from wood paste; it has the feel of cotton but is more absorbent and hangs better. Besides, rayon chiffon is just a third the price of silk chiffon. On Christmas Eve that year, during a cold front, Mia and Wanyu had a photo session modeling spring fashions for a magazine. It was a collection of cutwork rayon creating the image of the flying goddesses of the Duanhuang cave paintings. Mia agrees with Wanyu: earning money and supporting themselves is a matter of pride; spending the money of a man they love is happiness. These are different things altogether.

In damp, drizzling weather rayon turns moldy easily. Mia worried over the jars and bunches of dried flowers and dried reeds in her house, and Duan bought her a dehumidifier. Wind and rain darkened everything. Mia looked at the city skyline where black moss seemed to have grown. To counter the damp, she either drank hot ginger tea or put lots of powdered cassia into her cappuccino.

The smell of cassia and ginger was dissipated in the wind. The sun came out to shine on a purple ocean of Rococo and Baroque in the streets. That was the result of the film *Amadeus*. Mia looks back to the long summer and long autumn of 1985, when classical music cassette tapes topped the pop charts.

After the Irises broke a world record at auction, yellow, purple, and green became the main colors. Van Gogh led the way to Monet, and the brilliant blues, reds, and purples reflected in the waters of the twenty-four Giverny paintings came to life again in the form of clothes. Tahitian flowers and orange shades were also a hit; that was Gauguin. There was a retrospective exhibition of Gauguin in Paris with over 300 paintings; Duan and his younger son Weiwei happened to pass through there on their way back from the World Cup held in West Germany, and he gave her the painting "Jacob Wrestling with the Angels."

Because Gauguin was from Europe, he hesitated over the use of colors and spent a long time trying to decide. In fact it was simple: all he had to do was follow his will and paint the canvas with patches of red and blue. In the streams time flowed like glittering gold, so enchanting. Why hesitate? Why not pour the joyful gold onto the canvas? Plagued by his European habits, he dared not. It was the shyness of a regressive race, said Gauguin of his Tahitian period. Duan told her the story as though it were about an old friend.

Duan and Mia belong to two separate circles; the sections that overlap seem to occupy a very small amount of their time, but the quality is high. It is the time when they discard all worldly concerns, and one day is as good as a thousand years in crystallizing the essence of their relationship—it is like frankincense, a kind of resin originating from eastern Africa or Arabia, an expensive perfume.

Frankincense brings Mia back to 1986, when she was eighteen. She and her boyfriends made love with Nature. That was the year when Taiwan took a giant step forward and caught up with Europe, the center of high fashion. Mia's group signed up for a Madonna look-alike competition, which started her on her modeling career. She became keenly aware of her figure and gave up loose, long tops, favoring short and tight-fitting ones instead. The trend of sporting underwear as outer clothing started by Madonna had swept over Europe, and Mia, too, had several of these lovely things—in satin, see-through silk, linen, and Lycra. She wore them with suede miniskirts in the daytime; at night she changed into a sequined skirt and went dancing at KISS.

Like the expensive frankincense she acted as a cohesive force binding her boyfriends together. She was always the one to call for a gathering, and everyone came. Yang Ge, Ah Xun and his wife, Ou, "Ant," Kai, and the Yuan brothers. Sometimes she would call for a gathering at midnight while dancing wildly away; sometimes they were the last table to go after Yeru Restaurant was closed in the wee hours—they had paid their bills and as soon as everyone was there they were on their way. Kai had a car, so did Ou, and they drove to Mt. Yangming. First they bought all the food they needed at the 7-Eleven at the crossroads, then they headed for the mountain.

In the bamboo groves midway up the mountain they lay down side by side. A bottle of Chinese liquor was passed around and drained, and the lighted marijuana joint was an eerie red glowworm, which they inhaled in turn. After they had inhaled they relaxed and lay down, waiting. When their eyelids slowly closed from exhaustion, they no longer heard any heavy breathing; all sound had been vacuumed away and their surroundings expanded infinitely. In silent space the wind in the bamboos was like a bellows emitting, from the remotest distance, a mist that congealed into sand that swept together as waves. Dry, powdery, and cool, it approached from far, far away to cover them, and then—swoosh—it completely receded. In the naked, cool vacuum, the sky was suddenly filled with birdsong. Frankincense floated in the air; birdsong fell like rain to cover them. We're making love with Nature, Mia sighed sadly.

She definitely did not want it to end just like that. She was in love with Kai; he had caught her eye before June that year. That June, the magazine *Men's Non-no* brought out its first issue, and the young women of Taipei and Tokyo simultaneously found their Prince Charming—Abe Hiroshi. Since then she had collected twenty-one issues of *Men's Non-no*, all with Abe Hiroshi on the cover. Kai has the same manly eyebrows as Abe Hiroshi, the same guileless face sweating from exercise, the same clear, deep-set eyes born for romance. The only thing Kai lacked was a *Men's Non-no* and an agency to turn him into a star, Mia thought indignantly.

And so Mia and Kai developed a sense of comradeship; they were the best partners for magazine fashion features. Kai donned the heavy rebelliousness of London boys; a man-made leather jacket flung across one shoulder, she wore a high-waisted mini pencil skirt with a zip splitting her belly, and on either side of the zip two rows of eyelets going right down to the hem and tied together with two chains shoelace fashion right up to her ribs. It evoked the sound of motorbikes; the universe was on fire. Kai was so handsome that he loved only himself, and he treated Mia as his beloved brother Narcissus.

Mia was in love with Yang Ge, too. After the birdsong had stopped, they had rested for a while before the dampness of the heavy dew awoke them. They scrambled up and headed for the cars. Yang Ge held her hand as they wove through dead bamboo trees and sharp bamboo shoots, his warm, fleshy hand letting her know his intention. Mia did not want to make up her mind about anyone yet, despite her fondness for Yang Ge dressed in his perennial Levi jeans and khaki cotton shirt with its tail hanging out, and for the way he stuck his hands in his pockets, looking so bored that you expected him to vegetate. She was so infatuated with this air of nonchalance created by his old blue jeans and faded khaki that she would have impulsively married him. But Mia never answered the inquiring look in Yang Ge's eyes, never gave him any hint or any chance. They all got into the cars and drove up to the observatory.

The vapor and the clouds hung heavily in the air, like a river. The headlights courageously broke through the waters and worked uphill to the peak. A long wait. Ou took out a slip of paper the size of a fingernail and gave her half of it. She put it on the tip of her tongue where it slowly dissolved, and as it did she became so excited that she shook with uncontrollable laughter; even when the laughter turned to tears, she still could not control herself. Ou took an army coat from the trunk and wrapped her up tightly from head to legs, and then thrust her under the arms of the Yuan brothers so that she could stand steadily. She loved it when Ou pulled the doors of the car wide open and turned the music to its loudest: in the mist and vapor Billy Jean started dancing to the tune of Michael Jackson's "moon walk."

At last, look! What they had been waiting for is here. In the valley in front of them a mirage rose up. The water vapor was a mirror, reflecting in the darkness before dawn some part of the Taipei basin, a somber castle, quite clearly outlined.

Mia's eyes filled with tears. She vowed to the people sleeping soundly in that castle that she would have nothing to do with love. Love was too wishy-washy, too degrading—like Ah Xun and his wife, forever engaged in a mean-spirited tug-of-war. She did not even have time enough to feast her eyes on the world's many splendors; she decided that she'd create a brilliant future for herself whatever it might take. Material girl—why not? She'd worship things and she'd worship money. Youth and beauty were on her side; she worshiped her own beautiful body.

As they came down from the mountain they decided to have a bath at the hot springs. The headlights surged through the mist and falling petals, and soon it was dawn. Since they hadn't slept at all they could not stand the sunlight. Everyone put on sunglasses—the old-fashioned Franklin variety—and called themselves vampires. The vampires lay sleeping on the rocks after they had had their bath. Sulfuric vapor rolled upstream from the bottom of the valley, and the sun on their sunglasses looked like a metal biscuit. Mia pulled the reel out of the cassette tape and held it up against the wind; like a snake it whooshed out toward the sun. She held on to the reel, and the brown string became a trail taking her through the muddy yellow sky directly toward the metal biscuit. She felt that she was standing there alone, surveying all living things and the whole universe in a grand sweep of history.

From 1986 to the autumn of 1987, Mia and her boyfriends were absorbed in this kind of game, unaware of the brevity of youth. In October Pierre Cardin came to Taiwan to see how his products were doing. In the same month Abe Hiroshi wore a rose-red cashmere V-neck pullover and a turquoise necktie on the cover of *Men's Non-no;* he also starred in a film with Minamino Yoko playing a fashionable girl. For some reason all this seemed to have deprived Mia of something.

Overnight, she discovered that she was no longer in love with Abe Hiroshi. Her collection of his photos ended in February 1988—that was number 21. In a vast expanse of snowy plain Abe Hiroshi wore a white hat and a white outfit, hugging a white Japanese dog and smiling to show his healthy white teeth; so childish! It was an unfair relationship: one-way traffic. Even if she were to die for the love of Abe Hiroshi, he belonged to the public; he would not even give her the hint of a smile. She was surprised that she had been tricked. Abe Hiroshi was a narcissistic fellow who was so full of himself he had no room for anyone else. A narcissistic woman may be lovable; a narcissistic man is just unmanly.

Mia did not want any more games. Without her acting as convener, her boyfriends all dissipated like the mist to fight for their own careers. Quite a few of them became homosexuals, maintaining sisterly relations with Mia.

That was the watershed. The fear of AIDS led to a new fashion trend: feminine clothes for women and a gentleman's look for men; unisex clothes all disappeared. Mia, too, said good-bye to her hermaphroditic dress code, which had passed through phases of David Bowie, Boy George, and Prince.

Years ago, when she changed out of her school uniform, she wore an army-style outfit: khaki or beige, with badges. She walked around the West Gate district and the schoolgirls all swooned over her. At fifteen she had led the way in the beggary trend, wearing clothes with huge holes on the shoulders; her mother was no longer in a position to raise any objections. Although she did not know it at the time, she had always been ahead of her peers in following the trend set by Yohji Yamamoto and Issey Miyake. In 1984 Kou Kanuko created a new, country look with floral prints and layers of frills, but Mia just told her friend Baby to wear it. She herself donned a metal-gray riding jacket, bark-colored culottes, and a pair of cloth shoes on her unstockinged feet. The two of them went to McDonald's for the Valentine menu. Baby wore a gold-plated bracelet with Mia's name on it. They had a pair of moon and star earrings: one was on Baby's right ear, the other on Mia's left. That was the year when Baskin-Robbins came on the market—thirty-one different ice cream flavors in the form of colorful, solid little balls. Baby was an Aries, and on her birthday the two of them treated each other there. It was an icy cold place, but bright and airy like a greenhouse. Together they mapped out their dream-plan of opening a shop someday.

In the twenty-some years of her life, she owes Baby too much. When for the first time she wore a denim bra instead of a blouse under her jacket and a tight-fitting cotton skirt to show off her figure to her playmates. Baby was extremely displeased. In her overreaction she gave Mia a harsh scolding. Baby became more and more like Mia's mother, and the more she objected the more Mia rebelled. She was the one who led her playmates into the Madonna whirlwind. During the competition finals the mass media turned up in strength to photograph them. Afterward she saw a local MTV splicing shots of their group of Madonna look-alikes in with the publicity van of Wu Shuzhen, who was running for the Legislative Yuan on behalf of her husband, and with the yellow ribbons of Corazon Aquino's people-power revolution. In her red-hot circle there was a new group of people—her boyfriends. Baby drifted further and further away. When she occasionally looked back, she would see that from beyond where the ripples ended, Baby's lonely eyes were looking at her accusingly.

At twenty she was tired of fooling around. She became cruel like a queen bee; her only purpose was to make money. Romeo Gigli took the scene by storm; this Italian designer had great admiration for ancient Pompeii and used fabrics tightly wrapped around the body to conjure up a sense of nostalgia. Mia parted her permed hair in the middle and coiled it up at the back, showing her forehead, her shoulders, and her swanlike neck, like a nymph resurrected. She met Duan.

Baby asked her out for a long talk. She had heard that Mia was living with a married man and actually thought that she'd persuade her to leave him. Mia haughtily refused, treating Baby's sincere words as part of her selfish designs. Baby tried so hard to convince her, as if her life depended on it, but Mia just watched her as if she were some badly conceived character in a play who did not realize that her designs had been totally exposed. The air was filled with Baby's usual scent—Amour, Amour. What a moldy smell! It constantly reminded her of that dull, sweaty afternoon: outside the window the red blossoms of the cotton tree squatted on the branches like so many plastic bowls. Baby cried from sorrow; she left in a suppressed rage.

Soon after that she received a wedding invitation from Baby. The envelope was in her handwriting, but the card inside contained nothing but printed words. It was a most ordinary card with a cheap fragrance, an unknown name for the bridegroom, and common, a-penny-a-dozen names for the groom's parents. This was Baby's way of getting back at her. She was infuriated that anyone should sink so low, and refused to go to Baby's wedding.

They lost touch. Two years later, during the French Revolution bicentenary, she heard that Baby was staying at the maternity ward of the Veterans' Hospital. She went to Evergreen to get a box of "Revolution Candies" wrapped in the blue, white, and red of the tricolor flag, thinking that she would go and visit Baby, but then so many things happened and she never got around to it. Then she learned that Baby was divorced and had opened a flower shop; her daughter was just three.

The winter collection of '92 was still dominated by the Empire style: a flowing cape or poncho with tight trousers or thick stockings, or even a pair of knee-length boots. It is true that long boots are not suited to the Taiwan climate, but they can effectively correct the proportion of legs and torso and create a long, cranelike look. In the last three years "Revolution Candies" had ceased production and had therefore become antiquated editions, rare items.

It turned out that the flower shop also sold food. Baby was sitting on a black rattan stool; from the back her mature figure looked as stable as a huge piece of rock. She tiptoed in and covered Baby's eyes from the back, saying: This is rape. She had learned that years ago from some blue film and had done it to give Baby a fright; this had then become an intimate greeting between them. Baby struggled free and half hid herself behind the flower display unit, glad to see her and yet angry at the same time, saying that she should not have turned up unannounced and deprived her of a chance to make herself more presentable. At that moment Mia wished she had looked older, less glamorous, instead of looking as though she had cheated the years. Should she wait in the shop while Baby went home to do her hair and change, or should she come back some other day? Baby preferred to meet on another day. So instead of catching up, she blew a good-bye kiss at Baby, just as in the old days.

Now the flower shop has become the rendezvous for her girlfriends. It is in an expensive area, and all the shops along the lane are small boutiques. Mia can smell the shops; sometimes the smell is evoked by colors, sometimes by the decor and the use of space. Every time she walks down the lane it is like traveling through the world's ancient civilizations. The flower shop with its complex mixture of scents is like a Byzantine tapestry; the aroma of coffee wafts in the air, recalling the ancient age of handicrafts. Joey is responsible for the food served in the flower shop: homemade fruit cakes, cheese pie, oatmeal biscuits, and flower-petal puddings.

Mia had just made a decent sum and given it to Baby to invest in the shop. Baby only holds a third of the shares. The other two shareholders are her ex-husband and a potter friend, and they both declined Mia's offer because they did not know her. Though rejected, Mia felt happy. It seems that on the scales of her friendship with Baby, her side has gained back a little weight because of this.

By this spring the nostalgic trend had turned licentious. It was the licentiousness of the Orient, that of wearing embroidered jackets inside out. Mia had done that for years, so Paris and Milan were trailing behind her. She stood in front of the Christian Lacroix boutique opposite the flower shop: the display window shows a single Moroccan-style coat, its surface of rough ivory raw silk blends with the ivory-colored deco under the window lighting and turns into an expanse of desert sand—a color of sparsity. A corner of the flap is turned up to reveal the brocade lining of Damascus red with embossed patterns of purple and gold thread, which is also visible through the wide cuffs. Mia can smell the mysterious scent of musk.

Indian musk-yellow. Purple silk flings open to show a musk-yellow lining; dark blue cloth blows apart to reveal a scarlet blouse; emerald-colored satin is lined with a delicate pink. India boasts of a sense of mystery in its licentiousness, while China's is well controlled. As for Japan, everything is formalized; its is a stylized licentiousness.

Nostalgic splendor is just one side of the coin; the other is a repentant return to nature. In autumn and winter 1989 Christian Lacroix introduced his leopard hats, Moschino his leopard trimmings, and Ferre his coats of a combination of animal-fur patterns—tiger, zebra, giraffe, and snake. All this is reminiscent of the old British Empire two centuries ago; the stuffed animals they imported from their colonies swept through Europe like a wildfire.

These are fake furs, of course. Ecological protection is the byword now, so wearing the real thing will not just arouse public rage but is also unfashionable. Don't be a slave to fashion, be yourself; those are Moschino's famous words. That's a lie; Mia can almost see Moschino winking at her in his Milan workshop as he confesses.

Fake furs were the rage in the winter 1990 collections. They could pass for the real thing, and they did not violate the animal protection laws. But what's the point of imitating the real thing? It's just foolish. Much better for the fake items to be self-mocking, which is in line with the modern spirit, somewhat witty and quite cute. Even the three-tier string of man-made pearls Mrs. Bush wore, priced at $150, set a trend for pearl necklaces in the winter of '89. Mia's '91 anti-fur show, with its variations of fake furs dyed red and green, was cute and trendy.

Ecological consciousness began in the spring of '90: pale beach colors or soft desert tones. The subdued shades and cheerful grays are different from the neutral colors of the eighties: eggshell white, pearly gray, oyster black, ivory yellow, and seashell green. Natural is beautiful. Mia discarded her eyeliner with its clear definitions; eye shadows are no longer the focal point. One should emphasize personal characteristics: the natural shape of the face, high or low cheekbones untouched by blusher. Almond-colored or *café au lait;* the contrast of light and shadow disappears, and so do boundaries. All is clear and transparent. Foundations of the nineties are pear-colored, as opposed to the olive complexions of the eighties.

Mia has become quieter because of Duan; she is leaving behind her exaggerated queen bee stage. Slightly hanging breasts and a smooth curve at the waist are in line with the logic of environmental protection and are said to have real sex appeal.

Having become single again, Baby goes to her ex-husband's place to pick up her daughter every Saturday. The flower shop closes at 8:30 P.M., and a bronze candelabra with dark blue candles lights the place after closing; they sometimes have a night snack there with Mia. Sometimes they go to Mia's place to try her new concoctions of herb tea, and Duan is left sitting in a corner listening to music; there is no way he can break into their endless small talk. Baby's daughter is a Scorpio with a sting in her tail, a difficult child. When the three of them go out, Baby drives, and Mia either holds Baby's daughter on her lap or leaves her to play in the backseat with Baby keeping an eye on her in the mirror. Mia can foresee that this is the way of life Baby will choose for herself.

Christine proclaims herself a pajamas woman, one of a stubborn group who refuses to wear any kind of uniform such as the three-piece suits sported by successful career women. They cannot stand the pressure of a collar against their neck, and so they choose to wear the French-styled "Most Beloved"—long T-shirt-like dresses, or cotton-knit V neck, boat neck, and collarless blouses with lace trimmings.

Wanyu, on the other hand, is the pathetic woman of action. She is expert in fulfilling other people's dreams—her husband's, her lover's, her son's. She is constantly busy either because of a spirit of self-sacrifice or because she does not want others to be disappointed. They have great sympathy for Wanyu, this woman of action. She should leave some space for herself: have a good cry, go on a shopping spree, or just sit and stare; all this will do her good.

As for Mia, she's probably a witch. Her flat is filled with dried flowers and herbs, like a pharmacy. Duan often has the illusion that he is with a medieval monk. Her bathroom is planted with Chinese orchids, African violets, potted pineapples, Peacock coconuts, and all sorts of nameless ferns. On top of all that there are scores of different bath salts, bath oils, soaps and shower gels in glaring, poisonous colors; the room is like a magician's distillery. All this started with

Mia's sudden wish to retain forever the delicate pink color and fragrance of roses imported from Holland. Before the flowers were in full bloom, she took them out of the vase, tied them in a bunch and hung them upside down in the draft from the window; she looked helplessly at the pink color as it faded day by day. She had just moved out of her elder sister's home after they had a big row, escaping her sister's career-woman, two-income-family lifestyle and her mother's supervision. Like a goldfish suddenly set free, she was faced with the immediate pressure of fending for herself in the open sea, and she grabbed every opportunity to make money. On some occasions when she was hard up and could not afford to join in the fun, she put on a stern face of having seen through it all and said with an air of superiority that she had to go home to bed. And it is true that she had tried her best to build a warm nest. It was during this period that she developed a hard-times friendship for the bunch of dried roses.

She was witness to how the flowers lost their fragrance and how their colors darkened, until they turned into a different kind of matter altogether. That's fate; but there is still a chance, and her curiosity was aroused. She hung up a bunch of serissa for observation, and that was followed by cornflower, high-mallow, field mint. So the experiments started.

The first time Duan visited her place, there were no table and no chairs, no coffee and no tea, just five stunning cushions lying anyhow on the floor, several bunches of ferns and flowers hanging at the windows, a clay bowl filled with dried yellow rose petals, and a rattan tray containing the dried peel of lemons, oranges, and mandarins. They sat on the floor drinking 100 percent pure orange juice; Duan had a clean yogurt cup in one hand, which he used as an ashtray, and smoked and talked away. He asked her whether she had bought her cushions in three different places; Mia, surprised, replied in the positive. The two wax-dyed ones were bought as a pair, the two made of imported floral prints with tulip patterns were another pair, and the one with an embroidered elephant and little round mirrors was Indian; these two mugs were rather postmodern. Mia was glad that these household items, which she had selected with such care, had all been appreciated, and thought that maybe she should buy a good ashtray for the house. The next day she was also glad that her flat had no clear boundaries between the eating, sitting, and sleeping areas, for this made it natural for them to become lovers.

Duan had left the Soviet-made Red Star watch in her place. The next day he came back for it, only to forget again. He came again, and forgot again. For three whole days this man and this woman left their work unattended to; Mia almost missed an Armani autumn show at Sincere. They couldn't go on like that; they both said that it was right to break up. The Red Star watch was given to her as a memento; he had to resume working, too.

Mia's flat was filled with the sour-sweet taste of passion fruit; like golden-red larva it seeped through the cracks in the windows and the door and poured down from the balcony and the lift, until it filled the whole building. Just in case Duan might still phone her or come round, she sat there the whole day and finished a whole basketful of passion fruit. She dug at them with a spoon and fed herself mouthful after mouthful; by nightfall both the spoon and her teeth seemed to have been corroded by the sour juice. Only then did she stop. She buried her head in the pillow and fell sound asleep. The cleaned-out passion fruit shells were put on the balcony to dry—they're also called *arhat* fruit—the black shells look like rows and rows of *arhat* heads. Mia was extremely depressed. The next morning she took a large bag and left, having decided to ignore the notice for shooting a commercial that day even if it meant losing her job. She just would not sit around like a fool waiting for him to call; she would not turn into a worm gnawing at bitter fruit.

She bought a ticket and boarded a train, not caring where it was heading. When the train emerged from the railway station she was shocked by the ugliness of the streets along the railway: she had never seen Taipei from this angle. The train headed south, which was as strange to her as a foreign land; even the trees seemed unfamiliar. Her ticket was for Taichung, where she got out. She walked around till evening and then boarded a public bus. The bus was full, and she seemed an extraterrestrial among the passengers. The bus was bound for somewhere called Taiping Village. It was growing dark, and the wind carried a strange fragrance—a desolate foreign country. She got off, ran across the road, and found the stop for the return bus. She couldn't wait to get back to that city of indulgence and vice—her home. If she were to live alone away from the city, she would wither like an uprooted plant. She woke up in the express bus to see the huge display windows of Mitsukoshi Department Store and the clothes and accessories stands that lined the sheltered walkways. The bus turned into Chungshan North Road, where lights in the shops shone and glimmered through the camphor and maple trees. The bus went up the flyover, and she saw wall-size neon signs all around her. Like a fish back in water, Mia came alive again.

She went to see the Yuan brothers. Their father had a piano bar in a basement. By law they were not allowed to have a shop sign, so they hired a small truck, which they decorated as a shop sign and had it parked in front of the building every evening. A display board covered by neon lights; set against the background of silver and red lights are these golden words: Riddle in a Riddle. The elder of the Yuan brothers had the rotten luck to be called up for military service. When the younger Yuan saw Mia, he was elated, and proceeded to teach her a new way to have fun: he detached the electric wires connecting the neon lights to the building, switched them to the truck batteries and told her to get on. Decked out like a Christmas tree, their truck sped over the overpasses, took a detour to the East Gate and the Chiang Kai-shek Memorial before they turned back. Mia proudly showed Yuan her Red Star watch, took it off, and said he could wear it for a few days.

This is her homeland: a city-confederacy of Taipei, Milan, Paris, London, Tokyo, and New York. She lives here, steeped in its customs, well versed in its artistry, polished by its culture, ready to emerge as one of its preeminent representatives.

Faced with the trend toward femininity, Issey Miyake gave up his three-dimensional cutting and shifted his attention to the use of fabrics. Patterns are pressed onto silk and chiffon to create a stiff feel quite different from their original texture, giving a hard edge to soft femininity. Patterns of fish fins, seashells, palm leaves were pressed onto the fabric, creating a three-dimensional effect that replaced three-dimensional cutting. This effect is enhanced with crisscross stitching. The result is futuristic, typical of the wilful genius of Miyake.

When the Seoul Olympics was broadcast all over the world, Yves St. Laurent and Gianni Versace both frankly admitted that they had adopted for their day and evening wear the flamboyant Gravache's tight lace trousers and his cutting that allowed free athletic movements.

As a child Mia had seen Prince Charles and Princess Diana's wedding of the century. Everyone copied the Princess's hairstyle. It is sad that the fairy tale did not end there, that the story continued on, sad indeed.

Duan came to see Mia again. Mia ran up to him joyfully and clung to his neck; he was caught unawares and almost fell down laughing. She left her door wide open, hanging on to him in the elevator lobby like a baby monkey hanging on to its mother. Duan, a little overcome by her passionate behavior, had to quickly carry her into her flat. Mia loved to try lifting Duan, to see if she could get him one inch off the ground. Or else she would stand on his feet and they'd walk round the flat in an embrace. All this made Duan feel clumsy and embarrassed. They're lovers, but she's young enough to be his daughter.

When she gets married, Duan said, she could use his gold credit card to sign for everything, sign till he's broke. Mia listened quietly, saying nothing. The next day Duan made haste to correct himself: he should not have talked about her getting married; if he had kindled this idea in her, when the disaster came it would be his Achilles' heel, for Mia was his. Soon after that he corrected himself again: he's older than her and would probably die first. What would she do with the rest of her life? Better take things as they come. Mia listened to all this with the loving look of a mother, as if Duan were just a chattering child.

Just as summer wear is always replaced by autumn wear, passion cools and is replaced by a warmth like that of jade worn close to the body. Mia started with dried flowers, and continued her observations and experiments with herbal teas, bathroom accessories, pressed flowers, and handmade paper. All this was just to develop her reliance on the sense of smell, and to try desperately to retain the brilliant colors of the flowers.

Duan's company arranged for a tour to the national forest reserve for employees and their spouses, and while he was there he gathered a whole bag of pinecones, pine needles, and fir needles for her. She mixed two teaspoonfuls of cinnamon with half a spoonful of cloves, cassia, two drops of scented oil, some pine oil, and some lemon oil, and brushed a layer of the pine oil on the pinecone. Eucalyptus leaves, cork leaves, rose petals, and geranium leaves were tossed into this mixture, and dried red chilies, berries, and poinsettia were added. All this was put into a pine-colored, oval-shaped bowl: a festive bowl of fragrance reminiscent of Christmas for Duan's workshop.

Recently we have started using stones for corner areas. In the past it was all pebbles, but now we hope to use 30 percent Yilan stones. This way we can give a new look to old techniques and also overcome the shortage of tile workers. It was a development for DINKs and "single aristocrats." Duan had wanted to reserve one for Mia, but Mia prefers her own top-floor flat with the corrugated-iron structure on the roof. Here she can put her flowers, leaves, and peel out to dry, and she can stand against the railings to observe the sky, wearing a plain blue blouse that the wind blows open to reveal a bright red lining.

She is two years older than Duan's eldest. She has met the second son, Weiwei, who takes after his mother. The castle of clouds on the city skyline tells her that she will live to see Weiwei have a successful career, get married, and have children, but that Duan might not. And so she must learn to become independent of emotions, and she has to start now.

She put shredded wastepaper into water to dissolve the gluey substance and then transferred the paper into a food processor. The paste, mixed with water, was blended and poured onto mesh and pressed dry. Then the mesh was placed between white cotton cloth sandwiched between newspaper and wood boards, pressed repeatedly with a rolling pin, and then put under some heavy object for several hours. The sieve was then removed, and the cotton cloth with its contents was pressed evenly with a warm iron. A week ago Mia produced her first sheet of paper, paper she could write on. To prevent ink from penetrating it, she brushed a layer of alum on the sheet. This week she added some purplish rose petals into the food processor, and produced her second sheet of paper.

The castle of clouds is being blown apart, revealing a lake of Egyptian blue. Rosemary.

When she is old and her beauty has faded, Mia will be able to support herself with her handicrafts. The abyssal blue of the lake tells her that the world men have built with theories and systems will collapse, and she with her memory of smells and colors will survive and rebuild the world from here.

1990

Zhang Dachun (1957–)

LUCKY WORRIES ABOUT HIS COUNTRY

Translated by Chu Chiyu

On the evening he finished his "Proclamation to Soldiers, Civilians and Countrymen," Lucky Zhu opened his bottle of red-label rice wine with his teeth. He suddenly perked up. As usual, his wife was sending out snores from the bedroom behind the cane-fiberboard partition, and from time to time the bamboo bed creaked under her weight. His youngest son, Treasure, was playing his plastic harmonica by the window. Treasure's three brothers, Bliss, Fortune, and Longevity, were sitting around the other three sides of the dining table, dozing, studying English, and praising Baby Jesus respectively. None of these noises disturbed Lucky Zhu. He slurped up the spilled wine from the table and felt that the world was wonderful indeed, as if everything was about to start anew. "Yes, that's good!" He whisked off the peanut shells scattered on the table, picked up his proclamation and held it in both hands, then took a look at his four sons around him. "Yes, that's good!" he repeated emphatically and nodded in approval.

This feeling of satisfaction lasted three hours, during which he untiringly explained to his sons word by word the content, intention and spirit of his proclamation. At 11:40 the bed squeaked as Orchid got up. "A load of tripe!" she said to her husband. Over her arm hung a plastic apron, a rubber hose, and a bag of detergent. She cuffed Bliss on the back of the head, said, "Move it!" and mother and son stumbled out the door. Only then did Lucky hear the sound of Treasure's harmonica intermingled with the English sentences "He is a teacher. I am a student." and "We desire a better country, that is, a heavenly one—What does 'desire' mean, Fortune?" Fortune scowled and surlily snatched the simplified Bible from his brother, took a look at the phonetic symbols beside the characters, and said idly, "You don't even understand this? Didn't your teacher explain it?" "This isn't a schoolbook. Peter Wang lent it to me," Longevity answered, pursing his lips. Fortune tossed the Bible back to him and said, "When others have something you don't have, then you 'desire.' That's 'desire,' understand?" By this time. Lucky Zhu had fallen sound asleep. In his dreams, he whitewashed his walls again.

> Even if he had been able to discern the meaning of those words and what they referred to, he could hardly have had any better understanding of Eisenhower.

In fact, he had never whitewashed his walls. If his two ramshackle rooms were plastered with white paint and chalk, all the neighbors in the compound would laugh at him: "That old fool Lucky must have won the Patriotism Lottery." Their laughter would penetrate the whole area of illegal buildings, and spread across Jen-ai Road. Lucky Zhu would rather compete with every Zhang, Li, and Wang in the neighborhood in poverty, illness, and misfortune than show the slightest hint of being an upstart: whitewashing was out.

And so the Zhus' walls always looked the same as the neighbors', plastered with newspapers. Perhaps the only difference was that between the *Central Daily News* and the *National Evening Post*. Some years ago, although Lucky could hardly read, he did a favor to his neighbor Wang Changyuan, a paperboy from the front compound, by subscribing to the *Central Daily*. Wang Changyuan knew how to make a living. While delivering newspapers, he managed to get a part-time advertising job. Every Sunday he could get several dozen poster pull-outs from newspapers that ran pictorial sections. When he could not sell them all, he would go door-to-door and give them away to his neighbors. From then on, the walls of all the families in the compound turned colorful. There were pinups of Gina Lollobrigida, Audrey Hepburn, and later the Taiwan film stars Ling Bo and Le Di from the movie *Liang Shanbo and Zhu Yingtai*. At that time Lucky Zhu and Wang Changyuan were both still single. A dozen or so film stars in the two six-tatami rooms didn't look too crowded. Lucky's bamboo bed was bought at that time. It could put up with him whipping his horse on it all night in front of the film star pinups without making a squeak.

Except for those idle hours spent playing with himself, he was nothing if not respectful to the newspapers on the walls. When he did not have to carry night soil to the fields, he spent the better part of his time indoors, learning the characters on the walls. In fact his friendship with Yang Renlong developed out of his learning to read. Yang Renlong had studied at a teacher's training school back in his hometown on the Mainland. He could read out half an editorial in one breath without blinking an eye. He used to read like that, while Lucky listened and tried to make out the characters. Then Lucky would treat Yang

Renlong to a meal and wine or a couple of pots of strong tea, and that would be it. After Yang Renlong was poisoned by his adopted son, there was a long period during which Lucky felt he was not making much progress, as if he'd been thrown out of school and wouldn't be able to add to his knowledge anymore. This feeling, on top of pining for Yang Renlong, often caused him to invent some memories. He told Bliss, Fortune, Treasure, and Longevity, "No kidding! Your uncle Yang was a great scholar—you were born too late to have seen him. Just think how many books he had in him! Whole sheets of newspapers—news reports, editorials, he could write them all in a flash! No kidding!" Sometimes he would point to a smudgy old newspaper and say, "This was written by your uncle Yang."

The four brothers really were born on the late side—if Lucky hadn't overpowered Orchid and shaved off half her hair by force, tied her to the bamboo bed with shoelaces, and forced himself on her a few times, perhaps Bliss would never have been born at all.

He had been put up to this by Wang Changyuan—but two years later, after Wang Changyuan got married and followed his wife's example and became a Christian, he never admitted having taught Lucky Zhu this wicked trick. But once she got pregnant. Orchid stopped her frequent running back to her parents' home in Hualian. Lucky had tried to persuade Yang Renlong at that time, "Sell your gold and form a neighborhood savings association and get yourself a woman with whatever sum you can pool." "No, that's wrong!" Yang Renlong pointed at a pictorial above Lucky's bed. "They've got it all wrong!" He was talking about four pictures: starting from the left, the American president Eisenhower; Miss China, Liu Xiuman; a soldier wearing a homemade gas mask; and a five-hundred-kilo pig raised by Taiwan Sugar in order to promote the pig-raising industry. "Look!" Yang Renlong rapped his forefinger on the wall: "It clearly should be 'from the left' but it says 'from the right.' Now look, Eisenhower becomes a big pig, the one with the mask is Miss China, Liu Xiuman's wearing a gas mask, and the big pig becomes the president of the United States. Hah, what a joke!" Lucky handed him a cigarette and said, "I'm serious, Renlong. Even if you are a great scholar, you can't go on flogging your dick forever, can you?" Yang Renlong was still smiling, clenching the cigarette between his teeth. "Screwed up, it's all screwed up!"

After that, every time Lucky was humping Orchid, he would casually glance at the four pictures. He never felt there was anything wrong with Eisenhower and the big pig. Of course, he was clear on one thing: fixing his eyes on the soldier with the gas mask would make him hold out longer in his battle with Orchid than looking at Liu Xiuman.

> Peter Wang said softly, "Your family worships idols." Fortune asked, "What is an idol?" "An idol is an idol," said Peter Wang. Lucky Zhu jumped up from his knees and shouted, "What motherfucking idol!"—He guessed that "idol" must be something very bad.

Not until Yang Renlong died in the doorway, his eyes as wide as burst chestnuts, did Lucky learn that this holy sage also had his horny moments. His corpse was naked proof of this. Two rows of regular white teeth pointed skyward, bursting through dark purple lips which seemed about to swallow a big breast. A magazine full of big-breasted naked women had fallen at his side. Those hands, which had so often pointed at the newspapers on the wall, were clasped tightly around his big erect member. Wang Changyuan whispered in Lucky's ear, "Most likely he applied aphrodisiac lotion, and it swelled up till he died." Lucky pushed through the surrounding neighbors, took off his T-shirt, and then with great effort and difficulty pried open the dead man's fingers. By the time he finally managed to cover up the dead man's shame, Lucky was sweating all over. But the erection looked even more obtrusive under the white T-shirt. Someone even sniggered. A policeman arrived amid the laughter and immediately asked Lucky, "What are you doing? Who are you?" Then he turned to the people crowding round: "What the fuck are you gawking at? Get out, all of you!" Just then, another figure came rushing up and cried out, to everyone's amazement, "Dad, Dad, what's this all about? What happened?" The policeman did not so much as turn his head, but continued questioning Lucky Zhu: "Who are you?" "We're all neighbors." "When did you last see him?" "Yesterday, no . . . the day before." "What did he say?" Lucky scratched his bald head. Suddenly his sweating body started to feel chilly in the breeze; he shivered and said, "He said . . . he said that President Chiang Kai-shek's proclamation was really well written, that no one else could write so well."

On National Day the following year Wang Changyuan dragged Lucky Zhu to watch the military parade on television at a grocery store in the next street. As a 155-mm howitzer passed by the reviewing stand, Wang Changyuan nudged Lucky in the small of the back and said softly, "It's a nice store, isn't it?" Lucky responded with a perfunctory "Mm." "It'll soon be mine," Wang Changyuan said; one of his legs started to shake and his whole body seemed to be on a spring. After a long while, he finally said unhurriedly, "That widow's taken a fancy to me." Only then did Lucky Zhu shift his gaze from the ceremonial officer, across the knots of heads of the people who had come to watch television, to a point behind the counter. He saw on the wall a cross and a picture of Jesus, under which stood the kind-looking widow. "We can take care of each other, and if we put our two businesses together, we can get rich faster. Besides, it's more reliable to have your own son, after all, don't you think?" "What do you mean?" When Lucky asked this, instead of answering the question, Wang Changyuan fixed his eyes on the screen and then clicked his tongue a few times before he said, "Don't you read the papers? Yang Renlong's adopted son adopted a father again, a retired major. And he kicked the bucket, too, without rhyme or reason. Now it's come out. It was that adopted son who poisoned both his adoptive fathers." "For money?" Lucky asked very quietly, as if he feared he might offend somebody. "Why else? They stint themselves all their lives, but in the end their pensions, insurance, and gold all go to their adopted son."

The house left by Yang Renlong, which had stood empty for a year, was now taken over by Wang Changyuan. At the end of that year, the widow became a bride and moved into the compound and started, quite legitimately, addressing the neighbors as "brothers" and "sisters" and spreading the gospel. In the beginning, Lucky did not mind being called "Brother Zhu." Even when Orchid called him brother, the most he would do was say with a cheeky smile, "Call me 'sweet brother' if you want to call me brother at all." At the one-month celebration of Peter Wang's birth, the neighbors got together again in Yang Renlong's former house. When someone brought up the subject of Yang's tragic death, the former widow suddenly said, "That was because he was tempted by Satan! His heart was full of the devil, and he did not accept the words of knowledge. He was bound to end like that. My fellow brothers and sisters . . . " It was then that Lucky began to feel the woman was coming on too strong. He snorted disdainfully and began seriously missing Yang Renlong. He followed the others' example and reached into the cradle to pinch Peter Wang's tender, rosy cheeks, and said, "Better-looking than our Bliss and Fortune. What a strong boy! Has he been given a name?" "Peter, Peter Wang." Wang Changyuan said, "Peter is a good man in the Bible." "What?" Lucky was not really listening; he remembered instead that the cradle was sitting right on the spot where Yang Renlong's dead body had been. From that night Yang Renlong began appearing in his dreams. "I'm not really dead," he'd say.

He also told Lucky many other things. For example, he said that he would rather flog his horse while looking at the pictures on the wall every day than marry a badgering "imitation foreign devil" like Wang Changyuan had. He also said: The country is in danger and the communists will sooner or later attack Taiwan. If we want to fight our way back to the Mainland, we must raise more strong boys. It was just a shame that he couldn't face the expense of taking a wife early on; otherwise, he might have produced a few sons who could have fought. On the one hand, they could have served the country and on the other, he could have enjoyed offerings and memorial ceremonies on festival days. "If it's not too much trouble, on festive occasions, prepare me a cup of tea so we can have a good chat. What do you say?" Yang Renlong said with a sad smile. "It won't cost you much." "That's not the point. If I do that, I'll become your son," said Lucky, staring at Yang Renlong's bulging crotch: "Wow, you really aren't dead."

When Lucky Zhu woke up, Yang Renlong was dead, of course. He turned over, and the bamboo bed creaked, waking up Orchid. "Yang Renlong came back. He said the communists are going to attack Taiwan. He also wants me to make offerings to him." He sat up and fished a cigarette butt out from under the bed, lit it, and heaved a sigh. "Now we're in big trouble." Orchid rubbed her eyes and turned over to go back to sleep. It was a long while before she said, "Then make some offerings. In the end, we're the ones who'll eat them anyway." "I was talking about the communists. You're a nitwit." Lucky cast a sidelong glance at the soldier with the gas mask on the wall. In the dimness he could not see him very clearly. At first glance one actually could mistake him for Miss China. Orchid murmured, "I want to go to Hualian." Usually only after they had made love would Lucky allow her to go back to her parents' home. But this time nothing came out of his mouth except a smoke ring.

When Orchid came back from Hualian, she looked like an entirely different person: a thick wool cream-colored sweater, shiny black leggings, white leatherette shoes with two-inch heels, and permed hair as tousled as a chicken's nest. Her looks created a sensation in the compound. Everyone said she looked good—well, probably one had to squint at her out of the corner of one's eye to find her looks appealing. She also thrust two hundred New Taiwan dollars into Lucky's hand, saying that she had given some folk dance performances back home and the money was the tips from Japanese tourists. "There's nothing wrong with making money," said Orchid to two of her sons as she laid some boxes of local products on the dining table. "We're going to make a lot of money, so we can buy things, and we can also glorify God." "We can also do what?" Lucky tore open a box of yam cakes, took out one for himself, then grabbed another handful and put them on the small altar standing against the wall for the three generations of his ancestors and Yang Renlong. Orchid fluffed up her curly hair and said, "Glorify God!" That evening Orchid donated twenty New Taiwan dollars to God. Mrs. Wang said, "The Lord will answer your prayers." And she also told the brothers and sisters present that if she got enough donations, she would purchase some proper furniture and decorate the room as a "formal" house church.

Orchid's prayers were finally answered several years later: Lucky Zhu no longer had to carry night soil to the fields but became a street sweeper, a job that would arouse more sympathy or at least less revulsion. He had to assemble at the end of Jen-ai Road every midnight and then sweep the streets and sidewalks—instead of working on top of her.

By this time Bliss had already started primary school, and sometimes he could help his father read a character or two that he did not know. Peter Wang, though a few years younger than Fortune, knew a lot more than the dumb Bliss. He often came to Lucky Zhu's place after dinner to tell them how the earth was completely covered in water during the Flood. The whole family listened wide-eyed, almost drooling. Compared with him, Bliss and Fortune knew nothing. This put Peter Wang in a superior position and enabled him to come to the Zhus and tell them whatever came to his mind. Only once did he offend Lucky—on one Chinese New Year's Eve, Peter Wang pointed to the memorial tablets for Zhu's ancestors and Yang Renlong's photo on the small altar and whispered in Fortune's ear: "Your family worships idols."

After kicking Peter Wang out. Lucky rather regretted his action. Early the next morning, he hurried to the front compound; as it happened to be New Year's Day, he bowed several times to Wang Changyuan and greeted him, "Happy New Year!" Wang Changyuan put his forefinger to his lips, glanced indoors, and answered solemnly, "My family will not be celebrating the New

Year anymore." "Is that your wife's idea?" Wang Changyuan cocked his head and thought a little while before answering, "Not really. Just think, you come to see me and I go to see you, people tiring themselves out running about, what's the good of that?"

> That was really a bad year. First, the big storm out of the blue on the first of April, then the president died, the house was flooded, and Bliss was beaten up. Lucky grew into the habit of saying: "I'm down on my bloody luck!" The signboard of the house church did in fact fall down and break one of Lucky's teeth. For whatever reason he became a worried man from that time on.

The compound was hit by a flood several months after the death of the president. But, with the exception of Wang Changyuan's family, everyone, including Yang Renlong, said, "When the president is gone, everything goes wrong."

"I'm not really dead," Yang Renlong said in Lucky's dream the day before the flood. "I see very clearly that from now on, life will be harder and harder." "What did you say? I don't understand," Lucky asked. "Things are going rather well at the moment. In fact, I'm planning to buy a television set by the end of the year. Just a small one, black and white, but I don't mind. I would never have dared to dream about it before . . . " "Now that you have a family and have settled down, you don't want to go back, do you?" Yang Renlong cut in, wagging his finger. "Now that the old president has passed away, who is going to take us home? Tell me, who?" The question baffled Lucky, who almost woke up. Yang Renlong suddenly changed the subject and said, "The old president believed in Jesus, too. I didn't know that before." "So does my wife. She followed the example of Wang Changyuan's family and became a Christian, and a very devout one." "Well, it's good to be religious." "Of course it's good! I just didn't realize that before. Even the old president was a Christian, so of course it must be good."

But Lucky Zhu was not very pious after all. When the flood came, the following day, the first thing he did was rescue his idols: the memorial tablets of his ancestors, Yang Renlong's photo, and the portrait of the president, and stack them on his head. The rain kept darting in like glistening arrows through the roof and the cracks in the door and the wall board; the water soon rose to Orchid's hips. The bamboo bed floated slowly out from the bedroom toward the door. Fortunately, Bliss and Treasure managed to rescue it by a combination of dragging and pulling. They managed to put the dining table on top of the bed and the four of them squatted on the four corners of the table with their heads touching the main beam. They could only look on as the movie posters of Audrey Hepburn, Bruce Lee, and Zhen Zhen floated out, one after another, followed by the small altar. Orchid was holding a piggy bank in her arms, wailing out loud. Lucky forced a smile and said, "It's lucky we didn't buy the television." Orchid wept more resoundingly and sobbed as she counted the articles of furniture floating out: "Chair, electric pot, flask . . . my clothes, high heels . . . " Bliss chimed in excitedly, pointing to the far corner, "My school bag!" "Now you're in trouble," said Treasure, holding his own school bag tightly in his arms.

It was not solely because he lost his school bag in the typhoon that Bliss failed to make it to the next grade; and it was not only because he rubbed his snot on his classmate's clothes that he was beaten up at school. His teacher came and gave Lucky Zhu some tactful advice: it would be best for Bliss to receive special education; it wouldn't do to let him keep failing every year. But Lucky said: "Bliss has been doing great; he eats like a wolf and sleeps like a log, and gets stronger and stronger. Besides, he was already teaching me how to read last year. If you say my son is dull-witted, as his father, surely that makes me even more dull-witted? Teacher, let me tell you: it's a very bad year. I'm down on my bloody luck! As soon as this year is over, my luck will turn. Just wait and see, if you don't believe me. Next year, Bliss will come first in his class."

In trying to convince the teacher, Lucky Zhu convinced himself. As soon as he had seen the teacher off, he ran to Wang Changyuan's place. "He's gone to the shop. What can I do for you. Brother Zhu?" Mrs. Wang was all smiles. "How is Sister Gu?" Lucky answered perfunctorily and came straight to the point. "I've come to ask for a few old newspapers, the ones with the president's proclamations." "Pro-cla-ma-tions?" "Yes, proclamations." He twisted his lips, a little smugly. "Yang Renlong said that all the President's proclamations were good writing; nothing was better written. I want to have some of them and stick them on the wall in order to learn how to read them. Once I've learned the knack, I'll pass it on to my son. And when he learns he'll be number one in his class. And then we won't have to worry about repeating any grades." "But . . . but there have been no such proclamations for a long time." Mrs. Wang frowned and casually leafed through some recent papers. Then she smiled and said, "Are you interested in the Bible, Brother Zhu? It's good to read the Bible. You can find the words of knowledge. The old President often read the Bible." Lucky scratched his bald head. "Well . . . I still want the proclamations. I tell you what, when Changyuan comes back, ask him to find some for me. Whenever there's a portrait of the President there's a proclamation alongside it. Huh, if it hadn't been for the flood, there'd still be some on my wall. Damn it, how can we do without the proclamations! No wonder Yang Renlong says that life will become harder and harder."

Lucky Zhu left the Wangs', murmuring to himself as if under a spell. He thought to himself: That's it! Why hadn't I noticed it before? When the President died, the proclamations dried up. What are we to do? It was just at that time that the signboard with the words FOR GOD SO LOVED THE WORLD hanging outside the house church was blown down by the first autumn wind of the year. It fell right on the back of Lucky's head, neck, and shoulder, with one corner of it hitting his jaw, and clunk—out came a big tooth.

> Staring down Orchid's low-cut neckline at her big breasts, the man said, "You're really fortunate, Ma'am, you are so young and your son is already a man." When he said this, his eyes looked as if they were on fire—so did Lucky Zhu's.

One winter evening two years later, after Lucky Zhu had finished sweeping the streets and had stood in the cold waiting for the roll call, he quickly ran home. At the gate of the compound, he ran into a young man flirting with Orchid. The man wore a leather jacket with the collar turned up. He was sitting on a chair by the roadside, swinging his leg, while Orchid and Bliss were washing his white limousine. The man suddenly leaned over and stared down Orchid's low-cut neckline at her big breasts and said, "You're really fortunate, Ma'am, you are so young and your son is already a man." As he said this, his eyes looked as if they were on fire. Orchid said with a smile, "What fortune is there for us poor folks?" Lucky noted the smug expression on her face, her raised eyebrows and coquettish eyes. He wished he could run up and kick her flat on her face. But the back of his head, his neck and shoulder suddenly began to hurt terribly again. The pain gradually spread; so did his resentment toward the man with the car, toward Bliss, and toward himself.

At 6:30 that morning, when Orchid came into the room, pummeling on her back and hips to relieve the stiffness, Lucky suddenly grabbed her in the darkness, threw her on the bed, and said through clenched teeth, "I haven't screwed you for a long time, and you think I can't do it, don't you?" Orchid had never seen her husband like this before, and she thought that she might have entered the wrong house. She screamed; immediately a hand was pressed tightly against her mouth and she heard him say under his breath, "Screaming again! Don't think I won't dare shave your head again!" Orchid felt relieved: it was Lucky all right. He had it all planned out; he'd give his wife a taste of pleasure or pain. So he let out a grunt and pressed down. The bamboo bed started creaking again for the first time in years. This is how Longevity was conceived.

But this did not mean that he relaxed his watch on Orchid. On the contrary, he developed a habit of finding fault with her for talking to customers. It wasn't only his wife; he found fault with the customers, too. "Strange, how come it's only men who come to you to get their car washed?" he often said. "Are the women all dead?" Orchid supposed that her husband had become so irritable because the signboard that fell from the sky had damaged his brain. She secretly told one of her sisters at the gathering and asked her not to tell anyone else about it. The very next day Mrs. Wang told Orchid that she thought Brother Zhu's change of temperament had come about because he had been led astray by the devil. "We should love him, pray hard for him, and drive Satan out of his heart."

In fact, only Yang Renlong in Lucky's dreams knew what the problem was. "I suppose," Yang Renlong said, "you think too much. You know why you think too much?" Lucky did not reply; he just leafed through a magazine full of naked women. "You think too much because you read too much. Tell me, am I right?" Lucky still refused to answer. Yang Renlong heaved a sigh and said, "It's all my fault for teaching you to read newspapers. Who would have expected that you'd end up like this?" "Why do you say it's your fault?" Lucky finally spoke: "What's written in the papers is true. If I couldn't read, I'd be kept in the dark, and just be a dumb-cluck. Now after I've made all this effort, I'm able to understand something. I can see the light. So why do you say it's your fault?" He glanced at the newspapers on the wall: what vivid and lively headlines! He had learned to read some: "Revenge Killing," "Mistresses," "Lovers," "Affairs," "Perverts," "Love, Lust, Adultery," "Old Husband and Young Wife Tragedy" . . . As he scanned them they aroused shame and resentment in his heart.

He remembered that the talks he and his fellow street sweepers had when waiting for the roll call were on these very subjects. "It's not that I deliberately chose these to read. I just learned about them naturally from chatting with others, and so I knew about these things," he murmured, trying to explain. "It's not like the old days when you were here to tell me to read something like proclamations." Then he thought of another excuse and cried out, "Where can I find proclamations now? It's not like when you were alive." "Who says I'm not alive?" Yang Renlong rebuked him sternly. "Now the country is in danger, society is in such a state of chaos, and the communists will attack sooner or later. Look at yourself. Do you look like a man ready for battle?" "My head hurts, and my neck hurts, too . . . " "Shit!" Yang Renlong yelled. "You've got no bloody guts! Now you have a family and you've settled down. You don't want to go back, do you? Don't just try to look after your own woman! Think of more important matters: when the country is in danger, then society becomes chaotic; when society is chaotic, your wife will be in trouble; when your wife is in trouble, all other wives will be in trouble. It all follows. If you want to solve your own problems, you should solve the country's problems first. When the country is at peace, everybody can have a good life. Do you understand?" "Now I do."

> "I am in Grade Five. My elder brother is in Grade Two. My younger brother is too small to go to school. My youngest brother is even smaller, and he doesn't go to school, either. My dad learns to read with me. My mom washes cars. She believes in Jesus Christ. I sometimes believe and sometimes don't. It all depends."

The first time Lucky Zhu had the idea of writing articles himself was when Treasure was in his fifth year at primary school.

One evening, after drinking a couple of glasses of red-label rice wine, he happened to take up his son's composition book. As usual, he cursed a few times. Then he said, "If you can ever write an article half as good as your uncle Yang's, even if I'm dead I'll laugh myself back to life." "Uncle Yang died naked." Treasure could not hold back his laughter. Seeing this, five-year-old Longevity also laughed. Bliss grimaced and said, "What are you laughing about?" Lucky immediately chided, "What are you laughing about? Who told you this rubbish?" Treasure pouted without saying anything. Lucky poured himself another glass of wine and held it up to make a silent toast to his ancestors' memorial tablets, Yang Renlong's photo, and the portrait of the President on the shelf before he said, "No kidding! Your uncle Yang was a great scholar. You were born too late to have seen him. Just think how many books he had in him! Whole sheets of newspapers—news reports, editorials, he could write them all in a flash! No kidding!" "Can you write, then?" Treasure asked, cocking his head. Lucky Zhu was struck dumb, then he said, "You hold your tongue!"

In this way he bluffed his way through. After dinner, he took a nap leaning across the table, as he usually did until midnight, when he would go to the assembly point and sweep the streets. During this time, Yang Renlong burst in. His cheeks glowing red, he stumbled toward Lucky and slapped him hard across the side of his face where he had lost his tooth. Then he broke into a smile. "Treasure asked a good question: 'Can you write, then?' Tell me, can you write?" "I . . . can't." "Now that's the truth: those who should write won't write, and those who shouldn't write are writing. It's no wonder the papers carry that garbage about thieves and whores. Nobody understands the difficult situation the country is in. Let me tell you, Lucky, we're the ones who have read good articles. We must share those good points with others in order to make them understand. If you don't write, who will?" "What about you?" Lucky looked up and asked, "Why don't you write?" "How can I write when I'm dead?"

Dear Mr. Zhu,

Thank you for submitting your article to our newspaper. Whether in terms of topic, language or style, your article is superb. However, as our next few issues are already filled up, it would be impossible for us to publish your article in the near future. To avoid further delay, we are returning it to you. We are sorry that we are unable to publish it, and we hope you will understand. Thank you for your interest in our newspaper and we are looking forward to receiving further contributions from you.

Sincerely yours

"You've been in the newspaper business for so long, surely you can do me this small favor?" Lucky asked Wang Changyuan. The latter was busy photocopying some notes for a uniformed university student. Wang Changyuan said halfheartedly, "Can you hang on a minute? How many so far?" "Thirty-seven," the student answered. And Lucky said at the same time, "I've only written one." "Did you count it right? Otherwise I'll lose money," Wang Changyuan said as he wiped the sweat from his brow. "I wasn't talking to you." "Then you just listen." Lucky held up his proclamation in both hands, scanned it quickly, and continued, "Maybe it's not right to put this stuff of mine as high up on the front page as the old President's proclamations used to be. They can put it at the bottom. Besides . . . I'm not so good-looking, so I think we can forget about the photo. But the article has been revised again and again with Yang Renlong's advice. We're all mates. If you won't put in a word for me, you're letting our side down." "How many pages is it now?" "Forty-nine." "Are you sure? I'll lose money if you're off by even one page." "What do you say, Changyuan?"

Altogether Wang Changyuan copied eighty-six sheets of notes for the student. He counted them several times to make sure there was not one page too many before he was able to relax and collect himself. He then snatched the article from Lucky and asked, "How many copies do you want?" " . . . I didn't come to copy it. I thought . . . I'd like to ask you a favor, to help me to publish this in the newspaper. Don't you know all the press people?" The student leaned over, took a look at the article, and saw two pages of twenty-line manuscript paper; the heading was in big sprawling characters: "Proclamation to Soldiers, Civilians, and Countrymen." "What did you write something like this for?" Wang Changyuan narrowed his eyes and made a quick calculation. Then he said, "It will cost you at least ten thousand to get it printed in the paper. You stupid old fool, have you won the Patriotism Lottery or what?" "This costs money? I've spent so many hard days writing it, and now you tell me it costs money?" "Ads cost money. What do you expect?" I think you misunderstood him, sir." The student covered his mouth with his fist, held back his laugh and said gently, "I think this old gentleman wants to contribute this article. Do you want to have this—er—article published?" "That's right!" Lucky looked as if he had suddenly found someone who really understood him and said hastily, "As I said a moment ago, I only want to have this proclamation published. As for the photo, I don't think it's necessary." "In that case, I'm afraid, there's no use coming to him," the student said. "You should send it directly to the newspaper." "Why is it no use coming to me? I can make several dozen copies for you, so you can mail one to every newspaper." With that, Wang Changyuan was ready to start copying. The student stopped him hurriedly. "That won't do. You can't contribute an article to more than one publisher. That's the rule." "All right, we're all law-abiding folk. We'll follow the rules," Lucky said. "It's only in the case of a man like the old president, with articles like his, that every newspaper would want to publish them. Let's just start with one newspaper."

So, following the rules, Lucky Zhu mailed his proclamation to soldiers, civilians, and countrymen to one newspaper after another. Some newspapers returned it by mail after several days, some weren't heard from for six months or a year. But whatever the case, he always remembered Yang Renlong's instructions: If those who should write do not write, then those who should not write will write. He had written it out over thirty times, and every time he'd revised it several times from beginning to end and had copied it several times before he was satisfied. In the meantime, the signboard above the house church had been replaced by fluorescent lights in an acrylic frame, bright and secure. No chance of its being blown off by rain or wind again. Orchid had become excessively fat; few customers wanted to chat with her. Treasure had started secondary school. One day he said to his father, "I wonder if Uncle Yang was gay." Longevity asked Treasure how to pronounce and spell the word "John" and declared that he was "John the Apostle" and would follow Jesus' teachings to love God and love the people like "Brother Peter." It seemed that Bliss was the only one in the family who had not changed much. He washed different cars every day, and now and then scolded his three younger brothers. Only on rare occasions would he get confused and scold his father.

Lucky Zhu could stand his simpleton son's scolding, but there were times when he could not bear the consolation and encouragement from the newspaper editors. Every time his proclamation was rejected or vanished without a trace, he became more distressed. He knew that he wrote faster and faster, better and better each time, but the world outside the compound was getting crazier all the time, wasn't it? Every day he read from the newspapers he pasted on the wall about crimes with which he was getting more and more familiar, and about new crimes—crimes always went in sequence, one leading to another, and still another . . . Lucky Zhu began to dream that he was whitewashing his walls over and over again.

> Soldiers civilians and countrymen: These are no ordinary times. We are all no ordinary citizens. We must know that our country is in danger. The evil communist bandits may attack Taiwan any moment. The situation is very perilous. But we soldiers civilians and countrymen all have a lot of money. And we get more and more money every day. We can buy a lot of things. We can even afford to buy television sets. But we must know that being rich and glorifying God is not enough. Because people will make trouble even when they have money. Go to restaurants. Go to nightclubs. Fool around with women. Adopted son poisons adoptive father for money. What is the world coming to? So I say all soldiers civilians and countrymen must know that it doesn't matter not to have money. We do not bring money into this world when we are born. We do not take money away with us when we die. If we are poor we do not even fear flood. How can we be afraid of communist bandits? Another thing is the newspapers. Newspapers should carry more proclamations and more things that have got backbone. You can't say that without money you can't publish proclamations. Publish more proclamations. Publish less bad things and bad news so people will not learn to do bad things. Soldiers civilians and countrymen: let's work hard together to beat the communist

bandits liberate our compatriots recover the mainland and our sons and grandsons will have a good life. That's good.

Finally Lucky Zhu managed to have his proclamation published, using the money set aside for whitewashing his walls—he printed four thousand copies at Wang Changyuan's photocopy shop, and distributed them from door to door along the streets he swept. This time Orchid helped him a lot—every time she washed a car she gave the driver a copy along with her blessing: "God be with you." In the still of the night, from Lucky Zhu's house there still came the sound of the plastic harmonica, accompanying a boy's soft voice singing: We desire a better country, that is, a heavenly one. We desire a better country, that is, a heavenly one. . . .

1987

Zheng Qingwen (1932–)

REDEEMING A PAINTING

Translated by Jenn-Shann Lin and Lois Stanford

"When the country is chaotic, invoke severe punishment"
—*Qiu Official, Minister of Justice, Zhou Rites*

1

The person coming in the door was a balding, middle-aged man of medium height, about forty years old. He wore a deep brown shirt and purple-gray pants. He asked for me by name.

"That's me."

He told me that his last name was Zhang, first name, Yangxiu. Then, from the folder he was carrying, he took out a two-inch-square photo, a woman's photo, a little yellowed, and a Chinese painting, one foot long by two feet wide.

"Do you still remember this woman?"

I looked at the photo for a moment and shook my head.

"She was my mother, who brought in a painting to sell to you almost twenty-five years ago. This is her painting. It is like the one she sold to you—the size is the same and the theme is similar. Both depict a sparrow."

I examined the painting carefully. It could only be reckoned as a student's exercise, at best. Then I looked at the photo again.

"Oh, now I remember."

"Really?"

Yes, right. It was twenty years ago, not too long after Father had handed over this art gallery, Shangyi tang, Upholding Arts Hall, to me. I remembered that day; about eleven o'clock in the morning, a thin woman in her late thirties came in. She brought a painting for me to look at. At that time, although I had only taken over the gallery a short while before, I already knew a bit about painting because I had grown up in an art dealer's home and had worked in the gallery for more than five years. That painting, like the one before me now, had also depicted a sparrow and a bundle of rice stalks.

In Taiwan, those who specialized in traditional Chinese painting seldom painted sparrows, especially just one sparrow by itself. And also there were very few who painted rice stalks. Consequently, it made an especially strong impression on me. As a matter of fact, the woman did not paint well. The touch of her brush was crude, soft, and without vigor. The coloring was not right, either. I remembered that I had no intention of buying that painting and had pushed it back toward her.

"I know I don't paint well, but consider it to be like lending me two hundred yuan, and I won't come back again."

She glanced at me and looked down right away. Her voice was almost piteously entreating.

It is common for an art gallery to encounter matters of this kind. Sometimes artists who are just beginning bring their immature works into the store, either for financial reasons or because they know nothing about their own ability. The painting she had brought simply had not reached a proper standard.

Just then Father came out of the inside room with a cup of tea in his hand. As a matter of principle, he had never interfered with matters concerning the gallery, since he had handed it over to me. I would go inside to consult him if there was anything special.

"Just buy it, eh?"

Father glanced at the painting and spoke up. I was a bit surprised.

I handed two hundred yuan to the woman. She nodded her head again and again to express her thanks, to me and to Father as well, and then went out with her head down. I saw her eyes were reddened with tears.

"This painting isn't good, actually."

Father picked up the painting to take a look again.

"I know. But as an art dealer, sometimes you can't look just at the merchandise. This woman must have some real difficulties."

Father had been gone for more than ten years now, but I still remembered his words, which had been a great inspiration to me on how to be a man as well as an art dealer. In fact, after that I had had a better understanding of Father.

"As for this painting of yours . . . "

My first sense had been that he had come to sell his painting. I still remembered those words of his mother's: "I won't come again." But when I looked at him once more, I felt that he had not come for the purpose of selling his painting.

"I'm thinking of redeeming that painting of Mother's."

"Oh!" That was not what I had expected.

"My mother said that it would have been impossible to sell that painting. If it wasn't thrown away, it might still be in your gallery. But perhaps it has been too long."

In the lifespan of a painting, twenty years can be considered just a short time. In my gallery, there were works that were several hundred years old. No matter whether a painting was good or not, we would never throw one away. I realized that what he had meant by "throwing away" was different from what I meant. Sometimes, I would sort out a few comparatively immature paintings and sell them wholesale to smaller galleries. However, I had not sold that painting.

I remembered now that when I was straightening out the storage room several months ago, I had spotted it again. Originally, I had thought of selling it, but every time I looked at it, it reminded me of Father and his words. Therefore, I had kept it. The only thing was that I could not immediately put my finger on its exact whereabouts.

"If it was thrown away, my mother still wanted me to return the money to you."

"The painting is still here, but I have to look for it."

I went to the storage room, and looked sheet by sheet through several stacks of paintings that had not yet been mounted. It took me about ten minutes of searching before I finally found it.

"Got it." I took the painting into the gallery.

"Really?"

I passed the painting over for him to see. The theme, the style, and the size of the paper were all similar to the one he had brought with him. Even the signatures were the same, both signed with two characters, Jimei, meaning "suffering plum blossom." I compared the two paintings again for a moment. It seemed that the one in my store might even be slightly superior. His mother must have selected it carefully.

"I would like to redeem it."

"You don't need to do that. Just take it back home."

I seemed to see Father standing over there with a cup of tea in his hand.

"I can't do that."

He said that it was his mother's wish that even if the painting could not be found, the two hundred yuan plus interest should be returned to me.

I knew that some painters, having achieved fame, bought back at a high price immature works that had gotten into circulation early, just for the sake of maintaining a good reputation.

He said that his mother had thought it was a painting with absolutely no value at all, and that she was no painter either. However, she felt she had a debt to repay.

He said that he had gone to the bank to inquire. Somebody there had told him that those two hundred yuan, if calculated along with interest, had increased by thirty times; therefore, he wanted to give me ten thousand yuan. Since I had found the painting, he wanted me to quote him a price so that he could buy it back. If I did not want to give him a quote, he would pay me back ten thousand according to his calculation.

Otherwise, he said, he could exchange it for another of his mother's paintings—one that she had done later on.

This was precisely what interested me most. Although I felt that she had not painted well, that her foundation was not solid, that her aesthetic was not correct, people might, indeed, change. I had seen quite a few painters whose ability came from nonstop hard work. As an art dealer, I would not let any opportunity slip by.

"May I have a look at her paintings?"

2

At the appointed time, I went to his home, which was situated near a college town just at the foot of the mountains. It was a four-story house. On the main floor, there was a beef noodle bistro. When I arrived, it was already past two o'clock in the afternoon. Several customers, who looked like students from the university, were still eating noodles.

He said that this building, including the beef noodle bistro, belonged to him.

He took me to the fourth floor. The room in the back, the farthest away from the street, had been his mother's studio. It was a room of some three hundred and fifty square feet. Right beside the window there was a table, on which a painter's paraphernalia was laid out.

Looking from the window, one could see the line of low mountains.

On the wall, I saw an enlarged photograph of two people. One was his mother and the other, presumably, his father. Both were very young, almost like children. Judging from their clothing, the photo must have been taken in Mainland China. They were side by side, wearing small but natural smiles. In particular, his mother, who had full cheeks in this picture, looked quite different from the thin woman whom I had seen in my gallery.

In addition, on a corner of the painting table there was a smaller photo of his mother, showing the woman I had met, but taken much later. Wrinkles were visible on her face and her hair had turned gray. In this photo, I could see a pair of bright, piercing eyes, which I had not noticed before.

"In our home, no portraits of great men or their like are hanging on the walls."

He blurted out these words suddenly, which surprised me somewhat.

Also hanging on the wall was a mounted painting, a bit yellowed, depicting plum blossoms. You could tell from just a glance that it was very different from his mother's paintings. On it, an annotation read: "To commemorate Aimei's twenty-fifth birthday."

"Who painted it?"

"My father."

"Oh!"

I examined that painting carefully. It was a traditional Chinese painting. But its conceptualization and brushwork were nevertheless of a high order. The arrangement of parallel tree branches, the placement of flowers, the shades of color, and the utilization of blank space, all gave a feeling of freedom from conventionality. I looked at the name written on it—it was someone completely unknown to the local art circle.

"Is this your mother's name?"

The name his mother had written on her own painting was Jimei, not Aimei, which means "misty plum blossom."

"Yes."

"Did your father paint just this one painting?"

He did not reply. He walked across the studio silently, opened a closet, and took out a pile of paintings. He spread them out and carefully turned them one by one.

At first, I thought they were his father's paintings, but all he had brought out were his mother's.

His mother's paintings were also traditional Chinese paintings, but they were quite unlike the usual ones. Their subjects were different, and so was the manner of their expression. But even more important, it was clear that the artist's state of mind when she made these paintings was far different from that of an ordinary artist.

Traditional Chinese paintings ordinarily either depict landscapes, flowers, and birds, or human figures. Some artists may also paint animals—a tiger, a cat, or a horse.

His mother's paintings depicted mostly active subjects—men or animals. Sometimes she did paint flowers and plants, trees and grass, or a still life, but these things served as foils rather than themes.

Every picture she had painted, no matter whether it was of a human or an animal, was imbued with a sense of gloom and helplessness. The expressions and postures of her subjects were full of pain and misery. No message of the leisure, comfort, calm, or transcendence found in a traditional Chinese painting was to be seen here. The humans she had painted were not only full of pain but sometimes also showed grief or anger. The expressions of characters in traditional Chinese painting usually are lightly sketched, so that they appear as stereotypes—indistinct and incapable of communicating moods of happiness, anger, sadness, or joy. But she had worked in stark contrast to the tradition—she had done her utmost to intensify emotions. The feelings of her characters were very strong. Ordinary painters only wished you to comprehend the meaning of their paintings; she asked you to feel and experience it. This was not like traditional Chinese painting.

Furthermore, the flowers and birds that she painted were also different from those in the usual Chinese painting. She painted sparrows, Formosan bulbuls, Japanese white-eyes, and shrikes. There was a pair of shrikes perched on the tip of a bamboo branch, their mouths wide open and crying toward the sky. Trickles of blood came from the corners of their mouths. When I looked closely, I saw that the birds' feet were caught by bamboo sticks—the "bird trample" snare used to catch the black-headed shrike by people in the south. Although they were flapping their wings furiously, they could not get away. On the painting, a sentence of five Chinese characters read: "Miserable fate of migrating birds."

In another painting, she had depicted a pair of pheasants—Taiwan's native species, the vanishing Mikado pheasant. They were lying limp on the ground, in a puddle of blood.

The flowers and plants that she had painted were also different. In her paintings, no plum blossoms, chrysanthemums, or orchids were found; neither was the peony. The painting she had sold to me and the one her son had brought to my gallery depicted rice stalks. She had also painted sweet potatoes in bloom, with a kind of flower like a morning glory. I had never seen anybody paint sweet potatoes, nor was I aware that sweet potatoes blossomed. I even saw an insect resting on a leaf and nibbling it. The insect had grown a pair of horns and looked more like a dragon.

"Can you let me take another look at that painting of the sparrow?"

He spread out the painting. I looked at the eye of the sparrow, where a teardrop seemed to hang. At first, I thought she had not painted the eye properly but, in fact, the sparrow was weeping.

Word had it that there was once a painter who had finished a painting entitled "Looking to China, the Divine Land in the Distance," depicting a green dragon in tears. He had been arrested and imprisoned for many years.

Her paintings reminded me of Edvard Munch. Perhaps she had not actually seen Edvard Munch's paintings at all, or those by other expressionist painters from the beginning of the twentieth century—Franz Marc, Alfred Kubin, Ludwig Kirschner, Emil Nolde.

But her vision was like theirs. What she had pursued was not the beauty of elegance, leisure, and ease. What she wanted to depict was misery, helplessness, and despair—the deepest feelings and the saddest fate of human beings. I dared not say whether or not she had the capability and talent to do that; neither dared I say whether traditional Chinese painting was suitable for those themes. Nevertheless, her intentions were obvious. She had painted according to her individualistic vision, and this spirit of creation was what traditional Chinese paintings most lacked.

But what motives had driven her to embark on such a route? More significantly, was she thinking of opening a new direction for traditional Chinese painting? Or was she simply expressing her own inner feelings?

From those paintings of hers, I could see the trajectory of her progress. From the painting of the sparrow to the present, that progress was truly amazing. More admirable yet was that she had painted a world of her own. This was precisely what many ambitious artists tried but failed to achieve in their work.

The main question was whether or not, at this time, the conservative circle around traditional Chinese painting would accept her. Her paintings had really deviated very far from convention. She was even beyond the description of "guilty of heterodoxy."

"Your mother's paintings are really very unorthodox."

"When I bought this building, I intended to add a personal hall on the fourth floor, where she could worship Buddha. But she said that she wanted this studio instead. Once it was completed, she hid herself away in here and painted. Not until she died could anyone enter."

"She has passed away already?"

"Yes. How do you find her paintings?"

"They are full of gloom and misery."

"Oh!"

"Are there any special reasons?"

"Ah . . . "

"If it's not appropriate to tell me, you don't need to. I've only come to look at her paintings."

In fact, I did very much want to know. A painter's style is closely related to his life and thought. An understanding of that life and thought is very helpful in appreciating his work. I was aware, however, that many painters did not care to have their private lives exposed.

I looked through his mother's paintings again.

"Are there any more paintings by your father?"

Actually, I was really more interested in his father's paintings. He was an outstanding painter. Furthermore, I sensed from his words and actions that his father had died long before his mother.

He quietly brought out another pile of paintings. It looked as if this pile had only twenty or thirty pieces in it—in quantity, far fewer than his mother's. But in terms of content, I was much better able to appreciate them.

"Your father didn't paint much."

"He . . . he . . . he passed away very young."

He spoke a husky voice. I saw him lower his head, and his eyes reddened. It reminded me of the sparrow his mother had painted.

I looked at the photograph on the wall again. That couple was so young. But because I saw Zhang Yangxiu with such a heavy heart, I felt that it was inappropriate to ask any more questions.

I continued to look at both sets of paintings. As an art dealer, I would definitely pick his father's conventional paintings. The whole of his artistic production very naturally exuded the characteristics of great purity and graceful ease.

This was very praiseworthy. A critic once remarked that in this era of upheaval, it was not easy for this sort of style to emerge. A painter like this must have been endowed by Heaven.

"Are you willing to sell these paintings?"

"Do you think my father's paintings are good?"

"Very good. It's a pity that he didn't paint many more." I was sincere.

I knew that when some art dealers spotted good paintings, they did not speak up, in order that they might buy them cheaply.

"Because he died too early."

"Oh, it really is a great pity. Otherwise, he would be a famous master."

"How about my mother?"

"Her paintings are truly very different from most, so I dare not make a hasty judgment of their value."

"On her deathbed, my mother told me that you were the only person who ever bought one of her paintings. She very quickly realized that her paintings would not sell, and she had no more illusions. She chose to look for heavy manual labor. She once worked as a janitor and then as a maidservant. She led a hard life, but she never forgot painting."

"Did she ever think of selling your father's paintings?"

"That was impossible. She painted just to fulfill a cherished wish, my father's unfulfilled wish."

"Oh!"

"Truly, if you wish, you may pick a piece. This was my mother's idea."

"Your mother was unwilling to sell your father's paintings, but with regard to her own, it seems she didn't care."

"You're saying . . . "

"For example, she didn't forbid you to sell her paintings."

"No. She was unwilling to dispose of my father's paintings because of her respect for him, her feeling for him, and . . . My mother regarded my father's paintings as part of her body and her life. Even when she was in the greatest difficulty, she held fast to that position."

"What would happen if someone offered a very high price?"

"It has nothing to do with price. I honor my mother just as my mother honored my father."

I had been an art dealer for many years and had seen quite a few children who were only too anxious to dispose of their parents' works right away once their parents were dead. Some even sold them like wastepaper, by the catty. I was never quite sure whether they wished to extricate themselves quickly from parental shadows or were just eager to clear out some space. As art dealers, we were, of course, happy on the one hand, but watching the children's behavior, we felt pain on the other.

"Please pick one. Really."

"No."

"Why?"

"Keep them all together."

"Then I'll give you . . . "

"Don't ever mention money again. Although I don't know what has happened to your family, I can sense that it must be an extraordinary story. But let me tell you sincerely that if one day you're willing to sell the paintings, either your father's or your mother's, I would like you to let me know."

I spoke these words and went down the stairs to leave.

3

Three days later, Zhang Yangxiu came to see me in my gallery. At first, I thought that he was going to agree to sell the paintings. But I sensed immediately that this conjecture was not right. Nevertheless, I still expected something to occur.

"I have thought about it for a long time, and have finally decided to tell you about this matter."

He said that his father was a native of Jiangsu Province. During the war against the Japanese, he had responded to the call for "one hundred thousand youth, one hundred thousand soldiers" and left school to join the army. After the war, the Nationalist Army and the Communists once again engaged in civil war. His father had followed the Nationalist Army to Taiwan.

At that time, his father was already married.

When the Nationalist Army withdrew to Taiwan, their morale was quite low. They found many ways to vent their anger.

During that time, the army drivers purposely drove recklessly, speeding about the streets. In particular, the drivers of the so-called ten-wheeler military vehicles often got into trouble, knocking down and killing a number of pedestrians.

I still remembered this sort of thing myself. At that time, I was sixteen or seventeen years old and attending a junior high school and cycled to school every day. Whenever a ten-wheeler came down the street, I fled to the side of the road. Newspapers reported that these vehicles were called "tigers of the city," which made everyone panicky. I too, at that time, utterly detested these soldiers, who did not care about people's lives.

In light of these circumstances, the commander's office issued an order that any soldier was to be executed on the spot, without exception, if he ran over and killed a civilian.

His father had been driving down the street and had hit and killed a pedestrian. His father said that at that moment he had swerved to avoid a dog that had suddenly run across the street.

"Is the man's life more important or the dog's?" The military judge had asked his father.

"When I swerved to miss the dog, I didn't expect to hit the man."

In reality, the trial was just a formality. His father's plea did not reduce the charge; on the contrary, the judge thought that he had failed to admit his fault. But at that time, military laws were like mountains, and even an admission of fault would have been useless. His father was shot to death on the spot where the accident had taken place.

I still remembered that many civilians had regarded this as a good measure to suppress accidents. And in actual fact, the "city tigers," which had barged recklessly about the streets, disappeared almost immediately.

However, I did not expect to learn that his father had died in this way.

"My mother said that my father had greatly respected the commanding officer of that time, and that I had even been named Yangxiu to honor him. They never thought that my father would die at the commanding officer's order."

"Ah!"

"My father liked to paint," said he, and stopped for a moment. "When he was painting, my mother always kept him company. Sometimes, Father taught her one or two bits of brushwork technique. She admired my father very much, and said that he would have become an outstanding painter if times had been normal.

"When my father died, she not only lost the person she could depend on in life, but she also lost the support of his spirit. All of a sudden, we became orphan and widow.

"As soon as my father was executed, Mother moved us out of the military family compound. We completely lost whatever privileges a soldier then enjoyed. Not only that—because of the nature of what had happened, we really couldn't face other people.

"Although there were some people who sympathized with us, they also were helpless and, at most, could give us only a bit of moral support.

"When we left the military family compound, I was only two years old. I knew absolutely nothing of what had happened and did not even retain any real memory of my father's appearance.

"Mother worked first as a janitor and then as a maidservant. In fact, before that, she was a beggar. Because of our status and circumstances, even the heaviest and most menial laboring jobs were not easy to find. Later on, luckily, there was a fellow townsman, a seller of steamed buns, who took us in.

"I still remember that we lived in an illegal shack. When it rained, raindrops dripped in from the roof. We had to keep an umbrella open while we slept.

"Later on, that townsman's wife died. He wanted to marry my mother. My mother did not agree. One night, he came to the back of the shack and tried to take my mother by force. I made a desperate attempt to bite him. He beat me and beat my mother, too. We had to leave that very night.

"That was the period when we suffered the most. I didn't have any opportunity to go to junior high school. As soon as I graduated from elementary school, I went straight to work. But I was too little to do anything well. I pulled a three-wheel taxi first, but the passengers disliked me for being too young to move it very fast. I went to the Taipei Bridge to work as a truck attendant, but tumbled off and broke my two front teeth."

At this point, he opened his mouth. Sure enough, his two front teeth had been repaired at some time.

"I went to work at a fireworks factory, but Mother caught me and brought me back, saying that if I ever went there again, she would starve herself to death in front of me. At that time, we really could have starved to death.

"Later on, I went to a beef noodle bistro to work as a helper, starting out at first washing dishes. As luck would have it, the chef became very fond of me and taught me quite a lot. After three years, I became his assistant. After that, I went out on my own to set up a food stand for myself. Only when the business became passable could we finally settle down.

"As for my father's death, I knew nothing of it at all. Not until Mother was on her deathbed did she tell me.

"When Father died, he left behind only these paintings. The paintings and I were the only things that gave Mother enough courage to continue living. And not only did she want to keep the paintings, but she also wanted to add something to them. When Mother went to see you, it was at the time that we were driven to the last ditch of desperation. Even when I went to the fireworks factory to work, Mother was still naively thinking of relying on painting to support the family.

"But my mother very soon realized that it was almost impossible for a novice to survive in the art community. She painted all her life, but was only able to sell you that one piece. She told me that she had run into snags and had been turned down everywhere. Some art dealers even ridiculed her. In fact, she was quite aware that the reason you bought her painting was not because it was valuable, but because you had a noble sense of sympathy.

"But my mother never willingly gave up painting throughout her life. She wanted to remember my father in this way, to link with my father in this way, and even to express herself in this way.

"While she was painting, whether she was able to paint well or not wasn't the question, let alone whether she would be able to sell the painting.

"She always closed the door when she painted and wouldn't allow anyone to watch—not even me. I don't know whether she was afraid of infecting me with her sorrowful mood, or if she didn't want me to know that a huge misfortune and loss of honor had struck our family. Not until she was dying did she summon me to her studio.

"The first thing she charged me with was to redeem the painting in your hands. After that, she told me how my father had died.

"Of course, I understood her unwillingness to let those immature works circulate in public.

"She said that at the beginning she absolutely could not accept that Father had died so distressingly. She often felt that Father was still beside her. However, once she imagined him beside her, he would then seem far away. She said that every time she thought of Father, her heart ached as if pierced by something very sharp. She said that those bullets were actually hitting her own heart, and that she must paint out those feelings.

"But she herself didn't know whether she painted well or not.

"She wanted me to redeem the painting of the sparrow from you and then burn it immediately. As a matter of fact, she had already disposed of her earlier exercise works. She even went so far as to hint that if her other works were not good enough, they should be burned as well. She said that the reason she hadn't done it herself was because she had no way of judging them.

"Immediately before her death, she did something resolute. She burned Father's bloodstained clothes, which she had kept for almost forty years. She said that this was her own business, which should be brought to an end before she left. She had even thought that it was not right to tell me about this. But by that time, I already sensed that Father had not died a natural death. So I pressed Mother time and again for an answer until she was driven to the wall. She said that if the paintings were nothing but a venting of individual sentiments, they were worthless and should be burned as well. On the one hand, perhaps it was because I begged very hard, or on the other, perhaps it was because she still cherished some hope that the paintings reflected the lives and common sentiments of ordinary people—that is, some hope that they were real works of art . . . But she had absolutely no self-confidence. I know, too, that to some extent she hoped that through her work people would be attracted to my father's paintings. She hated to think that Father might have come to this world in vain. So I have come to see you more or less for the purpose of asking you to make an appraisal."

He had spoken disjointedly in telling about his father, his mother, and himself. Now he choked with sobs, barely finishing the last segment of his story.

I told him that I was only a businessman. I was afraid that to appraise the real worth of his mother's paintings was beyond my reach. He had to consult some other experts.

"This . . . "

"I know what you mean. I won't tell them what happened to your parents. I'll ask them to appraise the paintings from a purely artistic point of view. And as for your father's paintings, I have always had confidence in them."

1991

Tie Ning (1957–)

OCTDAY

Translated by Diana B. Kingsbury

MONDAY (WEEKDAY ONE)

An extravagance of sunshine bathed the street where a young boy with a book bag squirted water at the passing cyclists from a rubber ball. Smells—the face powder of women and the tobacco of men—enveloped the long stream of bikes like a cloud. The women's faces glowed white above yellow necks. Their reddened lips were parted, and fierce black streaks arched a thin line between eye and brow. Zhu Xiaofen brushed past thinking, Nothing wrong with that. You can't let cosmetic companies go out of business just so women can look natural.

Zhu Xiaofen was truly emancipated.

Zhu Xiaofen hadn't felt so at ease with herself in a long time, not since her wedding day. But now she was divorced, once and for all and just in time—she had just turned thirty-four. Every time she thought about her age and her divorce, she felt so happy she wanted to jump rope, do the "double twist" she had loved as a child. JUST-JUMP-THAT-ROPE! She pushed down hard on the pedals, tensing her thighs and tightening her hamstrings up to the buttocks, which had rounded out after the baby. But what did that matter? She could jump, which worked every part of her body: strengthening her nervous system, improving circulation, expanding lung capacity, enhancing digestion, and raising metabolism. She had to jump. Jumping was a prelude to flying; anybody who wanted to fly had to jump and jump and jump.

Zhu Xiaofen had a child, as already mentioned. While she had divorced the father, she had to keep her ten-month-old baby, loving it even more after the marriage had broken up. Her parents had taken over child care for her. Initially they had mentioned the baby as a reason to keep the marriage together. "For the child's sake," they would said. "But it is for the child's sake," she would respond. They knew whose child she meant.

Zhu Xiaofen hadn't always been so clever with words. In fact, she and her husband had hardly ever argued. She regretted agreeing to marry him the minute she said yes, but she was never interested enough in him to fight after they were married.

She worked as a fiction editor for a regional literary magazine and, after marriage, spent all her time away from home, scouting the country for new manuscripts. She had to be attentive not only to the mood of the writers but to their spouses as well, and she was kept busy calling upon brassy new stars and encouraging eager, embarrassed first-timers who were quietly budding in the corners. She loved her work, loved it so much she stopped breast-feeding after only two months to attend a writers' conference in Xinjiang. Dark wet stains blazoned across the front of her bulging blouse declared her spirit of selflessness. She was always pulling in second-rate manuscripts—people liked her sincerity—but then, out of the blue, a story by one of her new authors, published in her magazine, won a national award. Perfect timing. When they got around to reviewing activities, everyone in the editorial department agreed that an exception should be made for her promotion. And indeed she was later promoted to Associate Senior Editor.

Her husband was the last to hear the good news. Zhu Xiaofen liked to tell him only bad news, never good—hard to say whether it was to anger or depress him. At home all he could do was pick invisible bits of dirt from his clothes with his little finger. Watching him made her feel giddy.

At last the day came when she returned from a month on the road to a lockeddoor. Locked from the inside. She knew it then, standing on the doormat, knew she was about to break away, be freed, and all she could think of was to thank the door for its rebuff. When her husband finally swung it open, she saw one of those white-faced, yellow-necked women in the shadows.

They parted peacefully, although her husband had his say: "I knew you were waiting all along for the day when you came home to a locked door." She just smiled and thought that he might have had her figured out after all. He was good for more than just picking off lint with his little finger, after all. But understanding doesn't imply love. Maybe the more you understand someone, the more that someone disgusts you.

Zhu Xiaofen raced along, propelled, it seemed, by a thrust from behind, or perhaps it was by the force of her elation, the day's first wind whistling past her ears and stroking the fine golden hair on her tanned calves. She parked her bike in the shed and skipped upstairs to the editorial department, where she found her colleagues gathered in her office, either by coincidence or to await her arrival respectfully. The air hung with unspoken distress.

TUESDAY (WEEKDAY TWO)

"Utterly despicable!"

Those were Editor-in-chief Zou's words. Yesterday everyone in the department had taken turns sympathizing with Zhu Xiaofen. Today Big Sister Zou's "despicable" set off a round of public criticism directed indiscriminately at her husband.

The sympathy was naturally for her divorce. Though she wasn't psychologically prepared for it, she managed to endure the pity, reasoning that it was normal for colleagues to show concern at a critical juncture like this, when she was making important life changes. But, she thought, considering her own high spirits, they didn't need to feel that miserable. Besides, the group sorrow seemed so, well, rehearsed.

"Utterly despicable!" Big Sister Zou narrowed her attack. "His baby's ten months old, and he's willing to give it all up."

"That's what I call in-hu-mane," another voice chimed in.

Zhu Xiaofen tried to explain that her husband wasn't to blame, that it was she who had sought a divorce. Big Sister Zou interrupted her, saying that women of the eighties had sunk so low that they felt they must save face while shouldering incredible injustices; without pausing for breath, she asked Zhu Xiaofen if she had eaten breakfast, as if divorce meant she couldn't get a decent thing to eat in the morning. Zhu Xiaofen said thank you, she'd eaten, whereupon Big Sister Zou told the department clerk, "Crackerjack," to make her a cup of tea. She wasn't in the habit of morning tea, but Crackerjack had already presented her with the steaming cup and was explaining how she had bought this new health drink made from Yunnan Maifanshi black tea on last month's business trip to Liaoning Province. Whereupon everyone in the room gazed at Zhu Xiaofen and the cup, reminding her of the scene in Cao Yu's play *Thunderstorm* where Zhou Puyuan forces Fanyi to drink her medicine. She wondered for the longest time who was the German doctor, considering first Big Sister Zou, then Crackerjack, then the Yunnan Maifanshi black tea company. Finally, puckering her lips, she took a sip, afraid that if she waited much longer someone would kneel down and beg her to drink. With the hot liquid in her belly, she felt like laughing. She wanted to tell them all, calmly and sedately, that there was nothing to worry about. She was fine. In fact, she felt great—young and happy and ready to jump the "double twist" with the rope she had in her bag that very moment. But they didn't give her the chance. Big Sister Zou patted her shoulder, indicating there was no need to say anything. They understood everything.

Big Sister Zou's husband had died when she was young, and she knew the hardships of raising five children alone. One of her favorite stories was the sad plight of those five during her "cowshed" days during the Cultural Revolution. As the tale went, the oldest child put some pork ribs on to boil, but the five children cleaned out the pot, leaving only the bones and a thin broth, before the meat was even half-cooked. Everyone knew Big Sister Zou's rib story. It was a regular in the editorial department repertoire. She had won their respect, all right—one mention of her would inevitably call up a chorus of "it sure hasn't been easy." That phrase cut two ways: implied admiration, from which Big Sister Zou gained consolation, and superiority from experiences unknown to all the others. Now that Zhu Xiaofen was divorced—not widowed—but a single woman nonetheless, Big Sister Zou didn't feel so alienated. She had someone to share "it sure hasn't been easy" with. People need a common language, Big Sister Zou thought. Why should I have exclusive rights to that phrase?

Berating Zhu Xiaofen's husband, she thought of how she could help her get through the lonely days ahead. She would buy milk powder and fruit for the baby, and she could . . .

"Drink up." She pointed at the cup of tea in Zhu Xiaofen's hands.

WEDNESDAY (WEEKDAY THREE)

Two days of gifts later—melons, Coca-Cola, dried fruit, honey—and Zhu Xiaofen was beginning to hate the parcel-laden folks who came knocking at her parents' door. Busybodies like that disrupted the whole family.

It had every chance of being a quiet evening. But just as Zhu Xiaofen was stepping from the bath, her old comrade-in-arms Yu Zhen charged in. After graduation from college, the two had gone their separate ways, Yu Zhen taking a teaching job at the school and Zhu Xiaofen moving on to become an editor.

Yu Zhen had a beak for a mouth, a sharp, pointed thing from which emitted a long stream of her favorite word: "why, why, why, why." If you asked her if she'd eaten dinner, she had to first "why, why, why" before answering "yes," or "of course not." Rear end poised in midair above the couch, she stared in amazement at Zhu Xiaofen, as if a worm or a fly were crawling on her face.

"Why, why, why, why," she chirped. "It's been only a week since I last saw you, but you look terrible! Your face is sallow, your lips are dry, your neck is wrinkled, and your hair looks like it's been falling out. You can't go on like this. What will become of you? There are nutritive supplements, you know—ginseng root, donkey-hide gelatin, longan fruit. If you don't take better care of yourself, in another week I won't even recognize you. Why don't you use skin-tightening lotion, wrinkle-disappearing cream, foundation, eyeliner, mascara, all that? And a girdle. There's a new Japanese girdle for thirty-eight yuan you must buy. You have to change your hairstyle and do something about your wardrobe. You need bright colors. Those plain, simple clothes you wear look good on a teenager, but you're way over thirty now. The older you get, the more you have to make a statement with color. You have to open up a bit, think of your future."

Eyes glued to her pecking beak, Zhu Xiaofen thought how the only thing she'd left out was a 200-yuan bottle of 101 Hair Formula. "The way she talks, you'd think I'm over the hill, about to die of an incurable disease, too far gone to ask about! Why, why, why!" Zhu Xiaofen tried out Yu Zhen's word under her breath.

Yu Zhen knew all about Zhu Xiaofen's divorce. In fact, she was trying to get a divorce herself, but her husband wouldn't let go. He said it was her mouth. He loved that beak and wanted to keep the marriage together for its sake. Zhu Xiaofen was free, but Yu Zhen's beak was still held by her husband. That didn't seem fair. She felt as if she had been left behind. Why can't I get a divorce and you can? she thought. Besides, who's to say your divorce is a good thing? Don't you know that women over thirty have a hard time getting remarried? And look at you—with your sallow complexion, chapped lips, and wrinkled neck.

Zhu Xiaofen's complexion was fine, her lips pink and healthy, her hair strong and shiny, but to hear Yu Zhen go on . . . She knew that Yu Zhen was making things seem worse than they really were. More than good intentions lurked behind her concern. "You must think of your future," she was saying. "What will become of you?" What do you care what becomes of me? And why are you getting so excited anyway?

It may have been that Yu Zhen didn't mean to malign Zhu Xiaofen. Maybe she actually did see a sallow complexion, chapped lips, and thinning hair. Or maybe she thought she *ought* to see those things. Since she ought to have seen them, maybe they were really there for her to see. Existence determines consciousness. You stub your toe on a rock, but if the rock doesn't exist, then how could you have stubbed your toe? Ah, Yu Zhen, you pure materialist. Maybe you don't mean to slander me after all.

Zhu Xiaofen made up an excuse to get rid of her friend and, yawning, walked back into the bathroom. Peering at her reflection in the mirror, she patted her face and thought, If there's one thing I have to do tomorrow, it's jump rope.

THURSDAY (WEEKDAY FOUR)

The editorial department took a morning break at ten. Some did calisthenics, others practiced *qigong*, and the rest stood around to chat. Zhu Xiaofen went into the courtyard to jump rope under the walnut tree. At first she couldn't get it right. The rope caught at her ankles, twisted around her neck—what an awkward mess! But then she caught the rhythm and slipped into its natural easy beat. Why hadn't she done this sooner? She should have come out to jump on Monday. She should have jumped to let that crowd upstairs know how happy she was, how relaxed she felt. They might have then been able to avoid the scene of a few days before. She had to jump her best now, jump for all she was worth, as if to do right by that flurry of consolation touched off by Big Sister Zou. She was obviously fine. Look, there she goes with the "double twist," her bounce as springy as ever. Those large, flat walnut leaves look like the eyes of a giant Buddha, their scent faintly bitter.

She saw the calisthenics crowd and the *qigong* group stop what they were doing to watch her. She saw Big Sister Zou rush out of the building in a sweat, discreetly waving a pudgy white hand for her to stop. Stop jumping. Those deadpan eyes and that pudgy white hand—she felt as if they were watching her dance in iron chains, their mood deadly somber.

Big Sister Zou swooped in and cooed soothingly, "Don't jump, Zhu Xiaofen. Why are you still so upset? What's past is past. You have to let go. There's no need to come out and jump rope for our benefit. We feel bad enough for you as it is. Why can't you relax a bit, tell us your troubles? It will do you good. Give it a try, won't you?" Big Sister Zou pleaded so earnestly and with such grave concern that Zhu Xiaofen found it impossible to defend herself. She draped the rope over her shoulder and reluctantly gave in. What did they know about how she felt? Since when did jumping rope mean she was upset? What is relaxed, anyway? How was she supposed to act relaxed? Thursday already and we can't get past this business. It's true you should "think of others before yourself," as Chairman Mao said, but you have to let people live their own lives. Tell me how you think I should deal with this. Or maybe I'll just go on a business trip. I have to get away for a few days. I have to escape this confounding, smothering appeasement. I can't let them push me around.

FRIDAY (WEEKDAY FIVE)

Zhu Xiaofen took a day's train ride to a small, untarnished resort town along the coast where some writers had gathered with their work to pass the sweltering summer days.

High season meant huge crowds. It took nearly forty minutes of being squeezed through the human flood for Zhu Xiaofen to work her way to the station exit. Once there, she wasn't able to slip out and away—the ticket-taker was an old grade-school classmate. After all these years she could still pick out Zhu Xiaofen from the bobbing heads around her. "Hey, I hear you got divorced," she shouted. "They say that good-for-nothing dumped you. Well, no big deal. At first I couldn't believe it, but here you are, plain as day. Someone here to pick you up? Which hotel are you staying at? The Grand? Look, if you don't have anyone to drive you over, my husband's outside in his cab. He can take you."

Mouth and hands flapping at the same rate, she deftly ripped used tickets while Zhu Xiaofen stood to one side like a museum piece to be gawked at by the exiting passengers. Zhu Xiaofen knew that the extraordinary volume wasn't deliberate—railroad employees don't know how to speak softly. Working around clanking, chugging trains and mobs of people all day, if you don't speak up, no one will hear you. She could even forgive her classmate for jabbering on about her private life and for the caustic, malicious way she drawled "dumped." But if there was one thing she couldn't stand, it was that she assumed there was no one to pick her up. Why would she, Zhu Xiaofen, Associate Senior Editor for a regional publication, come all this way if there was no car? Don't tell me that once you're divorced you have to rely on a grade-school classmate's husband to get to a hotel! No, thanks. Don't trouble your husband. I have a car waiting for me, she shouted back. Her driver walked up at that opportune moment to take her bag, shutting up the ticket-taker once and for all.

She knew many of the people at the hotel, or rather, she knew many of the men. Most of the women had come with their husbands. They all treated Zhu Xiaofen with special warmth and concern, scrambling to fill her bowl that night at dinner. The cool sea breeze blowing in off the water beyond the restaurant swept the heat from Zhu Xiaofen's face. Shrimp and cuttlefish, her two favorites, fresh from the sea and cooked to perfection, were among the dishes that night. Her tablemates picked a few mouthfuls from those plates, then left the rest for her, making her feel like a glutton each time she reached out her chopsticks.

Zhu Xiaofen sensed they knew everything about her divorce and, seized by a bewildering anxiety, she couldn't figure out how she was supposed to act. All their comforting made her dizzy. Maybe it was the summer heat. She'd brought along her jump rope, but had a hunch that if she went skipping around the hotel courtyard, they'd say she was doing it for their benefit, to show she didn't care. Forget about jumping rope. Tomorrow I'll go swimming, she thought. Everyone here can enjoy the water. It doesn't matter if you're divorced, remarried, or single. You can be a bigamist and still go swimming.

She went back to her room and got a good night's sleep.

SATURDAY (WEEKDAY SIX)

It was a fine powdery beach. Zhu Xiaofen recalled how two years back, when swimming at a reservoir with gravel banks, she'd stumbled and twisted over the sharp rocks. Her husband had tried to pick her up, but she'd cried out as if insulted. I couldn't let him carry me around in broad daylight—better a stranger than him, she thought viciously. Her embarrassed husband had brushed himself off and moved away.

Zhu Xiaofen took a dip in the water and stretched out in the sun alongside two author friends. It suddenly occurred to her that neither of their wives was around. Hadn't the women said just yesterday that they went swimming every day at noon with their husbands? She politely inquired after their wives and was told that they had specifically told their husbands to accompany Zhu Xiaofen that day. They know you're on your own now, they explained, and they're afraid that the sight of couples would be painful. You see how well our wives understand you, even though you're not that close?

They had everything figured out. Zhu Xiaofen couldn't fathom how the waves stirred up by her editorial department had spread this far. What was she supposed to do? Thank the wives for their thoughtfulness or laugh at them for their brilliant good deed? Or perhaps shove fistfuls of sand down the throats of their clever husbands?

She stood up and, leaving the men behind, dove back into the sea. She had intended to strike up a light conversation with the men, knowing professionally she shouldn't let any opportunity pass, even when she wanted to be alone. Like right now. They had started the conversation, but she had tossed it aside and, without a second thought, taken to the sea. The sky was dark and gray, the water warm. An old woman over seventy was paddling gracefully by herself out by the shark barrier. Zhu Xiaofen headed toward her. She didn't give a thought to who the woman was, but admired the oblivious way she stretched out so easily along the waves. Her white swimming cap bobbed like a bouquet of vibrant but lonely flowers.

The two writers visited Zhu Xiaofen in her room that night after dinner. They came to talk business. Their most recent manuscripts, well, they were originally intended for so-and-so from such-and-such major literary publication. So-and-so had been trying to nail them down for eight years, or maybe nine, it's been so long it's hard to keep track, but now Zhu Xiaofen had come, and under such difficult circumstances. Ordinary folks could never understand how you feel. Ordinary folks? Not even second-rate writers can enter that realm of secret anguish and solitude. But we understand, you see, and so we've come. You don't need to tell us anything, Zhu Xiaofen. There isn't a single human emotion we first-rate writers can't comprehend. After much consideration, we've decided to make so-and-so wait another year (it's already been eight, after all, or maybe nine) and give you our latest work, the stories we finished this afternoon before dinner. What do you say to that? Let's just take it easy for the rest of the week. Don't worry, we won't ask about your you-know-what. And let's not talk about literature, or life, or any of that. Whoever brings it up is a son of a bitch. What do you say?

They pulled out two thick manuscripts and—*thunk*—set them solemnly on the tea table. Their faces shone with the august presence of knights delivering a declaration.

Zhu Xiaofen, you lucky thing. You didn't have to go out and commission these manuscripts—they walked right into your room on their own. Why are you in such a hurry to leave this cool, breezy place and get back on a hot, crowded train? You hold the work of famous authors in your hands.

SUNDAY (WEEKDAY SEVEN)

The hard-seat compartment steamed with the foul stench of packed bodies, but the passengers, long accustomed to train ordeals, remained placidly cool. Some perched on the sink in the bathroom. Others stretched out on the floor beneath the seats. Zhu Xiaofen stood in the aisle, her feet and ankles assaulted by the passengers, persimmon and watermelon remains on the floor.

She didn't mind. If she were down there, she'd do the same. She'd probably even spit on their shoes. Spitting sounded good right then; her mouth was suddenly full of saliva, rolling about under her tongue. Spitting was truly something satisfying, a grand sight, the fireworks of human experience. But she had to swallow to clear out her mouth for talking. She saw someone she knew. It was her old high-school principal.

The principal had been sitting by the window all along, but it wasn't until she was about to get off the train that she recognized her former student. With her gray hair and kind eyes, she looked like a sweet old grandma, but her voice still rang with severe force.

"Well, if it isn't Zhu Xiaofen! I heard about your divorce. Lots of rumors, all right. You're still so young, can't be much more than thirty. You have to straighten out your life. If you took things seriously, how could he leave you? You know I mean well. I like to see my students have a good future. Well, goodbye. I'm getting off at the next stop to see my grandson. Are you going into town? Here, take my seat."

Zhu Xiaofen sat down, watermelon seeds plastered across her ankles, and waved mechanically to the principal. Today must be Saturday. No, it's Sunday, she corrected herself. The ancient Romans had an eight-day week. Wouldn't that be nice? An octa-week. Eight days are better than seven, and tomorrow is Octday. Every week should have a day I could call my own. I need an eighth day.

Zhu Xiaofen determined to stay home and do whatever she liked on her Octday.

OCTDAY (WEEKDAY EIGHT)

A nasty odor wafted through the corridor. The water had been turned off for three days, and the toilets were backed up.

Trailing behind Zhu Xiaofen up the stairs, Crackerjack was explaining how no one knew when they'd have water again. The closest toilet was by the northern wall of the sweater factory compound, a good ten-minute bike ride away. She then apologized for asking Zhu Xiaofen into the office the first day back from her trip, but a woman from the Marriage and Family Research Center of the Municipal Women's Federation had come to see her.

The woman turned out to be an old acquaintance. Years back she had tried to get a job in the city, but the magazine had hired Zhu Xiaofen instead. Zhu Xiaofen had later rejected one of her manuscripts. They weren't close, but they weren't exactly strangers either.

The woman announced she had come to interview Zhu Xiaofen, then set out on a long discourse, sponging the sweaty fog on her glasses with a handkerchief as she talked. Her bulging eyes and thick lenses made her look like a large, diligent ant. She had already been to see Big Sister Zou, she said, and they agreed that Zhu Xiaofen's biggest problem was her refusal to relax and open up. She may not know Zhu Xiaofen that well, but she could see through her. Why make such a big fuss over who asked for the divorce? According to her research, men often claim it's the woman who initiates divorce in order to preserve her self-respect. Acquiescence on the woman's part is vanity, pathetic pride. Zhu Xiaofen, the crux of your problem lies right there. Why can't you admit that your husband didn't want you anymore? The Women's Federation stands up for abandoned women like you. But look how you've handled the problem. You go out to jump rope. You're obviously trying to hide your depression.

Zhu Xiaofen had to use the toilet.

Crackerjack held out a cup of her Yunnan Maifanshi health tonic. How could she make tea with the water off? This must be as precious as gold, Zhu Xiaofen thought, taking a sip.

Picking up where she'd left off, the woman from the research center said that everyone, but especially women, should cry when the time comes to cry and laugh when the time comes to laugh. Zhu Xiaofen, you're trying to escape reality. But how can you? You have a ten-month-old baby. You may never find another man who loves you, and even if you do, will you have his child as well? Ninety-nine point nine-eight-two percent of the men I've surveyed say they want their own child.

Zhu Xiaofen's eyes began to water from the urgent pressure in her bladder. Crackerjack reported this development to Big Sister Zou and the rest of the editorial department, who, upon hearing the news, let out a long communal sigh of relief—Zhu Xiaofen was finally going to cry. She was finally going to let it out. Their week of comforting and consoling had paid off. They jumped for joy, they sighed, they clasped their hands and paced the room.

No time for etiquette. Unable to hold it any longer, Zhu Xiaofen dashed out the door, leapt down the stairs, grabbed her bike, and sprinted toward the sweater factory.

She took a long time to drain herself empty. Reemerging in the sun, she wheeled her bicycle back to the factory gate. Her eyes, now dry, stung in the harsh morning glare. *Pa, pa,* she patted the bike seat. That wasn't her bike. Storming down the stairs a moment ago, she hadn't even pulled out her key. Whose bike could it be? Why wasn't it locked? A new, good model like that leaning dubiously against the bike shed made her wonder if the whole thing hadn't been planned.

She patted the seat again and, leaping astride, rode off with no particular direction in mind. Octday was her invention, she recalled. Monday has to come after Day Seven, and besides, it's not called Day Seven. It's called Sunday, the day of rest.

1989

Yu Hua (1960–)

ON THE ROAD AT EIGHTEEN

Translated by Andrew F. Jones

The asphalt road rolls up and down like it's pasted on top of ocean waves. Walking down this little highway in the mountains, I'm like a boat. This year, I turned eighteen. The few brownish whiskers that have sprouted on my chin flutter in the breeze. They've only just taken up residence on my chin, so I really treasure them. I've spent the whole day walking down the road and I've already seen lots of mountains and lots of clouds. Every one of the mountains and every one of the clouds made me think of people I know. I shouted out each of their nicknames as I walked by. So even though I've walked all day, I'm not tired, not at all. I walked through the morning, now it's the tail end of the afternoon, and soon I'll see the hair of dusk. But I haven't found an inn.

I've encountered quite a few people along the road, but none of them has known where the road goes, or whether there's an inn there. They all tell me: "Keep walking. You'll see when you get there." I think what everyone said was just terrific. I really am just seeing when I get there. But I haven't found an inn. I feel like I should be worried about that.

I think it's weird that I've walked all day and only seen one car. That was around noon, when I'd just begun to think about hitchhiking. But all I was doing was thinking about hitchhiking. I hadn't started to worry about finding an inn—I was only thinking about how amazing it would be to get a lift from someone. I stood by the side of the road waving at the car, trying my best to look casual. But the driver hardly even looked at me. The car or the driver. They hardly even looked at me. All they fucking did was drive right by. So I ran, chasing the car as fast as I could, just for fun, because I still hadn't started to worry about finding an inn. I ran until the car had disappeared, and then I laughed at myself, but I discovered that laughing too hard made it difficult to breathe, so I stopped. After that I kept walking, happy and excited, except that I started to regret that I hadn't picked up a rock before I started waving at the car.

Now I really want a lift, because dusk is about to fall and I can't get that inn out of my goddamned head. But there haven't been any cars all afternoon. If a car came now, I think I could make it stop. I'd lie down in the middle of the road, and I'm willing to bet that any car would come to a screeching halt before it got to my head. But I don't even hear the rumble of an engine, let alone see a car. Now I'm just going to have to keep walking and see when I get there. Not bad at all: keep walking and see when you get there.

The road rolls up and down from hill to valley, and the hills tempt me every time, because before I charge up to the top, I think I'll see an inn on the other side. But each time I charge up the slope, all I see is another hill in the distance, with a depressing trough in between. And still I charge up each hill as if my life depended on it. And now I'm charging up another one, but this time I see it. Not an inn, but a truck. The truck is headed toward me, stalled in the middle of the highway in a low point between two hills. I can see the driver's ass pointing skyward, and behind it, all the colors of the approaching sunset. I can't see the driver's head because it's stuffed under the hood. The truck's hood slants up into the air like an upside-down lip. The back of the truck is piled full of big wicker baskets. I'm thinking that they definitely must be packed with some kind of fruit. Of course, bananas would be best of all. There are probably some in the cab, too, so when I hop in I can eat a few. And I don't really care if the truck's going in the opposite direction as me. I need to find an inn, and if there's no inn, I need a truck. And the truck's right in front of me.

Elated, I run down to the truck and say, "Hi!"

The driver doesn't seem to have heard me. He's still fiddling with something under the hood.

"Want a smoke?"

Only now does he pull his head out from under the hood, reach out a black, grimy hand and take the cigarette between his fingers. I rush to give him a light, and he sucks several mouthfuls of smoke into his mouth before stuffing his head back under the hood.

I'm satisfied. Since he accepted the smoke, that means he has to give me a lift. So I wander around to the back of the truck to investigate what's in the wicker baskets. But they're covered and I can't see, so I sniff. I smell the fragrance of apples. And I think: apples aren't bad either.

In just a little bit, he's done repairing the truck and he jumps down from the hood. I rush over and say, "Hey, I need a ride." What I don't expect is that he gives me a hard shove with those grimy hands and barks, "Go away!"

I'm so angry I'm speechless, but he just swings on over to the driver's side, opens the door, slides into the cab, and starts the engine. I know that if I blow this opportunity, I'll never get another one. I know I should not just give up. So I run over to the other side, open the door, and hop in. I'm ready to fight if necessary. I turn to him and yell, "Then give me back my cigarette!" The truck's already started to move by now.

He turns to look at me with a big, friendly smile and asks, "Where you headed?"

I'm bewildered by this turnaround. I say, "Doesn't matter. Wherever."

He asks me very nicely, "Want an apple?" He's still glancing over at me.

"That goes without saying."

"Go get one from the back."

How am I supposed to climb out of the cab to the back of the truck when he's driving so fast? So I say, "Forget it."

He says, "Go get one." He's still looking at me.

I say, "Stop staring at me. There's no road on my face."

With this, he twists his eyes back onto the highway.

The truck's driving back in the direction I just came from; I'm sitting comfortably in the cab, looking out the window and chatting with the driver. By now, we're already the best of friends. I've found out that he's a private entrepreneur. It's his own truck. The apples are his, too. I hear change jingling in his pockets. I ask him, "Where are you going?"

He says, "I just keep driving and see when I get there."

It sounds just like what everyone else said. That's so nice. I feel closer to him. I want everything I see outside the window to be just as close, just as familiar, and soon all those hills and clouds start to bring more friends to mind, so I shout out their nicknames as we drive by.

Now I'm not crying out for an inn anymore. What with the truck, the driver, the seat in the cab, I'm completely at peace. I don't know where the truck's going, and neither does he. Anyway, it doesn't matter, because all we have to do is keep driving, and we'll see when we get there.

But the truck broke down. By that time, we were as close as friends can be. My arm was draped over his shoulder, and his over mine. He was telling me about his love life, and right when he'd got to the part about how it felt the first time he held a woman's body in his arms, the truck broke down. The truck was climbing up a hill when it broke down. All of a sudden the squeal of the engine went quiet like a pig right after it's been slaughtered. So he jumped out of the truck, climbed onto the hood, opened up that upside-down lip, and stuffed his head back in. I couldn't see his ass. But I could hear the sound of him fiddling with the engine.

After a while, he pulled his head out from under the hood and slammed it shut. His hands were even blacker than before. He wiped them on his pants, wiped again, jumped down, and walked back to the cab.

"Is it fixed?" I asked.

"It's shot. There's no way to fix it."

I thought that over and finally asked, "Now what do we do?"

"Wait and see," he said nonchalantly.

I was sitting in the cab wondering what to do. Then I started to think about finding an inn again. The sun was just falling behind the mountains, and the hazy dusk clouds looked like billows of steam. The notion of an inn stole back into my head and began to swell until my mind was stuffed full of it. By then, I didn't even have a mind. An inn was growing where my mind used to be.

At that point, the driver started doing the official morning calisthenics that they always play on the radio, right there in the middle of the highway. He went from the first exercise to the last without missing a beat. When he was finished, he started to jog circles around the truck. Maybe he had been sitting too long in the driver's seat and needed some exercise. Watching him moving from my vantage point inside the truck, I couldn't sit still either, so I opened the door and jumped out. But I didn't do calisthenics or jog in place. I was thinking about an inn and an inn and an inn.

Just then, I noticed five people rolling down the hill on bicycles. Each bike had a carrying pole with two big baskets on either end, fastened to the back. I thought they were probably local peasants on their way back from selling vegetables at market. I was delighted to see people riding by, so I welcomed them with a big "Hi!" They rode up to me and dismounted. Excited, I greeted them and asked, "Is there an inn around here?"

Instead of responding they asked me, "What's in the truck?"

I said, "Apples."

All five of them pushed their bikes over to the side of the truck. Two of them climbed onto the back, picked up about ten baskets full of apples, passed them upside down to the ones below, who proceeded to tear open the plastic covering the top of the wicker and pour the apples into their own baskets. I was dumbstruck. When I finally realized exactly what was going on, I made for them and asked, "What do you think you're doing?"

None of them paid the slightest bit of attention to me. They continued to pour out the apples. I tried to grab hold of someone's arm and screamed, "They're stealing all the apples!" A fist came crashing into my nose, and I landed several feet away. I staggered up, rubbed my nose. It felt soft and sticky, like it wasn't stuck to my face anymore but only dangling from it. Blood was flowing like tears from a broken heart. When I looked up to see which of them had hit me, they were already astride their bikes, riding away.

The driver was taking a walk, lips curling out as he sucked in deep drafts of air. He had probably lost his breath running. He didn't seem to be at all aware of what had just happened. I yelled toward him, "They stole your apples!" But he kept on walking without paying any attention to what I had yelled. I really wanted to run over and punch him so hard his nose was left dangling, too. I ran over and screamed into his ear, "They stole your apples!" Only then did he turn to look at me, and I realized that his face was getting happier and happier the longer he looked at my nose.

At that point, yet another group of bicycles descended down the slope. Each bike had two big baskets fastened to the back. There were even a few children among the riders. They swarmed by me and surrounded the truck. A lot of people climbed onto the back, and the wicker baskets flew down faster than I could count. Apples poured out of broken baskets like blood out of my nose. They stuffed apples into their own baskets as if they were possessed. In just a few seconds, all the apples in the truck had been lowered to the ground. Then a few motorized tractor-carts chugged down the hill and stopped next to the truck. A few big men dismounted and started to stuff apples into the carts. One by one, the empty wicker baskets were tossed to the side. The ground was covered with rolling apples, and the peasants scrabbled on their hands and knees like ants to pick them all up.

It was at that point that I rushed into their midst, risking life and limb, and cursed them, "Thieves!" I started swinging. My attack was met with countless fists and feet. It seemed like every part of my body got hit at the same time. I climbed back up off the ground. A few children began to hurl apples at me. The apples broke apart on my head, but my head didn't break. Just as I was about rush the children, a foot came crashing into my waist. I wanted to cry, but when I opened my mouth, nothing came out. There was nothing to do but fall to the ground and watch them steal the apples. I looked around for the driver. He was standing a good distance away, looking right at me, and laughing as hard as he could. Just so I knew that I looked even better now than I had with a bloody nose.

I didn't even have the strength for anger. All I could do was gaze out at everything that was making me so angry. And what made me the angriest of all was the driver.

Another wave of bicycles and tractors rolled down the hill and threw themselves into the disaster area. There were fewer and fewer apples rolling on the ground. A few people left. A few more arrived. The ones who had arrived too late for apples began to busy themselves with the truck. I saw them remove the window glass, strip the tires, pry away the planks that covered the truck bed. Without its tires, the truck obviously felt really low, because it sank to the ground. A few children began to gather the wicker baskets that had been tossed to the side a moment before. As the road got cleaner and cleaner, there were fewer and fewer people. But all I could do was watch, because I didn't even have the strength for anger. I sat on the ground, letting my eyes wander back and forth between the driver and the thieves.

Now there's nothing left but a single tractor parked beside the sunken truck. Someone's looking around to see if there's anything left to take. He looks for a while and then hops on his tractor and starts the engine.

The truck driver hops onto the back of the tractor, looks back at me, laughing. He's holding my red backpack in his hand. He's stealing my backpack. My clothes and my money are in the backpack. And food and books. But he's stealing my backpack.

I'm watching the tractor climb back up the slope. It disappears over the crest. I can still hear the rumble of its engine, but soon I can't even hear that. All of a sudden, everything's quiet, and the sky starts to get really black. I'm still sitting on the ground. I'm hungry and I'm cold, but there's nothing left.

I sit there for a long time before I slowly stand up. It isn't easy, because every time I move, my whole body aches like crazy; but still I stand up and limp over to the truck. The truck looks miserable, battered. I know I've been battered, too.

The sky's black now. There's nothing here. Just a battered truck and battered me. I'm looking at the truck, immeasurably sad, and the truck's looking at me, immeasurably sad. I reach out to stroke it. It's cold all over. The wind starts to blow, a strong wind, and the sound of the wind rustling the trees in the mountains is like ocean waves. The sound terrifies me so much that my body gets as cold as the truck's.

I open the door and hop in. I'm comforted by the fact that they didn't pry away the seat. I lie down in the cab. I smell leaking gas and think of the smell of the blood that leaked out of me. The wind's getting stronger and stronger, but I feel a little warmer lying on the seat. I think that even if the truck's been battered, its heart is still intact, still warm. I know that my heart's warm, too. I was looking for an inn, and I never thought I'd find one here.

I lie inside the heart of the truck, remembering that clear, warm afternoon. The sunlight was so pretty. I remember that I was outside enjoying myself in the sunshine for a long time, and when I got home I saw my dad through the window packing a red backpack. I leaned against the window frame and asked, "Dad, are you going on a trip?"

He turned and very gently said, "No, I'm letting you go on a trip."

"Letting me go on a trip?"

"That's right. You're eighteen now, and it's time you saw a little of the outside world."

Later I slipped that pretty red backpack onto my back. Dad patted my head from behind, just like you would pat a horse's rump. Then I happily made for the door, and excitedly galloped out of the house, as happy as a horse.

1986

Su Tong (1963–)

ESCAPE

Translated by Michael S. Duke

"If I ran to the ends of the earth, I could never escape." Those were my uncle's last words.

The next day my uncle left Maple Village. It was raining that night and everyone was sleeping soundly, so no one heard him open the door. After my aunt was awakened by the rooster crowing, she felt the blanket next to her, but it was empty, cold, and clammy. She called a few times in the direction of the outhouse, but heard only the drip drip dripping of water over the eaves. Pale blue sunlight squeezed in through the southern window, illuminating the sack of rice my uncle had carried in from the city and set upon the floor, but his pack was gone. My aunt sat on the bed and started crying, crying and pulling her hair. My aunt's hair was very black; black as black straw, it hung down to her breasts. She cried heartrendingly, then spoke to Grandfather and Grandmother: "Sanmai's gone. I've driven Sanmai away."

My grandfather asked, "Sanmai just came home yesterday. How did you manage to drive him away?" My grandmother said, "Cover your tits, you slut!"

My aunt said, "I didn't let him touch me. He picked up a filthy disease in town. I told him to get out and he really did. Oh, Sanmai, oh . . . "

Rats had gnawed a hole in the sack on the floor, from which rice was pouring out like sand, filling the room with the clean, fresh aroma of food grains. My aunt sat on the bed crying while my grandmother swept the rice up into a bamboo dustpan. My grandfather walked outside and saw Sanmai's footprints in the muddy ground. They resembled little boats full of rainwater. Where could Sanmai have run off to?

"That was in the autumn of 1951. It seems so strange talking about it today," my aunt said to me. "Just think how good that bastard Sanmai was at making revolution."

My uncle, Chen Sanmai, ran hurriedly in the night rain. The crooked outline of Maple Village grew smaller and smaller; our black dog ran over on the muddy road, barked a few times, and bit into Sanmai's pant leg. My uncle squatted down, petted the dog's soggy fur, and said: "Blacky, don't rub against me. Can't you smell my rotten odor?" The black dog held on tenaciously to Sanmai's pant leg. Sanmai addressed him again: "Even I can smell the stink. Haven't you smelled it yet?" Sanmai turned and looked at the far-off village and began to sob as he said: "My old lady doesn't even want me, so what're you tugging on me for?" Then he lifted up his pack and swung it at the dog. The blue pack with white floral pattern fell to the muddy ground. The black dog picked it up in his mouth and ran for home. Sanmai shouted after the dog, then stomped his foot, turned around, and walked on.

My uncle Chen Sanmai was empty-handed when he ran away. There was a torrential rain the night he left, but the sky did not fall.

My uncle went north, but my aunt went south in pursuit. She took the pack to Chen's Bamboo Goods Store and asked after Sanmai. The bamboo craftsman said, "Didn't Sanmai go home because he missed his old lady? Why would he leave again?" My aunt replied, "It's all your fault for ruining Sanmai. A decent man like Sanmai, and you taught him your filthy tricks. Where did he go? If you don't tell me, I'll burn your store down, and none of you can go on living the way you do!"

My uncle went north. No one had seen even his shadow. My aunt nearly went out of her mind searching for him for three days in that small southern city. On the fourth day, someone brought her news that Chen Sanmai had been spotted north of the Shanhai Pass begging by the side of the road. My aunt immediately boarded the train north for Manchuria. "That was the first time I'd been on a train," she said. "They told me I'd have to spend two days and two nights on the train before we'd be north of the pass. 'Isn't there any way to get there faster?' I asked, 'I'm so worried.' They said, 'Why don't you tie a rope to your back and pull the train, then?' and I said, 'If it would do any good, I really would pull it.'"

It was 1951. My aunt said, "Everywhere it was resist America, aid Korea and protect your family, defend the country. 'Hey la la la hey la la la!' everyone shouted in high spirits as the train boldly crossed the Yalu River. The rail lines were crowded with military trains; the men had put on new padded jackets, eaten their fill of fried bread, and headed off for the front. When the train stopped at Dandong and the doors swung open, everyone who jumped out was headed for the front. One young girl wanted to put a wreath of red flowers around my neck, but I immediately told her, 'I'm not a soldier, I'm looking for my man.' The station was packed with soldiers, all men. I squeezed my way through the crowd wearing a short padded jacket with a floral design. With so many people, where could I find Sanmai? I started shouting right there on the platform: 'Sanmai, Sanmai, Chen Sanmai.' No one could hear me. Dandong was too noisy; I couldn't even hear the sound of my own voice.

"A young man on his way to the war stuck his head out the train window and yelled in to me, 'I'm Sanmai. Are you my sister-in-law?' 'You've got the wrong person,' I said. 'I wasn't calling you, I was calling my man.' The young man, who looked about seventeen or eighteen, disappointedly scratched his shaved head: 'I guess I won't see my sister-in-law this time.' He looked so lonely and skinny, I felt sorry for him, so I smiled and said, 'I'll be your sister-in-law, O.K.? Call me Sis.' I took a big round piece of fried bread out of my bag and gave it to him. As he took the bread from my hands, he really did call me 'Sis.'"

My aunt just sat there on the platform waiting for Chen Sanmai to appear. For some reason she was certain he had run off to join the army. She figured that, having reached a dead end, Chen Sanmai must have joined the army. They feed you in the army, she reflected, and as shy as Chen Sanmai was, how could he possibly stand to beg for a living? My aunt just kept sitting there on the platform staring at the scene in Dandong as the sky gradually darkened, and when a line of cars moved slowly out of the station, she saw a face flash by, furtively looking at her from behind the transom window. She jumped up on the foot board, yelled "Chen Sanmai!" and leaped over to grab the car window. Chen Sanmai, dressed in an army uniform with an army cap on his head, stared woodenly at her with a weary and forlorn expression.

My aunt said, "Sanmai, Sanmai, get off this train." Sanmai could not hear her. She went on: "Have you gone soft in the head, Sanmai? Say something to me!" "I'm going off to die," said Chen Sanmai hoarsely. My aunt heard the engine roaring away like thunder and could not hold on any longer. She ran a few steps alongside the train shouting to Sanmai, "Don't go off and die. We've been given five *mou* of land to plant grain." Crying and shouting, my aunt watched the train pull away for Korea; there was no way she could hold it back.

My uncle Chen Sanmai had always been a timid and cowardly little man. This is the conclusion you would reach from the history of his many escapes. My grandfather said, "That bastard Sanmai is a useless good-for-nothing: he ran away when we asked him to eat; he ran away when we asked him to take a bath; if we beat him with the heel of our shoe, he ran away even faster. When he grew up and we found him a wife, he still ran away. Except for figuring out how to run away, you'd never know what else Sanmai wanted to do. He's really a good-for-nothing bum."

My uncle was nineteen when he married my aunt. At nineteen all he knew how to do was pedal an irrigation water wheel. His legs were short, thick, and powerful—like a couple of tree trunks. But his hands were as delicate and weak as a child's. Thinking back, my aunt said, shaking Sanmai's hand was just like shaking her little boy's hand. It never felt quite right. Sanmai's hand was cold and clammy. When she recalled her first night in bed with my uncle, she didn't know whether to laugh or to cry: "Sanmai said, 'I'm not tired; I still don't feel like sleeping.' Then he said, 'You go to bed first; I have to go to the outhouse.' Sanmai just ran out like that, still wearing his new shirt and pants. Where do you think he went? He went to pedal his water wheel. He took off his new shirt and pants, hung them on a tree, and pedaled that water wheel alone in the dark. When Grandfather and Grandmother found him, they were furious. What do you think he said? He said, 'You go on to bed. This stretch of land doesn't have enough water yet. I don't feel like sleeping.'"

My aunt said, "That bastard Sanmai, you couldn't tie him down even with a belt made of gold. Sanmai just couldn't live peacefully. That fall, when he went into Crowsbridge to sell sweet-potato vines and ran into some bamboo craftsmen from the city, he just pocketed the money and went off with them. Is a place like the city anywhere for someone like Chen Sanmai to be running off to?" my aunt asked. "Just think, Sanmai came back with some filthy disease; he got the punishment he deserved. Served him right, the bastard."

Maple Village was quite remote; the air in 1951 was damp, bitter, and permeated with the suffocating odor of rotting bamboo shoots. No one knew how the war in Korea was going. The men and women of our family shouted at an old bull as they plowed our five *mou* of land. You had to work if you wanted food to eat and clothes to wear, had to take good care of your five *mou*. There was no point worrying about Chen Sanmai. The local government stuck a red banner on our family's old cypress door frame: "Dependents of a protect-the-family, defend-the-nation revolutionary soldier." My grandfather said, "I wonder what the hell that bastard Sanmai looks like with a rifle in his hands. If he gives his life for his country, at least he'll have a glorious death." My grandfather ran his hand over the red banner and said, "If he dies, he dies. There's nothing to be too sad about. Dying with a full stomach is certainly a damn sight better than plowing the fields on an empty one."

"That was in 1951. It seems so strange talking about it today," said my aunt, who sat in front of the kerosene lamp every night making thick cotton socks, and was declared a "model female worker" when she sent them to the county government. My aunt's cotton socks were strong and lasting and were greatly appreciated when they reached Korea. She got blood blisters on her hands from all that sewing. At least one of those many pairs of cotton socks ought to have found its way to my uncle's feet. My aunt said she was preparing for Sanmai's sacrifice, that she was working so hard making cotton socks for the front just in order to prepare for Sanmai's sacrifice. My aunt said, "When someone dies, his feet shouldn't freeze; they should be nice and warm."

This is exactly the way my aunt described those days after my uncle Chen Sanmai ran away from home for the first time. The following winter, when he reappeared in Maple Village, his feet were bare. No one was more shocked than my aunt. As she knelt on the ground and rubbed his filthy, frozen feet, she asked, "The cotton socks, where are the cotton socks I made?" My uncle just shook his head; he was so cold he could not talk. At that my aunt started to cry. "Why didn't they give you some cotton socks? I made a trainload of cotton socks." Walking toward the house, supporting my uncle, she swore to herself she would never again make cotton socks for the front.

When my uncle Chen Sanmai came home to the village, he brought a peace medal with him. His lower abdomen also had a purple worm-shaped scar from a piece of Korean shrapnel. The way I see it, that, too, was a glorious decoration.

Back in 1952, my uncle Chen Sanmai was so elated and so admired by everybody that Maple Village slaughtered chickens and goats to welcome back the Chen family's hero. At the party celebrating Chen Sanmai's triumphs, my grandfather drank eight bowls of sorghum wine, laughed riotously without stopping until he laughed himself to sleep—he laughed himself to sleep and never woke up again. My grandfather was the first person in Maple Village ever to die of happiness; to this day the people still remember my grandfather's thunderous laughter just before he died, and they still remember his limply animated face beneath the red, square handkerchief. How could an old peasant who had lived sixty-one years die any happier a death than my grandfather did? Think about it.

After my uncle Chen Sanmai came back to the village, my aunt and my grandmother began to devote themselves to him. Two women supporting one man was a situation that violated traditional customs. But it was also bound up with the question of freedom in the family, and no one had the right to tell my uncle Chen Sanmai what to do.

If you had walked by the front of our house, you would have seen Chen Sanmai dressed in his unbearably filthy, dust-colored army uniform sitting against the wall basking in the sun. His face was skinny as a monkey's and looked like a rust-splattered piece of junk metal; his eyebrows were knit tightly together and his terribly bloodshot eyes had a pitiful, helpless expression. Many people heard that Chen Sanmai's right arm was injured, so he could not work in the fields. He rubbed his right arm with his left hand and told everyone, "The joint was crushed by artillery fire and I can't raise my arm." The others asked, "You can still pedal a water wheel, can't you?" Chen Sanmai answered with a laugh, "I can't pedal it. I can't do anything I should do." If you saw Chen Sanmai sitting there against the wall basking in the sun, his carriage and expression had both undergone a qualitative change from what they were before.

Chen Sanmai was, after all, someone who had lived through a harrowing experience.

A warm spring came to Maple Village at its accustomed time, and my uncle Chen Sanmai started to become obsessed with making kites. During the season of spring plowing, he avoided my family's five *mou* of land and preoccupied himself with making kites. Kites of every shape and kind hung all over the house—on the walls, the crossbeams, and bedposts. Kites decorated the serene skies of Maple Village, animating and enlivening this ancient and torpid rural village. Chen Sanmai led a group of children flying kites all around the village. The sacred five-colored phoenix swooped back and forth over the villagers' heads: it was an amazingly auspicious emissary from the Heavenly Kingdom; it came from the faraway, unfathomable realm of the immortals; it also came from my uncle's war-shattered hand. When Chen Sanmai ran wildly across the meadows clutching a kite string, his lethargic appearance grew heroically exuberant and his shouts of "Fly! Fly!" were full of wisdom and magic. Both Chen Sanmai and his kites fluttered along on the wind. I really did see him and his kites being blown along by the wind; he was about to take off into the air and fly right over the heads of the people doing the spring plowing.

It is definitely not a good thing for people whose fate is bitter to experience happiness. My aunt said she felt uneasy right from the start. As she watched Sanmai's kites soar higher and higher, she felt his soul was also drifting farther and farther away from her. My aunt said she was certain there was something that bastard Chen Sanmai was concealing from her. On April 21st, the day traditionally known as Rain in the Grain, my aunt was picking out seed grains in the front yard when she saw Sanmai running like mad toward the house. He stumbled along pulling an eagle-shaped kite as he ran up like a crazy man and pushed her into the house. He bolted the door and leaned panting against it; his face was nearly purple.

"What's the matter with you?"

"They've come. They've tracked me here."

"Who's come?"

"They've tracked me here. They're going to take me back to the war."

"Soldiers? When did you see them?"

"I was flying a kite on the hill of abandoned graves and I saw them stand up from behind the grave mounds."

"How many are there?"

"Two." My uncle's kite fell to the ground. "They hid behind the graves and then stood up like ghosts."

"We'll fight them off," my aunt shrieked. "One ruined arm isn't enough, you have to give your life, too?"

"If they take me back, it'll be a single bullet in the head for me. I know they'll shoot me. In Korea they specialized in hunting down deserters, and when they caught them they executed them."

"Sanmai, you're a deserter?" My aunt suddenly understood. Grabbing hold of Sanmai's collar, she shook him as he stood there stiffly. "Sanmai, you bastard, you're a deserter?"

Chen Sanmai closed his eyes tightly and let my aunt shake him. Suddenly, as he shook like a kite in the wind, he told her, "I didn't want to die, so I escaped and came home."

"Why did you go in the first place, if you were going to run away?"

"If I wanted to run away, why shouldn't I run away?"

My aunt collapsed to her knees on top of a winnowing basket full of grain. She started crying as she scooped up handful after handful of grain and threw it in Chen Sanmai's face. He just leaned there against the door, covering his face with his left hand without moving a muscle. My aunt did not see the turbid tears falling from Sanmai's eyes. After about two minutes had passed, my uncle Chen Sanmai unbolted the door and ran outside. My aunt followed him out and saw him grab that eagle-shaped kite and run. He bounded through the village like a gazelle, shouting all the way in a weak, hoarse voice: "Escape . . . escape . . . escape . . . !"

In just such a fashion my uncle Chen Sanmai went away and never came back. The lucky thing was that no one else saw those men who had come after him. Did they ever really come to Maple Village? This has long been a topic of conversation in my family. For a long time after my uncle ran away, you would regularly find big or small kites made by Chen Sanmai in the meadows, beside the irrigation ditches, or caught on chimneys. They were all kites whose strings had snapped in the wind, just like my uncle's unpredictable and ever-changing fate.

My aunt discovered she was pregnant. That was a month after my uncle disappeared. She wanted to cry, but had no tears left. She wanted to tell Chen Sanmai the news, but she did not know where he was. Just think, a woman carrying a baby who does not know where her man is; my aunt was in a wretched state.

"Chen Sanmai, you bastard, I'm going to find you and cut you into a million pieces if I have to chase you to the end of the earth going to cut your heart out and feed it to the dogs going to fry your skin in a skillet." That's what my aunt said to my grandmother as she swallowed back her bitter saliva. My grandmother, however, blamed my aunt: "You shameless girl, why couldn't you hold on to Sanmai's heart? No matter what you say, you're still the one who drove him away." At that my aunt jumped up, grabbed my grandmother by the hair, and butted her with her head. My grandmother hurriedly defended herself: wielding a bamboo strainer, she ripped open my aunt's blouse, exposing her breasts. My aunt, momentarily stunned, let out an earsplitting wail, covered her breasts with her hands, collapsed onto a pile of straw, and refused either to move or to eat for three days and three nights. They say the child in her womb starved to death that way; later, when they saw it was born dead, they said my aunt had starved it to death.

In 1952, my aunt suffered as though struck repeatedly by lightning; in that one year she lost both her beauty and her black hair, and from that time on she was a prematurely aged, hunchbacked, ugly woman. My aunt said that if she wanted to remarry she could never marry a good man. She wanted only to find Chen Sanmai, embrace him, and leap with him off a cliff; either that or they could hang themselves, or throw themselves into the river and drown, anything. "You tell me, what else can I do?" My aunt let down the graying chignon coiled around the top of her head and held out her aging hair for all to see: "Just tell me, what else can I do?"

Throughout the long drawn-out fifties, Maple Village experienced a mighty revolution just as the outside world did. Leading a bull and a dog and taking Chen Sanmai's peace medal and land certificate with her, my aunt joined a cooperative. Later, she became Maple Village's illustrious village leader. That was a stroke of miserable good fortune. People would point at the female village leader and say, "That's Chen Sanmai's woman; that's the woman Chen Sanmai abandoned." There was an unbreakable relationship between my aunt and my uncle: even if he ran away to the ends of the earth and no one knew if he was dead or alive, the spiritual bond between him and my aunt would remain unbreakable.

I once had a look at my aunt's land certificate; it was the first thing she ever wrote after attending a women's literacy class, and the characters were quite crooked. But what startled me was that she did not learn how to write her own name first—she wrote my uncle's name. This is what it looked like:

Land Certificate

Head of Household:	Chen Sanmai
Amount of Land:	Two acres
Household Members:	Chen Sanmai
	Me
	Child (who died)

But who could tell my aunt where Chen Sanmai had run off to, and why he did not come home?

It was many years later that she received my uncle's letter, although it can hardly be considered a real letter. My aunt said it was the autumn of 1960 when the postman delivered that heavy envelope. Only three words—Northeast, from Chen—were written on the outside. She opened it, and inside was a wad of food ration coupons from Heilongjiang Province, nothing else. My aunt said she instantly identified Sanmai's odor on those ration coupons. She said she really did smell Sanmai. "Chen Sanmai knew there was a famine here, so he mailed me enough Heilongjiang ration coupons to buy two hundred pounds of food." Her hands trembled as she spoke. "What do I want with Heilongjiang ration coupons? I want your heart, Chen Sanmai!" My aunt cried and laughed as she tried to make out the postmark on the letter. It was from a place completely foreign to her: Yichun, Heilongjiang.

The very next day my aunt took the train north to Yichun. Her description of this trip is truly heartbreaking; sometimes I even doubt its authenticity and would rather believe that my aunt just dreamed it up. I'll never believe that faraway Yichun is my uncle's final resting place. There's nothing there but forests and snow, and it's certainly not the sort of environment a person from Maple Village could survive in. But, according to my aunt's story, my uncle did indeed die in the forests of Yichun, and my aunt's story must be true.

It was snowing when my aunt arrived at Yichun.

No one in Yichun had heard of Chen Sanmai. They told her to go north. All the southerners worked in the forests, they said. "When you see lumberjacks, take a close look and see if your man's with them or not." So my aunt walked north through half a foot of snow, chewing her hard fried bread and asking after Chen Sanmai. Around dusk she ran into a group of workers transporting logs. They sized up my aunt for a moment, then asked bluntly, "Are you here to collect the corpse?"

"What? Is Chen Sanmai dead?" my aunt gasped.

"He's still barely breathing. Better hurry up."

"What happened to him?"

"He was crushed by a falling tree yesterday. They yelled at him to get out of the way, but he didn't hear them."

"Where is he?" my aunt shrieked. "Who tricked him into coming to this godforsaken place?"

"Walk toward that kite over there and you'll find him. You can ask him whatever you want."

My aunt saw a kite hanging from the top branches of a distant tree. She ran pell-mell toward that kite, and all the time she caught the scent of Chen Sanmai wafting over on the Yichun wind. Chen Sanmai's kite hung like a pennant on the top of a tree, as though it were a summons to his soul. By the time my aunt ran into the log cabin, her eyes were clouded with tears. She saw a man lying on the *kang* wrapped in filthy blankets, with only his shiny white head sticking out, facing the window.

"You caught up with me after all. If I ran to the ends of the earth, I could never escape."

My uncle uttered only this one sentence to my aunt on his deathbed. My aunt turned his head toward her and caressed it, as they enjoyed their final moments of conjugal affection. She discovered that my uncle's appearance had undergone a remarkable transformation since he ran away; although his hair was turning gray, his face had grown bright and youthful. Even on the verge of death, his black eyes still looked around in all directions, glowing with a rich, powerful vitality. My uncle struggled out of my aunt's embrace and, with his last ounce of strength, turned his face toward the window. My aunt asked, "Sanmai, who are you waiting for?" but he shook his head and pointed out the window.

Outside was the wind and snow of Yichun, the boundless forest covered with silver, and the sounds of power saws and trees crashing to the ground, which rose out of the stillness like the chanting of a prayer from somewhere beyond the sky. Outside the window, on a row of white birch trees hung a row of kites with broken strings: eight kites hung there silently in the wind and snow, their paper streamers blowing leisurely in the wind. My uncle stared at those eight kites. Who would you say he was waiting for? Perhaps he was waiting for those eight kites to float down from the trees.

My aunt attended my uncle Chen Sanmai's funeral in Yichun. In accordance with the customs of Maple Village, she wore a coarse hempen gown and walked behind the coffin as they trudged deep into the forest, she and four lumberjacks she had never met who carried the coffin. They walked along a snow-covered path, on both sides of which men were burning off the underbrush; the flames burned their way up the hillside, and the sky dropped heavy snow back upon the ground. It was a scene of fire burning snow: the world was snowy white, the flames were golden yellow, and the mourners were coal-black. Also in accordance with the customs of Maple Village, my aunt wailed for her husband for a distance of ten *li*. But, she said, when it was time to cry, she had no tears. She watched the snowflakes as big as goose feathers fall on the fire, watched the flames burn through the heavy snow, and thought it all wondrously beautiful. When she reflected that that bastard Chen Sanmai was dead, she felt her heart was completely cleansed. She had nothing left to worry about.

1991

Qiu Miaojin (1969–1995)

LETTERS FROM MONTMARTRE

Translated by Howard Goldblatt

LETTER ELEVEN, MAY 20TH

Xu:

My soul is so lonely, but I'm unwilling to describe that sort of loneliness for you, because I can't divulge the depth of my loneliness to anyone who'd cast away my soul, cast away my life, someone who'd cavalierly take me to the brink of death and who could, without a trace of emotion or sympathy for the pain and suffering I've experienced, cruelly exile me to a foreign country. I don't hate you as much as I did, but I am so desperately lonely.

I tried to reconcile the duality of love and hate that you had so painfully driven into my heart, and I had to do it silently, straining all alone, with no help at all. You seemed to be slowing down in all the ways you hurt and deceived me, but I still had no way of understanding or trusting you. You're getting more and more used to pessimism, hiding yourself more and more in silence; for you, even making an effort with words or actions to help me lessen the hurt became so difficult that letting me die was the most natural "peace" and "tranquillity." I never understood how you could've become so heartless and indifferent. Worse yet, you seemed to believe that your attitude was fair and that you had every right to treat me that way. You wouldn't even allow me to return to my homeland, lest I interfere with your life and "hurt you again." Please forgive me for saying this.

I often wonder if I still have the courage to see the element of "tragedy" recur? Qingjin once said that life is full of ruptures. Even if that's so, does it have to be so? Everyone I've loved in my life has treated me rudely and oafishly. I also treated others rudely and oafishly when I was young. But I wonder why we have to be so rude and oafish to those we love. Why can't we avoid hurting our loved ones by reflecting on ourselves more and by understanding ourselves and life better? I believe we can. The tragedy continues to occur and life is full of ruptures precisely because of the rudeness and oafishness between people. But I don't think this is the kind of life I want. There should be a rest in the composition of my life, not more tragedy or ruptures. I should also try to repair past ruptures and tragedies to lessen my sorrow and loneliness and lighten my baggage.

Xu, my beloved Xu, I now understand how to treat those closest to me, past or present. I understand everyone, but it's been a long process, off and on for ten years. In the future, when I meet people, I can clearly fit them into this structure. Three years have passed. I've finally squared accounts and figured out my mistakes, my deficiencies, and the right way to treat you. I hope to weave our future story into the traces of this process . . . Will I die young now that I've suddenly been enlightened on so many issues?

I longed to return to our former intimacy. I continue to ask myself how we'd lost that intimacy . . .

It must have begun after my move to Foyer, when our mutual understanding was no longer complete or thorough. My life in Paris has been unspeakably frustrating. I lost all confidence in my life and in whether we could be together (I reread my farewell letter to you from Foyer; such sad, pathetic love). I wavered between a strong desire to be with you at once and leaving you in order to put a stop to that desire, and that frustrated you. You didn't know how to face me and I, on the other hand, was hurt because you didn't know my true situation, and felt absolutely helpless because you could never make up your mind. I was indeed helpless in Foyer, feeling I could no longer continue to live a life of waiting, torn between desire and loneliness . . . I recall how disappointed I was when I returned to see you in April. I felt you didn't love me, that your reality—work and family—was more important than me. This was the kind of life I led. You didn't even want to come see me in Paris during your vacation. You were just humoring me when you said you would (this truly has a long tradition). Up till now, I've been right about the knowledge that came with those feelings. But back then you were at least willing to say you'd come see me. Now, all you wanted was for me not to return to bother you . . . Back then I had very limited resources in Paris; I didn't have many friends or fluent enough French to relieve the loneliness and frustration in my life. I exhausted all my resources and was running on empty, living a life of waiting all alone, missing and yearning for you. My choice was to cut off all ties, but it was only an attempt to escape my desperate desire for you.

But there was no escape. Like shackles, the desire trussed me up; like a gorilla trying to fight its way out, I failed and left with a bleeding head. So the lava of pain spewed forth to melt all the intimacy between us. Before you had a chance to know what you really wanted, before you had time to figure out how to treat me, my damned angel destroyed the baby-like trust you had in me. What followed was indifference toward me, which has lasted until today and seems less and less likely to diminish. I believe you hate me too, but your expression of hurt and hate is indifference. Now I've come to the core of the problem. It was at this point that your Eros toward me began a violent split and clash. You continued to give to me and care for me in real life where love was concerned, but the hate manifested itself in your indifference, closing yourself off and rejection, and my Eros went topsy-turvy. Unable to possess your Eros, I went crazy, absolutely crazy, crazy to the highest possible reach (ha ha) . . . Know why I'm laughing? Because what I have for you is a fatal, a life-threatening passion (that's why in the end I had no choice but to die or surrender to you unconditionally and belong to you for eternity). (The final rule of Eros is just this, sexual desire—emotional longing—death wish, which merge when they are at their strongest.) I am by nature a passionate person; with you as a fatal agent, I cannot escape death. Just thinking about it brings me pain. The thought that I can't have your Eros is enough to break my heart, break it into pieces (and not just leave it injured) . . . I received the love and care you gave me, but I continued to be confused by the feeling that deep down you didn't love me. I gave you stronger Eros, while, on the other hand, I kept doubting you, negating you, and oppressing you. I was inflicted with the illness of wanting, until the latent animosity inside you turned outward to become hurtful behavior, selfishness, and unfaithfulness, or to send messages of leaving and not loving me, which is the most extreme sign of indifference and animosity. By then, I'd turned into an attacker skilled at assault and destruction. The enemy relationship was established, so the most negative elements in our personalities were pushed to their extremes without constraints. What saddens me is that neither of us could stop this process; instead we tried hard to treat the other nicely (or love the other).

After having gone through so much, I have to mention as sincerely as I know how two very important matters, which also happen to be almost too hurtful to talk about. One was when I first hit you; I knew then that I'd lost you. I was crying pitifully inside, as I realized I could never get you back again. I began a life tortured by fear and nightmares. I was afraid to lose you, to be abandoned by you. My nightmares were all about your unfaithfulness. I couldn't control myself when I hit you, but I also killed myself in a more violent way . . . Even now I can't completely shake these dreams, which make me cry till I wake myself up. The second matter is that you all but completely resisted me sexually during the time we spent in Paris. I can even say that you didn't desire me at all, had no desire to make love with me. It wasn't until the past month that I could face and understand that. Just thinking about it often makes me cry . . . I can't face how we've let our relationship deteriorate to this point. It hurts so much I can't talk about it. Whenever memories of Clichy get too close, it's as if I'd received an electric shock. And oh how it hurts. . . .

At first I decided to forget you, to change myself completely and live a new life, to be someone totally different from my old self. That idea suddenly seemed both easy and imaginable. It now appears that I can rather easily shed those traits that have stuck to me and have been impossible to get rid of . . .

After returning from Tokyo, I began to sense that the nature of my sexual desire was changing, which seemed both miraculous and private, like the shifting of the earth's crust. I didn't know what to do; I wasn't even sure what had caused the changes. I felt that I was "becoming a 'woman' (based on the definition of a vulgar 'woman') or that I had the possibility of turning into a 'woman'." My periods became very regular. One early morning I dreamed about you. At the moment I woke up, intuition told me that I was having my period, which turned out to be the case. It was the exact day it was due, and I felt a sort of mysterious connection. I also saw in my dream what I looked like in long hair, a very feminine look. I had a premonition that I'd begin wanting to look pretty and that my face was getting beautiful (a sort of feminine beauty). One day, Qingjin looked at me and said I was pretty in a way that both men and women find attractive. I truly sensed that my face and my movements were becoming feminine. My sexual desires were also becoming more receptive. I still fantasized about you, but now it seemed that I wanted you to love me and give yourself to me, in contrast to the way I'd always loved and given myself to you . . . I also thought I could have sex with men (if it could be pure sex, that is). Or maybe I should say I started to believe that I could have perfect sex with a tender and sincere man (like Eric, in the doctoral program, who has pure male qualities) . . . I was scared, scared that I'd succumb to the attraction and become a real "woman" if an intellectual and spiritual man like Eric landed next to me. That was totally possible, and the transformed me was absolutely capable of doing it. What frightened me was that this was a way, the best way, for me to thoroughly abandon my desire for you and for Eros. I was afraid of that temptation, which was not a temptation of sex or of betrayal, but the temptation to leave you. It was a temptation of disappearing from you forever, of erasing myself once and for all, so that you'd never find me (I seemed to be always seeking an absolute way to love or be loved by you).

To me, it's horrifyingly pivotal to escape from the hopelessness and frustration related to your Eros. I believe it's the core of my death; sooner or later I will die or die again because of it. I'm afraid of this hopelessness and frustration, which haven't ended. I'm terrified that I will die for it again, and that creates a very ambiguous pain that I find hard to articulate. In Tokyo, Xiaoyong's single phrase was right on target; she quickly understood what sort of relationship had plunged me into death this time. I guess she understood what you meant to me when she saw your picture in Taipei. She must see things more quickly than I, and see more. In Tokyo she said that you had yet to comprehend what my passion for you meant, and that you could easily kill me. I think she wished I could give you up so I could live a peaceful life.

Eros, or the development of Eros, plays a very mysterious and crucial role in a romantic relationship. In the past, my relationships with Shuiyao and Xiaoyong were blocked with such great obstacles because I believed that they didn't desire me. I've always thought that, for them, Eros controlled and decided everything. Shuiyao unambiguously rejected me, so I walked away heartbroken. Xiaoyong, on the other hand, accepted me uncertainly, and her attitude always seemed to say that she really only needed a man's body. But she never clearly expressed herself either, until she wrote me a letter this year in which she said she now understood what it meant to have a "male" inside her. I cried all day, because her letter was proof that I was right about her. In the past, I'd sealed off my Eros for her over this issue of men's vs. women's bodies.

But it turned out that I was wrong, and that the opposite was true. It wasn't until later that Xiaoyong had a chance to tell me what she meant by "male." It turned out to be a maleness in personality, will, and soul, not physical maleness. Her reference to maleness meant me; it was because the maleness in me and in that person she loved was strong enough that she was able to desire, and also to block her desire for others. It took her three years to understand this; it took three years for her love for me to mature inside her body before she could understand this. The result was that she and I were in tune, equal and even in both love and sex. The extent of her passion was what I had always wanted, and I think it was because of the love and the sex she gave me that I was able to live on.

Shuiyao finally spoke up about "the thing I needed to know most," when I insisted that she tell me why she'd rejected me years ago. It was because of sex. She said that during the summer, when I ran away, she understood that I was afraid of sex. All of a sudden she understood everything. Then she thought about me every day, until one night her private parts began to bleed for no reason. She said she hated me after that night . . . Only then did things change and she completely rejected me. When she told me about this incident, which meant so much to her, I believe she was finally confronting her sense of the sinful and unclean nature of first-time sex. The classic hate that a woman experiences when her first love takes her virginity occurred in our story, and that was why I was sacrificed. When I returned, I witnessed how she and her new love had established a perfect sexual relationship. But I believe that where she was concerned, I was always the deepest, the purest, the most focused, and the least reserved object of her love. She could have a relationship with me now, but I don't want to interfere in her new life, so I refuse to have any intimate tie with her. Whatever I do, I can't coexist with her or love her enough. Others will suit her better, and I'll just treat her as a friend who lives in a faraway place.

Sex has never been a problem for me in previous relationships with women. I desire a woman's body and need to make love with the person I love. I think

I've always been someone who's been one hundred percent in love with women ever since Shuiyao and I were young together. My sexual desire for her was clear, and I desired only a woman's body back then. I'm positively in love with women. It was remarkable that my passion became more positive and stronger as I grew older. Xiaoyong was right about my having a strong maleness. As I naturally love women, the women I love do not need the prerequisite of a sexual orientation for loving women. So long as they have no prejudices against bodily organs, it's natural for us to reciprocate in love and sex. In a sexual relationship, the compatibility of positive (*yang*) and passive (*yin*) passion is the one thing that can remain strong and continue steadily. What I desire most are the gentlest, most passive women. I don't believe that my desire for, or union with, women is all that different from when a "man" wants a "woman."

I think that in true passion sex and love are one. I consider myself very lucky to have met you after Shuiyao. For me, someone whose sexual abilities and love have matured, you are truly someone I long for. It is an overpowering desire. The most positive life was strongly attracted by a passive life that took hold of her from the very first second, and the fire of mad love continued to burn till the third year. I ached for you every second and every minute, including the seven months in Paris. It wasn't at all a temporary passion like the night-blooming cereus flower. I can only be married to you and belong to you, or I absolutely can't be faithful to anyone. My passion is too strong and, if it weren't for you, I would be quickly tired of a person and live a life of abandonment out of dissatisfaction. Yes, there's no one else who could make my sex and love concentrated and pure to such an extent.

It's paradoxical that the person who needs to abandon herself to sexual gratification is often the one who can abstain from sex. Don Juan and a monk most likely are the same person. I can only remain chaste for you and give myself completely to you. I save myself for you because that's the way I love you. I need to love you so deeply and thoroughly. I don't know how to make you understand that my desire for you goes far beyond the satisfaction of being loved and sexual gratification. What I yearn for is the whole life, the union of body and soul. I long for more, "To find someone and then be absolute to this person." I've written this phrase in a previous letter and it's even more clear now—this is exactly what I want.

Where you were, you really didn't desire my body or feel like making love with me. Maybe you'd say that I've always been too "heavy" for you. It was probably even harder for you to stand me in Paris, as I wanted to be your lover twenty-four hours a day. Our differences in the expression of and demand for "passion" are the main reason why you couldn't live with me. Now I'm able to smile at this idea. Xiaoyong was even funnier when she said that in any case I've used you up so now you ran away. That's probably not so far from the truth. The degree of my passion and its expression was so high that even Xiaoyong couldn't take it. She's a very passionate person herself, but she also said that she could sense the strong desire inside me even though I didn't express it in front of her. Even she was overwhelmed by the pressure. Ai, she's pinpointed my problem, which was also the key issue that drove you away. You've often said I was too "heavy"; you said you wanted a less intense relationship. Every time I thought about this, I cannot help but hate myself, hate the traits in my personality, hate my overpowering passion and positive nature, hate my overwhelming longing and need for you, hate my strong desire to possess you, hate myself for being too male (and it's probably this hate that forces me to turn feminine), hate how my passion makes me ill and self-destruct so easily, hate how I suffer so easily, hate how my excessive demand toward you makes you nervous, suffocates and oppresses you . . . I hate how all these characteristics turn you away from me, as you can't stand me and don't want to be close to me. We lost our intimacy and you abandoned me and betrayed me. You didn't even want to look at me. When you were shouting on the phone, "I can't live with you," tears streamed down my face. If there's any hate, what I hate most is in fact myself.

P.S. I really lack the courage to confront all the details (the plot in a novel) concerning the sweetness and injuries of the past three years. The sweet sides were too wonderful while the injuries were too cruel. I went to see the movie *Landscape in the Mist* again yesterday. The little boy in the movie knelt in the center of the screen and wailed very sadly when he saw a donkey die. I cried my heart out with him, feeling as if I were the boy. I've truly become an innocent child who can cry so hard for the death of an animal . . . I walked out to Paris's magnificent evening wind with Baijing after the movie. She said the movie was so beautiful that she could die that night. I said, with someone who knew the beauty of that movie by my side, I could indeed die that night. Movies are like that, so is life, not to mention love, right?

I'm going to put this eleventh letter in my drawer, as I cannot face the details in it. I've reached the limit of the feeling that I can unearth and need to make you understand. As for our love, we'll save it for a better novel for the future, all right? I won't send it to you this time. J'arrive pas.

1996

Wang Anyi (1954–   )

GRANNY

Translated by Howard Goldblatt

Fu Ping showed up that afternoon at the house where Granny worked as a maid. Little girls were playing jump rope in the lane, creating a slight echo off the walls as their shoes scraped the concrete. Yellow rays of afternoon sun—it was three or four o'clock—shone brightly. The girls' skirts were beautiful in the light. Following the directions in Granny's letter, Fu Ping had walked to the gate at the end of the lane. Since it was open, she stood in the gateway, blocking the sun's rays. Some women were sitting by the compound footpath. She couldn't see their faces, but rays of light at their backs painted their silhouettes. One of them stood up. So, Fu Ping, you did come? Fu Ping said, Yes, Granny.

Granny was Li Tianhua's granny, but not by blood; she'd adopted him as a grandson. Back when the matchmaker had come to Fu Ping with a proposal, she'd stressed two points: first, Li Tianhua had attended middle school, and second, his granny was a housemaid in Shanghai. So even though Tianhua was the eldest in a large family, which kept them at the poverty level, it wasn't a hopeless case. Granny had been widowed early on and had no sons; her daughter was about to be married and become a member of someone else's family. That left an adopted grandson as her sole heir, and it was she who'd made it possible for him to attend middle school. Granny had come to Shanghai as a housemaid at the age of sixteen, thirty years before, long enough for her to be considered Shanghainese. She'd become an established nanny. Fu Ping, orphaned in childhood, and taken in by an uncle and aunt, placed great importance on her marriage prospects. Since it wouldn't have been right to speak directly to the subject, she had to be extremely vigilant. Whenever the matchmaker came to her door, she kept her head lowered; she wouldn't say yes and she wouldn't say no. If a suitor came to the house, she wouldn't show her face, spending the day at her girlfriend's house instead, and not coming home until whoever it was had left. Actually being taken to a suitor's houses was out of the question, so her aunt was forced to go alone. I can't delay the girl's marriage, she'd be thinking, or people might accuse her uncle and me of not caring enough about our niece's future. So when she returned home, she reported everything to Fu Ping: how the man had kind parents and well-behaved brothers and sisters, how the eldest of his younger sisters was already engaged, that the house was to be renovated the next year, and so on and so on. Still she wouldn't say yes and she wouldn't say no. But then, when Li Tianhua's name came up, that all changed. On the day he showed up, instead of hiding, she stayed to cook a meal and prepare tea. Looking out from under lowered eyelids, she saw a pair of black cloth slippers, held close together, not especially large, slightly narrow; the open fronts revealed white gauzy socks; the backs of the feet were on the high side. Those were not the feet of a man who tilled the fields, wide, archless feet made for standing in mud and water. She could tell he was not a man who made a living by the sweat of his brow. Before long, the matchmaker brought the betrothal gifts. In addition to the usual knitting wool, cotton fabrics, and colored threads, there was also some traveling money, which Granny had included so the girl could see the sights of Shanghai. And that was how Fu Ping arrived at the house where Granny worked.

Granny she may have been, but she looked younger than Fu Ping's aunt. Her hair was still black, and what appeared at first glance to be a receding hairline was actually a result of the way she tucked her bangs behind her ears. She wore a blue cotton jacket with long, looping buttons down the front and a stand-up collar. Granny lacked the fair complexion of most Shanghai residents, but didn't have the swarthy complexion of most country folk either; rather, her skin had a slight yellow cast. Since her face was full and round, the skin was taut, but not fine, no longer young, but not old—durable was more like it. Her hands, too, were like that: she had large knuckles, covered by skin that was starting to show its age. By this time, Granny had pretty much shed her hometown accent, but did not speak like a native Shanghainese. A hometown dialect with a Shanghai lilt. She maintained a healthy, erect posture, walking and sitting down, at the dinner table or at work; but when she bent at the waist, she rested on her haunches, legs apart, betraying signs of a country woman. Granny's features, too, were like that: sparse brows and pale eyes that weren't particularly noticeable on a woman from a privileged background, and she no longer looked like a country woman. But when she spoke, her lower lip protruded slightly, her upper lip hung back, exposing her teeth, and that look had a slight resemblance to one of those shrewish village women. A youthful injury in the corner of one eye had not left a scar, but did form a barely noticeable dimple at the tip. When she looked in a certain way, the dimple made her seem to be looking at something out of the corner of her eye, which invested her with a slightly shrewish charm. All in all, though she had lived in Shanghai for thirty years, Granny had not been transformed into a true urbanite, and yet she was no longer a rustic either; she was, instead, a hybrid—half urban, half rural. This half-and-half hybridity made her a special type. When she and women like her were out on the street, one look was all anyone needed to spot them for what they were: nannies.

Back home in the Yangzhou countryside, going into the cities as a nanny was a long-standing tradition. For some it was a lifetime occupation; for others a temporary job. Like Granny, there were women from various villages who'd lived in Shanghai for years and become full-fledged residents of the city. Most had been widowed while still young, or were married to shiftless or preposterous husbands, and had yet to bear a son. Such was the case with Granny. Bereft of family support, they were forced to be self-reliant. And the longer they were away from home, the less often they returned. And when they did, the visit was usually short-lived. They were no longer accustomed to their hometown environment, which normally led to bouts of diarrhea or rashes, and that sent them right back to Shanghai, often bringing along another woman or two, for whom they found work in a household. Sometimes they wrote letters home, urging one of the village women to come to Shanghai to find work. As time passed, a large number of country women were living and working in Shanghai, most in the same general area. Some employers were related or acquainted, and so they saw one another frequently, which made living away from home easier to get used to.

Granny had lived in Shanghai thirty years, virtually all that time on or near Huaihai Road in the flourishing Western District. Like all residents in a busy section of town, she viewed the quieter border sections as the wild countryside, when in fact those places, such as Zhabei and Putuo, were where people from her hometown had congregated, mostly as a result of wars or natural disasters, residents of Shanghai who had sailed down the Suzhou River. They found a spot of unclaimed land and threw up a rush tent, like the cabin of a boat, and moved in. Then it was off to the factories to find work. They constituted at least half of Shanghai's industrial workers. But Granny would not associate with those people. She had acquired the urbanite's prejudice of viewing Huaihai Road alone as the true Shanghai.

Working as a maid in Shanghai's Western District for decades, Granny had seen every type of person there was, and that made her a woman of broad experience. She once served a woman who played the old woman role in Shaoxing opera, and who was paid generous wages by the theater, while her husband was a plastic surgeon in private practice. Childless, they owned a large flat in a building reserved for foreigners, with an Indian doorman and an elevator operator who spoke English. And so Granny learned a few English phrases, like "good morning," "thank you," "come," "go," and the like. She wasn't expected to cook or do the laundry; her sole duty was to clean the carved mahogany furniture, with its mother-of-pearl inlays, with a feather duster. She didn't stay long, couldn't get used to the light work or the lack of human contact. Her next employer lived in a long lane at the eastern end of Huaihai Road. It was a pretty typical family, lots of children, where the husband, who worked in a bank on the Bund, was the sole breadwinner. She shared household duties with the wife, including looking after the children. The wife had a gaunt, sallow face and didn't dress well, giving the impression that *she* was the maid. Not a day passed that they didn't worry about the family finances, and they were often late with her wages. Granny hadn't been there long when the husband was diagnosed with TB and was confined to bed rest. Despite the woman's tearful pleas, she gave notice, not only giving up her last month's wages but even spending some of her own money to buy shirts and shorts for the children. Such a humiliating existence was not for her.

She'd also worked for a middle-class family in which husband and wife both worked and left their four children in her care. They were a loving couple; if anything, the husband was a little too cloying with his wife for Granny's tastes. He ordered a daily delivery of milk, which he warmed for her in the morning, and if she complained about the smell, he spoon-fed her. He was attentive to his wife at the expense of his children, who were drawn to Granny on the day she arrived. She liked them in turn, partly because they were so well behaved, yet she decided to give notice. She simply could not abide their father's nauseating behavior. Having lost her husband when she was quite young, she lived a chaste, widowed life, and was sensitive almost to a fault. But she hated to part with the children. Even after she went to work for another family, they often came to see her, and she introduced them to the children of her new employer as playmates, as friends.

The two families lived only a block apart, but the status of the new lane, with its apartment buildings, was a couple of rungs above the old one. The head of the family was a doctor; it was, by then, post-1949, so he'd closed his private clinic and now served as the head of a municipal hospital, traveling to and from work in a chauffeured automobile. He was a stern man who never once spoke to her nor ate at the same table with her. Yet he was actually the sort of man she held in high esteem, a dignified gentleman. His wife was a good woman as well, genial, generous, never cozying up to her husband in front of her or the children. If only the children hadn't been so insolent. The eldest, a girl, had barely started middle school and was already into modern fads—perms, brassieres, wearing her mother's nylons, and forever complaining that Granny ruined her clothes by scrubbing—a real young mistress. Her two brothers were a little better, but still haughty. They ignored the children of her former employer when they came to play, practicing the piano instead, always a fast number, while their visitors cowered off to the side, a sight that hurt Granny deeply. But they were, after all, children, who couldn't put on airs for long, and before long they were playing with their friends. One day, the husband came home early from work and noticed that someone else's children were playing in his house. He said nothing at the time, but later had his wife tell her to ask the children not to come anymore. Stung by this rebuff, a few days later she found an excuse to give notice. It wasn't that status meant nothing to her, but she had her pride, and could not abide arrogance in anyone.

She fit in quite nicely in Shanghai's circle of nannies, and was so self assured that she chose her families, they did not choose her. And she was firm in her insistence to work only on Huaihai Road in the Western District, and only for native Shanghainese. She would never have considered working for those speakers of the Shandong dialect who came south to work for the government. Someone had once recommended her as a nanny to an army commander in a Hongkou military compound. She went to take a look; though the promised salary was high, she chose not to take the job. The family lived in a sparsely furnished flat, with polished hardwood floors and a set of sofas against the wall, like a government office conference room. The large kitchen had clean pots and pans, and a cold stove. Not even water was boiled there; soldiers brought over boiled water from a communal vat. The family ate in not one but several dining halls, the commander in one, his wife—also in the military—in another, and the children in yet a third. Not what you'd call normal family life, and certainly not for her. She did not care for military surroundings in general, not for normal families, at least. So she walked out of the compound under an expanse of open sky, onto an expanse of open road. Not another person in sight, nor a single house—a bleak and dreary scene. Who can possibly live in a hellish place like that? she fussed. Back in the countryside we have ponds with ducks and geese, and farmers and their oxen in the field. She walked on until she neared a village, with chimney smoke and clucking hens and swallows coming from up north to nest. She gazed into the distance, where she saw one brick house after another. The coarse red bricks, fired only once, were porous and less solid than the green ones; but the red created a bewitching contrast to the lush green of the surrounding willows. Granny was reminded of all the colors in her home in the countryside. A passing army truck threw up a cloud of dust that coated her body and her face.

Her homesickness had weakened by the time she was back in the vicinity of North Sichuan and Haining Roads, where the streets narrowed again and shops, pedestrians, trolleys, and automobiles began to appear. Gazing down the lane, she saw laundry drying and children playing games, and she smelled a bit of cooking oil wafting in the air. Here was a life she understood better. The high-rises in Hongkou had been so tall. Little balconies with black wrought-iron railings hanging on red brick walls made those walls look especially large, broad, and steep. The lanes, too, were broad and large, and quite grand. But the terraces had an oppressive quality, and the residents were a jumbled lot, even in appearance, which led to a repellent feeling, overshadowing the occasional attractive individual; that was something she couldn't get used to. As she walked across the Haining Road Bridge, at the widest stretch of the Suzhou River, she saw a congested cluster of ships sailing toward her from far upstream. The stench rising from the river was unpleasant, that and the dampness carried on the wind, and she did not feel totally at ease until she was back on Huaihai Road; when the new-style, relatively squat, shallow houses came into view, she looked all the way to the end of the narrow lane, which twisted and turned, its storefronts crowded up against each other on nicely proportioned byways. There were high-rises, but not like those at Hongkou, which had the fortified look of the Central Post Office; the lobbies of the high-rises here were only as wide as single shops. Inside, an elevator rose and fell in view of people outside, and sunlight streamed in through a stained-glass window above the landing of the marble staircase beside the elevator. The elevator operator and the doorman were engaged in small talk, a word or two of their conversation reaching her ears as she passed. The street bustled with pedestrians, but they were orderly, locals for the most part, which is why it wasn't all jumbled. Everything was on a smaller scale here, and the frequent greetings could only occur in a residential area. The locals simply looked good, genteel, unlike the Hongkou residents, who were sort of gruff. The locals knew how to dress but were not slaves to fashion; precisely because they were familiar with the modern world, they were more staid, somewhat conservative even.

Granny walked along, no longer homesick. As we saw earlier, she'd taken on the attitude of city residents, including their prejudices. Could anyone say she wasn't one of them? She was more familiar with the city than some of the local youngsters. Listen to her relate all the strange things she'd seen and heard, things you could not make up. Plenty from this street alone. Like the child-slapping abductor, which is to say, someone slapped a child, who got all turned around, until all he could see was the street in front of him, and he walked off with the person, right out of sight. Then there was the story of the ghost that screamed in the middle of the night, and for this there was a name attached, that of a certain old lady from one of the lanes, who heard it every night for a full half year, and then died. And the man who ran off with his housemaid, and the woman who murdered her husband, and so on. And she knew lines from lots of plays: "The New Year's Sacrifice," "Wang Kui and Mu Guiying," "The Butterfly Lovers," "Third Sister Yang on a Bed of Nails," most of the lines coming from popular local plays or Shaoxing opera. She could even sing a few of them! You can believe me or not, that's up to you, but she had even seen Hollywood movies. Charlie Chaplin, for instance, she knew who he was. And she said his name like an American: "Chap-lin." But she didn't much like American movies, mainly because of the happy endings; she preferred tragedies. The mere mention of one of those sad plays had her in tears. Every child in her care had heard her tell stories in a manner perfectly suited to their young ears. She saw no need to faithfully follow the story line, preferring to hop from spot to spot, an episode here and an incident there, but always with powerful atmospherics. She specialized in exaggerated tales of terror and misery. In retelling "The New Year's Sacrifice," she focused on the scene where Xiang Lin's wife buys a threshold at the temple to avoid having her two husbands cleave her in half in the nether regions. In "Wang Kui and Mu Guiying" it was the episode where Mu Guiying reclaims her spirit, and in "The Butterfly Lovers" it was the final scene, where the graves split open. The episode from "Third Sister Yang on a Bed of Nails" was particularly horrific. The children, their faces turned ashen from fright, would crowd around to listen and to tremble, and to beg her over and over: One more, tell us one more.

Sometimes Granny would tell stories from her home in the country. They too were horror stories, but another kind of horror, the rural kind. Filtered through Granny's rural view of the world, they incorporated bewitching elements, and were not always simple and straightforward, which is why they sounded a bit like stage plays, full of color. One told of a beautiful bride in a phoenix headdress and embroidered cape, riding to her new home in a sedan chair; when she raises her head and looks behind her with a grimace, a demon's face appears. And with that she brings ill fortune into a farmer's home. There was also the story of the little demon incarnate. All the offspring of a certain couple died in infancy, never later than their first birthday, to the desperate consternation of their parents. Then one day a soothsayer advised them to cut the toes off the next child to be born so he could not walk to the door. They decided to take his advice: With the scissors poised to cut off his toes, the latest infant abruptly opened his eyes—they were the eyes of a grown-up! This was the story's terrifying climax. Then there was the story of the dying man who spotted generals sent by King Yama of Hell, carrying chains to lead him away. Granny made the rattling of the chains and the clanking of the weapons horrifying yet impressive, investing her tale with the vibrancy of a martial arts contest.

Those stories were all linked to Granny's own past. Widowed at a young age, mother of two sons who had died one after the other, she accepted her lot as a woman fated to suffer, someone with a tough karma, destined to be self-reliant. After years of domestic work she had accumulated some savings, but not enough for loans or handouts to a host of kin. Loans were no more than handouts that sounded a little nicer; the money never found its way back. How many people she carried on her back! Her daughter told her that her future husband wanted to attend high school, at her expense; her nephew was studying acting with a county drama troupe, room and board supplied for the first three years, and she had to help pay for his clothes; her younger sister's husband was stricken with cholera and had an operation—again, her money. Now her grandson was talking about getting married, at her expense, of course.

When she'd decided to adopt a grandson, the old Shanghai women had tried to talk her out of it. Now she was his meal ticket, but would the day come when he'd take care of her? He was just one more person with his eyes on her savings. The family she worked for had also urged her not to do it, saying she was better off holding on to her own money. They'd even taken her to a bank to open a savings account; then when people came for a handout, she could tell them it was in the bank and had to stay there until the account matured. But she went ahead with the adoption anyway. The so-called grandson was in reality the son of her late husband's older brother. Her own daughter was to be married this year, and when that happened, the family house would be claimed by her brother-in-law. But with a grandson, even though the place would belong to her family, it'd also be her house. When she was too old to work, she'd return to the countryside and move in, as reason dictated. To plan for that day, she cleverly arranged for her daughter to marry a nephew in her elder brother's family. That way, if her adopted grandson turned his back on her, her elder brother would have to take her in. Even after working in Shanghai for three decades and acquiring a Shanghai resident's card, she had no choice but to plan a return to the countryside, and that was why she was willing to lend money, even give it away; the grateful recipients would never abandon her. For a while, rumors of an affair between her future son-in-law and a classmate reached her ears from the countryside, so she asked someone to write a letter to ask him if it was true. He wrote back: "If you drink from the well, don't forget the well digger." She knew this came from the mouth of her son-in-law, but it struck a chord in her heart anyway. Wasn't she herself a well-digger?

2000

Alai (1959–)

FISH!

Translated by Howard Goldblatt

Owing to a minor illness, I stayed in the town of Tanggor to rest and do some writing for three days. A few doses of anti-inflammatory medicine put me back on my feet, and my three companions circled round to pick me up. Once we were back on the road, our Jeep headed west alongside the Yellow River. The morning sun glinted off of our reflectors. The rumble of the engine and the vibrations of the tires on the smooth highway traveled up to my hands through the steering wheel, and I felt my strength returning. After we'd driven some forty or fifty kilometers, the road veered off the broad grassy riverbank and began to climb.

I stopped halfway up a hill to turn the wheel over to our assigned driver.

Everyone climbed out of the Jeep, stretched, and squinted as we all aimlessly took in our surroundings. The town we'd just left had nearly disappeared in the deepest part of the prairie, the distance giving it an aura of beauty it didn't really possess. The bright sunshine lent slight warmth to the broad, gently flowing river at the foot of the hill. We sat on the ground, a soft rustle emerging from the autumn grass around us. That was the sound of the last thin layer of frost evaporating. The air was saturated with the fragrance of drying grass. After a cigarette break, we stood up, brushed the crushed grass off the seats of our pants, and were about to set out, when the rotund rump of a sleek-skinned animal lumbered into view. It was a giant marmot heading back to its dry mountain den after drinking from the river. The thick autumn grass parted as it made its way up the hill, and then closed behind it. I fetched my small-bore rifle from the car, took aim at the swaying movements of the inviting rump, and fired. The explosion flew off into the distance on the sun's rays, the fresh, stirring smell of gunpowder filling our nostrils. The marmot vanished without a trace, and I thought I'd hit it. But there was no blood at the spot where it had leaped at the sound before disappearing.

We climbed back into the Jeep and headed down the hill, continuing along the broad, grassy banks of the Yellow River until noon, when we started up another incline, where we stopped for lunch. On a big piece of army canvas, we laid out bottles of beer, some beef jerky, and some hardtack we'd bought at a Muslim café in a prairie town. Then, after eating our fill, we indulged in the languid pleasure of simply lying in the dry autumn grass. Warm, clean rays of sunlight from high in the boundless blue sky washed down on our hair, eyes, and bodies, like a special kind of bath. As windblown grass gently caressed our faces and hands, we felt as soft and spongy, body and soul, as the rich prairie soil beneath us. Crisscrossing streams at the foot of the hill fed placid bogs here and there, their watery surfaces glinting in the sunlight. They looked every bit as warm and as yielding as our sun-drenched bodies.

Inexplicably, I had a vision of the fish swimming lazily in all that water.

The ridges of their backs were black, their bellies light yellow. They made no sound as they hung suspended tranquilly beneath the surface, like dreamy shadows. Lacking scales on their bodies, they were known as naked carp. In the early nineteenth century, the Zoige and other local prairies were known collectively as the Songpan Prairie, and the fish were called Songpan naked carp. While I lay there lost in thought, my companions took fishing line, hooks, and bait out of the trunk of the Jeep Cherokee. As with rifles and ammunition, these are essential items for travel on the prairie.

We four had been sent out as a religious survey team, but were taking a break to get in some hunting and fishing. Two of my companions decided to head up the hill to hunt wild rabbits and marmots, leaving Gongpo Tashi and me to fish in the river.

Fishing was definitely the wrong assignment for me.

Water burials are common out on the prairie. Water and the fish that swim in it relieve the soul of its mortal body, which is why many Tibetans consider fish taboo. For this trip, I'd taken along a book sent to me by Professor Dhondup Wangbum of the Central Institute of Nationalities. Included in this book on popular Tibetan taboos and nature worship was a discussion of the taboo against catching and eating fish. The author wrote that in traditional rituals for exorcising ghosts and other unclean entities, it is essential to direct the incantations at invisible malevolent objects, driving them off of dry land, out of places of abode, and away from the depths of the heart straight into water. As a result, fish are a repository for inauspicious entities. Of course, I'd witnessed such rituals of exorcism and incantation, but had never linked them to the taboo against fish. And while the Tibetan tradition of neither catching nor eating fish has a long history, in the second half of the twentieth century, we began eating fish, and I confess that I am one of those fish-eating Tibetans. Still, what others describe as the mouthwatering tenderness of fish seems somehow rancid in my mouth.

And so, today's division of labor could not have been less appropriate.

The two Han Chinese, for whom the taboo against fish did not exist, picked up their rifles and began climbing at a crouch, the hilly expanse opening up ahead of them, while I followed Tashi down to the riverbank. The grassy ground at our feet rose and fell unevenly, since the prairie actually served as a covering for marshy earth below. Although the sky was so clear I could see for miles around, the bumpy ground and the menacing gurgles from the mud below unnerved this first-time fisherman.

Ever fished before? Tashi asked.

I shook my head. I was about to ask him the same thing. There was a hard edge to his obvious disappointment as he said, Well, I thought you had!

I didn't ask why he'd thought that, of course, since in the eyes of so many of my sinicized countrymen, I'm a bit more sinicized than they are, simply because I write in Chinese. Now that we were about to become fishermen, he must have assumed that I was more experienced than he.

Honest? Tashi asked again. You've never fished?

I shook my head vigorously.

He thrust the can of bait into my hand. Then I'm going hunting with the others. His powerful frame nearly flew across the grassy bank, nimbly yet with obvious reserves of strength, crossing one marshy spot and one little stream after another. The way he ran could make you swear he could race a cheetah if he had to. But now he'd placed all that power in the service of escape.

I stopped alongside a stream.

This particular stream was so shallow that the sun's rays dappled the riverbed. The banks were covered with red and white saw grass floating on the surface of the water. Shifting sand on the bottom, and not the water itself, produced a constant murmur. It was not a wide stream; in fact, it was squeezed so tightly at this spot that I could easily jump across it. I broke off a willow branch, tied on a line and some hooks, and was ready to fish.

What nearly stopped me was baiting the hooks. I opened the jar, and there, squirming in the rich black dirt and green leaves, were fat worms as thick as my pinkie. When I picked one up and pinched it in two, sticky muck oozed out, a mixture of red and green, and stuck to my fingers. Since the line came with two hooks, after baiting the first, I had to do it again—once I'd wiped my hands clean on the grass, that is. I heaved a sigh of relief after the second hook was baited; by then, my forehead was beaded with sweat.

I cast my line in what I thought was practiced style. Unfortunately, the stream was so narrow that the hooks and the worms impaled on them, plus a small lead weight, carried the line whistling over to the opposite bank, where it landed in the grass. Then, in jerking the pole back, I lost one of my worms, which meant I had to kill yet another one. With rising disgust, I watched as its sticky juices soiled my fingers again. The stuff was dark green, with some bright red spots. The color was less offensive after I put on my sunglasses. This time the hooks landed in the water, and I watched as the bait slithered through one dappled beam of sunlight after another before coming to rest on the clear bottom. Then it followed the sand drifting downstream. Tossing my army knapsack, with its bait, hooks, and what have you, over my shoulder, I followed the progress of the worms.

In the flow of the water, the worms quickly disintegrated; the gooey insides were the first to go, leaving behind shreds of pale skin, until they too floated off. That brought an end to the material essence of worm. Every couple of hundred meters, as I made my way downstream, I had to stop to re-bait my hooks. By the fifth or sixth time, I managed to calmly and casually pinch the worms and impale them on the hooks, causing hardly any distress, from my hands all the way up to my heart.

Two crisp gunshots from the far-off hill rocketed past me, hugging the ground as if they were the actual bullets. Even at that distance, I could see my companions running up the hill in the wake of the echoing gunshots. My hooks settled heavily in the water, the thin sound of shifting pebbles whispering in my ears. The last drops of moisture on the autumn grass hissed softly as they turned to mist. The water tugged gently at my line, the light quivers of the pole traveling down to my hand. The willow branch was rough on the skin, so I switched it to my other hand, and immediately felt the lingering heat from the sun. My companions had split up and were now making their way through the underbrush. Obviously, their shots had missed their target, allowing the marmot to return safely to its home. A moment later, green smoke curled skyward, the three men slipping in and out of the haze. They must have been choking as they stood around the opening trying to fan smoke down into the marmot's lair, hoping that would drive it out of its underground maze. But marmots build complex underground palaces, and even if this particular one had somehow neglected to equip its palace with ventilation tunnels, fanning smoke into a series of underground tunnels is a time-consuming process. Professional hunters always take air-blowers along with them. But not my companions, who were surely suffering more from their own smoke than the marmot ever would. At least where hunting land animals is concerned, I had plenty of experience.

Fishing was another matter altogether.

Suddenly I felt a tug. My heart skipped a beat. A fish? I looked down at the water. No longer lying on the bottom, the hooks and weight had been carried by the current to a spot not far from where I was standing, where the water formed a sizeable whirlpool. A noise like that of an ox being slaughtered rose from the whirlpool, the death rattle emerging from deep in its throat. It was a sound I sometimes heard from one of the city sewers. My hook had been sucked into the whirlpool, and when I tugged on the line, it tugged back.

Fish!

Enlightened lamas of the True Word sect once told me that when they are alone in their meditation chambers they have visions of a gleaming Tibetan word or some other image. I'd never been a True Word devotee, but the word *fish* streaked through my head, minus the gleam.

Fish! The word was swathed in the sticky sleek grayness of a scale-less body that, for some strange reason, instilled terror in me.

I heard myself blurt out the word, less from happiness than from amazement: Fish!

Just then a hulking fish broke the surface and whipped its glistening, watery body in the air; at the moment it left the life-sustaining water, it seemed caught up in feverish joy. Once I loosened my grip, the fish landed in the grass, and the watery sheen on its body vanished, replaced by a sticky sleek grayness. It was a color pregnant with misgivings. The closer I got to the fish, the stronger my sense of decay.

This was the first fish I'd ever caught.

Now that it was out of the water, it lay in the grass without moving. I knew that removing the hook would be a grisly process, and didn't dare look into the fish's sad bulging eyes. I gazed up into the sky instead, and as scattered puffy clouds floated in my eyes, I picked it up. It slipped right out of my hand. I don't know if that was because the fish put up a fight, or because its illusory slipperiness made me open my hand. It lay on its side in the grass, its mouth opening and closing frantically. Bloody froth gathered at the corners. The look of sadness in eyes that still somehow showed that it was resigned to its fate grew faint. Dropping the fish, of course, meant that I had to pick it up out of the grass again; this time I squeezed it so hard, its sharp fin cut my palm, and as I removed the hook from deep in its throat, its watery blood mixed with the thick blood from my cut hand.

Having watched other people fish out on the prairie, I knew that I ought now to snap off a flexible willow twig and thread it through one of the gills and out the mouth. That way I could string together all my fish, making it easy to carry the day's catch home. But all I'd really wanted to do was catch *a* fish on the prairie, not a whole string of them. That was why I'd been drawn to this shallow stream. Not far off, a river worthy of the name raised whitecaps as it rushed along.

Now the problem was, I'd caught a fish in my shallow stream without even trying! That was the last thing in the world I'd desired.

After re-baiting the hooks, I walked back and gazed at the spot where the fish had emerged. I saw nothing out of the ordinary. A little eddy, that's all, with the death rattle of the slaughtered ox vanishing into the grass at my feet. I stomped down hard, and the grass rustled briefly before returning to its stony silence. With surprising accuracy, I cast my hooks directly into the whirlpool. The bait made a few turns on the surface before sinking to the bottom.

It had no sooner disappeared from sight than my hand felt as if it had been stung, and the pole nearly flew out of my hand. Instinctively, I jerked it back, raising a raucous little geyser in the water. Another fish soared heavily through the air, and as it passed over my head in the sun's glare, its belly turned from the jaundiced yellow of earth to a blinding golden color. The shout that escaped from my lips could have been one of fright and could have been one of joy. This time the fish was separated from the hook in its mouth as it flew through the air and landed in the grass. It was lying there without moving by the time I reached it. The glare in its bulging eyes sent chills down my spine.

I returned to my spot alongside the stream and cast my hook. A fish took the bait almost immediately.

In hardly any time at all, I pulled a dozen fish out from under that whirlpool, one right after the other. They looked like a group of young adults, all the same age. I gazed down at them strewn across the grassy ground, and then turned to look at the marshy bogs around me, silent except for an occasional air bubble breaking the surface. I had the uneasy feeling that I was conspiring in the death wish of hordes of fish that had gathered in the same unlikely spot. A conspiracy! But this thought zoomed out of my head through a force of will. If I'd let it settle in, I might never have another chance to break free from the cultural taboo against fish.

We act so as not to have to stop and think about what we're doing.

My activity on this day was to cast baited hooks into a little pool (I'm convinced that a small but deep pool lay hidden beneath the stream's grassy covering), wanting to see how many stupid fish were waiting to fling themselves into the jaws of death. In the autumn fish settle low in the water, fat and lazy, and greedily swallow baited hooks all the way down to their stomachs. I turned to look at the fish lying lazily in the grass, waiting to die, and a strange mixture of loathing and fear surged inside me.

Inexplicably, I added another hook to the line and baited all three. They drifted slowly out to the center and were sucked down into the pool that may or may not have existed. I took a few deep breaths to calm myself. At the same time, I tried to imagine the bait slowly settling in the seemingly bottomless stream, floating in front of a fish suspended motionless in the water. Somewhat disappointed, the bait continued its way down into the darker water. With thoughts of that descent, I felt myself get lighter, as if *I* were floating; the surrounding darkness frightened me. But just as I was about to take my line out of the water, a fish pounced on the bait. Why, I wondered, had it attacked the bait so ferociously? Even if it was seeking death, there was no need to try so hard. It swallowed the bait and the hook hidden within it, then stopped moving and went still. I waited. A second fish took another hook, and then lay suspended calmly in the water, no fight in it, and no desire to escape death.

The third piece of bait went un-swallowed.

Knowing I'd feel it if another fish bit, I turned to take a leisurely look at my companions on the distant hill, still pointlessly trying to smoke out the marmot.

The smoke had thinned out, so apparently they'd abandoned their futile labor and had begun digging at the hole with an army-issue hoe we'd brought with us. If anything, this was even harder work, since the marmot's underground lair would begin a meter or so underground and then twist and snake along another hundred meters or two.

By all appearances a dull animal, the marmot is actually quite clever; by all appearances spry and responsive, these fish were unimaginably dull when confronted with a baited hook. See what I mean—a fish bit on the third hook! The pole bent nearly in half when I raised all three fish out of the water, and as they struggled, they all but pulled the pole into the stream. Their struggles were intended to return them to the water; that was something I could not agree to. With a shout and a mighty tug, I brought all three down onto the grass at my feet.

I took careful note as they stopped struggling the moment they hit the ground.

In fact, I took careful note of every facet of these fish, my prey. And not just careful note, but extremely careful note, with extreme sensitivity. I even took extremely careful and sensitive note of things that didn't exist.

At that moment, I took note of the cessation of struggle the moment the fish landed on the grassy ground. Some lay so close to the water that all they had to do was arch their backs, stiffen their bodies, and execute a flip any fish could manage to return to the stream. As the prairie turns a golden color, and the water begins to chill, flocks of migratory birds take wing. The fish, like a fleet of submarines, descend to the bottom of the stream, where there is little light but the water is warmer. As winter approaches, light is equated with freezing. But these fish, caught in the depths of the stream, now lay motionless in the grass, as if unaware that safety, that life itself, was so close. They lay there motionless, as if their deaths would test the limits of their killer's ability to justify his own actions. I was fishing that day in order to master myself. In this world we are often given incitements of many types, and mastering oneself is one of them. Mastering weaknesses in temperament, mastering a shyness or a fear of facing the unknown, mastering cultural or individual taboos. We then become unstoppable. I was now on my way to such mastery, and I wanted my companions to share in this moment. So I began waving my arms and shouting.

They stopped their laborious digging, straightened up, and stared in my direction. I picked up a fish and waved it in the air, shouting the whole time. They were a good two kilometers away, too far for them to see the fish in my hand, but I thought the sun glinting off its body would catch their attention. The sleek body did in fact glint in the sun's rays. The men were standing on the top of a little hill staring down at me, peaked rain clouds gathering in the sky at their backs. Lightning flashed from the clouds' dark, menacing centers, the sun adding a dazzling gold inlay to their edges. As thunder rumbled, the clouds moved eastward, toward us. Gusty breezes swept across the surface of the stream. The autumn grass, once standing proud, began to droop. And the wind caught my fishing line, which then formed a beautiful arc.

Another fish took a hook.

Deep down, I hoped it was the last one.

But then another one bit. Once again, I hoped it was the last one, but I had no illusions, knowing there were plenty of fish down there in some secret spot prepared to come looking for death. I was right—a third fish was now on my line!

When the three fish left the water, they put up a brief, symbolic struggle before lying motionless on the grass with the others. With all those dying fish on the ground around me, even though the sun was shining, relatively mild gusts of wind sent chills through me.

I shouted at my companions again, wanting them to bring their stuff down the hill to gather up all my fish. I couldn't wait to leave the bank of this stream. How could there be so many big fish in such a little bit of water? It seemed to me as if they were taking the hooks faster and faster. I followed each new catch with a series of shouts to my companions.

The dark clouds overhead caught me by surprise. By this time, I was baiting my hooks and taking the fish out of the water like a machine, not because I was a greedy fisherman but because there were so many fish queuing up to die. I already knew there were lots of people in this world who had given up on life, but I hadn't realized that fish could also have a death wish. They wore the look of disciples of some evil cult, wanting to place the responsibility for taking their lives on others.

The loathing I felt was on the rise.

The roiling black clouds quickly formed an arch above me, turning the surface of the water dark and dreary. I must have worn a fiendish look as I flung my baited hooks into the little whirlpool. When the flowing water turned as dark and menacing as the rain clouds overhead, the spot began to look like the entrance to Hell. The fish continued to ardently take the path to death.

My companions made their way slowly down the hill, stepping carefully around the boggy spots. Not because of rumors that if you stepped in the wrong place, your foot would be sucked into the quicksand-like mud, and you would be pulled under, but because these citified country boys were afraid of soiling their nice shoes in the sticky, stinky mud.

My feelings of isolation and fear increased.

Thunder rumbled overhead. Winds that were growing stronger tore at my hair and my clothes; they also churned up the surface of the water. Large raindrops pelted me in the face. I opened my mouth to shout, but the wind drove the air right back down my throat. Meanwhile, the fish kept lining up, more than ever. How bizarre! This is incredible! The grinning god of death has shown his true colors! I heard myself say through clenched teeth, Come on, you fuckers!

I heard myself say tearfully, Come on, you fuckers, I'm not afraid of you!

I heard myself say, Don't tell me you're not afraid too! I'm afraid, but if you're not, then come on!

Just as I was about to go over the edge, it ended, not because there were no more fish in the pool, but because the tin bait box was empty. I slumped down on the ground, dejected, and let go of my fishing pole, which was carried off by the water. I might have been crying, I don't know, because the crackling thunder overhead covered all other sounds. Then it was the noise of an enormous rain cloud overhead crashing down on me. Then, no more thunder and no more lightning, at least not for the time being. The heaviness of dusk surrounded me. My companions and the prairie were wiped off the face of the earth. I couldn't even hear the wind. Oppressive darkness everywhere. And a terrifying calm. Autumn grass that only moments before had bent before the wind sprang up noisily. Then I heard a deep gurgle, sort of like the cooing of pigeons. But I knew at once it wasn't the sound of pigeons, it was . . . it was the fish!

The fish were shouting!

I'd never known that fish could do that!

But I was immediately aware that they were shouting! A strained, low sound: *Gurgle, gurgle.* Not the cries of pigeons, but a heart-stopping sound like that of stepping on a rotting piece of leather. When you step on leather like that, it's as if you're walking on a corpse. At that moment, all those half-dead fish were calling out. Staring with those damned eyes that never close and opening wide their thirsty mouths, they strained to gulp down the moist air saturated with the heavy odor of gunpowder. They gulped down a breath and then opened their mouths: *Gurgle.* Another breath and their mouths opened again: *Gurgle.*

All those ugly fish strewn across the grassy ground, first one opening its mouth—*gurgle*—then another—*gurgle.*

I didn't want to think what it would be like if it hadn't rained, so I sat there motionless. The cloud pushed the sky down low. I was afraid I might bump into it if I stood up, or be struck by a coil of lightning snaking through the roiling black cloud. Another crack of thunder made the ground beneath me lurch upward, followed by a torrent of rainwater mixed with sleet, as if dumped on my head from an enormous leather pouch. Stabs of pain restored my normal feelings.

When the sleet turned into a routine rainfall, I lay down on my belly and gratefully let it wash over me. It felt to me that I was having a good cry, something no one else would witness, and that even I might not completely understand. To this day, I don't know if my tears had mastered me or if I was crying because I had mastered myself. Or if I was crying over other things I should have cried over but hadn't.

Very quickly, a western wind began pushing back the black cloud, with its vast energy and abundant supply of water. The sun reappeared in the sky above all living creatures. Warmth slowly returned to my frozen body.

My three companions finally made it to where I was waiting.

They walked around picking up my catch and putting it into a willow basket, which, crammed full, required two men to carry it. When I pointed out for them the little whirlpool hidden beneath the floating grass, they refused to believe that all those fish could have come from that one spot. We changed out of our wet clothes in the Jeep; the smell of dry clothes, plus the car odors of plastic and gasoline, made me feel safe. Once we were back on the road, I turned to look at my fishing hole. With so many streams flowing across the prairie and glinting in the sunlight, I couldn't be sure which of them was the one where that improbable encounter had taken place. You see, before a person even takes leave of a spot where something has occurred, that event has already vanished into nothingness.

2000

Chun Sue (1983–)

BORN AT THE WRONG TIME

Translated by Howard Goldblatt

SCHOOL

> No recess.
> You're in high school again.
>
> —*Nirvana, "School"*

West X High, the school I tried so hard to leave, and feared I never could. In my two and a half years of wallowing there, I felt like I was using up every ounce of energy and passion I had. Even up to the day I knew that I never again had to go back, it still invaded my dreams, turned them into nightmares.

I pushed my bike into the school yard on the first day of class and was immediately confronted by two class monitors, one named Li, the other called Big-Belly Wang. They were smiling, but I could see it was all an act, like maybe they were inspecting troops. "Hey, there, student. Take your bicycle outside and come back in again!" Big-Belly Wang said. What'd I do? Totally puzzled, I pushed my bike out the gate and watched to see how the other students entered: They all bowed to the teachers and greeted them with "How do you do, teachers!" The monitors "kindly" returned the bows. The two of them, a man and a woman, had mastered the imperial wave of national leaders, quite a pair. I got the picture. Swallowing my anger and embarrassment, 1 pushed my bike back inside. "How do you do, teachers!" They smiled. "Good morning." I was so goddamned disgusted I felt like puking.

The tuition there was high—thirteen hundred RMB—and with all the added fees, it came to nearly two thousand, which was a lot more than I'd paid for three years of middle school. The tuition was so damned high that I made up my mind to work hard at my studies. Brave words welled up inside me, and sort of hung around for a moment, before slipping away.

The morning and midday inspections during the first month were devoted to studying school regulations, a long-standing tradition. Every first-year student was given a twenty-four-page pamphlet, no exception, which we studied in the mornings and were tested on at midday. Its full title was "Beijing West X Vocational High School Rules of Student Governance," and it was divided into eleven chapters—Instruction, Character Standards, Proper Behavior, Classroom Study, Classroom Activity, Hygiene, Personal Property, Attendance, Student Status, Progress Awards, Discipline—plus the following appendices: (1) Evaluation and Selection of Outstanding Class, "Three Good" Students, and Outstanding Cadres; (2) Evaluation of Students' Daily Behavior; and (3) Evaluation of Classes' Daily Behavior.

The professional standards for Foreign Affairs PR Copy Secretary majors were:

Observe discipline and guard secrets; maintain good, positive work habits; greet others with a smile; be dignified and appropriate in appearance; and be refined and poised in behavior.

Possess complete mastery of vocational abilities: coherent, intelligible verbal skills; cordial, genial PR skills; ability to write practical, smooth official documents; relatively good English conversational skills; proficiency with machinery (including Chinese and English typing); relatively accomplished penmanship and calligraphy; and basic filing and stenographic skills.

Upon graduation, the following certificates would be awarded: General Secretarial, Typing, and Word Processing.

There was even a poem about proper behavior patched together by someone in the school's leadership, maybe by Principal Pan, who was an outstanding specimen:

Manner and looks crucial, you must know how.
Four rhyming-word codes, let's hear them now.
Sit proper legs crossed, knees ready to kowtow.
Stand squarely stretch tall, no jelly-bellied sow.
Stride steadily and strong, straight like a plow.
Face earthy and clean, do not paint your brow.
Nice natural hair style, not some furry chow.
Warmly cordial to others, say hello and bow.
Speak genially and softly, smile and say ciao.
Good to associate with, never cause any row.
Think pure noble thoughts, lofty goals a vow.
Be cultivated and polite, meek like a meooow.
Elegant and eternally poised, don't have a cow.

There were, in addition, the following absolutely incomprehensible regulations: No visiting other classrooms (Classroom Activity Regulation 7); Students from other schools may not wait for local students outside the school yard, and if they are caught, the students they are waiting for will be punished (Classroom Activity Regulation 11); Students must eat lunch at school, and may not go outside to buy food (same as above); Students who wish to go home for lunch must bring a note from their parents, who must make themselves aware of the students' lunch-hour activities (same as above); Students who go home for lunch must arrange for a special pass to be shown at the gate when leaving and reentering (same as above). Then there were slogans like "Neatness Is Discipline." No loitering in the hallways, no mail sent to school, no outside books; even missing class with cause or for sickness led to grade deductions. There were monthly schoolwide exams and no makeups. . . .

But the workload was light, and there was little homework. The first year in high school is supposed to be pretty relaxed, a time to enjoy life. And the pressure of exams is even lower in vocational high schools. Everything's always easy at first. There were, however, two courses that drove us nuts: Etiquette, and Posture and Fitness. Principal Pan personally taught the etiquette course. If you stared at her ghostly pale face long enough, she looked like an animal—a fox. For the P & F class, we had to wear tight gym suits, and there was never enough time between classes to change in and out of them. We hated it.

MY FIRST-YEAR CLASS (SECTION 6)

My life during that first year was a series of new beginnings. The time just flew by. There was more going on than I could deal with. The air in the western suburbs was clean, the sky blue every day, like silver. My class monitor was wonderful to me because I gained a reputation as a good student—I wrote poems, I painted, I studied, I organized activities, and I was determined to work hard and not waste my three years here, since I was intent on getting into the school of my dreams—Beida, Peking University. After the last two classes were over in the afternoons, I, along with my friend Xie Sini and some other girls, rode home on our bikes. It was autumn, Beijing's golden season. When the weather was fine and the air clean, outlines of the distant mountains sprang into view, and we sang Shen Qing's song: "A blue, blue sky above the red, red sun . . . " A distant, youthful joy enveloped us. It was like the brief honeymoon that launches a long marriage. Compared to the days that followed, this was the golden period of my entire school life.

Whenever I had the time, I went over to Beida or the Haidian Book City. Beida. Beautiful. That's it in a nutshell. Xie Sini said it was like a park. "It's much prettier than a park," I said proudly. At the time, Beida was even prettier than it had been when I visited it in the autumn of my third year in middle school. There was an exhibition of photographs by the Mountain Eagle Society, plus all kinds of charity sales and recruiting booths for clubs. Once again, I felt as clearly as was humanly possible that if I belonged to Beida (I no longer entertained the thought that Beida would belong to me), I would be unbelievably happy.

There were only twenty-seven students in my class, twenty-two of them girls. Five boys in a class was the lowest ratio in the school. But these five were special—they were active, funny, and they could talk a blue streak. And they all had a touch of melancholy.

We paid 120 RMB for lunch and got a card. Not the meal cards you got in college, the kind you swiped, but thin pieces of paper that a member of the student association checked each time you used it. And if you forgot yours, well, tut-tut, no food for you, and don't blame the school leadership. The one thing you didn't want to do was act put out and remind them that everyone had to pay the fee and eat campus food, because you'd be wasting your breath. Whether you ate or not was your business, and since you'd chosen this school, you were expected to follow its rules. Some of the students couldn't understand what the cards were for in the first place. Nothing, they were told, but you'd better show yours at lunchtime; and if you've lost it, you'll have to scrounge up five RMB for a replacement. Since our pitifully small cafeteria could only accommodate a few classes at a time on a rotating basis, we had to queue up on the basketball court to wait our turn to buy lunch. Objectively speaking, the food wasn't bad: two dishes, one meat and one vegetarian, and in every three-day period, we ate steamed buns twice and rice once. Sometimes we found sand and tiny pebbles in the rice, but that was no big deal, and even the occasional sliver of glass or small nail didn't raise an eyebrow.

About a month after classes began, a new student was assigned to Section 6. At our midday inspection, Teacher Wang walked in with a girl. "This is Du Yuan. Section 6 now has a new member." The new girl introduced herself in a low, throaty voice. She said she liked dancing and art, and that was all. Public speaking seemed to make her nervous.

The new girl acquired star status almost immediately. All the students in our school had to wear their hair short, and girls were expected to part theirs down the middle. Hers was short, but she parted it on the side. We all wore the same uniform, but she added a scarf around her neck, brown with white polka dots and probably no more expensive than those you can buy on street comers. But that silk scarf drew our attention like a magnet. It started a fad. And even though our silk or satin scarves might have cost more than hers, on her it just seemed more fitting, more natural. The truth is, I never got very close to her. She was an enigma. She didn't participate in any of our military drills. Someone said she was from Xi'an and that she lived in Beijing with her grandfather.

She reminded me of some of the characters I'd invented, and on several occasions I imagined her as a girl who existed only in my fantasies.

The school required each grade to organize a class activity with a special theme. The theme for first-year students was "I love my major." "I'm giving this assignment to you, Jiafu," Teacher Wang said to me. So I asked Ziyu to make a tape with Luo Dayou, The Beatles, Queen, Yu Dong, and Gao Xiaosong for background music, then I copied passages from novels about school, concentrating on stirring passages that glorified youth. Other students signed up to participate, thanks to the five to ten points awarded for each performance, and the show was a roaring success. Du Yuan performed a dance, and it wasn't until then that we realized how thin a waist she had. She wore this lovely expression while she danced, and had tied a ribbon of cloth around her waist, so thin it looked like it might fall off at any minute. It never did. The grade monitor and two outside judges, all male, stared at her, grinning from ear to ear. But our class monitor looked at me, not her, since I was her favorite, her most talented student.

Sometimes the school organized other activities in the current popular phrase of "going with a concept." Each had a clearly defined theme, such as "military training report-back performances" or "knowledge bowls," but the actual nature and substance were ignored. The problem was, I began to realize that the students at my school were extremely ill-informed. For example, during the knowledge bowl, if you asked who wrote the classic lines "Up to Heaven, down to Earth, on to the Yellow Springs / Two vast realms, in neither did he find her," the third-year students would sit there mute until someone would actually ask if such a poem had ever been written. If one of them managed to answer the question "What's the smallest bird on earth?" the audience would buzz. Shit, to think that someone so smart actually attends our school! It was astonishing! I was bored having to function in this environment. There was no campus culture to speak of.

Going to school every day eventually became exhausting, and all I wanted to do when I got home was sleep—a luxury I didn't have. In the summer following my graduation from middle school, I had interviewed four underground rock bands for a music magazine, and now I had to hurry and put the finished interviews into publishable form. And I had to practice the guitar to keep from lagging behind. Plus, every first-year student was required to write an "autobiography," a "self-confession" of a thousand words or more. "I want to chill out by myself, I don't want to go on living, I feel like lying down and never getting up again. . . . " They'd shoot me if I wrote that.

Hypocrisy was my only choice: "Life is bright and sunny, twenty-first century, a generation striding into a new century, the future . . . " You've got to be fucking kidding.

OLD ROSES IN A ROSE GARDEN

Another spring came and is on its way out.

Another spring wasted.

They'd just turned off the heating, and I was still wearing winter clothes. I hate being cold. Getting through the period when the temperature is rising but there's still a chill in the air just about does me in, even though winter is my favorite season. Little Yang from the band Faithless Babes said he'd had a lot of work recently, that his days were just packed, and I was glad to hear it. Energetic people with plenty to do should be out doing it. I had nothing special to do except indulge my fantasies and read books. For several weeks in a row I raced home on my bike on Thursday afternoons to catch the TV program *Very English*, hoping there'd be some rock music that I'd like. That was the only thing that broke up my boredom.

I've never been the sort of person who has goals. Never. And even with a rosy veil over my eyes, I couldn't see the future.

There was a slight drizzle one Wednesday morning, and after waking up, I sat in bed in my rumpled pj's, not wanting to move. . . . What to do? . . . True freedom has never existed in this world . . . should I transfer? . . . drop out of school? . . . The flowers in spring, the winds of autumn, and the setting sun of winter . . . these were the silly thoughts of a melancholy young girl. . . . Finally I managed to drag myself out the door, knowing that I was going to be late. It only took a second to decide what I was going to do. I pedaled past The Ark Bookstore, then circled back. It hadn't opened yet, so I rode over to the post office on Suzhou Avenue. Surrounded by the ringing of bicycle bells, I seemed to be the only carefree person around. At the post office I picked up the March issue of *The College Student* and flipped through it. My eye was caught by a poem written by the guy I'd run into at The Busy Bee, the "young poet" from the PLA Art Academy, Shi Jun. "What happened that night isn't something I ought to be talking about," he'd written. What a joke! He'd actually used words like "love" and "degenerate." No irony intended. I felt like calling him up and giving him this poetic line: "A shitty poem by a fucked-up person." The poet Yi Sha said it: In a rose garden an old rose like him will always be the enemy of rock 'n' roll.

I thought about calling up some friends that morning, but didn't. I wanted them to see me when I was cutting a sorry figure, all confused, and actually treat me to breakfast, then drag me off to relax with a book or take in some music, when in fact they'd probably be pissed off at being disturbed and pepper me with questions about why I wasn't in school, and end up trying to talk some sense into me.

For skipping school that day, I got my mother to write a note, and since my class monitor was partial to me, nothing happened. But in the days that followed, my disgust with the school grew stronger, and I regularly showed up late or cut classes, until the school laid down the law, requiring from me the "three musts" for an approved absence: a note from home, a note from a doctor, and a prescription, no exceptions.

FEEBLE SOBS

I was getting fed up with talking and all other forms of self-expression. I did everything possible to avoid contact with vacuous people.

I went out walking with Jelly. First we went to Earth Temple Park, where he'd interviewed the rock vocalist and songwriter Pu Shu a few days earlier. There was a chill in the air, so he took off his denim jacket and gave it to me. We found the bench where he'd conducted the interview, and Jelly told me Pu Shu had written some lyrics on the ground that day, but neither of us could find them, no matter how carefully we looked.

I brought up the name of a certain music critic. "Didn't you hear? He killed himself not long ago," Jelly said.

"He did?" I asked excitedly. "How come?"

"Don't know."

I really admired the guy's courage, and if I'd known he was thinking about suicide, instead of trying to talk him out of it I'd have had a good long conversation with him. I don't know why, but I've got this crude idea that anybody who fucking scorns life, who sees life as a pile of shit, who feels that life is meaningless and offers nothing but constant suffering, is fearless, courageous . . . in a word, cultivated. See, that's what gets me going. I'm a pessimist down to the marrow of my bones. Jelly once wrote an essay that I stumbled across one rainy day on the top floor of the Honghe Music School; it was in an old issue of a music journal. Here's part of what he wrote:

> *Whenever I'm about to leave the house, I check for my room key, my address book, which has the phone numbers of everyone I know in the city, the floppy disks with all my writing, my pager, and my bus pass. If any of them are missing, I can't leave the house. But then, once when I took a train on a long trip, I realized that not one of those things was absolutely essential.*
>
> *Sometimes I know of people who have passed on, and I grieve for the dead and for their loved ones. But the dead no longer exist and have taken their memories with them, while the ones they've left behind will cease their mourning one day and start getting used to life without them. As with a pebble tossed into a lake, the ripples will spread farther and farther until they disappear. At times like this, the realization comes to me that there is no absolute necessity for life.*
>
> *There is no absolute necessity for life.*

I don't much like Jelly's recent essays. He has lost the ability to turn common sentiments into serious writing. But in his early work, the depth of his sincerity is painful and exhilarating. He captures the beauty of desolation and annihilation. Reality makes people lose hope, so I think the way most men and boys hold passionately and stubbornly to life is disconcerting. How can they love life so much? When I read Jelly's essay, I picked up the phone and called him, since he was the first man I'd ever known who actually detested life. I liked that. Maybe I'm just naturally oversensitive, but I yearned to find a kindred spirit.

We went out to eat, and once we were in the taxi, a soft rain began to fall; the neon lights behind the rain made it incredibly visible. We went to a fast-food restaurant, where we sat down in a booth by a window. After the food came, Jelly asked me how things were at home.

"For me it's sheer torture, for them devastation." After a while I started talking about conducting interviews, and I got so emotional I started to cry. I was telling him about a time I went to interview the band Inductive Agency, alone and without knowing what I was doing, and all of a sudden I lost it. Jelly handed me a tissue, and I said, "Don't look at me!"

He smiled and, sounding both tired and caring at the same time, said, "I envy you. I haven't cried in a very long time. You're very mature."

"No, I'm not," I replied.

"Then life's going to be hard for you."

"I won't live long."

"How long do you plan to live?"

"Who knows? At least into the twenty-first century."

Jelly said I asked too much of life. But how was I to ask too little?

As we got onto the subway, he said abruptly, "Are you in a vocational high school?"

Sparks flew from my eyes.

"Yes, I'm in a vocational high school, but I want to go to Beida. You think that's bordering on the impossible? I want to become a top journalist, and I'm going to Beida."

Jelly looked down and took out an envelope. "Here," he said, "this is for you. You'll pass the entrance exam for sure. Beida's the school for people like you. If you can't get in, nobody can. Sensitive little thing." I opened the envelope. Inside were a photo of Xu Wei in a performance on April 8 and three blown-up publicity photos of him.

My future scared me; I didn't want to suffer. But suffering and joy have always been pretty much the same thing to me. Whenever I'm enjoying life, the cost is its opposite. So the only way to avoid suffering was to rid my life of joy. It all boiled down to one word: Death. No feelings. The land of ultimate bliss. Nirvana. I wanted absolute nothingness.

Instead I cried because I was going out on a date and had no new pants and no decent shoes.

I cried because an electric guitar cost fifteen hundred RMB, more than I could afford.

My room was an empty chamber. No friends. I hated lonely Sunday afternoons. I lay there and sobbed weakly, felt consigned to permanent weakness. I despised everything I saw. After I'd cried myself out, I felt cold. I hated myself.

I know there are lots of people who can't stand dark writing with a decadent tone, you know, like writing about yourself as if writing about others. If you're one of them, stop here. I'm not going to force you.

BORN TO BE A PILOT

I hated school more and more each day. I didn't want to study that shit anymore, didn't want to waste any more time there. I'd had about all I could take of the place. Just the thought of two more years there drove me up the wall. Thoughts of my final exam, plus exams on clerical work, shorthand, P & F, computer, made my head swell. I looked up at the mother hen standing at the front of the room and wondered what he'd come here for . . . I wanted to go to college, I wanted to go to college, I wanted to be alone, I wanted to be alone. If I stuck it out at this school, would there be anything left of me? Assigned a job, going to work, entrance exams . . . I'd die of exhaustion. The only subjects that interested me were language and politics, but my history teacher also taught second-year photography, so there was no history class my second semester. My life was like an unguided missile, and I figured that sooner or later I'd crash and be smashed to pieces.

I hated my school but liked the class I was assigned to. To be more precise, I liked the sluggish, decadent, somewhat sugary atmosphere, and I liked some of my classmates and teachers. I was grateful to the class monitor, Teacher Wang, for making so many things easy for me. In that harsh environment, I was relatively free, thanks to her. Despite the fact that I was no longer easily moved, I was touched. I think she must have understood my appreciation.

Toward the end of my fifteenth year, I bumped into painful reality time and again as I chased my dreams. I knew that my thoughts were all over the place, but they never lacked clarity. I knew exactly what I wanted and what I was doing.

What I needed now was to take care of myself.

I needed room to do what I wanted without interfering with anybody, free to do as I pleased.

I got to know a band from Kaifeng who called themselves SpermOva. The members of SpermOva sent me some black-and-white publicity photos, all featuring Jia Jia. The pictures were shot at a school, in condemned buildings, on Kaifeng streets, and in front of their homes. The band consisted of Bai Jianqiu (bass), Wei Ruixian (guitar), Jia Jia (lead singer, guitar), and Li Zhanwu (drums).

"Come to Kaifeng," they said. "We're here waiting for you."

I really, really loved that band and dreamed of walking down the streets of Kaifeng with them. I wanted to go there, I wanted to break out of this school, I wanted to go see them in Kaifeng, where we'd have a million things to talk about. My mind was made up. I was going there.

My mother found a guidance counselor for me, and wanted me to go see him on Saturday or Sunday, but I was defiant. There's nothing wrong with my head; why should I see a shrink? But then I thought, why not? If the psychiatrist could figure me out, who knows, he might talk my mother into giving me more freedom.

We wore short sleeves and hats on the blistering summer day we went to see the guidance counselor. After getting off the 375 bus, we had a long walk to the Qinghua University High School, where the counseling office was located. Some of the dorm students hadn't yet left, and we were treated to the sight of hot-blooded kids happily running around. We went to the third-floor mental health office in a small building, where we were greeted by a teacher with long hair. After we timidly took the seats we were offered, she poured us some hot water. We chatted a while, then she asked us to wait while she attended a meeting.

Mother and I sipped our water on the sofa, while I flipped through a stack of *Beijing Youth*. The green canopies of poplars bent in the wind and brushed against the window, and I could hear the shouts and laughter of students downstairs. I had a funny feeling: When had I lost my student's sense of innocence?

About an hour later, the teacher returned and said with an embarrassed smile, "Sorry to keep you waiting."

"No problem."

"Let's go into the other room," she said. The new room was much cozier than the first, and better furnished. "Would you like some coffee?" she asked.

"No, thanks, water is fine," I said. I liked her right off; she had a considerate, warm quality that earned my immediate trust. I told her about wanting to go to Kaifeng to see the band SpermOva, and she thought that was a good idea. Could I wait till summer vacation? I said I didn't want to wait even another day. She was on my side, but she tried to get me to compromise. I knew she was right, that she was just being practical, that waiting for summer vacation was the sensible thing to do. My mother even chipped in with the suggestion that the band could come to Beijing during summer vacation, at my parents' expense. But it didn't work.

The teacher reminded me how upset I would be if I went to Kaifeng and SpermOva turned out to be a disappointment, nothing like I'd expected.

I said I'd be prepared for that.

She smiled at Mother and just shrugged her shoulders.

I left Qinghua University High reluctantly. It impressed me as a terrific school. Big, beautiful, a great campus, lots of energetic students, and kind teachers. Just what I thought a high school ought to be.

KAIFENG, THE NIGHT IS STILL YOUNG

Mother and I went to buy train tickets. I filled my backpack with CDs and newspapers for the trip, but it seemed as if we'd traveled to hell and back before the train finally reached Shangqiu Station, just before Kaifeng.

The setting sun sent down beautiful golden rays of sunshine from the edge of the sky, reminding me of the classic lines: "A solitary plume of smoke in the desert / The rounded sun setting over the Yangtze." I went back to an empty car and sat down by myself, letting the sunbeams wash over my body, my face, and the cocoon of joy all around me, body and soul.

After I stepped down off of the train, my heart seemed about to burst out of my chest. I wondered where they might be waiting for me. "SpermOva!" I shouted.

No one answered in the darkness. Mother and I walked out of the station, then spotted four people at the foot of the steps. I rushed over. "Are you Jiafu?" one of them asked. I nodded and reached out to shake hands. That took him by surprise, but he stuck out his hand. I later learned that he was the bass player, Jianqiu. After my ID was checked, Jia Jia came up and hugged me, appearing warm and a little wary at the same time, maybe because my mother was there with me.

First we went to the home of Li Zhanwu, the drummer. Not a bad place, if you ask me. In some respects, an improvement over comparable apartments in Beijing. Li's mother was a typical middle-class urbanite. She spoke Mandarin pretty well, but I think she went a little overboard in welcoming us, which made me sort of uneasy. We all sat down to dinner at about nine o'clock. Obviously, there was a lot I wanted to say, and I finally got permission to spend the night with SpermOva in Li Zhanwu's apartment. We all walked there together. Kaifeng's streets are narrow and dark, and as I walked along I suddenly felt that something wasn't quite right. This was the city I'd dreamed about and fought to visit for so long; why wasn't I just about passing out from excitement? So I shouted, "Wow, here I am in Kaifeng! This is Kaifeng!"

To get to Li Zhanwu's place we had to cross some railroad tracks. The scene was new and magnificent, with trains passing through town and airplanes flying so low you could see their red lights. The apartment was aging but well equipped: a bed (including blankets and pillows), a balcony, a water heater, a toilet, even an old radio. As soon as I got there, I dumped all my CDs and newspapers on the bed, but that didn't get the reaction I'd expected. Here's how I wanted it to be: All of us lying in bed, arms around each other as we listened to rock music in the dark and talked about all sorts of things. That was the sort of intimacy I'd yearned for. But it's not how things turned out. I was sleepy, but they were still in high spirits, so they turned on all the lights and played loud music, each doing one thing or another, leaving me as the outsider, alone. What I wanted was to lie with my arms around Jia Jia or, for that matter, any of my friends. I really needed that feeling. A warm feeling. I touched Jia Jia's hand. "I want to hold your hand," I said. My mood was exactly like that in the Beatles' song. He was unmoved. Humiliation washed over me.

To hell with being rational—all I wanted was to follow my emotions. I understood that letting my emotions run free wasn't a good idea, that it could only mess things up. That was obvious, even then. But emotions are hard to control. Too hard, in fact. My heart was so spongy it sapped my energy. I felt powerless.

By about two in the morning everyone was tired. Li Zhanwu and Bai Jianqiu took the sofa. Jia Jia, Wei Ruixian, and I slept on the bed. The lights were turned off. Before we went to sleep, the lead guitarist, Wei Ruixian, told a bunch of dirty jokes, and we all laughed. I held Jia Jia's hand, hoping to feel something warm and dependable. He let me put it wherever I wanted, displaying no emotion whatsoever, which for me was sheer misery. The only possible explanation was that he (or they) had no feelings for me at all. God, what an idiot I was! Why was I always so sure of myself? Why were my feelings never appreciated? Why was I always the one who got hurt? Caught up in these thoughts, I drifted off into an uneasy sleep.

The moment my eyes opened in the morning, all 1 wanted was to get back to Beijing as soon as humanly possible. Just take off. But I knew that was out of the question. I felt like screaming, but I was in somebody else's goddamn apartment.

I felt like going up to Jia Jia and asking him: "Do you even consider me a friend?"

A FLASH

The next day felt even longer. Soon after I got up in the morning, Mother and Aunty Li (Li Zhanwu's mother) came over, and that was pretty awkward. We ate oil fritters, which made me thirsty. Jia Jia slept like a dead man, like there was no waking him.

Later that morning I went out onto the balcony to take in the view. Thick, tall parasol trees grew there, and the air smelled like tofu. Li Zhanwu later told me there was a pharmaceutical plant nearby.

Li, the drummer, and I got along great. He said his mother might send him to Kaifeng University in a few months to study computers. I gave him a ten-RMB Luo Dayou CD. I hit it off with Bai Jianqiu too. And yet I was still in a funk. The unity, purity, and infatuation you expect with a true comrade, they couldn't give me. I wanted nothing more than to talk openly about the tough issues of life, music, and ideals, or anything else, with people, but there was no one.

Before I had come here, every thought of the band had made me happy, had made me smile; now there was only fright and a sense of danger. How could it have turned out like this? It was real. My prior happiness was real, but so was my present distress.

The third day they took me to see their school, a vocational high school in a white building. The athletic field and the roof were covered with green moss, and both were a lot bigger than West X High. Students on the athletic field were in summer uniforms; the boys were playing soccer, the girls were just talking in groups. They were all so lively, so full of youth. The sun was bright as I walked up to their classroom and, gathering my courage, stepped inside. Some of the girls acted surprised when they saw me, probably wondering who this new girl was, since they'd never seen me before. Well, you won't be seeing me again, either, I thought.

A few minutes later, Bai Jianqiu came in with a fair-skinned, long-haired girl in a long skirt with shoulder straps. "Let me introduce you to someone, Gu Lingling. This is Jiafu. Jiafu, this is my girlfriend."

I looked at her. "I've heard him talk about you," I said.

"I've heard him talk about you, too," she replied as she twirled the jade bracelet on her arm.

I had to smile. She was cute, but certainly no pushover. Her reactions were quick. She answered my smile with one of her own, and I liked her immediately.

Their love seemed typical of middle-class boys and girls in any average-sized city—genuine and guileless.

Jia Jia and Bai Jianqiu took seats in the last row, off to the right. I sat down in front of Jianqiu. By myself. It was politics, one of my favorite classes back in Beijing. I hadn't taken a politics course for a very long time and was itching to get started. Deep down I hoped the teacher—a man, I expected—would raise some interesting topics for discussion, and that would give me a chance to display my talents, show them that I really was smart.

Well, class started—the teacher was, in fact, a woman—and instead of a lecture, she told them to review their lesson. What a bummer! I turned and looked behind me. Bai Jianqiu was asleep, head down on his desk. And Jia Jia? He was wrapped up in a book I'd given them called *Introduction to Sex* and wasn't even aware I was looking at him.

I sprawled out on my desktop and began memorizing words in an English textbook. This was so incredible.

After class, I went over to the school snack shop, where I tried a bottle of Kaifeng yogurt. Not bad, and cheap, only ninety fen. I also bought some chewing gum to give to them. The woman who ran the shop said that Kaifeng residents are all poor, so the cost of living is lower.

When school was out, Bai Jianqiu invited me over to his place. He and his family lived in a densely populated neighborhood of small apartment buildings, I met his father, a dark, skinny man who greeted me in the local dialect. Jianqiu's room was neat and clean, with a xylophone in one corner; some of his own paintings and some homemade posters of the band hung on the walls. "I'm going to buy my own bass guitar this year," he said.

He and Gu Lingling liked each other a lot, and goofed around quite a bit.

"I'll give you a jade ornament," she said with a smile, "and you and I can be sisters."

"Sounds too good to be true," I replied.

She took a tiny jade lock out of her purse. "I have a little jade key for this," she said. "They're a set. One for you and one for me. Starting today, you and I are sisters."

"They're real jade," Jianqiu said.

She pulled out a strand of hair to test it. It was real jade, all right.

"See, I told you." Jianqiu smiled proudly.

I spent the rest of the afternoon at Li Zhanwu's apartment before he took me to see the sights around town. First we went to a music store, where he told me it was where he used to buy copies of *Music and Video World* and *Punk Age*. It was the only music store in Kaifeng where you could buy rock magazines. They also sold audiotapes and pirated CDs. I did some window-shopping for clothes and checked out a Xinhua Bookstore.

The sun baked down on us. I was wearing a red T-shirt, a black-and-white-checked skirt, and red sneakers—dazzling youth. Li Zhanwu took me to a district where there was an abandoned auditorium; we climbed the cement steps to the top and sat down to talk. I bought a beer, and he told me he never drank, but the two of us shared the bottle anyway.

As evening fell, Li Zhanwu said we ought to get something to eat—his treat. At a busy marketplace we ate some ice cream and had a couple of soft drinks. I said, "Things here are really cheap!"

"That's right," he teased. "So are the workers' wages."

We went back after dark and got the other members of the band to go out on the town. Gu Lingling bought me some red silk thread for the jade lock. She strung it herself and draped it around my neck, and I made a silent vow not to ever take it off.

The next day I told them that I'd be leaving soon. "Where are you going?" Bai Jianqiu asked me.

"Home."

"Where?" He knew what I'd said, but he asked anyway. And I knew I'd rather not answer again, but I did.

"Home."

He just nodded absently. I turned to look at Jia Jia, but he hadn't stopped shooting hoops.

I went to find my mother at a guesthouse near the train station. After our first night in Kaifeng, when she'd stayed at Li Zhanwu's, she insisted on moving into the guesthouse. When I got there, she was drinking water and combing her hair; she seemed happy to me, maybe because she knew we were heading back to Beijing that night, that I no longer insisted on spending a month in Kaifeng, and maybe she was feeling happy that this trip had gone off without incident. Who knows? Whatever the reason, seeing her happy like that made me pretty happy too.

Jianqiu and Li Zhanwu went with us to the train station and watched our train pull away. But before we left, Li Zhanwu took a cross from around his neck and put it around mine.

LONELY HIGH-HEELED SHOES

Back to school.

My absence from school to visit Kaifeng greatly disappointed Teacher Wang. At night, when I walked home along the western section of Third Ring Road, I often ran into her, and it was awkward. When that proved unbearable, I finally made the following entry in my weekly journal:

A *hypothesis:*

Shall we continue to understand and support one another like good friends, or give one another the silent treatment?If the former, why don't we pick a time and talk this out? If the latter, then there's nothing I can say except that I'm guilty of a bad decision.

When the journals were returned, I found these lines at the bottom:

You want to talk it out? That's fine if you're willing to open up and speak honestly. I don't feel as if I was deceived as much as I don't think you've treated me as a true friend. There are simply some things you should talk to me about before you do them.

If you still want to talk, pick a time.

But the mutual esteem Teacher Wang and I had enjoyed was gone forever; we now kept each other at arm's length, not your ordinary student-teacher relationship.

Four students in our class left as a group for another school, one that specialized in teaching English. After completing the seven-year program, the students graduated with the equivalent of a college degree. The tuition was reputed to be exceptionally high. They were lucky, breaking out of this insane asylum of a school. None of us doubted that any school would be better than ours.

They had escaped. I, on the other hand, the one most desperate to leave, was still there.

That night I had a horrible nightmare.

The whole thing was filled with hopeless love, hopeless yearnings, hopeless flight, hopeless hopes. In the dream, someone I've always liked gives one of my young aunts a black liquid. "Don't drink that!" I scream. "Don't drink it!"

That was followed by flight and more flight, running madly, and when I finally awoke, I was overcome by a fear of death, a fear of freezing loneliness and of cold, and the understanding that no matter whether it's life or death, everything is controlled by something unknowable and mysterious.

A few days after returning to Beijing, I went silent, no longer going on and on about SpermOva. When I did speak, I began asking a bunch of childish questions: Do you have any true friends? Do you believe in love? Some of the people shook their heads, some nodded. When they asked me the same questions, I didn't have a clue.

Like the song says: *Take off your lonely high-heeled shoes and walk barefoot on the steps of the world's parks. My dreams are not of Paris, or Tokyo, or New York. My loneliness and I will meet in the quiet and stillness of midnight. . . .*

2004

PART FOUR

Poetry, 1918–1949

Xu Zhimo (1895–1931)

SECOND FAREWELL TO CAMBRIDGE

Quietly I am leaving
Just as quietly I came;
Quietly I wave a farewell
To the western sky aflame.

The golden willow on the riverbank,
A bride in the setting sun;
Her colorful reflection
Ripples through my heart.

The green plants on the river bed,
So lush and so gracefully swaying
In the gentle current of the Cam
I'd be happy to remain a waterweed.

The pool under an elm's shade
Is not a creek, but a rainbow in the sky
Crushed among the floating green,
Settling into a colorful dream.

In search of a dream? You pole a tiny boat
Toward where the green is even more green
To collect a load of stars, as songs
Rise in the gleaming stellar light.

But tonight my voice fails me;
Silence is the best tune of farewell;
Even crickets are still for me,
And still is Cambridge tonight.

Silently I am going
As silently I came;
I shake my sleeves,
Not to bring away a patch of cloud.

1925
Translated by Kai-yu Hsu

LOVE'S INSPIRATION

For a long time I have been gazing at death itself.
Since the day the bond of love was sealed in my heart
I have been gazing at death—
That realm of perpetual beauty; to death
I happily surrendered myself because
It is the birth of the brilliant and the free.
From that moment on I scorned my body
And even less did I care
For the floating glory of this life;
I longed to trust my breath to time
Even more infinite than it.
Then my eyes would turn into the glittering stars,
And my glistening hair, the clouds that are draped
All over the sky. Buffeting winds would
Whirl in front of my chest, before my eyes;
Waves would lap at my ankles, their sacred luster
Surging with each breaker!
My thoughts would be the lightning
That whips up a dance of dragons and snakes on the horizon;
My voice would thunder, suddenly awakening
The Spring and awakening life. Ah!
Beyond imagination, beyond compare
Is love's inspiration, love's power.

1930
Translated by Kai-yu Hsu

CHANCE

I am a cloud in the sky,
A chance shadow on the wave of your heart.
    Don't be surprised,
    Or too elated:
In an instant I shall vanish without trace.
We meet on the sea of dark night,
You on your way, I on mine.
    Remember if you will,
    Or, better still, forget
The light exchanged in this encounter.

1926

Translated by Pang Bingjun and John Minford, with Seán Golden

Wen Yiduo (1899–1946)

DEAD WATER

Here is a ditch of hopelessly dead water.
No breeze can raise a single ripple on it.
Might as well throw in rusty metal scraps
or even pour left-over food and soup in it.

Perhaps the green on copper will become emeralds.
Perhaps on tin cans peach blossoms will bloom.
Then, let grease weave a layer of silky gauze,
and germs brew patches of colorful spume.

Let the dead water ferment into jade wine
covered with floating pearls of white scum.
Small pearls chuckle and become big pearls,
only to burst as gnats come to steal this rum.

And so this ditch of hopelessly dead water
may still claim a touch of something bright.
And if the frogs cannot bear the silence—
the dead water will croak its song of delight.

Here is a ditch of hopelessly dead water—
a region where beauty can never reside.
Might as well let the devil cultivate it—
and see what sort of world it can provide.

1926
Translated by Kai-yu Hsu

ONE SENTENCE

There is one sentence that can light fire,
Or, when spoken, bring dire disasters.
Don't think that for five thousand years nobody has said it.
How can you be sure of a volcano's silence?
Perhaps one day, as if possessed by a spirit,
Suddenly out of the blue sky a thunder
Will explode:
"This is our China!"

How am I to say this today?
You may not believe that "the iron tree will bloom."
But there is one sentence you must hear!
Wait till the volcano can no longer be quiet,
Don't tremble, or shake your head, or stamp your feet,
Just wait till out of the blue sky a thunder
Will explode:
"This is our China!"

1927
Translated by Kai-yu Hsu

PRAYER

Please tell me who the Chinese are,
Teach me how to cling to memory.
Please tell me the greatness of this people,
Tell me gently, ever so gently.

Please tell me: Who are the Chinese?
Whose hearts embody the hearts of Yao and Shun?

In whose veins flow the blood of Jingke and Niezheng
Who are the true children of the Yellow Emperor?[1]

Tell me that such wisdom came strangely—
Some say it was brought by a horse from the river:
Also tell me that the rhythm of this song
Was taught, originally, by the phoenix.

Who will tell me of the silence of the Gobi Desert,
The awe inspired by the Five Sacred Mountains,
The patience that drips from the rocks of Mount Tai,
And the harmony that flows in the Yellow and Yangtze Rivers?

Please tell me who the Chinese are,
Teach me how to cling to memory.
Please tell me the greatness of this people
Tell me gently, ever so gently.

1927
Translated by Kai-yu Hsu

1. All legendary and historical heroes and sages of China.

Li Jinfa (1900–1976)

WOMAN ABANDONED

Long hair hangs down before my eyes,
Cutting off all glances of contempt and shame
And the rapid flow of fresh blood, the sound sleep of bleached bones.
Insects and the dark night arrive hand in hand,
Over the corner of this low wall
To howl behind my ears that never have been soiled.
They howl like winds in the wilderness,
Frightening many shepherds and their charges.

By way of a blade of grass I communicate with God in the deserted vale.
Only the memory of the roaming bees has recorded my sorrow.
Or I may pour my sorrow along with the cascades tumbling over the cliff,
And drift away among the red leaves.

At each of her motions she feels the weight of her sorrow increasing;
No fire of a setting sun can burn the ennui of time
Into ashes to float away through the chimneys and attach themselves
To the wings of itinerant crows,
And with them perch on the rocks of a roaring sea,
To listen to the boatmen's songs.

Sighs of her timeworn skirts,
As she saunters in a graveyard.
Never will she again drop a hot tear
On the lawn
To adorn this world.

1935
Translated by Kai-yu Hsu

NEVER TO RETURN

Go with me, child,
To an old city built in the Middle Ages—
It has lain asleep through the nights of the centuries;
There the creeks eternally sing songs of monotone—
Sighs of the poets from the East.
The cavernous hearts of the city
Are filled with lichens.

Still farther
Stands a dilapidated wall all alone,
Keeping vigil over a garden abandoned long ago,
Against a silence of black and dark blue.
These things befriend severe winters
And have no knowledge of the prime of summer.
In the thin layer of sand you may
Find chips of a wooden frame
(But hardly an appropriate gift for anyone).
Snails are chuckling in a shady nook.

There the birds are tired
And bees linger in their dreams,
And departing yellow leaves
Fly in the sky,
Nodding to the old pines,
To the flowing water.

You can only smell
The epilogue of the season—the odor of the rotting things.
Pale shades of the trees
Sometimes lull you to sleep,
With a little light from over the horizon
You may better discern their forms.
But their hearts are bleeding, rueful and cold.

If you want to hear our laughter,
Bring your lute
To play a "Never to Return."

1935
Translated by Kai-yu Hsu

Feng Zhi (1905–1993)

SONNET 2

Whatever can be shed from our bodies,
We'll let it be reduced to dust;
We arrange ourselves in this epoch
Like autumn trees, one by one

Handing over to autumn winds their leaves
And belated flowers, so they may stretch their limbs
Into the severe winter; we arrange ourselves
In nature, like cicadas emerging from earth

To abandon their shells in the dirt;
We arrange ourselves for the death
That lies ahead, like a song and

As the sounds fall from the body of the music,
There remains only the music's essence
Transformed into a chain of silent blue hills.

1941

Translated by Kai-yu Hsu

SONNET 4

Often as I ponder on the life of man,
I feel compelled to pray to you.
You, a cluster of pale-white weeds,
Never failed to deserve a name;

And yet you elude all possible names
To lead a life, insignificant and humble,
Never failing in your purity and nobility, but
Completing your life cycle in silence.

Of all the forms and all the sounds,
Some fade away, as they approach you,
And some become part of your quietude:

This is your great glory, though
Accomplished only in your self-denial.
I pray to you, for the life of man.

1941
Translated by Kai-yu Hsu

SONNET 27

From a pool of freely flowing, formless water,
The water carrier brings back a bottleful, ellipsoid in shape,
Thus this much water has acquired a definite form.
Look, the wind vane fluttering in the autumn breeze

Takes hold of certain things that cannot be held.
Let distant lights and distant nights,
And the growth and decay of plants in distant places,
And a thought that darts towards infinity,

All leave something on this banner.
In vain we have listened to the sound of the wind all night long,
In vain we watched the whole day the grass turning yellow and
the leaves red.

Where shall we settle our thoughts, where?
Let's hope that these verses will, like a wind cone,
Embody certain things that cannot be held.

1941
Translated by Kai-yu Hsu

Dai Wangshu (1905–1950)

RAINY ALLEY

Holding up an oil-paper umbrella,
I loiter aimlessly in the long, long
and lonely rainy alley,
I hope to encounter
a lilac-like girl
nursing her resentment.

A lilac-like color she has,
a lilac-like fragrance,
a lilac-like sadness,
melancholy in the rain,
sorrowful and uncertain;

She loiters aimlessly in this lonely rainy alley,
holding up an oil-paper umbrella
just like me
and just like me
walks silently,
apathetic, sad and disconsolate.

Silently she moves closer,
moves closer and casts
a sigh-like glance,

she glides by
like a dream
hazy and confused like a dream.

As in a dream she glides past
like a lilac spray,
this girl glides past beside me;
she silently moves away, moves away,
up to the broken-down bamboo fence,
to the end of the rainy alley.

In the rain's sad song,
her color vanishes,
her fragrance diffuses,
even her
sigh-like glance,
lilac-like discontent
vanish.

Holding up an oil-paper umbrella, alone
aimlessly walking in the long, long
and lonely rainy alley,
I wish for
a lilac-like girl
nursing her resentment to glide by.

1928

Translated by Gregory B. Lee

WRITTEN ON A PRISON WALL

If I die here,
Friends, do not be sad,
I shall always exist
In your hearts.

One of you died,
In a cell in Japanese-occupied territory,
He harbored deep hatred,
You should always remember.

When you come back,
Dig up his mutilated body from the mud,
Hoist his soul up high
With your victory cheers.

And then place his bones on a mountain peak,
To bask in the sun, and bathe in the wind:
In that dark damp dirt cell,
This was his sole beautiful dream.

1942
Translated by Gregory B. Lee

WITH MY INJURED HAND

With my injured hand
I grope around on this expansive earth:
This corner has already turned to ashes,
This corner is only blood and mud;
This stretch of water must be my old home,
(In the springtime, the dike-top flourishes like a tapestry,
The young willow branches broken in two emit a rare fragrance.)
I touch the coolness of the reeds and water;
The snowy peaks of Long White Mountain chill the bones,
The water in the Yellow River carries the sand and mud which
slip through the fingers;
Paddy fields south of the Yangtze, in those days your shoots
Were so fine, so tender . . . now there are only reeds,
The *lizhi* blossoms of Lingnan look lonely and weary,
And right over there, I dip my hand into the bitter water of a
South China Sea without fishing boats . . .
My formless hand flits over limitless rivers and mountains,
My fingers are stained with blood and ashes, my palm with gloom,
There is just that distant corner which is still whole,
Warm, bright, strong and flourishing.
Over there I touch lightly with my injured hand,
Like a lover's soft hair, like a breast in a baby's hands.
Putting all my strength into my hand
I hold it firm, I place love and all my hope there,
Because only there, is there sun, is there spring,
To expel darkness, and bring rebirth,
Because only there will we have a life different to animals,
A death different to that of ants . . . Only there, in everlasting
China!

1942
Translated by Gregory B. Lee

Bian Zhilin (1910–2000)

A BUDDHIST MONK

When day has done tolling its bells, it's another day,
        And a monk dreams a profound and pallid dream:
        Over how many years, shadows and traces are left behind,
In the memory seen only in a glimpse,
In the ruined temple, everywhere a vague scent pervades,
        Lamented bones are left in the censer as of old,
        Along with the sad fate of loyal youths, faithful maidens,
Wearily wriggling through the Buddhist sutras forever.

In a deep stupor, dream-talk foams out at the mouth,
        His head once again faces the skull-like drum,
        His head, the drum, are alike empty and heavy,
One knock after another, mesmerizing mountains and streams,
The mountains and streams slumber indolently in the evening mist,
And once more, he is done tolling the dolorous bell of another day.

1931

Translated by Eugene Chen Eoyang

A ROUND TREASURE-BOX

I have fantasized that from somewhere (the River of Heaven?)
I fished out a round treasure-box.
It contained several kinds of jewels:
Item: a crystalline drop of mercury,
Reflecting the image of the entire world,
Item: torchfire of golden yellow
Enveloping entire a festive feast,
Item: a fresh drop of rain
That holds all of your sighs last night . . .
Don't go to some watch shop,
Listening to your youthful spring being gnawed away by silkworms.
Don't go to some antique store
To buy your grandfather's old knickknacks.
Look at my round treasure-box
And go with me on my drifting boat.
We will go, although those in the cabin
Will be forever in the blue bosom of heaven,
Although your handshake
Will be a bridge. A bridge! But a bridge
Is also built inside my round treasure-box;
So, here's my round treasure-box for you,
Or for them, and perhaps they can just
Wear, pendant on the ears, these items:
A pearl—a precious stone—a star?

1935
Translated by Eugene Chen Eoyang

FEVERISH NIGHT

I really have a mind to say: "My heart will race with the clock."

Caught a cold, as twilight goes once again from the east,
Then comes back east, rushing back on two warm legs.
Squandering half a cold in the breezes of late spring:
Why are the eyes red? The nostrils raw?
Could be, lamp, lamp, lamp, you bother me.

In the end everything is lonely. You won't tell anyone, will you?
(At the time, you were drifting off to sleep.)
"Look, love, really, really,
I can't keep you company, with you listening to me snore."

You thought someone was about to ask discreetly,
Not knowing who sent those bouquets of fresh flowers.
You listened, patting dust off shirt and sleeve as you spoke,
"The flowers have bloomed? And I thought it was too early."

The two dilemmas are real: the heart outraces our years,
Then falls behind, by the wayside, by this much:
Those who "understand" say "Sick people think of their parents."
What? It's like a small child calling out for his big brother.
My thought intrudes: "My heart is racing with the clock."

There, there, there, we should be resting.
"Sleep, now, all is hope,
Sleep, now, all is hardship!"
It doesn't matter who sang the lullaby, and for whom.
The watch on the pillow sounds:
"Tick-tick, take your pick."[1]

1935
Translated by Eugene Chen Eoyang

---

1. Note: The original is onomatopoetic: *Ying-mian bo-bo;* it also puns on the cry of a hawker on the street: "Chewy noodles, fine pastries!"

Ai Qing (1910–1996)

SNOW FALLS ON CHINA'S LAND

Snow falls on China's land;
Cold blockades China. . . .

Wind,
Like a grief-stricken old woman
Closely following behind,
Stretching out her icy claws,
Tugs at the travelers' clothes.
With words as old as the land,
Her nagging never ends . . .
Coming from the forests
In horse-drawn carts,
You, there, farmers of China,
Wearing fur hats,
Braving the blizzard—
Where are you going?

I tell you,
I too am a descendant of farmers.
From your wrinkled faces etched with pain,

I understand deeply
The years and years of toil
Of the men who make their lives on the prairie.

Yet I
Am no happier than you
—Lying in the river of time.
Turbulent waves of hardship
Have so often swallowed me up,
Only to spew me forth.

I have lost the most precious days
Of my youth
In roaming and in prisons.
My life
Like yours
Is haggard.

Snow falls on China's land;
Cold blockades China. . . .

On the river of this snowy night,
One small oil lamp drifts slowly
In a rickety boat with a black canopy.
Who sits in there
In the lamplight, head bowed?

Ah, it's you,
Tousle-haired and grubby-faced young woman.
Wasn't it
Your home
—Warm and happy nest!
That was burnt to the ground
By the brutal enemy?
Wasn't it
A night like this
Bereft of the protection of a man
That, in the terror of death,
You were teased and poked by enemy bayonets?

On such cold nights as tonight,
Our countless
Aged mothers
Huddle together in homes not theirs—

Like strangers
Not knowing
Where tomorrow's wheel
Will take them.
And China's roads
Are so rugged
And so muddy.

Snow falls on China's land;
Cold blockades China. . . .

Passing over the prairies in this snowy night,
Over regions chewed raw by the beacons of war,
Countless, the tillers of the virgin soil
Lost, the animals they nurtured;
Lost, their fertile fields.
They crowd together
In life's hopeless squalor:
On famine's earth,
Gazing at the dark sky,
They reach out, trembling,
And beg for succor.

Oh, the pain and misery of China,
As long and vast as this snowy night!
Snow falls on China's land;
Snow blockades China. . . .

China,
The feeble poem I write
On this lampless night,
Can it bring you a little warmth?

1937
Translated by Marilyn Chin

THE NORTH

One day a poet from the grasslands of Ke'erqin said
to me, "The north is wretched."
Yes,
The north is wretched,
From beyond the frontier blows

The wind from the desert,
Scraping off the fertile greensward in the north,
And with it, the glory of the seasons
—Now a stretch of pallid ashen yellow,
Covered with a layer, an impenetrable miasma of
sand,
That howling gale that hurries over here from the
horizon
And brings with it a terror,
Maniacally
Sweeping over the land;
Vast and desolate hinterlands,
Frozen in the cold winds of December,
Villages, yes, mountainsides, yes, riverbanks too,
Crumbling walls and unkempt graves, as well,
All covered with a dusty mantle of misery. . . .
A solitary traveler,
His body leaning forward,
His hand shielding his face,
In the windswept sand,
Gasps hard for breath,
One step after another,
Still manages to move on . . .
A number of donkeys
—Those beasts with their mournful eyes
And drooping ears,
Bear the heavy weight
Of the suffering in the land;
Their weary tread
Steps laboriously
Over the north
And its interminable, desolate roads. . . .

Those streams have long since dried up,
And the riverbeds are lined with wheel tracks.
The people and the land of the north,
Are thirsty,
Oh, so thirsty for the fresh, life-giving spring.
The withered forests,
And low-lying houses,
Are sparse, forlorn,
Scattered under the dark-gray backdrop of the sky.
In the sky,
The sun can't be seen,

Just a flock of wild geese in formation,
Agitated, these wild geese,
Beat their black wings,
Cry out their uncertainty and distress,
And from this cold wasteland, flee,
Flee to
The south where green foliage blots out the
sky. . . .

The north is wretched.
The Yellow River, thousands of miles long,
Its waves, turbulent and muddy,
Has given this vast area in the north
Torrents of calamity and misfortune;
Oh, how the winds and frosts down through the
years
Have etched
The vast northern landscape:
Squalor and starvation!
And I
—I, this sojourner from the south,
Oh, how I love this wretched land in the north.
Its windy sands that pelt the face,
And its cold air that seeps into the bones,
Will not cause me to curse it,
I love this wretched land,
An endless stretch of desolate hinterland;
Yes, it brings out my devotion.
—I see them,
Our forebears,
Leading their flocks of sheep,
Blowing on the reed pipes,
Overwhelmed in this great desert dusk;
We have trod
This age-old, loamy brown layer of earth,
Where the skeletons of our forebears are buried,
—This earth that they first broke open with the
plow,
Thousands of years ago
They were already here
Battling the Nature that made them fight for
survival.
When they defended their territory,
They never once disgraced themselves.

They are dead now,
Leaving the legacy of the land to us—
I love this wretched country,
Her vast, barren soil,
Which gave us a language pure and simple,
And a capacious spirit as well.
I believe this language and this spirit,
Strong and sturdy, will survive on the land,
Never to be extinguished.
I love this wretched country,
This age-old country,
This country
That has nourished what I have loved:
The world's most long-suffering
And most venerable people.

1938

Translated by Eugene Chen Eoyang

He Qifang (1912–1977)

PROPHECY

It has finally arrived—that heart-throbbing day.
The sound of your footsteps, like the sighs of the night,
I can hear clearly. They are not leaves whispering in the winds
Nor the fawns darting across a lichened pass.
Tell me, tell me in your singing voice of a silver bell,
Are you not the youthful god I heard about in a prophecy?

You must have come from the warm and exuberant south,
Tell me about the sun there, and the moonlight,
Tell me how the spring air blows open the hundreds of flowers,
And how the swallow lovingly clings to the willow twigs.
I shall close my eyes to sleep in your dreamy songs—
Such comfort I seem to remember, and yet seem to have forgotten.

Stop please, pause in the middle of your long journey
To come in. Here is a tiger-skin rug for you to sit on.
Let me light up every leaf I have gathered in autumn,
Listen to me singing my own song.
Like the flame, my song will dip and rise in turn, again
Like the flame, will tell the story of the fallen leaves.

Don't go forward, the forest ahead is boundless,
The trunks of old trees show stripes and spots of the animals.
The serpentine vines intertwine, half dead and half living,
Not a single star can fall through the dense foliage above.
You won't dare to put your foot down a second time, when you
Have heard the empty and lonely echo of your first step.

Must you go? Then, let me go with you.
My feet know every safe trail there is.
I shall sing my songs without stop,
And offer you the comfort of my hand.
When the thick darkness of the night separates us,
You may fix your eyes on mine.

You pay no heed to my excited songs,
Your footsteps halt not for a moment at my trembling self.
Like a breeze, soft and serene, passing through the dusk . . .
It vanishes, and vanished are your proud footsteps.
Ah, have you really silently come, as in the prophecy,
And silently gone, my youthful god?

1931
Translated by Kai-yu Hsu

THINKING OF A FRIEND AT YEAR'S END

When a dried pinecone falls,
And the wings of low-flying birds rustle by
You pause in your solitary stroll in the woods;
When fish go hiding and the water is chilly
And your lonely fishing line floats in the pond,
When winter's white frost seals your window,
Hiding yourself in a long spell of illness
Do you still think of your house in the north?

In the old rattan chair in the corner,
In the shadow of the wall,
Stayed much of my unhappiness;
Often I had much unhappiness, but
Often yours was a congenial silence.
Often in the folds of the old cold cotton window curtain
There were lizards jerking their gray legs.
In the courtyard outside

The sound of a woodpecker, hollow and tremulous
Dripped from among the fine leaves of the elm tree.
You asked me if I like that sound.
If then were now, I would surely say I like it.

In the west wind a train of camels in their new coats
Lift their heavy hoofs
And let them down again, gently.
There is already a thin layer of ice in the street.

1931
Translated by Kai-yu Hsu

AUTUMN

Shaking down the pearls of dew that cloak an early morning,
The sound of a woodsman's ax drifts from a sequestered vale.
As sickles, saturated with the scent of new rice, are laid aside,
And bamboo baskets marched off to carry home fat pumpkins
  from the vine,
Autumn rests on the farm.

Casting a round net in the chilly fog over the river,
To bring in the shadows of black leaves like blue flounders,
While the mat canopy of the boat bears a layer of hoarfrost,
The boatman gently paddles his small oar, homeward-bound.
Autumn plays on a fishing vessel.

The grassy wilderness gets more desolate and broader with the
  crickets' chirping.
The water in the creek becomes more crystalline as it stoops to
  bare the rocks.
Where did they go, the notes of a flute that used to ride on a
  buffalo's back,
And the flute's holes whence the fragrance and warmth of a
  summer night used to flow?
Autumn dozes in the eyes of a shepherdess.

Between 1931 and 1933
Translated by Kai-yu Hsu

Zheng Min (1920–)

A GLANCE

REMBRANDT'S "YOUNG GIRL AT AN OPEN HALF DOOR"

Exquisite are the shoulders receding into the shadow,
And the bosom, locked up, rich as a fruit-laden orchard.
The shining face, like the flush of dream,
Echoes the hands resting on the half door, so slender.

The river of time carries away another leaf from the tree of
calendar,
Her half-closed eyes, like a riddle, speak of a blurred silence.
In the limited life the unchanging hurried pace is still too
hurried,
She casts, in a casual evening, a lasting glance at the
ever-changing world.

1949

Translated by Kai-yu Hsu

THE LOTUS FLOWER

ON VIEWING A PAINTING BY ZHANG DAQIAN

The one, with its apparently unfailing cup,
Holds the joy of blooming and stands
Like a towering mountain bearing an eternity
For which man has not words.

The young leaf, in no hurry to unfold itself,
Retains a hope in its untainted heart to loom up
Through the haze on water, gazing at the world
That wears, with reluctance, an old and faded costume.

But what is the real theme
Of this performance of pain? This bent
Lotus stem drooping its blossom
Toward its roots, it says nothing
Of the ravage of storms, but of the multiple life—
The solemn burden—it has received from the Creator.

1949
Translated by Kai-yu Hsu

PART FIVE

Poetry, 1949–1976

Ji Xian (1913–   )

SPRING DANCING

She flew out of the specimen exhibition room of the
National Research Institute
A skeleton, breaking the glass case without making
A sound, as the male deputy curator was taking a
siesta
After lunch. She was

O so lightly, lightly, lightly
Swinging with the choreography of Isadora Duncan
The subtle rhythm of Zhao Feiyan, in front of the
Commercial Building
A quiet, spring square. The square:
Azaleas bloomed and she danced. This dancer
Must have been love-crazed; and the napping curator
was apparently
A dreamless specimen according to a certain
definition
Specimen
Specimen
Spring dancing

(Dancing: skeleton
Dancing: young woman)
Specimen. Specimen. Spring dancing!

And when her mood was down, in an instant
She disappeared merrily, forgetting to fetch back
On the huge German hormone ad billboard
Awesome, the indelible shadow

1957
Translated by C. H. Wang

A WOLF

I am a lone wolf walking in the field

not a prophet
without any thought to sigh
but constantly with some extremely shivering howlings
shake that absolutely empty world
to make it tremble as if it had malarial fever
and blow its chilly wind that gets on my nerves

This is how I'm tough
        Sort of groovy

1964
Translated by C. H. Wang

Mu Dan (1918–1977)

SELF

Not knowing which world to call home,
He chose an arbitrary tongue and creed,
Pitched an improvised tent on sand.
Beneath the canopy of a little star,
He began his heart's commerce with things:
was that the real me?

By chance on his long trek he enountered an idol,
Assumed the semblance of a worshipper,
Calling these men friends, those men enemies,
Deploying emotions in their appropriate places.
The little shop of his life throve:
was that the real me?

After a spell of prosperity he went broke,
As if he had toppled his own dynasty.
The world cold-shouldered him, ridiculed him, punished him,
And yet all he had lost was his crown.
Lying awake at night he brooded:
was that the real me?

Meanwhile another world was posting bills for a missing person.
His disappearance surprised the vacant room
Where another dream was waiting for him to dream,
And numerous rumors were ready to give him a shape
Hinting at an unwritten biography:
was that the real me?

1976

Translated by Pang Bingjun and John Minford, with Seán Golden

SONG OF WISDOM

I have reached illusion's end
In this grove of falling leaves,
Each leaf a signal of past joy,
Drifting sere within my heart.

Some were loves of youthful days—
Blazing meteors in a distant sky,
Extinguished, vanished without trace,
Or dropped before me, stiff and cold as ice.

Some were boisterous friendships,
Full-blown blossoms, innocent of coming fall.
Society dammed the pulsing blood,
Life cast molten passion in reality's shell.

Another joy, the spell of high ideals,
Drew me through many a twisting mile of thorn.
To suffer for ideals is no pain;
But oh, to see them mocked and scorned!

Now nothing remains but remorse—
Daily punishment for past pride.
When the glory of the sky stands condemned,
In this wasteland, what color can survive?

There is one tree that stands alone intact,
It thrives, I know, on my suffering's lifeblood.
Its greenshade mocks me ruthlessly!
O wisdom tree! I curse your every growing bud.

1976

Translated by Pang Bingjun and John Minford, with Seán Golden

Zhou Mengdie (1920–   )

KINGDOM OF SOLITUDE

Last night again I dreamed myself
Sitting naked on the snowy peak.

Here the climate sticks on the grafting line between
    winter and spring
(Here the snow is soft as swan's down)
Here no disturbing city din,
Only the faint sound of time chewing time in rumination;
No spectacled snakes or owls, or human-faced beasts,
Only thorn apples, olive trees, and jade butterflies;
Here no language, no logic, no Buddha with a myriad of
    hands and eyes.
Everywhere is power poured out of primordial quiet.
Here daylight is mysterious and gentle as night,

Night more beautiful, more bountiful more splendid than day;
Here is coolness like wine, sealed with poetry and beauty,
Even the void can understand sign language, inviting the skyful
Of stars who forgot how to speak . . .

The past stands still without leaving, the future does not come;
I am the slave of the present, also its king.

1959

Translated by Angela C. Y. Jung Palandri, with Robert J. Bertholf

UNDER THE BODHI TREE

Who hides a mirror in his heart?
Who is willing to cross life in bare feet?
All eyes are blindfolded with eyes.
Who can from snow draw fire, and forge fire into snow?
Under the Bodhi tree a half-faced man
Raises his eye to the sky, and with sighs answers
That towering blue bending over him.

Yes, here someone did sit![1]
Grass congealed into emerald. Though it is winter,
Though the footfall of the seated one has faded,
You still could enjoy the quiet
And secret communion against moonlight and breezes.

How many springs have snapped
How many summers have ripened while you sat?
When you came, snow was snow, you were you.
Overnight, snow was no more snow, you were not you
Until this night of minus-ten years
When the first comet suddenly restored its flash

Then you are startled to see:
The snow is still snow, you are still you
Even the footfall of the seated one has faded
The grass remains emerald.

1965

Translated by Angela C. Y. Jung Palandri, with Robert J. Bertholf

---

1. According to Buddhist scriptures, Buddha sat under the Bodhi tree meditating and gained enlightenment by watching a comet.

Yu Guangzhong (1928–)

IF THERE'S A WAR RAGING AFAR

If there's a war raging afar, shall I stop my ear
Or shall I sit up and listen in shame?
Shall I stop my nose or breathe and breathe
The smothering smoke of a troubled air? Shall I hear
You gasp lust and love or shall I hear the howitzers
Howl their sermons of truth? Mottoes, medals, widows,
Can these glut the greedy palate of Death?
If far away there's a war frying a nation,
And fleets of tanks are ploughing plots in spring,
A child is crying at its mother's corpse
Of a dumb and blind and deaf tomorrow;
If a nun is squatting on her fiery bier
With famished flesh singeing a despair
And black limbs ecstatic round Nirvana
As a hopeless gesture of hope. If
We are in bed, and they're in the field
Sowing peace in acres of barbed wire,
Shall I feel guilty or shall I feel glad,
Glad I'm making, not war, but love,
And in my arms writhes your nakedness, not the foe's?

If afar there rages a war, and there we are—
You a merciful angel, clad all in white
And bent over the bed, with me in bed—
Without hand or foot or eye or without sex
In a field hospital that smells of blood.
If a war Oh such a war is raging afar,
My love, if right there we are.

1967
Translated by the author

NOSTALGIA

When I was young,
Nostalgia was a tiny, tiny stamp,
Me on this side,
Mother on the other side.

When I grew up,
Nostalgia was a narrow boat ticket,
Me on this side,
My bride on the other side.

But later on,
Nostalgia was a lowly grave,
Me on the outside,
Mother on the inside.

And at present,
Nostalgia becomes a shallow strait,
Me on this side,
Mainland on the other side.

1972
Translated by the author

THE WHITE JADE BITTER GOURD

SEEN AT THE PALACE MUSEUM, TAIPEI

Seeming awake, yet asleep, in a light slow and soft,
Seeming, idly, to wake up from an endless slumber,
A gourd is ripening in leisureliness,
A bitter gourd, no longer raw and bitter
But time-refined till its inner purity shows.

Entwined with bearded vines, embowered with leaves,
When was the harvest that seems to have sucked,
In one gulp, all that old China had to suckle?
Fulfilled to a rounded consummation,
Palpably, it keeps swelling all about,
Pressing on every grape-bulge of creamy white
Up to the tip, tilting as if fresh from the stem.

Vast were the Nine Regions, now shrunk to a chart,
Which I cared not to enfold when young,
But let stretch and spread in their infinities
Huge as the memory of a mother's breast.
And you, sprawling to that prolific earth,
Sucked the grace of her sap through root and stem
Till the fond-hearted mercy fondly reared,
For curse or for bliss, the baby bitter gourd
On whom the mainland lavished all her love,
Trampled by boots, hard trod by horses' hoofs,
By the rumpling tracks of heavy tanks,
There it lies, not a trace of scar remains.

Incredible, the wonder behind the glass,
Still under the spell of blessing earth,
Maturing in the quaint light all untouched
By time, a universe ever self-contained,
A mellowness beyond corruption, a fairy fruit
From no fairy mountain, but from our earth.
Long decayed your former self, O long decayed
The hand that renewed your life, the magic wrist
That with shuttling glances led you across, the smile
When the soul turned around through the white jade
A song singing of life, once a gourd and bitter,
Now eternity's own, a fruit and sweet.

1974
Translated by the author

Wang Xipeng (n.d.)

A GROUP OF URBAN YOUTHS IS ON ITS WAY

Chang'an Commune, Dengmai County

A hundred flowers bloom, and birds give song,
A group of urban youths is on its way!
With joyful news the children run along,
The old folks all rejoice, their spirits gay.

To Granny, they're her daughters and her sons,
A bowl of coconut milk she offers forth.
Old Grandpa strokes his beard, pokes up a thumb:
"New young'ns come to battle heaven and earth!"

New comrades welcomed to the farm with zest,
Hear how the gleeful chatter echoes now!
Excitement in a single line expressed:
"Let's take the road that's shown by Chairman Mao!"

The Party leader takes the youth aside
And makes the two line struggles crystal clear:
"In agriculture study from Dazhai
And we will plant red Dazhai blossoms here!"

Like eagles, youth must venture far and wide,
Not stay like fearful sparrows close to home;
We'll help to build a socialist countryside
Devote our youth to make new flowers bloom!

n.d.

Translated by Richard King

Luo Fu (1928–)

BEYOND THE FOG

An egret
In the rice field reading *Nourritures Terrestres*[1]
Encircling a certain fixed point, whirling like fog,
By chance bends down to bite a slice of cloud on the water.

Contemplation. No more than contemplating
Whether the sun is a nihilist,
Raising its left foot the whole body
Not knowing whether to stay in fog
Or beyond fog.

Spread your wings, the universe floats along,
Morning is a brilliant sound
Burning itself in the fog.

---

1. By Andre Gide (1941). The Chinese translation of the title affords a pun on the French words.

If the skyline is thrown up to fasten you
It will fasten your wings but not your flight.

1967
Translated by Angela C. Y. Jung Palandri, with Robert J. Bertholf

CITY: SAIGON, 1967

Must be, they must be growing and continuing to rise
To become buildings
To become rushing dust
To become the blank space of a painting in Chinese ink
All summer
The sun in the whole city sculpts a face on the wall
They are fiercely in love
Then, wiping their bodies
Then, raising a hand slowly
To draw a gush of black smoke from the throat
Bloom: the bars on Saturday
Bloom: the bombs on Wednesday
The tank walks chewing a hamburger
Whereas the machine-gun is a Dadaist
Elevating the stagnant water in the street
To become a stretch of twilight

Therefore
When a bunch of bullets fly from the southgate to
  the northgate
When we light up ourselves within
A furious lamp

1967
Translated by C. H. Wang

FOLLOWING THE SOUND OF RAIN INTO THE MOUNTAINS: NO RAIN

Holding an oil-paper umbrella
Humming "Sour is the Plum of March"
In the mountains
I am the pilgrims' only pair of shoes

Woodpeckers' empty
Echoes
A tree revolves up in the pecking pain

Into the mountains
No rain
The umbrella flaps over a blue rock
On which a man sits, head in his arms
Watching the cigarette stubs turn to ash

Down the mountains
Still, no rain
Three bitter pinecones
Roll along the roadsigns, toward me
Pick them up
A handful of chirping sound

1970
Translated by C. H. Wang

Ya Xian (1932–   )

SALT

The Old Woman had never seen Dostoyevsky at all. Spring, she just cried, "Salt! Salt! Give me a handful of salt." The angels were singing in the elm tree; that year, the garden peas hardly bloomed.

Seven hundred miles away, the Minister of Salt's caravan was moving around the sea. In the Old Woman's blind pupils, no sea weeds have ever grown. She just cried, "Salt! Salt! Give me salt." The angels were giggling, shaking down snow for her.

1911. The partymen have come to Wuchang, but the Old Woman has gone from her foot wrappings hanging on the elm into the breath of wild dogs and into the wings of bald-headed vultures. Many voices whined in the wind—"Salt! Salt! Give me a handful of salt." Nearly all the garden peas bloomed white that year. Dostoyevsky had never seen our Old Woman at all.

1958

Translated by the author

PARIS

The soft silk shoes from your lips
trample across my eyelids. In the evening, six o'clock in the evening
when a shooting star knocks me out
Paris falls to trifling away the night in bed.

Between the evening paper and the starry sky
someone is bleeding on the grass,
between the roof and the dew
a poppy blooms in the womb.

You are a valley
you are a good-looking mountain flower
you are a stuffed pastry trembling in the rat's-gray
as it rustles, chews and steals like a coward toward you.

How much truth can a blade of grass bear, God?
when the eyes are used to the midnight's poppy
and the silk sky of soles, when the veins are dodders
winding south from your thighs.

Did last year's snow remember those clumsy footprints, God?
when a baby cries, complaining of its umbilical cord,
next year when he hides his face passing Notre Dame
on his way to the beds' trifling years which will give him nothing.

You are a river
you are a blade of grass
you are last year's snow, remembering no footprints
you are perfumed, perfumed shoes.

Between the Seine and reason
who chooses to die,
between desperation and Paris
only the tower holds the sky.

1958

Translated by the author

THE COLONEL

It was a rose
Sudden
Born of fire
In a buckwheat field where they met the most decisive battle of the war
His leg was parted from him in 1942.

He has heard history and the laughter of history.
What is imperishable—
Cough syrup, a razor, last month's rent and the like?
During the skirmish of his wife's sewing machine
He feels the only thing that can capture him
Is the sun.

1960
Translated by the author

Zheng Chouyu (1933–)

PAGODA

Pagoda: spirits sit peacefully in the cell without mattress
As the spring wind tinkles the eavesbells
Spirits quietly lean over the lattices to enjoy a temple view

I and my buddy, among the crowd of the fallen
Also look around, recalling what happened in the last battle

Down there, the good old leaf-sweeper monk walks by
Then, as usual, there are the three woodcutters
Ah, can it be my son, grown up, one of the tourists?
He wears my old uniform, dyed apparently, and is
Arguing with his girlfriend (must be a science student)
How long a handful of ashes can last burning

1958
Translated by C. H. Wang

GRENZ-TAVERNE

Autumn earth is territoried under a common sun
Now sinking. Where the lands meet, yellow chrysanthemums stand
Silently. He came from afar, drinking in sobriety
Beyond the window there is a foreign country

Very much desiring to walk out; one step would create nostalgia
Sweet nostalgia which you can touch

Otherwise, let's get drunk alright
(He is an enthusiastic tax-payer)
Or by singing a couple of songs
He is better off than the chrysanthemums, standing
Within the border line

1958
Translated by C. H. Wang

CLEAR AND BRIGHT: IN THE GRAVE

I am still drunk, and the quiet night flows within me
As I stop up the ears, myth echoes around in my body
A smell of blossoms percolates through the skin
At this moment of ultimate beauty, I accept their worship
Receiving the sacrifice of a thousand streamers

Stars dropping down in strings, stirring up the vine between my lips
Fog is crystallizing, as cold as the prayerful eyes
So many so many eyes stream fast on my hair
I must return, to do something with these plants growing on limbs

I have returned: I have always been a stretch of blue hills

1959
Translated by C. H. Wang

Bai Qiu (1937–)

MOTH

A hungry silkworm
In my interior
Eats my heart

Forever discontent
Having eaten
Starts spinning his silk

Having spun his silk
In my dark interior
Dreams a dream

Dreams of a translucent sky
And wings to soar
Longs for an embrace

Biting through my exterior
Despite all my warnings
Rushes into the world

Says, The world is warm
The world is bright
Unlike this dark, cold interior

One night, above a candle
He tests again the world's warmth
Burns to ash
Never to return

1958

Translated by Pang Bingjun and John Minford, with Seán Golden

VAGABOND

Gazing at a distant cloud,   a silk fir
gazing at a cloud, a silk fir
a silk fir
silk fir

a

s
i
l
k

f
i
r

on the horizon   on the horizon

His shadow, short and lean. His shadow, short and lean
He's forgotten his name. Forgotten his name. Just
standing there.   Just standing. Standing
alone.   Standing.   Standing
Standing
Facing east
a solitary silk fir

1958

Translated by Pang Bingjun and John Minford, with Seán Golden

Ye Weilian (1937–   )

THE RIVER'S FANCY

Cloud layers bear down, drum sounds go up; white sun,
Why do you press my body and create streams,
Why when the wingless flight toward you
Rootlessly stands still, sightless,
Grasps that loftiness, do the two banks
Separate because of my body?

Enter an inside enter a between;
Which inside between which?

How is my interminable body moving about to regulate the earth?
Pondering the fact of my birth I wish to ask:
Did the clear water wait to receive the moon?
Did the trees grow by the attitude of the wind?
Since men introduced festive rites, their steps brought cities.

Those high cloud layers still bear down, drum sounds still go up,
The sea with its boundless trembling receives us,
With its colorless expanse quells rows of curious eyes.
White sun, when you die by the mountain, shameless women

Will wash the wind with their swinging breasts,
Will push out nature with their private parts.

(Man comes man departs
The same man
The same I
Man comes man departs)

Now after winter is refuted there is no name for seasons,
Also no chronology—those floating chronologies.
This time mountains are refuted, every instrument of sound
Becomes sky hue, becomes the motion of stars.
Enter an inside enter a between;
Which inside between which?
White sun, since I cannot drink myself up,
Tell me how can I see through my own eyes?
How not to be a river—
To be an unflowing surging river?

1963

Translated by Angela C. Y. Jung Palandri, with Robert J. Bertholf

THE PURSUIT

Confusion of cities and of villages in all directions
in the beginning creeps into an unprepared octagonal pen
sticking into
an insensible atmosphere suspended we too
twirl in the smoke on the bookcase in the church
producing steep tower in the world hurriedly
seeking for completion seeking in our expectation
sacramental union the sun helping
woods as though excessively carved things helping
our hands stretched out together touching a conflagration
rekindled incineration yellow red some nameable
dreading the birth of new life from joy
similarity and dissimilarity are both smoke of campfires cattle
sheep kangaroos
we also cannot forget yesterday and tomorrow unborn and again
killed today we also cannot forget the confusion in the union of
yesterday and today
without reality with shape similar to the self
from a curious position to the numerous recurrence of
historical changes

from thoughtful silence to shrubberies to birds to children's toys
or in today's completeness retreat to the boundless unconscious
  of the narrow heart

turn to the bamboo fence of the park the sound
is still vibrating:
    and I!
      and I?

1963

Translated by Angela C. Y. Jung Palandri, with Robert J. Bertholf

Dai Tian (1937–   )

THE STORY OF THE STONE

The time was 1969
The place, a certain colony
The character, I
The event:
Sudden
Birth and growth
Of a piece of stone
In my heart

It was a kind of
Night that didn't have an evening
It was a kind of
Decision
Of having to pull the brakes
It was a grain of sand
That exists
Nowhere in the eye

The fear people have
For a seed

Is that it might die
And, for a dream,
That it might be broken
And, for a stone,
That it just might keep on
Growing

If the mighty Mount Tai
Should find its place in the pupil
Then all its verdure
And colossal strength
Would become
In an instant
A mere
Emerald sphere

If the Great River
Should creep and surge
In the veins
Then, ah, all manner of fish therein
Would no longer
Be free
But would just
Freeze there

And so, like veins on a leaf,
The hand
Is gnawed
By a little bug
And so voices
Become unfamiliar
Like cries that come
From the other side of the river

A child
Comes along
And spits
Phlegm
On my face
And says:
"Never have I seen
Such an ugly stone statue"

1969
Translated by Diana Yue

DEBATE ON RUGGED MOUNTAIN[1]

They say Rugged Mountain is in the north
But in the south
In the south, too, there is
A mountain that is ever so rugged

You say on the top of the mountain
Stands a camelia tree
And he says the grassy slopes are
Encircled by frills of clouds and fog

Of course, there are also clear streams
That warrant our careful study
And stony crags
That deserve a decent trimming

But the problem is
What is a mountain
And, according to you, ultimately,
Does it exist or not

What is the rationale
Is it there or not there
Is it a noun or is it
Real substance

When formally the debate was over
He shows us the mountain haze
And when substance-wise the debate was over
You look into emptiness

They say Rugged Mountain is in the north
But in the south

---

1. *Trans. note:* Rugged Mountain—The original is Goulou Shan, also pronounced as Julu Shan. This mountain is situated in Hunan Province and is the main peak of the Heng Range, one of the centers of Taoism in China. The peak is famous as the site of an ancient stone stele said to be erected by the mythological emperor Yu. The word *goulou* does not carry any meaning. The translator is tempted to translate it as *guru*, to give it an association with ancient wisdom. But as the word is used adjectivally in line four of the poem, a safer translation would be *rugged*. *Rugged* probably has some visual and phonetic similarity with *goulou*, impressionistically speaking.

In the south, too, there is
A mountain that is ever so rugged.

POSTSCRIPT

One day in a certain month, I met my old friend Nonesuch. We talked first about Zen, and then about names. After "Zen" and "names," we talked about almost anything, drifting along and spitting out words almost amounting to madness, feeling we were ever so right and everybody else was shit, and that as big as the whole earth was it was no more than a tiny mustard seed! Oh what a show of scholarly conceit and subjectivity peculiar to us "scholar-officials"! Having got home, I had a few cups of booze, and, uh-oh, I began to understand. So here I wrote down this "rhyme nonsensical" as a joke about myself and also to record the incident. Call it debate or whatnot, it's really just trouble created out of nowhere by a bunch of stinking old literati, a game of words and nothing more! Nothing more!

1976
Translated by Diana Yue

Yang Mu (1940–)

SONG OF GRAY HAIR

In the beginning I thought time was a pool of
Stagnant water tinged with the sadness of civilization.
As night fell, spring chill touched off an explosion of my flesh:
Floods swelled and subsided. At last, I
Entered the Paleolithic Age of hunting.

I dreamed I was searching for a blue mountain faint as a lock of hair,
In which the pigeon had disappeared. When the wind stopped I saw
A group of women, clad in black, walking, then sitting down
In a circle, exchanging strange gestures.
Mysterious gestures indeed, but they expressed nothing more than
Grievances against the wars, which were
All excuses, they said, for my heroic entrance
Into the Neolithic Age.

A reckless man set fire to the mountain;
In the ashes we discovered copper.
Some I took to forge weapons to slaughter men by first cutting off
Their ears so as for me to become an arrogant, bragging king.
The rest I gave to my officials to make speculums

To impress their women, who did not have to comb their hair
By the river any more—
But I won't get into that.

Let me talk about another good-for-nothing with only one ear.
To avenge the shame he had suffered from the blood stained shoulder,
He spent ten years on a mountain, mining and extorting,
Before he discovered a harder substance than ever.
Grinding it, hammering it, singing to it with wine,
He created an icy, glowing sword. With that I entered
The Iron Age of combatant, martial display.

But that was when I began getting old.
During my worst years of decline,
Missionaries came from the West and presented to me a transparent
Goblet, a crystal vase,
And a vanity mirror, which shamed me
Each time I counted the rebellious gray hairs on my temples.

1975

Translated by Michelle Yeh and the author

AFTER THE SNOW

Bitter cold
After the snow,
Returning from the woods,
I cannot bring myself into the yard
To step on myth and poetry. I hesitate,
Standing at the foot of the silent bridge.
There is a light in the house. A broken tune
Drifts here and there. There is
A potted winter plum reclining
To gaze at its own slender shadow.

I hear a sigh
Coming from behind the door;
Someone is reading a book
On the interpretation of dreams.
After the snow—I suppose there is a fire
In the house, too, but I am a fire extinguished last year.
Someone is kindling me, poking me,
Like a handful of whispering stars.

I cannot help moving closer,
For I hear a sign
Coming to me like plum fragrance.
I hear the pages of the book turning—
Let me offer an interpretation for your dreams:
I have returned from a strange land to discover
How the temperature here changes between dawn and dark. If you
Are still cold, then put me on
The grate to make a fresh fire
For tonight.

1975
Translated by Michelle Yeh and the author

GEOMETRY: RIVER GODDESS

1

She who arrives across the water
Is a goddess. The distinct oars carry the boat along
Almost without a sound,
A chaste, white boat emerging
Between the pavilion and the willows

A goddess is coming, like the chimes of
A bell flitting across the water
Only to disappear in a moment—
Moonlight on her shoulder,
Frost on the prow and the stern.

2

And therefore, there is a lantern
To mark her trail
On the grid of the water:
Every two squares contain a water lily.
She is gliding, and yet she does not seem to come
Any closer, but afar lingering
There. For whom does she tarry on the islet in the middle
of the water?[1]

---

1. From "Goddess of the River Xiang," attributed to Qu Yuan (343?–278 b.c.).

Each time the lantern
Moves into a square, a water lily
Brightens up the moment,
Like her assenting smile.
Weaving in and out of darkness,
The boat leaves a flickering line in its wake
Between the distant pavilion and the nearby willows.
Is she a goddess? She must be
A goddess, moving like an aroused swan on the wing,
Gracefully, a dragon taming the elements, her beauty surpassing
Chrysanthemums in the autumn and pine trees in the spring.[2]
She is coming my way, but she is not any closer.
The slender oars skim the water
Quietly—a vision beyond reach.

3

Even so,
The moon shines on
The young tree, under which the goddess seems standing
Free, her tresses untied. I shall think of a new name
For the tree of lunar splendor.

The boat glides over the coordinates on the grid.
She begins to sing softly, like
A thin flower blooming and closing in the fog,
A fish net slowly sinking,
Willow leaves brushed by the moonlight,
And frost falling. The lyric of the song says:
> I hear the fair lady beckoning me.
> We shall fly away together
> And build a home in the midst of the water . . . [3]

She is coming, but she does not seem to
Get any closer. And as she tarries,
Her trail sparkles intermittently,
Scarcely analyzable—each light in bloom
Is a water lily.

1975
Translated by Michelle Yeh and the author

---

2. From "Goddess of the River Luo," by Cao Zhi (192–232).
3. From "Lady of the River Xiang," attributed to Qu Yuan.

Xiong Hong (1940–   )

THE DELUDED DREAM

The sacred horn suddenly loses its prophecy;
With no tortoise shells in the heart I cannot divine whether
Our meeting in the next existence is
North of the frontier or south of the River.
Say, old friend,
At parting did you rend the silk of the willow
Or the silk of hair?

The flat cypress weaves, the hair weaves,
The storybook also weaves, weaving an intricate net,
Netting me into a cocoon.
Beyond the cocoon is Zen, beyond Zen is a riddle;
The riddle is delusion, in delusion the net revolves.

Each revolution is an unpredictable dream
Because the book of dream interpretation was cast way
Into the dream of the illusive South.[1]

1968

Translated by Angela C. Y. Jung Palandri, with Robert J. Bertholf

---

1. South of the Yangtze River.

FIRE ON THE SEA FLOOR

The blue came howling,
Many precious illusions sadly
Retreating—
The sea floor will have a great fire,
        By the edge of the coral grove stand coral groves
        By their edges are more coral groves
But your name is the undying splendor.
You say:
"Raise your face and look at me—

Drink no more history's melancholy alone,
The rainy season is over, don't refuse the golden sunlight.
Design your tomb no more
Its crystal of 3,600 dimensions
Sits between the blinking of an endless dream.

"Raise your face and look at me—

The rainy season is over, restored
Behind the tired gray veil with
The ballerina's beautiful pose I wait for you, for you."

But illusions sadly retreat
From the cold muddy ground a tiny light-yearning plant
Timidly raises its face watching you—

1968

Translated by Angela C. Y. Jung Palandri, with Robert J. Bertholf

Chen Jinghua (n.d.)

OUR WILL TO SETTLE HERE WILL NEVER FAIL

Shatian Commune, Gaozhou County

The morning sky is filled with rosy clouds,
    To greet the sunrise in the eastern sky,
Toward that broad expanse of heaven and earth
    We open up our youthful wings and fly!

Steel becomes purer as it is refined,
    Knives become sharper still the more they're ground,
Successors to the revolution, we
    Will hone ourselves where storms and winds abound.

Legs deep in mud, our bodies drenched with sweat
    We labor daily with our peasant friends;
The feeling in our hearts is honey-sweet
    As, far before us, billowing rice extends.

We study with the peasants every night,
    Grasp weapons, wipe the scales from off our eyes;

We steel ourselves to battle Liu Shaoqi,
Denouncing all those tricksters and their lies.

Courage in revolution fills our breasts,
Youth is a fire whose valor always grows,
We open up the mountains, divert streams,
Our will expressed by wielding of our hoes!

How do we plan? Or write most stirring songs?
The answers from our peasant friends we find.
Flow down, our sweat! Again we tell you, flow
And wash away impurity from our minds!

The kapok trees before our doors bloom red,
Atop the mountains, mighty pines prevail;
We give this resolution to Beijing:
Our will to settle here will never fail!

n.d.

Translated by Richard King

PART SIX

Poetry Since 1976

Zhang Cuo (1943–   )

AUTUMN MEDITATION

1

A word from a faraway friend arrives, says
There is a separation, in autumn, quite Korean—
"In case you go away, please walk
On the path of fallen leaves which I have gathered for you."
Hundreds of fallen leaves,
As many as the varieties of mood;
The most heartbreaking is still the volume on the desk,
Collection of Ten Thousand Leaves,
Particularly the one by Kakinomoto Hitomaro:
"In the autumn mountains, yellow leaves are thick,
Mountain paths are misty,
Alas, where shall I seek my love?"
Thus we can see
Ten thousand leaves of words
Are actually ten thousand moods,
Drifting, unattached,
In a foreign land,
In autumn.

2

A message, following the autumn wind,
Sent from faraway,
Sadly reminding:
I finally dreamt,
Under a big tree,
The traveling you is autumn,
Leaves profusely falling
Covering your feet;
The solitary you is autumn,
The silent you is autumn.
The sound of autumn is the falling leaves,
The hair of autumn is the white reeds,
The love of autumn is the lonely pine deep in the
mountain.
Autumn is the dreamy season.
Only in the reunion after parting
Can one taste the dream and reality of life,
In the joy of staring at one another in silence.
Autumn is the reminiscing season.
Only after spring fades and summer withers
And maples turn red, and reeds white,
Can one be astonished by the stranger's face in the mirror,
And shaken by a flashing glimmer of white hair.
At last the age for reading Du Fu has come;
After the tribulations of wars,
The restlessness of feelings,
One is reminded of a lonely lantern in a northern mountain
In a solitary autumn night.
"I dare not wish for your chaste celibacy,
But I hope there is always me in you."
Since moving eastward,
There were too many undaring thoughts:
Not daring to look back,
Dreading deepening anger,
Not daring to look ahead,
Dreading regrettable thoughts;
There is only one daring thought:
On a night when the moon is bright and stars are sparse,
Putting on a coat and walking into the backyard to sharpen
my sword,
I softly recite the first half of a *waka:*

"Loneliness does not
Originate in any one
Particular thing . . . "

1983
Translated by the author

EARL GREY

Drink to you only with Earl Grey
I almost felt that my hair turned early grey
The tea is best consumed on an afternoon
In a white pavilion inside a rose garden;
Ladies with silk fans, tea silverware,
And ginger shortbread.
After the pouring of rich and thick cream
All are but tiny stirs of waves in a teacup:
Subtle, humorous jokes,
Occasional interruptions of an astonishing cry,
In a partial pre-Victorian era
With elegance and pride
Clinked the gold-rimmed cup
Along with the waltz of the silvery spoons
There are also prejudices
Insisted on visual gratifications
And on the intimate interactions between touch and taste
Before the final expression of a satisfactory sigh.
Such customs can be traced back to the sixteenth century
After the Portuguese princess married Charles the second
All the court was mesmerized with tea
A whole fleet resolutely steered toward Columbo!
Two hundred years later, Charles mixed with Grey
We then had Earl Grey
This Grey referred not to the color gray
Nor to Dorian of the portrait
Who worried about the loss of his youthful look
But to the prime minister of Great Britain
A Whig from head to toe
His anxiety, besides the voting rights of the bourgeois,
Was but a cup of Grey
Prepared specially for him
Earl—y on an afternoon.

1994
Translated by the author

Huang Guobin (1946–)

A NIGHT PRAYER

We believe too much in ourselves,
Like high and perilous walls
Perched on a cliff when a storm impends,
Confident and self-assured.
We refuse to groan when wounded.
We shed no tears when hurt.
We are so unlike our ancestors, who feared the thunder,
   the wind,
And the dark in the wilderness.
When they were helpless, they would pray to the earth,
   call upon heaven,
Gather round a totem,
Kneel down, prostrate themselves, confess their sins,
Telling of their anxieties, misgivings, and fears.

We believe too much in ourselves,
Like stubborn locks, deaf and dumb,
Refusing the probings of all keys;
Like mummies,

Locking themselves up in a tomb,
Refusing the moonlight that knocks at the door,
Refusing even more the dawn that comes over the
mountains.
In the quiet of the night, singing is heard from the galaxy,
But we lock our doors and windows fast,
Reluctant even to give ear to the wind that blows over
our roofs,
More reluctant to go out
Into the wilderness and look up at the starlit sky.

We believe too much in ourselves.
We never let our roots reach into the soil
To listen to the song deep in the ground
And the ore racing in the veins of igneous rocks.
We never stretch ourselves like seedlings
To put forth soft green tender leaf-tips
Into the deep, blue sky,
And, trembling in apprehensive delight,
Reach into the damp, cool mist of dawn,
Towards the morning star in the east,
And, finally, amidst the silence of lakes and mountains,
Hurl headlong into the boundless space beyond the
heavens.

1977
Translated by the author

WHEN YOU ARE NAKED, YOU HAVE EVERYTHING

Like the earth,
You must have nothing,
Except starlight, the water of streams,
And a dark night which is everywhere;
Like the reef,
Which has only the sound of billows, the spray of waves,
And the rise and fall of eternal tides;
Like the wind,
Which has only loneliness and solitude.

When you are naked,
You have everything;
Like the earth,
Which has rivers, mountain ranges, and forests;

Like the reef,
Which has the sea
And the pulse of the moon;
Like the wind,
Which has lofty mountains, towering ridges,
Boundless plains,
And vast oceans.

When you are naked, you have
The heavenly music beyond the nebulae
And the splendor beyond the heavenly music.

When you are naked, you have everything.

1978
Translated by the author

Luo Qing (1948–)

SIX WAYS OF EATING WATERMELONS

The Fifth Way: The Consanguinity of Watermelons

No one would mistake a watermelon for a meteorite.
Star and melon, they are totally unconnected;
But earth is undeniably a heavenly body,
Watermelons and stars
Are undeniably consanguineous.

Not only are watermelons and the earth related
Like parent and child,
They also possess brotherly, sisterly feelings,
Like the moon and the sun,
The sun and us,
Us and the moon.

The Fourth Way: The Origins of Watermelons

Evidently, we live on the face of the earth;
And they, evidently, live in their watermelon interior.

We rush to and fro, thick-skinned,
Trying to stay outside, digesting light
Into darkness with which to wrap ourselves,
Cold and craving warmth.

They meditate on Zen, motionless, concentrated.
Shaping inward darkness into
Substantial, calm passions;
Forever seeking self-fulfillment and growth.
Someday, inevitably, we'll be pushed to the earth's interior,
And eventually they'll burst through the watermelon face.

The Third Way: The Philosophy of Watermelons

The history of watermelon philosophy
Is shorter than the earth's, but longer than ours;
They practice the Three Don'ts:
See no evil, hear no evil, speak no evil.
They are Taoistically *wu-wei*,
And keep themselves to themselves.

They don't envy ova,
Nor do they despise chicken's eggs.
Watermelons are neither oviparous, nor viviparous,
And comprehend the principle
Of attaining life through death.
Consequently, watermelons are not threatened by invasion,
Nor do they fear
Death.

The Second Way: The Territory of Watermelons

If we crushed a watermelon,
It would be sheer
  jealousy.
Crushing a melon is equivalent to crushing a rounded night,
knocking down all the
  stars,
Crumbling a perfect
  universe.

And the outcome would only make us more jealous,
Would only clarify the relationship
Between meteorites and watermelon seeds,
The friendship between watermelon seeds and the universe.
They would only penetrate once again, more deeply,
  into our
  territory

The First Way:

EAT IT FIRST.

1972
Translated by Zhang Cuo

Bei Dao (1949–)

DECLARATION

for Yu Luoke[1]

Perhaps the final hour is come
I have left no testament
Only a pen, for my mother.
I am no hero
In an age without heroes
I just want to be a man

The still horizon
Divides the ranks of the living and the dead
I can only choose the sky
I will not kneel on the ground
Allowing the executioners to look tall
The better to obstruct the wind of freedom

---

1. A martyr from the Cultural Revolution.

From star-like bullet holes shall flow
A blood-red dawn

1980
Translated by Bonnie S. McDougall and Susan Ternent Cooke

RÉSUMÉ

Once I goose-stepped across the square
my head shaved bare
the better to seek the sun
but in that season of madness
seeing the cold-faced goats on the other side
of the fence I changed direction
when I saw my ideals
on blank paper like saline-alkaline soil
I bent my spine
believing I had found the only
way to express the truth, like
a baked fish dreaming of the sea
Long live . . . ! I shouted only once, damn it
then sprouted a beard
tangled like countless centuries
I was obliged to do battle with history
and at knifepoint formed a
family alliance with idols
not indeed to cope with
the world fragmented in a fly's eye
among piles of endlessly bickering books
calmly we divided into equal shares
the few coins we made from selling off each star
in a single night I gambled away
my belt, and returned naked again to the world
lighting a silent cigarette
it was a gun bringing death at midnight
when heaven and earth changed places
I hung upside down
on an old tree that looked like a mop
gazing into the distance

1979–1983
Translated by Bonnie S. McDougall and Susan Ternent Cooke

ANOTHER LEGEND

dead heroes are forgotten
they are lonely, they
pass through a sea of faces
their anger can only light
the cigarette in a man's hand
even with the help of a ladder
they can no longer predict anything
each weather vane goes its own way
only when they huddle
at the foot of their hollow statues
do they realize the depth of despair
they always come and go at night
suddenly illuminated by a single lamp
but difficult to distinguish nonetheless
like faces pressed against frosted glass
finally, they slip through the narrow gate
covered over with dust
taking charge of the solitary key

1983–1986

Translated by Bonnie S. McDougall and Susan Ternent Cooke

Shu Ting (1952–)

WHEN YOU WALK PAST MY WINDOW

When you walk past my window
Bless me
Because the light is still on

The light is on—
In the heavy, gloomy night,
Like a fisherman's light drifting.
You can think of my tiny house
As a tiny boat tossed by a storm.
But I have not sunk
Because the light is still on.

The light is on—
The curtains may reflect a shadow,
Showing me an old and feeble man,
With no expansive gestures anymore,
My back more hunched than before,
But what has aged is not my heart,
Because the light is still on.

The light is on—
It answers with fervent love
Regards sent from all around;
The light is on—
It looks with commanding pride
Down on seen and hidden oppression.
Oh, when did the light assume such strong character?
When you began to understand me.

Because the light is still on,
Bless me,
When you walk past my window . . .

1976
Translated by Eva Hung

A ROADSIDE ENCOUNTER

The phoenix tree suddenly tilts
The bicycle bell's ring hangs in air
Earth swiftly reverses its rotation
Back to that night ten years ago
The phoenix tree gently sways again
The ringing bell sprinkles floral fragrance along the
  trembling street
Darkness gathers, then seeps away
The dawning light of memory merges with the light
  in your eyes

Maybe this didn't happen
Just an illusion spawned by a familiar road
Even if this did happen
I'm used to not shedding any tears

1979
Translated by Eva Hung

ASSEMBLY LINE

On the assembly line of Time
Nights huddle together
We come down from the factory assembly lines
And join the assembly line going home

Overhead
An assembly line of stars trails across the sky
By our side
A young tree looks dazed on its assembly line

The stars must be tired
Thousands of years have passed
Their journey never changes
The young trees are ill
Dust and monotony deprive them
Of grain and color
I can feel it all
Because we beat to the same rhythm

But strangely
The only thing I do not feel
Is my own existence
As though the woods and stars
Maybe out of habit
Maybe out of sorrow
No longer have the strength to care
About a destiny they cannot alter

1980
Translated by Eva Hung

THE CRY OF A GENERATION

I do not complain
        About *my* misfortune
The loss of my youth,
The deforming of my soul.
Sleepless nights without number
        Have left me with bitter memories.
I have rejected all received truths,
I have broken free of all shackles,
And all that remains of my heart
        Is in ruins, as far as the eye can see . . .
But still, I *have* stood up!
I stand on the expanse of the horizon.
Never again will anyone, by any-means,
        Be able to push me down.

If it were me, lying in a martyr's grave,
Green moss eating away the characters on my headstone;
If it were me, savoring the taste of life behind bars,
        Debating points of law with my chains;
If it were me, my face haggard and pale,
        Atoning for my crimes with an eternity of labor;
If it were me, it would be
        My tragedy alone—
Perhaps I might already have forgiven
Perhaps my grieving and my anger
        Might already be at rest.

But,
For the sake of the fathers of the children,
For the sake of the children of the fathers,
So that we no longer need to tremble
        At the unspoken reproaches
        From beneath the gravestones everywhere;
So that we may no longer be faced
        Wherever we turn
        By the specter of the homeless;
So that innocent children
        A hundred years from now
        Need not guess at the history we leave behind.
For this blank in our nation's memory,
For the arduous path our race must travel,
For the purity of the skies
        And the straightness of the road ahead—
I Demand The Truth!

1980

Translated by Richard King

Wang Xiaolong (1954–   )

WHEN WE FINALLY TURN FIFTY

We'll be just as we are now
Kissing as we casually fix a meal
Getting by whether or not the laundry's been done
No talking allowed during reading time
No money in the bank
Having a spat once every three days on average
Making our walk home from the movies
Deliberately long and sad
Then pretending we haven't known each other for three whole days
So we can be especially intimate on Sundays
The weather getting strangely pleasant
During the night we dream with our heads stuck together
And see two small dogs
Running across the snow

When we finally turn fifty

1982

Translated by Fang Dai, Dennis Ding, and Edward Morin

SURGERY WARD

Even the geranium in the hall is crestfallen
Those who walk in here inevitably hang their heads
They trundle off to bed after dinner
Staring with one hundred percent sympathy at a body
That seems to lack something under a snow-white bandage
Later on they deliberately turn up the radio to a loud wah-wah
As they imagine they're the great Maradona[1]
Or some fucking football kicked against the goalpost
Nobody comes this afternoon
That girl who brought one boy oranges and little smiles each afternoon
Won't be coming back anymore
Last night that boy
Took advantage of everyone's sleeping and stealthily died
This morning one old sparrow turned up to sob a while
Now it hides under who-knows-what eave pondering a line of poetry
Nobody comes this afternoon
The nurse sits like a man with one knee to her bosom
Writing a long letter that never comes to the last line
She flicks on the light and instantly the sky is black
After dark the mosquitoes' mouths loom especially large
This world—if it had no mosquitoes—this world
In spite of everything wouldn't be a bad place.

n.d.

Translated by Fang Dai, Dennis Ding, and Edward Morin

1. Diego Armando Maradona is a famous Argentinean soccer player.

Shang Qin (1930–)

THE CAT WHO WALKS THROUGH THE WALL

Ever since she left, this cat has been coming in and out of my place as she pleases; doors, windows, even walls can't stop her.

When she was with me, our life made the sparrows outside the iron gate and windows envious. She took care of me in every way, including bringing me with her hands the crescent moon on nights hen there was a power outage, and emitting cool air by standing next to me on humid summer nights.

I made the mistake of discussing happiness with her. That day, contrary to my usual reticence, I said: "Happiness is the half that people don't have." The next morning, she left without saying good-bye.

She's not the kind of woman who would write a note with lipstick on the vanity mirror. She didn't use a pen either. All she did was inscribe these words on the wallpaper with her long sharp fingernails: "From now on, I will be your happiness, and you mine."

Since this cat started coming in and out of my place as she pleases, I have never really seen her, for she always comes at midnight, leaves at daybreak.

1987

Translated by Michelle Yeh

Yang Lian (1955–   )

TO A NINE-YEAR-OLD GIRL KILLED IN THE MASSACRE

They say that you tripped on a piece of skipping elastic
And you jumped out of the house of white chalk
On a day of terrifyingly loud rain

Nine bullet holes in your body exude a sweetness
They say that you lost the moon while you were playing
Green grass on the grave   Are new teeth

Sprouting where there is no need for grief
You did not die   They say
You still sit at the small wooden desk

Eyes crash noisily against the blackboard
The school bell suddenly rings
A burst of nothingness   Your death is killed

They say   Now   You are a woman and a mother
And each year there is a birthday without you
Just as when you were alive

1989

Translated by Mabel Lee

THE DEAD IN EXILE

This street is not real   Nor are the footsteps
Even though the moon still slowly rises
And falls   The light is not real
Pale yellow skeletons tapping on the ground
Round pebbles almost transparent

Night already silenced by decay
Even hatred   Softens
Warm earth beneath the coffin
Like forgetfulness spitting out seeds
Spitting out us

Does leaving Death's womb
Also need the stamp of a red birthmark
Inside the mother   Child
Clumsily wriggling like a lizard
Swims into the black river
Making the last day a day of birth

Thanks to homesickness   Thanks
To each collective assault on mother's abdomen
Blood flees from one body to another
Turns to water Dead water

Smallest body
Thus buried in the last tomorrow
In the moonlight the drop of semen still looks white from afar

We can only look from afar
Look at   Wandering shadows of our lives
Footsteps of the dead lengthen the street
The womb has no address
In the mirror names drown one by one
Heads are strangled by frames on walls
Brains excised like a cancer removed
Yet still living   Shouting
Look   Beyond thin memory beyond the yellow earth
A face gradually blurs
And all scenery is reflection

No one can transcend the prison of lies
No one knows   Who is a corpse
When the sun explodes   Sleeves
Are empty
Everywhere is a foreign land
Death gives no refuge

Laden with corpses a line of poetry drifts away
Drifts away
Storm on rotting leaves
Continues to rage
Wandering about lying in a grave
The corpse's eyes are pure white
Filled with invisible stars
Pure white flesh   Inside all blood and filth
Crawls from the dirtiest channel of the mother's body
Screaming and sliding towards Hell
Every morning
Dying more deeply

The days are not real   But as the days pass
We are distanced more from ourselves

1990

Translated by Mabel Lee

Gu Cheng (1956–1993)

AN ENDING

In the blink of an eye—
the landslide had come to a halt,
a heap of great men's skulls at the river's edge.

A schooner draped in mourning
passed slowly by
unfurling its darkened shroud.

How many graceful verdant trees,
their trunks deformed by pain,
are consoling the brave and strong with their tears.

God buries the broken moon
in heavy mists—
already everything is ended.

1979
Translated by John Cayley

CURRICULUM VITAE

I am a child of sorrow
from cradle to grave undergrown
from the northern grasslands
I walked out, followed
a chalk road, walked into
the town piled high with cogwheels
walked under lean-tos
in the narrow lanes
—into every trodden heart
wrapped in indifferent smoke
I still tell green tales
I believe my devotees
—the sky, and
the spuming drops of water on the sea
will shroud me completely
shroud my insituate
grave, I know that
at that time, all the green grass and small flowers
will all crowd round,
in the glimmer of the dim lamplight
softly softly to kiss my sorrow

1980

Translated by David Wakefield and Su Kuichun

Anonymous

MADWOMAN

Hiding all day in China's cell washing babies' diapers
    I
    have let thousands of years go by
Now I stretch wide open my body
And forge it into a knife   And slash apart the faces
    of this world
These faces of men

China, a father who has killed his own children
This very night is molesting his own daughter   China   China
You living coffin   I have stayed with you in your tomb for
    thousands of years   All for nothing
My breasts   Are now my own grave
And all over my body a moldy moss grows

This country is overrun with corpses   My naked body was soaked
In the flow of the Yellow River and the Yangtze   That
    oozes like bloody pus   Thousands of years
And they haven't made my skin any whiter
I lie on my bed   I whimper   I feel my body and torture myself

Ah China! Prim and sanctimonious men always disappoint me
Thousands of years have passed   But I am the only one who
    has climbed out of this living coffin
Discarding the ennui and the death which is nowhere absent
    Breaking the darkness
I have dark eyes   Dark hair   I wear a dark dress
I have black feet   And a black, black soul
But the color of my gloves is white
These white hands can kill our father

I am a hysterical woman in China
The first mad woman ever, so what of it!
In the middle of the night   I run away   From home
Leaving my husband behind
So what of it!
I am a mad woman   I have stripped myself naked
And I stand on a tree searching for the sun
At all the meetings that are called by men   I cast my
    vote in opposition
So what of it!

It's a country crawling with peasants
It's a country crawling with petty citizens
It's a country crawling with bureaucrats

They haven't achieved salvation through endless wars
In thousands of years throughout history and time
At death's turning point   At one with the structures of the earth
They move from slavery to slavery
The arms that once moved defiantly now hang down like
    drapes
And become plants

The newspapers founded on lies
And the Great Wall built on ashes   Are the same
The literary scholars with such refined airs   The old who refuse
    to be buried
And the young who are apathetic   They are the same
Squatting in the public toilets, the famous poets   the
    computerized children   Are the same
The teahouses and offices and research institutes
    Are all the same
I hate it all   Confucius   Zhuangzi   Stalin   Karl Marx
They nauseate me   I must swallow down all the deceits and

atrocities
I am dying I sprout wings But cannot become a myth and fly
to the moon
China's Dirty Starry Star-tattooed night
Like a fornicator Climbing all over me
Disgracing my lover I must kill you
From now on You cannot defile my body anymore
I am no mad woman I am human I am willing to take
punishment[1]

1989
Translated by Diana Yue

1. "Madwoman" was published anonymously in Hong Kong's *Chaoliu* (Tide) monthly, June 15,1989, less than a fortnight after the June Fourth Tian'anmen Square massacre in Beijing.

Chen Kehua (1961–)

THIS LIFE CAGE

it's true, we really are   prisoners of this life
getting up late one morning after   I'd turned thirty

it suddenly occurred to me that everything   had lost its meaning
including myself   poised this instant over the toilet bowl

childhood's somber fog still shuts me in on all sides   I realized then
that I had never grown any older   since that split-second in which I had
  become aware of myself

how used to myself I am   to prolonging myself   propagating myself
just like everyone else here   each in their own way

likewise imprisoned in lives determined unconsciously
but   in our collisions and sightings

how quietly   the bars of our cages
rattle . . .

1996

Translated by Simon Patton

CONTAINMENT

I once thought my heart was bigger
And so able to contain both you
And the other you hide in your heart

Like an oyster enclosing agony's pearl
But containment, I later realized,
Was only a spear in my side
That hurt me when I laughed

And you?
Have you ever secretly tried to contain me
And my sobbing laughter in a corner of some delightful evening? . . .

And has that other who is hidden away and rarely sighted
In a moment undetected by either you or me
Tried to brush the two of us ever so gently
From   his heart? . . .

1997
Translated by Simon Patton

Xia Yu (1956–)

THE RIPEST RANKEST JUICIEST SUMMER EVER

Summer sinks into the clock-face of the cat's eye
Sinks into chestnut colored limbs

A 17 franc basket of peaches
Day four and already summer has run from ripe to rank

All spring long we dined as if we had all the time in the world
Followed with interest the color, light and atmosphere

Observed the shadows of the grapevines advancing to this
Last evening of the postimpressionists

The dabs of light thicken on the hammock
Grow thin on the windblown curtain

Each stroke acquiring definition
Until the last stroke added bursts grape-skin

Must be August
Ripe for the Fauvists

Never again will mere light so delight us
And O how we weary of atmosphere

Our idle conversation spreads like vines in the arbor
In this ripest rankest juiciest summer ever

And O how we weary of style
Does style, after all, exist

So like the snow
Defiled at the merest touch

But even though the snow does not exist
The hammock is more manifest than ever

More than an April iris or an aperitif at six
Although compared to soccer broadcast live hardly anything exists

Our guest, an enthusiast of "Old Cathay," asserts that in these fallen days
Only armed revolution presents so many tragic implications

And then there is soccer
O how we dine as if we had all the time in the world

Smoked salmon, crab and lobster
And will you look at the size of this oyster

If we could but find the proper outlet and the sympathies
To release our leftist tendencies

1906, Cézanne, caught in a storm, returns to his studio
Removes his hat and coat and collapses by the window

Taking stock of the table, its overturned basket of apples, he notices
The "appleness of the apples" and their shadows, the three skulls

The wardrobe, the pitcher, the crock
The half-opened drawer, the clock

It occurs to him proportion is hardly worth making a fuss about
He will not fret over whether the table is level or not

He closes his eyes and dies
His eyelids trace a line pointing straight to three o'clock

Still, there is something wanting in all this
Must be time for Matisse

1999
Translated by Steve Bradbury

CONTINUING OUR DISCUSSION OF BOREDOM AND ENNUI

And so we must continue our discussion of boredom and ennui
Boring things are all so very
Boring
And any old boring thing is boring too
Only boring things are actually boring
Boredom doesn't need to be discovered it simply is

A sort of remote yet limpid sensation
A certain frenzy
A nostalgia and tremulous sentiment
Not all that far in fact from morality

So how would you describe the taste of boredom?
Only the most sophisticated waiter would say
"We cannot describe the taste of oranges,
We can only say there are certain tastes like oranges."

What entrances us is not its architecture
But its paralysis. There is an ambergris.
Amber-tinged. Nor is there any harm in
Comparing it to inept plumbing.
Brown-paper grocery bags.
A city made of recollections, desires, happy chance and mere coincidences
Sewers pursuing their backward course beneath the historical purview

It really is a problem of atmosphere
Boredom and ennui
Verging on the impressionists
At the sheerest threshold of ecstasy
Only light can express
Light in motion at every moment
The *luxe, calme et volupté* blasé
That siesta you imagine you will never awaken from
Verging on terrorism

Verging on cement and sand and iron
Scouring the bottom of a dish with a fork
Leaving behind bits of nail and skin

But what is least expected
Is that it appears in the form of a furniture store
It just so happens is named "Ennui and Ecstasy"

Utterly uncompromising in its low-key embellishment
All chairs surely undergo a process of design
Until they arrive at the point of no-return
Those wardrobes left unclosed
Verging on intuition

Bearing with them the congealing and wallowing night
Our subject is the odiousness of the ego
The differing forms of abandonment
The purposeless conclusion of the ornamental screen
And the irresolute decorativity of the violence of the lamplight

Who is the more sound or shall we say instead
Who has wandered further from the straight and narrow line
Who is the more radical
The more musically endowed
Who evinces the more festive air
Accords the more copious illustration
And the longer procession of marchers

Who is on the verge of the perfect bathroom
Who bears more comparison to a tub
How can you know if it is ecstasy or ennui
Who is the axis who the revolution

1999
Translated by Steve Bradbury

L'EMPIRE À LA FIN DE LA DÉCADENCE

For Qiu Jin, Qing dynasty revolutionary martyr

A waltz not without its possibilities of mutual destruction
Like your revolution

I discover I've appeared in the guise of a man
Like you

Dancing toward the nadir
Nadir *ad infinitum*

To the endless verge of toppling
The empire at the end of its decadence

But I am merely an androgyne
In a gloomy *salon*

Releasing my splendor
My clamorous masculinity

1991
Translated by Steve Bradbury

Wong Man (1971–)

OBDURATE

I see my own death
knocking on life
its strong rhythm challenging my senses
to dance, to offer sacrifice

it cries out—life
is intercepted at every street corner by desire
my tentative fingers try to make truth resound
excised by scissors, floating on ponds
told through word of mouth
truth   like my shut face
is resistant
sharp   hard   like teeth
obdurate
is the core of life

n.d.
Translated by Jane Lai

HOOVES OF MEMORIES

hooves of memories invade the archipelago
rivers expand
compasses of imagination   take over the lion on the bridge of the nose
sharp wings of frigate birds
slash open dawn

the month of March   moist faces in the south
curse the accelerator of youth
shredder of precious dreams

night truncated like a flag
like a body with lower limbs amputated
tarrying on the dark glasses of a barge-man

Grief   stretching on reality's imagined crane
Signal lights continue chasing death
The white flesh of trees luring the axe
The hand claims independence   heart and loose gums
disintegrating   ahead
festival queens prepare joyous
and soul-tiring life

n.d.
Translated by Jane Lai

Yip Fai (1952–)

LOBSTERS

—LOVE ACROSS SPECIES IN A PROSPEROUS AGE

Always you rely on your taciturnity and air bubbles
To regulate trendy loves and desires
Always you sink to the bottom in cold arrogance
To blend quietly with the passions of a prosperous age

Tortoiseshell spectacles, crocodile belts
Food and drink, men and women, so elegantly dressed
Bows and swallowtails on hair and neck
Demonstrate to foreign tribes the boundaries of propriety

The exoticism of the latest fashions
At times fits perfectly with the culinary landscape
At times squares off in silence with
The lusty laws of food and drink

The sense of taste transforms into the sense of sight
Species of different origins
Join in a murmur of meta-discourse
Deconstructing the theme across the water tank

An autumn for eyes ears tongue nose throat
Hails from afar summer's appetite
The caress of garlic, cheese and broth
The sizzling and torture of shell and meat

South of the throat and chest cannot suppress
The instinct north of the knees and legs
Primitive desires panting
Climb the ladder suspended from heaven

We size up the accessories on each other's outfits
Wondering what tricks they harbor
What underwear they allude to
What rhetoric they reveal

You are my Issey Miyake
An asymmetrical whirl-around wrap
I am your Master Chef Chan Dong
Countering the current with ancient recipes

2000

Translated by Martha Cheung

Luo Zhicheng (1955–)

SPRING 2001, UNREACHABLE CIVILIZATION

Spring
In the grass by a bamboo fence, someone
Finds a baseball from the year before
But can't remember where the mitt is

Gloom continues to hatch this city
Arid expressions in the eyes crowd into the narrow field of vision
Friends rush away, far away
Far away from our shared memories

Desolate, I walk to the edge of the city
then turn to gaze into the distance
Alas, there's a clear sense that
One careless step will take you out of Taiwanese history
Danger

Spring
The neighbor's kid takes a pail and a small shovel
To excavate the relics of a wooly mammoth in a wax museum

Perhaps because it's located on an active fault line, on the periphery of the
trade winds
The island is always shrouded in
An anxiety of loose connections with the earth

Dragging heavy steps, I
Cross the fast lane washed clean by the rain and the muddy dividing island
Accompanying a group of mediocre writers dressed in their best
To attend a crude, biased literary history
On page 282
Like a straggling giant-tusked mammoth
Scared that the ice age of civilization will submerge
The evidence of my own existence

In fact
Spring 2001
We exist only because
We witness each other's fear

n.d.

Translated by Sylvia Li-chun Lin

PART SEVEN

Essays, 1918–1949

Lu Xun (1881–1936)

EXCERPTS FROM *WILD GRASS*

Translated by Ng Mau-sang

EPIGRAPH

When I am silent, I am fulfilled; when I am about to speak, I then feel empty.

My past life is dead. At this death I greatly rejoice, because I know from this death that my life once existed. The dead life has decayed. I greatly rejoice, because I know from this decay that my life was not empty.

The soil of life has been cast upon the surface of the land. Tall trees do not grow from it, only wild grass. For this I am to blame.

Wild grass has no deep roots, it bears no pretty flowers, no pretty leaves. But it drinks in dew and water, sucks in the flesh and blood of long-dead corpses, and wrests its existence from each and every thing. When it is alive, it is always trampled on, cut down, until it dies and decays.

But I am at ease, joyful. I will laugh; I will sing.

Naturally I love my wild grass, but I hate the ground that uses it for decoration.

Under the crust the subterranean fire is blazing. When it erupts, its lava will consume all the wild grass, all the tall trees. Whereupon nothing will be left to decay.

But I am at ease, joyful. I will laugh; I will sing.

Heaven and earth are so still and silent, I cannot laugh or sing. Even if heaven and earth were not so still and silent, perhaps I still would not be able to do so. At this juncture of light and darkness, life and death, past and future,

I offer this clump of wild grass before friends and foes, men and beasts, the loving and the unloving as my witness.

For my sake, and for the sake of friends and foes, men and beasts, those loving and unloving, I hope that death and decay will come speedily to this grass. If not, then *I* will not have lived, and this would be an even greater misfortune than death and decay.

Perish, wild grass, and with it, my epigraph.

April 26, 1927

AUTUMN NIGHT

Through the window I can see two trees in my backyard. The one is a date tree, the other is also a date tree.

The night sky above is strange and distant. Never in my life have I seen such a strange and distant sky. He seems intent on forsaking the world and staying out of people's sight. But now he is winking—with eyes of a few dozen stars, utterly blue, and cold. A smile hovers around his mouth, seeming to him to be very profound, and thereupon he begins to spread frost on the wild flowers and wild grass in my courtyard.

I do not know the names of these flowers and grasses, or what people call them. I remember a plant that put forth a tiny flower—the flower is still in bloom, but she is even tinier, trembling in the cold, dreaming. She dreams of the coming of spring, of autumn, of a skinny poet wiping his tears on her last petal, telling her that autumn may come, winter may come, but eventually spring will come, when butterflies will fly gaily about, and the bees will sing their spring song. Thereupon she smiles, although she has turned red in the piercing cold and remains curled up.

The date trees have shed all their leaves. Some time ago, a boy or two still came to beat them for the dates that others had left behind. Now, not a single one is left; even the leaves have all fallen. The date tree understands the dream of the tiny pink flower, that after autumn spring will come; he also knows the dream of the fallen leaves, that after spring there is still autumn.

He has shed all his foliage, leaving only the trunk; he is relieved from bending under his load of leaves and fruit, and now enjoys stretching himself. But a few boughs are still hanging down, nursing the wounds caused by the poles that struck him for his dates, while the longest and straightest of his boughs are like iron, silently piercing the strange and distant sky, making him wink his wicked eyes; piercing the full moon in the sky, making her go pale with embarrassment.

The wickedly winking sky turns an even deeper, perturbed blue. He seems intent on escaping from men, on avoiding the date tree, leaving only the moon behind. But the moon has secretly hid herself in the east. Only the naked trunk is still like iron, silently piercing the strange and distant sky, determined to pierce it to death, regardless of how and how often he winks his seductive eyes.

With a sharp shriek, a vicious bird of the night flies past.

I suddenly hear a slight tittering in the middle of the night, so soft that it seems not to want to awaken those who are asleep, though the titter echoes across the surrounding air. In the dead of night, there is no one about. I instantly recognize that this laughter is coming from my own mouth. Put to flight by the sound, I go back into my room and immediately raise the wick of my lamp.

The glass pane of the back window rattles; many insects are still blindly battering against it. Shortly afterward, a few squeeze in, probably through the holes in the paper covering. Once inside, they knock against the glass lampshade, making yet more rattling sounds. One plunges in from above, and runs into the flame. It is a real flame, I think. But two or three rest panting on the paper lampshade. The lampshade was replaced only last night, its snow-white paper folded in a wavelike pattern, with a sprig of scarlet jasmine painted in one corner.

When the scarlet jasmine blossoms, the date tree will again dream the dream of the tiny pink flower; it will grow lushly and bend in an arc. I hear again the midnight laughter, and immediately cut the train of my thought. I look at these little insects still resting on the snow-white paper—their heads big and tails small, like sunflower seeds, only half the size of a grain of wheat. How lovely and pitiable they are in their emerald hue.

I yawn, and light a cigarette, puffing out the smoke. I stare at the lamp and pay silent tribute to these dainty heroes in emerald green.

HOPE

My heart is exceedingly lonely.

But my heart is at peace, without love or hate, without joy or sorrow, without color or sound.

Perhaps I have aged. My hair has turned gray, is this not very clear? My hands shake, is this not very clear? Then, the hands of my soul must also shake, and its hair must have turned gray.

But these are events of many years ago.

Once, my heart was filled with songs that reeked of blood: blood and iron, flame and poison, recovery and revenge. Suddenly these songs all became empty, though sometimes I deliberately tried to fill this emptiness with vain, self-deceiving hope. Hope, hope—I had used this shield of hope to fend off the attack of that dark night of emptiness, but behind this shield lurked the same dark night. In this way my youth gradually wasted away.

Hadn't I accepted long ago that my youth had passed away? But I had thought that the youth outside me still existed: the stars, moonlight, stiff, fallen butterflies, flowers in the dark, the ominous hoot of the owls, the cuckoo weeping blood, the faint smiles, the swirling dances of love. . . . Mournful and elusive though this youth may be, it is nevertheless youth.

But why am I so lonely now? Can it be that all the youth outside me has also passed away? That the young people have also become old and feeble?

All I can do now is to fight this empty dark night with my bare fists. I put down this shield of hope, and hear the song "Hope" by Sandor Petöfi (1823–1849):

> What is hope? but a prostitute:
> She seduces everyone into giving her their all;
> After you have offered your greatest treasure—
> Your youth—she abandons you.

Seventy-five years have gone by since this great Hungarian patriot and lyric poet died for his country on the spears of the Cossacks. Sad though his death was, even sadder is the fact that his poems have not died.

Life, how miserable you are! Even Petöfi, gallant and unyielding, finally halted in the dark night and, looking back at the hazy east, said:

> Despair is like hope, in that both are vanity.

If I still have to spin out my life in this "vanity" that is neither light nor darkness, I will go and search again for that mournful and elusive youth that has passed away. It matters not if this youth is outside me. Because once the youth outside me has perished, the decrepitude inside me will also wither away.

But now there are no stars, no moonlight, no stiff, fallen butterflies, no faint smiles or swirling dances of love. Yet the young people are safe and sound.

All I can do now is to fight this empty dark night with my bare fists. Not finding the youth outside me, I myself will try to shake off this decrepitude inside me. But where is this dark night? There are no stars, no moonlight, no faint smiles or dances of love; the young people are safe and sound; and in front of me, if the truth be told, there is really no dark night.

Despair is like hope, in that both are vanity.

1927

THE EVOLUTION OF THE MALE SEX

Translated by D. E. Pollard

To call the coupling of birds and beasts "love" would verge on impious, one has to admit. But it cannot be denied that birds and beasts do have their sex life. When male and female come together in the mating season, we have to expect a bit of flirtation to go on. Indeed, the female does sometimes put on an act of coyness, running away and then looking back, even calling out, and may keep this up right until "cohabitational love" is put into effect. Although there are many species of birds and beasts and their forms of "love" are complex, one thing is beyond question: the male has no special rights to speak of.

That mankind is the lord of creation is evident in the first place in the capabilities of the male. To begin with nobody was very fussy, but owing to children "knowing their mother but not their father,"[1] the distaff side "ruled" for a period; at that stage the matriarch was probably a more imposing figure than the clan head of later days. Afterward, for whatever reason, women ran out of luck: round their necks, on their hands, and on their feet shackles were secured, rings and bands were fixed—though several thousand years later the rings and bands were changed to gold and silver and set with pearls and gemstones, these necklaces, bangles, rings, and so on are still today symbols of female subjugation. Since women had been turned into slaves, men no longer

1. "Knowing their mother but not their father." The quotation is from a description of primitive communities in *The Spring and Autumn Annals of Lü*.

needed their consent to "love" them. As a result of tribal wars in olden days, captives would become slaves, and women captives would be raped. By then the mating season had long been "abolished," and the male master could rape female captives and female slaves at any time and in any place. The practice of present-day bandits and toughs and their ilk not to regard women as human actually harks back to the warrior code of the tribal chiefs.

But although the capability of rape put mankind one step ahead of birds and beasts on the ladder of "evolution," in the end it was still only half civilized. Imagine how off-putting all that women's crying and sniveling, wringing of hands and contortions of body must have been. It was after that wonderful thing called money made its appearance that the evolution of the male sex was really impressive. Everything on earth could be bought and sold, sexual gratification naturally being no exception. At the expense of a few coins men could get what they wanted of a woman. On top of that he could say to her, I'm not taking you by force, you are doing this of your own free will; if you want to earn some money, you have to do thus and thus, and submit to my every wish. This is a fair exchange between us! Having debauched her, he required her to say "Thank you, sir." Are birds and beasts up to this? Whoring then marks quite a high stage in men's evolution.

At the same time, the old-style marriage made "at the behest of the parents and after consultation between matchmakers" was superior even to whoring. Under this system, the man came into a piece of live property that was his to hold forever. From the time the bride was deposited on the bed of the bridegroom she had only duties and obligations to perform; even the freedom to haggle over a price was denied her, let alone love. Like it or not, in the name of the Duke of Zhou[2] and the sage Confucius, you had to cleave to one man for all your days, and you had to preserve your virtue. The man could use her whenever he pleased, yet she had to abide by the morality of the saintly fathers: even "to conceive an unclean thought is to be guilty of adultery." If the dog had used such ingenious and harsh measures against the bitch, you may be sure the bitch would have "jumped the wall" in desperation. But the woman's only resort was to jump down a well and earn a reputation as a virtuous wife, a pure woman, or a martyr to chastity. The evolutionary significance of a marriage made according to religion needs no elaboration.[3]

As to men's resorting to the "most scientific" theory to make women willingly bind themselves to lifelong fidelity without the benefit of religion, and firmly

---

2. The Duke of Zhou is said to have been the author of the *Classic of the Rites,* which sets out rules for a marriage ceremony but has little or nothing to say about the relations between husband and wife after the ceremony.

3. The original word *lijiao* means more exactly "ethical teachings," but as they were in China ultimately based on scriptural authority and upheld by the power of the state, they had the force of the religious tenets of an established church. Moreover, wisely or not, Lu Xun does bring in Christian teaching.

believe that sexual desire is "animal lust," not the precondition for love, thus inventing "scientific chastity"—that of course is the acme of civilized progress.

Ah me, the difference between the ways of man—the male sex—and those of birds and beasts![4]

1933

4. This is an unfinished quotation from *Mencius*.

Zhou Zuoren (1885–1967)

IN PRAISE OF MUTES

Translated by D. E. Pollard

There is a proverb that runs: "The dumb man chews on yellow rue,"[1] the point of which lies in the matching line, "Bitter as gall, but he can't tell you." But another proverb says, "Under the rue bush strumming a tune," which indicates that making merry when things look black is common enough too. Though the mute is afflicted by not being able to express himself, doubtless he has his own private pleasures, which may be superior to those of us who can wag our tongues: how are we to say?

It is commonly held that dumbness is a form of disability, on a par with being eyeless or having one leg. This is very unfair. A dumb person's mouth is neither unformed nor infirm, he just cannot speak, that is all. The *Shuowen*[2] says, "Dumbness: the ailment of not being able to speak." Even accepting, as Mr. Xu would have it, that inability to speak is an ailment, it is quite an unimportant one, which does not much detract from the main uses of the mouth. When we look into the uses of the mouth, roughly speaking we find them to be the following: (1) eating; (2) kissing; (3) speaking. Actually the mouth of a mute is perfectly all right: it is not short of a tongue, neither are the upper and

---

1. The plant *huanglian* is not actually rue, but to English speakers, rue is about the only plant proverbially associated with bitterness.

2. Compiled by Xu Shen of the Han dynasty, *Shuowen* is the first dictionary of the Chinese language.

lower lips joined together. So if he wants to eat and drink, no matter if it is foreign fare or "Chinese menu," he can indulge himself to his heart's content, without the slightest inconvenience. Therefore we can take it as read that dumbness does not cause the least impairment to a person's constitution.

What about kissing? Given a mouth that, as explained above, can drink and munch at will, it will of course meet no difficulty with this line of work, for as the Dutchman, Dr. Van de Velde, says in chapter 8 of *Ideal Marriage,* the business of kissing is confined to the three senses of smell, taste, and touch, and has no connection with sound, which shows that the mute's inability to speak by no means stands in the way.

When all's said and done, the so-called ailment of dumbness is still only in respect of "not being able to speak." As I see it, that is neither here nor there. That mankind can speak is in fact surplus to requirements. Consider the teeming life on this earth, all sentient beings. None does not act out its destiny, each fulfills its nature. When have they ever spoken a word? It was said of old, "The chimpanzee can speak, yet it remains a beast; the parrot can speak, yet it remains a bird." How sad that these creatures, having painfully learned a few of somebody else's catchphrases, are still the same creatures they ever were, and have become the butt of the sage's jibe to boot. Honestly, has it been worth it?

When in time past the four-eyed Mr. Cang Jie[3] officiously invented script, it set the kindly ghosts howling a whole night through, and I fear that when among the ape-men the first one stretched his larynx and learned to speak it might well have made the primitive gods heave a profound sigh. To what end do we toil and scheme in life? "Drinking, eating and sex: men's great desires reside in these."[4] Assuming that they do not encroach upon these great desires, may not other matters then be allowed to look after themselves? The most important clause in the Chinese philosophy of practical living is, "The less you get involved in, the better." With regard to the mute, you might say he is able to dispense with one involvement.

The saying goes, "Sickness enters through the mouth, calamity issues from the mouth." That speech is not only of no advantage to people, but on the contrary is harmful, is here plain to see. Once you utter something, your words imply a judgment, which is dangerous, these days. People cannot always be saying "I love you" and such sweet nothings; what is more, when you look into it carefully, "I love you" carries implications like "I do not love her," or "I won't let him love you," and so might sow the seed of ruin. It is not for nothing that your wise man in chatting to visitors will only say, "The weather today . . . ha ha ha," without elaborating further, for though the weather is insensible, yet to

3. The legendary being accredited with the invention of Chinese characters to replace knotted string. His four eyes betoken discernment.

4. "Drinking, eating, sex": a quotation from the *Liji.*

call it good or bad is ultimately rather imprudent; hence he passes the matter off with a laugh.

Years ago, I read Yang Hui's (d. 54 B.C.) letter to Sun Huizong.[5] I only remember a few sentences like "I planted a field of beans and was left with acres of stalks." I was privately much taken by it, little suspecting that Mr. Yang was actually cut in half for writing these words. It is as beyond comprehension as fifteen- or sixteen-year-old girl students in Hunan being shot for reading *Fallen Leaves* (Guo Moruo's, not Xu Zhimo's).[6] But this world is beyond comprehension, and we, alas, are at its mercy. Our forefathers, who were subjected to these experiences over the last few thousand years, have left us this parting advice: "The man of foresight practices self-preservation." The teahouses, which have grown accustomed to this situation over the last few decades, are plastered with slogans saying "Do not discuss national affairs." The gold statue in our family's history had its lips thrice sealed,[7] and for 2,500 years has been an example to the world, his reputation second to none. Now, should we not suppose the mute is the gold statue of our time?

Ordinary people regard the ability to speak as a virtue, but there are those who have achieved renown through pretending dumbness. I might add that high and low, past and present, people of this kind have been very few, which very fact goes to show what a rare and estimable thing dumbness is. Pride of place goes to the illustrious Lady Xi.[8] By virtue of her looks, which were of a kind to "cause kingdoms to fall," she was twice made consort. She bore the King of Chu two sons, but never spoke a word to him. The littérateurs of China who like to give the glad eye to dead and gone beauties of olden times then went to town writing poems about her; some said she was good, some said she was bad, all flaunted their frowzy finery. But still Lady Xi's fame thereby grew great. Quite frankly, hers was truly a tragedy in a woman's life: it did not simply concern one person in one place at one time; you could almost say it symbolized the fate of all women. Nora, the heroine of Ibsen's play *A Doll's House*, says she had never imagined she could have borne two children to a man who was a stranger to her: this was precisely the fate of Lady Xi. In fact, could one deny that it is the fate of all women under capitalism?[9]

---

5. Yang Hui was an official at the court of the Han emperor Xuan. He was elevated to the nobility for exposing a plot, but was later schemed against in turn and reduced to commoner status. His letter to his friend Sun Huizong stating his grievances was the cause of his execution. It survives in the *Wenxuan*.

6. *Fallen Leaves* is the title of an autobiographical novel by the left-wing Guo Moruo and a poem by the right-wing Xu Zhimo.

7. According to the *Kongzi jiayan*, Confucius encountered a gold statue on a visit to the state temple of Zhou; three times he stopped its mouth, and inscribed on its back the motto "The man of antiquity most chary with words."

8. Lady Xi was the wife of the ruler of Xi in the Spring and Autumn period (770 B.C.–476 B.C.). When Xi was conquered by Chu, King Wen took her as part of his booty.

9. By "capitalism," Zhou seems to mean a form of social organization that is not communist,

There is another nontalker: I mean the hermit at the end of the Han dynasty called Jiao Xian.[10] My fellow provincial Jin Guliang [fl. 1661] included this hermit in his *Register of the Peerless*; he also wrote this judicious encomium:

> Xiaoran lives alone
> Seals his lips, does not speak
> Quietly hidden till the end
> A joke to creatures of the wild

Moreover, as was said, "In this wise he lived out his days, and passed the hundred ere he died." In which case, by pretending dumbness you can both gain a reputation for high integrity and enjoy the fortune of a long life. The praiseworthiness of dumbness is thus blindingly clear.

Manners are in decline, men's hearts are not as pure as of yore. Nowadays the dumb have actually affected certain gestures and begun to speak. However, these still cannot be used in the dark; they cannot speak then. Confucius said, "When the state has lost the way, actions may be bold but words should be modest."[11] Could it not be that the mute is conforming to the ancient ways?

1929

---

specifically a system based on the notion of property. In relation to women, he is thinking of them as being treated as their husbands' chattel, as opposed to companions or equals. Zhou restated his long-held grievance against "capitalism" in this regard in his 1951 letter to "the responsible member of the Central Committee," published in *Xinwenxue shiliao*, 1987, 2:214–215.

10. Jiao Xian (named Xiaoran) went into voluntary seclusion in the age of turmoil following the fall of the Han dynasty. He lived in the barest poverty but nevertheless observed the nicest proprieties. His story is told in the *Sanguo zhi* (*History of the Three Kingdoms*).

11. This passage is in Book 14 of the *Analects*.

THE AGING OF GHOSTS

Translated by D. E. Pollard

I am as a rule quite eager to learn about the business of ghosts, but what, you might ask, is the use of such knowledge once gained? Probably none: at bottom it may be mere curiosity. The Ancients said, only the sages can know the condition of ghosts and spirits, which shows it is hardly an easy matter. I repent myself that in my youth I did not meddle with metaphysics: now that that avenue is closed, all that is left to me is to make good use of a passion for digging for textual evidence, and seek material in chronicles ancient and modern; perhaps in that way one can get a hint or two, one never knows. But the hundreds and thousands of years they go back is an unconscionable time, the records have multiplied endlessly, and the uninitiated are unlikely to stumble on the scent. What is more, the world of ghosts seems absolutely full of conundrums, quite enough to occupy the gentlemen of the academies of science for a lifetime. Here I raise only one question, namely that mentioned above, the aging of ghosts. If I may be allowed, I will make light work of a heavy task, and sketchily set out my myopic view, all the time "respectfully awaiting the favor of instruction."

After a person dies and becomes a ghost, does the ghost in the shades or some other place actually continue to grow older year by year as before? That one would like to know. There are two approaches possible. One would be in accordance with our unregenerate theory that ghosts do not exist, but that would scarcely be to the point, and would moreover be too unsporting. The other would follow the common line that ghosts do exist. Now the question whether there can be aging or not arises only if ghosts do exist, so when you come down to it, we are stuck with this single approach. However, though the existence of ghosts is an article of faith for all believers, whether they age or not is a question on which different people have different views, and on which there is no hallowed doctrine.

Ji Yun of the Qing dynasty says in chapter 4 of his *Thus Have I Heard It Said*:

> Ren Zitian reports that someone out at night in his locality saw in the moonlight two people sitting together on a cemetery path amid the cypresses. One was a young man of sixteen or seventeen, of pleasing and handsome aspect, the other a woman whose white hair hung down to her shoulders, whose back was stooped and who carried a stick: she appeared to be in her seventies or eighties. They were billing and cooing, apparently delighting in each other's company. Wondering to himself of what provenance this old hussy could be that she was so saucy with the youth, he went nearer to them, whereupon the figures melted away. The next day he inquired whose graves they were, and only then discovered that this certain person had died in his youth, and his wife survived to maintain a virtuous widowhood for another fifty years. When she died she was interred with him in this place.

One must suppose from this that ghosts never grow old: their appearance and age are tied to the time of their death. But when you reflect on the implications of this, you discover many awkwardnesses. The young husband and old wife is one such. Then, too, there is the eventuality of the son being old and the father being young: according to etiquette, the duties of keeping the parent warm in winter and cool in summer, of tucking up at night and inquiring after comfort in the morning, may not be neglected, but they would impose a crippling burden on the son, and he would deserve all our pity. Again, as our mundane law permits remarriage, consider the poor scholar who takes a new wife when widowed in order to continue his line: after death he would then be responsible for supporting quite a few households, and this old fellow too would have to command our sympathy. On the other hand, the wife who remarries is according to popular belief sawn in half: when the former husbands come in for their share of an old body, what are they supposed to do with it?

Shao Bowen of the Song dynasty writes in chapter 18 of his *Records of Things Seen and Heard*:

> When Madam Li gave birth to Master Kangjie, a girl twin was stillborn. Over ten years later, the mother saw in the moonlight from her sickbed a girl curtseying to her from the doorstep. The girl said, weeping: "Unbeknown to you. Mother, the ignorant doctor poisoned me with his drugs. Woe is me." Madam Li replied: "It was fate." The daughter said: "If it

> was fate, how is it that my brother survived and I did not?" Madam Li answered: "That is just what was fated, that you should die and your brother survive." The girl departed, still in tears. Another ten years or so passed, and Madam Li again saw the girl come to her, weeping. She said, "Having missed my chance because of an ignorant doctor, I have had to wait these twenty long years before being born into the world. Mindful of the maternal bond, I am come to say good-bye." Then she left, once more in tears.

Mr. Quyuan[1] quotes this passage in chapter 8 of his *Commonplace Book of the House of Tea Fragrance, Series Three*, and comments:

> This matter is most peculiar. Since the girl died in her mother's womb, she was just a lump of flesh quite without consciousness. But after ten years or so she could both curtsey and speak. How could it be that after dying she could still mature with the passing years, as in normal life?

As I see it, going by what Mr. Shao says in *Records of Things Seen and Heard*, it is indeed indisputable that ghosts do mature with the passing years. If you apply this assumption to Ji Yun's account, the young man of sixteen or seventeen ought to have become an old gent of seventy-odd, in which case the story would not get off the ground, as a pair in their seventies or eighties canoodling in the moonlight, though one would have to reckon it a case of "long in the tooth but young at heart," is not particularly outlandish. And there is another thing: ghosts can observe people, but people cannot observe ghosts. When at last they met among the cypresses, the man-ghost would be sure to recognize his wife, but I fear the wife-ghost, assuming no one reintroduced them, could by that time have hardly recognized her spouse of half a century before.

The viewpoints of Shao and Ji both have their strengths and weaknesses. We ordinary people would find it extremely difficult to choose between them. Probably we can only allow them to coexist: whether in the underworld the ghosts are divided into warring camps, each choosing to grow old or not grow old as they wish, that we have no means of knowing. The theory that ghosts do not grow old seems to be the common one, the theory that they do grow old is slightly eccentric, but I have turned up some other supporting evidence. The one-volume *Supplement* to *The Trials of the Wangxinglou*, printed in 1899, was written by Qian Hejin of Wuxi, to commemorate his son Xingbao. The main volume is unfortunately unobtainable. The *Supplement* contains a *Diary of Conversations via the Planchette*, which records Qian's written communications with his children. His third son, Dingbao, was born in 1879 and died within forty days; his fourth son, Xingbao, was born in 1881 and died at the age of

1. Quyuan is the assumed name of Yu Yue (1821–1906), a favorite author of Zhou Zuoren.

twelve; his third daughter, Ezhen, was born in 1887 and died five days after birth. They all responded at the séances. The diary reads:

> 21st of 12th month, 1896, evening: Xingbao came at last. I asked: "When you left us you were twelve. Have you grown physically since then?" He replied: "I have."
>
> 17th, 1st month, 1897: I rose early and took my place at the planchette. My late brother Yunsheng and my sister Run and Xingbao were all in attendance. I asked my brother: "You were only twenty-seven when you passed over, now you are over fifty. Have you grown older in appearance?" He replied: "I have." "Have you grown whiskers?" He replied: "I have."

From this it can be seen that ghosts are no different from the living in aging with the passing of the years. There are several other entries:

> 29th, 1st month: Question: "At what age did you achieve consciousness?" Answer: "At three." Question: "For how many years did you take suck?" Answer: "Three." (This to Dingbao)
>
> 21st, 3d month: My sister Run came. Question: "Was there something?" Answer: "Glad tidings." Question: "What glad tidings?" Answer: "On the fourth of the fourth month Xingbao is taking a wife." Question: "How old is his bride?" Answer: "Thirteen." Question: "Are we invited to wish them happiness?" Answer: "No." Question: "Are you going?" Answer: "Yes." Question: "Are wedding presents required?" Answer: "They are." Question: "Is Dingbao married?" Answer: "Yes." Question: "Has he any children?" Answer: "Two sons, one daughter."
>
> 29th, 5th month: I asked Xing: "Is your wife Shannan well?" Answer: "There is to be a happy event." This meant she was pregnant. "When did she become pregnant?" Answer: "The fifth month." "What month is she due to give birth?" Answer: "The seventh month." Subsequently I asked my departed brother: "People give birth after ten months. Do ghosts all give birth after three months?" He replied: "Yes. Such are the differences between people and ghosts. Girls are ready for marriage at the age of eleven."
>
> 12th, 6th month: I asked my second daughter, Yingke: "How many children have come with you?" Xingbao replied for her: "Ten." I was greatly surprised, and thought there must have been a mistake. I repeated the question over and over again, but the answer was as before. I called on my sister Run and asked her, but she replied in the same terms as Xingbao. I asked how it could come about that she could have produced so many children after having been married for only five years. Did it mean she gave birth more than once in a year? The answer came: "Yes." Only then did it come home to me how wide the gulf is between ghosts and people—they seem in this respect to be practically the same as cats

and dogs. When I had heard previously that Xingbao had married a wife eleven years old, I had thought it make-believe, but now when I piece it all together, I realize that the ways of ghosts are not to be fathomed by the reasoning of men.

19th: I asked Xingbao, "Is your great-uncle Shouchun still with you?" He replied: "He is dead." "How long has he been dead?" Answer: "Three years." "When someone dies, are they buried in coffins, as here?" Answer: "Yes." Till now it had not dawned on me that ghosts also die. The ancients used a special word for the death of ghosts, evidently not without reason. No doubt the children born in the shades receive their souls from those who die there.

The above excerpts all contain discoveries about the nuptials, obsequies, birth, and death of ghosts, and as material for a treatise on the life of ghosts is very precious. I discovered this volume in the spring of 1933 on a bookseller's pitch in Changdian.[2] It was printed with wooden movable type on white paper, with corrections made in ink: a pleasingly elegant production. The *Diary of Conversations via the Planchette* and *Supplement* are most interesting; their account of conditions down below is quite detailed, but lack of space prevents me from quoting more. Though it is a matter of regret that I was not able to get hold of the main volume, it would not appear to contain any record of planchette sessions, so its value is not as great as it might have been otherwise. My reaction on reading this compilation was that Mr. Shao's theory had received endorsement, and the case that ghosts grow up thus could not be denied.

I do not believe in ghosts, yet I like to hear tell of the affairs of ghosts; this is a great contradiction. Nevertheless, though I do not believe people turn into ghosts after death, I do believe that there is a human being behind every ghost. I do not understand what the "natural function of yin and yang"[3] is all about, but the idea that ghosts are the projections of the hopes and fears of living people is surely sound.

Tao Yuanming is one of the great free spirits in history. His "Going Back to Live on My Land" says, "Human life is like a passing pageant / In the end we return to nothingness," and "Spirit explains" has "When the time comes you have to make an end / There's no point in making too much fuss." Yet his "Dirge for Myself" says, "I want to speak but my mouth utters no sound / I want to see but my eyes have no sight / Formerly I slept on high couches / Now my nights are passed in the wild grassland." One would not expect Master Tao to cling to illusions about life and death, yet he does write in this vein with great strength of feeling. However, to deduce the nature of life after death from the

---

2. A seasonal street market in Peking.

3. This is the formula Zhang Zai (ca. 1020–1077) devised to account for the phenomena of ghosts and spirits.

sensibilities of one's lifetime is after all the inclination of humankind, and is quite natural.

The average person is more bent on survival, and neither can nor will believe that he or his loved ones will simply fade into oblivion, so he comes up with all sorts of conjectures, on the assumption that existence must continue. The conditions of this existence differ slightly with the race, the locality, and even individual likes and dislikes. These are revealed not deliberately but unwittingly; in fact, listening to people talking about ghosts is tantamount to listening to people discussing their most private thoughts. It would seem that the view that ghosts exist is the opium for a life of trouble and care, a form of comfort for those helpless in the face of the greatest sorrow and fear: "Amorous young men and women can continue unfinished romances; of dauntless heroes it is said, 'In another twenty years they'll be back again as other brave fellows.'" It is those who hold to materialism who are in for a hard time: as with those of powerful wills for whom anesthetics are ineffective, they have to look on wide awake as their flesh is cut into. Guan Yu's "scraping of his bones"[4] certainly counts as heroic, but really involved uncalled-for suffering, and is not something the ordinary person could stand up to; so it is not surprising that the majority turn to anesthetics for deliverance.

The *Diary of Conversations via the Planchette* says:

> 1st, 8th month: A stray ghost responded to the planchette. He announced that Ezhen had been reborn into the human world. I asked when, and it was written, "20th of the 7th month." I asked where, and the answer came, "In the city." I asked her name, but the stylus wrote, "Not known." All of my kith and kin who have been awaiting rebirth for so long have departed one after another in the space of a few months. Am I to presume that mortal births have been exceptionally numerous this year, and so they have all gone to make up the quota? It really passes understanding. After Xing, only Ezhen remained to respond to my summons. If this report is true, then henceforward my dealings with the planchette are over and done with.

When I read this section I could not help my spirits drooping. The *Supplement* to *The Trials of the Wangxinglou* is one of the saddest books I have read, and I have this sensation every time I leaf through it. It is as if one were suffering agony from a wound and found relief in taking morphia, but that morphia was actually brewed from homemade fudge: the passerby observing this would not know whether to laugh or cry.

---

4. In the novel *Sanguo yanyi*, Guan Yu carries on with a game of chess while the surgeon cuts his arm open to the bone to draw the poison from an arrow wound.

I myself do not believe in ghosts, but like to hear about ghosts, and have great sympathy with the superstitions of the old way of life. This shows that I am already an old man, for those with one foot in the grave tend either toward harshness or toward tolerance.

1934

READING ON THE TOILET

Translated by Don J. Cohn

The fourth volume of Hao Yixing's *Jottings from the Studio of Drying Books in the Sun* contains a section entitled "Reading on the Toilet":

> An old story tells of a woman who was such a devout Buddhist that she never for a single moment stopped chanting the sutras, and continued this practice even when she went to the toilet. Though she reaped the rewards of her piety, she finally passed away in the privy one day. This story is told as a caution, and though it belongs to the moral teachings of Buddhism, the story itself is not necessarily true. However it does make the point that holy scriptures are not to be canted in unclean places.
>
> *Guitian lu*[1] quotes Qian Sigong as saying: "Reading has always been my favorite pastime. When seated I enjoy the classics and histories; when recumbent, I prefer reading anecdotes and fiction; and when in the toilet I like to read popular *ci* poems."
>
> The same book quotes Xie Xishen as saying that when Song Gongchui went to the toilet he would take a book along with him, and the sound of his chanting could be heard far and wide.
>
> Personally I find all of this quite ridiculous. Squatting in the toilet, pants down, with a book in one hand is not only a desecration but an acrobatic feat. Must a man pursue learning to this extreme?

---

1. By Ouyang Xiu (1007–1072).

> Elsewhere Ouyang Xiu quotes Xie Xishen's statement that he prefers to do his writing "on" three different places: on horseback, on his pillow, and on the toilet, since these are the only places where he can concentrate properly. This is a clever observation, personal without being overly frivolous.

Although Hao Yixing's essay is most interesting, I differ somewhat with his opinions, since I myself am quite in favor of reading on the toilet.

When I was a boy, my grandfather told me that male servants in Beijing had a saying that went like this:

> Our masters may eat quickly, but we servants shit quickly.

This is a bit of a cheap shot, yet it contains an element of truth. Of course it's difficult to be precise about the amount of time one spends on the toilet, but it can never be all that short. And defecating differs from eating in that even the few moments spent on it seem to be wasted, and one feels compelled to make good use of them. For instance, in my native place, the common folk usually get through a pipe of tobacco when they go to the outhouse. And if someone is washing rice or clothing on the stone steps on the bank of the river, or if an acquaintance happens to pass by carrying a shoulder pole, this is an ideal opportunity to engage in a bit of conversation. They might shout at the top of their voices: "How many cash per pint did you pay for that rice?" or "Where are you going?" In this context, reading seems to me about the same as smoking a pipe.

Having said this much, I might add that certain types of toilets are conducive to pipe smoking rather than reading. The outhouses along the rivers in Zhejiang referred to above are one example.

When I was in Nanjing, I lodged for a while in a bookstore run by a friend from Hunan, a man named Liu, who had been introduced to me by Zhao Boxian. The district examinations were being held that year, and Mr. Liu had opened his bookstore in the vicinity of the Flowery Memorial Gate. Being ill at the time, I found it very uncomfortable living in the Academy, and Mr Liu kindly invited me to stay in his shop, where he cooked rice gruel and prepared my medicine for me. Though he made his living selling books to candidates preparing for the district examinations, he also worked for the underground revolutionary movement. I always had the greatest respect for his indefatigable spirit. I slept to the rear of the bookshelf that stood behind the shop's counter, and ate my gruel and took my medicine there as well. However, there was no toilet in the shop, and one had to go into the street and past a couple of houses to where there was a large heap of garbage piled up against a wall in an empty lot. Getting there was a hardship for me; first, because I was in poor health and walking anywhere was quite a task; and second, even if I had been in good health, that toilet was not the sort of place I would have relished visiting too often. This is the second example of a place better suited to pipe smoking than reading.

In the summer of 1919 I was in Hyuga, Japan, visiting a friend, and stayed for a while in a mountain village named Kijo. The toilet there was of the common variety, with a roof and wooden door and windows, but it stood some thirty or forty meters from the house all by itself in the middle of a field. At night one needed a lamp to light the way, and when it rained an umbrella was necessary; it rained a lot there. As I recall, during my five-day visit to Kijo, it rained all but one day. This is the third sort of place unfit for reading.

Last there are the typical latrines of Beijing, which consist simply of a hole in the ground and two bricks to stand on, with no protection whatsoever from the wind, rain, or sun. I had an opportunity to visit [Sun] Fuyuan in Dingzhou last year. The toilets there are designed like those in the Ryukyu Islands. You stand on the platform and do your business with a bunch of hogs snuffling and snorting in the pit below. This tends to frighten the uninitiated. Who could read in such a place? This is my fourth example.

According to the *Yulin* [*Forest of Tales*, written ca. fourth century] the toilet in the mansion of Shi Chong [?–300] was furnished with a large couch with a red silk curtain behind it, and fine straw cushions. In addition, there were two servant girls in attendance holding embroidered perfumed sachets. I would find such a luxurious setting quite unsuitable for reading. My own personal requirements are quite simple. All a toilet needs is a roof, walls, windows, and a door, as well as a light in case one has to go at night; if there is no electricity, a candle will do. It can be twenty or thirty steps away from the house, and though you may need an umbrella on rainy days, it rains very little in the North anyway. With such a toilet, I see no harm in bringing a book along if you feel like it.

In Tanizaki Jun'ichiro's *Setsuyo zuihitsu* there is a section entitled "In Praise of Shadows," the second part of which discusses the virtues of toilet design in Japan. In the temples of Kyoto and Nara, the toilets are all constructed in the ancient style. Though dark inside, they are kept spotlessly clean and are usually located in a grove where one can smell the fragrance of leaves and moss. These toilets are normally placed at a distance from the main residence, but connected to it by covered corridors. Squatting in such a dark place, with only the light filtering in through the paper screen walls to see by, one can indulge in reverie or gaze through the window at the scene in the courtyard. The feelings engendered in such a setting are indescribably pleasant.

Tanizaki continues:

> As I have said there are certain prerequisites: a degree of dimness, absolute cleanliness, and quiet so complete one can hear the hum of a mosquito. I love to listen from such a toilet to the sound of softly falling rain, especially if it is a toilet of the Kanto region, with its long, narrow windows at floor level; there one can listen with such a sense of intimacy to the raindrops falling from the eaves and the trees, seeping into the earth as

> they wash over the base of a stone lantern and freshen the moss about the stepping stones. And the toilet is the perfect place to listen to the chirping of insects or the song of the birds, to view the moon, or to enjoy any of those poignant moments that mark the change of the seasons. Here, I suspect, is where haiku poets over the ages have come by a great many of their ideas. Indeed one could with some justice claim that of all the elements of Japanese architecture, the toilet is the most aesthetic.[2]

Tanizaki is, after all, a poet, so that in speaking so eloquently he may be prettifying his subject somewhat. But I am referring only to his use of language. What he is trying to say here is quite right.

During the "Warring Country" period [15–16 cents.] in Japan, the Gozan monasteries became the exclusive domain of nearly all efforts in preservation and creativity in the traditional arts. This brought about changes in artistic style, such as the evolution of "palace painting," characterized by bright colors and hard edges to monochrome ink painting, with its gnarled trees, bamboos and rocks. Naturally, similar changes took place in architecture. This is particularly evident in the traditional teahouse, and the "aestheticization" of the toilet is simply a side effect of this trend.

Followers of Buddhism have from the earliest times been very particular about toilets. Having read some early Buddhist discipline books from the Hinayana and Mahayana traditions, I have gained the greatest respect for the thorough concern shown by the ancient Indian worthies for every aspect of human behavior. Concerning the matter of going to the toilet, the *The Great Monk's Three Thousand Prescribed Ways of Austere Deportment*, translated during the Eastern Han dynasty, contains "twenty-five matters concerning the outhouse." In the sixth part of the *Sarvastivada Vinimatrka*, translated into Chinese during the Song dynasty, there are thirteen entries on the subject, ranging from "placement downwind" to "building design." In the second part of "Transmission of the Inner Dharma," in *Letters from the South Seas* by the Tang monk Yi Jing, item number 18 treats "matters relating to the convenience." These texts all contain extremely detailed rules, some of which are both rigorous and extremely funny. After reading them I always feel the greatest respect for their authors.

Lu Zhishen's rise in the monastic hierarchy from kitchen assistant to toilet cleaner in the novel *Shuihu zhuan* suggests the importance of the toilet in Chinese Buddhist monasteries in the past. Unfortunately this concern seems to have waned in modern times. In 1921 I spent six months in the Western Hills near Beijing recuperating from an illness. I was staying in the Shifang Hall of the Temple of the Azure Clouds. Nowhere in the vicinity of the temple was a

---

2. Translation of this section quoted from *In Praise of Shadows*, trans. Thomas J. Harper and E. G. Seidensticker (New Haven: Leet's Island Books, 1977), pp. 3–4.

single decent toilet to be found. As I wrote at that time in *Miscellaneous Letters from the Mountains:*

> My ramblings have taken me as far as the springs on the eastern side of the temple, an area I really find quite appealing. In fact, I take a stroll there every morning before the crowds arrive, and am always enthralled with the scenery. My only regrets are the presence of garbage everywhere, and the noxious odors that greet me wherever I turn—rising from the countless specimens of what is referred to in the *Pharmacopia* as "human brown stuff." Sometimes I feel that China is a land of great contradictions. On the one hand, Chinese people never get enough to eat; on the other hand, they don't dispose of their feces properly,

Under these conditions, a Chinese Buddhist temple with even the most rudimentary toilet facilities should be a cause for celebration. And thus perhaps it's unreasonable to hope to discover a quiet place for contemplation or study. If Buddhist monks are so slovenly, can we expect much more from the common people?

A clean toilet may be an acceptable place to read, but hardly appropriate for writing. When choosing what to read, it matters little whether the book is one of the Classics, Histories, Philosophers, or Anthologies; any book at all will do. As a general rule I prefer not to bring rare editions or books that are difficult to understand to the toilet; often I'll just choose a grammar book. Essays appear to me to be the most suitable genre for the toilet, and novels or short stories the least. As for reciting texts out loud, few people read the Eight Great Prose Masters of the Tang and Song dynasties anymore, so perhaps we need not chant their works on the toilet.

1936

Lin Yutang (1895–1986)

MY TURN AT QUITTING SMOKING

Translated by Nancy E. Chapman

Anyone who has been a smoker has, in moments of confusion, made the grand resolution to give it up. For a certain period of time they vow to wrestle with the demon of tobacco to see who will be the victor and who the vanquished, only coming to their senses after ten days or so. I too once strayed down this path, declaring in a sudden fit of excitement that I was going to quit smoking. It was not until three weeks later that, pricked by conscience, I came to regret my foolishness. I swore that never again would I allow myself to become so dispirited or so lacking in self-control, and that hereafter I would be a faithful believer in smoking until the day I reached senility. At that point I might very well be swayed by the heresy of those busybody women from the temperance society of the YMCA to give it up altogether, since in old age people become fainthearted, are unable to control themselves, and cannot be held responsible for their actions. However, as long as I am in possession of my faculties and am still able to tell right from wrong, I will never again submit to this kind of temptation. Having learned my lesson, I have come to the realization that to give up smoking for no reason, thus depriving my soul of ease and carefree comfort, is an immoral act that shortchanges me while bringing no benefit to others. According to the famous British biochemist, Professor John Burdon Sanderson Haldane (1892–1964), smoking is one of four major inventions in the course of human history that have had the greatest impact on our lives. Of the other three inventions, I remember that one was treatment with animal hormones for the purpose of postponing the onset of old age. But that is another story.

I am ashamed to recount how muddleheaded and timid I was in those three weeks, knowing full well how much good one small cigarette would do my body and soul, yet lacking the courage to go enjoy it. Thinking back, now that this is all a thing of the past, I cannot fathom how I could have been so deluded for three full weeks. Indeed, were I to give a detailed account of my psychological odyssey during those three weeks, I would need paper from a forest of trees. The first thing I would mention would naturally be that there is something altogether addled about this notion of quitting smoking. Why should anyone want to do it anyway? Needless to say, even now I can still come up with a conventional answer to this question. In truth, however, we humans are often irrational in our behavior, sometimes intentionally doing what we should not do and sometimes, in moments of idleness when we have nothing else to occupy us, intentionally setting tasks for ourselves that test our mettle, starve our bodies, and sap our strength. This we do in order to confound our natural inclinations and prepare ourselves thereby to assume the responsibilities of worthy men. Aside from this, I cannot imagine how I managed to come up with such a wretched idea. It's a bit like Tao Kan's habit of moving bricks,[1] or the calisthenics that people do nowadays—as scholars with no wood to chop, no water to draw, and no carts to pull, they swing their arms up and down for no apparent reason, just for the sake of exercise, without making any contribution at all to social and economic productivity. This thing known as quitting smoking is probably just a way for wise men and sages to give their souls a little exercise.

Not surprisingly, I experienced a strange and unbearable sensation in my throat, mouth, and even my upper bronchial tract for the first three days—it was rather like an itch and yet not quite. This, it turned out, was relatively easy to deal with. I ate some mint candy, drank strong tea, and sucked on top-quality French Valda lozenges, and in three days I managed to overcome that strange itchiness. However, this was but the first stage of the saga, involving a purely physiological struggle that was in no way unusual. Anyone who thinks this is all there is to quitting smoking has forgotten that smoking is a matter of the soul; indeed, failing to understand this principle disqualifies a person from even addressing the issue.

It was only after the first three days had passed that I entered the second stage of my ordeal, the struggle of the soul. I suddenly came to realize that, when one gets right down to it, there are two types of smokers in this world. The first are fakes—social smokers who are only interested in joining the crowd. Since for them quitting smoking does not involve the second stage—the psy-

---

1. Tao Kan (259–334), a general of the Jin dynasty, maintained his physical strength by carrying bricks out of his courtyard in the morning and moving them back in at night.

chological struggle—it doesn't tax them in the least to give it up. Once they decide to quit and succeed in doing so, they are praised as being of "strong will." Can we consider them as ever having been true smokers? If a person can give up an addiction as easily as if he were selling some old clothes, it obviously was never an addiction in the first place. Indeed, for people like this, smoking is a physical activity like washing their faces or brushing their teeth—they can choose to brush or not—but it touches no inner need and holds no spiritual meaning for them. Apart from washing their faces, eating their meals, and returning home to hug their children, their souls impose no other demands. They can rest easy at night, having read through a few Aesop's fables with the women from the temperance society—the lyrics of Xin Qiji (1140—1207), the poetry of Wang Wei (701–761), the music of Beethoven, and the tunes of Wang Shifu (ca. 1250–1300)—all are irrelevant to them. To these people, the waterfalls on Mount Lu are nothing but water flowing from up above to down below. Let me ask you: is it conceivable that one could read Xin's lyrics and Wang's poems without smoking at the same time?

For people who really appreciate smoking, quitting presents a problem that is thoroughly beyond the imagination of men and women from the temperance society. It takes less than three days of abstinence for bona fide smokers to realize how pointless it all is and how cruelly we have treated ourselves. Rationality and common sense lead us to ask: is there any good reason—political, social, moral, physiological, or psychological—why people should refrain from smoking? Why should they knowingly use their intelligence and will to violate conscience and harm their good nature, thus depriving themselves of a carefree and serene state of mind? Everyone knows that writers must be energetic and free-spirited, uninhibited in mind and unobstructed in perception, if fine writing is to emerge. When reading, one must also let mind and spirit converge, ridding the heart of obstacles and allowing the spirit to roam; only then can it qualify as true reading. Can such a mental state be attained if one is not smoking? At the moment of greatest inspiration, reaching for a cigarette is really the only reasonable thing to do. Slipping a piece of chewing gum in one's mouth, by contrast, would be unbearably vulgar. For now, I will present two incidents to illustrate my point.

One time, my friend B came to Shanghai from Beiping [Beijing]. It had been three years since we last met. In Beiping, we had often spent whole days together and would frequently share our evenings smoking and conversing about literature, philosophy, modern art, and various problems related to reforming mankind and the world. When he came to Shanghai, we sat around the stove at home talking about old times. Our conversation touched on news of our old friends in Beiping and the ups and downs of human affairs. Whenever we came to a particularly interesting point, I felt like reaching out to take a cigarette but ended up only making a pretense of standing up, sitting down, and fidgeting in my seat. My friend B, by contrast, continued to puff away in comfort, looking as if he could not have been more contented. Since I had already told him that I had quit smoking, I was too embarrassed to break my vow in his presence. Nevertheless, I was feeling quite unsettled deep down, as if something were somehow missing. My mind was clear: whenever B reached a particularly high point in his comments, I had no trouble agreeing with him by commenting "You can say that again!" all the while wishing I could be as excited and absorbed by the conversation as B was. We continued to chat in this peculiar manner for an hour or two, but I persisted in keeping my vow and my friend eventually took his leave. In terms of "strong will" and "determination," I suppose one could say that I had triumphed, but I could not help feeling a bit sick at heart. Several days later, B wrote to me en route saying that I had changed—I was not as animated or easygoing as I had been in the past. Even my conversation had suffered; maybe, he said, it was due to the air pollution in Shanghai. To this day I regret that I did not join him in smoking that night.

On another evening, a group of us were at a meeting that we convened regularly once a week. It was our custom to have one person present a paper to serve as a starter for discussion after dinner, and the meeting would then become an orgy of smoking. This time, it was C's turn to read a paper. His topic was "Religion and Revolution," and his essay was full of witty observations. I remember him saying that Feng Yuxiang had joined the northern branch of the Methodist Church, while Chiang Kai-shek had joined the southern branch. Someone then said that if that were the case, Wu Peifu would probably soon be joining the Western branch.[2] As we continued to banter, the smoke grew ever thicker, layer by layer. Its fragrance pervaded the room, and inspiration began to burst forth. H, a poet, sat in the middle of the room reclining in his chair and practicing blowing smoke rings. Each ring wafted slowly upward, and his poetic musings were most likely following suit, floating higher and higher. Unfortunately, his ease of countenance was something that cannot be described to the uninitiated. I was the only one not smoking, and I felt like an outcast, exiled beyond the pale of civilization. By then, quitting smoking had come to seem more and more meaningless, and I suddenly came to the realization that I had been completely deluded. I searched for the reasons that had initially led to my vow to quit smoking, but could not summon up a single one.

Aside from all this, my conscience also nagged me from time to time, because I reckoned that the highest state of thinking is to be found in a divine sense of inspiration. But if one is not smoking, how can the soul ever hope to reach this state? One afternoon, I went to visit a Western woman friend. She sat at a table, one hand holding a cigarette, the other resting on her knee. Her body listing slightly, she cut an entrancing figure, and I felt that my moment of awakening had arrived. When she extended her box of cigarettes to me, I withdrew one slowly and calmly, knowing that from this moment onward I would again attain salvation.

---

2. Feng Yuxiang and Wu Peifu were Chinese warlords in the 1920s.

When I got home, I immediately asked the servant to go out and buy a pack of English cigarettes. There was a burn spot on the right-hand side of my desk where I had always rested my cigarette in the past. Since in those days I had rarely been without a cigarette, I had carved next to the burn the inscription, "The Dent of Bygone Time." At first, I thought it would take some seven or eight years before I would burn through the two inches of tabletop. When I decided to give up smoking, I was sorry to note that the dent was only half a centimeter deep.

I was therefore overjoyed to place my cigarette there once again. Although the road ahead was long and broad, I would travel it without flagging. Later on, I moved to a place with a smaller study, and ended up selling the desk. "The Dent of Bygone Time" was thus no more. This I regret more than anything in life.

1932

THE MONKS OF HANGZHOU

Translated by Nancy E. Chapman and King-fai Tam

We once took a sightseeing trip to Hangzhou. Being fearful of bedbugs, we decided upon arrival to act like upper-class Chinese and stay in the Xiling Hotel, even though by doing so we would perhaps have to rub shoulders with Western loafers who might be staying there. When our car passed along Silk-Rinsing Road, I saw a woman kneeling by the side of a small river, but she was washing clothes, not rinsing silk. I was reminded of Xi Shi, the legendary beauty of the Spring and Autumn period (770–480 B.C.), who, I now realized, owed her fame to her work as a silk rinser and especially to her distinctive pose as she knelt beside the river.

It was raining gently when we arrived at West Lake. After checking into our room, we gazed out of our window. Everything was laid out before us like a painting—the inner lake, Lone Hill, the long causeway, and the Baozhu pagoda, as well as sightseeing boats and people visiting the lake. The rain had left the trees outside our window unusually verdant and lustrous, and the grass was a velvety green. One could barely see for the rain and mist, but raindrops were audible on the grass and pathways, melding to a steady patter. There were five or six small dwellings at the foot of the hill. Though humble in themselves, they were surrounded by a pleasing array of footpaths and patches of grass, and trees and bushes that grew unfettered at a comfortable distance from one another. A scene of no deliberate design, it far surpassed in beauty the mansions and villas on Yu Yuan Road in Shanghai. I thought of the city people there who need hundreds of thousands of dollars just for the purchase of a small lot. Once they get to that point, they proceed to bulldoze it flat, trim the greenery into pyramids, cones, and other three-dimensional shapes, form flower beds in strange geometric patterns, and construct five-foot-high artificial mountains and seven-foot-wide fishponds. Having accomplished all of this, they seem immensely pleased with themselves. It's a sight to wrench one's heart.

That night I was kept awake by the merrymaking of the idle Westerners and their women. Early the next morning we hired a car to tour Tiger Spring. Driving along the Su Causeway, we could see the lake shimmering in the sunlight on both sides. Green islets seemed to float on the water's surface, their reflections clear as a mirror image. The distant view was obscured by the mist, and behind the islets all was a boundless void: who could say if it was a mountain or a lake, the human world or a supernatural one? This sense of vastness is the hardest thing to paint, but it is easiest to portray it in a lake scene, especially a lake in the rain. As long as one can capture this vision of glimmering light and distant shades, one will have brought the mood to life.

In the midst of this natural scene, there intruded a structure resembling a lighthouse that was ugly beyond belief and thoroughly offensive to the eye. Seeing a building like this at West Lake is like finding a festering sore on the face of a beautiful woman. I asked the driver what it was, and he said that it was a commemorative hall left over from some exhibition. Heaven keep us from heinous crimes such as this committed by shameless students returned from overseas! I vowed that, were I ever to command a battalion occupying Hangzhou, I would target first this insult to the face of West Lake and blow it to smithereens. People of future generations would remember the event with these lines:

> Green are the trees along West Lake's shore
> Only this blemish the senses abhor.
> General Lin, his anger unbounded
> With his cannons this eyesore pounded.

Halfway up the hill sits Tiger Spring, and the half-mile trip from the foot of the hill to the door of the monastery was beautiful beyond comparison. We therefore decided to leave our car behind and proceed on foot. On both sides of the road were tall trees whose names I did not know—suffice it to say they were very tall. There were flowers, too, and I did not know their names either, but I found them very beautiful. We were not taught botany or zoology in primary school, and I felt the loss now. A few hundred steps from the entrance to the monastery a small stream gushed down the hillside. Little waterfalls appeared where it flowed over hanging rocks, making a delightful sound. A man was imploring his six-year-old son to come look at the waterfall, but the "little master" refused, protesting that his clothes would get all wet. Besides, he complained, the mud was dirty, and what was so special about a waterfall anyway?

When we came to the entrance of the monastery, a Buddhist incantation escaped my lips unwittingly, just as people who do not believe in Jesus often say, "Oh, Lord." Tiger Spring tea from the temple is renowned, and we of course wanted to try some, believing this the genteel thing to do. Some men and women were busily drinking tea and taking pictures: one in particular was raising his cup for the camera, but after it clicked, I didn't see him drink from it. I was sure, though, that there would be a picture in his photo album with the caption "On such and such a day, the Master of the Serene Abode savored tea at Tiger Spring." The thought of it was enough to discourage me from having any myself. Just then, a young monk asked if I would like to buy some tea leaves, and I resolved to leave without doing so.

There are two things at Tiger Spring that visitors should not miss: the latrines and the teakettles, both of which are ingenious inventions of the monks there. While one may choose to forgo the tea itself, the kettles in which it is brewed are worth taking a look at. If European monks are expert at making wine, there is no reason why the monks of Tiger Spring should not be able to devise good teakettles. (Perhaps this kind of kettle already existed in southern China. If so, I have never seen one before.) They are made of copper, and resemble the kind used in homes, except that they are considerably larger. They are in fact over two feet high and about three feet in diameter, with two long, cleverly designed pipes on top. In the center is a cavity for charcoal that heats water in the surrounding compartment. Even though the kettles have a handle and spout, it was hard to imagine how anyone could manage to pour tea from such an unwieldy vessel. I asked a monk to explain to me how it worked. Using a cast-iron pot, he ladled some spring water from a large urn and poured it down one of the pipes. Almost immediately, boiling water began to flow from the spout of the kettle. I understand that this is what is known in physics as water pressure equilibrium. Thus, when the cold water was added to one end, hot water was naturally pushed out the other. Moreover, cold water sinks and hot water rises. After seeing the demonstration, I felt it would be pretentious of me to explain its operation to the monk in technical terms. This method of obtaining hot water is a perfect model of convenience: the same amount of water always flows out of the kettle as is added to it, and the kettle remains full as a result.

Whenever I visit West Lake, I always make a point of going to Jade Stream to view the fish there. I enjoy watching them swim around, but I also lament that they have been deprived of the happiness of swimming freely in deep lakes and steep ravines. If monks respect life enough to set fish free here, why not go a step further and release them into the Qiantang River? Even if they then meet premature death, they will not have lived in vain. Viewing fish is indeed a refined pastime, but there is no evading the charge that people are in reality accumulating religious credits for themselves by setting living things free.

While I was watching the fish, a monk came over to talk with me. He spoke quite elegantly, with a Henan accent, and it occurred to me that, though vegetarianism is in theory quite conducive to good health, I had yet to see a monk with a ruddy complexion. Instead, most are sallow and scrawny in appearance and sluggish in their movements, clearly a sign of malnutrition. This prompted me to raise the question of sexual desire with him, inquiring if there was a connection between vegetarianism and abstinence. He seemed to feel uncomfortable answering, since my wife was with me, so, in our local dialect I asked her to go to the other side of the pond to look at the fish. The monk and I then covered a number of topics about modern marriage. He seemed to be a forthright person, so I decided to put some questions to him:

"Take that woman in red over there, for example," I said. "Would you monks feel aroused if you looked at her?"

My impudent question brought forth an unexpected lecture from the monk on the subject of celibacy of a sort one rarely hears. The gist of it was similar to Plato's belief that a thinker should refrain from marrying.

"Why wouldn't we feel aroused?" he responded. "However, if you read the Buddhist scriptures, you will understand how destructive carnal desire can be. At one moment a person feels nothing but happiness, but later on he experiences all sorts of cares and tribulations. Why do you suppose so many young men drown themselves in rivers nowadays? For love—for women. So many people are divorced these days. How is it that at one point a man cannot live without a woman, but now he thinks of nothing but separation? Look at me, a man on my own. I am free to go to Mount Tai or Mount Miaofeng, Pudu, Shantou—wherever I want."

I could see that he was of the same mind as Saint Paul, Kant, and Plato. And, wasn't it true that many of Schopenhauer's insights about women were derived from Buddhist scriptures? As I mulled over these thoughts, an old woman from the temple happened to pass by. I would not have thought anything of it except that the monk hastened to explain, "She's here because pilgrims who come to the temple often bring their womenfolk, and it's awkward for us to serve them. So we hired her to keep things tidy."

It hadn't actually occurred to me to think otherwise. After all, Schopenhauer and Plato had never had anything against women serving as housekeepers.

1941

Zhu Ziqing (1896–1948)

PROSE SELECTIONS

Translated by Howard Goldblatt

HASTE

The swallows may go, but they will return another day; the willows may wither, but they will turn green again; the peach blossoms may fade and fall, but they will bloom again. You who are wiser than I, tell me, then: why is it that the days, once gone, never again return? Are they stolen by someone? Then, by whom? And where are they hidden? Or do they run away by themselves? Then, where are they now?

I do not know how many days I've been given, yet slowly but surely my supply is diminishing. Counting silently to myself, I can see that more than 8,000 of them have already slipped through my fingers, each like a drop of water on the head of a pin, falling into the ocean. My days are disappearing into the stream of time, noiselessly and without a trace; uncontrollably, my sweat and tears stream down.

What's gone is gone, and what is coming cannot be halted. From what is gone to what is yet to come, why must it pass so quickly? In the morning when I get up there are two or three rays of sunlight slanting into my small room. The sun, does it have feet? Stealthily it moves along, as I too, unknowingly, follow its progress. Then as I wash up, the day passes through my washbasin, and at breakfast through my rice bowl. When I am standing still and quiet, my eyes carefully follow its progress past me. I can sense that it is hurrying along, and when I stretch out my hands to cover and hold it, it soon emerges from under my hands and moves along. At night, as I lie on my bed, agilely it strides across my body and flies past my feet. And when I open my eyes to greet the sun again, another day has slipped by. I bury my face in my hands and heave a sigh. But the shadow of the new day begins darting by, even in the midst of my sighing.

During these fleeting days what can I, only one among so many, accomplish? Nothing more than to pace irresolutely, nothing more than to hurry along. In these more than 8,000 days of hurrying what have I to show but some irresolute wanderings? The days that are gone are like smoke that has been dissipated by a breeze, like thin mists that have been burned off under the onslaught of the morning sun. What mark will I leave behind? Will the trace I leave behind be so much as a gossamer thread? Naked I came into this world, and in a twinkling still naked I will leave it. But what I cannot accept is: why should I make this journey in vain?

You who are wiser than I, please tell me why it is that once gone, our days never return.

1922

SPRING

Oh, the waiting, the waiting! Finally the east winds begin to blow, and spring is just around the corner. The world seems to have awakened from its slumber as, excitedly, it opens its eyes.

The mountains take on a luster, the waters start to rise, and there is a blush on the face of the sun.

In the gardens and in the countryside new grass, tender and green, secretly threads its way up through the earth; everywhere you look the ground is covered with it. Some people are seated, some are lying down, and others are turning somersaults; then there are games of ball, footraces, and hide-and-seek. The breezes are gentle; the grass, soft as cotton.

Peach trees, apricot trees, and pear trees jostle each other, all of them in magnificent bloom, each trying to outdo the other. There are fiery reds, pinks like the sunset, and snowy whites—and always the abounding fragrance of flowers. Close your eyes, and the trees seem already heavily laden with peaches and apricots and pears. Beneath the flowers a teeming host of bees fills the air with the sound of their buzzing, as butterflies, large and small, flit to and fro. Everywhere there are wildflowers of many kinds, those with names and those without, scattered throughout the thickets and looking like countless eyes or like stars, here and there winking at you.

"When the willows are green, the winds that touch your face carry no chill." Oh, how true! They are like the caress of your mother's hand. And the winds bring an aroma of freshly turned earth mixed with the scent of new grass and the bouquet of myriad flowers, all blended together in the slightly moistened air. Birds make their nests among the luxuriant flowers and tender leaves, and in delight they blend their voices; from their throats come the crisp, boastful strains of their songs of enchantment, which merge with the sounds of gentle breezes and flowing water. Then you can also hear a lilting tune from a shepherd boy's flute, played the day long as he sits astride his bullock.

Most prevalent are the rains; a single rainfall can last two or three days. But don't be distressed! Just look—it is like the fine hair of a bullock, like delicate embroidery needles, or fine silk, densely slanting downward as woven strands, covering the roofs of houses with a blanket of fine mist. The leaves of the trees are so green they sparkle, and the grass is so green it hurts your eyes. Toward evening the lamps are lit, giving off a pale yellow glow that accentuates a night of tranquility and peace. Off in the countryside, on the small paths and at the sides of stone bridges, people stroll leisurely under their raised umbrellas. Then there are the farmers who work the soil clad in their grass cloaks and hats, and whose grass huts are scattered around the countryside, standing silently in the rain.

In the sky the number of kites slowly increases as the number of children on the ground grows. In the city and in the countryside the populace seems to come to life; the old and the young emerge in spirited animation, flexing their muscles and stirring up their spirits, each occupying himself in his own pursuits. Spring is the time when plans for the year ahead must be made; when starting out, there is an abundance of time, and everywhere there is hope.

Spring is like a newborn child, brand-new from head to toe, starting out in life.
Spring is like a blossoming and graceful maiden, laughing and then walking on.
Spring is like a robust youth with limbs of iron, leading us on the road ahead.

1924

THE SILHOUETTE OF HIS BACK

It has been more than two years since the last time I saw my father, and the memory that has stayed with me the longest is the silhouette of his back.

It was during the winter of that year; Grandmother had just died, and Father's temporary appointment with the government had been terminated. Truly those were days when "calamities never come singly." I traveled from Beijing to Xuzhou, planning to return home with my father for the funeral. When I reached Xuzhou, I met my father, and I noticed that his garden was in complete disarray. I thought again of Grandmother and was unable to hold back the flow of tears. Father said, "Things are as they are; you shouldn't be sad, for happily there is nothing under Heaven that is hopeless."

On our return home, by selling and pawning our things. Father was able to clear up his debts; then he borrowed money to pay for the funeral. During those days the situation in our home was a pathetic one, partly because of the funeral and partly because of Father's unemployment. After the funeral ceremonies were completed, Father set out for Nanjing to look for work, and since I intended to return to Beijing to study, we took to the road together.

When we reached Nanjing a friend invited us to go on an excursion, so we stopped over for a day. At noon on the next day we had to cross the river to Pukou in order to board the afternoon train headed north. Owing to his busy schedule, Father had originally decided not to see me off and had asked a hotel attendant whom he knew well to accompany me. He enjoined the attendant time and again to be extremely attentive. But in the end he could not dispel his anxieties, fearing that the attendant would prove to be unreliable; he was unable to make up his mind for some time. Actually, at the time I was already twenty years old and had journeyed to and from Beijing two or three times, so it wasn't such a major affair. He vacillated for a while, then finally decided that he would see me off after all. I tried to persuade him, two or three times, that he need not go, but he simply said, "No matter, having them go isn't a good idea."

We crossed the river and entered the train station. I bought my ticket while he busied himself with the luggage, of which there was so much that he found it necessary to offer a tip to a porter before we could pass on. He then busied himself with bartering over the charges. In those days I thought I was as smart as one could be, and, feeling that his speech wasn't all that elegant, it was necessary for me to interject some words of my own. Finally, however, he arrived at an agreed price and escorted me to the train. He located a seat next to the car door for me, over which I draped the purple fur-lined overcoat that he had had made for me. He instructed me to be careful during the trip, to be on my guard at night, and to avoid drafts. And he also charged the attendant with taking good care of me. I was laughing to myself over his absurdness; all they're concerned with is money, so asking them for favors is absolutely useless! What's more, was it possible that a fellow as old and mature as I was would be unable to take care of himself? Ai! As I think back on it now, I was really too smart for my own good then!

I said, "Papa, you go on now." He glanced out of the train car and said, "I'll go buy you some oranges. You wait here; don't go anywhere." I could see there were several peddlers waiting for customers over beyond the railing of a distant platform. To get to that platform you had to cross the tracks by jumping down and then clambering back up the other side. Father was a stout man, so crossing over there would be no mean task. At first I wanted to go myself, but he wouldn't allow it, so all I could do was let him go. I watched him hobble over to the tracks in his black cloth cap, black cloth gown, and dark blue outer jacket, and slowly ease himself down without too much trouble. But when he had crossed the tracks and was trying to climb up to the other platform, that was no easy matter. He grabbed hold of it with two hands, then hoisted up both of his legs, his stout body listing to the left and showing the great strain he was exerting. It was then that I noticed the silhouette of his back, and tears promptly coursed down my cheeks. I hurriedly wiped away the tears, afraid that he might notice, and afraid also that others might be watching. When I looked out from the train car again he was already on his way back, carrying a load of deep-colored oranges. To cross the railroad tracks he first tossed the oranges to the ground and slowly lowered himself down, then picked up the oranges and started out again. When he made it over to this side, I quickly went over and gave him a hand. Then the two of us walked back onto the train, and he dropped the whole load of oranges on top of my leather overcoat. Then he brushed the mud off his clothes, his mind having taken on a relaxed mood. After a moment he said, "Well, I'm going now; write when you get there." My gaze followed him as he walked away. He took several steps, then turned around to me and said, "Go on in, there's no one inside." When the silhouette of his back had merged with those of the people coming and going, when I could no longer spot him, I went back in and sat down. Once again tears welled up in my eyes.

These past few years my father's and my paths have failed to cross, and our family situation has worsened each day. From his youth he had struck out on his own and had supported his family by himself, undertaking several important jobs. How could he have envisioned such ruinous times in his advanced years? He was a witness to unhappy times, so naturally could not help giving vent to his feelings, and trifling family matters often aroused his anger. His attitude toward me gradually came to differ from earlier days. But not having seen me in the past two years, he has come to lose sight of my shortcomings, and thinks only of seeing me and my son.

After I came to Beijing he wrote me a letter in which he said, "My general health is good, but I am bothered by a rather painful shoulder that makes it difficult to raise my chopsticks or lift a pen; probably the hour of my passing is not far away." When I read to this point, through the shining translucence of my tears I saw once again the silhouette of that stout back covered with a dark blue outer jacket and black cloth gown. Ai! I do not know when I shall be able to meet him again.

1925

THE MOONLIT LOTUS POND

These past few days I have been exceedingly restless. This evening, as I sat in my courtyard enjoying the cool night air, I suddenly thought of the lotus pond along which I was used to taking daily walks, and I imagined that it must look quite different under the light of this full moon. Slowly the moon climbed in the sky, and beyond the wall the laughter of children playing on the road could no longer be heard. My wife was inside patting Run'er[1] as she hummed a faint lullaby. I gently threw a wrap over my shoulders and walked out, closing the gate behind me.

Bordering the pond is a meandering little cinder path. It is a secluded path; during the day few people use it, and at night it is even lonelier. There are great numbers of trees growing on all sides of the lotus pond, lush and fertile. On one side of the path there are some willow trees and several varieties of trees whose names I do not know. On moonless nights this path is dark and forbidding, giving one an eerie feeling. But this evening it was quite nice, even though the rays of the moon were pale. Finding myself alone on the path, I folded my hands behind me and strolled along. The stretch of land and sky that spread out before me seemed to belong to me, and I could transcend my own existence and enter another world. I love noise, but I also love quiet; I love crowds, but I also love seclusion. On a night like tonight, all alone under this vast expanse of moonlight, I can think whatever I wish, or think of nothing if I wish. I feel myself to be a truly free man. The things I must do and the words I must say during the daytime I need not concern myself with now; this is an exquisite secluded spot, a place where I can enjoy the limitless fragrance of the lotuses and the light of the moon.

On the surface of the winding and twisting lotus pond floated an immense field of leaves. The leaves lay high in the water, rising up like the skirts of a dancing girl. Amid the layers of leaves white blossoms adorned the vista, some beguilingly open and others bashfully holding their petals in. Just like a string of bright pearls or stars in a blue sky, or like lovely maidens just emerging from their bath. A gentle breeze floated by, bringing with it waves of a crisp fragrance like strains of a vague melody sent over from distant towering buildings. When that happened the leaves and blossoms trembled briefly, as though a bolt of lightning had streaked across the lotus pond. The leaves themselves were densely crowded together, pushing back and forth, and they seemed to be a cresting wave of solid green. Beneath the leaves restrained currents of water flowed, imprisoned beneath them, the color forever hidden, while the stirrings of the leaves were even more pronounced.

The moon's rays were like flowing waters, gently depositing their moisture on the layer of leaves and blossoms. A light green mist floated just above the lotus pond. The leaves and blossoms looked as though they had been bathed in milk, or like a blurred dream swathed in airy gauze. Although the moon was full, a light covering of clouds in the sky prevented it from shining brightly; yet I had the pleasant feeling that I had come to a fine spot. For just as one cannot do without deep slumber, still a light sleep has its own delights. The moon's rays filtered down through the trees, and dark, uneven shadows of varying shades were cast by the dense foliage on the high ground, perilously dark and spooky.

---

1. The name of one of the author's children.

The bewitching shadows cast by the sparse, twisted willow trees seemed to be painted on the lotus leaves. The moonlight on the pond was spread unevenly, but the rays and the shadows were a concert of harmony, like a celebrated tune played on a violin.

On all sides of the lotus pond, far and near, on high ground and low, there are trees, most of them willows. These trees completely envelop the whole of the lotus pond; only by the side of the path are there gaps, here and there showing through, seemingly left there just so the moon can shine in. The colors of the trees are uniformly dark. At first glance they resemble a bank of fog and mist, but the slender, graceful forms of the willows can still be distinguished in that fog and mist. Above the treetops a row of mountains can be seen ever so indistinctly, just the hint of their shapes, while one or two faint glimmers of roadside lamps seep through the openings of the branches, appearing like the weary eyes of a tired man. Now the spot was at its noisiest, if you count the chirping of cicadas in the trees and the croaking of frogs in the water. But the noise was theirs alone; I added nothing to it.

All of a sudden I was reminded of lotus gathering. The gathering of lotuses is an old custom south of the Yangtze, whose origins probably date from very early on but that flourished during the Six Dynasty period.[2] This we know from the poems and ballads of the time. The lotus gatherers were young maidens who drifted in small boats and sang their songs of love. It goes without saying that there were great numbers of lotus gatherers as well as those who came to watch them, for that was a festive and a romantic occasion. "The Lotus Gatherers" by Emperor Yuan of the Liang dynasty[3] tells it well:

Princely lads and alluring maidens
Adrift in a boat, their hearts in accord;
The boat's prow describes a slow turn
As they exchange wine cups;
The oars become intertwined,
And the boat moves across the floating duckweed;
The maidens with their slender waists simply bound
Cast glances behind them.
Summer begins where the spring leaves off;
The leaves are tender, the flowers in bloom.
Protecting their dresses from the dampness, smiles adorning their faces,
They gather up their skirts, taking care not to capsize the boat.

This paints for us a picture of the pleasant excursions of those days. They

2. A.D. 317–588.
3. A.D. 552–555.

must have been truly memorable events; it is a pity that we can no longer enjoy such pastimes.

> I then recalled the lines from
> "Tune of the West Isle".
>
> Gathering lotuses at Nantang in the fall,
> The lotus blossoms rise above our heads.
> Bending over to pluck the lotus seeds,
> Lotus seeds as transparent as the water.

If tonight there were lotus gatherers, the lotus blossoms here too would "rise above their heads." But it is not enough to have before me only these rippling shadows. All of this stirred up in me a sense of longing for the South. With these thoughts in my mind I suddenly raised my head and found that my steps had carried me to my own gate; I softly pushed it open and entered. I was greeted by complete silence; my wife had long since fallen fast asleep.

1927

Feng Zikai (1898–1975)

BOMBS IN YISHAN

Translated by D. E. Pollard

The first time Yishan was bombed would have been in the autumn of 1938, when I was still in Guilin. It was said the target was Zhejiang University, and countless bombs were dropped. The university dormitories were out in Biaoying district, which is crisscrossed by ditches, and the students knew what to do in air raids. By lying low in the ditches, they escaped without a single casualty. One student, however, was suffering from a mental illness; in his deranged condition, he refused to take cover, and stayed in a building that was bombed. The shock brought an immediate end to his symptoms, and he afterward was restored to health and was able to resume classes. His story was often told at Zhejiang University, as a matter for celebration.

I encountered the second bombing, which took place in the summer of 1939. This time, though, it was anything but a matter for celebration. Quite a lot of people were killed by the bus station, quite a lot injured, and quite a lot more were frightened out of their wits. I was one of those frightened out of their wits. Ever afterward I blanched at the sound of an iron wok lid being banged, or the hiss of steam from a kettle. I was such a bundle of nerves that when the old lady next door called her little boy Jinbao, I used to think she was shouting "Jingbao!" (Air raid warning!), and was poised to jump to my feet and run for cover. Now that it is over and I can lick my wounds, I still get angry at the thought of the vileness of the Japanese warlords. Thankfully, our final victory has been won, the Japanese have surrendered, and their warlords are being executed. And I have come through safe and sound. If I look back here on bygone days, it may actually help to lay some old ghosts to rest and contribute to the festive mood.

We ran into trouble when we first arrived in Yishan. When the Zhejiang University bus carrying my own family of ten and a few other passengers, plus a load of baggage, got to the East Gate, we were stopped by two policemen, who said an air raid alert was in force and we weren't allowed into the city. That explained why the gate was completely deserted. The driver immediately turned the bus round and drove back a mile or so, stopping under a big tree out in the country. We all got out and sat on some rocks in a gully. By then it was past noon, and stomachs were rumbling. Luckily we had a basket of *zongzi* to stave off our hunger.[1] It happened to be the Qingming holiday time, and though we were traveling we still kept to our old custom of making some "Qingming *zongzi*" to take with us. So now all of us, that is, my whole family of ten, the driver, and the other passengers, tucked into the *zongzi* and sat around talking. The sun was shining, the breeze gentle, the day was perfect. If we had been able to forget we were in Yishan taking cover from an air raid, and imagine we were picnicking by the West Lake in Hangzhou, that afternoon would have been pure bliss! The whole family mustered, from the two-year-old to the over-seventies, out on a spring excursion, and a few friends along besides—how exhilarating, how civilized! Alas, the sad truth is that in this life we are sometimes obliged to make believe like that.

When we had finished the *zongzi*, the sun was slanting in the sky, as if to tell us we could enter the city now. Thereupon we got back on the bus and headed back. This time we were indeed allowed to go through the East Gate. But no sooner had we alighted than a crowd of people started rushing in our direction. When we asked in alarm what was up, we discovered it was another air raid alert! Being newcomers we did not know the geography of the place, and had to flee blindly in the wake of the crowd. Our children and old folk were not very mobile, so they made for the nearest cover of a thicket outside the East Gate. I fled with other people across the river and hid in a cave. The all clear did not sound till it was nearly dark. Fortunately when we got back to the bus, we found the luggage was all still intact, and the rest of the family eventually straggled back, all accounted for. Then we had to find lodgings and somewhere to eat. We did not get to bed till late at night. We learned that there had been three alerts that day, those that we encountered being the second and third. We were also told that the thickets outside the East Gate concealed the station and the military command post. These would have been the prime targets for the bombers. Imagine, my family was hiding from an air raid right in the target area!

---

1. *Zongzi* are little packets of sticky rice with meat and vegetable flavoring wrapped in bamboo leaves; they are normally eaten during the Dragon Boat Festival.

Our relationship with Yishan was measured in air raid alerts: we became acquainted in the middle of one, and afterward parted in one. In between we had alerts practically every day, and experienced one bombing.

To begin with, we lived over the Kaiming Bookshop in town. Later on we could not put up with all the running about occasioned by the great number of air raid alerts, so we rented a small cottage some distance from the city, and the family moved out, leaving me and one small son in the Kaiming Bookshop. One day, it happened to be market day, I was idly gazing down from an upstairs window on the hawkers' pitches at the roadside. I saw a crepe fabric seller suddenly pack up his goods. The hawker on the neighboring pitch, without inquiring into the reason why, did likewise. A third followed suit, then a fourth, and in no time all the hawkers along the street were packing up, telling each other, "It's an air raid!" They all made off helter-skelter in search of safety. Quite befogged, I took my son downstairs to look for shelter myself. But once outside, I found everyone all smiles. In fact there was no air raid warning; it was only much ado about nothing. The alarm was sparked off, it transpired, by the fabric seller packing up early for reasons of his own. His movements were quite hasty and abrupt, which led the hawker next to him to think an air raid was coming, with the farcical consequences I have described. As the old saying goes, if three people say there is a tiger, there *is* a tiger. But behind the farce could be seen the real fear of air raids at that time. I found it impossible to settle down to anything in this jittery atmosphere, where people were afraid of their own shadows, so I took my son to join the rest of the family in the cottage in the country.

This thatched cottage was pitifully small; just three rooms of ten square feet each. We needed to buy two bunk beds to sleep the ten of us. The beds doubled as seats, the dining table doubled as a desk, without too much trouble. If you looked upon it as a boat rather than a house, it was in fact rather spacious. And there was the scenery as well: pavilion, terrace, escarpment, hills, stands of bamboo. These were originally the Dragon's Ridge Gardens, and where we lived was originally the gardener's cottage. The escarpment was quite rugged, with lots of clefts and fissures. We hid in those clefts during the air raid alerts. At the first alarm we all stayed put, and waited for the emergency alert before taking cover in the clefts. But the enemy planes never came, and every time we returned peacefully to our little cottage. But later on, some days before the fall of Nanning, the neighboring county was bombed and Yishan took flight. We ourselves came to think the rock clefts gave inadequate protection, and we ought to find a safer refuge. But inertia prevailed, and we did nothing about it.

One day I fully intended to go out and look for a cave, but the weather was quite unsettled, alternating very oddly between sunshine and rain. Everyone said it was unlikely there would be an alert. My native indolence persuaded me to put off my expedition. Suddenly the alarm bell sounded. The people taking flight past our house seemed unusually panicky, and the clanging of the bell was unusually ominous. On top of that, the emergency alert followed swiftly. I had to stop an acquaintance of mine to find out that reliable report had it that the enemy planes were especially active that day, and the chances were Yishan would be bombed. Applying the test of air raid alerts to my family, they could be divided into two factions: the bold faction, namely my wife, my mother-in-law, and the youths over sixteen; and the timid faction, my older sister and the two girls, I could be said to be sandwiched in between, belonging to no faction; or you could say I was a fence-sitter, a misfit, or a member of both factions, because after a drink I belonged to the bold faction, but before I'd had a drink I belonged to the timid faction. That day the bold faction took cover in the nearby rock clefts. As I hadn't had a drink I joined the timid faction in going farther afield.

Going farther afield did not mean we had a safer objective in mind, it was just a belief akin to that of people who bought joss sticks to worship the Buddha, namely, "to fork out money is a virtue in itself." Likewise we thought to go further afield must be a good thing in itself. We happened to fall in with some people we knew who were making resolutely for the open fields; they assured us there were caves up ahead. So we pushed on with our guides, getting bootfuls of water. Our cross-country trek ended in a spot where there really was a formation of towering rocks, and we hurriedly searched for the cave. These rocks were in the shape of a V laid out horizontal on the ground, allowing you to pass through the open end to the apex, but there was no cover overhead—actually it was no cave at all! Still, by this stage we could not move on elsewhere; if we were to die, we would die here.

Lots of men and women squeezed into the V. I crouched at the mouth of the V. Now able to take in the surroundings, I uttered an exclamation of dismay. In fact we were only a few hundred feet from the prime targets of the station and the sports field! It was a whole lot more dangerous here than among the rocks of the Dragon Ridge Garden. As I was getting all worked up I heard a heavy droning noise, and the people in the V shouted:

"The Jap bombers are coming!" Whereupon they all ducked down and camouflaged themselves with the ferns that sprouted from the rocks. What was I to do, stuck outside the opening, with no protection at all? Suddenly I spotted on the outer slope of the V formation a slight depression overgrown with ferns. On the inspiration of desperation, I laid myself flat in the hollow underneath the ferns.

I lay still and watched the sky through the leaves of the ferns above me. A squadron of enemy bombers appeared in the distant sky heading toward me, the drone of their engines growing louder all the time. I thought to myself, There are only three possible outcomes today: one, I will get up and go home unharmed; two, I will be injured and be carried to hospital; three, I will be killed in this hollow. Any way, I had to take what came. I seemed to see one of those shakers used for drawing lots in front of me, with three spills in it: one marked 1, one marked 2, one marked 3. I stretched out my hand and drew one . . .

As this thought was going through my mind, three bombers came up over my head. Suddenly they slowed and hovered. Then a black spherical object fell from the aircraft straight toward me. I could not bear to look, and covered my face, waiting for it to explode. First there came a whistling noise, followed by a "crump." The earth shook and the rocks shook. The blast lifted me from the ground. Yet I seemed not to have been injured. Peeping out, all I could see was a spreading pall of smoke, and the three planes circling over it. Another black spherical object fell from a plane, and a second whistled down from a different plane. The objects were right overhead. I covered my face with my hands, and heard "crump," "crump" all around me.

I pictured a bomb landing right in the middle of the V, going off bang, and all of us—men, women, young and old—blown to smithereens in a flash: an end like this would have been clean and straightforward, and would have put us out of our misery at least. But the latest bombs did not do that: they just demoralized us with their more powerful blasts. This proved the bombs were getting closer, and our danger was increasing. Suddenly I heard a woman howl from inside the V, followed by the sound of whimpering. I could not work out what was going on. Fortunately the enemy planes were moving on, the drone of their engines fading. We all began to breathe again. I got up, covered in dust, and crept over to the opening of the V. They were surprised to see me, not knowing where I had got to, or whether I was safe or not. Seeing them all unscathed, I asked why the howl. It turned out there was a wasps' nest in the V. One young woman had knocked against it, and had been stung, hence the howl and whimpering.

The enemy planes dropped a dozen or so bombs and, their bloodlust satisfied, returned to base. Long afterward the all clear sounded. We filed out of the V but could not see far for the dust and smoke, which still hung in the air. The girl who had been stung by the wasp set off home through the haze, her hand held to her swollen face.

My terror had dissipated by the time I got home after my false alarm, but it had been replaced by a sense of grievance. This just wouldn't do! I hated to have my right to life controlled by the enemy! But what could I do about it? I was still pondering when my daughter came back and reported that numerous bombs had fallen around the station, on the sports field, by the river, and in the park; so many people had been killed and so many injured. One woman had been killed under a tree, her head half blown off while her body remained sitting erect. Lots of people had been carted off to the hospital shrieking and groaning. When I heard this report, I realized how lucky we had been. It was clear the enemy had deliberately bombed the outskirts rather than the city center, anticipating that the city would have been evacuated by the time they arrived. In that case our V had presented them with a nice target! I don't know what good deeds our little band had done to have saved us from harm. As I think back on it now, perhaps that V foreshadowed the V that appeared on the night of 10 August 1945, the symbol of final victory.[2]

That night I could not contain my indignation. I felt that to kill people by "air raid" was too unmanly. If there is honor among thieves, there is also an honorable way of killing. If we are both on level ground, and you come to kill me, I run. If I can't get away, I am killed by you. This kind of killing, simply in terms of killing, is fair enough, and one would die without complaint. But if they come to kill you from above and you have to get away from below, they are bound to have the upper hand, and you are bound to be on the losing end. The matter of dying was secondary; what was intolerable was the moral injustice and affront to one's feelings. I had to think of a way to render the killers from the air powerless against me and to save myself from further indignity.

The next day I had my solution. After breakfast I gathered together some fellow spirits from my family, and we set out for the hills, taking with us reading matter and victuals. We walked over a mile to the Nine Dragon Cliffs, sat in the entrance of a big cave, and read.

Having spent a carefree day, we returned at dusk. I was totally unaware of whether there had been an air raid or not. This style of life continued for over a month, during which time I was indeed free from further subjection to indignity. Nor was the city bombed again. But before long there came the news of the fall of Nanning. I had no choice but to take the refugee trail, carrying my sense of injustice along with me.

1946

2. The actual date of the Japanese unconditional surrender was August 14, 1945; the signing of the documents of surrender took place on September 3.

Liang Shiqiu (1901–1987)

SICKNESS

Translated by D. E. Pollard

Lu Xun once conjured up the picture of a gent coughing up half a mouthful of blood while being helped onto his porch by two maidservants to look at the autumn begonias, pretending that this was a paradigm of high culture and refinement. In fact, while there are any number of things that are cultured and refined, illness is the great exception. One can understand that those who have not the good fortune to be able to view autumn begonias propped up by two maidservants might find that condition enviable, but to add the circumstance of "coughing up half a mouthful of blood" seriously diminishes its enviability: I would not be surprised if marching off alone and unaided to a vegetable patch to look at turnips and cabbages might not be thought preferable.

I recently read an article that referred to pregnancy as a "physiological abnormality"; to me it was the author who was "psychologically abnormal." The true form of physiological abnormality is illness. Just the sight of an invalid's face is hard enough for most people to stomach: as yellow as a notice of bereavement, or as green as a freshly unearthed ancient bronze; a layer of skin stretched over a skull, or just a flicker of an eyelid more than a mask. Illness is a change from normality, a necessary part of the process of changing from a living person to a dead person. Because illness is abnormal it is also ugly. They say that the picture of the Chinese Helen[1] clutching her heart and furrowing

1. The "Chinese Helen" was Xi Shi, a legendary beauty of the fifth century B.C. There is a

her brow is beautiful, but if the truth be told, that view is but a personal quirk; it may be safely discounted when one remembers the story of the man driven away from home because of his repulsive body odor who found a warm welcome at the seaside.

I once had a very long spell in hospital because I myself fell ill. I came to the conclusion that we Chinese men are extremely maladapted to staying in hospital. When he is in good health every man can be a little local despot. Servants, needless to say, are his hired slaves, his wife is only a slave who is provided with bed and board, and his parents are self-enlisted slaves. Accustomed as he is to living in the lap of luxury and having people at his beck and call, when one day his eminence finds himself subject to an indisposition and is carried off to hospital, he will not be content until he has moved his entire household (including the kitchen!) in with him. Once installed in the hospital, he acts as if he is in his own country villa and has people running about buying watermelon, making lotus-root drinks, fetching water for him to wash, filling his thermos flask. Actually it would be more accurate to say the hospital is treated as a hotel rather than a home, principally on account of the noisiness. The fact that a patient in Ward 4 is about to peg out does not stop the visitors in Ward 5 from holding forth in loud voices; neither does the fact that the patient in Ward 6 has just swallowed a big dose of sedatives prevent the man in Ward 7 from hollering for his amah at the top of his lungs.

A hospital is the battlefield over which life and death fight for final victory; as such it will resound with groans and lamentations, shouts and jubilations—for human beings are not made of stone, and even a saint could not be expected to restrain himself in such circumstances. Those who get short shrift are those who thought a hospital was a place where they could recuperate in peace.

But there was one occasion when I found it in my heart to excuse the noise that came from the next ward. It was the middle of the night, and the voice was a woman's. First the bell rang, then came a call of "Nurse!" Thereafter a ring, followed after an interval by a call, the tempo rising from largo to allegro, the tone becoming more and more urgent, the pitch more and more shrill. Everyone in the hospital, apart from those resting in the mortuary, must have heard, but no one brought her what she wanted. The calls gradually turned to sobs, desperation gradually turned to entreaty, and by the time all the correct procedures had been followed and the thing had passed down the chain of command to finally reach her, its hour had passed, and it was of no more use.

---

famous anecdote about her habitual frowning in Zhuangzi [Chuang Tzu]: "The beautiful Hsi-shih [Xi Shi], troubled with heartburn, frowned at her neighbors. An ugly woman of the neighborhood, seeing that Hsi-shih was beautiful, went home and likewise pounded her breast and frowned at her neighbors. But at the sight of her the rich men of the neighborhood shut tight their gates and would not venture out, while the poor men grabbed their wives and children by the hand and scampered off" (*The Complete Works of Chuang Tzu*, trans. Burton Watson [New York: Columbia University Press, 1968, p. 160]).

The old-style notice of bereavement liked to use the phrase "passed away at the end of his/her allotted span in the bosom of his/her family," not without reason. If you nurse an illness at home you may not get the best of treatment, but you won't be bothered by extraneous irritations. Supposing the illness were incurable and you had to slip this mortal coil, to do so in the bosom of your family is something that may justifiably be mentioned with pride, for it means the death would have been a comfortable one.

Serious illness may profoundly alter one's outlook on life. When I was at death's door, I was overcome by a sense that one could take nothing for granted in this life, and consequently took a more tolerant attitude toward everything. For instance, I normally made no allowances for one man I knew who drew a rice ration on false pretenses, but when, after several injections of heart stimulants, I saw him blithely turn up again, I could not help softening toward him: it seemed to me he could after all be admitted to the human race. Lu Xun's last words were that he "forgave no one, nor sought forgiveness from anyone." This stand one can accept, but those of less than his great stature are likely when their strength ebbs to come to terms with humankind. After I had lain flat on my back for many days, I came to see everyone in a sympathetic light, and this old world of ours didn't seem such a bad place after all. However, when my temperature and pulse had nearly returned to normal, my old standards reasserted themselves and the scales fell from my eyes.

It is the weak who need sympathy. Sympathy extended at times of weakness is the kind most readily appreciated. If someone comes to visit you when you are so sick that you cannot feed yourself, that token of sympathy is taken in immediately, like gentle rain falling on parched ground. The invalid will be reassured that man can still reach out to man, that man acts more tenderly toward his fellow men than beasts do. However, to inquire after an invalid's state of health is an art: it is not the same as a journalist's interview, nor yet the same as offering condolences to the bereaved. My latest illness took a tortuous course, so much so that the story required half an hour to tell, or rather more if one used a Europeanized form of the Chinese language. Yet my visitors inquired with such earnestness and solicitude that I had no choice but to make a detailed report. When my repeat performances passed the thirty mark they began to pall, and I felt embarrassingly like those old professors who mount their podium year after year and put on the same record. My solution was to offer relatively extensive coverage to those visitors who had come a long way, and to stress the dangerousness of the illness, in order to persuade them that their journey had been really necessary and save them from disappointment; while local friends got a severely truncated version, with due apologies. Then there were those excessively warmhearted people who would not leave until they had helped you in some way—or if they had to leave without helping you, felt very put out about it. To please them, I asked them to pour me a glass of water though I wasn't thirsty, putting on an act of appealing helplessness. Lastly there were the very straitlaced who, judging me about to depart this vale of tears, were induced to ponder on the eternal truths of the great religion, and assumed an ever more serious expression: they sat there wordless, plunged in deepest gloom. On these friends I will in future make the heaviest demands, for I realized that they could be not only relied upon to attend the sick; they were also were the right people to hold a wake.

1949

HAIRCUTS

Translated by Nancy E. Chapman

Getting a haircut is by no means a happy event. Anyone who has been to the dentist to have a tooth pulled inevitably feels a great sense of trepidation upon seeing a barber's chair, the two types of chairs being very much alike. We can't expect barbers' chairs to be ornately carved of sandalwood or in the style of Louis XIV, but at least they shouldn't be as ugly as they are. Not square, not round, dead and hard—sitting in one makes you feel as if you're on a butcher's block about to be slaughtered. The stand on which the itinerant barber at your door carries his tools is even more frightening: the rods from which he hangs small flags and bells must originally have been designed for severed heads!

A visit to the barber is, however, one of those bothersome things a person cannot avoid. As the saying goes, "A gentleman should be neat in attire and respectable in appearance. Why are only those with tangled hair and dirty faces considered sages?" The way one cuts one's hair has a lot to do with one's appearance. The Sikhs of India, for example, traditionally refrain from cutting their hair or shaving their beards, believing these to be "gifts of their parents that are not to be harmed." That is why it isn't at all unusual that whenever you see them, their heads and faces are covered with hair. This would simply not do in our society. If a person walks around with his hair all a rat's nest, others suspect he is in mourning for his parents or has just been released from prison. Even more annoying is the issue of a man's beard. If you allow your beard to grow long, it will spread and intertwine this way and that, but that won't matter, since hair on a man's face tends to inspire respect. Shaving it clean, which leaves your skin with a certain slightly greenish hue, is also acceptable and likewise respected. The only time people will keep their distance from you is if you grow a stubbly beard that is neither one thing nor the other—a beard that resembles fur on the neck of an animal, or a porcupine's quills, or freshly cut rice stalks. Among the heroes in the Ming novel *The Water Margin*, Lu Zhishen's sudden growth of stubble on his shaven face was half the reason why people feared him. The beard of Zhong Kui, the ghost-gobbler, was a mass of spears. Since we have no desire to scare people or feed on ghosts, nor do we have the courage to flout the customary tidiness of the gentleman, do we have any choice but to make frequent trips to the barber?

There is nothing at all disreputable about being a barber. As with executioners and butchers, theirs is a profession of service to others. What is more, barbers appear particularly respectable, their Western suits being a virtual symbol of their status as high-class Chinese. If you have a friend who is an executioner, he will size up your neck whenever he sees you, looking for the best place to aim his blade. This is just part of his profession. Similarly, a barber, after you sit down in his chair, rolls up his sleeves and surveys your hair, showing no interest whatsoever in the person to whom the hair belongs. He drapes over you a white sheet, which is usually not particularly clean but is more likely to be spotted like tiger skin. Then he puts a strip of cloth around your throat and yanks it tight. This won't kill you, of course, but it is certainly plenty tight. Were it his own neck, chances are he would not apply quite so much pressure. The point of all this activity is, of course, to have your hair cut, but there is no avoiding also having some of your hair yanked out at the roots in the process. The best form of protest is to screw up your face at the mirror and hope the barber sees you. While it is true that the human head, balanced atop the neck, enjoys a considerable degree of freedom to turn in different directions, there will always be some angles that are hard to manage; yet barbers don't seem to pay much heed to this point. They always seem to think that the position of your head is not quite right, and proceed to pull and twist it this way and that to the convenience of their scissors. I suspect that most barbers must have Herculean strength; otherwise, where did they get such powerful arms?

A large mirror is placed in front of the barber's chair for good reason. It is not so much for you to admire your reflection as to let you know what the barber is doing to your head—and who could fail to be concerned about that? People who wear glasses, however, are left in a blur once they take them off, unable to see much of what is happening. This is a special problem when, as the scissors are brandished before you, you sit there stiff as a corpse, not daring to move and unable to see the other customers sitting around you. It's a pity, because you end up missing out on a lot of things. For example, there may be a customer on your left sitting bolt upright having a shave. The sound is like that of grass being cut, and you conclude that he is a very big fellow. In fact, this is not necessarily so—the customer might even turn out to be a woman. The one sitting to your right, on the other hand, appears to be applying perfume and vanishing cream, and you think she must be a real beauty. This may not be the case, either—perhaps it's actually a man! You might as well forget about looking at all, since it only makes you uncomfortable to do so. In the end, the best thing for it is just to sit there twiddling your thumbs.

The most enjoyable part of this entire experience is having your hair washed. As the thick soapy suds drip down your head, you feel as if you had been doused with the sobering lotion administered in a Buddhist ceremony. The barber scours your scalp with both hands, and though he is no Ma Gu,[1] his fingers still resemble the claws of a bird. What can be downright tantalizing is when he works most of your scalp so hard that it hurts yet leaves untouched a spot in the southeast corner that is itchiest of all. When he rinses your hair, he sometimes floods your ears as well. But, since most people limit their daily washing to the facial area and fail to reach the corners and distant borders, undergoing such a thorough cleansing ends up being an event to be remembered. Harder by far to endure is the next step—the blow-dryer—which hisses out a cold stream of wind, punctuated at times with belches of unbearably hot air. It all comes to seem like some sort of punishment.

The most intolerable part of this entire experience is having your face shaved. A razor as sharp as can be skitters over your throat and brow and beside your ears, and all you can do is close your eyes and bate your breath amid a pool of sweat. Robert Lynd (1879–1949), in his "A Sermon on Shaving," wrote:

> As the razor touched my face, I was not always free from such apprehensive thoughts as: "Suppose the barber should suddenly go mad?" Luckily, the barber never did, but I have known other and comparative perils. There was that little French barber, for instance, who shaved me during a thunderstorm and who sprang into the air at every flash of lightning. There was also the drunken barber who felt for my cheek with the razor as a drunken man reaches out for something and misses it. Having at last brought the razor down on my face, he leaned on it to steady himself, and by leaning hard, even succeeded in shaving a certain patch on my right jaw. I did not dare so much as to utter a protest while the razor was on my skin. Even a whisper, I felt, might unnerve and overbalance the man, and my jugular would be severed before he knew he had done it. No sooner, however, was the razor temporarily withdrawn from my face—*reculer pour mieux sauter* is, I think the way the French describe it—than in a nightmare voice I gasped out: "No more. No more. That will do, thank you."

Experiences as frightening as this are indeed rare, but anyone can get the jitters if, in the midst of having a shave, they happen to think of that funny

1. A Chinese goddess well known for her beauty as well as for her clawlike hands.

episode in the comedy routine that tells of a barber's apprentice practicing his trade on a fuzzy winter melon. Whenever he is called away, he parks his razor in the melon with one deft jab. Later on, when his apprenticeship is over and he has entered the profession, he often mistakes people's heads for that melon!

After all is said and done, though, the actual physical danger involved in having your face shaved is of secondary consequence. What is most insufferable of all is when the barber, having finished your shave, takes his hands and impudently rubs them all over your face—and you're still required to pay up!

1949

PART EIGHT

Essays, 1949–1976

Liang Shiqiu (1901–1987)

ON TIME

Translated by King-fai Tam

The Greek philosopher Diogenes often slept in a clay urn. One day, Alexander the Great went to see him, and, in his usual imperial tone, asked, "Is there anything you want me to do for you?" The irreverent philosopher rolled his eyes and said, "I just want you to step aside a bit and stop blocking the sunlight."

The significance of this well-known little anecdote is perhaps a matter of individual interpretation, and different people have come to different conclusions. It has usually been taken to suggest that Diogenes viewed honor and respect as no more valuable than some discarded shoe, and wealth as nothing but a passing cloud. He regarded even the emperor as no different from any other man: not only was there nothing that he hoped to gain, he also saw no need to treat the emperor in any special way. Dr. Johnson, however, had a different interpretation, asserting that one should focus on the sunlight in the story. Sunlight is not an emperor's to bestow, and Diogenes' request was that Alexander not take away something that was beyond his power to give. This request is hardly excessive, but its implications are profound. In his discussion of the story, Dr. Johnson thus proceeded from a consideration of "light" to one of "time." Extremely precious as time is, we may not realize how often it is snatched away by others.

The saying that "human life does not exceed a hundred years" is not far from the truth. Of course, some people are so old that it almost seems as if they will never die, but the average mortal cannot expect to live beyond a century. Even then, sleep occupies a very large part of the many summers and winters that make up our lives. Though Su Shi (1037–1101) might have exaggerated somewhat when he said it takes up half a lifetime, it certainly amounts to about one-third. As for childhood, however we might choose to describe it—as guilelessly innocent or bumbling and benighted—we spend it obliviously and unthinkingly. Then, once we reach advanced age, our wits grow dim and our senses dull, even to the point that "a man cannot avail himself of the company of a beautiful woman." At that point, with only a breath of air separating us from death, there is not much joy in life to speak of. The beginning and ending having thus been snipped away, very little of life is left. And, even in the short span that remains, time is not necessarily ours to control. To be sure, the uninvited guests that Dr. Johnson complained about, who come to the door on the slightest pretext and make themselves at home regardless of how busy their host might be, leave one not knowing whether to laugh or cry. In my view, however, they don't really amount to serious "time-thieves"; it's just that they have collected a small tax on our limited capital. We still have ourselves to blame, I am afraid, for the largest drain on our time.

Some people assert that "time is life," while others say that "time is money." Both have a point, since there are people who equate money with life. On closer consideration, however, it becomes clear that we cannot have money without life. After all, when life is no more, what use is money? To be sure, many people choose money over life, but parting with money instead of life is still the wiser course. That is why it is said in the Han Taoist classic *Huainanzi* that "the sage does not value a foot of jade but rather an inch of time, because time is hard to come by, but all too easy to lose." Who among us as children did not write compositions with titles like "Valuing Time"? How many of us, though, were able early on to comprehend that time "is hard, to come by but all too easy to lose"? When I was young, our family engaged a private tutor. My elder sister and I often took advantage of our tutor's inattention to turn the clock on the study desk ahead half an hour in order to get out of class early. After a while, our teacher found us out. He then marked a spot on the paper windowpane in red ink and would not dismiss class until the sunlight reached it. It took this to put an end to our schemes for playing hooky.

Time flows on unceasingly, and no one can detain it for even a moment. Just as Confucius said, "It passes swiftly by, mindless of day and night." Every day, we tear a page from the calendar, which grows ever thinner. When we have almost reached the last page, we are inevitably startled to find the end of the year again approaching. If we were to bind all of these calendars into a single volume, it could serve to symbolize our entire life. If we then went on to rip out page after page, I wonder how we would feel inside. Truly, as Shelley said, "If winter comes, can spring be far behind?" But how many times can any person witness the passing of winter and coming of spring?

Just let go what you cannot detain. The problem remains, however, how to spend the time that has not yet fled and is still within our grasp. What the noted scholar-statesman Liang Qichao (1873–1929) most detested was to hear the word *diversion*, asserting that only those who are tired of life have the heart to "kill time." In his view there was never enough time to do all the things a person needed to do: how, then, could there still be room for diversions? Everyone has his own way of using time, however. When Emperor Qianlong of the Qing dynasty was on a tour of the south, he saw boats busily coming and going on the Grand Canal and asked the people around him, "What are they so busy bustling about for?" His favorite attendant, He Shen, happened to be standing next to him and intoned, "Either for fame or for profit." This answer was very much on the mark, and shouldn't be dismissed because the person who made this statement was of questionable character. What I fear, though, is that, since the Golden Age of the three dynasties,[1] people have cared little about reputation. Of fame and profit, profit has probably counted more. "People die for money just as birds die for food," and the notion that time is money still rings true. The poet Wordsworth had this to say:

> The world is too much with us, late and soon,
> Getting and spending, we lay waste our powers.

This is why some people would rather retire to the mountains to live an upright, reclusive life, enjoying the fresh breezes and the bright moon, and "keeping company with fish and shrimp and befriending does and bucks." Keats delighted in spending long hours watching a flower to see its petals slowly unfold, deeming this one of the great joys in life. Ji Kang (223–262) enjoyed wielding a hammer to fashion metal artifacts under a big shady tree, now and then "taking a sip of wine and playing a tune on the zither." His contemporary Liu Ling was likewise carefree and uninhibited, "keeping a jug of wine by him when he was idle, and carrying a wine pot when up and about." Each of these eccentrics embodies a unique way of whiling away one's time. The most extreme example of transcendent living is found in the Buddhist collection of anecdotes and sayings *The Record of Passing the Lamp*:

> Monk Nanquan asked Lu Heng, "How do you spend your days?"
> Lu replied, "Not wearing a shred on my body."

By this Lu meant that he was free of all attachments. As the Sixth Chan Master Hui Neng said, "Since there is nothing to begin with, whereon for the dust to settle?" This state of understanding is lofty indeed: one could say it is like "treating the whole universe as one morning, and a million years as a single moment." For all of these men, time was never a problem.

Indeed, as the Persian poet Omar Khayyám said, we cannot know from whence we came or where we are going. We neither will our coming to this

---

1. The Xia, Shang, and Zhou dynasties.

world, nor are we consulted when we leave it. As we stumble through our sojourn in life, should we surrender our hearts to the demands of our bodies in the time allotted to us? Should we try to attain immortality through virtue, actions, and words? Should we investigate the meaning of life and death, and then transcend the three realms?[2]

1973

2. The realms of sensuous desire, form, and the spirit. These are matters for each of us to decide.

SNOW

Translated by Nancy E. Chapman and King-fai Tam

Li Bo once wrote that "the snowflakes on Mount Yan are as large as straw mats." This statement is, of course, as much a poetic conceit as "white hair thirty thousand feet long." Poets tend to exaggerate. Science tells us that the structure of snowflakes varies with weather conditions, the largest being no more than three or four inches in diameter. If they were as large as straw mats, would a person then be completely covered by a single snowflake?

The more snow there is, the better, as long as it does not cause any damage. As it falls, it flutters gently down, like salt cast into the air or dancing willow catkins. How could anyone fail to enjoy such an appealing sight? Indeed, though some people like rain and others detest it, I have never heard of anyone disliking snow. Even in frigid places enveloped in white, Eskimos use large chunks of ice to build igloos that are quite warm to live in.

A person can't appreciate snow on an empty stomach. Pressed on all sides by hunger and cold in drifting snow and a howling wind, one might be more concerned with the problem of staying alive. How could one have the leisurely mood of counting "one by one by one . . . snowflakes waft amid the plum blossoms and are seen no more"? In the later Han period (A.D. 25–220), there was once a man named Yuan An (A.D. ?–92). One day, a blizzard blocked his door and all the roads were cut off, so people assumed he must already have died. When the magistrate of Loyang ordered that the snow be removed from the streets, they discovered Yuan An lying inside his house, frozen stiff. When asked why he had not come out, he replied, "When there is a blizzard, everyone goes hungry, and it would not have been right for me to trouble other people." What a dear dumbbell to have assumed that because he was hungry, everyone else must be, too! I don't suppose that as he lay there freezing he could ever have come out with a line such as "Snowflakes in the wind like petals fall."

One winter evening, when Wang Huizhi (A.D. ?–388) of the Jin dynasty (A.D. 265–420) was living in Shanyin,[1] the snow tapered off and the moon was clear and bright. Wang suddenly thought of his friend Dai Andao in the far-off Shan area, and set out in a small boat to visit him, traveling all night before reaching his destination. Upon reaching Dai's door, however, he turned back without going in. Had it not been for the snowfall, he would not have been seized by this sudden refined impulse. If, on the other hand, he had had to worry about where his next meal was coming from, he would not have had the equanimity to take the trip in the middle of the night, only to abandon the purpose of his visit after getting there. It seems that Xie An's (A.D. 320–385) genteel practice of gathering his sons and daughters together to compose poetry on snowy days is a luxury that only noble and wealthy families can afford.

Each clump of snow has numerous crystals, and each crystal has many surfaces. Snow is as white as it is because each of these surfaces reflects light. When I was young, I heard that people sometimes brewed tea from melted snow. Curious about how it would turn out, I went into the courtyard, scooped up the top layer of some fresh snow, and put it in an urn to melt. I then boiled it, and after cooling it for a minute or two, poured it over some "Big Red Robe" tea leaves in a Yixing teapot to brew. I then poured the tea into a teacup and savored it. After I had finished, I raised the cup to my nose and took several sniffs. However, I failed to feel the uplift—"the wind under the wings"—that one is supposed to experience; on the contrary, my tongue felt stiff and wooden. I took a second look at the water remaining in the urn, and thought that it could probably use some sodium carbonate to purify it. In these days of polluted air, I suppose it's too much to expect that snow will still be clean and white.

One year, I was traveling between Kaifeng and Luoyang, and my car broke down in the middle of a snowstorm far from any town or village. My stomach was grumbling, so I stopped at a roadside stall to buy something to eat. To my delight, the owner went to the trouble of cooking some noodles for me. Since there was no water around, however, he scooped up some snow from the side of the road with a washbasin and cooked the noodles in this muddy slush. Although it's sometimes said that a hungry person can make a meal of anything, this particular bowl of noodle soup I found a little hard to stomach. From that point on, I began to think of snow as something to be admired from afar, not toyed with up close. When Su Wu was reduced to eating his blanket and gulping down snow to quench his hunger and thirst, however, it was a different story.[2]

---

1. Modern-day Shaoxing.

2. Su Wu was sent as an envoy from the Han court to the court of the Xiongnu, where he

Snow is quite appealing in its ability to spread over a vast expanse, covering everything indiscriminately. On some winter nights I fall asleep curled up under a quilt, not daring to move for fear of the bone-chilling cold. Upon opening my eyes in the morning, I can see hints of an unusually bright sky shining through the window lattices and gaps in the shade. I get up to open the window, and exclaim with delight at the white, silvery world outside. Bamboo branches and pine needles alike are weighed down with snow, and the bare limbs of balding trees are outlined in silver. Everything is engulfed without discrimination—the rich man's vermilion gate and the poor man's grass awning; elegant carved railings and humble clay walls; ornamented steps and rough wooden hinges. Ditches and holes in the ground, twigs and branches on the ice, bits of grass and dirt on the road—all are buried under a cloak of crane feathers sent from heaven: such is the impartiality of snow. It enhances what is beautiful, and conceals what is repulsive, if only for a little while.

It is in agriculture that snow proves of greatest benefit to human beings. We depend on the natural elements for our livelihood, and since time immemorial have been beholden to heaven's every caprice. As is written in the *Book of Songs:*

> The heavens gather the clouds together mixing rain and snow . . .
> The snow is enriching and abundant, nourishing a hundred kinds
> of grain.

Or, as it is commonly said, "The gift of snow portends a bounteous year." That is to say, if snow is plentiful in the winter, the following year will see a bumper crop. Snow does not have to be "so deep as to reach a cow's eye"—one foot is quite enough nourishment to last the season. Some even say that snow is good for wheat and to ward off locusts. This is because locusts lay their eggs in the ground, but a foot of snow can seep through ten feet of earth, thus drowning the eggs and eradicating the scourge.

I too have experienced the blessings of snow. My living room opens out onto two rows of peonies, and a patch of daylilies sits beneath the eaves of my study. I once shoveled snow that had accumulated from several snowfalls onto the flower beds. The snow helped to protect their roots from freezing and provided nourishment for them when it melted the following spring. Sure enough, when the earth awoke from its winter slumber, new sprouts burst forth and grew into sturdy stems, with clusters of flowers like embroidered brocade. I remember thinking how much more meaningful this was than if I had used the snow to make a snowman.

I have heard it said that a certain strongman once composed a doggerel about snow that went:

---

was then held hostage for nineteen years. During this time, he led the life of a shepherd on the freezing northern plain.

The yellow dog sports white fur,
The white dog dons a thicker hide.
Stepping outside, I sigh and gasp,
The world is unified.

If it is true that "poetry comes easily to high officials," how much more so this must be for our hero at the height of his confidence and power. Not that the doggerel is without a trace of wit, only that it is laughably uncouth. Perhaps this has something to do with the social background and temperament of our poetaster. Legend has it that Louis XIV was once very proud of a poem he had composed. He sought the view of the critic Boileau, who replied, "Nothing is beyond Your Majesty's power. Your Majesty set out to write a bad poem, and has succeeded brilliantly!" Perhaps our little czar's ditty on snow has the same distinction of mediocrity.

1973

Yu Guangzhong (1928–)

THUS FRIENDS ABSENT SPEAK[1]

Translated by D. E. Pollard

To get letters from friends, especially airmail letters from overseas that bear the stamp of exotic climes, is unquestionably one of life's greatest pleasures, provided, that is, that they do not call for a reply. Answering letters is a heavy price to pay for the enjoyment of reading letters. The inevitable consequence of tardiness or infrequency in answering letters is a corresponding reduction in, and ultimate cessation of, the pleasure of receiving letters, in which case friendship is prematurely broken off, until the day in sackcloth and ashes you summon up the willpower to put pen to paper again. Through this dillydallying the pleasure of receiving letters has turned to the misery of owing letters. I am an old lag in this respect: practically every one of the friends I have made in my comings and goings can recite from my crime sheet. W. H. Auden once admitted that he was in the habit of shelving important letters, preferring instead to curl up with a detective novel; while Oscar Wilde remarked to Henley: "I have known men come to London full of bright prospects and seen them complete wrecks in a few months through a habit of answering letters." Clearly Wilde's view was that to enjoy life one should renounce the bad habit of answering letters. So I am not the only one to be fainthearted in that regard.

---

1. Since the Chinese title "Chi su cun xin" (A foot of plain silk, an inch of heart) is untranslatable, I have substituted the quotation from John Donne's "To Sir Henry Wotton."—Trans.

If it is conceded that replying to letters is to be dreaded, on the other hand not replying to letters is by no means a matter of unalloyed bliss. Normally a hundred or so letters are stacked on my bookshelf, of diverse maturity of debt outstanding, the longest being over a year. That kind of pressure is more than an ordinary sinner can bear. A stack of unanswered letters battens on me like a bevy of plaintive ghosts and plays havoc with my smitten conscience. In principle the letters are there for replying to. I can swear in all honesty that I have never while of sound mind determined not to answer people's letters. The problem is a technical one. Suppose I had a whole summer night at my disposal: should I first answer the letter that was sent eighteen months ago, or that one that was sent seven months ago? After such a long delay even the expiry date for apology and self-recrimination would surely have passed. In your friends' eyes you have already stepped beyond the pale, are of no account. On the grapevine your reputation is "that impossible fellow."

Actually even if you screw up all your moral courage and settle down at your desk to pay off your letter debt come what may, the thing is easier said than done. Old epistles and new missives are jumbled up together and stuffed in drawers or strewn on shelves; some have been answered, some not. As the poet was told about the recluse he was looking for: "I know he's in these mountains, but in this mist I can't tell where." The time and energy you would spend to find the letter you have decided to answer would be several times that needed to write the reply itself. If you went on to anticipate that your friend's reaction to receiving your letter would be less "surprised by joy" than "resentment re-kindled," then your marrow would turn to water, and your debt would never be cleared.

To leave letters unanswered is not equivalent to forgetting friends, no more than it is conceivable that debtors can forget their creditors. At the bottom of such disquietude, at the end of your nightmares, there forever lurks the shadowy presence of this friend with his angry frown and baleful looks: no, you can never forget him. Those whom you really put out of your mind, and do so without qualm, are those friends who have already been replied to.

I once held forth to the poet Zhou Mengdie in this wise: "You must immediately acknowledge new publications friends send you. After the usual thanks and congratulations you can conclude with the sentence 'I will get down at once to a close and reverential perusal.' If you delay these congratulatory letters for a week or a month, then you are in trouble, because by that time you would be under an obligation to have read the book and could not get away with these general compliments." Mengdie was quite overcome. Unfortunately I have never followed my own advice and must have lost many friends as a consequence. But I do remember sending in a fit of enthusiasm a new book of my own to some friends. One of them took a couple of months to send a note of thanks, explaining that his wife, his daughter, and his wife's colleagues had all been desperate to read this great work, and he was still waiting his turn, which showed how fascinating the book was, etc. To this day I don't know whether to believe this story of his, but if he was lying one has to own that his was a stroke of genius.

It is said that the late Dr. Hu Shi not only responded to all requests, he even personally answered letters from schoolchildren asking for advice. On top of that he wrote his famous diary, never missing a day. To write letters is to be considerate to others; to keep a diary is to be considerate to oneself. That such an éminence grise could after his intellectual labors be so thorough and methodical on both counts leaves one lost in admiration. As for me, having already confessed myself unable to cope on the epistolary front, diaries would be a sheer luxury.

I am inclined to think that few of my contemporaries can hope to emulate the natural and easy-flowing style of the older generation of writers and scholars in their exchange of letters. Mr. Liang Shiqiu, for example, is burdened with great fame, and because of his many connections naturally has a great deal of correspondence to deal with, but in the more than twenty years I have known him he has always replied promptly to my letters. Moreover, his own are unfailingly witty and written in elegant hand, revealing a different side of him to the joviality that characterizes our tête-à-têtes. Given my fear of writing letters, I can't say I correspond with him very frequently. I also have to bear in mind the fact that he stated in one of his *Cottager's Fascicles* that there are eleven kinds of letters that he does not keep—no doubt mine are number eight on the list. As far as I know, his most frequent correspondent is Chen Zhifen. When Chen was young he was always exchanging letters with celebrated writers like Hu Shi and Shen Congwen, and he built up a voluminous collection of famous men's autographs. Mr. Liang has humorously called him a "man of letters": perhaps by now his own turn has come to have his letters collected.

My friends fall into four schools on the basis of their letter style. The first school's letters are shot off like telegrams: just a few lines, maybe twenty or thirty scribbled words, with the momentum of a blitzkrieg. The trouble is that the recipient has to spend a lot more time puzzling out and deciphering the message than it took the sender's pen to gallop across the paper. Peng Ge, Liu Shaoming (Joseph S. M. Lau), and Bai Xianyong are representative of this school. The second school writes letters like a young lady embroiders flowers, finely drawn, the characters handsomely formed, a true study in calm and unhurriedness. As for content, apart from their practical function they express the writer's feelings and have an engaging tone that it is a pleasure to listen to. Song Qi and Xia Zhiqing (C. T. Hsia) can be said to typify this school, especially Xia Zhiqing: how comes it that a great scholar writes such copybook tiny characters, and always uses economical aerogrammes? The third school comes between the first two and follows the golden mean: their letters are neither tepid nor fiery, their pace is well modulated, and they are written in big bold characters, open and candid in mien. Yan Yuanshu, Wang Wenxing, He Huaishuo, Yang Mu, Luo Men are all "exemplary characters." One might mention especially He Huaishuo for the wide sweep of his discussion, while Yang Mu spaces his characters far apart and leaves large gaps between lines, at the same time indulging his liking for parchment-gauge notepaper: his cavalier disregard for postage puts the rest of our gallant band in the shade. The fourth school employs the hair brush[2] and covers the page with loops and whorls, the form of the characters being somewhere between the running and the "grass"; these are the celebrities who scorn to conform. Luo Qing is of their number.

Of course those who put on the most style are Liu Guosong and Gao Xinjiang: they don't write letters at all, they simply telephone from the other end of the earth.

1967

2. This refers to the writing brush made of goat/rabbit/weasel/mouse and other animal hair; it should not be confused with a hairbrush.—Trans.

Yang Mu (1940–)

NINETEEN SEVENTY-TWO

Translated by Joseph R. Allen and Han Haiyan

1

So this is what it means to live in the Northwest: fleeting days and endless winter nights, and always waking up to the sound of rain. Darkness hangs beyond the dripping eaves, even though the clock on the floor says it's already eight in the morning. The blinds open up onto waves of mist caught in the debates between the depth of night and the coming of dawn. And there is always the rain, but sometimes it is quite unlike rain, rather it is like snow that has not quite crystallized, floating lightly down.

Rain that falls with the demeanor of snow.

Here we are in Seattle, a coastal city in the upper latitudes: the Northwest famed for forests and salmon. We have fallen into this dark, dank winter. Out in the yard a naked, leafless tree stands; I am not sure what kind of tree it is but I suppose it might be an apple tree. At least when we were living in California we often heard that this part of the country was famous for its apples. We heard the same thing when we were living in New England. When I get up and wander over to the window, I am surprised to see the lawn covered with a thin blanket of snow that is just now beginning to melt.

The University of Washington stands above a large lake. On a clear day from one of the vantage points on campus you can see the floating bridge below with its constant stream of traffic. I understand that there are times when you can also see sailboats out on the lake, but I suppose that is only in the summer.

Beyond the lake is another lake, and then off in the distance are the mountains, which stand tall and snowcapped, arrayed along the horizon in hues of white and blue, somewhat like the mountains above Denver. Yet there is something different about them too. The boulder-strewn slopes of the Rockies stand larger and more majestic; looming among the neon lights of the city, they seem arrogant and overbearing. They are really quite nice, although not very elegant. Even though the mountains in Seattle are also tall, expansive, and snow-covered year-round, they are not as desolate as the Rockies; they have instead a certain elegance about them. Perhaps this is because of their proximity to the lakes and ocean.

The sun is, however, not a common sight in Seattle, especially in the depth of winter, such as we are today. And if the sun does come out, it is never before 9:30 in the morning. While I sit typing in front of my office window on the fourth floor of this Gothic-styled building, I lift my eyes every so often to either gaze out into the distance or to watch the people who bustle along the damp stone pathways below. Across the campus, there are rooms where I can see the lights burning brightly. Winter in Seattle is in the turning on of lights.

Suddenly I am overwhelmed by a melancholy like that of a teenager, an unknown, inexplicable sadness. Suddenly there is this flutter of unhappiness. By now I should have outgrown the age when I could dash off a twenty-line poem at the drop of a hat, when the setting sun or breaking dawn could sink me into a fit of melancholy; I should have outgrown the age when I was always sad but did not know why I was sad. But suddenly I am filled from on high with these brooding and confusing emotions; gazing far off into the distance, I am unsure how I might dispel this mood.

And now there is occasionally this fatigue. When we first came here, I felt a belated grievous sense of renewal, like Dante without his guide. I rediscovered a sensitivity to the imagery of things, as real and as uplifting as a return to Florence. Even the clamor of the city was beautiful. Whenever I came to an intersection I would glance to the west, back across the sea, the never changing sea. I knew that each time I looked, the sea would be the same, but I always turned to look nonetheless, trying to make it appear a casual gesture, an everyday glance to the west.

I no longer awoke terror-stricken in the middle of the night. When I had my tea, I liked to sit by the lamp near the fireplace, but that was not necessarily a sign of old age. No, there was this resistance in me, a feeling of confronting myself, of fighting with myself. I had no idea what my friends were doing—no doubt some were off wandering, some wounded, and some weeping. At first I was concerned for them, and missed them; I even invented lives for them: fascinating, novel lives, lives as serene as temples and as persistent as clocks. But in the end I grew tired; one might even say that I grew tired of them. One might imagine that long ago we had run into each other and spoken briefly, met and then parted. Now, having parted, we are indeed apart.

In a similar way, I left behind my life of the last ten years. As if once I had decided to wade the stream, the trees and flowers instantly lost their natural fragrance; once I put out the light, the room sank into darkness. Caught in this cold and solitude, I questioned myself until I grew bored with the questions. Perhaps a new life lay at the far end of hopelessness. Perhaps we can be like the wind, without form or substance, blowing from one valley to the next, letting the size and configuration of the valleys determine our form.

2

Sometimes I wonder if I miss New England. Perhaps not, but New England is, after all, New England, a place not easily forgotten. I was there from September 1970 to December 1971. When I left there still was no snow on the ground, which was very rare. Yesterday I received a letter from a friend who said it had been below zero ever since the first of the year.

Days of cold can also be unnerving. During my first winter in New England, we lived in a small house in the woods outside town. Once we returned from New York around midnight to find the woods blanketed in glistening snow. The snow lay deep on the walk, untouched in our three-day absence. Wading through the knee-deep snow, we headed toward the front door. It took ten minutes just to go the thirty yards to the house. When we got to the house, there was a cedar tree bent over blocking the door. I gave it a shove, it shook off some snow and sprang upright, sending a shower of snowflakes into the air. Swaying back and forth, it then stood still and tall again: a cedar dimly glistening, backlit by the light off the midnight snow. The cedar is called a "tree of shadows." Unlike other plants that turn toward the sun, the cedar tends toward shades and shadows. Thinking that it had been leaning against my snow-bound door in the dead of the night made me feel uneasy.

Throughout that dark, gloomy winter, the snow continued to fall outside my window. Inside, the fireplace burned without warmth. Through it all, I felt chilled and listless. If not snow, then sleet—raining and snowing together, turning the ground into a thick sheet of ice. In my room I typed, worked on my dissertation, every once in a while coming upon lines such as "We march along, rain and snow falling on the mire."[1] Spring came very late. Way into March the sky was filled with blowing snow as the wind howled through the woods. At the end of the month the snow still lay in a forgetful winter sleep, which even the April sun could not budge. The snow did not melt, the lilacs did not emerge from the dead land, and without the spring rains mixing desire and memory, April is *not* the cruelest month. This lasted up into May, when sud-

1. From poem 168 of the classical anthology *Book of Songs* (ca. 600 B.C.), which was the subject of the author's doctoral dissertation.

denly one night the spring wind began to blow, and when we arose in the morning the last little patch of winter's snow was gone. Only then did we notice that the lilies were about to blossom, the woodpeckers were hammering away, and the bugs were out in droves. But before we had prepared ourselves for spring, it was already gone and we were into a summer of buzzing bees and chirping crickets. Farmers placed bunches of garden asparagus by their front doors for sale. They sold it throughout the summer, right up until fall arrived with its dead sunflowers, shriveled cornstalks, and gigantic pumpkins piled high in fields, porches, and sheds. The fall foliage that filled the town and surrounding hills was so beautiful that it made your heart ache, made you feel faint; it was so beautiful that it filled you with anger and suspicion. It was so beautiful it made a believer out of you; you sought for some god to lean on, to worship for making all this possible.

By the time of the first snows of November, you weren't quite so intent upon finding God. By December, you were shivering and cursing, having returned to being a dyed-in-the-wool atheist.

3

The natural beauty of New England was such a shock to me that I could never find the words to describe it. One could never be ready for a world so full of change. You just could not grasp it. When you thought of a line to describe that world, it had already changed into something else, abandoning you, making you feel that its swift changes were there to tease you, to scorn you, to expose how your imagination was too weak to capture its ever-changing light.

There is a beauty in the world that humbles, and this was it.

Now I suspect that perhaps beauty can bring us pain beyond all other pain; one might say it is a pain that does not just attack one's mind. Perhaps it is something like a slow poison that, once it affects the senses, seeps slowly into the blood, circulating throughout the body. There it stays, lodged permanently in the system, part of its very chemistry, making it impossible to resist or to escape.

Pure beauty can drive one to madness. As it did the old aesthetician who collapsed on that sunlit beach in *Death in Venice*. His sole purpose in being in Venice was his pursuit of perfect beauty. This reflects the spirit of the German cultural tradition with its preoccupation with the Mediterranean world. Ever since Winckelmann, there had been this tendency to look southward in their pursuit of beauty; in this way, Goethe's travels to Rome were a search for his spiritual home. Under the spell of that young, godlike boy of perfect form, what was originally merely a trip to the south was transformed into a tragedy emblematic of an entire culture. The high culture of the Mediterranean appeals directly to the senses rather than to the intellect. That the beauty of ancient Grecian statues and painted vases of Rome could be found in the body of a young boy is beyond the comprehension of the German intellect, with its penchant for logic and argument. For them this is a destructive and deadly beauty.

Death in Venice, moreover, contains love tainted by a primeval offense. Perhaps the earliest manifestation of that is in the madness and infatuation on the beach. Classical Platonic infatuation of one man for another is not to be found in the heroic form of David, rather it is in the desire for complete and perfect "beauty," which turns the aesthetician into a symbol of ugliness against that southern backdrop. Over and over again, we see in the contrast of the guileless young boy and that pensive old man the alternation of god and demon, the cruel devouring of a mind of great intellectual power.

In this sense, the intellect is pointless and irrelevant: it is as if one were trying to appreciate a peony in a purely analytical light.

Furthermore, there is also something suspect about our understanding of "love." According to traditional explanations, love is mysterious, reverent, and above criticism; thus, it should exist in a state of complete independence—free from value judgments and beyond the imposition of analysis or generalization. That being so, then love should offer sustenance to all things as the wind and rain do. It should sweep over and fill them without distinction or qualification. One thinks of those such as Gide who, alienated from their own sexuality, seek spiritual and even physical sustenance in the homosexual world. Then when one thinks of the criticism that these people suffer, one realizes that "freedom" is in the end a very limited liberation. A well-known scholar of comparative literature once said, "Homosexuality is perhaps quite natural; many people discover only in middle age that their early aversion to homosexuality was in fact the repression of a manifestation of their own sexuality." Within my first week in Seattle a friend and I happened to start talking about the problems of love and life. He said to me, "I am a man, but there seems to be no way for me to approach a woman. The objects of my love are other men; when I am with them I am happy. But people are disgusted by these feelings."

4

This winter Seattle suffered the most severe snowstorm it had seen in twenty years. It snowed for two days and two nights; the roads were impassable, cars were abandoned everywhere, the fence in the yard was crushed under the weight of snow, and the pipes in some people's houses burst. The University of Washington closed down for two days and there was no talk of making up the classes; it just closed. This was unheard of here.

After the storm all was quiet and restful. We thought, well, tomorrow it will probably rain all day and wash away the snow. But no, it did not rain at all—instead we had more than a week of crystal-clear skies. This was when we first actually saw the surrounding mountains, tall with their blue-green forests covered in blankets of glistening snow.

The first time we went out after the storm, we turned right heading down the street; there they were, standing on the horizon, mountains as tall and imposing as the mountains above Denver. After this, whenever we went out, either for a walk or a drive, we were always looking at the mountains. Now that I think about it, that obsession with looking at the mountains was probably dangerous. But to stand by the lake on campus looking at the mountains felt natural and comforting. The lake was empty; at the most there might be an occasional motorboat speeding along the shore. The sailboats were all stored away; they would have to wait until spring to sail again, or at least until warmer weather.

One day, after an entire afternoon of being holed up in my basement study, I went out to buy some beer. On the way back to the house, I was driving along a hillside near the lake when I suddenly raised my eyes and saw right in front of the car a towering mountain—we had been in Seattle for a month and I had never seen this mountain before. It is hard to say, perhaps it was not so much that I raised my eyes to it as that it moved into my line of sight; I didn't see it, it saw me. At first I didn't believe it was real; it was just too huge and awe-inspiring. I really wondered if it might not be some sort of winter mirage caused by the reflection of the evening light in the cold mists. I stopped the car by the side of the road and got out to look at it more closely. Yes, it was real. Lofty and majestic, from its delicate peak, the mountain sloped gently off to both sides. Halfway down was bathed in the golden light of the setting sun, which was just about to disappear.

More imposing and more real than Jesus Christ himself. Mount Rainier, standing some 14,400 feet tall, the most important peak in the Cascades, a coastal range that threads through the northwestern corner of the United States. This mountain was my epiphany.

1972

PART NINE

Essays Since 1976

Ba Jin (1904–)

REMEMBERING XIAO SHAN

Translated by Michael S. Duke

1

Today is the sixth anniversary of Xiao Shan's death. The events of six years ago still appear quite clearly before my eyes. When I returned home from the crematorium that day, everything was a mess. After three or four days, I gradually settled down; sitting alone at the desk, I wanted to write something in remembrance of her. For fifty years, it has always been my custom, when I have nowhere else to express my feelings, to turn to pen and paper; but during those days in August 1972, every day I sat for three to four hours staring at the blank paper lying before my eyes and could not write a single sentence. Painfully I thought of myself: "Being locked in the 'cowshed' for several years, had I really turned into a 'cow'?"[1] It seemed that my head was being pressed down by a huge stone and my thoughts were frozen. I simply put down my pen and did not write anything at all.

Six years have passed. Lin Biao, the Gang of Four, and their minions certainly did treat me terribly, but I lived through it and, in spite of everything, still live in comparative health; my mind is not befuddled. And sometimes I can even write a few essays. I have been going often to the Longhua Crema-

1. During the Cultural Revolution, Chinese intellectuals were reviled as "cow [or 'ox'] devils," and the rural areas where they were sent for labor reform were known as "cowsheds."

torium lately to participate in the ceremony of laying to rest the ashes of old friends. In that great hall, I remember many things. The mourning music is playing the same, but my thoughts wander from that big hall full of people to the middle room where there were only twenty or thirty people, and we were just bidding farewell to Xiao Shan's body with the sound of our crying. I remember something Juexin said in *The Family*: "It seems that with Jue's death there is another unlucky ghost." When I wrote that sentence forty-seven years ago, how could I have ever thought that I was writing for myself? I did not shed a tear, but I felt as if countless sharp claws were tearing at my heart. I stood beside her dead body, stared at her pale white face and those lips that swallowed back the expression of a thousand sorrows, gritted my teeth tightly, and silently called out her name. "I am thirteen years older than she," I thought. "Why couldn't I be allowed to die first?" I thought it was so unfair! What crime had she ever committed? She too had been locked in a "cowshed," had borne a little sign reading "cow devil," and had swept the streets! What for, really? The reason was very simple: she was my wife. She was ill and could not receive medical care; this too, all because she was my wife. I tried everything, but not until three weeks before she died—relying on "going through the back door"[2]—was she finally able to enter a hospital; but the cancer cells had metastasized, bowel cancer had become liver cancer.

She did not want to die. She wanted to live. She could have lived on . . . if only she was not the "Black King's stinking old lady!"[3] I involved her in everything, and I ruined her.

Throughout all the years that I "stood to the side,"[4] she suffered all of the same spiritual indignities that I did. I was never physically beaten, however, but the blows she suffered from a brass-buckled belt wielded by the "Red Guard from Peking" left a black welt over her left eye that did not disappear for many days. She was beaten for protecting me. When she saw those young people rush in in the middle of the night, she was afraid they were going to drag me away; she sneaked out the front door and across the street to the police station to ask the "people's police" comrades to help out. There was only one man on night duty there, and he did not dare interfere. Right then and there she was cruelly lashed with a brass-buckled belt and forced back home to be locked in the toilet with me.

She not only shared my suffering, but also gave me much comfort and encouragement. While the "four calamities"[5] were raging, in my original work

---

2. "Going through the back door" is PRC slang for using personal influence in order to obtain special services.

3. The "Black King" was the worst category of the "five black" classes of counterrevolutionary enemies of the people during the Cultural Revolution, viz, the intellectuals.

4. "Stand to the side" is PRC slang for being relieved of one's employment while under political investigation and attack.

5. "Four calamities" are, of course, the Gang of Four.

unit [a sub-unit of the Writers' Union], people treated me as a "criminal" and a "despicable person." Life was extremely uncomfortable; sometimes it was nine or ten o'clock at night before I could return home, but as soon as I entered the house and saw her face, a sky full of dark clouds scattered away. If I had any grievance or complaint, I could tell her about it. There was a period when every night before we went to bed we had to take two sleeping pills before we could close our eyes, but just as the sky grew the least bit light we woke up. I would call her and she would call me. Plaintively I would say, "This life is so hard!" and she would use the same tone of voice to reply, "Yes, this life is very hard"; but she would immediately add a sentence, "We've got to endure it," or "Endurance is our victory." I said "life is so hard" because at that time every day at the "cowshed" I had to do physical labor, study, write explanations of my actions, investigative reports, and overall reports on my thoughts. Anyone there could curse me, admonish me, or give me orders. People who came from outside to coordinate the Writers' Union could call me out as "an example to the masses" anytime they felt like it, and I had to report orally on my own crimes. There were no fixed working hours; they were decided arbitrarily by the "surveillance group" that ran the "cowshed." Anyone could barge into my home and take anything that he felt like taking. At that time large-scale mass criticism attacks and assembly-style television criticism attacks had not yet begun, but they were coming closer and closer.

She said "life is so hard" because she was dragged in twice by the authorities to "stand to the side" and do physical labor, and after that often endured being attacked along with me. A big-character poster criticizing my criminal activities was put up on the criticism board on Huaihai Central Road with the names of every member of my family written out "to inform the masses"; needless to say, the "stinking old lady's" name occupied the most prominent position. Those words gnawed at her heart like maggots. When she was suddenly attacked and dragged into the Writers' Union by the "fanatical faction" of students from the Shanghai Drama Academy, a big-character poster also appeared on our front door detailing her so-called criminal activities. That night, fortunately, our son tore it down; otherwise that poster might have killed her!

People's dirty looks, cold ridicule, and hot abuse gradually wore away her body and spirit. I noticed that her health was gradually deteriorating. Her surface calm was false; underneath, the pain in her heart was seething like a boiling cauldron. How could she hide it! How could she possibly calm it down! She constantly comforted me, expressed confidence in me, and felt indignant on my behalf; but as she saw my problem grow more serious day by day and the pressures on me increase day by day, she was extremely worried. Sometimes when she would walk me to work or come to see me after work, as she walked into Julu Road and drew near the Writers' Union, she could never manage to hold her head up. I understood her, sympathized with her, and very greatly feared that she could not withstand those heavy blows.

I remember one night when it came to regular quitting time, we were not held back for punishment; returning home, she was rather happy and went into the kitchen to cook dinner. I skimmed through that day's newspaper, and on the third page was an article by the two worker authors who were then the headmen of the Writers' Union: "Thoroughly Exposing the True Face of Ba Jin's Counterrevolutionary Activities." I read a couple of lines and then quickly hid the paper away for fear that she would see it. When she brought out the finished meal, she had a smile on her face and she even talked and laughed while we ate. After dinner, she wanted to read the paper; I tried to lead her attention elsewhere, but to no avail. She found the paper and her smile completely disappeared. That night she did not say another word and went into the bedroom early; later I discovered her lying on the bed quietly sobbing. Another peaceful evening was ruined. Today when I think back to that scene, her tearstained face is perfectly clear before my eyes. At that time how I wished I could make those tear streaks disappear and make that smile reappear on her careworn face! Even if it meant taking a few years off my span of life, I would be more than willing if only to retrieve one quiet peaceful night of family living. But during the time when the "four calamities" raged, that was impossible.

2

I heard Zhou Xinfang's[6] daughter-in-law say that before she died Zhou's wife was regularly dragged out by those whose work it was to beat people, thrown back and forth like a football, and beaten until her whole body was scaly with welts. When people urged her to hide, she replied, "If I hide, they will take it out on Mr. Zhou the same way." Xiao Shan never suffered that new style of punishment, but spiritually she was tossed back and forth like a football. She had the same idea that if she suffered more emotional harassment it would lighten the pressure on me. Actually, that was just a kind of wishful thinking that only resulted in more suffering for her. I watched her waste away day by day, watched the spark of her life gradually being extinguished, and I felt so sick at heart! I tried to dissuade her, to comfort her, even wanted to hold her back, but all to no avail.

She often asked me, "When will your case ever be decided?" I would laugh and say, "There's bound to come a day when it'll be decided." She would sigh and say, "I'm afraid I won't be able to wait until that time." Later, when she became ill, some people urged her to telephone me to come home; I don't know how she found out, but she said, "He's writing an investigative report, and we should not disturb him. His case is probably going to be decided." By

6. Zhou Xinfang (1895–1975), well-known Beijing opera performer.

the time I finally came home on leave from the May Seventh Cadre School,[7] she could no longer get out of bed. She still asked me how my report went and whether my case could be decided. At that time I really was writing such a report, and, as a matter of fact, had already written it several times. They wanted me to write simply to waste my life, but how could she ever understand?

That was only two months before her death; we did not know, but the cancer cells had already metastasized. We wanted to find a doctor to give her a real examination; there was just no way. Usually one went to a hospital and signed up for a general registration, waited a long time before finally seeing a doctor or an intern, who casually filled out a prescription and closed your case. Only if you had a temperature of 102 degrees were you qualified to register for emergency treatment; otherwise you still might wait around in an observation room full of sick people for a day or two. At that time finding transportation to the hospital was also very difficult. Most often my son-in-law would borrow a bicycle and let her sit on it while he slowly pushed it along. One time she hired a small, three-wheeled cart to go to the hospital, and when she came out she could not hire another cart; all she could do was walk slowly back home with the friends who had gone with her to the hospital. Alternately walking and resting, by the time she arrived at our street corner she was about to collapse and had to ask a passerby to go to our house and tell us. A niece of hers had just come to visit with her and so she carried her home on her back. She hoped to be able to take an X-ray and find out just what sort of bowel illness she had, but it was impossible; later on, relying on a relative of hers to "open the back door," she had two X-rays and finally learned that she had cancer. Still later, another friend pulled strings to "open the back door" and get her into the hospital. She was very happy and thought that she had been saved. She was the only one who did not know the true nature of her illness; in the hospital, she only lived three weeks.

After my first leave period was up, I got two more short leaves in order to stay home and take care of her, less than a month altogether. Seeing that her illness was growing more serious by the day, I really did not want to leave her unattended; but when I requested a leave extension, a "worker's propaganda brigade" leader of my unit forced me to return to the Cadre School the next day. When I got home and she asked me, there was no way I could keep it from her; she sighed and said, "You go on and don't worry." She turned her face to the side and wouldn't let me see her. When my daughter and son-in-law saw what was happening, they went angrily and bravely to Julu Road to explain things to that "worker's propaganda brigade" leader in hopes that he would agree to allow me to stay a few more days in the city area and take care of her;

7. May Seventh Cadre Schools were set up in accordance with a directive by Mao Zedong on that date in 1966. Their purpose was ostensibly to reform rightist cadres and intellectuals through laboring with the peasants in the countryside.

but he adamantly carried out the law. He even said, "He's not a doctor; what's the use of his staying at home! Staying at home would not be good for his reform." They came home indignantly and merely said that the authorities did not agree; only later on in answer to my questioning did they pass on that "famous remark." What could I say? The next day I'd go back to the Cadre School!

She slept poorly that entire night, and I slept even worse. What a surprise, the next day my rusticated son turned up in our house; he had arrived in the middle of the night. He had received my letter and asked for leave to come home and visit his mother, but he had not imagined that his mother was so very ill. I greeted him, passed his mother along into his care, and then returned to the Cadre School.

I felt very bad on the train. I really could not understand why things had to be the way they were. At the Cadre School for five days, I had no way to receive news of home. I had already guessed that her illness was very grave, but they would not let me ask about her condition. How hard it was to make it through those five days! On the fifth day, the head of the Cadre School informed us that the entire collective was going into the city early the next morning for a meeting. In that way I could finally go home and see my wife. Relying on a friend's assistance, she was to move into the hospital's liver cancer ward; everything was all ready for her to move in on the following day. She wanted so much to see me again before she moved into the hospital, and I finally made it home. Even I had not imagined that her illness would worsen so quickly. We looked at each other; I could not even say a word. Finally she said, "I'm finally going into the hospital." I answered, "You just don't worry and get well." Her father came to see her. The old man was blind in both eyes, so going to the hospital would be very difficult; he had probably come to say farewell to his daughter.

I finished lunch and then went to participate in the big meeting where everyone would attack me and criticize me as a counterrevolutionary. I was not the only one being attacked. Among the others was a friend of mine, Wang Ruowang; he used to be a writer, but he was younger than I. We were locked up together in a "cowshed" for a while. His crime was being an "ex-rightist."[8] He would not give in, would not obey; he put up big-character posters announcing that he would "liberate myself by myself." On that account the crimes he was accused of grew greater and greater. It was not enough that he was locked up for a time; he was also accused as a counterrevolutionary and sentenced to forced labor under guard. During the entire meeting, I felt as if I

8. Wang Ruowang, a Shanghai writer, was purged during the anti-rightist campaign of 1957. Branded a "rightist element," he was sent to a farm for labor reform; in 1962 the designation "rightist element" was rescinded, but as an "ex-rightist" (literally, "with hat removed") he was still in trouble throughout the 1960s.

were dreaming strange dreams; when I came home after the meeting ended and saw Xiao Shan, I felt a special intimacy, as if I had finally returned to the human world. But she was uncomfortable and did not want to talk; once in a while she would say something. I still remember something she said twice, "I won't be able to see it." I asked her several times what she would not be able to see. Finally she answered me, "I won't be able to see you liberated."[9] What could I say!

My son stood there by our side looking very dejected and in low spirits; he only ate half a bowl of rice for dinner and seemed to have a cold. She suddenly pointed at him and said softly, "What is he going to do?" He had already been rusticated in a farming village in the mountains of Anhui Province for three and a half years; no one paid any attention to him politically, but he could not support himself physically, and, because he was my son, he had lost many of the rights of a citizen. First he learned how to be silent, then he learned how to smoke. I looked at him with a guilty feeling in my heart. I regretted that I had ever begun to write fiction, and I never should have had children. I remember a couple of years ago during a particularly difficult-to-bear period she had said to me, "The children say their daddy has done bad things and hurt our whole family." That was like using a dagger to cut away my flesh; I did not say anything and only swallowed my bitter tears. Waking up from a nap, she suddenly asked me, "Are you going back tomorrow?" I said, "I'm not going." That "workers' propaganda brigade" head had informed me that day that I did not have to go back to the Cadre School, but could just remain in the city. He had also asked me, "Do you know what Xiao Shan's illness is?" I'd answered, "I know." Actually, the family had kept things from me and not allowed me to know the true situation; I guessed what it was from that question of his.

3

For about twenty days, I went to the hospital every day for most of the day. I took care of her, sat by her bedside and watched over her, and talked briefly with her. Her illness worsened, and as she grew weaker every day, her abdomen grew larger day by day and her movements grew more and more difficult. At that time there was no one on the ward to help her; except for food and drink, she had to take care of everything else herself. Later on I heard her fellow patients praise her for being "strong and resolute." They said that every morning she would quietly struggle to get out of bed and go to the washroom.

The doctor talked to us. He said that the patient's health was not good enough to operate, that what was most to be feared was bowel obstruction; if there was no obstruction, it would be possible to prolong things for a while.

9. "Liberated" here means released from political investigation.

That half a month after she went into the hospital was the one period since August 1966 in which I felt both painful and fortunate; it was the last peaceful time that she and I spent together, and I cannot forget it to this day.

After half a month, though, her illness grew worse. One day during lunch, the doctor told my son to bring me in to talk. He told me the patient's bowels had become obstructed and it was necessary to operate. The operation would not necessarily be successful and there might be trouble during the procedure, but the consequences of not operating were even more horrible to contemplate. He wanted me to decide and then to persuade her to agree. I decided and then went to the ward to explain it to her. After I finished talking, she said just one thing. "It looks like we are going to have to part." She looked at me, her eyes full of tears. I said, "That's not possible. . . . " My voice choked up. Just then the head nurse came in to comfort her and said to her, "I'll be with you. It's all right." She answered, "If you're with me, it'll be all right." Time was very short. The doctors and nurses made all of the preparations very quickly, and she was taken into the operating room; it was her niece again who wheeled her through the operating room doors. We waited outside in the hallway for several hours, waited until she was safely sent out; our son wheeled her back to the ward. Our son stayed at her side overnight. In a couple of days he too fell ill, and an examination showed that he had hepatitis; he had brought it back from the farm village in Anhui. At first we wanted to keep the news from his mother, but we inadvertently let her find out. She kept asking repeatedly, "How is our son?" At night when I came home and walked into my quiet empty room, I almost wanted to cry out, "Everything, fall down on my head! Let every sort of calamity come at once!"

I ought to thank that friendly and kind head nurse. She sympathized with my plight and told me to let her handle everything relating to my son's treatment. She arranged everything, went with him to see a doctor, to be examined, and allowed him to move into a quarantine ward in another part of the hospital where he could receive prompt care and treatment. He waited bitterly in that quarantine ward for his mother's illness to improve. His mother lay on her sickbed and very weakly said a few words. She always asked, "How is Tangtang?" I understood from her tear-filled eyes just how badly she wanted to see her most beloved son, but she no longer had the energy to give it much more thought.

Every day she had transfusions and saline injections. When she saw me come, she would keep on asking me, "How many cc's of blood? What are we going to do?" I would comfort her, "You just take it easy. There's no problem; getting well is the important thing." More than once she said, "This is hard on you." What hardship did I have? If I could do things for the person I loved most, even if it was just some small thing, I would be happy! The doctor gave her oxygen, and she had tubes stuck into her nose all day long. She asked several times for them to be taken out because she was in pain, but after we talked to her she finally put up with them.

She only lived five days after the operation. Who could have thought she would go so fast? During those five days, I stayed at her bedside all day silently watching her suffer (I could really feel her suffering), but except for requesting two or three times for that huge oxygen tank to be moved away from the front of her bed and expressing her anxiety about using too much blood and not being able to pay the medical bills, she never once complained about anything. When she saw people she knew, she often seemed to want to convey the feeling "Please forgive me for causing you all so much trouble." She was very peaceful, but did not doze off; she always had her eyes wide open. Her eyes were very large, very beautiful, very bright. I watched and watched as though watching a candle that was about to flicker out. How I yearned to make those two eyes continue to shine! How I feared her leaving me! I even wanted to suffer ten thousand tortures because of my fourteen volumes of "evil books"[10] if only to make her keep on living peacefully.

I was not at her side when she left this world. It was a Sunday. The Anti-Epidemic Station of the Hygiene Department sent someone to disinfect our house because we had hepatitis in the family. Her clan sister had the time to go to the hospital and look after her; we had agreed that we would go after lunch and relieve her. We never imagined that as soon as we sat down to lunch we would receive a message telling our daughter to go to the hospital and saying that her mother was "in trouble." It was truly a bolt out of the blue! I hurried with my daughter and son-in-law to the hospital. Even the mattress had been removed from the sickbed that she had occupied. Some people told me she was in the morgue. Then we ran downstairs and met her clan sister there. It was she who had got some people's help to bring the patient who had "breathed her last" into the morgue. The dead one had not yet been placed in a metal box and put in the freezer; she was lying on a stretcher, but had already been tightly bound up in a white sheet and her face was not visible. I could only see her name. I bent over and embraced that white linen package that still had a human shape. I was weeping and calling her name. Only a few minutes passed. What kind of a last farewell was that?

According to her clan sister, at the moment that she left this world, her clan sister did not know it. She had once said to her clan sister, "Bring the doctor." The doctor had come, but there was nothing special. After that, she just gradually sank into sleep. Her clan sister still believed she was sleeping. A nurse who came to give her an injection first discovered that her heart had already stopped beating. I had not been able to say a last good-bye to her; I had a great deal of things that I had not yet expressed to her. She could not have left me without leaving behind even one word of farewell! When she told her clan

10. The fourteen-volume *Collected Works of Ba Jin,* containing his pre-1949 writings, was branded "a great anti-party, anti-socialist poison weed" during the Cultural Revolution.

sister, "Bring the doctor," most likely it was not "Bring the doctor (yisheng)"; but rather "Bring Mr. Li (Li Xiansheng)." She usually called me that. That morning of all mornings why was I not in her sickroom? None of us were at her side; she died so very sadly!

My son-in-law immediately telephoned our few relatives. Her younger sister-in-law hurried over to the hospital and immediately fainted. Three days later, we held the final parting ceremony at the Longhua Crematorium. Not one of her friends came, firstly because we did not notify them and secondly because I had been the target of nearly seven years of investigation. There were no mourning songs and no mourners, just the sound of crying and grief; I warmly thanked those few friends who came to the ceremony and my daughter's two or three fellow students who especially helped out. Finally I bid farewell to her remains. Her daughter stared at her face and wept mournfully. In his quarantined room, the son whom she regarded as her very life did not yet know that his mother had already died. It is worth mentioning that the son of a deceased friend whom she had looked after like her own son hurried down all the way from Peking just to see her one more time. This technician who worked all day with steel certainly did not have a heart of steel. After he received our telegram, his wife told him, "You better go. If you don't go, your heart will never be at peace." I stood there beside her transformed body a while, and someone took our picture. I thought painfully to myself that it was the last time; even if the picture turned out terribly, I would still want to treasure the scene.

Everything was over. After a few days, I went with my daughter and son-in-law to the crematorium again to pick up the jar containing her ashes. After storing them in the storage room for the required three years, I brought the jar back to the house. Some people advised me to give her remains a peaceful burial, but I would rather put the jar in our bedroom where I can feel that she is still with me.

4

Those nightmarish days have finally passed. Almost in the blink of an eye six years have been left far behind. It certainly was not the blink of an eye! So many days of blood and tears were contained in those years. Not only six years. Half a year has passed since I first began to write this short essay, and during that half a year I have regularly gone to the crematorium to stand in the big hall and mourn silently, bow ceremonially, and memorialize my friends who were hounded to death by the Gang of Four.

Every time that I put on the black gauze armband and the paper flower, I think of my own dearest friend: an ordinary lover of literature; a not-too-successful translator; a good-hearted person. She was a part of my very life; her ashes contain my own blood and tears.

She was one of my readers. I met her for the first time in Shanghai in 1936. Twice, in 1938 and 1941, we lived together like friends in Guilin. In 1944 in

Guiyang we were married. When I first met her, she was not yet twenty, and I must bear a great deal of the responsibility for her growth and development. She read my novels, wrote me letters, and then later met me and fell in love with me.

We courted each other for eight years, and when we finally married in Guiyang, we only made one announcement and did not even have a banquet. From Guiyang we moved to Chongqing, where we lived in one room in a seven- or eight-room house under the stairs of the sales department of the Cultural Life Publishing Company on Minguo Road. She had someone buy four glasses and began to organize our little family. She stayed with me through all kinds of difficult trials. During the War of Resistance against Japan, we escaped from Canton only about ten hours before the Japanese troops entered the city; we went from Guangdong to Guangxi, from Kunming to Guilin, from Jinhua to Wenzhou; we were separated and met up again, and after we met up we parted again. Part of the record of that sort of life is included in my *Report of Travels*. Forty years ago a friend criticized me, saying, "What sort of writing is this!" After my *Collected Works* was published another friend thought that I should not have included those essays. What they said made sense; for the last two years, I have told my friends and my readers more than once that I have decided not to allow my *Collected Works* to be published again. For my own sake, however, I often read over those reports. In those days when I fell into difficulties and my friends all went on ahead making their fortunes, she would always whisper very intimately in my ear, "Don't feel bad. I won't leave you. I'm right here at your side." That was for certain. Only just before she was wheeled into the operating room did she ever say, "We are going to have to part."

I lived with her for over thirty years, but I really did not help her very much. She was more talented that I was, but she lacked the spirit to do difficult and meticulous studies. I enjoyed very much her translations of Pushkin and Turgenev's novels. Even though the translations were not appropriate and were not in the style of Pushkin and Turgenev, they were rather works of creative writing, and reading them, for me, was a kind of enjoyment. She wanted to change her life, did not want to be just a housewife, but she lacked the courage to accept patient suffering through hard work. On the advice of a friend, she received the permission of comrade Ye Yiqun—later also hounded to death by the Gang of Four—to go to *Shanghai Literature*[11] to "perform voluntary labor." She did a little work there, but then during a "campaign,"[12] she came under attack. They said she only sought articles from older writers and also that I had sent her there to be a spy. When I was just about to "stand to the side," she was also

11. *Shanghai wenxue* was originally titled *Wenyi yuebao*. It was the house organ of the Shanghai Writers' Union; Ba Jin was the titular chief editor, but the real power was Ye Yiqun.

12. A Communist Party–directed attack on some individual or tendency.

called back to the Writers' Union to participate in a "campaign." It was the first time she had ever participated in that kind of stormy struggle, and participating as the household member of a reactionary authority, she really did not know how to handle it. She was completely flustered and, in a panic, could neither sit nor stand; afraid for me, she worried about her children's future. She looked for someone to hold out a helping hand to her, but her friends deserted her and her "fellow workers" used her as a target; some even thought that by attacking her they could attack me. She was not a regular employee of the Writers' Union or the publication, but still she was ordered to "stand to the side," stand in line and wear a sign; after she was sent home, she was also dragged before the authorities.

After a while, she wrote an admission of guilt. The second time she was sent home, the leader of the "rebel faction" in our area[13] even notified the neighborhood committee members that she should be punished by sweeping the streets. Afraid that someone would see her, very early she would get up in the morning and go out with the broom, sweep until she was exhausted before coming back home, close the door, and heave a great sigh; but sometimes she would run into children on their way to school who would curse her as "Ba Jin's stinking old lady." On occasion when I would see her returning with the broom, I did not dare to look her in the eye because I felt so guilty. The sweeping was a mortal blow to her. In less than two months, she fell ill; after that she did not go out to sweep the streets again (my younger sister carried on her sweeping for a while), but she never completely regained her health again. Even though she continued to hang on for four years, right up to her death, she was not able to see me regain my freedom. These were her last days, but certainly not her final denouement. Her final denouement will be intimately related to mine.

When I lose the ability to work anymore, I hope that Xiao Shan's few translated stories will be there on my sickbed. Then when I close my eyes for eternity, please mingle my ashes with hers.

1979

---

13. The term *rebel faction* is, of course, a post–Cultural Revolution anachronism; at the time, they were the Maoist orthodoxy carrying out the policies of the Cultural Revolution.

Wen Jieruo (1927–   )

LIVING HELL (FROM HER MEMOIRS)

Translated by Jeffrey C. Kinkley

August 27, 1966,
early in the morning

I brought my mother a pot of chicken soup. When they raided the home where I lived with my husband, Xiao Qian, and my third elder sister, the people in the red armbands from the neighborhood factory had commanded my sister to slaughter her chickens—all of them, a good two dozen. We couldn't eat them all at once and there was no one to take them in. So she dug a trench and buried them—all save two, which she used to make this broth. It was she who thought of sending it over to Mother, for I had noticed, in passing by Mother's little cookroom on the morning of the twenty-sixth, that her briquette stove had never been lit. Maybe she hadn't eaten for days.

When I entered Mother's dark little room, the soup was still warm. I watched her swallow every mouthful until it was finished. Surely this wasn't my mother, she who was always so bright and cheerful? The trembling old lady before me, clasping the casserole of soup, was wretched and alone, without a soul to protect her. She had aged ten years in the space of a few days: her hair was disheveled, her face haggard and pallid, her eyes sunken.

In the days when the family was well off, Mother had been fond of Beijing opera and mahjong. But she could stand adversity and hardship, too. During the eight years of the Japanese occupation, she had stitched together all the clothes and padded shoes that we children ever wore, brothers and sisters alike—clothes for each season in succession, seam by seam, sole by sole. Every piece of jewelry she owned was sold off to pay our school fees. Finally she had to mortgage our house. She was never able to pay it off. We had to rent our rooms after the Liberation. Came the time when we could scarcely afford food enough to see us through to the next day, I promised her: "Someday, when I've graduated from college, I'll earn money and support *you*."

I'd kept my promise, through sixteen years of work. Besides supporting her, a duty I shared with my younger brothers, my royalties had got her a Simmons bed, a fur coat, and other comforts. And so, in this "great political revolution by which the proletariat overthrew the bourgeoisie and all oppressor classes," the "red armbands" made her into a target of struggle.

As I was about to leave, Mother handed me a jar of cocoa powder and a can of mandarin orange sections. "Give them to the children," she said. In the midst of all this, she hadn't forgotten her grandchildren. She also gave me a tiny parcel, a square of paper folded up into a little homemade envelope. She explained that it contained leftover grain ration tickets.

That day was already particularly upsetting. I hadn't been able to think up a single damning thing to write down against my family. I thought of Akutagawa Rynosuke's novella, *Hell Screen*. The protagonist, a painter named Yoshihide, looks on helplessly, in terror, while a feudal lord burns his daughter alive. I felt the same, knowing full well that Mother was not long for this world under these cruel and savage beatings. Still, I could not save her. I pleaded with one of the "red armbands" at the publishing house where I worked to come with me to the scene of the torture—otherwise, my mother's life surely could not be sustained. "Think how many revolutionary martyrs have been sacrificed," he barked, "without your giving a hang about them. Here we are in a time of crisis, and you're worried about a few people in your own family!"

In that instant I felt that I was no longer living in a human world. All society had become one giant mangle iron. It could press people like Mother and me into powder at any time.

THE NIGHT OF THE TERROR

It was already nine o'clock when I left the office on the night of August 27. The rules were that we could go home at eight, but after supper one of the "red armbands" insisted I turn in some damaging information exposing my family. I promised I'd write out something that night and turn it in first thing the next morning. So I stayed behind an extra hour to work on it.

I had just reached the gateway to the compound on Douzui Lane when I was caught off guard by a "Halt!" and surrounded by a band of ruffians. Some of the men snatched away my cloth tote bag, which carried the cocoa powder and canned oranges Mother had given me that morning. They also stripped off my watch. Then two women patted me down from head to foot. I was wearing only a white linen blouse made over from an old Chinese-style long gown of

Yakko-san's[1] and blue trousers, with an undershirt and panties on underneath. They found nothing.

With the women on either side and beefy men surrounding me in back and in front, I was led under guard in the direction of the Army Hospital. A woman brushed past us in the doorway. In the light of the traffic signal I recognized her as Elder Sister. Then it dawned on me: they had dragged her out to be struggled against, with Mama. Because I was not at home, a contingent had lain in wait at my doorstep. My sister and I exchanged glances, but neither of us dared acknowledge the other.

They shoved me into the main courtyard of No. 30, Alley Eight, and forced me to stand at attention facing Mama's dwelling. She had two small rooms off a tiny courtyard at the northwest corner. The wooden fence-gate leading to her corner was shut tight. It was pitch-black inside, deserted and silent. Was she holding her breath, listening intently to the uproar in the courtyard? The thugs interrogated me from the start as if I were a spy for a foreign power. They said they'd discovered a radio transmitter and receiver in a storeroom off the front courtyard at No. 11 Douzui Lane. I told them that those rooms on the south side of the courtyard were purchased in 1962 from the Chen family in the compound. There had been two lavatories there, each with double trenches serving as latrines; we'd filled up the holes in one lavatory, turning it into a storeroom. The ground might be a little loose in the filled-in places, but it could not possibly have radio broadcasting apparatus. The Chen family had bought the place right after Liberation; before that, we didn't know—why not ask the Chens?

Then they all shouted at once, "Your eldest sister, the one who lives in America, is a spy. The old witch (meaning Mama) is a veteran spy, and you're her apprentice spy. You're one whole family of foreign agents." They pressed me to reveal the hiding place of our transmitter.

Next they said, "What kind of person was your grandfather on your father's side? Your grandmother? Your father? Your uncle? Fucking class enemies, all of them—ten *thousand* deaths would have been too good for them!"

I thought to myself: How fortunate for them that they never lived to see this day.

From the interrogation I learned that after Liberation my mother, trusting the policy of the Party, had on her own initiative come clean with the police all about how her eldest daughter had become an American citizen. That had sown the seeds of her destruction. During the 1951 movement to suppress counterrevolutionaries, she had handed over to the local police station three rusty

1. Japanese for "that fellow," used by Wen Jieruo and her family as an indirect reference to Xiao Qian while he was courting her, as an English girl might refer to her beau in French as *lui*. After the marriage, the phrase, often shortened to "Ya," became Wen Jieruo's favorite term of endearment for her husband.

old swords that belonged to Grandfather when he was a county magistrate under the Qing dynasty. This had now become a crime on her part, of "keeping secret weapons after the Liberation." She also confessed that her younger brother, who had attended the Whampoa Military Academy, was liquidated at the beginning of the fifties. As a result, she was classed a Dependent of a Counter-revolutionary. How could she have known that he would be exonerated one day, after the Third Plenum of the Eleventh Central Committee (the one that put Deng Xiaoping in power)? And that a memorial plaque reading "Former Home of Wen Xuru" would be nailed over the door where he lived? On top of this, there was the charge that her husband had been a diplomat for twenty years—before the war.

My interrogation continued until midnight. Then someone shouted, "Drag the *veteran* spy out here, too, so we can struggle against them together!"

Two of my tormenters ran out angrily, pushing open the wooden gate leading to Mother's little yard. The light went on in her room. One of them rushed back and whispered something; suddenly five or six others dashed off.

One of the thugs smacked me on the back with his fist and bellowed, "The old spy alienated herself from the people and hanged herself to avoid being punished. We didn't watch her closely enough. This gets her off the hook too easy. Get your ass over there and look at her!"

When I entered her room, dear Mama had already been taken down and parked on her cot, the one Yakko-san had fashioned in the fifties for the old spinster cousin who had been half a mother to him. The cousin had slept on it when she entered our household; Yakko-san gave it to my mama after he returned from the farm where he was sent down.

I had been told that a person's face becomes contorted and purple after death by hanging, but Mama in death was as serene and composed as if in a deep sleep; any expression of terror had vanished. She was wearing a hand-sewn seersucker cheongsam with short sleeves. Her lips were slightly parted, as if her eyes might open at the softest word in her ear.

A thought flashed through my mind: Whether Mama had gone to heaven or to purgatory, she had at least escaped this hell on earth forever.

In a deafening roar, the ruffians all shouted at once that I must swear out loud, "She deserved to die! This rids the world of a piece of rotten flesh!"

Could people be any crueler, any less human than this, anywhere in the world? Having driven Mama to death, they were forcing me to curse her. Mama, I said to myself, forgive me. Good it is that calumnies and curses have no more power to hurt you.

Under the force of their threats, I haltingly spit out the words they had commanded.

"Louder! Now swear, '*I* deserve to die, too. It would rid the world of another piece of rotten flesh!'"

I repeated the words, louder this time.

"Now this: 'All people in the Seven Black Categories[2] deserve to die. It would be wonderful. The world would be rid of a great pile of rotten flesh!'"

I began to wonder if the hoodlums surrounding me were men or beasts.

Even the Nazis hadn't been so vicious when they persecuted the Jews, had they?

Later I heard that in another province they had sailed one boatload after another of the Seven Black Categories people into a river and sunk them, drowning all on board. Among them were pregnant women and children.

The Japanese militarists massacred vast numbers of my countrymen. Their crimes were too numerous to record. But all that happened in wartime. And they didn't kill their own compatriots. The Americans dropped atomic bombs on Hiroshima and Nagasaki, but they'd never contemplate setting them off on their own soil. If all the people killed in the "Cultural Revolution" were added together, from Liu Shaoqi, the president, on top, to the plainest of ordinary citizens like my mama at the bottom, the total might far outnumber the victims of the Rape of Nanjing and the two atomic bombs.

On that terror-filled night in the Red August of 1966, I cursed the corpse of my mother, not yet fully cold, as the hooligans commanded. I cursed myself, and everyone in the Seven Black Categories, thinking that there would be an end to it, that they would release me to go home. But there was no end. They knew that Mother was a housewife in their neighborhood; this gave them the power of life and death over her. Yet I was a cadre in a government organ. It was not so easy for them to go ahead and work their violence on me (not daring to go to the publishing house where I worked to seize me, they had ambushed me outside my home). So they rounded up a group of Red Guards, telling the "little generals" that a veteran spy had killed herself to escape punishment, that I was her daughter and part of a family conspiracy, and that they had better beat me until they got the whole story out of me. The hooligans from the street factory even gave the Red Guards the self-winding gold Movado watch they'd stripped off me during their body search, saying that it was peculiarly big and heavy, and sounded funny, being one of my espionage tools. In truth Yakko-san had bought it in Switzerland; his name was still engraved on the case in English, with the year of purchase—1945.

I found it impossible to blame that band of young people, even in this moment of my deepest despair. I knew they must be middle-school students from somewhere in the neighborhood, not much older than my own daughter

---

2. Landlords, rich peasants, counterrevolutionaries, and bad elements were the original Four Black Categories; rightists were added in 1957, and, early in the Cultural Revolution, capitalist roaders and "cow or 'ox' demons and snake spirits," to make seven. Subsequently there was a revision; to the earlier five were added renegades, spies, capitalist roaders—and intellectuals, who brought up the rear, as "stinking ninth elements."

and son. At that age, they ought to be in a classroom, soaking up learning. And at that time of night, they ought to be peacefully asleep, at home. But they had been assigned, or tricked, into committing mayhem all night long—into leading a life of crime.

Having been given the duty of torturing me, the "little generals" surrounded me in a circle. They rolled up their sleeves one by one and lashed me with the brass buckles at the ends of their belts. Crack, crack, without end. "Aw, we're being easy on you," they said as they whipped me. "Go look at all the piles of corpses at the No. 1 Middle School. Their eyeballs were gouged out!"

I thought they were just trying to scare me. Afterwards I learned from reading some "revolutionary" Red Guard tabloids that the Municipal No. 1 Middle School really did set up a water dungeon. Written on the wall there in flowing fresh blood, and in formidable big characters, were the words "Long Live the Red Terror."

They also pressed me to find out where my "big brother" was. When I said I just had two younger brothers, that my single older one had died at the age of three, they retorted, "Don't play dumb, 'big brother' means your superior in the spy agency."

They wanted me to come clean about my code name, "big brother's" code name, and where my radio transmitter was located.

I don't believe they really thought I was a spy. But they had red bands around their arms, and that strip of cloth represented absolute authority. Now that those "red armbands" from the street factory had handed ready-made prey over to them, they naturally pounced on me like hungry wolves thirsty for the taste of blood.

My tortures continued until the morning light. Smearing ink all over my face, the Red Guards made me walk barefoot from the Eighth Alley of Dongsi Street to the Broad Street Inside Chaoyang Gate. They shouted slogans and lashed at me with their belt buckles the whole way, never letting up.

After the "little generals" had conducted my torture parade to the publishing house where I worked, they punished me by having me bend over in the reception room, while they plucked clumps of hair from my scalp, using the frame of my eyeglasses as tweezers. That went on forever. My colleagues at the press would come out the door and walk by in groups of twos and threes, but no one dared make a sound.

I'd never resisted during my night of torture, but now that I was in my workplace, I felt a little braver. Even if its Party committee had already fallen, the place had a work team that could not let this go all the way. Boldly straightening up, I glared at them and yelled, "If I've committed a capital offense, beat me to death immediately! What you are doing now is the death of a thousand slices, in disguised form!"

I do not know how many of them understood that old imperial term for slow execution by gradual dismemberment. In any case, I plunged on ahead, which actually threw them for a loss, and they suddenly dispersed.

Just then the sound of sobbing came from the flight of steps leading up to the doorway. An editor who worked in my own office retorted, "You're not allowed to cry! You didn't weep for the warriors who shed blood and were martyred. An old witch has died, that's all. What the hell are you wailing about?"

It was my elder sister who was weeping. Afraid of the corpse decomposing, neighbors in Mother's courtyard had rushed to tell my sister, demanding that she send it to be cremated. Mama's bank books had been taken away during the raids on her home. Her cash on hand wouldn't cover the 28-yuan cremation fee, and neither would my sister's. Yakko-san and I had seen all our bank books confiscated, too; without proof, I couldn't even withdraw my own savings. Luckily I had taken several bills out of our home before the first raid and put them in my desk drawer at work, hoping to take Mother back home to the country. I went upstairs to fetch one, and to ask some comrades in the publishing house to accompany my sister to bear away the body. I was not allowed to go myself, for from that day forward I lost my liberty. They kept me confined there.

When Sister removed Mother's name from the household registry, she had to turn in all the grain ration tickets Mother had left behind. As I unfolded the little paper parcel with the ration tickets she had handed me the day before, I saw, written in neat little characters with pencil on the inside surface, "Farewell." All of a sudden I realized that to preserve the dignity of her character, Mother had decided to end her life by the morning of the twenty-seventh.

Later, Elder Sister told me that the crematorium had ceased sending out the usual hearses that picked up one body at a time. It sent around a big truck piled high with a dozen other corpses, each one wrapped up in just a cotton sheet, lying where it fell when it was heaved up onto the back. Nor would they permit you to keep the ashes. I thought about it: With so many corpses burned at the same time, even if you could, how would you know that they were from *your* loved one? How were these crematoria any different from ovens in the Nazi extermination camps?

While she was waiting for the truck to arrive, Elder Sister heard talk of two other cases of attempted suicide in our lane. People whispered to each other: "Just a while ago she was here sweeping the street, and then in the blink of an eye—" That was another woman that Elder Sister had known very well. She had entangled herself in the power lines; it hadn't killed her outright, but charred her hands and chest. Then there were the Feis, mother and daughter. They had swallowed something and been in a coma for days.

In that Red August of 1966, the most worthless thing in China was a human life.

1990

Xiao Wenyuan (1933–)

A BIZARRE KIND OF ROBBERY

Translated by D. E. Pollard

In the ninth century A.D. at the ferry crossing where the Wanshui joins the Yangtze River there occurred a most singular case of robbery. As the poet Li She's boat was passing through, its way was barred suddenly by desperadoes. They shouted: "Who goes there?" Li She's retainer replied in haste: "The Grand Scholar Li!" The chief of the desperadoes responded: "Excellent! Since it is he, we have but one demand: we would that he compose a poem for us, no more." On hearing this, Li She, who was hiding in the cabin, put brush to paper:

> The dark rain sweeps the riverside village
> Heroes of the greenwood honor my name by night
> No use to try to avoid you another time
> The world nowadays is half populated by you gentlemen

Lord-a-mercy! A false alarm, passed off in the end with no harm done. "The world nowadays is half populated by you gentlemen" indicates that "bandits" were as thick as fleas on a dog's back. He might run into them any day. But when that came about, desperation would beget inspiration: he would dash off a spell in the form of a quatrain, and the danger would be averted. This is a safer way than having a pistol-packing troop of bodyguards.

The newspapers often carry Western news of such-and-such a museum being burgled; however, the objects lost are mostly things like famous paintings worth a king's ransom or crowns encrusted with gems. The ancients had a saying: "A place attracts crowds by virtue of an individual, the worthy man is honored only by later generations." You have to be an old fossil to be worth anything. But Li She was, as plain as a pikestaff, still living and breathing. The desperadoes did not steal gold, did not steal silver, of all things they wanted to fleece him of a poem. This "fleecing" was both novel and neat. I imagine it must be an extremely rare case in the annals of crime.

I think this lot of desperadoes must have once been law-abiding folk who were driven by lack of alternatives to take to a life of crime. In order to keep alive, their first needs were for food to fill their belly and clothes to cover their frame, yet on this occasion they sued for a poem: why should that be? Perhaps this indicates that prior to the incident Li She's poems had already spread among the people and found favor with humble men and women, to the extent that his fame had reached even these illiterate desperadoes.

Li She's poetry is comparatively fresh and perspicuous, flowing clear and easy to chant; at the same time it shows some originality. His "Herdboy Song" goes:

> Herding oxen by day, herd the oxen to the river bend
> Herding oxen by night, herd the oxen through the village valley
> Out from the woods, in cape and hat, fresh rain fine
> Lying flat, playing pipes, sedge grass green
> Belt bristles with arrows, a riot of tall weeds
> No fear of the tiger getting better of the calf

The style is natural and ingenuous, and has a childlike charm, which makes it different from the hectoring, pock-faced works we are accustomed to. This kind of poem children can chant, and adults appreciate. His "Yellow Sunflower" poem goes:

> Do not subject this flower to the vulgar gaze
> Just dyed gosling-yellow, the color not yet dry
> It will rise to heaven on the autumn wind
> The lady in the Purple Sun Palace wants a cap

Poems about sunflowers abound, but their theme is usually that "the character of things doesn't change." Li She has devised something of his own making. He makes the association between the shape of the flower and the cap of the Purple Sun Palace lady, a novel and ingenious comparison that has its roots in personal experience. In his lifetime he was several times demoted, more than once fell foul of mutinous soldiery, and for ten abject years plumbed the depths of adversity. After he shook loose the dust of the world, his wife was powerfully moved by his example and entered a Taoist convent. Looking at his wife's Taoist cap he thought of the sunflower; seeing the sunflower he recalled his wife's

Taoist cap. There's no telling how many times this figure formed in his mind in this circular fashion.

Of course, there is nothing very startling about Li She's poetry, and there can be no thought of comparing him with the stars in the literary firmament. Nevertheless in his heyday in the mid-Tang his fame spread far and wide. If his poetry had been abstruse and dessicated, and no one had understood it, how could the desperadoes have come to know of his great name? Running into the heroes of the greenwood as on this occasion, even if his life had not been imperiled, his being stripped of all possessions was no more than could have been expected. On the other hand, supposing that his poetry had been plain and simple and in popular vein, so that the country yokel could take it in at first glance, but mild as water and about as appetizing as chewing wood, then it would not have given as much honest pleasure as the jingles the herdboy or the carter might make up as they went along. If the heroes of the greenwood had paid their call in those circumstances, not only would they not have extorted just one poem, even the present of a boatload would not have got him off the hook.

Perhaps desperadoes can't write poetry, but that is not to say they can't tell fair from foul. If some poetaster thinks your humble man and woman can be hoodwinked, and cleverly prinks up crude and coarse, base and ugly stuff to force upon them, even if he goes to the length of enlisting the aid of celebrities, arranging a publicity circus, and creating an almighty hullaballoo, the result will still, I fear, not be all that was hoped for.

To encounter the heroes of the greenwood on one's travels is of course a misfortune in life, but to be fleeced, to be blackmailed, to be robbed on account of one's poems, how can one tell that this might not be an inestimable blessing for the poet?

1985

Xi Chuan (1963–)

SALUTE

Translated by Maghiel van Crevel

ONE: NIGHT

In the noise of trucks passing through the city: how hard it is to make the blood be quiet! How hard to make the draught animals be quiet! What persuasion, what promise, what bribe, what threat will make them quiet? But they *are* quiet.

Stone beasts under the archway are breathing moonlight. The knife-grinder's rickety body is bent like the crescent moon. He is exhausted but he will not go to sleep; he whistles, to call the birds from sleep to the end of the bridge, but forgets that on the cliff, silvery as the moon, there is a pregnant leopard that no one's looking after.

The spider intercepts an imperial edict, thus going against the wish of the road.

In hemp fields, lamps have no right of residence.

Someone is about to arrive and knock on the door, sheep are about to appear and roam in the meadow. The wind is blowing on apples which have never yet entered its dreams, a youth is singing in the basement, surpassing himself. . . . It's night, needless to say. Memory can create brand-new things.

How vast the sky, higher than memory! Climb high to see far, and the spirit will know no limits. Ever-burning lamps, two or three, look like will-o'-the-wisps. For the soul that cannot sleep, there is no poetry. One needs to stay awake and be on guard, but in the face of death one cannot ponder.

I have brought you a searchlight; there must be fairy maidens flying over your head at night.

I chose this record player for the warehouse, to play you a song, to cure your old affliction.

In this night, with the stars in battle array, my hair stands on end and the black mole on the left side of my chest is blacker still. God's grain is plundered; beauty comes under attack from large, vengeful birds. On nights like this, if I fly into a rage, if I retaliate, then do not speak to me of mercy! If I pardon your crimes, then take to the road right away and do not stop to thank me.

Please clean your wounds with the juice of the ginger root.

Please leave a way out for the weasel.

How powerless the heart when the lights go out, when street sweepers get up, when crows take off into the sunlight shining on this city, proud to have their luxurious wings no longer confused with nighttime writing.

A face flushed red, all the body's blood. The bugle blows, dust trembles: the first note always sounds bad!

TWO: SALUTE

Dejection. Dangling gongs and drums. Dozing leopard in the basement. Spiral staircase. Nighttime torch. City gates. Cold, below the ancient stars and reaching to the grass's roots. Sealed-off body. Undrinkable water. Ice floes drifting like ships. Birds for passengers. Waterways closed. Children unborn. Tears unformed. Punishment unbegun. Chaos. Equilibrium. Ascension. A blank . . . how does one speak of dejection and not be in the wrong? Face to face with a crown of flowers left at the crossroads, please realize the price one pays for recklessness!

Pain: a sea, unmovable.

On the seventh page of suffering, civility is written.

To want to scream, to force the steel to shed a tear, to force the mice used to living in secret to line up and appear before me. To want to scream, but in the softest possible voice, not like curses but like prayers, not like the roar of cannon but like the whistle of the wind. A stronger heartbeat accompanies a greater silence, helplessly watching how the stored-up rain will all be drunk—well, then, scream! Oh, how I want to scream, with hundreds of crows clamoring, I have no mouth of gold, no words of jade—I am an omen of no good.

Too many desires, too little seawater.

Illusions depend on capital for their preservation.

Let the rose redress our errors, let thunder reprimand us! On this endless road, there is no asking where the journey leads. When the moth flies into the flame, that is no time to talk of eternity, and it is hard to find proof of a man's moral flawlessness.

Memory: my textbook.

Love: unfinished worries.

Happiness is like clouds over our heads. Clouds over our heads are like the angels' chariots of war: chaotic peace! Dangerous undertakings! A man goes deep into the mountains and miraculously survives. In winter he hoards cabbage, in summer he makes ice. He says: "One who will let nothing move him is not real, nor the place where he comes from nor his present life." Therefore we crowd around the peach blossom to sharpen our sense of smell. Face to face with the peach blossom and other things of beauty, one who knows not how to doff his hat in salute is not our comrade.

But we do not hope for an outcome in which souls are made to lie idle and words blackmailed.

Poetry guides the dead and the next generation.

THREE: ABODE

Clocks let on the sounds and sights of spring, the cricket on its manor sings. What I will not allow has happened: I am slowly changing into someone else. I must call out three times, I must call myself back.

With the props that I've collected, I decorate the room. Every night, I have the good fortune to enjoy a play staged purely by props.

The kitchen is a place for knives and forks to sleep, the square is a place for the goddess to stand.

The world in the mirror is my world's equal but its opposite, too: if it isn't hell, it must be heaven. A man exactly like me, but my opposite too, lives in that world: if he isn't Lucan[1] he must be Saint John.

I rarely touch my cheeks or my ankles. I rarely touch myself. Therefore I rarely criticize myself, and I rarely beat myself up.

This often happens: Liu Jun makes a phone call to find another Liu Jun.[2] As if I am talking to myself, cradling the phone.

The smile of one who suffers from a mental illness. The reproductive organ he bares to the sun and to women. The sound of him banging his head against the wall. His underdeveloped brain. "Am I right? Am I right?"—the question he persists in asking, over and over again.

There is no guard at the door of my house. If I hire a guard, I must guard him with all my might.

If three thousand beauties came to sit in this room, would you be excited or afraid? Three thousand beauties, they might be three thousand fox spirits, the only way to cope with them would be to get them drunk.

A man whose axe has chopped his fingers off come to tell me the story of his love.

Experiences of others may to us well be taboos.

---

1. Roman epic poet (39–65), author of *Pharsalia*.

2. Xi Chuan's official name.

The lilac in the inkwell is slowly turning blue. It hopes to remember this night, it would do anything to remember this night, but that is impossible.

I nourish this flower seed with my innermost secret: when the lotus blooms, it will be summer.

FOUR: THE MONSTER

The monster—I have seen it. The monster has bristly hair, razor-sharp teeth, it is close to going blind. The monster breathes its husky breath, it shouts of calamity, yet its feet move without a sound. The monster has no sense of humor, like someone trying hard to cover up humble origins, like someone destroyed by a calling; it has no cradle offering memories, no goal offering direction, not enough lies to defend itself. It beats on tree trunks, it collects infants; it lives like a rock, it dies like an avalanche.

The crow seeks allies among scarecrows.

The monster hates my hairdo, hates my smell, hates my regret and my overcautious ways. In short, it hates my habit of dressing up happiness in pearls and jade. It bursts through my door, tells me to stand in a corner, will not let me explain and falls through my chair, shatters my mirror, rips my curtains and all protective screens around my private soul. I beg it: "When I am thirsty, don't take away my teacup!" Right then and there it digs out water from a spring: that must be its answer.

A ton of parrots, a ton of parrot talk!

For the tiger we say "tiger," for the donkey we say "donkey." But how do you address the monster? It has no name, so its flesh melts into its shadow, so you cannot call out to it, so you cannot determine its place in the sun nor foretell the fortune or misfortune it may bring. It should be given a name, like "sorrow" or "shyness," it should be given a pond from which to drink, it should be given a roof over its head for shelter from the rain. A monster with no name is scary.

A thrush bumps off all the king's men!

The monster is exposed to temptations too, but not those of the palace, not those of female beauty and not those of sumptuous candlelit banquets. It is coming toward us, but surely there is nothing about us to make its mouth water? Surely it will not try to suck emptiness from our bodies? What kind of temptation is that! Sideways through a shadowy passageway, the monster collides head-on with a glint of steel, and that smallest of injuries teaches it to moan—to moan, to live, not to know what faith is. But as soon as it calms down, it hears the sesame stalks budding once again, it smells the Chinese rose's fragrance once again.

Across a thousand mountains flies the wild goose, too timid to speak of itself.

This metaphor of a monster goes down the mountainside, picks flowers, sees the reflection of its face in the river, in its heart of hearts feels unsure who that is; then it swims across, goes ashore, looks back at the haze above the water, finds nothing, understands nothing; then it charges into the city, follows the trail of a girl, comes by a piece of meat, spends the night under eaves, dreams of a village, of a companion; then it sleepwalks fifty miles, knows no fear, wakes up in the morning sun, discovers it has returned to its earlier place of departure: still that thick bed of leaves, hidden underneath the leaves the dagger still—what is about to happen here?

Dove in the sand, you are awakened by the shine of blood: the time to fly has come!

FIVE: MAXIMS

Strike down shadows, and it will be people that stand up.

Trees listen to trees, birds listen to birds; when poisonous snakes raise their bodies upright to attack people passing, they become people themselves.

To scrutinize the face in the mirror is to affront a stranger.

The law says: those who go looting at the scene of a fire must die, those who put up a sheep's head to sell dog meat must get what they deserve, those who gaze and peer to left and right will find a trap beneath their feet, those with narrow chicken minds must meet with scorn. But I can't stop myself from adding something here, for I have seen that women whose star is rising are just as competent as men whose star is rising, just as muscular, just as ruthless.

The sunflower is after all a flower too!

Why have cats not tigers become our pets?

Tiny pain, like the feeling of sand pouring into the rims of eyes—from whom does one seek compensation?

A book will change me, if I want to take it in; a girl will change me, if I want to sing her praises; a road will change me, if I walk it to the end; a coin will change me, if I want to own it. If I change someone else who lives beside me, I change myself: my single conscience makes the both of us suffer, my single selfishness makes the both of us blush.

Truth cannot be public. Thoughts without echo are difficult to sing.

Anger puts incantations out of order.

To the shipwrecked sailor, what use is a compass?

Don't ask too much of the world; don't sleep with your wife in your arms while dreaming of high profits; don't light lamps during the day; don't do business with the night; smearing black on other faces will not make your own face any whiter. Remember: don't piss in the wilderness; don't sing in cemeteries; don't make rash promises; don't be a nuisance; make wisdom into something useful.

Motionless shadows may be held in contempt, but one must stand in awe of moving shadows.

The sunbirds all suddenly take off; who is giving chase?

What kind of luck will make your left eyelid stop twitching?

SIX: GHOSTS

The air embraces us, but we have never noticed. The dead have withdrawn from us, into the fields, into the moonlight, but we know exactly where they are—in their joy they will not run farther than a child.

The treasures buried deep and unknown to anyone have all been spent by Time, with nothing in return.

The dead buried deep and gradually forgotten—how can they take care of themselves? They should be moved out of their graves.

The death of others makes us guilty.

Sorrowful winds surround the dead and ask for consolation.

There is to be no death by lightning, no death by drowning, no death by poison, no death in battle, no death by disease, no death by accident, no death by unending laughter or unending crying or gluttonous eating and gluttonous drinking or an unstoppable flow of words until one's strength is exhausted. Well—how then is one to die? Noble death, ugly corpses; a death without a corpse is impossible.

We break up roads and build high-rises to make the ghosts lose their way.

Things left behind by the dead sit in a circle, holding their breath and waiting to be used.

How will the ghosts appear? Unless hats can be transformed into hat ghosts and clothes be transformed into clothes ghosts, flesh-turned-ghosts must be naked, but the appearance of naked ghosts is not in keeping with our current morality.

In the dark, someone reaches out a finger and taps me on the nose.

The tinkle of the devil's chimes is just what I need.

SEVEN: FOURTEEN DREAMS

I dream of lying on my back with a sparrow standing on my chest telling me: "I am your soul!"

I dream of a swimming pool lined with sheets of iron. I lie flat, singing to my heart's content while my feet are kicking the iron and keeping time, but suddenly there is no one left in the pool.

In my dreams I steal things. How can I protest my innocence to the sun?

I dream of a pile of letters on my doorstep. I stoop to pick one up. But this is a love letter I wrote to a girl, years ago! Why has she returned it?

I dream of a woman calling me on the phone. A stranger, a woman who seems as if she is already dead, in a tone of the utmost concern urges me not to attend tonight's party.

I dream of vanishing from the face of the earth. In a subway station, I hear an old lady sobbing.

I dream of Haizi,[3] grinning at me and denying his death.

I dream of Luo Yihe,[4] luring me into a garage, its floor covered in oil stains. In a corner stands a single bed with white sheets. That is where he sleeps, every night.

I dream of entering a meeting room, the air inside thick with smoke. The room is full of men and women seated in chairs, with blurred faces, not saying a word. As I sit down, a man comes storming through the door, his face covered in blood, screaming and shouting: "Who's the traitor?"

I dream of a child falling from a high-rise. Without wings.

I have dreamt of twisted steel, I have dreamt of poisonous leaves—this is a city in the midst of collapse: fires rage, hooded men emerge and vanish. But one small building is left in peace. I am keeping my appointment, sitting on the stone steps outside the entrance, but the person I'm expecting never shows up.

What kind of horse is called a "Horse of Fortune"?

What kind of meteor will set the sea on fire?

I dream of lying on my back, the waves outside my window crashing ever louder. On this solitary island even the seagulls have nowhere to roost, but who is that man, whose is the face that flashes past my window?

EIGHT: WINTER

This is the time when the hair turns gray, this is the time when Orion passes by us, this is the time when the soul loses its moisture and the snow descends on the factory's reception office. A girl sitting down is invited and takes to the dance floor in flickering light, a spare-time writer stops writing and starts to prepare food for the birds of dawn.

Snow is falling, horse dung is freezing.

Village accountants are dancing into the city.

A cat stops en route and enters into debate with itself, in two voices.

A painting incomprehensible to a child remains incomprehensible to this day.

The taxi covered in snow is pure white, like a polar bear. Its engine doesn't work, its body temperature drops to zero. But I can't stand watching it give up,

---

3. Chinese poet (1964–1989) whose literary career has been closely associated with that of Xi Chuan and Luo Yihe. Haizi's suicide in March 1989 shocked the mainland Chinese poetry scene and made him into something of a martyr. In the original, the "child" three stanzas down is to the ear indistinguishable from the poet's name. There is an abundance of texts by and on Haizi; see for example the special section in *Shi tansuo* 1994: 3, 88–119 and *Haizi: The Complete Poems*, ed. Xi Chuan (Shanghai: Sanlian chubanshe, 1997).

4. Chinese poet (1961–1989) whose literary career has been closely associated with that of Xi Chuan and Haizi. Luo Yihe died on 31 May 1989 of a brain hemorrhage. See *Luo Yihe: The Complete Poems*, ed. Zhang Jue (Shanghai: Sanlian chubanshe, 1997).

so I write "I love you" on one of its windows. As my finger moves across the glass, it makes a happy, squeaking sound, just like the forehead of a girl expecting a kiss will start to glow.

Diseases do not go around in winter, diseases do as they please.

Frozen taps save on every drop of water, frozen oceans save on our deaths.

Whenever I wake up in the dead of night, that is when the fire in the stove goes out. Barefoot, I get out of bed, walk toward the fire-stove, rattle the fire-tongs, and fire-flames—gone without saying good-bye—come crackling back into this world to warm the night's saliva and breath. For the one just now dreaming of wolves, my lighting the fire means rescue. How I want to tell him that even in the midst of cold, fire will burn one's hand; wolves' fear of fire must go back to when one among them was burnt by fire.

Oh you hero who break through my door, you can take the money jar from under my bed, take the fire from my stove, but you cannot have my glasses and you cannot have my slippers—you can't live in this world pretending to be me.

An address with no name has made me silent for a long time, a face has been forgotten: another life, another way of killing time, have formed an Other of my flesh and blood. With the address in my hand, I walk into a street full of wind and snow: by what sort of people shall I be admitted, rejected?

Spit marks: there are people living here.

The cold has underrated our endurance.

1992

Syman Rapongan (1957–   )

A FATHER AND SON'S BOAT FOR THE BLACK CURRENT

Translated by Terence C. Russell

A DAY IN OCTOBER, 1990

Night ever so lightly shrouded the island of the Yami people in several layers of black gauze. Fine strands of rain fell intermittently from the sky's pitch-dark clouds and were blown askance by the autumn wind.

In Yama and Yina's[1] public housing residence the clean white walls had been blackened by months and years of wood fires. Even the tube of the single fluorescent lamp had turned black. Yama gently opened the old and shabby door leading inside. "Ah! It's raining outside . . . " He slowly leaned his back against a wall that was as black as his skin and took a deep drag on his cigarette. From the look in his eyes and the expression on his face it was impossible to tell if he was happy or sad. For a Yami man advanced in years it seemed as though everything was determined according to the fatalistic attitude of "we work when the sun comes out and we rest when it sets." But although I say that, they were yet so strong and they had never bowed their heads before anyone on account of life's hardships. Even when they became gravely ill and their lives were coming to an end, in those last few days they still had to labor. What was certain was that there were still a good many years of labor ahead for my father. What brought him joy was that the day had finally come when he

1. Yama and Yina mean "father" and "mother" in the Yami language.

and I would build a boat together. He would educate me in how to select the materials and how to pay homage to the spirits of the mountain forest . . . and so forth. Yama was really anxious for me to learn the traditional and ancient survival techniques. He often told me, "My deepest and greatest shame in life as a father is that you have abandoned the traditional work of our people." He exhaled a large cloud of smoke and quietly hummed a poem that he had composed.

He asked himself apprehensively whether or not the father of his grandchildren was willing to go up the mountain with him to cut wood to build a boat. Besides that, the grandchildren urgently needed money to buy powdered milk. Did they need money or did they need to build a boat? Disconsolately, he hummed another of his songs:

> In his youth he is as sure of himself as I was
> Under the scorching glare of the blazing sun
> He goes back and forth between Big and Little Orchid Isle . . .

"You're not the only Yami who's gone out in the scorching heat of the sun. What're you singing that arrogant song for . . . ?" Unable to bear listening to such a beautiful song, Yina mocked him. Outside, pitch-black clouds filled the sky so that the moon was no longer visible. Resting against the wall, my father spread his palms beneath the fluorescent light and counted the days. He calculated that this was an auspicious night and that he could go and discuss the matter of building a boat with the father of his grandchildren. That is what Yama thought.

The growl of my motorcycle engine shattered the nighttime tranquillity of the village, so I turned off the engine as soon as possible. Tonight that dog of mine, who loved to eat but not to move around, was waiting attentively outside in the rain for me to return from fishing. The sound of his bark drew my father out of the house and into the soaking rain. "Father of my grandchildren, from tonight onwards don't go diving and fishing by yourself. The demons now are a thousand times worse than they were back in my day."

"Yama, every time before I go diving I leave two cigarettes on the shore to beg any dead relatives haunting the shore to protect me," I responded affably to my father.

"Ever since the Chinese came, there have been so many that you can't count them, and also Japanese evil spirits that have come to live on our island. The ones that really will take a person's life are the evil spirits from abroad. So if you are diving at night you must be careful, father of my grandchildren," Yina added.

It was always demons. They were always talking about demons. In my mind there were no demons, but when they spoke to me this time I was a little bit afraid. In my heart I felt extremely unhappy. "Wow, what a lot of fish!" that slightly plump woman of mine exclaimed gleefully. Naturally, although my parents spoke of demons, when they had fresh fish in their stomachs they were endlessly gratified.

Middle of the night. The fine strands of rain continued to swirl down during the night. Nights of autumn wind and rain were the ones I loved the best. I gazed at the scene made visible by the light radiating from the streetlamp. The rain was beautiful indeed. In my hand I held a large bowl of fish soup and I carefully savored the fruits of my own labor. Looking at my children lying every which way on the bed in deep slumber, I thought I was still really a little bit like my father. Shortly afterward, my father stepped out onto the veranda with a cigarette in his mouth. He said, "I've waited over ten years. Do you want to build a boat together with me? The flying fish season is going to be here soon, and a family without a boat is the same as a family without a man."

"Have you still got the physical strength to go up into the mountains and chop wood?" I ventured to ask.

It was as though I could see my father's smiling face through the darkness of the night. He seemed to be ridiculing me for saying the wrong thing. The night breezes carried with the autumn wind brought a slight chill. He was seventy-four years old, but even on a night like this he was naked from the waist up—truly a great father.

"If I've got the nerve to talk to you about building a boat, I've got what it takes to climb the mountain and chop down trees. On the contrary, I'm just afraid that you won't learn the skills of boat building from me," Father was saying.

To be sure, trimming a tree down to a three- or four-centimeter-wide plank was no easy task. On top of that, the plank would be curved, and roughing out the form on the mountain would take not only skill; even more importantly it would be a test of the strength in our arms. As to whether I had more strength than my father, it was just like he said: "Going on external appearances, you are stronger and better developed than me, but compared to when I was your age, you've got a long way to go, my child. Besides, chopping wood doesn't depend entirely on strength. It depends on your technique in wielding the axe . . ."

"If you've still got the strength, then we'll build a boat together," I said.

"It's not a question of whether or not I have the strength; it's whether a man without a boat can be called a Yami man."

He continued, saying, "You look as though you're going to turn into a Taiwanese. If someone says that my son is a sinicized Yami, I'd rather be dead."

Yama was a very traditional man and he had a lot of character. He refused to eat any food that had been fried in salad oil. His favorite food was thus fresh fish. In fact, the thing I had most longed for since returning to live in my native place was to build a boat with my father. Now it was he who had suggested it first. This brought me inexpressible joy.

"It is already very late at night and you are tired from fishing. There are so many things that can wait until we go up the mountain, then I can slowly teach you."

After my father went back into the house, Yina asked him, "Our grandchildren's dad was in Taiwan for over ten years. Is he up to it?"

"If he's not up to it he'll still have to be up to it. He's not Chinese. Someone who uses money to buy fish from someone else is the most useless kind of man . . ."

"True enough, but does our grandchildren's father have the strength and the heart to learn how to build a boat?" In the undisturbed night, no matter how quietly Yina spoke, I could still hear her very clearly. She was right to be concerned. There were many of our young people, who, after they had wandered about in Taiwan for many years, would return home to see their families for three or four days. During that time, all that the older generation could smell on their bodies was the scent of makeup, cologne, and the heavy odor of alcohol. There was not a hint of the smell of seawater or fish on them. The reason my mother questioned my strength was not because I had been tarnished by bad habits, but rather, in her eyes, because I had the qualities of a Chinese,[2] and not the flesh and blood of the Yami people. I had become estranged from the trees and no longer smelled of the soil. These things that Yina said proved that in their hearts I belonged to Generation X, and did not have the status of a traditional laborer.

A CERTAIN DAY AT THE BEGINNING OF NOVEMBER

For our Yami people, boat building was the most important skill and survival tool, and was affirmed by the clansmen to be truly a man's work. Aside from simply making the boat, whether your workmanship was fine, whether the boat was fast or not . . . etc., all was evidence of your abilities. The accumulation of those abilities over a long period of time defined your position in society.

Look! That flow of surging billows on the Black Current, it flows at different rates in winter and summer, and the difference is even greater between the inshore and offshore waters. When there is a full moon or a partial moon, a spring tide or neap tide, the conditions are also never completely the same. Yama and I stood halfway up the mountain where the Yami ancestors, the Stone Man, and the Bamboo Woman met. As we gazed into the distance at the black tide, which looked like a winding river, he gave me this brief explanation.

"When your grandfather was a boy there were twenty-some-odd boats that went fishing from our Yimuluoku Village. If you add the forty-some-odd boats

---

2. Meaning that the Chinese are relatively skilled at manipulating others and their intentions are relatively malicious.

from Yiladai Village, there was a total of almost seventy boats. Where the ocean current passes, those are also the places where the fish are most abundant. One day, the morning waves were quiet. It was in the summer, just at the time when the tidal flow was about to change, so the fish took the bait especially well and our people who were fishing were especially happy. Just at the moment the tide was about to ebb, a strong wind came up and a heavy rain began to fall. Everything more than ten oar lengths away turned pitch-black. The ocean water was flowing to the southeast, which is in the direction of the Philippines. In the blink of an eye, the surf was raging and the currents surged. At the time, any inexperienced people, or any who had not heard the elders talk about how to deal with the powerful sea, were swallowed up by the great ocean. Those who had experience, or who often talked to the old people, were able to follow the current and slowly row toward shore. After the angry, crazy winds, the pelting rain, and the towering waves suddenly subsided there were only sixteen boats from the two villages that were able to follow along the shore reefs and make the return trip. One of them was your great-grandfather's. As for the rest, we could only give blessing to their souls. So, father of my grandchildren, please never forget, when young people are out rowing a boat they must by all means learn to observe the changes of the cloud formations on the ocean horizon to both east and west. When there are spring tides and neap tides, the ocean currents have a direct relationship to the moon. Although you are pretty good at diving and spearfishing, that is completely different from rowing a boat offshore to fish. If you don't have strong arms and thick calluses on your palms, you can't do battle with the sea." Father taught me like this as we were in the process of looking for timber.

"Father of my grandchildren, this tree is *apnorwa*, and that one is *isis*. That tree is *pangohen*. . . . They are all excellent timber for building boats. This *apnorwa* has been waiting for you for more than a decade; it is the best timber for the section of the two sides of the hull. This kind of timber rots the most slowly. This tree is a *cyayi*, and it's the one we will cut down today for the keel . . ."

Before my father cleared away the brush and creepers around the boat's keel he kept reciting something. Then he knelt on the ground and prayed, saying,

> Mountain spirits of the forest
> I am already an old man who is a grandfather
> My voice and the scent of my body
> Are all familiar to you
> The father of my grandchildren has also come to bless you
> Do not allow the knives and axes in our hands to go from
>   sharp to dull
> So that you may be in the ocean sooner
> Crashing through the waves and tall breakers, displaying
>   your heroism.

Pi! . . . With one stroke of the axe the gray-faced egrets and tree leaf butterflies on the peak of Mount Li Baduke were startled into flight. They cried out and chattered, but my father did not give these birds so much as a single glance, fearing that he might catch sight of the *tazkok* bird (an inauspicious bird). As he trimmed the trunk of the tree he prayed again:

> I have waited for you for more than a decade
> Now I trim away the chips of wood that surround you[3]
> Leaving your firmest and strongest parts
> This is a piece of timber filled with the smell of flying fish
> and tilefish[4]

After my father had chopped one third, he handed the axe to me and asked me to recite the last line, "a piece of timber filled with the smell of flying fish and tilefish." . . . The more I recited, the more vigorously I worked until, before long, the tree fell to the ground smoothly. My father then said:

> You are the master of my grandchildren's father
> I beg you to protect my son in the sea
> The glory of a full load of flying fish belongs to you

"Yama, is it necessary to say so much when you are cutting the trees to build a boat?" I asked.

"Trees are the children of the mountain; boats are the grandchildren of the sea. All living things in Nature have a soul. If you don't bless the spirits of Nature in prayer you are not one of the living things on this island. . . . Since we have these rituals, Nature will not thin out our people." What did this have to do with thinning out? I wondered.

"Syman, you lived an aimless life in Taiwan for sixteen years, you have no way of grasping this. You have no way of believing in the way we old people revere all living things on this island. You got an education in Taiwan, but the teachers in Taiwan absolutely did not understand that the souls of the trees have the privilege of being venerated. They only taught you knowledge that has no relevance to the life of our people on this island. I am already well advanced in years. In these final years, while I still have some work left in me, I hope only that you will not cast away these things that your father tells you. Only people who constantly labor can have clear thoughts . . . "

The more we trimmed the tree trunk, the thinner it became. My father looked like someone suffering from malnutrition; his muscles were all atro-

---

3. Meaning to cut away the evil spirits that interfere with good fortune.

4. When beseeching the boat spirits to bring good fortune, the Yami language represents the idea of good fortune with the smell of fish.

phied. But the muscles that remained clung tightly to the bone and were covered with thick veins. They were so clearly defined, I am afraid that muscles built in a body-building gym could never be so beautiful. Carefully, and with the utmost respect, I observed my father slice upward and then down, trimming the wood. He showed not the slightest hint of fatigue. In the deep recesses of my heart I naturally felt very much his inferior.

"*Pi . . . ba, pi . . . ba.*" The sound of the axe rang out crisp and clear over Li Baduke Peak. The calls of the birds, sounding exactly like the immaculate laughter of girls, brought a sense of expansive joy to my heart.

"When you are in the mountains don't be gazing off east and west. The evil spirits in the mountains can easily tell that you are a newcomer, and afterwards things won't go smoothly for you when you work up here . . . "

Why was it that there was not a moment when the specter of ghosts did not float into the elders' thoughts? When the work was going smoothly they would be grateful for the assistance of the demons. When things were not going well, they would use the most severe, the most virulent language to curse the evil spirits. With the first tree—the boat's keel—my father's attitude was very grave. A boat is a grandchild of the sea. Why was that, I wondered? He was a man of seventy-four years, just what kind of divine power drove my father to want to build a boat? Was it the pride of old age, or was it that he wanted me to personally experience the difficulties of building a boat and the pride of finishing one? As I trimmed away at the wood, these things ran through my mind.

"Son, the keel of the boat must be a little higher in the bow and stern. You have to be constantly thinking and rethinking the curvature of the boat, because that determines whether your first boat is fast or not. You have to continually . . . " My father was beside me giving directions. In this way, from the time we cut down the first tree until we cut down the twelfth tree, I learned so much from Yama's words. At the same time, I discovered that the pride gained from living on the island was exactly equal to the extent of my own efforts. During the month and a half that we had been going up the mountain to cut lumber to build the boat I had also learned how to fear and respect the mountain forest, how to say prayers of blessing to the ancestral spirits, and how to love and cherish the basic life essence of the mountains and the sea. What made me ten thousand times more respectful was the survival wisdom that the elders had obtained in exchange for their physical labor. They would bow their heads in humility before the mountain forests and the waves of the great ocean, but they would never be meek and submissive toward others of their people who were equally strong for labor as they. On soil of equal quality they would compete in a good-natured way, either furtively or overtly. They would compete on the same ocean and pass on their determination for survival. Through this process, I came to understand that the character of my people, which seemed to be peacefully weak and fiercely rational, was formed completely through the influence of their environment. The adverse conditions for survival (the environment) had, in the end, instilled in the Yami people their humble character.

THE LAST WEEK IN DECEMBER, 1990

The sun pierced the murky wrinkles of the dark night, and then its reddish skull pushed above the tranquil horizon of the ocean. The sky had finally turned white. My father and I were like obedient children of the sea as we went together to the seaside to bless our boat. The boat floated on the surface of the water like a hero, gazing proudly across the limitless ocean. We squatted at the upper edge of the tide line, where the water lapped on the shore. The stream of ripples rolling in was like the smiles of the Ocean God's multitude of children, all come to welcome our boat enthusiastically.

"Father of my grandchildren, the hull has a slight list to the left. That is because we trimmed relatively less from the left side of the wooden planks. Heavy on the left and light on the right, that's exactly the kind of boat that I wanted. That's because both of us are right-handed and our right arms are stronger. So when we row we will go in a straight line." My father finally broke into a smile as he spoke.

I looked like a solitary hero with no honor guard, or welcoming masses. I sat in my newly built boat and enacted the ritual of a trial voyage. My father was on the shore admiring the speed of the boat and my manner of rowing it.

In two more months flying fish season would begin. The people in the village had long ago sent off the young Yami people who had come from Taiwan to visit their families. All that remained, scattered around the island, were old people with very few years of work left in them, and a few young people who were unfit to make a living in Taiwan, which included me.

One and a half months after the Great Boat and Fish Festival was the Small Boat Ceremony, the most solemn, stately festival to pray for the flying fish. My father wore a silver headdress, and I followed behind him as he walked toward the sea. On my head I wore an *ovay*[5] made of pieces of gold, silver, and bronze foil, and other things considered most precious by our people. In his right hand he held a ceremonial knife and a piece of tender bamboo about a meter and a half long. In his left hand he held a tender leaf of the tropical almond tree that had been boiled in water. Inside were wrapped three newly grown ears of millet that symbolized unending reproduction. My father announced, "On the sea your boat is your life, so the first ear of millet is to bless the soul of the small boat. The second ear is to bless and beseech the spirits of the black-winged flying fish. The third ear is to pray that you, the flying fish, and the hull of the boat will all exist together on the ocean as a single soul that unifies the three in one. You must make supplication, saying: 'With purest heart and the freshest sacrificial blood I bless you (flying fish). I will respectfully obey all the rules of the flying fish season. I wish only that you will fall like drops of rain and fill my new boat so that we may all be blessed together.'" Afterward he cut the bamboo

---

5. Pieces of gilt foil are the tangible commodity most valued by the Yami people.

into three sections. He stuck two of the sections—roughly ten centimeters long—into the rope that secured the oars. The longer section he placed on the right side of the bow. Finally, I stood in the boat facing the limitless, broad ocean and took off my silver headdress. I pointed the open end of the headdress toward the sea and prayed: "I use this silver headdress to call to you and to bless you—food bestowed by the heavenly spirits. I shall forever respect the taboos passed down by your ancestors. My heart has been filled with all of these blessings, just as you alone will fill the hull of my boat, without any other kind of fish mixed in with you."

On the following day I instructed my family members to ask for a day off from school. At dawn, when the sky was just becoming light, everyone in the village who had a boat gathered again on the seashore. They also brought along their fishing gear and waited for the most senior warrior—the leader of the men who would fish for devil's head dagger fish. When all the seafaring men were accounted for, and after the fishing gear had been doused with seawater under the direction of the elders, they all called out to the souls of the flying fish. Following this, the most aged elder was the first to cut through the waves of the Sea God. Then one boat after another struck out toward the area of the sea where they would pursue the schools of devil's head dagger fish. I was the youngest boatman and, naturally, was the last to go out. This was also something that I loved best, because I could enjoy the grand spectacle of one boat after another crashing through the waves. My admirable people, they were all ocean-going worthies well advanced in years. In their slack muscles they carried a determination to survive. They carried the survival skills and culture passed down for more than a thousand years by their ancestors. Their attitude was so resolute, so stable. Just what kind of divine force drew my esteemed elders to go out year after year without fail to observe the rituals of the flying fish season? Was it custom? Was it glory? Was it status? Was it competition? I was constantly mulling over these questions. The whitecaps on the breaking waves were the welcoming smiles of the Sea God's multitude of children. I could hardly wait to follow the elders' trail. I was the last one.

"Go, Son! By respecting the taboos you will bring both you and me peace of mind." My excitement was filled with joy, and my joy was filled with seriousness. My seriousness anticipated a haul of fish, a haul of fish that would bring me, my father, and my family the highest honor. The first oar stroke, the second oar stroke . . . I plunged through the crests of the waves. I scanned the crests for the finned backs of the devil's head dagger fish, with eyes as sharp as an eagle's. A distance of one hundred meters, one kilometer, two kilometers, but my father still stood erect on the pebbles with his hands cupped over his eyes, concentrating on the progress of the boat that we had built together. Perhaps he was giving me his sincere blessing. We went farther and farther. It was as if my father had undergone a chemical reaction and transformed from a human body into a black dot of flesh. But from the ocean I could still see his hands cupped over his brow. Finally, in the rhythm of the rising and falling waves, the black dot that was my father disappeared at the same instant the dawn sun rose in the east and cast its bright rays on the gravel road in the village.

Drifting on the ocean, I felt as though I was a little bit like a Yami man. The boats carrying the old men of stout determination but slack muscles intermittently brushed against each other as they went, moving in parallel. The men's faces expressed an inner happiness at being on the sea, which moved me tremendously. "Syman, be careful of the waves. We warmly welcome you into the Mataw fleet, a tradition passed down from our ancestors." At that point I had truly shed the false, hollow garb of my decade or more in Taipei, so it seemed. The sunlight leapt over the peak of Mount Du Se'ente. Strands of its radiance scorched my seemingly strong, mature flesh.

Wow, a devil's head dagger fish burst through the surface of the ocean and into the air beside my boat. When it plunged back into the water, the spray it threw up soaked my shirt. Wow! That's my big fish! I quickly grabbed hold of my fishing line, thus beginning my battle of wisdom and physical strength against the big fish. This was no joke. That was a huge fish! In order not to be disgraced before the fleet, in order to demonstrate that I was a Yami man, and in order to show my strength, I did not give the devil's head dagger fish an opportunity to collect itself, but hauled in the line for all I was worth. However, the fish was, after all, a creature of the sea, and its strength was no less than mine. It took ten minutes, but I finally defeated that big fish. Just as I was dragging the fish into my boat a lot of people noticed that I had caught a devil's head dagger fish, and I was only the second to do so. There was still no news from the other forty or fifty boats. The old men complimented me on my good luck with their smiling faces. I was now dripping in sweat on account of the ten-minute-long test, so I took off my shirt, at the same moment shedding the false, artificial outer garments of my sinicization. Now I could absorb the scorching ultraviolet rays of sunlight and the drenching of the waves on an equal basis with my people. Hey . . . I was a Yami, truly, and absolutely not a civilized Yami youth. I stroked the rolling ocean current with both hands and recited to myself, "You recognize me now, Ocean." Then I communicated with the soul of my boat, saying, "May you and I always be sons of the Sea God and display our heroism on the ocean."

Three kilometers, two kilometers, one hundred meters, ten meters . . . we drew closer and closer to the shore. My father and the elders who came to welcome the fleet had been on the shore chatting for a long time. Long ago, in the years of their prime, on days like today they had been called heroes. All of them had their hands cupped over their brows as they tried to guess who the first boatman of the returning fleet would be. (On the first day of Mataw[6] anyone

6. Mataw takes place after the second ceremony to call the fish. There is a period of five days when it is permitted to angle only for flying fish and devil's head dagger fish. All other fishing activities are prohibited.

who has not caught a devil's head dagger fish cannot be the first to return home.) They hoped that he would bring back good news. The closer the boats came, the clearer the shrunken forms of the elders became. Naturally, during the journey back they had been engaged in animated discussions of who, in their opinion, that person would be. In his heart, Yama must have known long ago that it would be me, but the rest of the elders, no matter how they tried, could not guess that it would be a novice like me leading the return journey. They thought that under such conditions, for a novice, if the fishing line did not get tangled, he would have absolutely no patience. My father's heart beat furiously in his breast, fearing only that I was bringing bad news.

Sybon[7] is the grandson's father. Wow . . . as I was rowing *mapaboz*, backing the stern toward the shore,[8] I could see the expression on my father's face. He was completely puzzled. The other elders had all straightened up and were looking left and right to see if there was the tail of a big fish in the bow of the boat. The tide had gone out a long way and there were reef rocks jutting above the surface of the water. This meant that as I rowed for shore I had to follow a snaking path. I pretended that I had not caught a big fish, deliberately looking very disappointed, rather than smiling broadly. But I was holding my joy under the tip of my tongue. Four or five elders strained their necks to try to see into my boat. At that moment my father, who had stepped into the water some time before, took hold of the *morong*[9] on my stern. He finally showed those teeth of his that had been stained by sixty years of betel nut juice. As for me . . . my smile was the highest form of tribute I could give the elders. It showed that this year there might be a good catch of fish. Not bad, eh! For a novice to return without an empty boat was good luck! Syman Rapongan had not been sinicized. . . . Syman had caught a fish to give in tribute to the soul of the moorage harbor. They were truly grateful for the good news that I had brought. . . . Through the homage paid by the elders I reaped the most sacred of blessings and confirmed that I was a brave Yami warrior of the sea. At noontime, as the Mataw fleet returned to shore, one boat after the other, all of the braves had also scored well. Under the noontime sun, I did not know if my grandfather's soul had also given me his blessing in the underworld. Yama, Yina, my wife, and my children all flocked around me joyfully smiling. I thought, this is something that can be much admired in people without civilization—they use accomplishments gained from their labor to build up their social position. Next year, the year after, and even if I am fortunate enough to still be breathing at eighty, I will always want to respect the taboos of the flying fish and take part in the fishing procession.

1993

---

7. Sybon refers to the grandfather's generation.

8. This manner of beaching a boat is referred to as *mapaboz* in the Yami language.

9. The top section of the boat's decorative mast.

PERMISSIONS

Grateful acknowledgment is due to the following individuals and publishers for permission to reprint copyrighted material. Minor emendations (orthography, punctuation, etc.) have occasionally been made for the sake of consistency.

Arcade Publishing, for story by Mo Yan, "Iron Child," from *Shifu, You'll Do Anything for a Laugh,* trans. Howard Goldblatt (2001).

Center for Chinese Studies, the University of Michigan, for the story by Chen Yingzhen, "My Kid Brother Kangxiong," from *Exiles at Home: Stories by Ch'en Ying-chen* (1986), trans. Lucien Miller.

Center for Taiwan Studies, University of California, Santa Barbara, for the story by Tzeng Ching-wen, "Redeeming a Painting," trans. Jenn-shann Lin and Lois Stanford, from *Magnolia: Stories of Taiwanese Women* (2005).

Chinese PEN, for the story by Xi Xi, "A Woman Like Me," trans. Howard Goldblatt (Spring 1984).

Chinese University Press, for poems by Dai Wangshu, "Rainy Alley," "Written on a Prison Wall," "With My Injured Hand," from Gregory Lee, *Dai Wangshu: The Life and Poetry of a Chinese Modernist* (1989).

Chiu Ko Press, Taipei, for the poem by Yu Guangzhong, "The White Jade Bitter Gourd," from Yu Kwang-chung, *The Night Watchman* (1992), trans. the author.

Columbia University Press, for stories by Yu Dafu, "Sinking," trans. Joseph S. M. Lau and C. T. Hsia; Shen Congwen, "Xiaoxiao," trans. Eugene Chen Eoyang; Ling Shuhua, "The Night of Midautumn Festival," trans. Nathan K. Mao; Zhang Tianyi, "Midautumn Festival," trans. Ronald Miao; Ding Ling, "When I Was in Xia Village," trans. Gary Bjorge; Wu Zuxiang, "Young Master Gets His Tonic," trans. Cyril Birch; Xiao Hong, "Hands," trans. Howard Goldblatt, from *Modern Chinese Stories and Novellas: 1919–1949* (1981), ed. Joseph S. M. Lau, C. T. Hsia, and Leo Ou-fan Lee; and by Pai Hsien-yung (Bai Xianyong), "Winter Nights," trans. John Kwan-Terry and Stephen Lacey; Wang Chen-ho, "An Oxcart for a Dowry," trans. the author and Jon Jackson, from *Chinese Stories from Taiwan: 1960–1970* (1976), ed. Joseph S. M. Lau, with Timothy A. Ross; Huang Chunming, "The Fish," trans. Howard Goldblatt, from Huang Chunming, *The Taste of Apples*, trans. Howard Goldblatt (2001). Wang Jo-wang [Wang Ruowang], "A Visit to His Excellency: A Five-Minute Movie," from *Literature of the Hundred Flowers*, Vol. II: *Poetry and Fiction* (1981), ed. and co-trans., Hualing Nieh; poem by Luo Qing, "Six Ways of Eating Watermelons," from *The Isle Full of Noises: Modern Poetry from Taiwan* (1987), ed. and trans. Dominic Cheung; and poem by Shang Qin, "The Cat Who Walks Through the Wall," from *Frontier Taiwan: An Anthology of Modern Chinese Poetry* (2001), ed. Michelle Yeh and N. G. D. Malmqvist.

Commercial Press, Ltd., Hong Kong, for the story by Ye Shaojun, "A Posthumous Son," trans. Bonnie S. McDougall, from A *Posthumous Son and Other Stories* (1979), trans. Bonnie S. McDougall and Lewis S. Robinson; poems by Xu Zhimo, "Chance"; Mu Dan, "Self," "Song of Wisdom"; Bai Qiu, "Moth," "Vagabond," from *100 Modern Chinese Poems* (1987), ed. and trans. Pang Bingjun and John Minford with Seán Golden.

Doubleday, a division of Bantam Doubleday Dell Publishing Group, for poems by Xu Zhimo, "Second Farewell to Cambridge," "Love's Inspiration"; Wen Yiduo, "Dead Water," "One Sentence," "Prayer"; Li Jinfa, "Woman Abandoned," "Never to Return"; Feng Zhi, "Sonnet 2," "Sonnet 4," "Sonnet 27"; He Qifang, "Prophecy," "Thinking of a Friend at Year's End," "Autumn"; Zheng Min, "A Glance," "The Lotus Flower," from *Twentieth-Century Chinese Poetry: An Anthology* (1963), trans. and ed. Kai-yu Hsu.

Fiction, for the story by Wang Zengqi, "Small-Hands Chen," trans. Howard Goldblatt, vol. 8, nos. 2 and 3 (1987).

Foreign Languages Press, Beijing, for poems by Ai Qing, "Snow Falls on China's Land," "The North," from *Selected Poems of Ai Ching* (1982), trans. Eugene Chen Eoyang; and Mao Dun, "Spring Silkworms," trans. Sidney Shapiro, from *Chinese Literature*.

Green River Press, Inc., for Ba Jin, "Remembering Xiao Shan," trans. Michael S. Duke, from *Perspectives in Contemporary Chinese Literature* (1983), ed. Mason Y. H. Wang.

HarperCollins, for the story by Gao Xingjian, "The Accident," trans. Mabel Lee, from *Buying a Fishing Rod for My Grandfather* (2004).

Harper's, for the story by Wang Zengqi, "A Tail," trans. Howard Goldblatt (April 1989).

Heat 4: New Series, Burnt Ground, for story by Alai, "Fish!" trans. Howard Goldblatt (2002).

Indiana University Press, for material by Lu Xun from *The Complete Stories of Lu Xun* (1981), trans. Yang Xianyi and Gladys Yang, "Preface to the First Collection of Short Stories, *Call to Arms*," "A Madman's Diary," and "Kong Yiji."

Mei Ya Publications, Inc., Taipei, for the poem by Yu Guangzhong, "If There's a War Raging Afar," from Yu Kwang-chung, *Acres of Barbed Wire* (1971), trans. the author.

Micromegas (vol. 5, no. 3), Department of Comparative Literature, University of Massachusetts, for poems by Ji Xian, "Spring Dancing," "A Wolf"; Luo Fu, "City: Saigon, 1967," "Following the Sound of Rain Into the Mountains"; Zheng Chouyu, "Pagoda," "Grenz-Taverne," "Clear and Bright: In the Grave," guest ed. and trans. Ching-hsien Wang.

New Directions 45 (1982), for poems by Bian Zhilin, "A Buddhist Monk," "A Round Treasure-Box," "Feverish Night," trans. Eugene Chen Eoyang.

New Directions Publishing Corporation, and Anvil Press Poetry (London), for poems by Bei Dao, "Declaration," "Résumé," "Another Legend," from *The August Sleepwalker* (1990), trans. Bonnie S. McDougall and Susan Ternent Cooke.

Northwestern University Press, for the story by Can Xue, "Hut on the Mountain," from *Dialogues in Paradise* (1989), trans. Ronald R. Janssen and Jian Zhang.

Renditions, a Chinese-English Translation Magazine, published by the Research Centre for Translation, Chinese University of Hong Kong, for copyrighted material by:

Chen Jinghua, "Our Will to Settle Here Will Never Fail," trans. Richard King, no. 50 (Autumn 1998).

Chen Ruoxi, "The Tunnel," trans. Chi-chen Wang, no. 10 (Autumn 1978).

Feng Zikai, "Bombs in Yishan," trans. D. E. Pollard, no. 38 (Autumn 1992).

Hua Tong, "Yan'an Seeds," trans. Mark Caltonhill, no. 50 (Autumn 1998).

Lao She, "An Old and Established Name," trans. William A. Lyell, no. 10 (Autumn 1978).

Li Ang, "Curvaceous Dolls," trans. Howard Goldblatt, nos. 27 and 28 (Spring and Autumn 1987).

Lu Xun, "Epigraph," "Autumn Night," "Hope," from *Wild Grass*, trans. Ng Mau-sang, no. 26 (Autumn 1986); "The Evolution of the Male Sex," trans. D. E. Pollard, no. 31 (Spring 1989).

Luo Zhicheng (Lo Chih-cheng), "Spring 2001, Unreachable Civilization," trans. Sylvia Li-chun Lin, no. 61 (Spring 2004).

Shu Ting, "The Cry of a Generation," trans. Richard King, no. 50 (Autumn 1998); "When You Walk Past My Window," "A Roadside Encounter," and "Assembly Line," trans. Eva Hung, nos. 27 and 28 (Spring and Autumn 1987).

Wang Xipeng, "A Group of Urban Youths Is on Its Way," trans. Richard King, no. 50 (Autumn 1998).

Xi Chuan, "Salute," trans. Maghiel van Crevel, no. 51 (Spring 1999).

Xiao Wenyuan, "A Bizarre Kind of Robbery," trans. D. E. Pollard, no. 31 (Spring 1989).

Zhang Dachun, "Lucky Worries About His Country," trans. Chu Chiyu, nos. 35 and 36 (Spring and Autumn 1991).

Zhou Zuoren, "In Praise of Mutes" and "The Aging of Ghosts," trans. D. E. Pollard; "Reading on the Toilet," trans. Don Cohn, no. 26 (Autumn 1986).

Renditions Books, Hong Kong, for copyrighted material by Huang Guobin, "A Night Prayer," and "When You Are Naked, You Have Everything," trans. the author, from *Trees on the Mountain: An Anthology of New Chinese Writing* (1984), ed. Stephen C. Soong and John Minford.

Renditions Paperbacks, Hong Kong, for copyrighted material by Gu Cheng, "An Ending" and "Curriculum Vitae," from *Selected Poems by Gu Cheng* (1990), ed. Seán

Golden and Chu Chiyu; and Yuan Qiongqiong, "Cat," trans. Howard Goldblatt, from *Contemporary Women Writers: Hong Kong and Taiwan* (1990), ed. Eva Hung.

M. E. Sharpe, Inc., for the story by Liu Yichang, "Wrong Number," trans. Michael S. Duke, from *Worlds of Modern Chinese Fiction: Short Stories and Novellas from the People's Republic, Taiwan, and Hong Kong* (1991), ed. Michael S. Duke.

Stanford University Press, for the story by Li Rui, "Electing a Thief," trans. Jeffrey C. Kinkley, from *Furrows: Peasants, Intellectuals, and the State* (1990), ed. Helen F. Siu.

Taiwan Literature: English Translation Series, for stories by Lai Ho (Lai He), "The 'Steelyard,'" trans. Howard Goldblatt, and Wu Zho-liu (Wu Zhuoliu), "The Doctor's Mother," trans. Sylvia Li-chun Lin, no. 15 (July 2004); and Ch'iu Miao-chin (Qiu Miaojin), "Letters from Montmartre," trans., Howard Goldblatt, no. 11 (July 2002); and essay by Syman Rapongan, "A Father and Son's Boat for the Black Current," trans. Terence Russell, no. 17 (July 2005).

Tiananmen Publications, Kingston, Australia, for poems by Yang Lian, "To a Nine-Year-Old Girl Killed in the Massacre" and "The Dead in Exile," from *The Dead in Exile* (1990), trans. Mabel Lee.

University of California Press, for poems by Zhou Mengdie, "Kingdom of Solitude" and "Under the Bodhi Tree"; Luo Fu, "Beyond the Fog"; Ye Weilian, "The River's Fancy" and "The Pursuit"; Xiong Hong, "The Deluded Dream" and "Fire on The Sea Floor," from *Modern Verse from Taiwan* (1972), ed. and trans. Angela C. Y. Yung Palandri, with Robert J. Bertholf.

University of Hawaii Press, for poems by Wang Xiaolong, "When We Finally Turn Fifty" and "Surgery Ward," from *The Red Azalea: Chinese Poetry Since the Cultural Revolution* (1990), ed. Edward Morin, trans. Fang Dai, Dennis Ding, and Edward Morin.

Zephyr Press, for poems by Xia Yu, "The Ripest Rankest Juiciest Summer Ever," "Continuing Our Discussion of Boredom and Ennui," and "L'Empire à la Fin de la Décadence," from Hsia Yü, *Fusion Kitsch* (2001), trans. Steve Bradbury.

ZYZZYVA, for stories by Wang Meng, "Tales of New Cathay" ("Disputatiasis," "Little Little Little Little Little," and "Right to the Heart of the Matter"), trans. Howard Goldblatt, vol. 1, no. 2 (1985); Yuan Qiongqiong, "A Lover's Ear," trans. Howard Goldblatt, vol. 1, no. 3 (1985).

OTHER WORKS IN THE COLUMBIA ASIAN STUDIES SERIES

TRANSLATIONS FROM THE ASIAN CLASSICS

Major Plays of Chikamatsu, tr. Donald Keene 1961

Four Major Plays of Chikamatsu, tr. Donald Keene. Paperback ed. only. 1961; rev. ed. 1997

Records of the Grand Historian of China, translated from the Shih chi of Ssu-ma Ch'ien, tr. Burton Watson, 2 vols. 1961

Instructions for Practical Living and Other Neo-Confucian Writings by Wang Yang-ming, tr. Wing-tsit Chan 1963

Hsün Tzu: Basic Writings, tr. Burton Watson, paperback ed. only. 1963; rev. ed. 1996

Chuang Tzu: Basic Writings, tr. Burton Watson, paperback ed. only. 1964; rev. ed. 1996

The Mahābhārata, tr. Chakravarthi V. Narasimhan. Also in paperback ed. 1965; rev. ed. 1997

The Manyōshū, Nippon Gakujutsu Shinkōkai edition 1965

Su Tung-p'o: Selections from a Sung Dynasty Poet, tr. Burton Watson. Also in paperback ed. 1965

Bhartrihari: Poems, tr. Barbara Stoler Miller. Also in paperback ed. 1967

Basic Writings of Mo Tzu, Hsün Tzu, and Han Fei Tzu, tr. Burton Watson. Also in separate paperback eds. 1967

The Awakening of Faith, Attributed to Aśvaghosha, tr. Yoshito S. Hakeda. Also in paperback ed. 1967

Reflections on Things at Hand: The Neo-Confucian Anthology, comp. Chu Hsi and Lü Tsu-ch'ien, tr. Wing-tsit Chan 1967

The Platform Sutra of the Sixth Patriarch, tr. Philip B. Yampolsky. Also in paperback ed. 1967

Essays in Idleness: The Tsurezuregusa of Kenkō, tr. Donald Keene. Also in paperback ed. 1967

The Pillow Book of Sei Shōnagon, tr. Ivan Morris, 2 vols. 1967

Two Plays of Ancient India: The Little Clay Cart and the Minister's Seal, tr. J. A. B. van Buitenen 1968

The Complete Works of Chuang Tzu, tr. Burton Watson 1968

The Romance of the Western Chamber (Hsi Hsiang chi), tr. S. I. Hsiung. Also in paperback ed. 1968

The Manyōshū, Nippon Gakujutsu Shinkōkai edition. Paperback ed. only. 1969

Records of the Historian: Chapters from the Shih chi of Ssu-ma Ch'ien, tr. Burton Watson. Paperback ed. only. 1969

Cold Mountain: 100 Poems by the T'ang Poet Han-shan, tr. Burton Watson. Also in paperback ed. 1970

Twenty Plays of the Nō Theatre, ed. Donald Keene. Also in paperback ed. 1970

Chūshingura: The Treasury of Loyal Retainers, tr. Donald Keene. Also in paperback ed. 1971; rev. ed. 1997

The Zen Master Hakuin: Selected Writings, tr. Philip B. Yampolsky 1971

Chinese Rhyme-Prose: Poems in the Fu Form from the Han and Six Dynasties Periods, tr. Burton Watson. Also in paperback ed. 1971

Kūkai: Major Works, tr. Yoshito S. Hakeda. Also in paperback ed. 1972

The Old Man Who Does as He Pleases: Selections from the Poetry and Prose of Lu Yu, tr. Burton Watson 1973

The Lion's Roar of Queen Śrīmālā, tr. Alex and Hideko Wayman 1974

Courtier and Commoner in Ancient China: Selections from the History of the Former Han by Pan Ku, tr. Burton Watson. Also in paperback ed. 1974

Japanese Literature in Chinese, vol. 1: *Poetry and Prose in Chinese by Japanese Writers of the Early Period*, tr. Burton Watson 1975

Japanese Literature in Chinese, vol. 2: *Poetry and Prose in Chinese by Japanese Writers of the Later Period*, tr. Burton Watson 1976

Scripture of the Lotus Blossom of the Fine Dharma, tr. Leon Hurvitz. Also in paperback ed. 1976

Love Song of the Dark Lord: Jayadeva's Gītagovinda, tr. Barbara Stoler Miller. Also in paperback ed. Cloth ed. includes critical text of the Sanskrit. 1977; rev. ed. 1997

Ryōkan: Zen Monk-Poet of Japan, tr. Burton Watson 1977

Calming the Mind and Discerning the Real: From the Lam rim chen mo of Tsoṇ-kha-pa, tr. Alex Wayman 1978

The Hermit and the Love-Thief: Sanskrit Poems of Bhartrihari and Bilhaṇa, tr. Barbara Stoler Miller 1978

The Lute: Kao Ming's P'i-p'a chi, tr. Jean Mulligan. Also in paperback ed. 1980

A Chronicle of Gods and Sovereigns: Jinnō Shōtōki of Kitabatake Chikafusa, tr. H. Paul Varley 1980
Among the Flowers: The Hua-chien chi, tr. Lois Fusek 1982
Grass Hill: Poems and Prose by the Japanese Monk Gensei, tr. Burton Watson 1983
Doctors, Diviners, and Magicians of Ancient China: Biographies of Fang-shih, tr. Kenneth J. DeWoskin. Also in paperback ed. 1983
Theater of Memory: The Plays of Kālidāsa, ed. Barbara Stoler Miller. Also in paperback ed. 1984
The Columbia Book of Chinese Poetry: From Early Times to the Thirteenth Century, ed. and tr. Burton Watson. Also in paperback ed. 1984
Poems of Love and War: From the Eight Anthologies and the Ten Long Poems of Classical Tamil, tr. A. K. Ramanujan. Also in paperback ed. 1985
The Bhagavad Gita: Krishna's Counsel in Time of War, tr. Barbara Stoler Miller 1986
The Columbia Book of Later Chinese Poetry, ed. and tr. Jonathan Chaves. Also in paperback ed. 1986
The Tso Chuan: Selections from China's Oldest Narrative History, tr. Burton Watson 1989
Waiting for the Wind: Thirty-six Poets of Japan's Late Medieval Age, tr. Steven Carter 1989
Selected Writings of Nichiren, ed. Philip B. Yampolsky 1990
Saigyō, Poems of a Mountain Home, tr. Burton Watson 1990
The Book of Lieh Tzu: A Classic of the Tao, tr. A. C. Graham. Morningside ed. 1990
The Tale of an Anklet: An Epic of South India—The Cilappatikāram of Iḷaṅkō Aṭikaḷ, tr. R. Parthasarathy 1993
Waiting for the Dawn: A Plan for the Prince, tr. and introduction by Wm. Theodore de Bary 1993
Yoshitsune and the Thousand Cherry Trees: A Masterpiece of the Eighteenth-Century Japanese Puppet Theater, tr., annotated, and with introduction by Stanleigh H. Jones, Jr. 1993
The Lotus Sutra, tr. Burton Watson. Also in paperback ed. 1993
The Classic of Changes: A New Translation of the I Ching *as Interpreted by Wang Bi*, tr. Richard John Lynn 1994
Beyond Spring: Tz'u Poems of the Sung Dynasty, tr. Julie Landau 1994
The Columbia Anthology of Traditional Chinese Literature, ed. Victor H. Mair 1994
Scenes for Mandarins: The Elite Theater of the Ming, tr. Cyril Birch 1995
Letters of Nichiren, ed. Philip B. Yampolsky; tr. Burton Watson et al. 1996
Unforgotten Dreams: Poems by the Zen Monk Shōtetsu, tr. Steven D. Carter 1997
The Vimalakirti Sutra, tr. Burton Watson 1997
Japanese and Chinese Poems to Sing: The Wakan rōei shū, tr. J. Thomas Rimer and Jonathan Chaves 1997
Breeze Through Bamboo: Kanshi of Ema Saikō, tr. Hiroaki Sato 1998
A Tower for the Summer Heat, Li Yu, tr. Patrick Hanan 1998
Traditional Japanese Theater: An Anthology of Plays, Karen Brazell 1998
The Original Analects: Sayings of Confucius and His Successors (0479–0249), E. Bruce Brooks and A. Taeko Brooks 1998

The Classic of the Way and Virtue: A New Translation of the Tao-te ching *of Laozi as Interpreted by Wang Bi*, tr. Richard John Lynn 1999

The Four Hundred Songs of War and Wisdom: An Anthology of Poems from Classical Tamil, The Puṛanāṇūṛu, ed. and tr. George L. Hart and Hank Heifetz 1999

Original Tao: Inward Training (Nei-yeh) *and the Foundations of Taoist Mysticism*, by Harold D. Roth 1999

Lao Tzu's Tao Te Ching: *A Translation of the Startling New Documents Found at Guodian*, by Robert G. Henricks 2000

The Shorter Columbia Anthology of Traditional Chinese Literature, ed. Victor H. Mair 2000

Mistress and Maid (Jiaohongji), by Meng Chengshun, tr. Cyril Birch 2001

Chikamatsu: Five Late Plays, tr. and ed. C. Andrew Gerstle 2001

The Essential Lotus: Selections from the Lotus Sutra, tr. Burton Watson 2002

Early Modern Japanese Literature: An Anthology, 1600–1900, ed. Haruo Shirane 2002

The Sound of the Kiss, or The Story That Must Never Be Told: Pingali Suranna's Kalapurnodayamu, tr. Vecheru Narayana Rao and David Shulman 2003

The Selected Poems of Du Fu, tr. Burton Watson 2003

Far Beyond the Field: Haiku by Japanese Women, tr. Makoto Ueda 2003

Just Living: Poems and Prose by the Japanese Monk Tonna, ed. and tr. Steven D. Carter 2003

Han Feizi: Basic Writings, tr. Burton Watson 2003

Mozi: Basic Writings, tr. Burton Watson 2003

Xunzi: Basic Writings, tr. Burton Watson 2003

Zhuangzi: Basic Writings, tr. Burton Watson 2003

The Awakening of Faith, Attributed to Aśvaghosha, tr. Yoshito S. Hakeda, introduction by Ryuichi Abe 2005

The Tales of the Heike, tr. Burton Watson, ed. Haruo Shirane 2006

Tales of Moonlight and Rain, Ueda Akinari, tr. and introduction by Anthony H. Chambers

MODERN ASIAN LITERATURE

Modern Japanese Drama: An Anthology, ed. and tr. Ted. Takaya. Also in paperback ed. 1979

Mask and Sword: Two Plays for the Contemporary Japanese Theater, by Yamazaki Masakazu, tr. J. Thomas Rimer 1980

Yokomitsu Riichi, Modernist, Dennis Keene 1980

Nepali Visions, Nepali Dreams: The Poetry of Laxmiprasad Devkota, tr. David Rubin 1980

Literature of the Hundred Flowers, vol. 1: *Criticism and Polemics*, ed. Hualing Nieh 1981

Literature of the Hundred Flowers, vol. 2: *Poetry and Fiction*, ed. Hualing Nieh 1981

Modern Chinese Stories and Novellas, 1919–1949, ed. Joseph S. M. Lau, C. T. Hsia, and Leo Ou-fan Lee. Also in paperback ed. 1984

A View by the Sea, by Yasuoka Shōtarō, tr. Kären Wigen Lewis 1984

Other Worlds: Arishima Takeo and the Bounds of Modern Japanese Fiction, by Paul Anderer 1984

Selected Poems of Sō Chōngju, tr. with introduction by David R. McCann 1989
The Sting of Life: Four Contemporary Japanese Novelists, by Van C. Gessel 1989
Stories of Osaka Life, by Oda Sakunosuke, tr. Burton Watson 1990
The Bodhisattva, or Samantabhadra, by Ishikawa Jun, tr. with introduction by William Jefferson Tyler 1990
The Travels of Lao Ts'an, by Liu T'ieh-yün, tr. Harold Shadick. Morningside ed. 1990
Three Plays by Kōbō Abe, tr. with introduction by Donald Keene 1993
The Columbia Anthology of Modern Chinese Literature, ed. Joseph S. M. Lau and Howard Goldblatt 1995
Modern Japanese Tanka, ed. and tr. Makoto Ueda 1996
Masaoka Shiki: Selected Poems, ed. and tr. Burton Watson 1997
Writing Women in Modern China: An Anthology of Women's Literature from the Early Twentieth Century, ed. and tr. Amy D. Dooling and Kristina M. Torgeson 1998
American Stories, by Nagai Kafū, tr. Mitsuko Iriye 2000
The Paper Door and Other Stories, by Shiga Naoya, tr. Lane Dunlop 2001
Grass for My Pillow, by Saiichi Maruya, tr. Dennis Keene 2002
For All My Walking: Free-Verse Haiku of Taneda Santōka, with Excerpts from His Diaries, tr. Burton Watson 2003
The Columbia Anthology of Modern Japanese Literature, ed. J. Thomas Rimer and Van C. Gessel, vol. 1, 2005

STUDIES IN ASIAN CULTURE

The Ōnin War: History of Its Origins and Background, with a Selective Translation of the Chronicle of Ōnin, by H. Paul Varley 1967
Chinese Government in Ming Times: Seven Studies, ed. Charles O. Hucker 1969
The Actors' Analects (Yakusha Rongo), ed. and tr. Charles J. Dunn and Bungō Torigoe 1969
Self and Society in Ming Thought, by Wm. Theodore de Bary and the Conference on Ming Thought. Also in paperback ed. 1970
A History of Islamic Philosophy, by Majid Fakhry, 2d ed. 1983
Phantasies of a Love Thief: The Caurapañatcāśikā Attributed to Bilhaṇa, by Barbara Stoler Miller 1971
Iqbal: Poet-Philosopher of Pakistan, ed. Hafeez Malik 1971
The Golden Tradition: An Anthology of Urdu Poetry, ed. and tr. Ahmed Ali. Also in paperback ed. 1973
Conquerors and Confucians: Aspects of Political Change in Late Yüan China, by John W. Dardess 1973
The Unfolding of Neo-Confucianism, by Wm. Theodore de Bary and the Conference on Seventeenth-Century Chinese Thought. Also in paperback ed. 1975
To Acquire Wisdom: The Way of Wang Yang-ming, by Julia Ching 1976
Gods, Priests, and Warriors: The Bhrgus of the Mahābhārata, by Robert P. Goldman 1977
Mei Yao-ch'en and the Development of Early Sung Poetry, by Jonathan Chaves 1976
The Legend of Semimaru, Blind Musician of Japan, by Susan Matisoff 1977
Sir Sayyid Ahmad Khan and Muslim Modernization in India and Pakistan, by Hafeez Malik 1980

The Khilafat Movement: Religious Symbolism and Political Mobilization in India, by Gail Minault 1982

The World of K'ung Shang-jen: A Man of Letters in Early Ch'ing China, by Richard Strassberg 1983

The Lotus Boat: The Origins of Chinese Tz'u Poetry in T'ang Popular Culture, by Marsha L. Wagner 1984

Expressions of Self in Chinese Literature, ed. Robert E. Hegel and Richard C. Hessney 1985

Songs for the Bride: Women's Voices and Wedding Rites of Rural India, by W. G. Archer; ed. Barbara Stoler Miller and Mildred Archer 1986

The Confucian Kingship in Korea: Yŏngjo and the Politics of Sagacity, by JaHyun Kim Haboush 1988

COMPANIONS TO ASIAN STUDIES

Approaches to the Oriental Classics, ed. Wm. Theodore de Bary 1959

Early Chinese Literature, by Burton Watson. Also in paperback ed. 1962

Approaches to Asian Civilizations, ed. Wm. Theodore de Bary and Ainslie T. Embree 1964

The Classic Chinese Novel: A Critical Introduction, by C. T. Hsia. Also in paperback ed. 1968

Chinese Lyricism: Shih Poetry from the Second to the Twelfth Century, tr. Burton Watson. Also in paperback ed. 1971

A Syllabus of Indian Civilization, by Leonard A. Gordon and Barbara Stoler Miller 1971

Twentieth-Century Chinese Stories, ed. C. T. Hsia and Joseph S. M. Lau. Also in paperback ed. 1971

A Syllabus of Chinese Civilization, by J. Mason Gentzler, 2d ed. 1972

A Syllabus of Japanese Civilization, by H. Paul Varley, 2d ed. 1972

An Introduction to Chinese Civilization, ed. John Meskill, with the assistance of J. Mason Gentzler 1973

An Introduction to Japanese Civilization, ed. Arthur E. Tiedemann 1974

Ukifune: Love in the Tale of Genji, ed. Andrew Pekarik 1982

The Pleasures of Japanese Literature, by Donald Keene 1988

A Guide to Oriental Classics, ed. Wm. Theodore de Bary and Ainslie T. Embree; 3d edition ed. Amy Vladeck Heinrich, 2 vols. 1989

INTRODUCTION TO ASIAN CIVILIZATIONS

Wm. Theodore de Bary, General Editor

Sources of Japanese Tradition, 1958; paperback ed., 2 vols., 1964. 2d ed., vol. 1, 2001, compiled by Wm. Theodore de Bary, Donald Keene, George Tanabe, and Paul Varley; vol. 2, 2005, compiled by Wm. Theodore de Bary, Carol Gluck, and Arthur E. Tiedemann; vol. 2, abridged, 2 pts., 2006, compiled by Wm. Theodore de Bary, Carol Gluck, and Arthur E. Tiedemann

Sources of Indian Tradition, 1958; paperback ed., 2 vols., 1964. 2d ed., 2 vols., 1988

Sources of Chinese Tradition, 1960, paperback ed., 2 vols., 1964. 2d ed., vol. 1, 1999, compiled by Wm. Theodore de Bary and Irene Bloom; vol. 2, 2000, compiled by Wm. Theodore de Bary and Richard Lufrano

Sources of Korean Tradition, 1997; 2 vols., vol. 1, 1997, compiled by Peter H. Lee and Wm. Theodore de Bary; vol. 2, 2001, compiled by Yŏngho Ch'oe, Peter H. Lee, and Wm. Theodore de Bary

NEO-CONFUCIAN STUDIES

Instructions for Practical Living and Other Neo-Confucian Writings by Wang Yang-ming, tr. Wing-tsit Chan 1963

Reflections on Things at Hand: The Neo-Confucian Anthology, comp. Chu Hsi and Lü Tsu-ch'ien, tr. Wing-tsit Chan 1967

Self and Society in Ming Thought, by Wm. Theodore de Bary and the Conference on Ming Thought. Also in paperback ed. 1970

The Unfolding of Neo-Confucianism, by Wm. Theodore de Bary and the Conference on Seventeenth-Century Chinese Thought. Also in paperback ed. 1975

Principle and Practicality: Essays in Neo-Confucianism and Practical Learning, ed. Wm. Theodore de Bary and Irene Bloom. Also in paperback ed. 1979

The Syncretic Religion of Lin Chao-en, by Judith A. Berling 1980

The Renewal of Buddhism in China: Chu-hung and the Late Ming Synthesis, by Chün-fang Yü 1981

Neo-Confucian Orthodoxy and the Learning of the Mind-and-Heart, by Wm. Theodore de Bary 1981

Yüan Thought: Chinese Thought and Religion Under the Mongols, ed. Hok-lam Chan and Wm. Theodore de Bary 1982

The Liberal Tradition in China, by Wm. Theodore de Bary 1983

The Development and Decline of Chinese Cosmology, by John B. Henderson 1984

The Rise of Neo-Confucianism in Korea, by Wm. Theodore de Bary and JaHyun Kim Haboush 1985

Chiao Hung and the Restructuring of Neo-Confucianism in Late Ming, by Edward T. Ch'ien 1985

Neo-Confucian Terms Explained: Pei-hsi tzu-i, by Ch'en Ch'un, ed. and tr. Wing-tsit Chan 1986

Knowledge Painfully Acquired: K'un-chih chi, by Lo Ch'in-shun, ed. and tr. Irene Bloom 1987

To Become a Sage: The Ten Diagrams on Sage Learning, by Yi T'oegye, ed. and tr. Michael C. Kalton 1988

The Message of the Mind in Neo-Confucian Thought, by Wm. Theodore de Bary 1989